# The Complete Book of
# Handicrafts

# The Complete Book of

# Handicrafts

Edited by Jill Blake and Joan Fisher

**Book Club Associates**

London

# ACKNOWLEDGEMENTS

All photographs by Robert Belton except those on :

Pages 9, 34, 35, 121, 122, 130, 200, 201, 202 and 257 by courtesy of Syndication International

Pages 31 and 33 by courtesy of J & P Coats Ltd

Page 127 by courtesy of Trans-World

Page 254 collages by courtesy of U-Spray and Power Pack

This edition published 1976 by Book Club Associates London

By arrangement with Octopus Books Limited
59 Grosvenor Street London W1

Reprinted 1977

© 1973 Octopus Books Limited

ISBN 0 7064 0157 3

Printed in Czechoslovakia

# CONTENTS

# INTRODUCTION

Most people – and that includes men as well as women – gain enormous pleasure from making attractive and useful things for themselves, their homes, their families and friends. This book is designed to inspire beginner and enthusiast alike with practical handicrafts ideas both traditional and modern. Children have not been forgotten either – there are special things for young people to make, requiring a minimum of parental supervision.

Each chapter is concerned with a different handicraft. With each new subject a comprehensive lesson in the craft is given first, followed by special designs on which to practise your newly-acquired skills. As your knowledge increases so the designs become more sophisticated.

Of course, if you already know how to knit, sew, embroider, crochet and tat; do tapestry, feltcraft, patchwork and appliqué; knot macramé; make hats, toys and lampshades; create collages; frame your own pictures; and do leatherwork and basketwork, you can make our special designs without following the lesson first.

You will find our lessons easy to follow and complete in every detail. A carefully-planned index will help you answer questions quickly.

This invaluable work of reference will last a lifetime, give you endless hours of creative pleasure, teach you new skills and remind you of old ones and, hopefully, give satisfaction to those who make and those who wear or receive.

The Editors

# EMBROIDERY

## Lesson One:
## Flower motifs from simple stitches

## The stitches . . .

### Chain stitch

Bring the thread out at top of line and hold it down with the left thumb. Insert the needle where it last emerged and bring the point out a short distance away. Pull the thread through, keeping the working thread under the needle point (A).

### Stem stitch

Work from left to right, taking regular, slightly slanting stitches along the line of the design. The thread always emerges on the left side of the previous stitch. This stitch is used for flower stems, outlines and so forth. It can also be used as a filling, rows of stem stitch worked closely together within a shape until it is filled completely (B).

### Satin stitch

Take straight stitches across the design, keeping stitches close together. If wished, running stitch or chain stitch may be worked first to form a padding underneath and give a raised effect. Care must be taken to give a neat edge. Do not make stitches too long (C).

### Buttonhole stitch

Bring the thread out on the lower line of the design, and insert the needle in position in the upper line, taking a straight downward stitch with the thread under the needle point. Pull up the stitch to form a loop and repeat (D).

### French knots

Bring the thread out at the required position. Hold the thread down with the left thumb and encircle the thread twice with the needle as at E1. Still holding the thread firmly, twist the needle back to the starting point and insert it close to where the thread first emerged (see arrow). Pull thread through to the back and secure for a single French knot or pass on to the position of the next stitch as at (E2).

## THE MOTIFS

### TAKE ONE TULIP

The colour illustration on page 9 shows how from one basic motif and just three simple stitches, it is possible to create a variety of attractive eyecatching

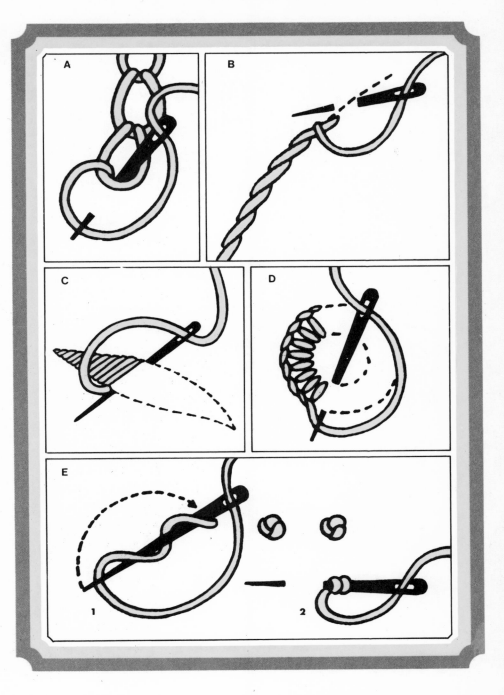

designs. In fact there are eight different versions of the tulip shown in our illustration. Each uses a combination of satin, chain and stem stitches—some motifs use all three stitches, others just two. On the next page you will find the outline of the basic tulip motif in actual size, and a guide to the stitches used for each variation.

### How to use your tulip motif

Embroider the tulip as a single motif on to a guest towel or dressing table mat, or work rows or groups of motifs (all the same or different variations) on to a tablecloth, trolley cloth, runner or chair back cover.

### MATERIALS

For each motif you will need 1 skein of Clark's Anchor Stranded Cotton in each of chosen shades: tulip B uses Magenta 064, Moss Green 0264 and Forest Green 0216; tulip A uses Scarlet 046, and two shades of Forest Green 0216 and 0218; tulip D uses two shades of Magenta 060 and 064, Moss Green 0264 and Forest Green 0216; tulip C uses Amber Gold 0305, Geranium 010, and two shades of Forest Green 0216 and 0218; tulip E uses Geranium 010, and two shades of Forest Green 0206 and 0218; tulip F uses Rose Pink 053, Gorse Yellow 0301, and Snuff Brown 0375; tulip H uses the same threads as tulip F plus pale Rose Pink 048; tulip G uses canary Yellow 0290, Ecru/Cream 0386, and two shades of Muscat Green 0278 and 0281. A crewel needle No. 7. Fine embroidery linen to suit purpose for which finished design is intended, or other suitable fabric. The motif can also be worked directly onto a guest towel, handkerchief or runner.

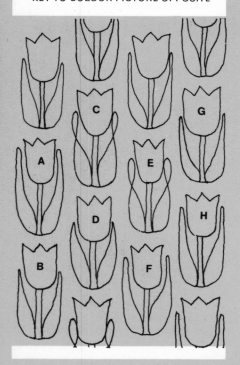

## DIAGRAMS

Diagram, left, shows the motif as used for tulip D in actual size. The diagrams below give a guide to the threads and stitches used to work each variation on the basic motif, and also indicate how the basic motif can be easily adapted to give the variations.

throughout. Trace the motif as given in diagram, left, or adapt it to work one of the other variations, on to your linen, positioning it to suit your particular design.

Now work the embroidery, following the guide to stitches and colours as given in the diagrams below, for the motif you are working.

## TO MAKE

**Note.** Use 3 strands of thread

## TO FINISH

Press embroidery on the wrong side.

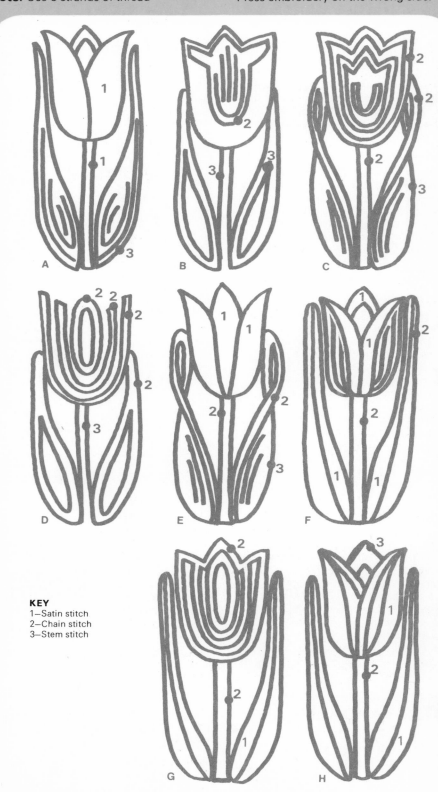

**KEY**
1—Satin stitch
2—Chain stitch
3—Stem stitch

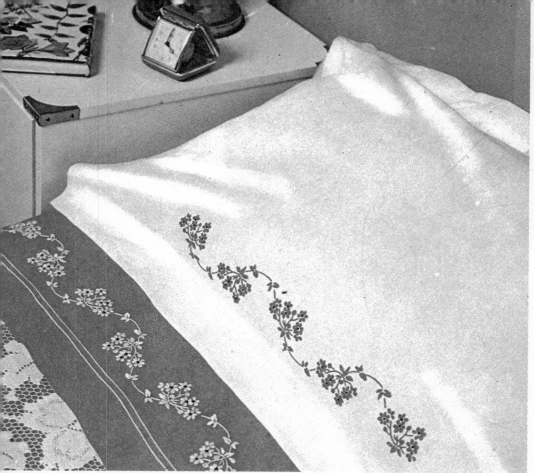

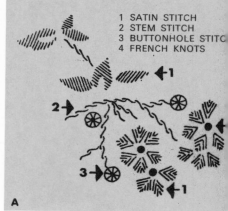

1 SATIN STITCH
2 STEM STITCH
3 BUTTONHOLE STITC
4 FRENCH KNOTS

A

# AND SO TO BED

**Pretty for a guest room—bed linen embroidered with sprigs of flowers.**

## MATERIALS

Of Clark's Anchor Stranded Cotton—4 skeins White 0402, 2 skeins Carnation 029, and 1 skein Black 0403. A sheet in deep pink, and a white pillowcase. A Milward 'Gold Seal' Crewel needle No 7

## DIAGRAMS

Diagram B gives a section of the design in actual size. Diagram A gives a guide to the stitches used.

## TO MAKE

**Note.** Use 3 strands of thread throughout. Work embroidery on the sheet in white cotton, with black French knots. Work embroidery on the pillowcase in carnation cotton, with black French knots.

Fold sheet in half lengthwise, and fold pillowcase in half widthwise. Crease lightly to mark folds. Trace section of design as given in diagram B on to the sheet, making first tracing centrally across fold and 2¾in. down from top edge of sheet. Trace the section twice more on either side of the central motif, positioning each tracing close to the previous one, so complete tracing gives a continuous line of motifs. Trace the design on to the pillowcase, making the first tracing so the right-hand cluster of flowers is centred on the fold, and the motif is 3in. down from top edge of pillowcase. Trace section of design as given once more to the right of the first tracing. To complete the design, trace one small cluster of flowers on to the left-hand side to correspond. Work embroidery, following the guide to stitches as given in diagram A. All unnumbered parts on the diagram are worked in the same stitch as the numbered parts most similar to them.

## TO FINISH

Press embroidery on the wrong side.

B

# EMBROIDERY

## Lesson Two: Counted-thread work

Embroidery, in very general terms, is divided into two distinct groups: free-style work and counted-thread work. In free-style embroidery, a design is usually worked over a traced or ironed-on transfer, and the design can take almost any form. In counted-thread embroidery, no tracing or transfer is required; instead a design is worked on an evenweave fabric by counting the threads of the fabric, and working each stitch over an exact number of these fabric threads. For this reason, as the stitches are restricted by the mesh of the fabric, designs tend to be geometric in form.
There are a number of stitches which are used only for free-style embroidery, and a number which are used only for counted-thread work, but there are a number of stitches common to both techniques.
Drawn-thread and drawn-fabric work are both traditional forms of counted-thread embroidery.
In drawn-thread work, threads are withdrawn from the fabric, and then embroidery is worked over the edges of the space of the withdrawn threads. Decorative stitches may also be worked over the loose threads which are left when the warp and weft threads of the fabric are withdrawn.
In drawn-fabric work, groups of threads of the fabric are drawn together. The actual stitching is not the main feature of this embroidery: it is the open pattern formed on the fabric by the pulling together of the threads. The stitches are worked over a regular number of threads of fabric, and the working thread is always pulled firmly with each needle movement, so that an open-work effect is achieved.
In any form of counted-thread embroidery, the initial preparation of your fabric is all-important. As the embroidery is really a mathematical exercise, it is essential that the threads of the fabric are counted out as accurately as possible. A beginner should start with a fairly coarse mesh fabric, as the warp and weft threads are then easier to see and count. Begin by marking out the centres of your fabric, both horizontally and vertically, with basting stitches. As a further guide to accurate counting, mark out threads in groups of ten along the top and down one side of fabric. Use basting stitches, taking each stitch over a group of ten threads, then under the next group—and so on.

## Counted-thread stitches

### BACK STITCH

Bring needle out at the right-hand side of area where stitching is to appear, but 3 threads from the edge. Take a backward stitch over 3 threads of the fabric, bringing the needle out 3 threads in front of the place where the needle first emerged. Continue in this way, working from right to left in the required direction (A).

### FLY STITCH

Bring needle out at top left-hand side of area where stitch is to appear. Holding the thread down with the left thumb, insert needle to the right-hand corner of area. Keeping the thread below the needle, bring needle out on lower line of stitching, and take a straight vertical stitch downward over one thread of fabric (B).

### SATIN STITCH

This stitch which is simply a straight vertical or horizontal stitch, may be worked from right to left, or left to right, and over any number of fabric threads (C).

### HOLBEIN STITCH

Sometimes called double running stitch.

Work from right to left, working a row of running stitches over and under 3 threads of the fabric, following the outline of the design. On the second row, worked from left to right, fill in the spaces left in the first row (D).

### HEMSTITCH

This is a drawn-thread stitch. Measure required depth of hem, plus the turnings and withdraw required number of fabric threads. Do not withdraw the threads right across the fabric, but only to form a square or rectangle. Cut threads at the centre and withdraw gradually outwards on each side to within the hem measurement, leaving a sufficient length of thread at corners in order to darn the ends invisibly. Turn back the hem to the space of the drawn threads, mitre corners and baste. Bring the working thread out 2 threads down from the space of drawn threads through the folded hem at right-hand side, pass needle behind 4 loose threads, bringing needle out 2 threads down through all the folds of the hem ready for the next stitch. The number of threads may be varied to suit the fabric or design (E).

### LADDER HEMSTITCH

This is worked in a similar way as hemstitch, above, with the hemstitch being worked along both edges of the space of drawn threads (F).

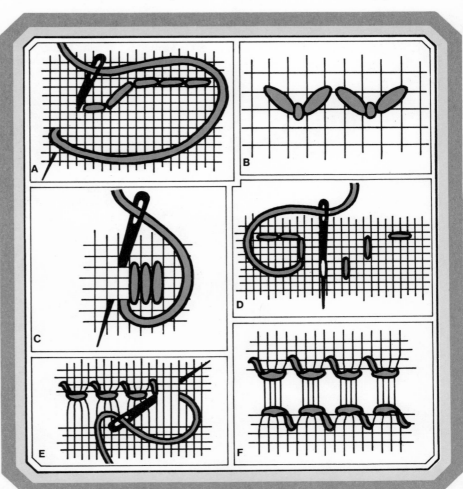

# YOUR COUNTED-THREAD MAKE

# TROLLEY CLOTH

## MATERIALS YOU WILL NEED

Of Coats Anchor Tapisserie Wool—2 skeins Amber Gold 0309; of Clark's Anchor Stranded Cotton (USA: J & P Coats Deluxe Six Strand Floss)—5 skeins Orange 0326, 4 skeins Periwinkle 0119, 2 skeins Jade 0188, and 1 skein Indigo 0127. ½ yd. evenweave embroidery fabric, 21 threads to the inch, 59 in. wide. Milward 'Gold Seal' tapestry needle No. 19.

## TO MAKE

*Note: Use 6 strands of stranded cotton throughout.* Cut a piece from fabric 17½ in. by 25½ in. and mark the centre both ways with basting stitches. Diagram A, below, shows a section

of the complete design. Each of the background lines on the diagram represent the threads of the fabric, and the blank arrow should coincide with your crosswise basting stitches. Diagram B gives a complete corner section of the design.

With one long side of fabric facing you, begin the embroidery with satin stitch at the blank arrow on diagram A, 154 threads down from crossed basting stitches. Work the section of design in diagram A first, following stitch and colour key as a guide to the different stitches and thread colours used. Repeat this section six times more to the left, then work corner section as given in diagram B.

Turn fabric and continue border to lengthwise basting stitches. Work other three quarters of the design to correspond.

## TO COMPLETE

Press embroidery carefully on the wrong side. Turn back ½ in. hems on all edges, mitre corners, and slipstitch neatly in place.

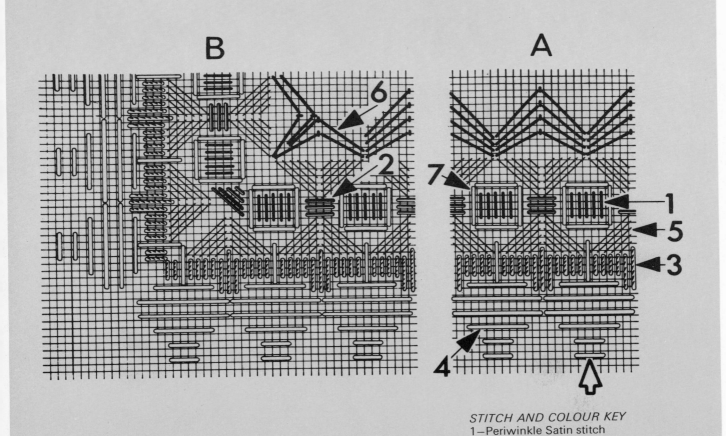

STITCH AND COLOUR KEY
1—Periwinkle Satin stitch
2—Indigo Satin stitch
3—Jade Satin stitch
4—Amber Gold Satin stitch
5—Orange Satin stitch
6—Periwinkle Fly stitch
7—Amber Gold Back stitch

# EMBROIDERY

## Lesson Three:
## Transferring designs to fabric

A design for a free-style embroidery can be transferred to your fabric in any of several ways, depending on the fabric, the design to be worked, and whether the design is in the form of a printed transfer, or it has to be traced from another source on to the fabric.

## Transfers

There are two types of transfers, the single impression and the multi-print. The single impression transfer may only be used once. The multi-print can give up to eight impressions, depending upon the type and weight of the fabric used.

### SINGLE IMPRESSION TRANSFERS

Cut away all lettering from the transfer. Heat iron to a fairly hot temperature. Place transfer sheet, face downwards on the fabric in required position and secure with steel pins. Apply iron for a few seconds and remove.
Carefully lift a corner of the transfer paper to check that the design has come off satisfactorily. If it has not, then re-apply iron. Be careful not to move either the transfer or the fabric, otherwise the impression will smudge.

### MULTI-PRINT TRANSFERS

Cut away all lettering from transfer. Heat iron to a hot temperature, and then transfer design to fabric in a similar way as for a single impression transfer. If necessary, protect the fabric from the direct heat of the iron by placing tissue paper round the transfer.

## Tracing methods

### CARBON PAPER

This is the simplest method, but not generally considered to be the most satisfactory. Use light-coloured carbon paper for dark fabrics; dark carbon paper for light-coloured fabrics.
Place carbon paper in position face downwards on the fabric, then place the drawing or tracing of the design you wish to use on top. Draw over all the lines with a sharp, fairly hard pencil. Take care to press only on the lines of the design, otherwise the carbon may smudge the fabric.

### POUNCING

This is a fairly lengthy method, but is probably the best of all. Trace the design on to firm tracing paper, then with a needle prick small holes over all the lines, spacing the holes evenly about 1/16th in. apart. Rub the back of the pricked design with fine sandpaper to remove the roughness. Place the pricked design on to the fabric and keep in position with weights. Rub powdered charcoal (for light fabrics) or powdered chalk (for dark fabrics) through the holes. Remove the tracing paper and blow off the surplus powder from the fabric. Paint over the dotted lines of powder with watercolour paint, using a fine paintbrush.

### BASTING TO TISSUE PAPER

Trace the design on to fine tracing or tissue paper. Place the tissue paper in position on fabric, and stitch along the lines of the design, taking small running or basting stitches. Carefully remove paper, leaving stitches in position on the fabric. Remove the stitches as work progresses and they are no longer required.

### TRACING ON TO FABRIC

If you are using a fine transparent fabric, such as organdie, nylon or silk, simply place the design underneath the fabric and paint over the lines with watercolour paint and a fine paintbrush.

## Some more free-style stitches

### BACK STITCH

Work from right to left. Bring needle through on the stitch line, then take a small backward stitch through the fabric. Bring the needle through again a little in front of the first stitch. Take another stitch, inserting the needle at point where it first came through (A)

### FLY STITCH

Bring the needle through at the top left of area to be covered, hold the thread down with the left thumb, insert the needle to the right on the same level, a little distance from where the thread first emerged and take a small stitch downwards to the centre with the thread below the needle. Pull through and insert the needle again below the stitch at the centre and bring it through in position for the next stitch. This stitch may be worked singly or in horizontal rows (B1) or vertically (B2).

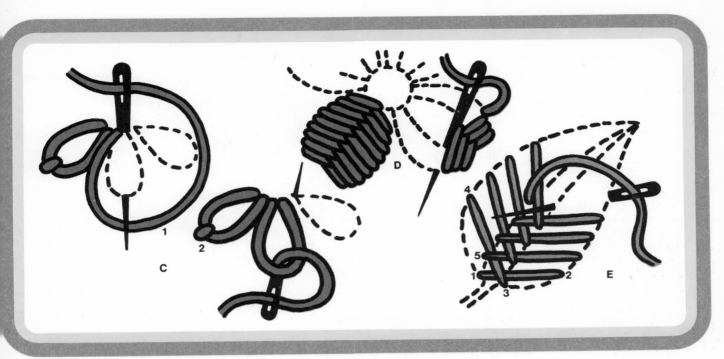

## DAISY STITCH

This is sometimes known as detached chain stitch. Work in a similar way as for chain stitch (see Embroidery, lesson one) but fasten each loop at the foot with a small stitch. This stitch may be worked singly or in groups to form flower petals (C1 and 2).

## FLAT STITCH

Take a small stitch alternately on each side of the shape to be filled, with the point of the needle always emerging on the outside line of the shape. Two lines may be drawn down the centre of the shape as a guide for the size of the stitch. The stitches should be close together and fold into one another (D).

## LEAF STITCH (Fig. E)

Bring the needle through at 1 and make a sloping stitch to 2. Bring the thread through at 3 and make a sloping stitch to 4. Bring the needle through at 5 and then continue working alternate stitches on each side in this way until the shape is lightly filled. When this stitch is used there is normally an outline of stem stitch or chain stitch worked round the shape.

## YOUR FREESTYLE EMBROIDERY MAKE

## GUEST TOWEL

## MATERIALS YOU WILL NEED

Of Clark's Anchor Stranded Cotton (USA: J. & P. Coats Deluxe Six Strand Floss)—1 skein each Petunia 093, Violet 0102, Spring Green 0237. ¾ yd. white huckaback towelling, 18 in. wide. Milward Gold Seal' crewel needle No. 7.

Diagram A

## DIAGRAMS

Diagram A (previous page) gives one repeat of the design in actual size. Diagram B gives a guide to the stitches and thread colours used throughout the design.

## TO MAKE

*Note:* Use 3 strands of thread throughout.
Fold the fabric across the centre lengthwise and crease lightly. The broken line on diagram A indicates your centre fold.
With narrow end of fabric towards you, trace the design as given in diagram A centrally on to fold, 3¼ in. up from raw edge.
Trace the design once more on each side of the central motif, spacing the motifs ¼ in. apart.
Work the embroidery, following diagram B and the stitch and colour key. All unnumbered parts on the diagram are worked in the same stitch and colour as the numbered parts most similar to them.

## TO COMPLETE

Press embroidery on the wrong side. Stitch a ½ in. hem at top of towel, a 1½ in. hem along lower edge (below embroidery).

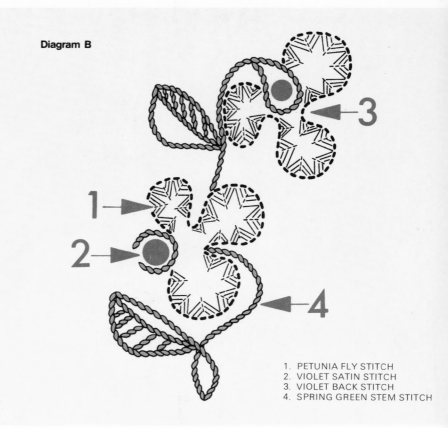

**Diagram B**

1. PETUNIA FLY STITCH
2. VIOLET SATIN STITCH
3. VIOLET BACK STITCH
4. SPRING GREEN STEM STITCH

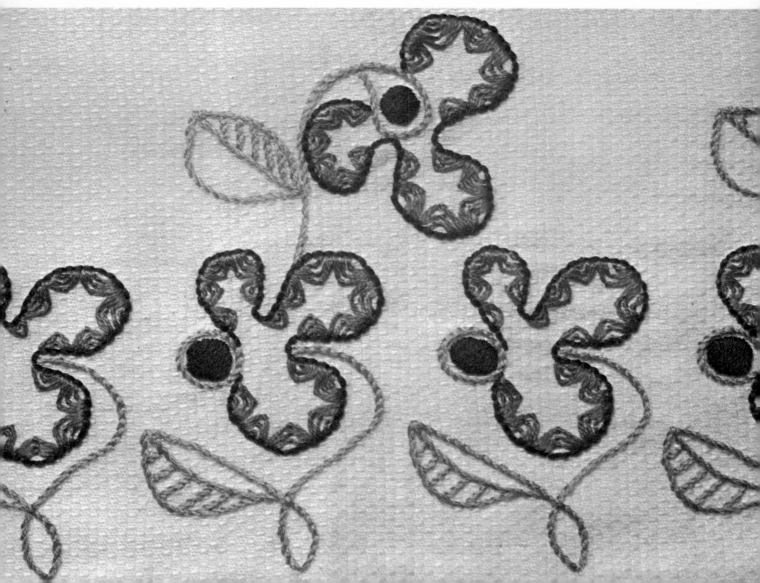

# EMBROIDERY

## Lesson Four:
## Decorative darning

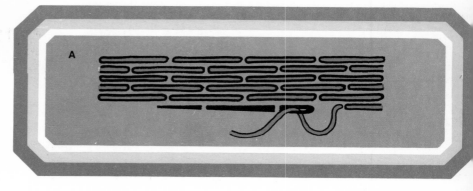

The simple utilitarian darning stitch can be most effectively used in embroidery work. An evenweave fabric should be used, and ideally the design should be worked solely in darning stitches. Evenweave embroidery linen makes a suitable background, but so does net, canvas and huckaback. A traditional design uses bright colours of thread to darn fairly simple patterns in and out of the meshes of the fabric.

## To work darning stitch

Really the darning stitch is simply a long basting stitch worked to give a decorative effect. Work from right to left, picking up only one thread of the fabric with each stitch (A). The fabric threads which are picked up should form a pattern, as well as the darning stitches themselves. It is important to space stitches evenly, and for this reason an open-mesh fabric has to be used, so the fabric threads can be counted out. Darning stitches may be used to create a pattern motif, or may be used to fill in a background, thus forming a pattern motif from the fabric left unstitched.

### DARNING ON NET

This technique can be used to make patterned net curtains, fine bedspreads and even a bride's or bridesmaid's veil. The important rule to bear in mind with this form of darning is that the thread used should be thick enough to fill the mesh of the net exactly—neither too thin, so it drags the net, or too thick so it distorts it.
With a coarse-mesh net, wool is the best yarn to use; with finer nets, stranded cotton is suitable, as then the appropriate number of strands can be used to fill the mesh of the net exactly.

### DARNING ON HUCKABACK

As huckaback has a pronounced and regular weave, this makes an ideal background for darning embroidery. Attractive towels can be quickly and

*Lagartera tablecloth, worked entirely in satin and back stitch—making instructions start overleaf*

inexpensively made in this way. Stranded cotton again is the best yarn to use. Work darning stitches, just taking the stitches under the loops of the fabric. Nearly all the stitching will then be on the surface of your work.

## TO WORK DOUBLE DARNING STITCH

This is a variation of the basic darning stitch which is useful for building up a flat surface filling. Work one row of darning stitches from right to left, spacing the stitches evenly so the length of the stitch and the length of the fabric picked up are equal. Now work a second row of stitches from left to right, filling in the gaps left on the first row. On this return journey the needle should be inserted into the fabric and brought back out at the same holes as on the first row (B).

# TWO TRADITIONAL TABLECLOTHS

## Swedish darning tablecloth

*(illustrated overleaf)*

### MATERIALS YOU WILL NEED

Of Clark's Anchor Stranded Cotton—11 skeins Cyclamen 088, 3 skeins Muscat Green 0281, and 1 skein Black 0403; 2¼ yd. beige evenweave embroidery linen, 21 threads to 1 in., 59 in. wide. A Milward 'Gold Seal' tapestry needle No. 21.

### TO MAKE

*Note: Use 6 strands of stranded cotton throughout.*

Mark the centre of the fabric both ways with lines of basting stitches.

The diagram below gives a little more than half the complete motif. Each of the background lines on the diagram represent the threads of the fabric, and the blank arrow should coincide with your crosswise basting stitches. The design is worked throughout in darning stitch; the diagram shows the arrangement and

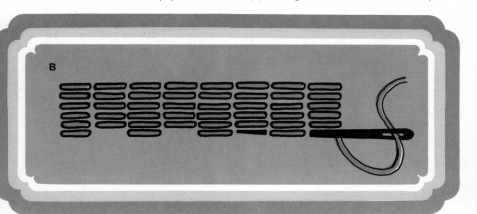

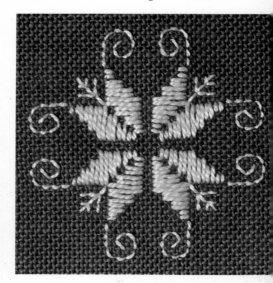

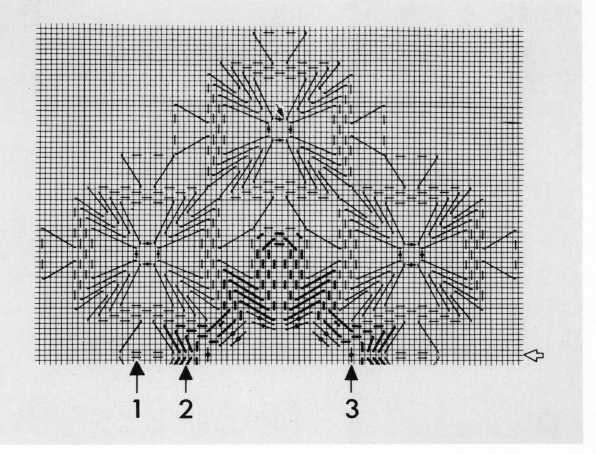

**COLOUR KEY**

1. Cyclamen

2. Muscat Green

3. Black

1  2  3

length of individual stitches on the threads of the fabric.

Commence the embroidery with one short side of fabric facing you, and beginning stitching at small black arrow 28 threads down and 127 threads to the right of crossed basting stitches. Work section of design given in the diagram, following key to thread colours given. Work in reverse from blank arrow to complete the motif. Repeat the motif three more times immediately below as shown, leaving 22 threads between, and complete lower right-hand quarter.

Work lower left-hand quarter to correspond. Turn fabric and work other half in a similar way.

## TO COMPLETE

Press embroidery on wrong side. Turn in 1-in. hems on all edges, mitre corners and slipstitch neatly in place.

# Lagartera tablecloth

## MATERIALS YOU WILL NEED

2 balls Clark's Anchor Pearl Cotton No. 5 in White 0402, and 1 ball Clark's Anchor Pearl Cotton No. 8 in White 0402; 1½ yd. dark green evenweave embroidery linen, 21 threads to 1 in., 54 in. wide; Milward 'Gold Seal' tapestry needles Nos. 20 and 24.

## TO MAKE

*Note:* Use No. 8 Pearl Cotton and No. 24 needle for back stitch throughout; use No. 5 Pearl Cotton and No. 20 needle for satin stitch throughout. Mark the centre of your fabric both ways with basting stitches. Diagram A (opposite) gives an eighth of the central section of the design; diagram

# LAGARTERA TABLECLOTH

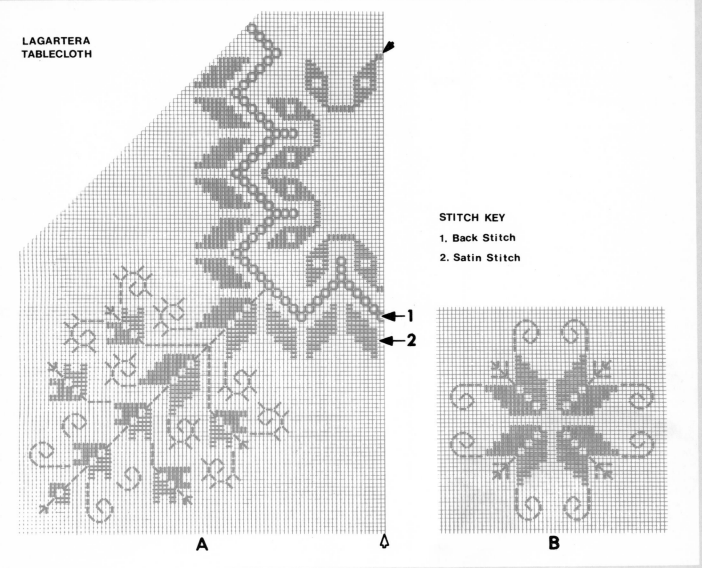

**STITCH KEY**

1. Back Stitch
2. Satin Stitch

A

B

B gives one complete motif. Each of the background lines on these two diagrams represents the threads of the fabric. The blank arrow on diagram A should coincide with your basting stitches.

Diagram C gives one quarter of the design, showing the position of central section and motifs. The broken lines on this diagram should coincide with your basting stitches. The numbers represent the threads of the fabric between the central section of the design and the motifs.

Commence the embroidery at blank arrow on diagram A, 40 threads down from crossed basting stitches, and work the section as given, following the stitch key given—only back stitch and satin stitch are used throughout the design.

Complete one quarter of the design, following diagram C for position of motifs. Work other three quarters to correspond.

## TO COMPLETE

Press the embroidery on the wrong side. Turn in 1-in. hems on all edges, mitre corners and slipstitch neatly.

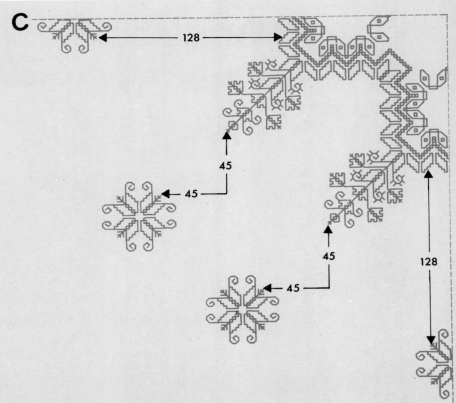

# EMBROIDERY

## Lesson Five:
## Lettering and monograms

Embroidering decorative letters on to household linen and fashion accessories can add an attractive personal touch to your work.

Any style of letter may be used, and a variety of stitches to work the letter. If two letters are arranged so one is interwoven with the other this is known as a cipher; when the letters share the same upright stroke—so neither is quite complete in itself—this is a monogram. The style of lettering chosen should obviously be in keeping with the item it is to decorate—sheets, pillowcase and guest towels, for example, which provide a plain linen base can take fairly ornate letters, but if it is wished to embroider letters on to a modern scarf, blouse or other fashion accessory then a slightly plainer type of letter may be more appropriate.

Experiment with lettering on squared paper to find styles that appeal to you. Look through newspapers and magazines at headings and if you see letters which you think could be adapted to give a basis for embroidery, then trace them off and transfer to your squared paper, so measurements of each letter can then be accurately assessed, and letters worked out to harmonise with each other.

## The stitches

Any type of stitch may be used to work your lettering, but the simpler stitches are usually the most effective. Cross stitch, for instance, looks pleasing when used to work a fairly plain style of letter. Other stitches which work well are chain stitch, double back stitch and stem stitch. Satin stitch however is probably the most popular and widely used stitch for lettering and can be used on its own, or combined with other stitches.

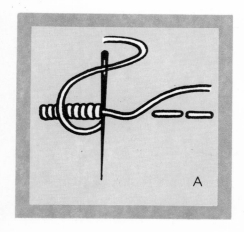

A

### PADDED SATIN STITCH

This gives a good rich appearance to your embroidery and is particularly suitable for the more ornate style of letter. Work an outline round the letter first with chain or running stitches, then fill in the areas between the outline lines with chain stitches until every part of the letter is covered. Finally work satin stitches over the padding of chain stitches, keeping stitches close together, very regular and all slanting in the same direction.

### CORDING

This technique is suitable for small, fairly plain letters. Lay a thread along the line of the letter (this is the cording thread), then with another thread, known as the top or working thread, work vertical stitches close together over the cording thread until it is completely covered. Cording looks most effective when worked in a thick, well-twisted thread (A).

# YOUR LETTERING MAKES

## Guest towel motif

### MATERIALS YOU WILL NEED

Clark's Anchor Stranded Cotton in colour as wished. Plain-coloured linen or huckaback guest towel. Milward 'Gold Seal' crewel needle No. 6.

### TO MAKE

*Note. Use 3 strands of cotton throughout.*

Diagram A overleaf gives the alphabet in a scaled-down version, and B the decorative circle which can be used to ring round your letter. Prepare a full-sized diagram following instructions in Sewing, lesson one.

Diagram B shows the arrangement of satin stitches used to form the letter 'R' and also the circle motif. From this guide it should be an easy matter to adapt the arrangement of satin stitches for the other letters. Trace the circle motif in one corner of the guest towel, or position it as wished, then trace the chosen letter centrally within the circle. Work the embroidery in satin stitch. If wished, the letter may be padded first with chain stitches.

### TO COMPLETE

Press embroidery lightly on the wrong side.

## Tunic motif

### MATERIALS YOU WILL

Clark's Anchor Stranded Cotton in colour as wished. Plain-coloured tunic top with long ties. Milward 'Gold Seal' crewel needle No. 6.

### TO MAKE

*Note. Use 3 strands of cotton throughout.*

The letters are taken from the alphabet design for Guest Towel Motif, but the decorative circle motif is omitted. Trace group of letters as wished on to one tie of tunic. If it is wished to combine a group of letters into a cipher or monogram experiment on a piece of paper first to find the best linking arrangement of the letters before tracing on to your tunic.

Work embroidery and complete as described for Guest Towel Motif.

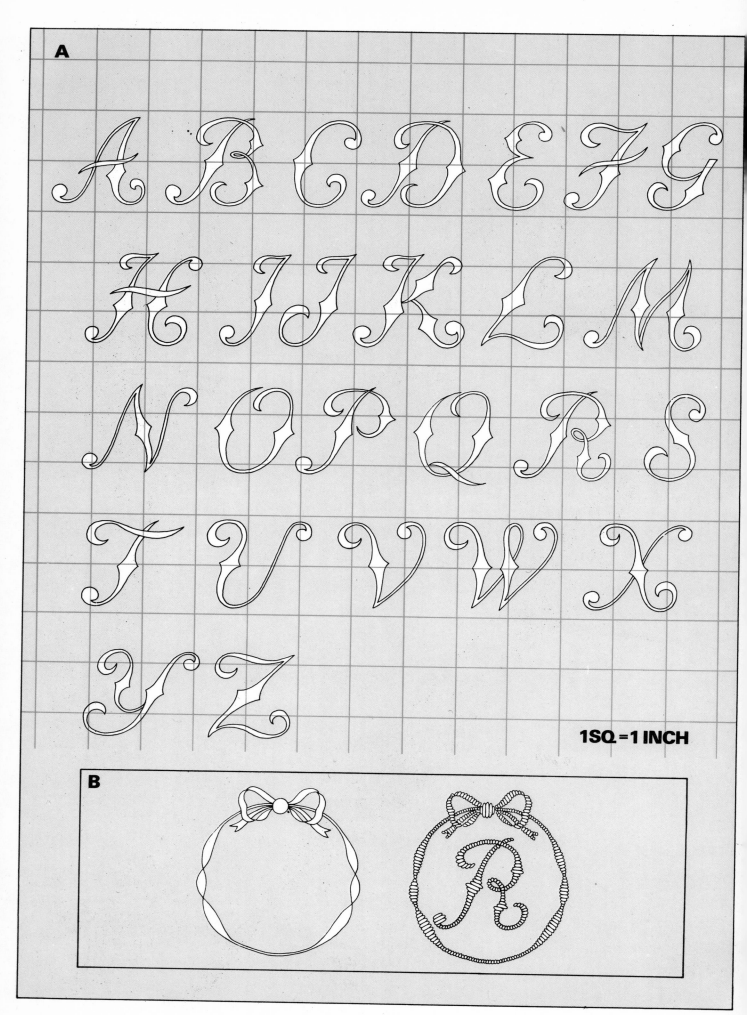

**A**

**1 SQ. = 1 INCH**

**B**

# Handkerchief motif

## MATERIALS YOU WILL NEED

Clark's Anchor Stranded Cotton in colour as wished. Plain linen handkerchief. Milward 'Gold Seal' crewel needle No. 7.

## TO MAKE

*Note. Use 2 strands of cotton throughout.*

Diagram C gives the complete alphabet in actual size, and D the decorative circle which can be used to ring round your letter, if wished.

Diagram D shows the arrangement of satin stitches used to form the letter 'A' and also the circle motif. From this guide it should be an easy matter to adapt the arrangement of satin stitches for the other letters. Trace the circle motif diagonally across one corner of the handkerchief, then trace chosen letter centrally within the circle. Work the embroidery in satin stitch. If wished, the letter may be padded first with chain stitches, as described on previous page.

## TO COMPLETE

Press embroidery lightly on the wrong side.

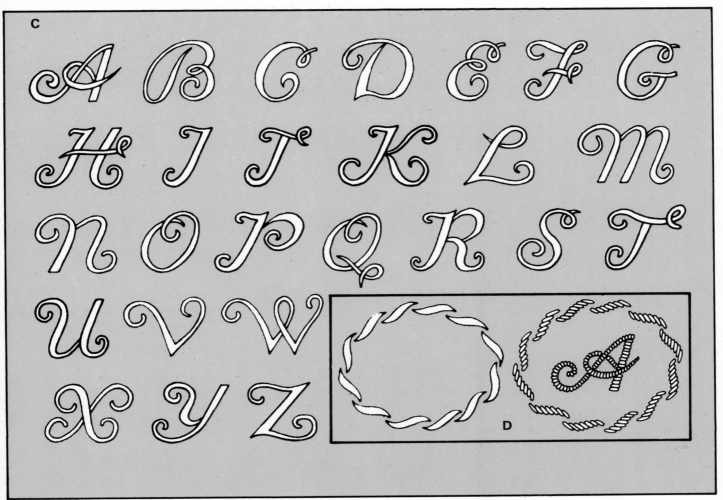

# EMBROIDERY

## Lesson Six:
## Cushions

### Making up your cushions

Whatever the shape of the cushion design you are making—square, oblong, round, triangular—the basic method of making up is similar.

Place back and front sections of your cushion right sides together, making sure the edges are even. Stitch round three sides for square or oblong cushions, or with circular cushions stitch round, leaving a 6-in. gap anywhere in the seam. Trim seams carefully, and clip into seam allowances on curved and shaped edges. Turn cushion cover right side out. Now insert your cushion pad, or suitable stuffing— a well-shaped cushion should be tightly stuffed with no loose folds of fabric at all. Finally turn in seam allowance on remaining open edges, and slipstitch neatly together. If preferred this seam may be left unstitched, and the opening closed instead with press fasteners, or with a zip fastener. This means the cover can be easily removed for cleaning.

### MORE STITCHES
#### Double knot stitch
Bring the needle through at 1 on diagram A. Take a small stitch across the line at 2. Pass the needle downwards under the surface stitch just made, without piercing the fabric as at 3. With the thread under the needle, pass the needle again under the first stitch at 4. Pull the thread through to form a knot. The knots should be spaced evenly and closely to obtain a beaded effect. (A).
#### Up and down buttonhole stitch
Begin as for ordinary buttonhole stitch. Pull thread through. Insert the needle on the bottom line and take a straight upward stitch with the thread under the needle point. Pull thread through first in an upward movement, then downwards to continue (B1 and 2).
#### Rosette chain stitch
Bring the thread out at the right end of the upper line and hold down with left thumb. Insert the needle into the upper line a short distance from where it emerged and bring out just above the lower line, passing the thread under the needle point, draw the needle through and then pass the needle under the top loop without piercing the fabric (C1 and 2).
#### Couching
Lay a thread along the line of the design and with another thread, tie it down at even intervals with a small stitch into the fabric. The tying stitch can be of a contrasting colour to the laid thread.

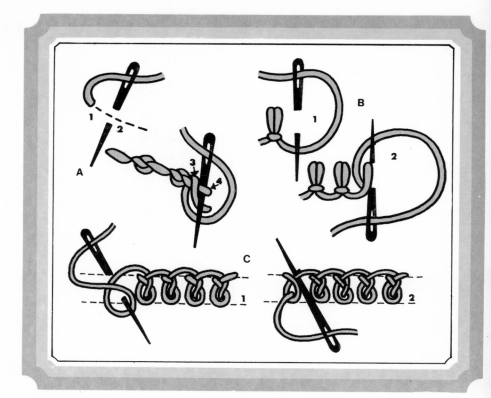

## YOUR CUSHION MAKES

### Twin cushions

#### MATERIALS YOU WILL NEED

**For kingfisher cushion**—of Coats Anchor Tapisserie wool 2 skeins each Yellow 0296, Orange 0314 and Cream 0386. **For orange cushion**—of Coats Anchor Tapisserie Wool 2 skeins each of Jade 0188, Amber Gold 0306 and Cream 0386. **For both**—½ yd. furnishing fabric for each cushion, 48 in. wide. Milward 'Gold Seal' chenille needle No. 19. A cushion pad 15 in. square, or suitable stuffing for each cushion.

#### DIAGRAMS *(overleaf)*

**Diagram D** gives a reduced version of ¼ of the design. Prepare a full-sized diagram, as in Sewing, lesson one.
**Diagram E** gives a guide to the thread colours and stitches used.

#### TO MAKE

Cut 2 pieces, each 16½ in. square, from each piece of fabric. Trace the design as given in diagram D centrally on to one piece of each colour of fabric. Work embroidery following diagram E and stitch and colour key. All unnumbered parts on the stitch and colour diagram are worked in the same stitches and colours as the numbered parts most similar to them.

#### TO COMPLETE

Press embroidery on the wrong side. Make up cushions as described in lesson, stitching seams with ¾ in. turnings.

## Circular cushion
*Illustrated overleaf*

#### MATERIALS YOU WILL NEED

Of Clark's Anchor Soft Embroidery—1 skein each Lilac 0107, Peacock Blue 0169, Muscat Green 0281, Gobelin Green 0223 and White 0402, plus 3 skeins of Gobelin Green 0223 for tassels. Of Clark's Anchor Stranded Cotton—1 skein each Cream 0386, Grey 0399, Kingfisher 0161 and Forest Green 0218. ½ yd. furnishing fabric, 48 in. wide. Milward 'Gold Seal' chenille needle No. 19 for Soft Embroidery, 'Gold Seal' crewel needles Nos. 6 and 7 for Stranded Cotton. A circular cushion pad with diameter of 16 in., or suitable stuffing.

#### DIAGRAMS *(overleaf)*

**Diagram F** gives the complete centre circle of the design and one quarter of the outer motifs in actual size.
**Diagram G** gives a guide to the stitches and thread colours used throughout the design.

#### TO MAKE

*Note. Use 4 strands of Stranded Cotton and No. 6 crewel needle for blue chain stitch, 2 strands and No. 7 needle for rest of embroidery in stranded cotton.*

Draw 2 circles, each with a 17 in. diameter, on fabric and cut out. The easiest way to do this is to draw out a circle of this size on stiff paper with a pair of compasses, cut out and use as a pattern for cutting the fabric. Alternatively, if you do not have compasses, tie a piece of string to a pencil, cut the string to half the diameter of the circle (i.e. 8½ in.), fasten the free end to the centre of the paper with a drawing pin.

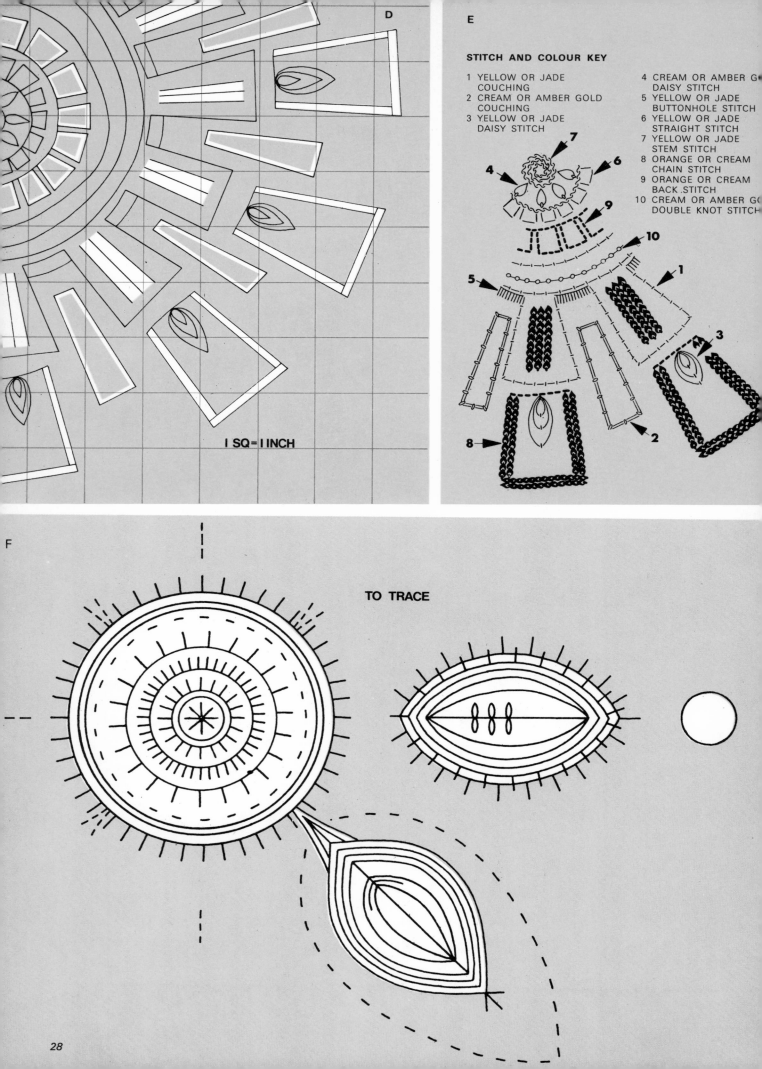

**D**

I SQ = I INCH

**E**

## STITCH AND COLOUR KEY

1 YELLOW OR JADE
  COUCHING
2 CREAM OR AMBER GOLD
  COUCHING
3 YELLOW OR JADE
  DAISY STITCH

4 CREAM OR AMBER G●
  DAISY STITCH
5 YELLOW OR JADE
  BUTTONHOLE STITCH
6 YELLOW OR JADE
  STRAIGHT STITCH
7 YELLOW OR JADE
  STEM STITCH
8 ORANGE OR CREAM
  CHAIN STITCH
9 ORANGE OR CREAM
  BACK .STITCH
10 CREAM OR AMBER G●
  DOUBLE KNOT STITCH

**F**

TO TRACE

28

Hold the string taut with the pencil perpendicular and move the pencil round, drawing out the circle. Trace the design as given in diagram F centrally on to one circle of fabric, repeating the motifs alternately round in position indicated by dotted guide lines to complete the whole design. Work embroidery, following diagram G and stitch and colour key. All unnumbered parts on the stitch and colour diagram are worked in the same stitches and colours as those parts most similar to them.

## TO COMPLETE

Press embroidery on the wrong side. Make up cushion as described in lesson, stitching seam with ½ in. turnings. Make 8 tassels with green soft embroidery thread, and stitch round edge of cushion, spacing evenly.

### STITCH AND COLOUR KEY

1. LILAC STRAIGHT STITCH
2. FOREST GREEN RUNNING STITCH
3. PEACOCK BLUE RUNNING STITCH
4. MUSCAT GREEN CHAIN STITCH
5. CREAM CHAIN STITCH
6. GOBELIN GREEN CHAIN STITCH
7. KINGFISHER CHAIN STITCH
8. FOREST GREEN ROSETTE CHAIN STITCH
9. CREAM ROSETTE CHAIN STITCH
10. WHITE ROSETTE CHAIN STITCH
11. GREY UP AND DOWN BUTTONHOLE STITCH
12. LILAC DOUBLE KNOT STITICH
13. LILAC BLANKET STITCH
14. PEACOCK BLUE BACK STITCH
15. GREY COUCHING (2 LAID THREADS)
16. GREY COUCHING (1 LAID THREAD)
17. WHITE COUCHING
18. LILAC DAISY STITCH

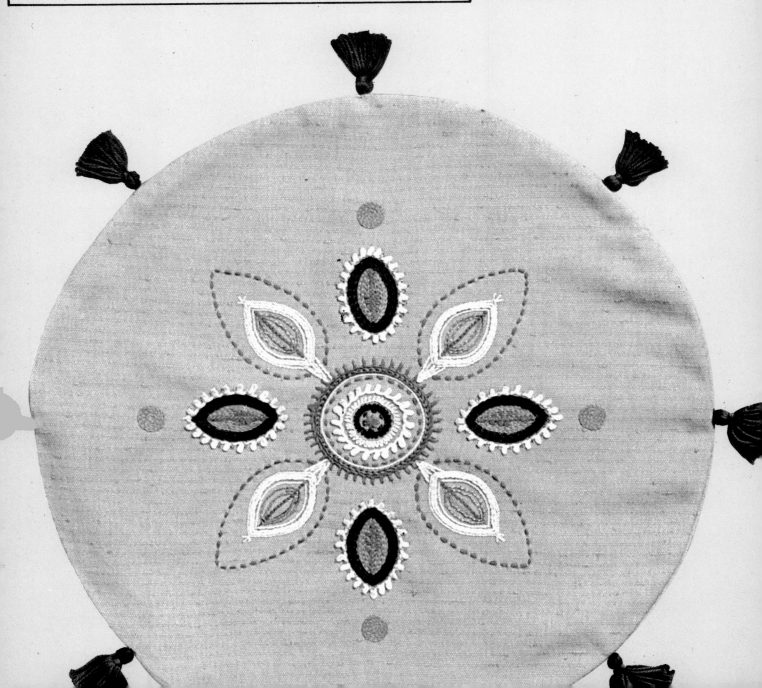

# CROSS STITCH WORK

## Lesson One:
## The basic stitches

Cross stitch is one of the most ancient of all embroidery stitches. Work carried out entirely in cross stitch or in one of its many variations, often in brilliant colours, has been found in nearly all parts of the world, and particularly in peasant embroideries. For this reason, cross stitch work has become almost a separate 'branch' of embroidery. Cross stitch can be combined with other stitches, but it can also most effectively be used on its own to create an attractive and interesting design. The stitch, and its variations, may be worked on evenweave linen or on canvas; half cross stitch is simply the first half only of the complete cross stitch, and is useful when the thread you are working with is too thick or bulky to work a complete cross stitch.

## The basic cross stitch

Bring the needle out at the lower right-hand side of area where stitching is to appear, then insert the needle 4 threads up and 4 threads to the left, and bring out 4 threads down, thus forming a half cross stitch.
Continue in this way to the end of the row. Work second row from left to right and complete other arm of each cross (A). Cross stitch may be worked either from left to right or from right to left. It is important that the upper half of all the stitches lies in the same direction.
When working cross stitch on canvas, in order to prevent distortion of the canvas, it is best to complete each stitch before moving to the next one. In this case bring needle through at lower right-hand side, as before, and insert 4 threads up and 4 threads to the left. Bring out 4 threads down and complete the cross by working a stitch across the first stitch to top right-hand corner. Continue in this way. Cross stitches may be worked over a single intersection of fabric or canvas threads, or over 2 by 2 or 3 by 3 threads, or even more. For intricate designs, however, the smaller the individual crosses worked, the more effective will be the finished embroidery.

## The variations

### DOUBLE CROSS STITCH

Work a basic cross stitch, then bring needle out 4 threads down and 2 threads to the left. Insert needle 4 threads up and bring out 2 threads to to the left and 2 threads down. Insert the needle 4 threads to the right and bring out 2 threads down and 4 threads to the left ready for the next stitch (B).

### LONG-LEGGED CROSS STITCH

This is always worked from left to right. The first arm of the cross is worked over 8 threads; the second arm worked over the usual 4. Diagram (C1). shows the method of working the stitch; diagram (C2) shows 3 stitches completed.

### RICE STITCH

This consists of a basic cross with each of its corners crossed by a small straight stitch. The basic cross is usually worked over 4 by 4 threads, in a fairly thick yarn; a finer yarn, often in a contrasting colour, is used for the crossed corner stitches. Work the basic crosses first across area to be covered. Over the corners of each basic cross work small diagonal stitches at right angles over 2 threads each way of fabric or canvas, so that these small stitches also form a cross (D).

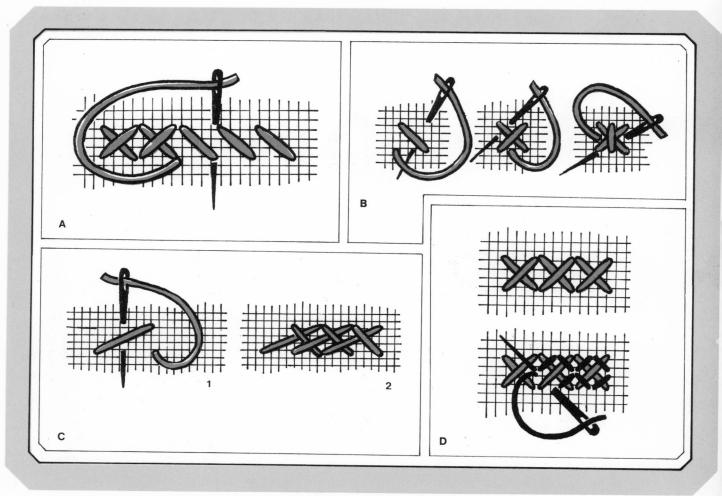

30

## STRAIGHT CROSS STITCH

This is worked over 2 by 2 threads, and consists of a straight vertical stitch crossed by a straight horizontal stitch. When working in rows, it is usual for stitches to be worked between stitches of the previous row, to give an interlocked appearance (A).

## DOUBLE STRAIGHT CROSS STITCH

Work a straight cross stitch, as described above, but over 4 by 4 threads. Over the centre of the straight cross, over 2 by 2 threads, work a basic cross stitch (B).

## LARGE AND STRAIGHT CROSS STITCH

This is another combination of basic cross and straight cross stitches. Work basic cross stitches over 4 by 4 threads alternately with straight cross stitches over 2 by 2 threads (C).

## OBLONG CROSS STITCH

This, as its name implies, is an elongated version of the basic cross stitch. It is worked over 4 horizontal and 2 vertical threads of fabric or canvas (D).

## YOUR CROSS STITCH MAKE—

# BIRDS AND TREE PICTURE

Our picture is worked on an evenweave linen, but the design may be embroidered equally successfully on canvas. If canvas is used, however, then the whole of the background area will have to be covered with stitching, as no canvas should ever show through a finished tapestry needlework design.

## MATERIALS YOU WILL NEED

Of Clark's Anchor Stranded Cotton (USA: J & P Coats Deluxe Six Strand Floss)—two skeins each Cyclamen 089, Laurel Green 0212, Parrot Green 0256, and Flame 0333, one skein each Rose Pink 053, Muscat Green 0279, Gorse Yellow 0303, Coffee 0380, and Ecru 0388; for canvas only: six skeins Cream 0386. ½ yd. cream evenweave embroidery linen, 21 threads to the inch, 59 in. wide; alternatively a single-thread tapestry canvas, 21 threads to the inch, may be used (if preferred, a coarser mesh canvas and tapisserie wool can be used, although this will give a larger finished design). Milward 'Gold Seal' tapestry needle No. 24. A picture frame with backing board, 9 in. by 14 in.

## TO MAKE

*Note: Use 3 strands of cotton throughout for fabric or canvas.*
Cut a piece from fabric or canvas 14 in. by 20 in. Mark the centre both ways with basting stitches. The design is worked throughout in cross stitch, each stitch worked over 2 by 2 threads of fabric or canvas.
The diagram overleaf gives the complete design, each square on the diagram representing 2 threads of fabric or canvas. The centres are marked by the blank arrows, and these should coincide with your basting stitches.
Begin embroidery centrally, and follow colour key as a guide to thread colours used in the different parts of the design. If working on fabric, then the background should be left unstitched so the cream-coloured linen becomes an integral part of the design.
If working on canvas, then fill in background area with cross stitches worked in cream thread. Extend background at sides, and at top and bottom, so total embroidered area measures approximately 8½ in. by 13½ in.

## TO COMPLETE

If using fabric, then press embroidery carefully on the wrong side. If using canvas, then stretch the canvas if necessary (see Tapestry Needlework, lesson two).
Place embroidery centrally over backing board. Secure on all sides with pins into edge of board. Secure at back by lacing from side to side, vertically and horizontally, with strong thread (for more detailed instructions for framing, see Picture Framing, lesson one). Remove pins and mount picture in frame.

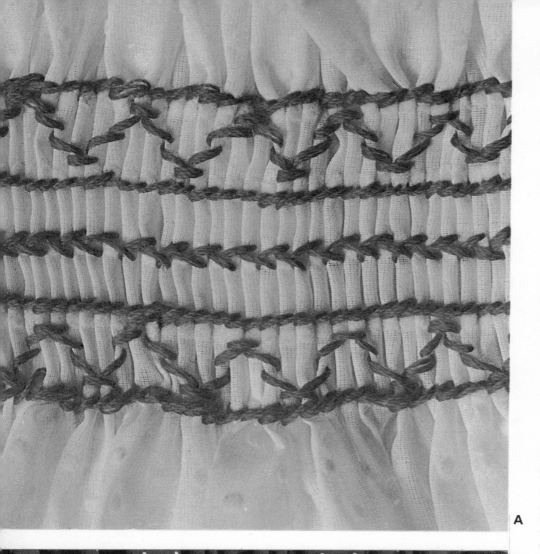

A

B

# SMOCKING

## Lesson One:
### Learning to draw up the work; some basic stitches

Traditionally smocking was a decorative needlework used on the centre front and sleeves of the 'smock'—the garment which is probably the only one which could be considered as the National Costume of Great Britain. Apart from the smocking, these garments would have symbolical embroidery on the collar, yoke and side of the smock to show the occupation of the wearer. Farmers would have symbols of the land, gardeners flowers and leaves, milkmaids churns and butter pats, shepherds crooks, hurdles and sheep and gravediggers' smocks were decorated with crosses!

The art of smocking became rather unfashionable—it was regarded as too rustic, not delicate nor elaborate enough for clothes of quality, until it began to reappear as an integral part of children's clothes—usually as smocked dresses and sundresses for little girls and smocked rompers and shirts for little boys. But suddenly smocking has become fashionable as a way of decorating dresses, lingerie, blouses, and it even appears on evening and party dresses.

Basically, smocking is 'a kind of needle-work used for holding gathers in place' as the dictionary says, but it is much more than that, properly done it is long-lasting as well as extremely decorative and it gives natural elasticity to the fabric which enables this to be made up very easily into garments of many types, shapes and sizes.

## How to smock

### PREPARING THE FABRIC

The smocking is worked with embroidery thread on the gathered fabric, and it is *absolutely essential* to prepare the fabric properly first. The gathers must be uniform, and are made in the ratio 2½:1, so allow 2½ in. of fabric for every 1 in. finished work. If you are working with plain fabric you need to apply a smocking transfer first. These are sold in different widths, depths and spaces between the dots. Make your choice according to the size the finished work is to be. Press the fabric first, tack the transfer in position on the *wrong* side of the fabric and iron off with a warm iron, or a cool one if the fabric is very delicate or synthetic (C), then remove the paper. Dotted or checked fabrics can be gathered without the use of a transfer, but they may have to be gathered on the right side of the fabric if the design is not printed through. Each individual dot *must* be picked up on the needle. Use a fine sewing needle and bright or contrasting coloured cotton, and as the running threads cannot be joined, each thread should be the width of the fabric. Knot at one end, then make a back stitch to prevent the knot from pulling through, and, working from right to left, put the needle in one side of every dot and bring it out the other, carry the thread to the next dot and continue to the end of the row, taking care you put the needle in each side of the dot and not through the middle (D). When all the lines have been threaded with running thread, pull up the work carefully to the required width (with very deep gathers pull up a few at a time) and tie the loose ends to prevent the gathers from slipping (E). Even out Although the gathers were made on the *wrong side* of the fabric, the smocking is worked on the *right side*.

## BASIC RULES

Every gather must be picked up in the needle if the work is to look good. Smocking stitches are usually worked from left to right with the exception of honeycomb smocking which is done from right to left. When working down, the thread must be *over* the needle. When working up, the thread is *below* the needle. For top level stitch, the thread is *above* the needle. For bottom level stitch the thread is *below* the needle (F).

Before starting to smock, plan the design carefully, a true sense of balance between the different types of stitches should be maintained. Avoid monotony, try to intersperse straight stitches with those which form a diamond pattern and do not overcrowd the work, leave a blank line here and there. Also plan for an attractive blending of colours which will tone or contrast with the fabric, such as red on white, autumn colours on cream, turquoise, white and lilac on purple (as our samples).

## FABRIC SUGGESTIONS

Almost any type of fabric can be smocked, but the lighter weight fabrics are the most successful, organdie, voile, lawn, fine cotton, poplin, silk, shantung and lingerie fabrics. Heavier weights can be smocked successfully such as linen, some fine wool fabrics, and what

C

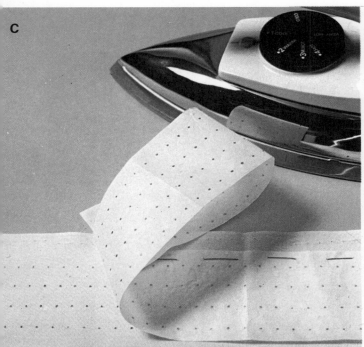

D

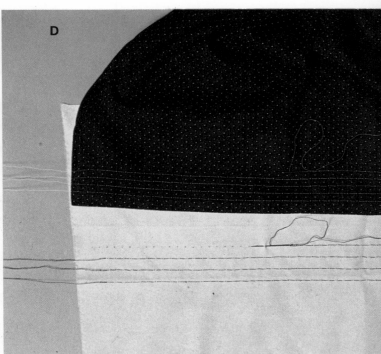

E

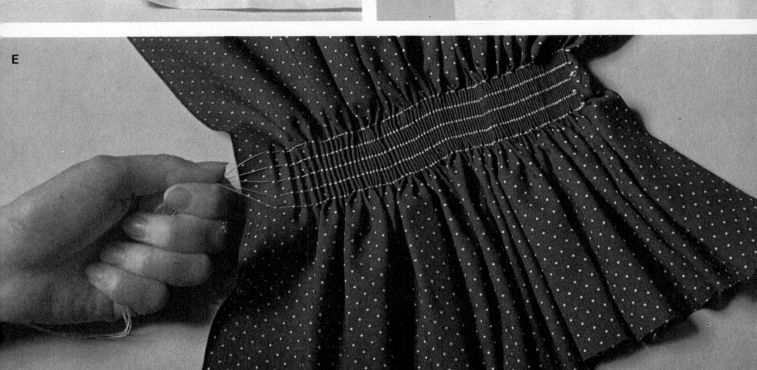

looks nicer than a Viyella smocked dress on a baby or a velvet party dress on a little girl? Avoid textured fabrics as they do not gather well.

## THREAD

Stranded embroidery cotton is the usual thread used for smocking and it is split to make a thinner strand depending on the weight of fabric used. Four strands are used for heavy fabric (wool, velvet etc.), 3 strands for normal fabrics and 2 strands for light fabric (voile, organdie and fine lingerie fabrics). Linen can be smocked with linen thread and silk and shantung with silk thread. It is not wise to use wool as this is too heavy and breaks too easily.

## OUR SMOCKING DESIGNS

You can experiment first and make a 'test' piece, or use these designs on blouse, shirt or dress. Remember the

basic rules. Every pleat *must* be picked up in the needle. Work from left to right and secure the thread on the back of the first gather with a knot and firm backstitch before bringing the needle through to the right side and starting the first stitch on the first pleat. When working down, thread must be over the needle, when working up the thread is below the needle. Do not pull work up too tightly.

## RED AND WHITE SMOCKING (A)

This uses only 3 basic stitches, yet the finished work looks far more complicated.

**First row—outline stitch**
Keep the needle level with gathering thread at all times, and with embroidery thread below needle, pick up the top of every single pleat.

**Second row—quarter wave stitch**
This is worked upwards. Start with a level stitch, thread *below* needle, take the second stitch on the next pleat quarterway, third stitch at half-way or dot row, finish with top level stitch with thread *above* needle. Now work down to form other side of triangle with thread *above* the needle, use the same spacing as going up and finish with bottom level stitch.

**Third row—outline stitch**
**Fourth row—cable stitch**
Work as outline stitch, but keep embroidery thread alternately *above* and *below* the needle, keeping the needle level with the gathering line.

**Fifth row—outline stitch**
**Sixth row—quarter wave stitch**
**Seventh row—outline stitch**

## PURPLE, LILAC AND TURQUOISE SMOCKING (B)

This uses only 4 basic stitches, but the combination of colours adds variety and makes a much more interesting design.

**First row—outline stitch**
**Second row—cable stitch**
**Third row—outline stitch**
**Fourth and fifth rows—baby diamond stitch**
This is made from two rows of baby wave stitch. Start half-way between rows with level stitch, with the thread *below* the needle, but pick up 2 pleats in the needle. The second stitch is taken on next pleat on the dot row with thread *below* the needle, then make top level stitch with thread *above* the needle. Keep the thread *above* the needle and go back down to half-way for fourth stitch. This completes a unit. Start again, picking up two pleats on level stitch and continue as before. Work the lower row so the top level stitch of bottom row meets the bottom level stitch of the top row, again picking up 2 pleats in the needle.

**Sixth row—outline stitch**
**Seventh row—cable stitch**
**Eighth row—outline stitch**

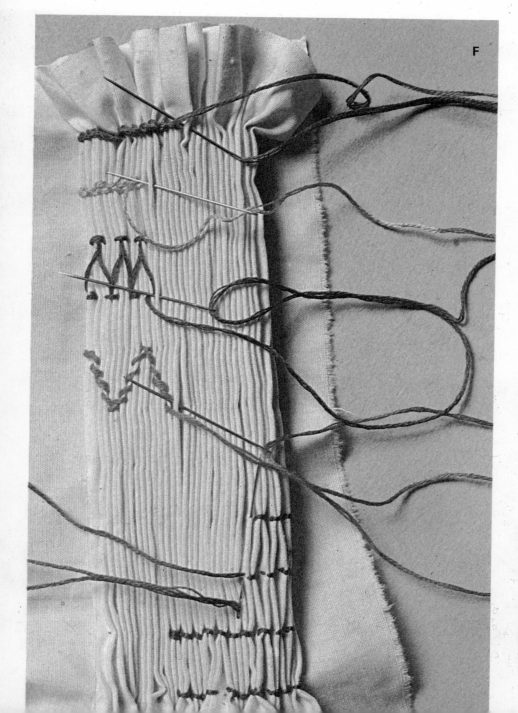

| AGE | ROWS | SKEINS STRANDED COTTON |
|---|---|---|
| 1–2 years | 11–13 | 4–5 skeins |
| 3 years | 13–15 | 6 skeins |
| 4 years | 17–21 | 8 skeins |
| 5 years | 23–25 | 9 skeins |
| 6 years | 26–27 | 10 skeins |
| 7–8 years | 29–31 | 12 skeins |
| 9–10 years | 31–33 | 14 skeins |

CHILDREN'S SMOCKED DRESSES—GUIDE TO QUANTITIES

# SMOCKING

## Lesson Two:

### More basic smocking stitches, honeycomb smocking, and a sundress to make for a little girl

In Smocking, lesson one, on previous pages, we showed how to draw up the work in preparation for smocking and how to work the first basic stitches. The instructions on drawing up the work are repeated in the instructions for making the sundress, and to recap here are the basic rules to remember when smocking:

1. Draw up the work so gathers are uniform in the ratio $2\frac{1}{2}:1$.
2. Every gather must be picked up in needle when smocking.
3. Smocking stitches are usually worked from left to right, except honeycomb smocking which is covered in this lesson.
4. When working up, the thread is *below* the needle.
5. For top level stitch, the thread is *above* the needle.
6. For the bottom level stitch the thread is *below* the needle.

## Honeycomb smocking

This type of smocking is used where the gathers need to be held together but no design is required, as the thread shows only where the stitches are taken. Traditionally, it should be worked with embroidery thread just as shade lighter or darker than the material. As this would not have shown up very well in the photograph we used apricot on cream, but there is no reason why you

*A pretty sundress for a little girl—instructions start overleaf*

should not use a contrasting colour, or if a patterned fabric is being honey-combed, choose one of the colours in the material and match to this. Only a small stitch on the surface is seen, and in order to make a really deep honeycomb the pleats are heavier and deeper than regular smocking.

Gather up the work as lesson one. Working from right to left (unlike other smocking which is worked from left to right), start in the first pleat. Take a stitch through the top of the *second* and *first* pleats together, catch them together with a second stitch, this time bring the needle down at the back of the *second* pleat to the second row of gathering, missing out the first pleat on the right-hand edge. Catch together the *second* and *third* pleats with a stitch, then make a second stitch over the top. Take the needle back under work to the first gathering thread. Catch together the *third* and *fourth* pleats with two stitches, take the needle down at the back to the second row of gathering threads and catch together the *fourth* and *fifth* pleat. Continue this way, up and down, until the row is complete. Now work from right to left again on the second and third rows of gathering and so on until the smocking is as deep as required (see diagram 1). The thread, as in all smocking is *above* the needle for top level stitch and *below* the needle for bottom level stitch. Honeycomb can be worked from top to bottom, but most people find it easier to work from the bottom upwards.

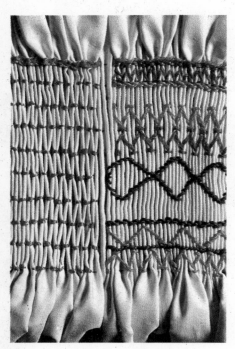

## Our sample

The left hand side is honeycomb stitch as described above, with a row of chain stitch at the top. To work a row of chain stitch, work from left to right (it may be easier to turn the work so you actually work from top to bottom)

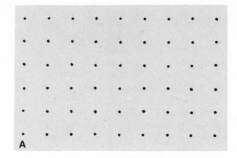

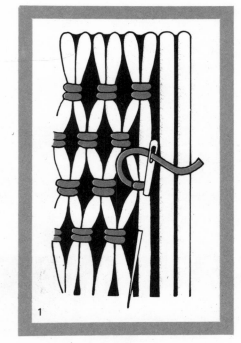

and work as for chain stitch in embroidery, picking up each pleat in the needle (for chain stitch see lesson one Embroidery). Do not pull the work too tight or the gathers will not be elastic enough.

The right hand side of the sample is a combination of simple and slightly more advanced stitches. All are worked from left to right.

### First row—outline stitch
Keep the needle level with gathering thread at all times, and with embroidery thread *below* the needle, pick up the top of every single pleat.

### Second row—turret stitch
This is one of the oldest smocking stitches known and is usually worked between two rows of cable stitch, but it is equally pretty on its own.
Start on the lower row of dots, bring the needle up from wrong to right side of the material on the first pleat and take over to the second pleat with a level stitch. The thread is taken up on this same pleat (second) to top row of dots, to do another level stitch over to a third pleat. Repeat up and down and level stitches to end of pattern.

### Third row—cable stitch
Work as outline stitch, but keep embroidery thread alternately *above* and *below* the needle, keeping the needle level with the gathering line.

### Fourth and Fifth rows—baby diamond stitch
This is made from two rows of baby

wave stitch. Start half-way between rows with a level stitch, with the thread *below* the needle, but pick up 2 pleats in the needle. The second stitch is taken on next pleat on the dot row with the thread *below* the needle, then make a top level stitch with the thread *above* the needle. Keep the thread *above* the needle and go back down to half-way for fourth stitch.
This completes a unit. Start again, picking up two pleats on level stitch and continue as before, working the lower row so that the top level of the bottom row meets the bottom level stitch of the top row, again picking up 2 pleats in the needle.

### Sixth row—link stitch
Link is made up of cable stitches, each one above the other on consecutive pleats to form a diamond pattern. To work, take a regular first level stitch, thread *below* needle, take the second stitch on the next pleat, third stitch on the next pleat slightly higher up and the fourth stitch on the next pleat on the dot row, thread at all times *below* the needle, finish with a top level stitch with thread *above* the needle. Work down, keeping the thread *above* the needle, using the same spacing as going up, finishing with a bottom level stitch, repeat across work, then to complete the diamond, work the second row so the top level stitch of the second row meets the bottom level stitch of the previous row.

### Seventh row—cable stitch
### Eighth row—quarter wave
This is worked as link stitch, to form a triangle instead of a diamond and usually only three stitches are made between the bottom and top level stitch.

### Ninth row—outline stitch
### Tenth row—baby wave stitch
Work as half baby diamond stitch (fourth and fifth rows).

**YOUR FIRST MAKE—**

# A SUNDRESS FOR A LITTLE GIRL

Our dress was made to fit a 5-year-old, but the instructions can be altered to fit any size. As with all smocked designs, the main fabric pieces are cut and smocked first before the work is made up.

## MATERIALS YOU WILL NEED

$1\frac{1}{8}$ yd. 36-in. wide fabric (we used fine blue lawn); 1 reel sewing thread to match fabric; Clark's Anchor Stranded embroidery cotton—2 skeins Kingfisher 0163 (split and use 3 strands throughout); Milward 'Gold Seal' crewel needle No. 7 for smocking;

bias binding to match dress fabric (optional).

## TO MAKE

Cut two pieces from the fabric 21 in. by 36 in. (with the short side to the selvedge) for the dress, and cut 4 pieces 12 in. by 1½ in. for the shoulder ties. Cut curves for armholes by cutting out semicircles at the upper corners of the two large pieces of fabric about 3 in. in depth and 2 in. in width. Leave edges raw for the time being. Make a small hem along the top edge of the fabric, either by hand or machine. Trace the section of the full-size drawing of the smocking dots (A) on to the *wrong* side of the fabric, 1 in. down from the top edge, and ¾ in. in from the armhole. Repeat this section as required across the fabric to within ¾ in. of the other armhole. If preferred an iron-on smocking transfer in the same scale can be used, also ironed on to the *wrong* side of the fabric. Repeat on the second piece of fabric. Working on the *wrong* side of the fabric, gather up the rows of dots as explained in Smocking lesson one, and as shown in diagram B, taking care to pick up every dot, and starting each row with a knot and a small back stitch to secure the thread. Use a separate thread for each line, long enough to gather right across the width, as knots must not be made across the work. Leave a loose thread at the end of each row.

Draw up the lines of stitching, easing gently to form pleats, but do not pull too tightly as the pleats must be flexible—our finished smocked area measures 7½ in. wide by 1½ in. deep. Tie the loose ends firmly in pairs close to the last pleat.

*Note:* When working smocking stitches do not pull too tightly as the finished work must have elasticity. Now work the smoking on the *right* side of the fabric. Diagram C gives a section of the smocking which is repeated across the fabric; the dotted lines at the left-hand side indicate the rows of gathers and show the placing of stitches in relation to rows; the broken lines between the stitches indicate the pleats.

**The first row** is cable stitch, as diagram D.

**The second and third rows** are double chevron stitch, as diagram E.

**The fourth row** is wave stitch as diagram F.

## TO WORK CABLE STITCH

Secure the thread at the left-hand side and bring the needle through to the left of first pleat on lower line; take a stitch through second pleat with the thread *above* the needle; take a stitch through the third pleat with the thread *below* the needle, continue to end of row 1. Lower section of diagram D shows two rows of cable stitch worked together as one row, which we used on our dress.

## TO WORK CHEVRON STITCH

Secure the thread at the left-hand side and bring the needle through to the left of the first pleat on the lower line. Draw the needle horizontally through the second pleat with the thread *below*, insert the needle horizontally through third pleat on upper line. With the thread *above*, insert the needle horizontally through the fourth pleat on upper line; with the thread *above* insert the needle through fifth pleat on lower line; continue to end of row.

*Note:* This stitch is also known as baby wave, double rows are worked as diagram C.

## TO WORK WAVE STITCH

Secure the thread at the left-hand side and bring the needle through to the left of the first pleat on the upper line, take a stitch through second pleat, on same level, with thread *above* the needle; take a stitch on the third pleat slightly lower, with the thread still *above* the needle. Insert the needle horizontally through fourth and fifth pleats, finishing the last stitch with the thread *below* the needle. This completes the downward slope. On the upward slope, work in the same way, with the thread *above* the needle, making each stitch level with the corresponding one on the downward slope.

When you have worked both pieces of smocking, lay them on an ironing board and place a damp cloth over the embroidery and pass a hot iron lightly over it.

*Note:* Smocking should *never* be pressed firmly or ironed as the pleats flatten and the whole purpose of the work is ruined.

Make up the dress by removing all gathering threads. Join the side seams with a French seam (see Sewing, lesson three); face the armholes using the small remnants of fabric cut off, or use matching bias binding. Turn up the hem and slipstitch. Press the hem and seams and armhole taking care not to flatten the smocking. Fold ties in half lengthwise, machine stitch the long side and one short side ½ in. from edge, trim seams and turn to right side. Turn in raw edges and slipstitch, then press. Attach ties to dress at shoulders.

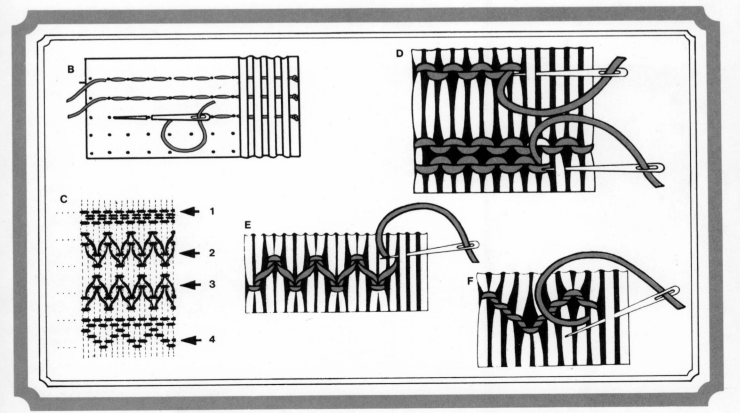

# SMOCKING

## Lesson Three:

## Tips on technique

**SOME MORE DIFFICULT STITCHES AND A SMOCKED NIGHTDRESS TO MAKE**

If you have followed lessons one and two you will already be familiar with the basic techniques of drawing up the work and working the various smocking stitches. In this lesson we show you how to work some slightly more difficult stitches but first of all here are some tips on technique.

The tension of smocking stitches will vary with each individual, and generally the finished smocking will be less wide than the prepared and pulled-up gathers. Do not pull the smocking stitches too tightly when working the design, otherwise you will gradually close up the pleats. This is why we have suggested trying basic samples, like ours, before you actually start working on a dress, nightdress or whatever. The tendency is usually to work too tightly so remember this when smocking and say to yourself 'elasticity'! If you do pull the work up too tightly, all may not be lost! You may be able to remedy the fault by steaming the smocking and then gently stretching it with your hands. However, if it definitely is too tight, keep the work for something else—it may be suitable for a child's garment or as one front half of a blouse, or a cuff to an attractively full sleeve. When smocking, always cut the

material so the selvedges are at the side and *never* at top and bottom—in other words the pleats run the length of the fabric. If you are working with fabric which frays easily (like our nightdress), machine stitch, or whip over by hand, all the raw edges to prevent them from becoming hopelessly unravelled—these fraying threads really would become a nuisance, tangling with the drawing-up and embroidery threads. When smocking the back of a dress, start your design at the centre back, that is on one side of the placket allowance, and work to the armhole and underarm. Then to have a perfect match, reverse the work and start the other side of the centre back and work to the opposite armhole and underarm. If you have a large motif in your smocking design, be sure that it is centred in the middle of the dress. To do this, count the pleats to get the exact centre, run a piece of coloured thread down the middle of the work, then start the motif from the centre and work towards the outside. Reverse the work to do the other half, and continue the design to the opposite edge. Once the large main motif is established, carry on in the usual way, working from side to side. Once you have smocked a garment, and it has been worn and washed, remember that smocking (washed or not) should *never* be ironed. While the garment is still damp pull the gathers firmly back into place, and if possible dry flat so the weight of water does not pull the work out of shape. If smocking does become a little over-stretched and shapeless with constant wear and washing it is possible to restore the shape by whipping the back of the pleats with two or three rows of fine Latex thread at a tension suitable to restore the elasticity.

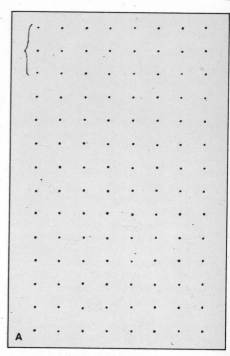

A

### YOUR SECOND MAKE

# A SMOCKED NIGHTDRESS

This pattern can be easily adjusted to fit any size. We used a turquoise nylon lingerie fabric, smocked in cerise and white, but you can choose any suitable fine fabric and the smocking can tone or contrast with the material.

### MATERIALS YOU WILL NEED

2⅝yd. 36-in. wide fine fabric (muslin, voile, lawn, chiffon, nylon, etc.); 1 reel sewing thread to match fabric; Clark's Anchor Stranded embroidery cotton—1 skein Cerise 035 and White 0402 (split and use 3 strands throughout); 1 Milwards 'Gold Seal' crewel needle No. 7 for smocking; bias binding to match fabric (optional).

### TO MAKE

Cut the following pieces from the fabric: One piece 47 in. by 36 in. for front, one piece 47 in. by 30 in. for back. Two pieces 1½ in. by 24½ in. for ties, two pieces 1½ in. by 15½ in. for shoulder straps. If the material is likely to fray whip raw edges (see lesson).
Trace the given section of smocking dots (A) on to the *wrong* side of the larger pieces of fabric ½ in. from left-hand edge and 6 in. down from the top. Repeat this across the width of the fabric to within ½ in. of the right-hand edge. Trace section within brackets only in same way, ½ in. from the top edge of the fabric. Gather up the rows of dots (B) as described fully in lesson one. Draw up the rows of stitches, easing gently to form pleats. Do not pull up too tightly, and tie loose ends firmly in pairs close to the last pleat. *Note:* When working smocking stitches do not pull too tightly as the finished

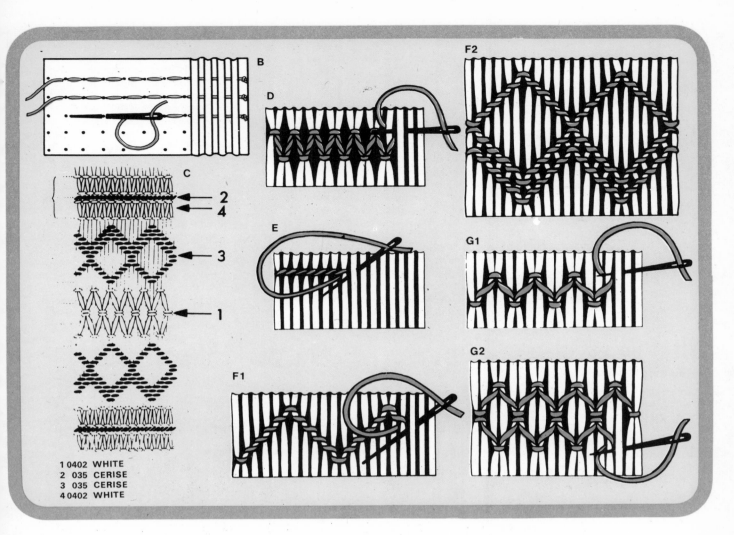

1 0402 WHITE
2 035 CERISE
3 035 CERISE
4 0402 WHITE

work must have elasticity (see lesson one), and work stitches on the *right* side of the fabric.

The diagram (C) gives a section of the design which is repeated across the fabric—the dotted lines on the left-hand side of the diagram indicate the rows of gathers and show the placing of stitches in relation to rows. The broken lines between the stitches indicate the pleats. The section within the brackets is repeated along the top edge of the work. 1 is worked in white, 2 and 3 in cerise and 4 in white.

**The first row** is chevron stitch as *diagram D*.
**The second row** is outline stitch as *diagram E*.
**The third row** is chevron stitch.
**The fourth and fifth rows** are wave stitch as *diagram F*.
**The sixth and seventh rows** are honeycomb stitch as *diagram G*.
**The eighth and ninth rows** are wave stitch.
**The tenth row** is chevron stitch.
**The eleventh row** is outline stitch.
**The twelfth row** is chevron stitch.

## TO WORK
## CHEVRON STITCH

Bring the needle through to the left of first pleat on upper level. Draw the needle horizontally through the second pleat with thread *above* needle; with thread still *above*, insert needle

horizontally through the same pleat on lower line; with thread *below*, insert needle horizontally through third pleat and still with thread *below*, insert needle through same pleat on top line. Continue in this way.

## TO WORK
## OUTLINE STITCH

Secure thread at left-hand side and bring the needle through to the left of first pleat; pick up the top of next pleat, inserting the needle with a slight slope and having the thread *above* the needle. Continue in this way.

## TO WORK
## WAVE STITCH

Secure thread at left-hand side and take a stitch through second pleat on the same level with thread *below* the needle; take a stitch in third, fourth and fifth pleats, each slightly higher than previous stitch and having thread *below* needle in each case; insert the needle horizontally through the sixth pleat, thread *above* needle. This completes the upward slope. On downward slope, work each stitch to correspond with upward slope, but with the thread *above* the needle in each case (F1). F2 shows the second row worked in the reverse direction and also a third row worked closely under the second row.

## TO WORK
## HONEYCOMB STITCH

Secure the thread at left-hand side and bring the needle through to the left of first pleat on lower line; draw the needle horizontally through the second pleat with the thread *below* needle; with the thread still *below*, insert the needle horizontally through third pleat on upper line; with thread *above*, insert the needle horizontally through the fourth pleat on upper line; with the thread *above*, insert the needle through fifth pleat on lower line. Continue to end of row (G1). G2 shows a second row worked in reverse below first row. When the smocking has been completed, lay on an ironing board, wrong side up, place a damp cloth over the smocking and pass a warm to hot iron (depending on the fabric) *lightly* over it, *but do not press*. Remove all the gathering threads. Make up $\frac{1}{2}$-in. ties, turn right side out and press. Join front to back of nightdress down sides, using a french seam and inserting the ties at the waist. Gather the top back edge to fit individual requirements and bind all round the top with a bias strip cut from the remaining fabric or with bias binding. Make up the straps, turn right side out and press, and sew to top edge. Press side seams. Try on nightdress and mark and turn up hem by hand.

# SEWING

## Lesson One:
## Making your own pattern

Each lesson of your sewing course includes a garment to make, and the pattern for each of these garments is given in the form of a miniature pattern on a squared grid. From this miniature diagram, it is an easy matter for you to prepare your full-size paper pattern. Our step-by-step instructions and diagrams show you exactly how to do this.

## What you will need

### For making a pattern . . .

Suitable paper—large sheets of fairly stiff paper which ideally should be ready marked out in 1-in. squares. You can buy rolls of graph paper marked out in 1-in. squares from most art material shops. Alternatively use plain strong white paper (cartridge paper is excellent and this is usually available, also from art material shops, in extra wide and long rolls). Ordinary brown wrapping paper can be used if wished. If you cannot find big enough sheets of paper then use transparent self-adhesive tape to join several sheets together to give the required length and width.
A yardstick is essential for drawing straight lines, and if you use plain or brown paper for ruling out into 1-in. squares.
Pencil and rubber—choose a medium pencil, neither too soft nor too hard.
Tracing or greaseproof paper—for tracing off facings.
A suitable working surface—this should be a clean, hard, flat surface, big enough for you to spread out your paper. A long kitchen table or a decorator's pasting table is ideal. Alternatively, if you do not have a suitable table, then you can work on the floor, provided it is hard-surfaced (not carpeted). If necessary, cover the area first with a sheet of clean paper so your pattern stays clean and dustfree.

### For cutting-out . . .

A sharp pair of scissors.
Pins—good-quality steel ones are best.
For transferring marks—tailor's chalk, or dressmaker's tracing wheel and carbon paper, depending on method chosen.

### For sewing . . .

Basting thread to contrast with fabric.
Sewing thread to match fabric.
Needles.
Tape measure.

## Making your pattern step by step

1. If you are using plain or brown paper, your first step will be to mark out the total area of your paper into squares. Check the pattern you are using. Normally diagram patterns are given on a 1-in. grid (i.e. each square on the miniature diagram represents 1 in.), in which case mark out the entire area of your paper into 1-in. squares (A). Sometimes however a pattern will be given on a 2-in. grid. In this case, mark out your paper into 2-in. squares. If you are using paper already printed with 1-in. squares, mark it into 2-in. squares by drawing over the appropriate lines.
2. Next check the size of the pattern as given against your own measurements. If the pattern is for, say, a bust size 34 in. and hip size 36in., and you are bust size 36in., hip size 38in., then an extra ½in. will have to be added to all side

edges (B) (½in. added to each side edge of front of garment, and ½in. to each side edge of back adds up to a total of 2in. extra). On the other hand, if you are a size smaller than the measurements given, then you will have to deduct the appropriate amount from the side edges. Mark the new cutting lines to suit your size on the miniature pattern. If further fitting adjustments are necessary, follow instructions in lesson two for adapting a pattern to fit.
3. Now copy the pattern as given on the miniature diagram on to your full-size squared grid, remembering that each of the squares on the small diagram represents one square on your grid. Follow the outlines and positions of curves, angles and lines in relation to the squares as closely as possible (C).
4. If there are shaded areas marked on the pattern sections, these usually represent the facings of neckline, armholes and front edges. When you are satisfied your outlines are accurate, mark in the shaded areas to your diagram (D).

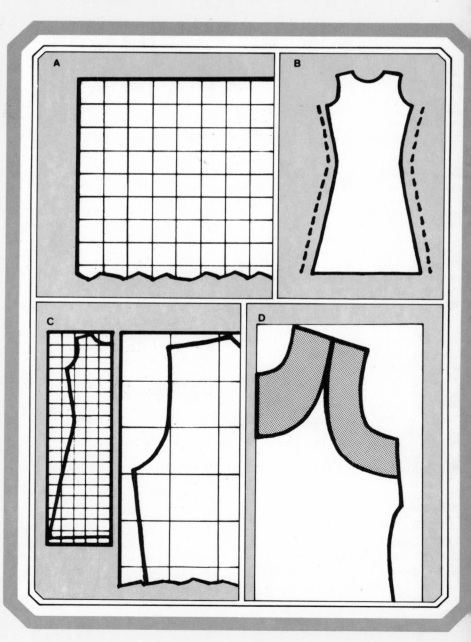

5. Place tracing or greaseproof paper over the facings as marked on your diagram, and trace off these sections (E).
6. Write the appropriate names on your pattern pieces, including the traced facings, e.g. Back, Front, Sleeve and so on, and transfer any other markings as indicated on the small diagram. For instance, dart markings (usually indicated by dotted or broken lines). centre front and centre back edges, and any notches (F). It is important when cutting out your fabric that the pattern pieces are placed straight on the lengthwise grain of the fabric—usually this grain line is indicated on a pattern by a lengthwise arrow, showing the direction in which the pattern piece should be placed on the fabric. Mark this arrow on your pattern pieces.
7. Cut out your pattern and facing pieces. You are now ready to cut out your fabric.

## Preparing and cutting out

1. Before you begin to cut out from your fabric, it is essential to check that the fabric is straight. Sometimes if a length of fabric has been cut unevenly from the roll, this crooked line can mislead you into placing your pattern pieces at an angle, and not on the true straight grain of the fabric. It is best therefore to straighten the cut edge before beginning work. This can be done by any of the following methods, depending on the fabric being used:
**a.** If the fabric has a prominent rib or woven pattern or check, merely cut along a thread in the design.
**b.** Loosely-woven fabrics can have a crosswise thread drawn out—clip into one firm side edge of the fabric (known as the selvedge) with scissors and pick out one or two crosswise threads with a pin. Continue working across the fabric, pulling and cutting and following the course of the threads you started with, until you reach the opposite selvedge. Cut along this line.
**c.** Some fine and medium weight fabrics can merely be torn across their width to straighten. Check first on a corner of the fabric to see if it will tear easily. If it will, clip into one selvedge of the fabric, about an inch up from the cut edge, then quickly and firmly tear fabric right across as far as other selvedge. You will need to cut through the selvedge as before, as normally this will not tear easily.
**d.** On pile or napped fabrics, threads can be unravelled until one thread can be drawn off across the entire width, then trim away the uneven fringed edge.
2. If fabric is creased press it before you pin pattern pieces in place. If you are using a fabric which you think might shrink, preshrink it by pressing it with a moderate iron over a damp cloth. Allow to dry.
3. Check against the cutting-out layout given for your pattern. Normally pattern pieces are cut from double thickness fabric, and the fabric as a rule is folded in half on the lengthwise grain with the selvedges meeting, and right sides of fabric facing. Sometimes however it is necessary to fold fabric crosswise. Fold fabric as indicated by the cutting-out layout you are using, and as a further aid to keeping fabric straight, pin the selvedges together all the way down (G).
4. Place your pattern pieces on folded fabric, positioning them as indicated on cutting-out layout. Pin them firmly and evenly in position, taking care not to pucker them or pull them out of shape. They should be perfectly flat. If you are using leather, or a heavy fabric which will not take pins then anchor pattern pieces in position with weights, and mark round the outline of the pieces with tailor's chalk. Sometimes a cutting-out layout will indicate that certain pattern pieces should be placed on the folded edge of the fabric, to avoid a seam at this point
Place the pattern piece carefully along the fold being sure to line up the edge of the pattern and the fold exactly. Pin in place along fold, then pin round remaining edges of pattern piece (H).
5. Cut out, cutting with long strokes of the scissors. Never use pinking shears for cutting out as they give an unreliable line.
6. After cutting do not remove the pattern pieces immediately. The next step is to transfer the markings on the pattern pieces to the fabric itself. This includes all markings except the grain line (which is only a cutting-out guide). The markings should be made on the wrong side of the fabric and there are several methods to choose from:
**a.** Tracing wheel and dressmaker's tracing paper—this method is good for firm, smooth fabrics, but not tweeds, laces or sheers. Dressmaker's carbon paper is available in a good range of colours—choose a shade lighter or darker than your fabric colour. Place carbon between fabric and pattern and then 'draw' tracing wheel over all the pattern lines, rolling wheel away from you (J). Put a sheet of cardboard under fabric to protect your working surface. With lightweight and sheer fabrics, you can use the wheel on its own without any carbon paper—the little teeth on the wheel will leave visible marks.

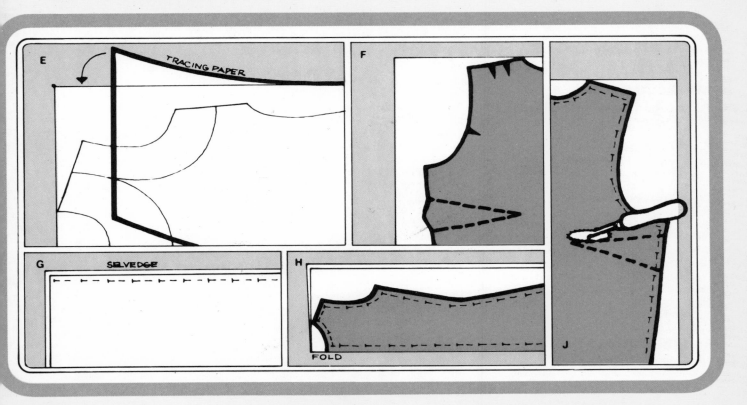

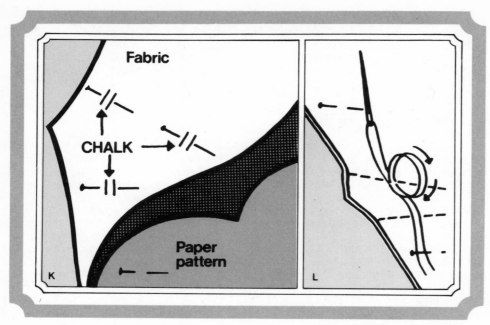

b. Pinning—marking by pinning is fairly quick, but pins are inclined to drop out so this is not such a reliable method as some of the others. Insert pins through markings on pattern vertically until they come out of fabric on the other side. Mark that point with another pin. After placing all the pins, pull the two sides of fabric apart, and carefully repin on each piece, picking up a thread

or two of fabric so pin lies flat.

c. Chalking—this too is a quick method, and the chalk marks are easy to remove afterwards, but on some fabrics the marks do not show up very clearly. Pin on markings through pattern and fabric, then carefully take pattern piece away from pins, easing it over the heads and points of each pin so you do not tear the pieces too much. Mark with tailor's

chalk at point which has been pinned on both sides of fabric (K). When pins are removed you will have tiny chalked markings. For a dart or similar marking involving a row of chalk markings, join these markings together to give a continuous line.

d. Tailor's tacks—this is the slowest method, but an accurate one for all fabric types. Thread a needle with a long double thread of tacking or darning cotton. Do not knot the end. At each marking take a small stitch through the pattern and both fabric layers, leaving thread end 1in. long. Take a 2nd stitch over the first, leaving a long loop (L). Cut thread leaving a 1-in. end. Cut through the top of the loop. When you remove the pattern pieces, do so very carefully so as not to pull out the threads. Separate the fabric layers, clip the threads between to leave thread tufts on both layers.

7. When all marks have been transferred to the fabric, unpin pattern pieces, taking care not to tear them. Fold them carefully, and place them in a polythene bag or other suitable container so the pattern can be used again when required.

8. Pin fabric pieces together, pinning darts in place where marked, and try on to see if any further minor adjustments to the fit are necessary. If all is well, then you can proceed with the sewing.

## YOUR FIRST MAKE—

# A TWO-WAY DRESS

From the same basic pattern, you can make a useful pinafore dress for everyday wear, and an elegant long dress for parties and special occasions.

## MATERIALS

**For pinafore dress:** 1¾yd. of fabric, 54in. wide, or 2½yd. of fabric, 36in. wide.
**For long dress:** 3½yd. of fabric, 36in. wide, or 3yd. of fabric, 45in. wide.
**For both dresses:** matching thread; a 22-in. zip fastener; a hook and eye.
**For belts:** bought belts may be used, or if it is wished to make belts, a 2-in. buckle will be required for pinafore dress. For long dress belt, a length of ready-beaded trimming (from a haberdashery store or department), 2in. wide, and equal to your waist measurement plus 1in. will be required, also a strip of lining material 1in. bigger all round than the beaded strip, and 3 hooks and eyes.

## FABRIC SUGGESTIONS

**For long dress:** printed cotton, wool tweed, any lightweight woven fabric, corduroy.

**For long dresses:** printed cotton, satin, brocade, Tricel jersey, Tricel surah, cotton jersey, silk.

## SIZE NOTE

The pattern as given will comfortably fit bust size 34in., hip size 36in. To adapt pattern to fit your size, follow instructions as given in Step 2.

## TO MAKE YOUR PATTERN

The diagram overleaf gives the pattern pieces you will need. One square on the diagram equals 1in. Following our step-by-step instructions, prepare your full-size pattern on squared paper. To make pinafore dress, follow hemline as marked on pattern; for long dress, use full length of pattern. Armhole facings and back neckline are the same for both versions of the dress, but the front neckline and its facing are different. Follow appropriate line for the style you are making. Transfer dart markings (bust and back shoulder), straight grain indication and notch marked A on centre back edge to your pattern pieces.

## TO MAKE DRESS

Cut out fabric pieces, following cutting-out layout overleaf and the step-by-step instruction. Centre front of dress front and of front neck facing should be placed on fold of fabric. If you are making a belt from the same fabric then the belt section should be cut from single thickness of

fabric as shown.
Unless otherwise stated, all seams are stitched ⅝in. from the edge of fabric (this is referred to as a ⅝-in. turning, or as a ⅝-in. seam allowance).

1. Stitch one bust dart: crease along the centre line of marking, right sides of fabric facing. Fold dart to bring outside lines together. Begin pinning at point of the dart, pinning with heads of pins towards fold of dart. Baste in place, then stitch either by machine or hand from the wide end of the dart to the point. At the point, make the last stitches right on the fold. Clip thread ends to about 2in. long and tie in a neat knot. Press dart down. Stitch other bust dart in a similar way.

2. Stitch one shoulder dart: bring the marked lines together, right sides of fabric facing. Pin, tack then stitch along this line. Press dart towards centre back. In a similar way stitch other shoulder dart.

3. Place centre back sections together, right sides facing, and stitch centre back seam from notch A to lower edge. If your machine does not have a seam guide on it, before stitching any long straight seam, pin edges carefully together, then with a ruler and chalk pencil mark the ⅝-in. seam allowance all the way down. Stitch along this line.

4. Press seam open, using a steam iron or a moderate iron over a damp cloth. I

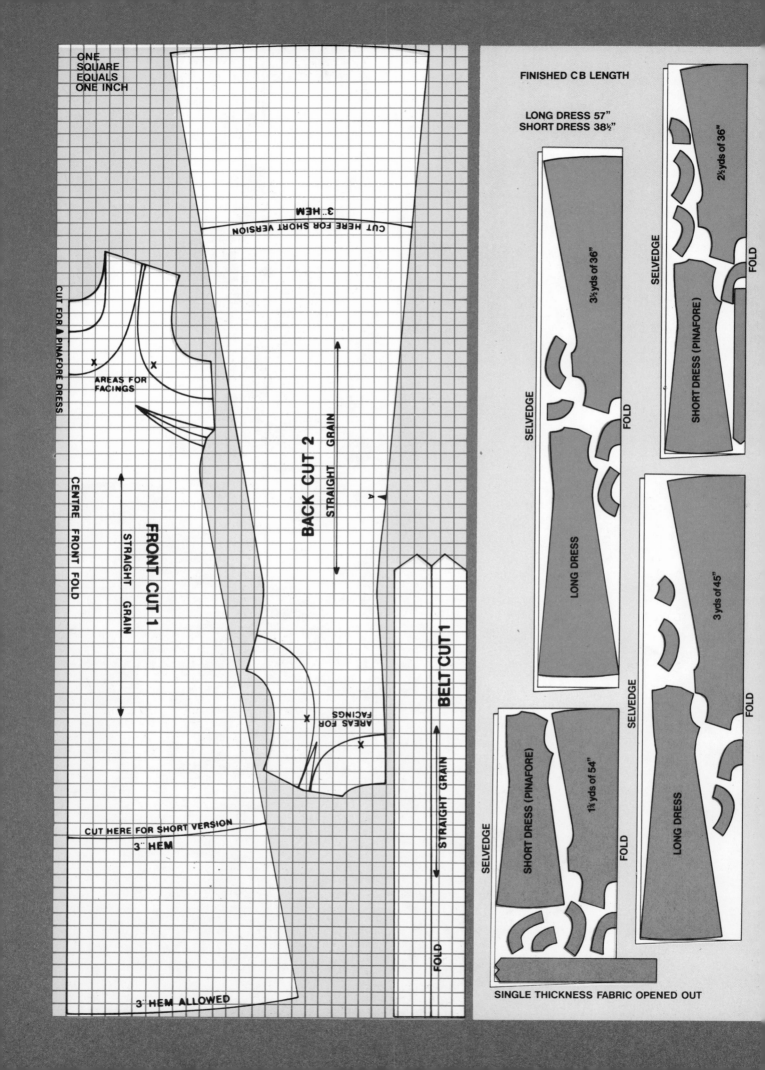

ONE
SQUARE
EQUALS
ONE INCH

CUT FOR A PINAFORE DRESS

AREAS FOR FACINGS

X          X

CENTRE FRONT FOLD

FRONT CUT 1

STRAIGHT GRAIN

CUT HERE FOR SHORT VERSION

3" HEM

3" HEM ALLOWED

BACK CUT 2

STRAIGHT GRAIN

CUT HERE FOR SHORT VERSION

3" HEM

AREAS FOR FACINGS

X

X

BELT CUT 1

STRAIGHT GRAIN

FOLD

FINISHED CB LENGTH

LONG DRESS 57"
SHORT DRESS 38½"

SELVEDGE

3½ yds of 36"

FOLD

LONG DRESS

2½ yds of 36"

SELVEDGE

SHORT DRESS (PINAFORE)

FOLD

SELVEDGE

3 yds of 45"

LONG DRESS

FOLD

SELVEDGE

SHORT DRESS (PINAFORE)

1⅜ yds of 54"

FOLD

SINGLE THICKNESS FABRIC OPENED OUT

is important to press seams carefully as you go along.

5. Baste remainder of centre back seam together above notch A. Insert zip into this part of the seam. The zip can be machine-stitched in if your machine has a zipper foot, or if preferred, for a neat, couture finish, it can be sewn in by hand. Press basted seam open, then remove basting thread. Place closed zip under the back opening so right side of zip is against pressed seam allowance, and the tab end of zip is ½in. below neckline edge. Working on right side of fabric, pin fabric to zip tape down one side, so edge of fabric fold is at centre of zipper teeth. Pin down other side easing edge of fold up to meet edge of first fold at zip centre. Now baste, taking basting down one side, across lower end of zip, and up the other side, keeping stitches about ¼in. from centre opening. Stitch zip in place. Use a single strand of regular or heavy duty thread, silk or buttonhole twist, and begin sewing at bottom end of zip opening, securing end of thread on underside. Bring needle up through all thicknesses, just inside the seamline. Make tiny backstitches, picking up only a thread or two of the fabric at a time, and spacing stitches equally. Remove basting. Press. For reinforcement, machine-stitch zipper tape only to the seam allowance on inside.

6. With right sides together, join dress front to back by stitching along side and shoulder seams. Press seams open.

7. With right sides together, join back neck facing to front neck facing along shoulder edges. Neaten raw edges along outer edges of facings by turning the seam allowance to wrong side of fabric and stitching neatly in place.

8. Right sides together, place facing in position to dress. Pin, baste then stitch right round neckline edge. Trim seam allowance to about ¼in. (to make finished seam less bulky), then snip into the seam allowance at intervals on the curved areas, taking care not to snip through the actual stitching. This will help the curve to lie flat. Turn facing to the inside and press carefully.

9. Join one front armhole facing to one back armhole facing, with right sides facing, at shoulder and underarm edges. Join other pair of armhole facings in a similar way. Neaten outside edges of facings, in the same way as you neatened raw edges of neck facings. Press seams open. Place each armhole facing in position on dress, right sides together and matching shoulder and underarm seams. Pin, baste then stitch. Trim seam and snip into curves as you did for neckline facings. Turn facings to inside. Press carefully.

10. Slipstitch facings neatly to dress along zip, at shoulder seams and under-arm seams to keep them securely in place.

11. Turn up hem at lower edge to required length, and stitch neatly (see hints on stitching hems, in lesson two).

Sew hook and eye to fasten centre back opening at neck edge, above zip.
12. To make fabric belt, fold fabric strip in half lengthwise, right sides together. Stitch down the long side and one short side. Trim seam, and turn strip right side out. Press. Fold the unstitched end of the belt over centre bar of buckle

to the wrong side. Turn under raw edge and sew in place by hand.
13. To make beaded belt, turn in ½in. round all edges of lining strip and place to back of beaded strip, wrong sides together. Slipstitch together round edges. Stitch hooks and eyes to fasten short edges of belt together edge to edge.

# SEWING

## Lesson Two:
## Making a paper pattern fit.

Whether you work from a bought paper pattern or one you have made yourself, if your garment is to have a professional finish, it is essential that the pattern is adjusted to suit the exact shape and size of your figure—very few of us are exactly 'stock size'. Adjustments should be made to the paper pattern pieces before placing on fabric to cut out. The first step is to take your own measurements accurately, compare these with the measurements given for the pattern, and establish where your figure differs from stock size.

Once you have prepared one paper pattern to fit your figure precisely, this can be kept as a sort of master pattern and used as a guide to adapting all future patterns you use. The following instructions show how a few of the more common figure adjustments can be simply dealt with.

Remember when taking your measurements to allow for ease of fit—no garment should ever be skin tight.

### LONG-WAISTED

If you are long-waisted, the waistline of a stock size pattern will fall above your natural waistline, so it must be lowered. Both back and front pattern pieces must be adjusted in a similar way. If you are using a bought pattern, an alteration line will be printed on the pattern pieces. Cut the bodice pattern along this line. If you are using your own pattern, measure up from the waistline and draw a line straight across the pattern about 1 in. up from the waistline. Cut along this line. Place both sections of the pattern on a flat surface, with a strip of tissue paper under the area which has been cut apart. Spread pattern pieces apart to give the required amount of extra depth. Keeping centre front edges of pattern straight, and the cut edges parallel, pin or tape pattern to paper (A). Trim edges to continue lines of pattern.

### SHORT-WAISTED

If you are short-waisted, then bodice pattern pieces will have to be shortened. Fold along the alteration line, or if using your own pattern draw in a line as for long-waisted alteration, above, then fold along this line. Measure up from this fold the amount by which the pattern has to be shortened, and draw a line at this point. Bring folded edge up to meet this line. Pin, and trim edges straight (B).

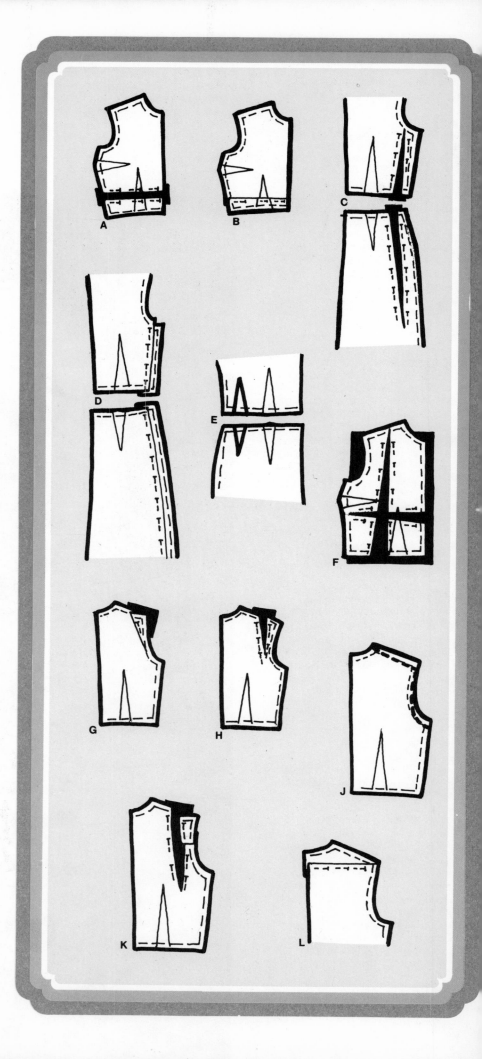

# HEMLINE

To shorten or lengthen a skirt, simply add to, or subtract from, the hem edge. With a bought paper pattern sometimes an alteration line is indicated on a skirt piece. In this case adjust on this line, and not at hem edge.

# WAISTLINE AND HIPS

**To enlarge:** slash pattern pieces for bodice and skirt sections about 2 in. from side seams. Spread over tissue paper allowing the extra width needed. Pin and trim (C).

**To reduce:** pin vertical folds on bodice and skirt sections about 2 in. from side seams, taking up the required amount. Trim pieces if necessary so the edges are straight (D).

**Reduce waistline only:** make extra darts on front and back of bodice and skirt sections, about 2 in. from side seams—the size of each dart should be equal to a quarter of the total amount you wish reduced. For instance, if you want to reduce the waistline by 4 in., then each dart should be 1 in. across at widest point (E)

# LARGE BUST

Slash front bodice section up from centre of waistline edge to just below shoulder, and again across front below bust dart. Spread over tissue paper to give extra measurement needed, letting vertical slash taper to nothing towards shoulder. Pin and trim. Shorten waistline dart to avoid horizontal slash. Mark an extra waistline dart in slashed space, so waistline will be the original size (F).

# SHOULDER

**To make narrower:** pin a fold over tissue paper to take up extra width, from the midway point of shoulder edge on back and front bodice sections letting the fold taper down towards armhole edge (G). Clip armhole seam allowance. Trim shoulder edge straight.

**To make wider:** draw a diagonal line from the midway point of shoulder edge towards armhole. Slash along this line, and spread pattern on tissue paper to give extra width needed. Pin, then trim to new shape (H).

**For sloping shoulders:** on back and front bodice sections draw in new seamlines sloping down the required amount. Lower armhole seam by the same amount (J).

**For a broad back:** slash pattern piece for back bodice from shoulder edge straight down for about 10 in. Spread over tissue paper to give extra width required. Bring shoulder edges together. Pin and trim edge straight. Clip armhole seam allowance (K).

**To avoid wrinkles across back:** lower the back neckline by pinning a horizontal fold right across pattern piece, from about an inch below neckline at centre back and tapering to nothing at shoulder edges (L).

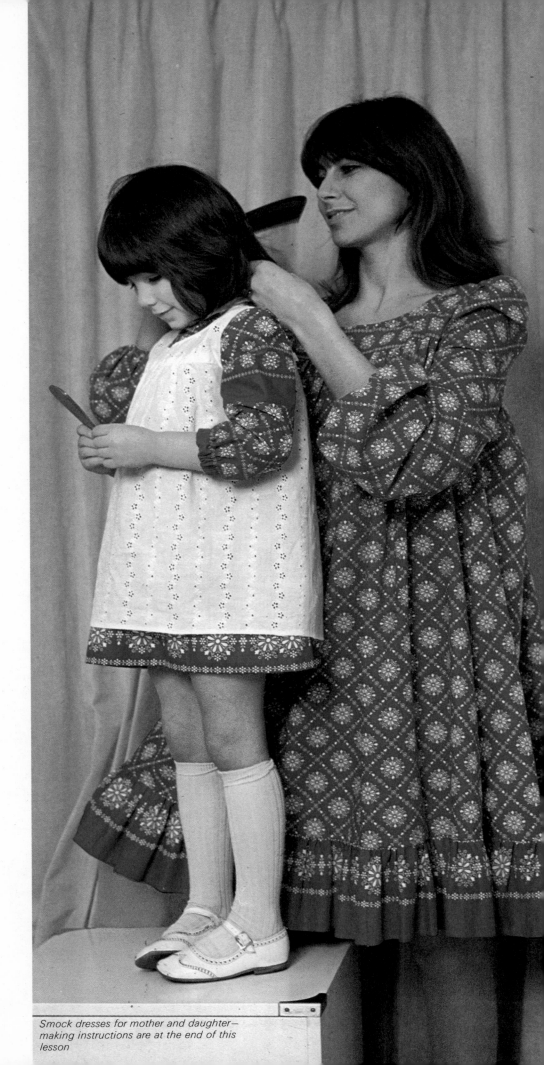

*Smock dresses for mother and daughter—making instructions are at the end of this lesson*

## SLEEVES

**To lengthen:** find the elbow point on your paper pattern, then place this against your arm to see how much extra length is required. Slash pattern above and below elbow point, then place the pattern pieces over tissue paper, spacing the pieces out to give the extra length required. Pin tissue to pattern pieces, and trim away excess at sides to give the new piece (M).

**To shorten:** make horizontal folds above and below elbow point to reduce length by the required amount. Pin and trim outer edges of pattern piece so they are straight (N).

# Techniques for a professional finish

## SEAM FINISHES

Unless you intend to line a garment, all seams should be finished by one of the following methods to prevent fraying, and to strengthen the seams.

**1. Pinking.** Probably the easiest seam finish of all—simply trim seams with pinking shears (O).

**2. Pink and stitch.** Stitch $\frac{1}{4}$ in. from the edge of seam allowance, then trim edges with pinking shears.

**3. Turnings.** This method is good for fabrics that fray easily, and for lightweight fabrics. Turn under edges of seam allowance for about $\frac{1}{8}$ in., and then stitch close to the edge. Alternatively, stitch $\frac{1}{8}$ in. from the edge, turn edge under on stitching line, and stitch again close to the folded edge (P).

**4. Overcasting.** This is good for heavy fabrics that fray easily. Work from right to left, making neat, small over stitches along the edge of seam allowance, pushing needle from wrong side to right side of fabric. Alternatively, machine stitch along seam allowance $\frac{1}{8}$ in. from the edge, then make overcasting stitches as for previous method, but insert needle just under the line of machine stitching (Q).

**5. Binding.** This is good for heavier fabrics, particularly if the garment is not lined. Fold bias seam binding in half lengthwise and use to enclose edge of seam allowance. Stitch so that both edges of the seam binding are caught with the one row of machine stitching (R).

## HEM FINISHES

First, use chalk to mark your hemline to the length you require, making sure the hem is even all the way round—if possible, get someone else to help you. Turn hem to wrong side of skirt or dress along the marked line and pin, inserting pins at right angles to the fold to make a smooth line. Baste and press after the pins have been removed. To prevent an impression of the hem showing on right side of fabric when using heavy fabrics, place a piece of cardboard or brown paper between

the hem and the garment. Measure and mark hem depth and cut away excess fabric.

Neaten raw edge of hem by any of the seam finishing methods listed above, then stitch hem in place by any of the following methods:

**Tailor's or couture hem.** This gives a good flat finish and the stitching is virtually invisible on the right side of the garment. Baste hem in place about $\frac{1}{2}$ in. from top edge. Fold hem back against the outside of the garment and slipstitch in position as follows: insert needle in neatened hem edge and then pick up one thread in the fold of the garment fabric. Take the next stitch in the neatened hem edge and the following one in the fold (S). Continue in this way. Press hem flat over the stitching.

**Catch-stitch hem.** This hem is ideal for heavy fabrics. Work from left to right. First catch one thread in the hem inserting needle from right to left. Next pick up one thread in the garment, inserting the needle below the hem edge the same distance that the first stitch was above the edge. Take next stitch in hem, and the following in the garment, and so on. Do not pull stitches tight (T).

**Seam-taped hem.** Stitch bias seam binding tape to neatened hem edge, about $\frac{1}{4}$ in. from the edge. Hemstitch other edge of tape to garment (U).

**Lockstitch hem.** Work from left to right: take a small stitch through one thread in the garment, and then take a stitch of two or three threads in the top edge of the hem about $\frac{1}{4}$ in. to the left of starting point. Draw needle through, over the looped thread. Continue in this way round the entire hem. This gives a hardwearing hem, and is particularly suitable for children's clothes.

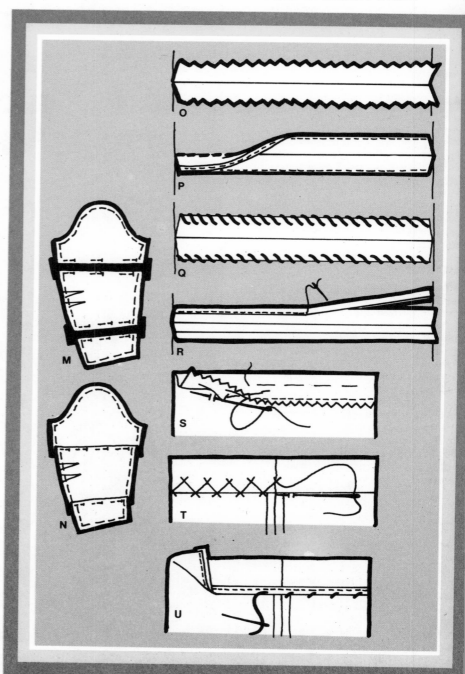

# SETTING IN SLEEVES

Normally a sleeve has more fabric round its 'head', or top shoulder section, than the armhole of the garment—the fuller and puffier the sleeve, the more fabric there will be. In order to make the sleeve fit neatly into the armhole, it is necessary to 'ease-stitch' the head of the sleeve, before stitching it in place. A pattern will normally have notch markings to indicate where this ease-stitching should be done. Ease-stitching may be done by machine or by hand: if using a machine, then use 6—8 stitches per inch for heavy fabrics, 8—10 stitches per inch for lightweight fabrics. If worked by hand, then simply work a row of neat running stitches. Work your stitching between the notch markings first of all exactly on the seamline, then work a second row of stitching $\frac{1}{4}$ in. from the first row, but within the seam allowance. Leave about 3 or 4 in. of thread loose at each end of both rows

of stitching.

The secret of success in setting in sleeves is in the way you hold the garment. Have the bodice with the inside of the armhole of the sleeve towards you. Pin the sleeve into the armhole, right sides together, matching underarm seams, notches and marks, and placing the mark at the head of the sleeve to the shoulder seam of the bodice.

Ease in the fullness between the notches on the head of the sleeve by drawing up the loose threads until the edge of the sleeve matches the edge of the garment armhole edge.

Distribute the material evenly between the pins. Pin carefully into place. Hold easing threads secure by winding the thread ends round a pin at each end of stitching. Always place pins at right angles to seam line when pinning a sleeve into place, never along the seam line.

When a sleeve has a great deal of fullness at the head (e.g. see our smock

dress overleaf), distribute the gathers evenly making little pleats if necessary between the notches. Avoid having tucks or gathers exactly on the shoulder seam line. When the sleeve is accurately pinned in place, baste and remove pins. Stitch with the sleeve side up, and starting at the underarm. In this way you can ensure that the seam does not become puckered as you work.

When first row of stitching is complete, work another row of stitching about $\frac{1}{8}$ in. away from the first row, within the seam allowance. Between the notches at underarm, trim close to stitching. Do not trim the sleeve head. Press in the following way: with wrong side upwards, lay the top of the sleeve seam on an ironing pad or sleeve board, with edges of seam allowance together and sleeve side up. Press the seam allowance only, between the notch markings (keep rest of garment clear of the ironing pad). This will ensure the allowance turns into the sleeve. Do not press underarm section.

## MOTHER'S SMOCK DRESS PATTERN  I SQ = I INCH

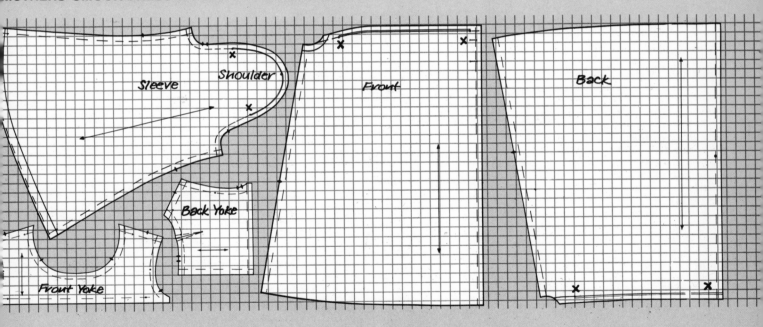

## CHILD'S SMOCK DRESS PATTERN  I SQ = I INCH

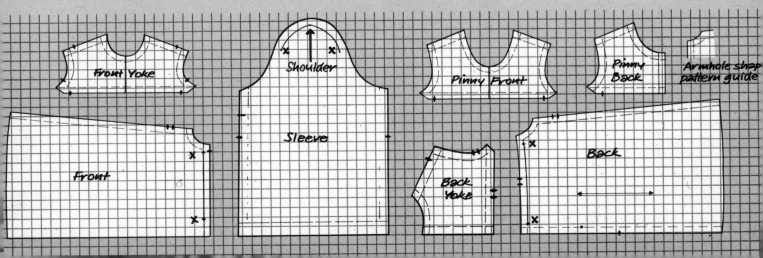

# MOTHER AND DAUGHTER SMOCK DRESSES

This attractive smock can do double duty as a maternity dress for Mother—for daughter, there is a pretty over-pinny to wear with the smock.

## MATERIALS YOU WILL NEED

**For the mother's smock dress only:** 4⅝ yd. fabric, 36 in. wide, or 4 yd. fabric, 45 in. wide.

**For the child's smock dress only:** 1¾ yd. fabric, 36 in. wide, or 1⅝ yd. fabric, 45 in. wide, or 1⅛ yd. fabric, 54 in. wide.

**For matching mother and daughter smock dresses:** 6¼ yd. fabric, 36 in. wide.

**For the child's over-pinny:** ⅝ yd. fabric, 36 in. wide.

**Also required:** matching sewing thread, a hook and eye (for each dress), a 20-in. zip (for mother's dress), a 10-in. zip (child's dress), ½ yd. elastic (mother's dress), ⅜ yd. elastic (child's dress), ⅜ yd. ready-folded braid for neck edge of child's dress, and 1 yd. ribbon for over-pinny ties.

## FABRIC SUGGESTIONS

**For smock dress:** printed, plain or polished cottons, cotton lawn, Terylene lawn, voiles, other synthetics, linen, poplin, denim, gingham.

**For over-pinny:** broderie anglaise, cotton, pique, gingham, denim, seersucker, calico, lawn, broadcloth, linen, cotton sateen.

*Note:* Our mother's dress was made from a border-printed cotton. If you wish to use a similar border or one-way print, you must allow extra fabric for matching of the pattern—you could need up to ¾ yd., depending on fabric width and the particular pattern on it. With our fabric, we cut off one border to make the hem frill, used another border for the yokes, and re-arranged the pattern pieces to fit.

## SIZE NOTE

The mother's smock is very generously cut and should comfortably fit bust size 36 in., with plenty of room for expansion if the dress is to be worn as a maternity dress. The child's dress should fit size 4, chest size 23 in. Finished back length at centre back: mother's dress 37½ in., including frill; child's dress 20 in. To adapt the pattern to fit different sizes, follow instructions given in Sewing lesson one.

## TO MAKE YOUR PATTERNS

The diagram on previous page gives the pattern pieces you will need. One square on the diagram equals 1 in. Following our step-by-step instructions in lesson one, prepare your full-size pattern on squared paper. Transfer dart markings, notches and crosses, and straight grain indication to your paper pattern pieces. Unless otherwise stated, all seams should be stitched ⅝ in. from fabric edge.

## TO MAKE MOTHER'S DRESS

Cut out fabric pieces, following cutting-out layouts below (choose the layout to suit the fabric width you are using).

1. Stitch darts at neck edge in back yokes: right sides of fabric facing, fold each dart, matching outside lines, and begin pinning at the point. Baste, then stitch from the wide end of the dart to the point, making the last stitches right on the fold. Tie thread ends in a knot before clipping. Press each dart towards centre back.

2. Place front and back shoulder seams of yoke together, right sides facing. Pin, matching notches. Stitch. Press seams open.

3. Join front and back yoke facing sections together, right sides facing, as above. Press seams open.

4. Right sides facing, pin the facing sections to the yoke front and back. Match notches. Baste in place. Stitch at neck edge. Grade the seam: this means trimming the facing seam allowance to ⅛ in., and trimming the dress yoke seam allowance to ¼ in. Grading reduces bulk and gives a neater, flatter finish. If you have more than two thicknesses, trim the fabric to graduated widths between ⅛ in. and ¼ in.

5. Clip at right angles into the seam allowance of the neck curve, to within about a thread of the stitching line. This will allow the seam to lie flat when you turn the facing to the inside. The greater the curve, the more clips are required in order to make it lie flat.

6. Understitch facing to seam, to stop the facing rolling to show on the outside of the garment: open out facing and seam allowance, turn seam allowance under facing. Right side up, machine stitch on the facing, close to the seam, through all the thicknesses of fabric. Turn facing to inside of garment. Baste close to the neck edge. Press.

7. Right sides together, join centre front seam of dress. Press seam open.

8. Gather along upper edge of dress fronts between crosses. Make 2 rows of gathering, one on the seamline and one about ¼ in. away within the seam allowance. You can gather by hand, using small even running stitches, or by machine. Use a longer machine stitch and draw the thread ends through to the underside. Tie threads in a knot at one end of the stitching line. At the other end, draw the threads to adjust the gathers to the correct length.

9. Pin dress front to front yoke with right sides facing, matching any marks or notches and leaving the yoke facing free. Draw up the gathers to fit the yoke and tie ends of thread in a knot. Pin then baste carefully, adjusting the gathers as you work. Stitch. Press the seam upwards towards the bodice.

10. Right sides facing, put back sections of dress together, pin along centre back seam, then baste from lower edge to mark. Stitch. Press seam open.

11. Gather along the upper edge of dress back sections between crosses. Make two rows of gathering, one on the seamline and one ¼ in. away within the seam allowance. Gathers should end ⅝ in. away from centre back opening.

12. Leaving yoke facing free and with right sides together, pin back skirt sections to each back yoke, matching marks or notches and centre back. Draw up the gathers to fit and pin,

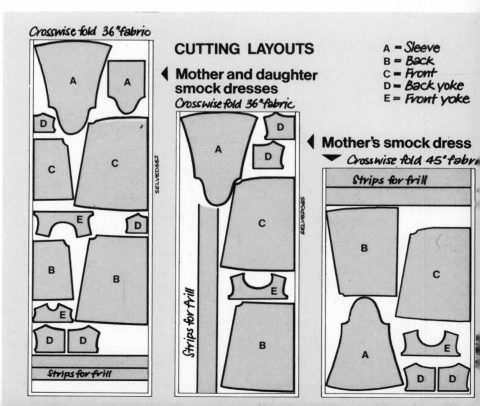

**CUTTING LAYOUTS**

◀ **Mother and daughter smock dresses**
*Crosswise fold 36" fabric*

◀ **Mother's smock dress**
▼ *Crosswise fold 45" fabric*

A = Sleeve
B = Back
C = Front
D = Back yoke
E = Front yoke

*Crosswise fold 36" fabric*

*Strips for frill*

SELVEDGES

then baste, adjusting the gathers as you work. Stitch. Press seam upwards.

13. Pin then baste edges of back opening together, right sides facing, above mark on the seamline. Leave yoke facing free. Press seam open.

14. Stitch zip in position to this seam, following instructions as given in the two-way dress pattern, lesson one.

15. Turn under ⅝ in. seam allowance on lower edge of the yoke facings and slipstitch over the seams.

16. Make ⅝ in. turnings at centre back edges of yoke facings, and slipstitch to zip tapes. Press.

17. Stitch hook and eye at neck edge above zip to fasten centre back neck edge.

18. Baste yoke and yoke facings together at armhole edges.

19. Gather along the upper edge of each sleeve between crosses. Make two rows of gathering stitches, as described in techniques for a professional finish (see previous pages).

20. With right sides facing, pin then stitch each sleeve seam. Press seams open.

21. Turn up the lower edge of each sleeve on line indicated, turning in ¼ in. along raw edge. Stitch to sleeve, leaving an opening in the seam at the sleeve seam. Cut a piece of elastic the measurement of your wrist plus about 1 in. Thread the elastic through the hem just stitched (fasten a safety pin on to the elastic and gradually ease pin through the hem taking the elastic with it). Lap ends of elastic over each other for about ½ in. and sew firmly together. Stitch the opening in the hem closed so the elastic is hidden.

22. Set sleeves into armholes, following instructions given in techniques for a professional finish.

23. Right sides facing, stitch together strips of fabric, each 6 in. wide, to make frill at hem of dress. You will need

twice the measurement of the dress hem for fullness. Press open each seam as you stitch it. Now gather along one edge ⅝ in. from the edge. Make a second row of gathers ¼ in. away from the first row within the seam allowance. Before drawing up the gathers, mark carefully into four equal sections—this will make it easier to attach the frill to the dress hem edge, matching the markings to side seams and to front and back seams. Pin carefully. Working one section at a time, draw up the gathers to fit the hem and pin. Baste each section. Stitch. Press seam upwards towards dress.

24. Finish lower edge of frill by making a ½ in. turning and pressing up; turn in ¼ in. round raw edge, pin then slip stitch in place. Press well.

## TO MAKE CHILD'S DRESS

*Note:* If you are making matching mother and daughter dresses, the child's dress has a centre front seam. If you are making the child's dress on its own, then follow the separate cutting-out layout in which the centre front edge is placed on fold of fabric. There will then not be a centre front seam.

Make up the child's dress in a similar way as described for the mother's dress with the following differences:

Follow the instructions for the mother's dress through to step 18, but do not stitch side seams together. Gather upper edge of each sleeve between marks. Pin the sleeve to the armhole edges, right sides together, matching notches and marks. Draw up gathers to fit sleeve. Pin and baste, adjusting gathers. Stitch. Turn seam toward sleeve.

Now join the dress side seams and the sleeve seams, matching notches, underarms and marks, in one operation,

thus making one long seam starting at hem and finished at wrist at each side of dress.

If you cut the dress without a centre front seam, placing fabric to fold, ignore instructions for joining dress fronts. Gather straight across top edge of front. Neckline trim: insert neck edge into ready-folded braid. Pin. Slipstitch in place on right side and wrong side. Turn in ends at back opening, and stitch neatly in place.

As there is no frill on child's dress, simply turn up hem to length required and stitch in place (see techniques for a professional finish.

## TO MAKE OVER-PINNY

From ⅝ yd. of fabric, 36 in. wide, cut two strips: one to measure 7 in. by 36 in., the other to measure 15½ in. by 36 in. From the 7-in. strip cut out pinny yoke, front and backs, as indicated on cutting-out layout. Fold the other strip of fabric into four, by folding first in half, and then in half again.

Cut away curved area from one top corner, using the armhole shape pattern guide and following the diagram below. Make two rows of gathering along the three top edges of pinny skirt, thus forming one front section, two back sections (see diagram below). Draw up gathers to fit yoke backs and yoke front. With right sides together, pin, then baste in place, matching centre backs. Stitch. Press seams upwards. With right sides facing, pin yoke back and yoke front together at shoulders. Stitch. Press seams open. To neaten edges, make tiny clips into curves where necessary. Make ¼ in. turning and machine stitch. Turn up ¼ in. again, and slipstitch to pinny. Divide ribbon into four equal lengths. Sew at back neck edges and at lower edge of back yokes. Press.

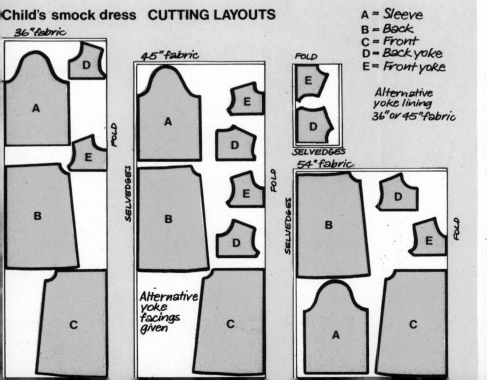

**Child's smock dress CUTTING LAYOUTS**

36" fabric

45" fabric

54" fabric

A = Sleeve
B = Back
C = Front
D = Back yoke
E = Front yoke

Alternative yoke lining 36" or 45" fabric

Alternative yoke facings given

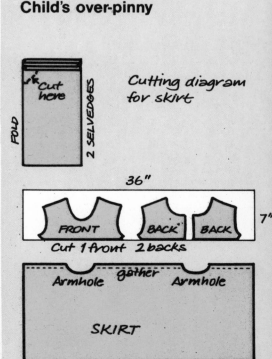

**Child's over-pinny**

Cut here

Cutting diagram for skirt

36"

FRONT   BACK   BACK

Cut 1 front 2 backs

7"

Armhole   gather   Armhole

SKIRT

# SEWING

## Lesson Three:
## Buttons and buttonholes

## Buttons

Buttons are made in all kinds of materials, from plastic and wood to metal and glass. Basically, however, there are only two types of button: the shank button which has a solid top and a 'neck' or stem beneath, and the pierced button which has two, three or four holes. Choose a button size suitable for the lapping extension edge of the garment where the button will be stitched—the button should not overlap the edge of the fabric. A decorative button—i.e. one stitched to the outside of a garment merely for ornamental purposes—does not need a shank but a button which has to go through a buttonhole does need a shank to allow the fabric to lie smoothly.

If you want your buttons to stay firmly in place on your garment you must choose your sewing thread to suit the material. Normally, a No. 40 mercerised thread is suitable for mediumweight fabrics. Use a coat of beeswax (pass the thread through the wax three or four times) for sewing on buttons on coats and woollen dresses and jackets. This makes the thread stronger and more slippery so the actual sewing is easier too. Silk buttonhole twist or sewing silk is better for finer fabrics, while heavy button thread is best for thick fabrics when you need more strength. Multipurpose threads can be used for all fabric types.

### MEASURING AND PLACING BUTTONS

To estimate the length of buttonhole you should make for a particular button, cut a $\frac{1}{4}$ in. wide strip of paper, wrap it round the button at its widest part (not round the shank) and pin paper ends under button (A). Remove strip without taking away pin. Smooth flat, so the fold is opposite the pin. The distance from the fold to the pin is the length of the buttonhole required. To determine the exact position for sewing on the buttons to your garment, lap the garment edges over each other matching centre front or centre back markings (depending on where the button opening is to be). Line up neck and hem edges then pin carefully. If you are making horizontal buttonholes then place a pin at the outer edge of

the buttonhole into the fabric beneath (B). Position the button $\frac{1}{8}$ in. to the left of this pin mark. If you are making vertical buttonholes then the top and bottom of each should be marked in a similar way; the button is then placed halfway between the two pin marks.

### MAKING A SHANK

A thread shank can be made for a button which does not already have one. The length of the shank you make will depend on the thickness of the fabric on your garment. A fine fabric will need a very small shank, but a heavy fabric such as a thick tweed may need a shank of up to $\frac{1}{2}$ in. To make the shank, first position the button on your garment then bring needle and thread to the right side of the fabric, and take a small stitch to secure the thread. Always use double thread and knot the ends. Bring the needle through the button and place a matchstick across the top of the button to allow for the shank. Take

thread over the matchstick then back through the button and back into the fabric (C). Continue sewing back and forth in this way always taking stitches over the matchstick. When the button is firmly sewn to the garment, remove the matchstick and wind the sewing thread firmly round the threads under the button, thus forming a shank. Finally draw the needle to the wrong side of fabric and secure with a few stitches. Cut the thread—do not break it.

### REINFORCING BUTTONS

If the button is to be used under heavy strain, or if it is to be used on soft fabrics which might tear easily, it should be reinforced. On the inside of the garment, directly under the button location, place a small flat button or a square of firm fabric. Sew through the button or fabric when attaching the outside button (D). A square of iron-on interfacing makes a good reinforcement for light and medium-weight fabrics. Cut a small piece of interfacing slightly smaller than the

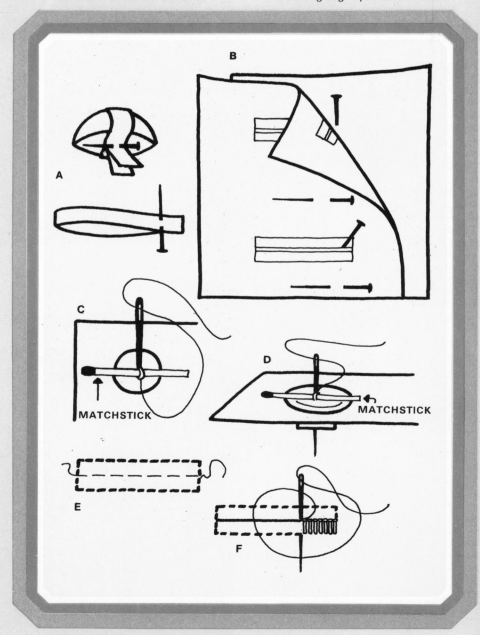

button and press on to wrong side of garment between fabric and facing. Stitch through button, backing material and fabric together.

## BUTTONHOLES

There are four basic methods of making buttonholes: the tailor's or hand-sewn buttonhole; the machine worked buttonhole; the piping buttonhole and the bound buttonhole. The last two methods look similar when finished. Some buttonholes tend to stretch with use, especially in fine, soft fabrics. Bear this in mind when you calculate the length of your buttonhole. Buttonholes should be slightly larger than the buttons for easy fastening, but never more than $\frac{1}{8}$ in. for normal buttons. When very small buttons are used, the difference should be less then the $\frac{1}{8}$ in.; when a thick or heavyweight fabric is used, and the button is covered with the same fabric, or the button has a high design (such as a ball button), the buttonhole should be slightly larger than the $\frac{1}{8}$ in. difference.

## MARKING BUTTONHOLE POSITIONS

Transfer the position of each buttonhole from the paper pattern you are using; if you have altered the pattern it may be necessary also to re-space the buttonholes. Make the markings by chalking, basting or pinning. Alternatively, mark the buttonhole lines with dressmakers' tracing paper on interfacing. Pin the interfacing to the garment and baste-mark through to the right side of the fabric.
Buttonholes should be on the straight grain of the fabric. They are placed horizontally on a coat or dress front, vertically on a strap opening or on a light blouse or shirt. Use sharp, pointed scissors for cutting the buttonhole slit.

## HAND-SEWN BUTTONHOLES

These are worked after the garment is finished. Mark the buttonhole positions on your fabric. Using a single thread and small running stitches, stitch about $\frac{1}{16}$ in. from the buttonhole marking line in a 'letterbox' shape (E). Alternatively, a row of machine stitching can be worked. Insert pointed scissors at centre of marking and slash buttonhole on the centre mark to the ends. Overcast the edges of the slit to stop the material from fraying.
Now work buttonhole stitch over the neatened edges, working from right to left as follows:
Start at the end and insert needle into slit bringing it out below stitching. Bring thread from needle eye around and under needle point, from right to left. Draw needle up to form a 'purl' on the edge. Do not pull the thread tightly. Continue in this way, placing

stitches close together so the purls will cover the edge (F). At end towards garment edge, form a fan as shown in diagram, keeping the centre stitch of the fan in line with the cut. Make a bar at the end opposite the fan by taking several stitches across the end and working blanket stitch over the threads and through the garment cloth. To finish run the thread under a few stitches before cutting (G).

A vertical buttonhole has two bar tacks, one at each end. A tailor's buttonhole is sometimes worked with strands of thread lying along each side of the slit, working buttonhole stitch over them. This type of buttonhole is suitable for sheer fabrics, lightweights and materials that fray.

## MACHINE BUTTONHOLES

These are made with a buttonhole attachment or on zigzag or semi-automatic machines. Follow instructions in the machine guide book and test buttonholes first on a scrap of the same material you are using. Machine worked buttonholes are suitable for children's or casual clothes.

## BOUND OR PIPED BUTTONHOLES

Both these buttonholes are neatened with self-fabric and are made on the fabric and interfacing only, before the facing is applied to the garment. They give a neat, professional looking finish on jackets and coats.

**Bound buttonholes.** For each buttonhole, cut a strip of fabric, 2 in. wide and 1 in. longer than the buttonhole size for lightweight fabrics, up to 3 in. wide on thicker materials. This strip can be cut on the straight grain or on the bias of the fabric. Mark centre with iron crease. Right sides together, matching crease to buttonhole mark on fabric, baste patches in place. Baste along the crease to stop the patch slipping (H). Using small machine or hand stitches, stitch a rectangle 'frame' round centre line, with the horizontal lines of stitching each $\frac{1}{8}$ in. from the centre line. Slash along the buttonhole line, inserting scissor points in the centre and cutting through patch and garment to within $\frac{1}{4}$ in. from ends of stitching. Clip diagonally into the corners, to form triangles—be careful not to clip the stitching (J). Remove any basting. Push the patch through the opening carefully to the wrong side of the garment. Smooth out, making sure the folds or 'lips' are equal. Stitch down the small inverted pleats formed by the patch on the inside with a few running stitches (K). Press buttonhole with steam iron or damp cloth. Now work tiny back stitches into the buttonhole stitch line working on the right side. After completing all the buttonholes, attach the garment facing. From the right side put pins straight through centre of

each end of the buttonhole to mark the length on the facing. Slash facing on a straight line between the pins, and make a short clip at centre of each edge of slash. Turn in the edges and hem securely in place making an oval on the facing side. If wished, the facing may be slashed and clipped in the same manner as the outside of the garment was done. In this case, the marking pins should be put into the four corners of the buttonhole; the edges and triangular ends are then turned and hemmed in place to make a rectangle.

**Piped buttonholes.** These are also worked through fabric and interfacing only. Cut a length of fabric about $\frac{1}{2}$ in. wide. Fold strip along centre and press. The strip should be long enough to pipe both sides of each buttonhole. Or cut one long strip and prepare it for all your buttonholes at the same time. The strips may be cut on the straight grain or bias of the fabric. Cut strip into buttonhole sections—i.e. length of buttonhole plus 1 in. Wrong sides together, fold each strip lengthwise and stitch $\frac{1}{8}$ in. from folded edge. If wished, piping cord may be encased in the strip. Trim edges $\frac{1}{8}$ in. from stitching (L).

Right sides together, place strip on garment lining up raw edges of strip with buttonhole line. Place another strip on other edge of buttonhole, in a similar way (M). Stitch $\frac{1}{8}$ in. from raw edges the exact length of buttonhole.

This stitching will be directly over the previous stitching on the strips. Slash buttonhole, clip and turn piping inside, and complete as for bound buttonholes.

## YOUR THIRD MAKES—

# SHIRTS FOR FATHER AND SON

## MATERIALS YOU WILL NEED

**For man's shirt:** 3 yd. fabric, 36 in. wide; 8 medium buttons; $\frac{1}{2}$ yd. interfacing.

**For boy's shirt:** $1\frac{3}{4}$ yd. fabric, 36 in. wide; 7 medium buttons; 1 yd. interfacing.

## MEASUREMENTS

**Man's shirt:** to fit chest size 40 in., neck size $15\frac{1}{2}$ in.

**Boy's shirt:** to fit boy of about 7–8 years old, neck size 12 in.

To make bigger or smaller size shirts, allow $\frac{1}{4}$ in. either less or more at centre back edges of body, yoke and collar pattern sections. Add or subtract $\frac{1}{4}$ in. on side seams and underarm sleeve seams.

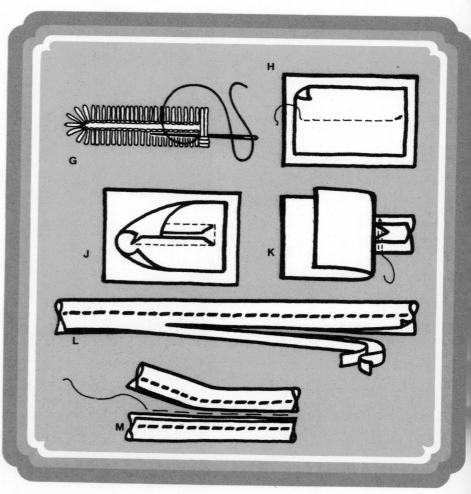

## FABRIC SUGGESTIONS

Woven cottons, gingham, cotton mixtures, brushed cottons, Terylene voiles, lawns, Viyella.

## TO MAKE YOUR PATTERN

The diagram right gives the pattern pieces you will need. One square on the diagram equals 1 in. Following instructions in lesson one, prepare your full-size pattern. Cut out pattern pieces from fabric, following the correct cutting-out layout as given overleaf. **Note.** Unless otherwise stated stitch all seams $\frac{5}{8}$ in. from fabric edges.

## TO MAKE BOY'S SHIRT

1. Begin with yokes. With the back shirt right side towards you, pin one yoke along the seamline, right sides facing. Stitch.
2. Now turn the back of the shirt so the wrong side is towards you, and pin the other yoke along the seamline. But this time, right side of yoke should face the wrong side of the back bodice. Take care to pin and stitch along your original row of stitching. Press up both yokes. You have now sandwiched the shirt back turnings between the two yoke pieces.
3. Join the shoulder seams of the under yoke to the front shirt pieces. Stitch and press. Press in the turning of the top yoke. Pin and edge stitch along the shoulder seam.
4. Baste interfacing to wrong side of one collar piece. Right sides facing, pin two collar pieces together. Baste and stitch collar. Trim away seam allowance evenly to about $\frac{1}{8}$ inch. turn out collar and press carefully.
5. Press back front facings along the fold lines as marked on pattern. This forms three layers of fabric for extra strength for button and buttonholes. Do a row of edge stitching along inner fold of facing.
6. Pin one layer (undercollar and facing) to neck edge of shirt, right sides facing. Baste and stitch.
7. Turn in seam allowance on top collar and either slip stitch down or edge stitch by machine through all the layers.
8. Fold front facings on to outside, creasing on marked foldline. At neck edge, stitch from fold as far as centre front notch. Fasten off securely. Snip into neck turnings at end of stitching. Fold facing to the inside. Baste and press.
9. Slip stitch remainder of facing to collar.
10. Neaten edge of sleeve facing by turning under $\frac{1}{4}$ in. and stitching on the folded edge. Press. Stitch round point of slash very close to edge.
11. Right sides together, pin facing round the slashed opening on the sleeve. Stitch very carefully a seam allowance of $\frac{1}{4}$ in. graduating to nothing at the point of the slash. Turn facing to inside. Press.
12. Pin sleeve head to armhole edge,

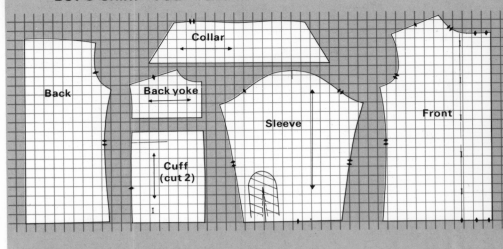

BOY'S SHIRT  I SQ = I INCH

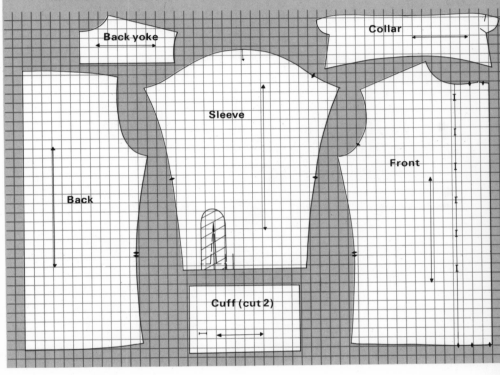

MAN'S SHIRT  I SQ = I INCH

matching notches and shoulder point and easing where marked on pattern. Stitch with lapped seam. Press.
13. Pin underarm seam of body and

sleeve all the way down, matching underarm point and any other notches. Stitch with lapped seam. You must work from the hem up to the cuff in order to get into the sleeve as it narrows. Press.
14. Pin cuff interfacing to one half of cuff on the wrong side. Tack. Fold cuff, right sides together. Press. Stitch short ends. Trim seam and turn out to right side. Press.
15. Pin one layer of cuff with interlining to sleeve edge, matching notches. Stitch. Trim seam. Press. Turn in other layer of cuff and hem on to sleeve or stitch by machine.
16. Check centre front lengths are equal and trim if necessary at bottom edge. Then neaten edge of shirt with narrow hem. Press.
17. Press the whole garment.
18. Mark buttonholes as indicated on pattern. Make worked buttonholes by hand or machine on front and cuffs. Sew on buttons.

and stitch collar. Trim away seam allowance evenly to about $\frac{1}{8}$ in. and also clip in where marked on pattern. Turn out collar and press.

Follow step 5 as Boy's Shirt.

6. Man's shirt has a neckband in one with collar. Therefore it extends to the end of button stand and does not finish at the centre front point as the boy's shirt. So pin one layer under collar and facing to the neck edge of shirt, matching centre front notches. Baste and stitch. Trim and press.

Follow step 7 as Boy's Shirt.

Omit steps 8 and 9.

Follow steps 10—18 as Boy's Shirt.

## Hints to help

### FLAT FELLED (OR LAPPED) SEAM

This is the basic seam used in shirtmaking because it is neat, strong and flat and has no raw edges to fray in frequent washing. Two rows of stitching show on the right side. Make a plain seam, wrong sides together, so the turnings are on the outside. On one seam allowance only, trim the turning about $\frac{1}{8}$ in. Fold in the top seam allowance to half its width. Baste and press. Edge stitch on fold to the garment.

### FRENCH SEAM

A neat seam which also encloses all the raw edges, and which can be used on very fine fabrics. It is not suitable for curved or shaped seams or for fitted dresses.

Stitch seam, with wrong sides of fabric together. Trim both seam allowances to approx $\frac{1}{8}$ in. Fold fabric right sides together, pressing along the stitched join. Baste $\frac{3}{4}$ in. in through the double thickness from fold edge and stitch by machine.

## TOP STITCHING

A feature of men's shirts. This is also used for outlining seams, pocket edges or collar edges. It is simply a row of extra stitching placed at an even distance from the edge of a seam, following the line or shape of the seam or collar edge. This gives added definition.

## COLLARS

When making shirt collars, accuracy of stitching and good pressing are all-important. It is important that the points of the collar are absolutely even to give a really professional look. One of the simplest methods to achieve this is to mark your stitching line with a chalk or pencil. To do this, when you have pinned the three layers of collar together, carefully measure in from the outside edge of the collar the exact turning and mark with a fine line. It will show up better if marked on the interfacing and if you stitch carefully on this line, when you have trimmed away your turning and turned out and pressed the collar, the result should be perfect.

Always check that the collar points are the same length—make any necessary corrections before putting the collar on to the shirt.

### TO MAKE MAN'S SHIRT

Follow instructions for Boy's Shirt for steps 1—3.

4. Baste interfacing to wrong side of one collar piece. Right sides together, pin two collar pieces together. Baste

# CUTTING LAYOUTS

## Man's shirt

**3 yards of 36″**

**SELVEDGES**

**FOLD**

**SELVEDGES**

**FOLD**

**SELVEDGES**

**INTERFACING $\frac{1}{4}$ yard of 36″**

**SELVEDGE**

**SELVEDGE**

## Boy's shirt

**INTERFACING $\frac{1}{4}$ yard of 36″**

**SELVEDGE**

**SELVEDGE**

**1$\frac{3}{4}$ yards of 36″**

**SELVEDGES**

## Lesson Four:
## Rouleau button loops

Button loops, or rouleau fastenings as they are sometimes known, are used when a decorative finish to a garment is required. They are also useful for fine fabrics, such as lace, where bound or worked buttonholes would not be suitable. It is usual to make the loops from strips of bias cut fabric, or if preferred from ready-made satin tubing or fine braid. They combine best with ball buttons.

## To make the loops

Cut bias strips of fabric, $1\frac{1}{8}$ in. wide (see Quick Tips, overleaf). Fold bias in half lengthwise with right sides together. Stitch $\frac{1}{4}$ in. from fold, stretching the bias slightly while stitching. Slant the stitching toward edges of bias at one end.
Turn the bias right side out. To do this use a heavy needle threaded with 4 or 5 in. of heavy thread. Knot the thread ends and fasten securely to one end of bias. Insert needle, eye forward, through bias fold. Work the needle through the tube, turning bias inside out (A1 and 2).
**Corded loops.** If you are using a lightweight or delicate fabric, it may be desirable to fill the tubing with piping cord for added strength. Use a cord of suitable size for the fabric. Determine the width of the bias strip by folding fabric over the cord and pinning it snugly. Cut $\frac{1}{2}$ in. beyond the pin. Unpin and measure the width of the cut piece. Cut true bias strips of this width and of the required length.
Cut a length of cord twice the length of the bias. With right sides together, fold strip over one half of the cord. Secure end of bias at centre of cord either by hand or by machine. Stitch close to cord, using a zipper or cording foot on your machine. Start the stitching about $\frac{1}{4}$ in. from cord and taper in, stretching bias slightly as you stitch. Trim seam allowance to $\frac{1}{8}$ in. (B). Turn bias right side out over cord by pulling the cord end that is covered and working bias back over the uncovered cord.

## Attaching the loops

Use cut loops when the buttons are large or the loops are spread some distance apart along the edge of the opening.
Cut individual loops, adding $1\frac{1}{4}$ in. to each length for seam allowance. On the right side of fabric, baste loops on the seam allowance in the correct location with the ends even with the garment edge (C).
Stitch across ends of loops, stitching $\frac{1}{16}$ in. from seamline inside seam allowance. With right sides together,

pin facing over loops. With garment side up, stitch on $\frac{5}{8}$ in. seamline, using the first line of stitching as a guide. Trim seam allowance.
Fold facing to inside along the seamline and press. Loops will extend beyond garment edge.

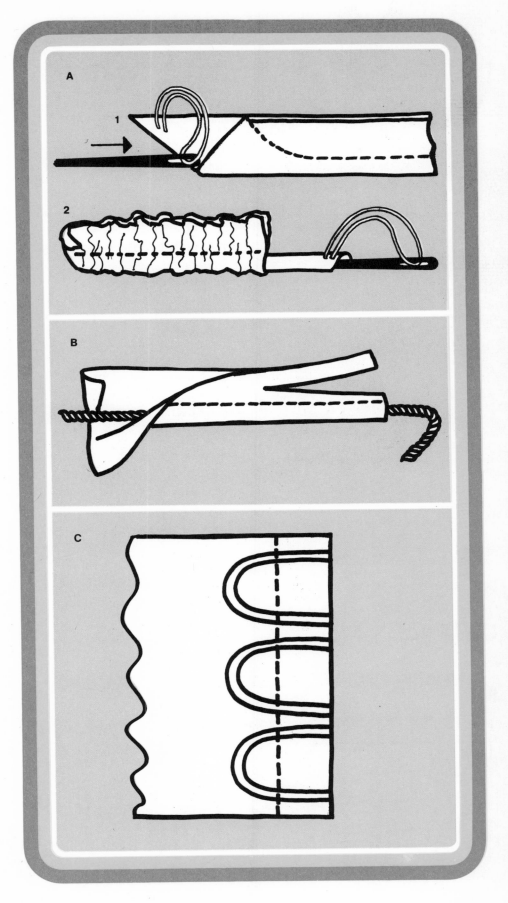

**Alternative method.** When the buttons are small and placed close together, use a continuous strip of narrow tubing. On a strong piece of paper, draw a line $\frac{5}{8}$ in. from one edge to represent the seamline. Draw another line to the left of the first one. The distance between the two lines equals the width of the loop. Across these two lines, draw lines equalling the length of each loop. Form loops between markings. Baste along seamline to secure loops (D).

Pin the paper with loops to the right side of the garment, matching edges and with loops facing away from the edge. Stitch over loops on seamline. Tear away paper; attach facing and finish as for first method.

**Quick loops.** Loops can also be sewn to the garment after it is finished. Make a continuous tube dividing it into correct lengths for the buttons. Mark garment edge. Matching the marked points, sew loops with small stitches, making sure that the seam of the tubing is turned to the underside (E).

## Quick tips

**Cutting on the bias.** The term bias means crossways. The true cross or bias of a fabric is an edge running at 45 degrees to the straight thread. Fabric on the true cross has maximum amount of stretch and 'give'. To find the bias of a length of fabric, lay the fabric flat with its grain running straight up and down and side to side. Fold the lengthwise grain diagonally so it is lying across the material or along the weft thread. The crosswise threads of the fabric should now be running in the same direction as the lengthwise threads. The diagonal line formed by the fold is the true bias. Press this fold, then cut away the triangular section of fabric above it. For bias cut strips, cut the strips parallel to this cut edge.

**Waistline stay.** This is a strip of tape or petersham which is hand stitched into the waist of a fitted dress to prevent the waistline stretching or sagging. It can also help to take the weight of an extra heavy skirt, and is essential for any style with a bloused bodice. After the dress is complete, cut a piece of petersham, $\frac{1}{2}$ in. wide, the measurement of the dress waistline plus seam allowance. Neaten each end by hemming and stitch on a hook and eye, this forms a sort of belt. Pin into the waistline on the inside seam, leaving about $1\frac{1}{4}$ in. each end free under the dress opening.

### YOUR FOURTH MAKES

# A FITTED DRESS

In long and short versions, with alternative neckline finishes, and fastening with rouleau button loops.

### MATERIALS YOU WILL NEED

**For long dress:** $4\frac{1}{4}$ yd. of fabric, 36 in. wide, or $2\frac{3}{4}$ yd. of fabric, 54 in. wide; 1 hook and eye; $\frac{1}{2}$ yd. interfacing, 36 in. wide.

**For short dress:** $3\frac{1}{8}$ yd. of fabric, 36 in. wide, or $3\frac{1}{8}$ yd. of fabric, 54 in. wide; 2 hooks and eyes; $\frac{1}{4}$ yd. interfacing, 36 in. wide.

**For both dresses:** matching sewing thread; a 6-in. zip fastener; a 1-in. buckle; seam binding; 11 ball buttons.

### FABRIC SUGGESTIONS

**For long dresses:** moss crêpe, wool crêpe, fine wools, Crimplene.
**For short dress:** printed raschel jersey, Acrilan, lightweight synthetic jerseys.

### SIZE NOTE

The pattern as given will comfortably fit bust size 34 in., hip size 36 in. To adapt pattern to fit your size, follow instructions in Sewing, lesson one.

### TO MAKE YOUR PATTERN

The diagram overleaf gives the pattern pieces you will need. One square on the diagram equals 1 in. Following the step-by-step instructions in Sewing, lesson one, prepare your full-size pattern on squared paper.

Cut out fabric pieces. following cutting layout overleaf, and using the instructions given in that lesson. Unless otherwise stated, all seams are stitched $\frac{5}{8}$ in. from the edge of the fabric.

### TO MAKE LONG DRESS

**Step 1.** Prepare bias loops (see lesson). Cut into 11 equal pieces, each $2\frac{1}{4}$ in. long. You will need a total of $24\frac{1}{2}$ in. of rouleau which can be made up in long lengths or short pieces, as you wish. This rouleau is made from the left-over cuttings of the dress and must be on the true bias.

**Step 2.** With the right front bodice, right side towards you, pin and baste the loops into position as marked on pattern. The loops must face away from the centre front and the raw edges must line up with the raw edge of the centre front bodice. Stitch into position.

**Step 3.** Right sides together, pin and baste front facing on to right bodice front. Stitch centre front edge (Note. In the case of the short dress, continue stitching along neck edge as far as notch indicated for tie neck. Clip in seam). Repeat with left front bodice. Trim seams and press facing on to the inside of the bodice. Loops will now be facing the correct way.

**Step 4.** Pin and stitch front bodice darts and press. These are curved darts therefore they should be well marked and basted first to keep the correct curve.

**Step 5.** Pin and stitch back bodice darts and press towards centre back.

**Step 6.** Pin and baste shoulder seams and bodice side seams taking care to match notches. Stitch and press open.

**Step 7.** Pin and baste interfacing on to wrong side of under collar. Right sides together, pin and baste collars together and stitch outer collar edge. Trim seam evenly to $\frac{1}{8}$ in. all round outer edge. Turn out collar and press carefully.

**Step 8.** Pin and baste neck edge of undercollar to neck edge of bodice. on right side.
Stitch and press. Turn in neck edge of top collar and hem or machine stitch to wrong side of seam just stitched.

**Step 9.** Run gathering thread or large machine stitch between the notches as indicated on head of each sleeve. and cuff edge. Join underarm sleeve seams. Draw up gathering thread at cuff edge. Join short ends of cuff band to form a

# FITTED DRESS   I SQ = I INCH

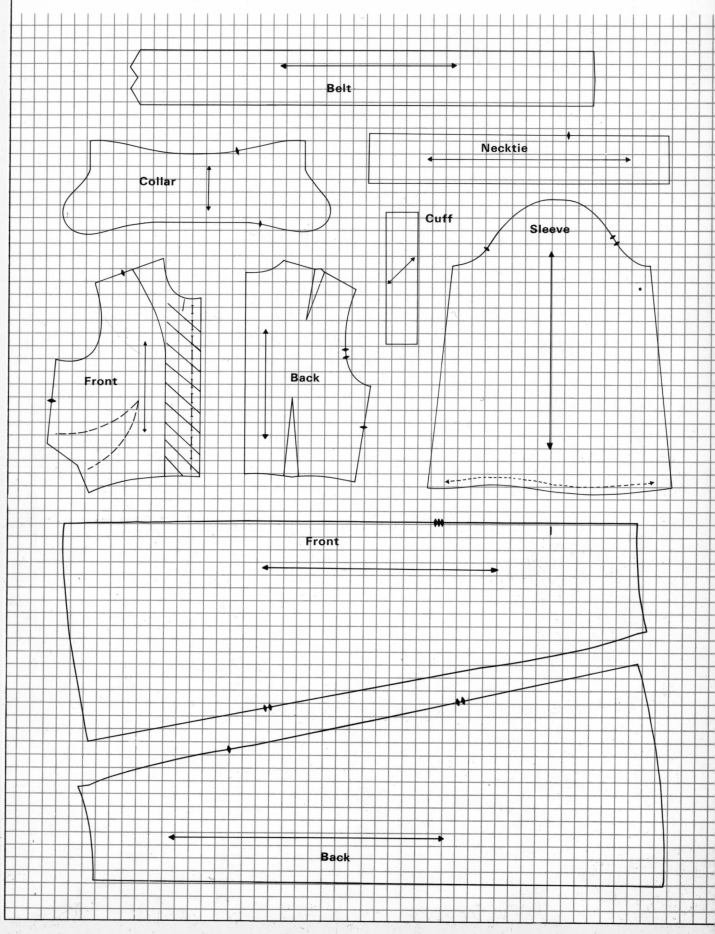

Belt

Necktie

Collar

Cuff

Sleeve

Front

Back

Front

Back

ring. Right sides together, pin cuff band to sleeve edge (working inside the sleeve), keeping gathers evenly spaced. Baste and stitch. Turn under the edge of cuff band and hem to sleeve. Repeat with second cuff.

**Step 10.** Pin sleeve head into armhole (working from inside of the garment). Take care to match notches and underarm seams. Ease in head of sleeve. Baste and stitch. Repeat with second sleeve.

**Step 11.** Right sides together, join front skirts at centre front seam, leaving top open 7 in. for zip as indicated on pattern. Press centre front seam.

**Step 12.** Insert zip.

**Step 13.** Right sides together, join side seams and press. Take care to match notches.

**Step 14.** Pin and baste bodice to skirt at waistline, matching skirt centre front and centre back seams and side seams, to bodice centre front and centre back and side seams. Stitch. Press seam upwards.

**Step 15.** Neaten front bodice facing by overcasting or machine stitching and attach at the front waistline. Hem to bodice at front waistline inside.

**Step 16.** Pin and stitch seam binding to hem edge. Press up hem carefully, pin and hand-stitch.

**Step 17.** Fold belt piece in half lengthwise and press, wrong sides together. Now open out and on the wrong side pin and baste interfacing.

**Step 18.** Right sides together, fold belt lengthwise, stitch along the long edge of the belt and the mitred (pointed) end leaving the other end open for turning out. (Note. A good tip to make it easier to turn out your belt is to baste stitch a piece of tape slightly longer than the belt to the pointed end, near the tip, leaving it inside but taking care not to catch it in with your machine stitching. Baste it below the machine stitching line. When you have finished stitching, the end of the tape should be just visible in the open end of the belt. Pull the tape and the belt will turn itself right way out. Remove tape.) Press belt flat carefully, rolling seam between finger and thumb to get it absolutely on the edge. Stitch buckle to the other end and neaten.

**Step 19.** Mark button positions on left front and stitch on eleven buttons.

**Step 20.** Handstitch in waist stay and sew on hook and eye at centre front waist. For short dress sew hook and eye at centre front neck, too.

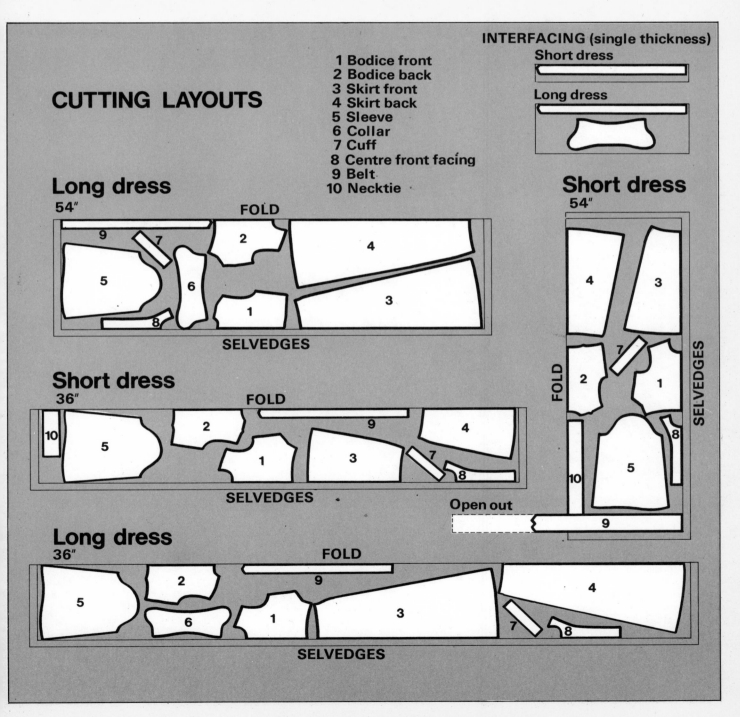

# CUTTING LAYOUTS

1 Bodice front
2 Bodice back
3 Skirt front
4 Skirt back
5 Sleeve
6 Collar
7 Cuff
8 Centre front facing
9 Belt
10 Necktie

**INTERFACING (single thickness)**
Short dress
Long dress

**Long dress** 54"
**Short dress** 54"
**Short dress** 36"
**Long dress** 36"

Open out

FOLD  SELVEDGES

**Step 21.** Make belt carriers at side seams. Mark position by laying belt at waist so that it is half above and half below the waistline seam. Carriers should be $\frac{1}{4}$ in. wider than belt. To make chain carriers, use double strands of thread knotted together and fasten the thread securely on the wrong side with a stitch or two. The idea is to make a loop of thread covered with blanket stitch. Make a small stitch above the waist and another at the marked position below the waist on the side seam. Work back and forth three or four times. Leave the necessary looseness or slackness in the loop to allow the belt to pass through easily. Now work blanket stitch over the threads. Fasten off.

**Step 22.** Give the garment a final press paying particular attention to collar, armholes, waist and hem.

## TO MAKE SHORT DRESS

Make as for Long Dress but omit step 7 and replace with step 7 as given below.

**Step 7.** Right sides together, join neck band at centre back seam. Press open. Fold neck band in half lengthwise, right sides together. At each end of the tie, stitch short ends and along the long edge as far as the notch mark. Clip in as indicated at notch point. Turn out the tie ends and press flat. Pin one edge of the neck edge of the neck band to the neck edge of the bodice (between the notches indicated on pattern for tie neck style). Baste and stitch. Turn in seam edge of top layer of neck band, hem to bodice along neckline on the inside.

# SEWING

## Lesson Five: Making a lining

There are two basic methods of lining a garment: mounting (also known as underlining or backing) and loosening. Although the pattern for cutting out is usually very similar to main pattern pieces, loose linings for jackets or coats are generally made a little looser.

## Loose lining

A loose lining for a jacket usually has a release pleat down the centre back for ease. Baste this pleat and press it to one side. Leave the basting in until garment is finished. Jacket lining should be about ¾ in. shorter than jacket when finished. The lining should be sewn over the raw edges of the facings. It is a good idea to stay-stitch back and front necklines, shoulders, armholes initially for strength ⅝ in. away from edges. Catch-stitch the release pleat at centre back at waist, hem and neck. Make up the linings for back and front of garment and press. Do not stitch shoulder seams. Make up sleeve linings and press.

**Attaching.** You can do this by hand or machine (The machine method is suitable for simple clothes and children's wear).

**Hand method.** Place jacket on table wrong side out and lay lining on top, right side of lining uppermost. Wrong side of jacket is against wrong side of lining. Match centre back pleat of lining to centre back neckline, and match side seams of lining to garment at armholes. Pin in place. Open out the garment so side seams are facing you. Now pin the side seam allowance of the lining to the side seam allowance of the jacket and baste loosely from about 2 in below armhole (A). End about 3 in. above hem.

Baste the lining all round armhole (B). Begin at underarm and work up each side, front and back to within an inch of the shoulder seam. Pin lining front shoulder edge to jacket seam. Sew. To neaten, turn under back shoulder edges of lining (along seamline) and pin over front at shoulder (C). Baste the lining across the back of the neck, taking seam allowance, and slip stitch or work felling stitch in place. To fell: work from right to left using a very small sharp needle. Catch up one thread of the fabric, then slip the needle in the fold of the turned-down edge (about ¼ in.) and bring it up again to make another stitch, catching the two pieces together, by picking up a thread below the fold. This makes a stitch invisible from both sides of garment.

**Sleeves.** Turn lining and jacket sleeves wrong side outwards. Keeping top edges even, match underarm seams and pin the seam allowance on the lining to the seam allowance on the jacket. Sew seams together with running stitch, leaving 3 in. free at top and bottom (D). Now slip your hand and arm inside lining sleeve from the armhole, grasp lower edges of jacket sleeve and lining and draw them through, turning lining to the right side over the jacket sleeve (E). Pin lining to armhole, placing top of sleeve to shoulder seam. Draw up ease thread on shoulder of lining sleeve, making fullness even, then turn under the edge of lining on the seamline. Pin in place. Sew to armhole with tiny hemming stitches, finishing carefully.

**Machine method.** Stitch lining shoulder seams. Pin and stitch lining sleeves into lining armholes, and trim the seam allowance underarm between the notches. Press the seam open above the notches. To make it stay flat, clip seam allowance on curves. Slip sleeve lining over jacket sleeves, wrong sides together, matching shoulder seams. Pin at armhole and neck.

**To finish lining.** Pin over front facings (with seam allowance pressed under) at front and back neckline. Sew with small slip stitches, easing lining over bust. Leave 3 in. at hem free.

**Hem.** Baste lining and jacket 3 in. above the hem all the way round. The bottom hem of lining should already have been pressed on seam allowance. Pin it over the jacket hem, but match the two raw edges inside (F). The lining will be shorter, of course, than the jacket. Baste and slip stitch. There will be some fullness; press it down over the hem. Sew the last bit of lower front lining to facing.

**Sleeve finish.** Baste jacket sleeve and lining together approximately 3 in. above the hem, basting all the way round. Pin and baste the pressed edge of lining over the sleeve hem. This leaves ½ in. of sleeve showing. Slip stitch in place (G). You need fullness to stop pulling. Coat linings should be

*Smart separates, right for any occasion. Instructions start overleaf.*

left loose at the hem, so hem lining separately and make it about an inch shorter than coat. In this case sew the ends of lining to front facing and attach lining to coat at seamlines with a few neat stitches.

## Mounting

Lining and fabric are cut the same and handled as one layer. To underline, put markings on lining only, and pin then baste the two fabrics together all the way round, with wrong side of dress fabric to wrong side of lining. Pin and baste along the centre line. If fabric is slippery or loosely woven, work rows of long basting stitches up and down to hold material together. Leave all the stitches in place until you have finished making the garment.
Backing a garment gives it more body and helps to prevent seating and creasing. It is particularly good in the case of loosely-woven tweeds.

**YOUR FIFTH MAKES**

# A WARDROBE OF SEPARATES

## LONG WAISTCOAT/TUNIC
## STRAIGHT-LEGGED TROUSERS
## TIE-NECKED BLOUSE
**make it with long or short sleeves, or extend the pattern and make a classic dress**

### MATERIALS YOU WILL NEED

**For tunic:** 1¼ yd. of fabric, 58 in. wide, or 2 yd. of fabric, 36 in. wide. 1½ yd. of lining fabric, 36 in. wide. 3 medium buttons.
**For trousers:** 2 yd. of fabric, 54 in. wide, or 2½ yd. of fabric, 36 in. wide. A 7-in. zip fastener. ¾ yd. of petersham ribbon, 1 in. wide. 1 hook and eye.
**For blouse:** 2⅞ yd. of fabric, 36 in. wide (for long-sleeved blouse with tie), or 2½ yd. of fabric, 36 in. wide (for short-sleeved blouse without tie). A 20-in. zip fastener. 1 hook and eye. 4 medium buttons (for cuffs).
**For dress:** 3 yd. of fabric, 36 in. wide, or 2 yd. of fabric, 54 in. wide. A 20-in. zip fastener. 1 hook and eye. 4 medium buttons.

### FABRIC SUGGESTIONS

**For tunic:** tweed, velour, velvet, jersey, lightweight wools. We used a Digoloom wool velour.
**For trousers:** jersey, wool tweed, worsteds, denim, sailcloth. We used a mediumweight Digoloom checked wool.
**For blouse:** lightweight supple fabrics such as crêpe, synthetic lightweight jerseys, surahs, Viyella.

**For dress:** wool challis, jersey, surah, crêpe, Viyella.

### SIZE NOTE

The pattern as given will comfortably fit bust size 34 in., hip size 36 in. To adapt the pattern to fit your size follow instructions given in Sewing, lesson one.

### TO MAKE YOUR PATTERN

The diagrams opposite give the pattern pieces you will need. One square on the diagrams equals 1 in. Following the step-by-step instructions in Sewing, lesson one, prepare your full-size pattern on squared paper.
To make blouse, cut along cutting line marked on dress front and back pattern pieces. To make dress, use full length of the pattern. For short-sleeved blouse cut sleeve pattern piece on cutting line marked. Cut out fabric pieces, following layouts on following page. Unless otherwise stated all seams are stitched ⅝ in. from the edge of fabric, and should be pressed open after stitching.

## Tunic

1. Pin, baste and stitch darts on front tunic. Press. If the fabric is thick, cut open the darts on the fold line and press open. Repeat with neck darts on the back tunic.
2. Right sides together, pin and baste centre back seam, matching notches. Stitch and press seam open.
3. Right sides together, pin and baste together shoulder seams and side seam of tunic. Stitch and press seams open.

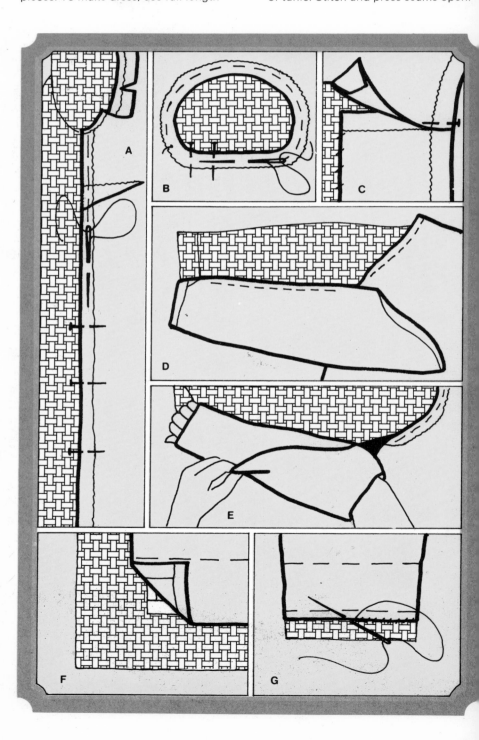

4. Right sides together, pin and stitch shoulder seams of front and back neck facings. Press.

5. Working on the outside of the garment and with right sides together, pin the facing into position, matching relevant points. Baste and stitch.

6. Trim neck and front edges to an even $\frac{1}{8}$ in. all round and turn facings to inside. Press.

7. Press up the hem of the tunic and pin. Slip-stitch the facing to the hem at the points where they meet. Slip-stitch the hem of the tunic. Press again.

8. Pin and stitch darts in the front linings. Right sides together, pin, baste and stitch shoulder seams and side seams of lining. Press seams open.

9. Turn tunic inside out and with wrong sides together pin and baste lining on to tunic. Turn in and slip-stitch lining round facing and hem. Press.

10. Clip the seam allowance at intervals round tunic armhole so that the $\frac{5}{8}$ in. may be pressed to the inside of the garment and lie flat. Repeat with the armhole of the lining and then pin and slip-stitch the lining to the tunic armhole. The armhole is then faced out by the lining itself.

11. Make hand stitched or machine buttonholes in positions marked on pattern.

12. Stitch on buttons and give final press.

## Trousers

1. Right sides together, pin and baste front crutch seams as far as zip opening (as marked on pattern). Stitch and press open, clipping seam where necessary.

2. Working on the outside of the trousers, place zip face down on the position as indicated on pattern. Using a zipper foot on the machine, stitch along the righthand tape of the zip about $\frac{1}{8}$ in. in from the teeth and stitching through single fabric of trouser front only. Turn back on centre centre fold line (see pattern) and pin and baste through all thicknesses along indicated stitching line, also pinning and basting zip into position on other side of centre front seam. Complete zip insertion and press.

3. Make darts at front and back waists and press towards centre front and centre back.

4. Right sides together pin and baste back crutch seam. Stitch and press open.

5. Right sides together pin and baste front and back trousers together along side seams and inside leg seams, taking care to match notches and crutch seams. Stitch and press open.

6. Cut waist petersham to correct size allowing 2 in. extra for hems and over-lap for hook and eye fastening. Make $\frac{1}{2}$ in. hem at each end of petersham and pin and baste along waistline of trousers, working on the outside of the garment and pinning the lower edge of

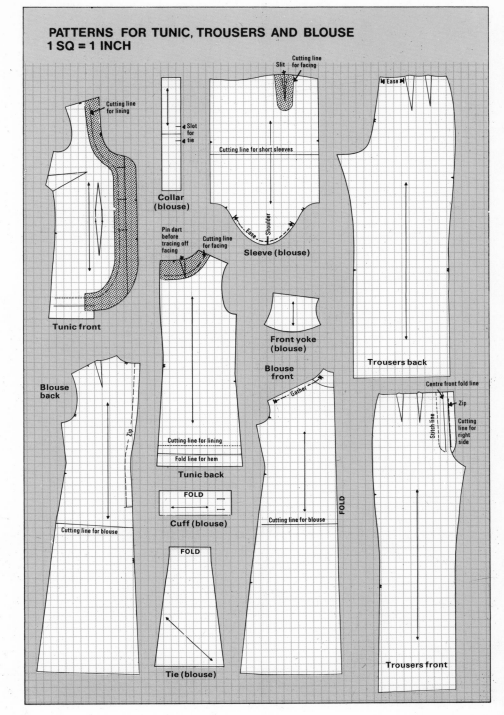

**PATTERNS FOR TUNIC, TROUSERS AND BLOUSE**
**1 SQ = 1 INCH**

Cutting line for lining

Collar (blouse)

Slot for tie

Cutting line for facing

Slit — Cutting line for facing

Cutting line for short sleeves

Ease — Shoulder

Sleeve (blouse)

Ease

Pin dart before tracing off facing

Cutting line for facing

Tunic front

Front yoke (blouse)

Trousers back

Blouse back

Blouse front

Gather

Centre front fold line

Zip

Stitch line

Cutting line for right side

Zip

Cutting line for lining

Fold line for hem

Tunic back

FOLD

Cuff (blouse)

Cutting line for blouse

FOLD

Cutting line for blouse

FOLD

Tie (blouse)

Trousers front

the petersham on the seamline so that the petersham extends upwards beyond the seam allowance of the trousers waist. Stitch and turn the petersham on to the inside of the trousers and press downwards.

7. With neat handsewing catch the petersham to waist darts and seams so that it is held in position.

8. Pin and press up trouser hems; neatly hem-stitch and press again.

9. Attach hook and eye at centre front waist.

## Blouse

1. With large machine stitch run gathering threads on front bodice as indicated on pattern. Draw up threads, spacing gathers evenly.

2. Right sides together, pin and baste front yokes on to front bodice and stitch. Press turnings upwards.

3. Machine a second row of stitching along yokes $\frac{1}{4}$ in. from the seamline.

4. Right sides together, pin front neck facing to outside of bodice front at the neck edge and stitch. Trim seam allowance and press to inside of bodice.

5. Make back shoulder darts and press towards centre back.

6. Right sides together pin and stitch centre back seam as far as opening for zip. Press seam open.

7. Right sides together pin and stitch shoulder seams. Press open.

8. Pin short ends of neck collar band and stitch. Turn out and press.

9. Clip in seam allowance at points

indicated for slot for tie.

10. Right sides together, pin one layer of neck edge of collar band to the bodice neckline, leaving free where indicated for the tie slot. Stitch and press turnings upwards.

11. Pin and slipstitch top layer of collar neck to blouse neckline, slip-stitching the collar to itself between marks for the slot.

12. Insert zip at centre back seam bringing it to the top of the collar band.

13. Pin, baste, stitch and turn out tie. Press.

14. Right sides together, pin and stitch side seams. Press open.

15. Neaten outer edges of facings and, right sides together, pin sleeve facings on to outside of sleeves. Stitch, press and turn back on to inside of sleeve.

16. Right sides together, pin and stitch sleeve seams. Press open.

17. Run gathering thread along cuff edge of sleeve. Draw up evenly, spacing gathers.

18. Right sides together, pin and stitch short ends of cuff. Turn out and press.

19. Pin one long edge of cuff to sleeve edge and baste, keeping gathers evenly spaced. Stitch and press turnings downwards.

20. Hem top layer of cuff to sleeve edge neatly.

21. Pin sleeve head into armhole, matching shoulder point and underarm seam and easing in head as indicated on pattern. Stitch and press. Repeat with second sleeve.

22. Make narrow hem on blouse body.

23. Make hand-sewn or machine buttonholes on cuffs.

24. Stitch on buttons, hook and eye at centre back neck and slot tie through front neck of blouse. Give final press.

**Alternative versions**

To make blouse or dress without tie, omit instructions for tie and also those indicating leaving the collar band free between notches. Apply collar band to neckline all the way without a space. Short-sleeved blouse has 1-in. hem instead of cuffs. Follow cutting line as marked on pattern. Dress has 2-in. hem.

Follow cutting line as marked on the pattern. Make self-belt for dress or use a bought belt.

## TROUSER TIPS

**Stay-stitch** $\frac{5}{8}$ in. from waistline and $\frac{1}{2}$ in. from side seams at top part of trousers (not legs).

**Easy fitting method** to ensure trousers fit you properly—baste centre front and back crutch seams and inside leg seams. Then pin side seams on right side of fabric. Slip trousers on and make adjustments before stitching.

**Set** the creases before you seam trouser fronts and back together, after you have made sure that fitting is correct. Crease should be at the centre of each front and back piece, ending just below waist darts in front. Baste crease markings and fold. Use steam iron and cloth, and get a sharper crease by pounding edge with a block or back of a wooden clothes brush after steaming.

**Stitch** the crutch seam with a continuous line of stitching, when making trousers with a side zip. Place one trouser leg inside the other, right sides together. Use smaller sewing stitch than usual or narrow zig-zag or stretch stitch. Reinforce with a second row of stitching over first line.

**Permanent creases**—stitch narrow tucks, wrong sides together. Stitch very close to the fold edge, stopping just below waist darts in front.

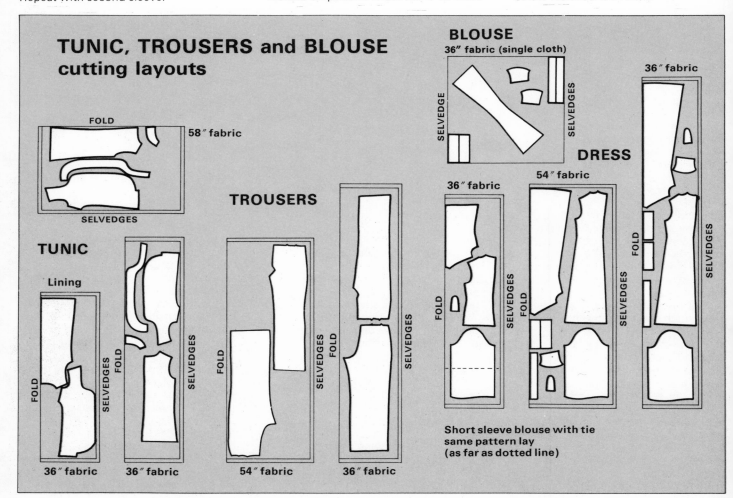

# TUNIC, TROUSERS and BLOUSE cutting layouts

**BLOUSE**
36" fabric (single cloth)

SELVEDGE

SELVEDGES

36" fabric

**DRESS**

FOLD — 58" fabric

SELVEDGES

**TROUSERS**

**TUNIC**

Lining

54" fabric

36" fabric

36" fabric

54" fabric

36" fabric

36" fabric

**Short sleeve blouse with tie same pattern lay (as far as dotted line)**

# SEWING

## Lesson Six:

## Giving a couture finish to your garments

## Trimming ideas

**Sew pretty ribbon or braid** to trim where facing and lining meet inside a jacket or coat. Use narrow width for your decorative finish to go round corners easily. Alternatively, use ricrac braid or lace edging. Sew in by hand.

**A chain weight** across the back of a suit jacket helps the jacket to hang better, and looks decorative. Buy chains specially for sewing—they have flattened links. A chain should be long enough to extend across the back of the jacket below the lining, and beyond the side seams. Overcast gold chain in position along the top of the hem. Make sure stitches do not go through to front of garment. Remove chain before dry-cleaning because pressing it will cause an impression on jacket front.

**Covered hooks and eyes** give a nice finishing touch to a garment. Use large hooks and eyes and work blanket stitches closely over them with button-hole twist thread.

**Covered snap fasteners** are also attractive, especially if they are used in a position where they may show when worn. Use lightweight matching fabric. Cut circles about twice the diameter of the snap and gather round the edge. Put snap in middle, draw up threads and fasten off, then sew on snap in the usual way. When you fasten snaps, the ball part will automatically make the centre hole in the fabric (it doesn't need any special finishing).

**Sunken snaps** are good with loosely woven materials. Place the ball part of the fastener behind the fabric—slip it between fabric and facing. Stretch fabric threads to push ball through to right side. Now stitch.

**Make ribbon belt** using beautiful ribbon backed with a strip of iron-on non-woven interfacing. Cut strip slightly narrower than width of ribbon and 1 in. shorter than your waist. Round off corners, centre interfacing and press in place. Cut ribbon ends diagonally.

## Tailoring tips

### FOR A PERFECT FINISH

**Padding stitch** is used to hold interfacing and underlining to the fabric at places like collars. On the wrong side, baste interfacing to fabric round edge.

Hold material with left hand and with needle make stitch, picking up small amount of interfacing and only a thread or two from the fabric underneath. Do not pull thread too taut—keep it loose otherwise you will get an impression of pad stitching on the right side. Make long diagonal stitches about $1\frac{1}{4}$ in. apart in rows. Stitches should be barely visible on right side.

**Interfaced hem** for tailored jackets. Open out facings on coat or jacket at lower edge. Cut a bias strip of interfacing $1\frac{1}{2}$ in. wide, the measurement of hemline between front interfacings, plus 1 in. Piece together interfacing strips if necessary. Place bias strip along hemline centred to the fold of the hem so that the strip is folded in half when hem is turned up. Extend ends of bias $\frac{1}{2}$ in. over front interfacing each side. Sew interfacing to underlining or to fabric of garment with invisible herringbone (feather) stitching. Turn up lower edge of hem along hemline. Baste close to fold. Finish as usual and press lightly. Sew up hem. This can also be used for jacket sleeve edges.

**Interfacing** is a third layer of fabric used between fabric and facing and helps to provide crispness, shape and support for a garment. Interfacing is generally used for necklines, cuffs, collars, down the fronts of jackets, to reinforce buttonholes and to add body to hemlines. There are many types and weights of interfacing available.

**Iron-on interfacings** tend to make a fabric stiffer, so they are often recommended for use in smaller areas. But **iron-on tailor's canvas** is proving a boon for use on suits and coats because it saves a great deal of work. Just press on and pad stitch round the edges instead of all over as you normally would. Iron-on, non-woven interfacings can be used on all fabrics, except the one hundred per cent synthetics. Use sew-in interfacings for these fabrics, choosing a weight to suit the weight of the fabric.

A useful aid is a **fusible fleece** which bonds fabric to fabric without sewing—good for hems, pockets, sleeves, motifs collars, repairs and patching. It can also be used as a backing to preserve the shape of lace knitting and crochet. To eliminate collar padding, just cut the fleece to the shape of under collar. Apply with a hot iron. When cool, remove the transfer paper, place interfacing on top and steam press.

**Collar canvas** can be bought already cut on the cross. **Hair canvas** for tailoring can be cotton or wool but although wool is more expensive, it has more spring.

**Shrink sleeve head** to fit in tailored armholes. There is sometimes a lot of fullness on the head of a sleeve to ease in when sewing woollen coats and jackets. Run a gathering thread round top of sleeve between notches, marking the ease. Draw up threads to fit armhole, spreading fabric between finger and thumb so that it does not go

into pleats. (Do this first before stitching underarm sleeve seams.) Lay sleeve on ironing board or sleeve board, and with damp cloth and steam iron, gently press head of sleeve to shrink away fullness.

## Pressing

### LIKE A PROFESSIONAL

With tailoring—as with other aspects of sewing—your skill with pressing makes all the difference to the finished look of your garment. You must press before, during and after making up your garments. Press seams before starting to stitch one garment section to another. If you are not sure about the effect of heat on a particular fabric, it is best to check-press a scrap first.

### EQUIPMENT

A steam-dry iron is best, with a variable temperature control for synthetics as well as cotton and wool. Pressing cloths prevent shine on a fabric and are best made of muslin or cheesecloth. Use damp if you need extra moisture as well as the steam from iron. Heavier drill fabric protects your clothes from shine, while wool pressing cloths are best used with wool materials to prevent flattening the texture.

A sleeve board looks like a miniature ironing board and is essential for reaching awkward corners on sleeves. Keep the cover clean and padded.

A **velvet board** is also useful. You put the pile side of the material over the wire side of the board to prevent it from flattening.

A **seam roll** is a long, narrow bolster shape, about 3—5 in. longer than your iron. It is used for pressing small sections or seams and stops ridges on the outside when you press seams open.

A **tailor's clapper** or pounding block is a smooth, shaped piece of wood which you use to flatten seams and facing edges as you steam them. You steam-press, then slap down the clapper on your seam and hold for a few seconds. It gives sharp edges. Use in tailoring, buttonholes, collars, lapels, facings, pockets, hems, pleats, not on zip.

A **tailor's ham** is a firm rounded cushion and is used for pressing shaped sections of the garment, such as curved darts or shoulder and bust seams.

**Make do** . . . if you haven't got any heavy, suitable drill cloths to hand while pressing and need one to prevent shine, you can improvise by using heavy brown paper. A stiff clothes brush can be used instead of a velvet needle board for small areas.

## Good grooming hints

**Hang** your clothes on a strong,

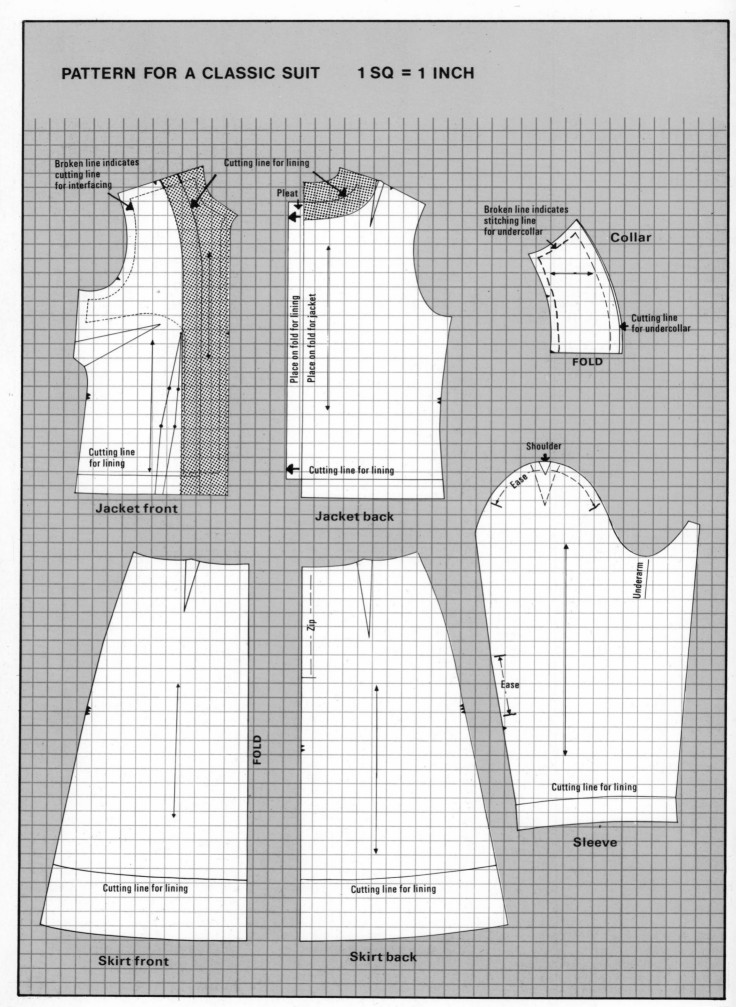

# PATTERN FOR A CLASSIC SUIT    1 SQ = 1 INCH

Broken line indicates cutting line for interfacing

Cutting line for lining

Pleat

Broken line indicates stitching line for undercollar

**Collar**

Cutting line for undercollar

**FOLD**

Place on fold for lining

Place on fold for jacket

Cutting line for lining

**Jacket front**

Cutting line for lining

**Jacket back**

Shoulder

Ease

Ease

Underarm

Zip

FOLD

Cutting line for lining

**Sleeve**

Cutting line for lining

Cutting line for lining

**Skirt front**

**Skirt back**

contoured hanger and you will not have to iron so often. Fasten the buttons and zips and remove belts and heavy objects from pockets.

**Remove** shine and over-pressing by holding your steam iron about an inch away from material, letting the steam go through it. Apply white vinegar with a thin paint brush—test first—then steam press, to remove creases and shine.

**Press** after washing, ironing on the wrong side first to open up seams.

**Take care** that you press according to the type of material. For instance, dark coloured cottons need a dry cloth with steam iron if you press them on the right side. Lighter cottons may need a heat setting like silk, but heavier cottons could need the higher linen setting. Rayon needs low heat; press on wrong side with a dry cloth. Linen needs higher heat and more dampness; continue to press until it is dry. Do not leave damp.

Wool is rather sensitive and needs moisture and heat. Use a clothes brush to raise the nap while the fabric is still a bit damp. Take the greatest care with synthetic fibres and silk. You need the least amount of pressure, moisture and heat. Test a scrap first to see that the material does not spot with water (a danger with silk). Try placing a strip of tissue paper between fabric and iron.

As a rule, you do not need to use a cloth, but if you decide to use one, it should be thin. Dull fabrics should be pressed on the wrong side, or use a pressing cloth for the right side. It is very difficult—almost impossible—to remove iron-shine from acetates.

**Dampness.** A wet cloth may cause over-pressing and may spot fabric. To make sure your cloth is just the right dampness, wet about a third of it, then roll it up and wring.

**Pressure.** Have the weight of the iron in your hand and use only light pressure on material. Never rest the weight of the iron fully on the garment. Lift and lower with care. You only need more pressure when pressing firm weaves and crease-resistant fabrics.

## YOUR SIXTH MAKE

## A CLASSIC SUIT

The edge-to-edge jacket is semi fitted, and has a neat roll collar; the skirt is a flattering A-line style. The blouse is the short-sleeved version of blouse pattern given in Sewing, lesson five.

## MATERIALS YOU WILL NEED

2⅜ yd. of fabric, 54 in. wide, or 2⅜ yd. of fabric, 60 in. wide, or 2¾ yd. of fabric 45 in. wide (all without nap). 2⅞ yd. of lining fabric, 36 in. wide; ¾ yd. of interfacing, 32 or 36 in. wide. A 7-in. zip fastener; 1 hook and eye. A waist length of petersham ribbon plus 2 in.; seam binding tape for hem.

## FABRIC SUGGESTIONS

Worsted, mediumweight wool and wool mixtures, tweeds, cotton velvet, corduroy.

## SIZE NOTE

The pattern as given will comfortably fit bust size 34 in., hip size 36 in. To adapt the pattern to fit your size, follow instructions given in Sewing, lesson one.

## TO MAKE YOUR PATTERN

The diagrams on page 70 give the pattern pieces you will need. One square on the diagrams equals 1 in. Following the step-by-step instructions in Sewing, lesson one, prepare your full-size pattern on squared paper.

Cut out fabric pieces, following the cutting layouts.

Unless otherwise stated, all seams are stitched ⅝ in. from edge of fabric, and should be pressed open after stitching.

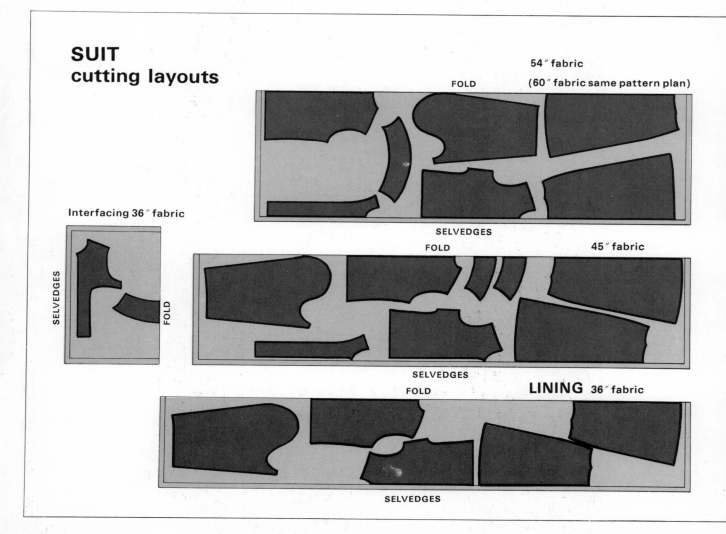

**SUIT cutting layouts**

lesson on previous pages).

13. Pin sleeve into armhole. Baste and stitch. Press. Make second sleeve in a similar way.

14. Stitch seam binding to sleeve hems and jacket hem. Press up hems and stitch with neat, loose stitches.

15. Make darts in lining and press.

16. Right sides together, pin and stitch shoulder seams and side seams of lining. Press.

17. Pin and stitch lining sleeve seams, right sides together.

18. Turn jacket inside out and, wrong sides together, pin in jacket lining round jacket facing.

19. Anchor lining round armhole by attaching to seam allowance of jacket armhole with running stitches (see Sewing, lesson five).

20. Slipstitch lining to jacket all round facing edge, pleating lining for ease of movement (see Sewing, lesson five) at centre back as indicated.

21. Right side out, slip sleeve lining over jacket sleeve and pin round armhole, easing in fullness round head. Slipstitch sleeve lining to jacket lining on armhole seam. Pin lining to sleeve hem and slipstitch neatly all round.

22. Turn jacket right side out and give final press.

## TO MAKE SKIRT

1. Make waist darts in back and front skirt pieces. Press towards centre back and centre front.

2. Right sides together, pin and baste centre back seam as far as zip opening, as marked on pattern. Stitch and press open.

3. Insert zip at centre back.

4. Right sides together, pin and baste side seams. Stitch and press open.

5. Make darts in skirt lining and press.

6. Right sides together, pin and stitch centre back and side seams in lining using French seams if the cloth is inclined to fray.

7. Wrong sides together, pin lining to skirt along waist line. Anchor with a row of machine stitching and turn in and hem round zip opening.

8. Cut petersham to correct size for waist measurement plus 2 in. and make $\frac{1}{2}$-in. hem at each end.

9. Pin petersham along waistline working on the outside of the skirt and pinning the lower edge of the petersham to the seamline, so that the width of the petersham extends beyond the seam allowance of the waist seam.

10. Stitch and turn petersham on to inside of skirt and press.

11. Attach with neat hand stitching to darts and seams to hold petersham in position.

12. Apply seam binding to hem edge.

13. Press up skirt hem and stitch neatly by hand.

14. Press up lining hem and stitch neatly by hand.

15. Sew hook and eye at centre back waist.

16. Give final press.

## TO MAKE JACKET

1. Pin and tailor-pad stitch interfacings on to front jacket and under collar (see lesson on previous pages).

2. Make darts as indicated on front and back jackets. Press. Where a thick fabric is used, clip darts and press open.

3. Right sides together, pin, baste and stitch shoulder and side seams. Press open.

4. Right sides together, pin and baste neck edge of under collar to neck edge of jacket. Stitch and press open. Clip seams where necessary.

5. Pin and baste shoulder seams of facings, right sides together, and stitch. Press open.

6. Right sides together, pin neck edge of top collar to neck edges of facings. Stitch and press open.

7. Working on the outside of the jacket and right sides together, pin and baste facings and top collar to centre front edge and outside collar edge of jacket, taking care to match notches.

8. Stitch carefully along centre front edge and along outside edge of collar.

9. Trim turnings away evenly to $\frac{1}{8}$ in. all round and turn facings to inside of jacket and press carefully.

10. Right sides together, pin sleeve seams, easing in where marked on pattern. Baste, stitch and press open.

11. Stitch dart on sleeve head and press open.

12. With large stitch, run retaining thread round head of sleeve between the arrows on pattern indicating ease. Draw up. Shrink away fullness (see

# APPLIQUÉ

## Lesson One:

## The art of Appliqué

**Jill Blake tells you how this attractive craft can be adapted for pictures, curtains, cushions and clothes.**

Appliqué as defined by the dictionary means 'applied' or 'cut from one material or fabric and applied to the surface of another'—a rather heavy and unattractive way of describing a most attractive and decorative art. In appliqué, areas of fabric are cut out and applied to the background fabric in a variety of ways depending on the use of the finished work, whether it is to be practical or decorative, and also depending on the materials used. If the finished piece of appliqué is to be a picture, then the areas of applied fabric do not have to be extremely well fastened, but it is usual to use decorative embroidery stitches to enhance the work. Where the finished work will have to withstand washing, ironing and constant wear and tear, such as on children's clothes, aprons, etc., then they must be extremely securely fastened. Methods of fastening are different, hand or machine embroidery can be used, or matching stitching, or in some cases neat handstitching, but non-fray materials such as leather, plastic and felt can be stuck in position.

## Fabrics and threads

As far as possible, the pieces of material to be applied to the background should be cut to follow the same grain as the background fabric. This helps to prevent the shapes puckering when the work is finished. It is usual to tack the shapes in position first and the raw edges can be treated in different ways. If the work is a picture, which will eventually be mounted under glass, the appliqué design can be caught down every $\frac{1}{2}$ inch or so with a minute stitch, using a fine needle and a thin thread such as machine embroidery cotton. Alternatively, a sewing machine may be used. If the picture is not to be mounted under glass, then a more secure method of fixing will be needed, such as satin, herringbone, buttonhole or feather stitch, and this embroidery also enhances the work,

as previously mentioned. You can use stranded embroidery cotton for this, although other threads, including metallic ones, give a very decorative quality to the work, and where very heavy fabrics are being applied, linen thread or tapestry wool can be used very effectively.

## Texture

Texture is important in appliqué work. If you are making a picture, a rich variety of textures can be added to the background fabric to create a sumptuous effect, but washable clothes should have other washable fabrics, in the same weight, applied to them—and it is very important to see that they are colour-fast! Items such as cushions, curtains, bedcovers and garments which are likely to be dry-cleaned can have a variety of fabrics such as silk, satin, velvet, wool, or lamé appliquéd on to the background. Loosely woven fabrics such as hessian, nets, tweeds, open-weave furnishing fabrics and other materials which fray easily, should be used with care unless they are intended to give a shaggy texture to the work. They can be treated with rubber solution or millinery glue—a

light coating should be applied to the edges on the back of the fabric and allowed to dry before placing on the background fabric. Alternatively, iron on to the iron-on type of self-adhesive bonded fabric which is really a stiffener (Vilene), so the pieces will keep their shape and remain perfectly flat, although stitching will be a little harder with shapes treated in this manner.

Felt, leather and plastic are very easy to work with which is why some of these have been used for our aprons. They do not fray at all so the edges do not need to be turned in. They can be sewn in place by any of the methods previously mentioned, or they can be stuck on using a special fabric adhesive which will not mark the fabric (Copydex). As these materials are not woven they do not have any grain so they can be cut in any direction and placed any way on the background without fear of puckering.

## Blind appliqué

Blind appliqué is the technical name for appliqué where the raw edge of the shapes is turned under then hemmed down. Obviously the shapes in this

type of appliqué cannot be too complicated and it is usual to cut a straight or simple curved edge, otherwise the raw edges would be difficult to turn under. Make a paper shape or template first, rather like patchwork. The paper shape is then pinned and tacked to the right side of the fabric to be applied. The edges of the shape are turned under and tacked to the wrong side of the fabric. The shape then looks like a neat piece of paper with fabric turnings on the wrong side. The shape is then applied to the background, right side uppermost, paper and all, and the paper and tacking threads are then removed from the front. The stitches used for this type of appliqué should be invisible from the front of the work and are not used to enhance it at all. It is possible to use an interfacing material such as felt, Vilene or paper. This is tacked or ironed on to the **back** of the fabric shape to be applied, and the raw edges, where necessary, are turned over the interfacing. They are then tacked, any curves are clipped and the appliqué shape is slipstitched with the background material. The interfacing is not removed and consequently the appliquéd design has a slightly raised effect.

## Appliqué using the sewing machine

This is worked using the foot of the machine and a zig-zag stitch. Cut out the fabric shape and tack to the background, use a zig-zag stitch all round the edge of the shape to secure. The stitches must not be very close together otherwise the work will pucker. This method is generally used for appliqué pictures. For clothes a more complicated way of fixing is necessary. Iron on the material from which the applied shape is to be cut to mending tape or self-adhesive fabric stiffener (Vilene). Tack to the background fabric and turn the two materials upside down. Mark the shape to be appliquéd on the back of the work and follow round with a fine, not too close, zig-zag stitch. Turn the work the right way up and cut away the surplus material round the applied shape. Zig-zag round once again with a slightly wider and closer satin stitch.

**YOUR FIRST MAKES—**

# APPLIQUÉ APRONS

The apron shapes have been drawn out on squared paper without allowing for turnings. Each square represents 1 in. First make a paper pattern using brown paper or newspaper for the aprons and for the motifs.

# Man's gardening apron

## MATERIALS YOU WILL NEED

1 yd. 48 in. wide hessian or canvas; 2 yd. cotton binding 1 in. wide; small felt squares for appliqué; sewing cotton; in suitable colour.

## TO MAKE

Using the pattern, cut apron shape and pocket. Allow ¾ in. turning all round plus a 2 in. hem at the bottom of the apron. Cut two apron strings 43½ in. long (these are especially long so that they will tie at the front of the apron) and a neckband 25 in. long from the binding. Turn the edge of the apron over twice, inserting apron strings and neckband underneath the turned edge at the same time. Tack edge all around. Machine sew the turned edge with a double row of stitches. Cut out appliqué motifs in felt following the diagrams. Do not allow turnings as felt does not fray. Tack motifs in position on bib front and pocket. Machine sew round the edge of the appliqué. Tack the pocket in position turning raw edge under. Machine with double row of stitches. Turn up hem and stitch. *Note:* the appliqué motifs on this apron could be made of strong cotton material. In which case the shapes must be cut out slightly larger and a narrow edge turned under and tacked so that the material will not fray. When the shapes are placed in position on the apron the selvedge grain of the material should run downwards so that it will correspond with the background. This is important because the tension is then the same and the fabric is much less likely to pucker.

# Little girl's felt appliqué apron

(To fit 3-4-year-old)

## MATERIALS YOU WILL NEED

½ yd. felt; ½ yd. cotton material for lining; 2 yd. cotton binding 1 in wide; ¾ yd. coarse cotton lace; ¾ yd. thin white cotton cord; small felt squares for appliqué; 'invisible' thread; fabric adhesive (Copydex) optional.

## TO MAKE

Using the pattern, cut out apron and lining. Cut two apron strings 26½ in. long and neckband 18 in. long from the binding. Turn in edge of felt ½ in. all round and tack. Insert apron tapes under the edge of the turning at the same time. Cut out felt appliqué shapes, following the diagrams. arrange in position and tack them carefully onto apron. Small pieces can be stuck lightly in position with fabric adhesive (Copydex). Slipstitch round the shapes with 'invisible' thread. Cut and arrange white lace and cotton cord in position. Tack and hand sew. Turn in ½ in. edge around the lining. Lay the wrong sides of the apron and lining together. Tack and slipstitch the two together.

# Boy's work apron

(To fit 4-5-year-old)

## MATERIALS YOU WILL NEED

½ yd. 36-in. wide plastic coated fabric; 3½ yd. decorative cotton braid for edging and apron strings; ¼ yd. contrasting plastic coated fabric for name appliqué; reel Trylko or other sewing thread suitable for man-made fibres; all-purpose adhesive (Evo-stick or Bostik).

## TO MAKE

Following the pattern cut apron shape. Cut neckband 17 in. long and two apron strings 20 in. long from the braid. Turn ½-in. edge onto right side of material all way round apron, and stick down lightly with a clear all-purpose adhesive. Tack the braid on top of this turning all round the edge of apron. At the same time tack apron strings and neckband on to apron underneath the main braid outline. If a straight braid is used it must be eased round the armhole curvature with a series of small tucks. This problem will not arise if a bias binding is being used, but in this case a stronger, thicker, braid will be required to make the neck and apron strings. Machine stitch the braid. Design and draw the lettering for the name on paper and trace on to the contrasting plastic coated fabric. Cut out and fix the letters on the apron with strips of adhesive tape (Sellotape), (tacking stitches would be difficult

due to the thickness of the fabric). The edges of the letters do not need turning in. Machine stitch round the letters and then carefully remove the tape.

# Apron

## MATERIALS YOU WILL NEED

1 yd. 36-in. wide plastic coated fabric; ½ yd. 2 contrasting plastic coated fabrics, one plain, one patterned; 2 yd. coloured tape 1 in. wide for strings; reel Trylko or other sewing thread suitable for man-made fibres; adhesive suitable for plastic coated fabric (Evo-stick or Bostic).

## TO MAKE

Using pattern, cut out the apron shape and turn in ½ in. all round. When turning this fabric it helps to stick in position with adhesive tape (Sellotape) or adhesive before sewing as the fabric is too thick to tack properly and can show needle marks. Machine sew edges.

Cut out and turn in pocket edge all round, Sew top edge with double row of machine stitches. Place pocket in position on apron and machine in place with two rows of stitches.

Cut out motifs following diagrams. Make sure surface of the plastic coated fabric is clean and dust free. Stick motifs in place with clear adhesive (Evo-stick or Bostic), or for extra strength an impact adhesive

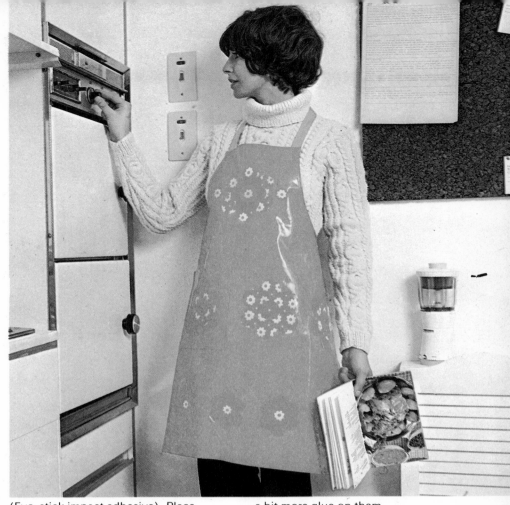

(Evo-stick impact adhesive). Place apron very flat with weight on top of the motifs and if possible leave overnight. Check that edges of the shapes are glued down firmly. If necessary use

a bit more glue on them.

Cut tapes into three 18-inch lengths and machine stitch to apron for neck tape and strings. Finish strings with neat hem.

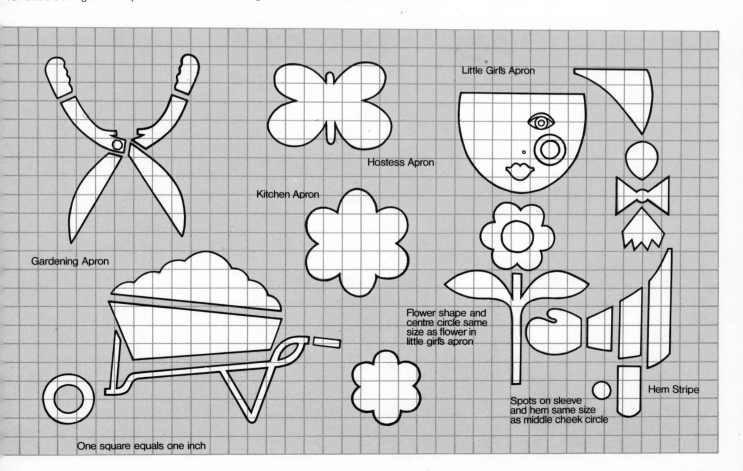

Gardening Apron

Kitchen Apron

Hostess Apron

Little Girls Apron

Flower shape and centre circle same size as flower in little girls apron

Spots on sleeve and hem same size as middle cheek circle

Hem Stripe

One square equals one inch

# Hostess apron

## MATERIALS YOU WILL NEED

1 yd. 36-in. wide pink cotton fabric;
1 yd. 36-in. wide white cotton fabric
(for lining); 4 yd. white lace edging;
1½ yd. daisy edging (daisies about
1 in. wide); 1 small white lace edged
handkerchief (for butterfly), or 30 in.
white lace and ¼ yd. white cotton
lawn; reel Sylko or other sewing
thread.

## TO MAKE

Cut two strips 26 in. by 36 in. one in
pink and one in white lining fabric
for the skirt of the apron. Turn in ½ in.
hem down sides and bottom of pink
fabric and tack. Gather lace edging
slightly and tack to wrong side of pink
fabric, so a small frill shows on the
right side. Machine stitch round
stitching through lace and hem.
Cut white daisy edging into separate
flower heads, arrange on front of
pink fabric, tack and sew in place by
hand. Leave four daisies to decorate
the butterfly.
To make the butterfly, cut out the shape
following the diagram, from the plain
part of the handkerchief or lawn,
turn in a very small hem and tack.
Edge the wing with the lace from the
edge of the handkerchief or separate
lace, and tack in position. Hand sew a
daisy head in the centre of each wing.
Tack shape on apron, machine stitch
round the solid edge of the butterfly and
hand sew lace edge. Make antennae
of lace and hand sew on apron.
Lay apron and lining wrong sides
together, tack a ½ in. hem round lining,
slipstitch to apron. Remove tacking
threads. Gather top of apron and
lining to fit front of waist (about 15 in.).
For the waistband and strings, cut
each 9½ in. strip of fabric lengthways
into two 4½-in. pieces. Cut one into
two and join each end to the larger
strip. Sew seams by machine and
press on wrong side. Place lining and
material right sides together and fold
lengthways. Turn in ¼ in. hem, tack
and press.
Place centre of gathered apron to
centre of waistband. Tack (baste)
into place and stitch in front with
machine. Sew bands onto skirt on
reverse side. Join edges of remaining
tie strings and press.

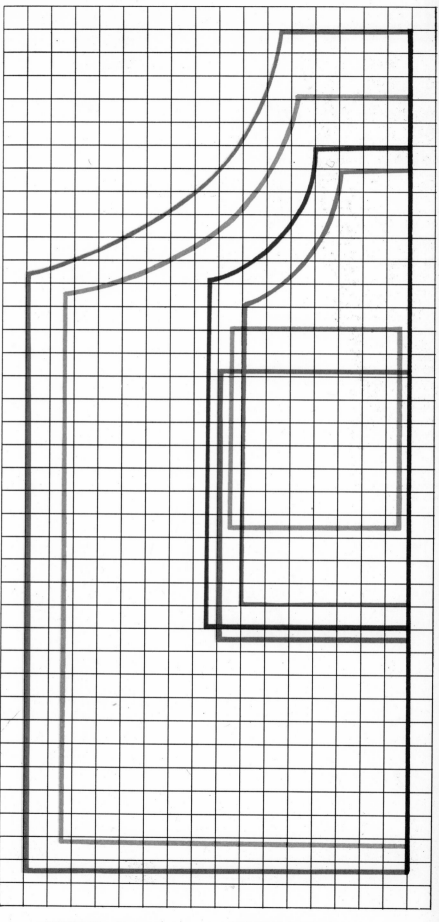

GREEN: Gardening Apron  PURPLE: Felt Apron
RED: Kitchen Apron  BLUE: Boys Apron

# APPLIQUÉ

## Lesson Two:

## Making appliqué pictures and belts

**Jill Blake tells you more about this attractive craft**

Appliqué can be such an intensely creative art, each picture as individual as an oil painting, so it is not possible to give precise instructions for our appliqué picture, but if you followed our first appliqué lesson you will already know the basic principles of the art and this lesson will inspire you (we hope) to make your own pictures.

## Framing up

If you plan to make a large picture or hanging, then it is wise to use an embroidery frame to hold the background fabric in position, and rigid, while you work on it. Cut the backing or background fabric at least 1 inch larger all round than the finished work is to be, with the selvedge grain running from top to bottom. Mark the centre. Fold down $\frac{1}{2}$ inch top and bottom, and on the two sides fold the $\frac{1}{2}$-inch turning over fairly fine string. Stitch with a running stitch with the occasional back stitch for extra

strength (A1). Next, take the rollers (B2) and mark the centre of the webbing on each. Put the marked centre of the fabric wrong-side down to these two points and pin outwards towards the sides. Using strong thread, such as button thread, overcast the edges of the backing fabric to the webbing. Slip the slats through the slots at the ends of the rollers. If your fabric is considerably longer than the side pieces, wind the extra fabric round the rollers before slipping in the slats (B3). Put in the pegs or split-pins making sure the distance between the rollers on each side is even. The pegs are adjusted to keep the fabric absolutely taut for transferring on design or for actual embroidery, but it is left slack when the fabric to be applied is positioned. Use a length of string long enough to do one side without a join and lace through the backing and over the slats (B4). If you are using a backing fabric and the *background* fabric has to be placed on top of it, stitch the background fabric to the backing, first the top, then bottom and then sides. Tighten up the frame and lacing and tie off the string. For really large work a quilting frame may be used.

## Variety in colour and texture

It is very important to use different colours and textures skilfully, and in lesson one we told you how to cope with fabrics which fray or are likely to pucker. As most fabric pictures are

likely to be framed under glass it is not always necessary to have every piece of applied fabric fastened down securely, but embroidery does greatly enhance this type of picture, and in fact our picture was made entirely by embroidering the shapes in position. Because embroidery is likely to be used on at least part of the picture it is most important to choose the background fabric carefully—ideally a linen or linen-like fabric, scrim, crash, closely woven cotton, hessian (burlap) or fine wools make the best background fabric. Avoid anything which will stretch too much or which is loosely woven.

## Designing the picture

There are several ways of designing an appliqué picture. One way is to sit down and draw out various ideas until you achieve a design which you like and then colour it. This design can then be transferred to the background fabric and also be used to cut out the fabric which is to be applied to the background (see notes on transferring the design). But this method is really for the professional designer, and it is easier for the amateur to use printed fabrics for the appliqué design, which can be simply cut out following natural outlines in the fabric. Move these about on the background until a good blend of shapes and colours is achieved, press, then pin in position (C1) and tack (C2), starting with pieces which go at the back of the picture. Remember

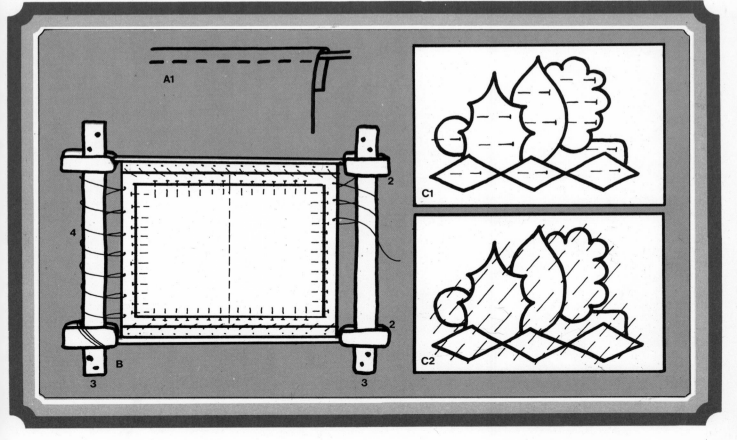

when pinning, if all the shapes are to be fastened to the background by embroidery, it is wise to allow a little space between the shapes, otherwise it can be difficult to embroider over three thicknesses of fabric. If the fabric is to be partly machine or hand stitched, then fabrics can overlap, and in some cases fragile fabrics, such as net and lace, can be used very effectively to overlap each other and thicker fabrics. Another way of designing appliqué is to use pieces of coloured paper which correspond in tone to your fabric scraps. Cut these into interesting shapes and move them about on plain paper, the colour of your background, until you get a pleasing design. You can then carefully draw round each shape, move them one by one and use them as a pattern to cut each fabric piece. It is wise to stick the coloured paper in position on your background paper, so you have a chart to work from.

For a really random appliqué design, one which will give an abstract picture as an end result, you can cut out interesting shapes from pieces of fabric, as varied in weight as possible, perhaps adding some braid or cord for texture interest. These can be moved about on the background fabric until the desired result is achieved and they can then be pressed, pinned and tacked in position.

Remember a picture needs to have a focal point. This can be achieved by using one boldly patterned or coloured piece of fabric, or by lines or shapes leading the eye towards one point in the picture. If embroidery is being used, this can help draw attention to the focal point. Start with the large shapes first when planning your design and remember a large shape need not necessarily be a large piece of applied fabric—it could be created by a collection of small ones, or by a mass of embroidery stitches worked into a shape. It is sometimes possible to help a weak design by clever use of embroidery stitches on the finished picture.

## Colour

Colour is very important, and you may well decide the picture is to go into a certain room and will need to complement the colour scheme—if this is the case then it should not be too difficult to work out what colours you want to use. If, on the other hand, you are starting with no particular colour scheme in mind, remember some of the most effective pictures are created by the use of different tones of one colour with perhaps a bright accent colour used in moderation. For example, a picture based on leaf shapes in tones of brown, gold and beiges on a creamy-white ground can have sharp accents of orange and turquoise, or a picture in plums, purple and pinks can be dramatically enhanced by the use of lime or emerald green as the accent

colour. Naturally, to a certain extent you will be limited by the pieces of fabric which you have available, but it is better to use several pieces of the same fabric than risk spoiling the appliqué by using lots of clashing colours.

## Transferring the design

If you have worked out the design on paper or by using coloured paper stuck onto a background you will need to transfer the design onto your foundation fabric. One way is to trace the design on to tracing, tissue or greaseproof paper and transfer this to white paper. The white paper can be used as a pattern for the shapes, and the original design used as reference. Tracing or tissue paper can be tacked to the background fabric and used as a guide to placing the shapes, and can be torn away before the stitching and embroidery are started. It helps to go over the shapes with a dressmaker's tracing wheel before starting to apply the fabric, as then the paper is more easily torn away.

More complicated methods can be used, such as pricking through the design and then rubbing in black or white pounce, but this is only really necessary where the design is very intricate.

Dressmakers' carbon paper can also be used to transfer a design. Place this face down on the background fabric, place the tracing, or original design, over this and outline with a very sharp point. When the carbon

paper and design are removed, the design is repeated on the fabric, but this method is only suitable for light coloured backgrounds.

## Our picture

Our picture was made on a background of pinky-purple linen-like fabric (Moygashel) and the applied shapes were cut out from cotton furnishing fabric. These came from a furnishing shop who were pleased to sell the book cheaply as the designs were being discontinued at the end of the season (Sandersons fabrics). But it is possible to use remnants, which are often sold off very cheaply, in the same way. The shapes were cut out, following the natural outline of the fabric design, but some were left large and others were cut down into a more interesting smaller shape. The shapes were moved about on the background fabric until the desired result was achieved and then the outlines were lightly marked round with a white pencil (chinagraph), the pieces of fabric were then pressed, pinned and tacked in position on the background fabric. A mixture of embroidery stitches were used to secure the shapes in place; satin stitch, buttonhole stitch and blanket stitch. The work was further enhanced by the use of chain stitch, stem stitch, cross stitch, couching, lazy-daisy stitch and French knots. Stranded embroidery cotton was used, split in half to give three threads.

(These stitches have appeared in Embroidery, lesson one; Felt and Fabric craft, lesson one; Fabric craft, lesson two).

felt cut the two smaller pocket shapes (F) and from the bright contrasting felt cut 2 large stars (G). Turn in the larger pocket shapes across the top and tack. Turn in $\frac{3}{8}$ in. across the top of the smaller pocket shapes, finish with a double row of stitching $\frac{1}{8}$ in. from the edge. Arrange the stars (1 large and 4 small) on each small pocket shape and stitch or stick with all-purpose fabric adhesive (Copydex). Place the front of the pocket (smaller shape) wrong side down onto the right side of the larger pocket shape, so that the serrated edge shows evenly behind. Stitch the pockets together $\frac{1}{8}$ in. from the edge, starting at one corner and working down the side, around the bottom and up to the top corner. Press, turn pockets right way out, press if necessary. To attach the pockets to the belt, place the pockets onto the outside of the belt so that the inside corners of each come at a point 2 in. on either side of the centre front fastening, and the top corners of each pocket touch the top of the belt. Tack in position starting and finishing at the top of the contrasting band, so that the pockets hang freely from the belt as illustrated. Try on to make sure belt fits properly and pockets hang well. Stitch.

## Child's safety purse on a belt

### MATERIALS YOU WILL NEED

$\frac{1}{8}$ yd. strong canvas, 36-in. wide; $\frac{1}{2}$ yd. denim, 36-in. wide; 4 yd. ric-rac braid; sewing threads to tone; small oddment fabric same colour as braid to cover buckle and fasteners; buckle kit to cover your own buckle (Picaby Buckle Kit) or bought buckle, $1\frac{1}{2}$ in. wide; $\frac{1}{4}$ yd. heavy-weight interlining (Vilene); button snaps (Trims) for fastening.

### TO MAKE

Make the belt first. Measure the waist and allow at least 6 in. extra for turnings and buckle threading. Cut a $1\frac{3}{4}$ in. strip across the width of the canvas to the required length. Cut a $3\frac{1}{2}$ in. strip of the denim to the same length. Lay the canvas on the wrong side of the denim, touching one edge and tack. Fold denim in half length-ways with right sides together. Stitch $\frac{1}{4}$-in. seam. This will hold the canvas inner strip. Turn the belt to right side and shape one end. Press. Sew on ric-rac braid as illustrated. Cover the buckle and attach to the non-shaped end of belt. Now make the purse. Lay the patterns (H) on the denim and cut *two* of each pattern shape. Cut interlining (Vilene) from the same pattern—only *one* of each shape. Fold one of the large denim pieces in half, right sides together, so that the purse shape is formed. Stitch $\frac{1}{4}$-in. seam round the outside of the purse shape from point *a* to point *c*. Turn to right side and tack $\frac{1}{4}$-in. turning both

## YOUR SECOND MAKES

# BELTS FOR CHILDREN

Appliqué belts can look most decorative and even a small boy would accept a belt designed as a holster, which would also be a practical, safe place for dinner or 'bus money. Different designs can be used to taste—just give free rein to your imagination!

## Holster belt
### MATERIALS YOU WILL NEED

 yd. 36-in. wide strong canvas; $\frac{1}{4}$ yd. 6-in. wide felt in the main colour; ewing thread to tone; $\frac{1}{4}$ yd. 36-in. wide elt in contrasting colour; sewing thread o tone; 3 small squares of different oloured felt; hooks for fastening; ll-purpose fabric adhesive (Copydex) ptional.

## TO MAKE

Measure the waist and allow an extra 3 in. for overlap and fastening (or measure hips if it is to be worn as a hipster belt). Cut a strip of canvas 2 in. wide to the length required. Cut a strip of the main colour felt $4\frac{3}{8}$ in. wide to the length required. Cut a strip of the contrasting felt $\frac{5}{8}$ in. wide to the length required. Tack and stitch this narrow strip to the main coloured felt strip so that, when the canvas is covered with the felt, the bright strip will be on the centre of the outside of the belt. Cover the canvas with the felt in this way and stitch by hand on the wrong side. Press if necessary. Machine stitch a line of stitches round the belt $\frac{1}{4}$ in. from the edge, leaving one of the ends plain for the overlap. Attach the hooks. Now make the pockets. Cut two large shapes from the squares of felt following diagram (D) and 8 small appliqué stars (E). The two large shapes, which form the back of the pockets can be cut with pinking shears to give a decorative edge. From the main colour

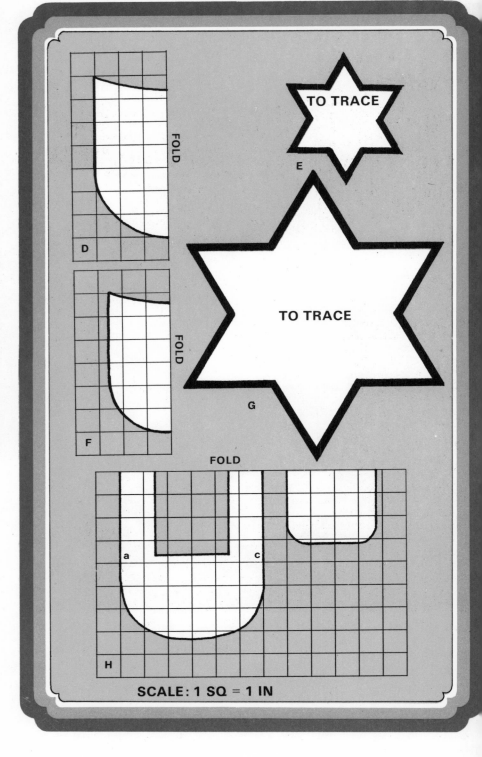

Included in image 2:

FOLD

D

FOLD

F

TO TRACE

E

TO TRACE

G

FOLD

a    c

H

**SCALE: 1 SQ. = 1 IN**

sides of strap from front to back and across the top of the purse opening. Make up the second large denim shape in the same way inserting the interlining (Vilene) at the same time. Place the two shapes together, one inside the other, so the inner shape becomes a lining. Tack and stitch strap edges together. Stitch across top of purse. For flap of purse, take one small denim shape and place interlining shape on wrong side, turn in $\frac{1}{4}$ in. all round. Turn in $\frac{1}{4}$ in. all round the second small denim shape. With the right sides facing outwards, place the two pieces together and stitch round $\frac{1}{8}$ in. from the edge. Fold this shape in half and stitch one half onto the outside back of the purse to create a pocket. The other half folds over the front to form the front flap. Sew on ric-rac braid as illustrated. Attach the snap fastenings to front flap and purse, so they close the purse firmly. Thread pocket onto belt.

## MORE SUGGESTIONS FOR TRIMMING A BELT AND PURSE

There are many different ways of trimming the basic belt and purse, instead of using the designs we show. There are a large variety of embroidered appliqué motifs available in the shops, ready to sew onto material. Butterflies in a fairly large size on the purse and smaller ones on the belt could look very pretty. Brightly coloured or patterned cotton braids are as effective

as the ric-rac braid on our denim belt. For a more dainty belt and purse, use a natural linen and decorate with machine-embroidered ribbon.
It is easy to cut appliqué shapes out of fabric in the same weight as the belt and purse. Or again you could use felt for the belt and appliqué shapes. Keep to simple shapes—for example a repeating flower and leaf motif; a row of hearts; hearts, diamonds, spades and clubs in red and black on a white belt; on a wider belt, letters can be used spelling out the child's name, or the purse can have just the initials. Abstract patterns look attractive too,

circles, diamonds, squares and triangles can all be used effectively. It is best to cut the shapes out of paper first and arrange on the belt and purse to judge the effect. The fabric shapes can then be cut slightly larger than the paper patterns and a small edge turned under to prevent fraying. Arrange the shapes on belt and purse so that the weave of the appliqué shape corresponds to that of the belt and purse material, to avoid tension and the puckering of the fabric. Tack and sew shapes in position with matching sewing thread. Felt shapes do not need a turning and can be stuck in place if preferred.

# KNITTING FOR ALL

## Lesson One:
## Back to Basics

### First steps to successful home knitting

## What it's all about

Knitting is an exciting craft, easily and quickly mastered and capable of producing an astonishing variety of different results. In its simplest form, you can use the craft to make gay scarves, colourful patchwork squares, dainty baby garments and easy sleeveless tops and boleros. When you are familiar with more advanced techniques and patterns, you can go on to make superb fashion outfits: coats, suits, dresses, long evening capes, trousers . . . there is virtually no limit to the range of garments and practical household articles too which can be produced with just a pair of knitting needles and a ball of wool! Surprising as it may seem when you look at an intricate piece of colour work, or an exquisitely fine lacy pattern, there are only two basic stitches in knitting: every pattern is based on a different combination or arrangement of these stitches. In this first lesson we show you how to do one of the two basic stitches, we also talk about the tools of the trade, and introduce you to the important techniques of casting on and off, and shaping by decreasing.

## Choosing the right yarn

To a novice knitter, a knitting wool store with its vast array of yarn types, colours and weights, can be bewildering. And as yarn manufacturers are constantly bringing out new and different types of yarn, the choice becomes even more confusing. . . Where do you begin to select the right yarn for your purpose? Why are there so many? What is the advantage of one over the other? In fact, most of these yarns can be divided into one of two categories: either a yarn made from natural fibres (wool or cotton) or a yarn made from man-made fibres (nylon, Acrilan and so forth). Sometimes however you will find a yarn in which natural and man-made fibres are combined so you get

the benefits of both in the same yarn. Every yarn has a particular characteristic which is useful for a different purpose: for example, cotton yarns are ideal for fine tablecloths and for beachwear, where a crispness of texture is attractive; wool is best for a baby's vest where softness is of paramount importance; and nylon, or a mixture of nylon with wool, gives a hardwearing, easy-to-wash finish suitable for a schoolboy's sweater. For luxury, long-lasting classic garments, cashmere or even pure silk yarns will give beautiful results.

When you buy a knitting pattern, a specific brand name and type of yarn will be recommended, and it is a rash knitter indeed who ignores this recommendation. Standard weights of yarn—for instance, three-ply or double knitting—even vary from one yarn manufacturer to the other. One

manufacturer may produce a double knitting weight which is somewhat fuller than average. This yarn will be heavy and so the length of a 1-oz. ball will be less than that of a 1-oz. ball in a lighter yarn. In other words, if you buy the wrong yarn you may need more than the quantity specified in the pattern.

When yarn is dyed (and this applies to black and white yarns as well as to colours) the makers number each batch in what is called a dye lot, and that number is printed on the band round each ball of yarn. It is important to check this dye lot number when you buy, and always to choose all the yarn needed for a particular garment from the same dye lot. Unfortunately small discrepancies between one dye lot and the next are as inevitable with

*Gay garter stitch bolero to knit, instructions start after lesson*

professional dyeing as they are with home dyeing. If you make a garment from two different dye lots, you may end up with an unattractive patchy effect.

Yarn is often named by the ply: two-ply, three-ply, four-ply and so on. The ply number indicates how many strands are twisted together to make the yarn. Although a two-ply yarn is usually very fine, it need not necessarily be so, if the individual strands are thick—a rug wool, for instance, could be made up of two very thick strands. In general terms, however, two-ply is very fine, three-ply a little thicker, four-ply a popular fine weight for thin sweaters, socks and children's wear, and double knitting (about twice the weight of three-ply) is a heavier weight which is quick to knit but not too bulky.

From time to time yarns are produced which are based on these standard weights, but have special finishes. Angora, for instance, is roughly equivalent to a four-ply yarn, but it knits up with a fluffy surface, and mohair—also equivalent to four-ply— gives a long shaggy surface. In crêpe yarns, which are available in different weights in both natural and man-made fibres, the plies are twisted a certain way in the spinning to give a slightly crinkled surface finish to the yarn. Bouclé yarns, which give a knobbly, tweedy look for suits and coats, are produced by tightly over-twisting the plies in the spinning until they cockle up into clusters. These clusters are then bound in place by the other plies of ordinarily spun yarn.

There are also many 'fancy' and novelty yarns available which are produced by the clever combination of different yarn types and colours. For instance, by combining several plies of yarn each dyed a different colour, an attractive multicoloured yarn is produced. There are glitter, jewelled and sparkling yarns, too, which are lovely for party dresses and accessories.

# Knitting needles

Knitting needles are usually made either of lightweight coated metal or of plastic; extra thick needles are sometimes made in wood for working big, loose patterns. Needle sizes are graded by a numbered system from very fine through to thick. In the UK sizing range, the lower numbers indicate the thicker needles, the higher numbers the thinner ones. This system works in reverse for the American and Continental sizes—e.g. size 1 needle in the USA is the equivalent of a UK size 12.

Each size of needle is normally available in a choice of lengths, and the particular length you choose will depend on the garment you are making. A skirt, for instance, which takes a lot of stitches, is more comfortably worked on a long needle, while an edging for a cardigan, perhaps taking only eight or nine

stitches, is better knitted on a pair of very small needles.

In addition to pairs of needles, set of four needles are available for working in rounds. These needles have points at both ends, and can produce a continuous tube of knitting.

This is useful for fairly small items where seams are not wanted—such as socks, gloves, polo necklines. For larger tubular items, such as skirts and trouser legs, where working with four needles would be unwieldy, it is best to use a single circular needle. This is a very long, flexible needle with a point at each end—knitting is worked round and round on this one needle. Circular needles are available in a much wider range of lengths than ordinary straight needles, and it is important to choose the length which will hold the minimum number of stitches in a particular pattern so the stitches reach from point to point without stretching.

# Importance of tension

Every knitting pattern quotes a tension measurement, and it is on this vital factor that the success of your work depends. The tension measurement refers to the number of stitches and rows produced in each square inch, using a certain yarn weight and knitting needle size. For example, it is commonly

accepted that most four-ply yarns when knitted on UK size 10 needles (USA size 3) give 7 stitches and 9 rows to the inch. So if you want to make a baby's dress to measure, say, 10in. across the front of the chest and 10in. long, you will need to cast on 70 stitches and to work 90 rows. But if you are a tight knitter, or use the wrong size needle, you may produce 8 stitches and 10 rows to the inch, in which case 70 stitches and 90 rows will make a piece of fabric roughly 8¾in. by 9in. When you sew the back of the dress to the front you will have lost at least 2¼in. all round, and it is unlikely the dress will fit the baby for whom it was intended! This is why it is vital to check your tension before you start.

**To make a tension check,** using the yarn and needle size quoted in the pattern, knit a square of about 3 or 4in. in the stitch pattern given. Press the square lightly and leave for a few hours to settle back to its natural size. Now lay it on a flat surface, carefully measure out a 2-in. square in the centre of your knitted piece, and mark this area with pins. Count the number of stitches and rows in this area, and check against the measurement quoted in the pattern. If the pattern quotes a tension measurement of 7 sts. and 9 rows to the inch, then you should have 14 stitches and 18 rows in your 2-in. square.

If you find you have more stitches and rows than the number given, try another sample square using a size bigger needle. If you have fewer stitches and rows, then try a smaller needle. Continue to work sample squares until you achieve the correct tension. Some experienced knitters know that they habitually knit somewhat tighter than average, and so automatically use a size larger needle than the one recommended, but until you have tried a few times you cannot know this. It is impossible to overstress the importance of tension checking—time spent getting it right at the beginning is never wasted, but one of the guarantees of success.

# Holding the needles and yarn

For practice purposes, choose a fairly large size needle (UK size 8 or 9; USA size 6 or 5) and double knitting yarn in a bright colour (so stitch detail will be easy to see). During work the stitches will be on the needle in your left hand and you will transfer them one at a time to the needle in your right hand. The right-hand needle is then put into the left hand and the whole process repeated.

The left-hand needle should be held with the fingers and thumb above it, so that the needle is held gently but firmly against palm (A). The right-hand needle is held between thumb and forefinger, resting on the division

between them, and the tip of the second finger is held against the needle (B). The usual way to hold the yarn is to pass it round the little finger of the right hand, under the ring and middle fingers and over the index finger (C). However any method of holding the yarn, providing it is comfortable for you, and the yarn can be paid out evenly, is acceptable.
Try to achieve the correct grasp of the needles early, neither grasping them too tightly or too loosely, and practise working so the right hand is not taken off the needle each time a stitch is made—a common fault with children and many beginners.

# Casting on the stitches

Casting on is the term given to putting the first row of stitches on the needle. There are several methods of doing this.
**Thumb method.** This method uses only one needle, and is suitable for most garments, as it gives a firm springy edge. Undo a length of yarn from the ball (equal to at least three times the width required of finished item). Make a slip loop near the ball as follows: hold the yarn in your left hand and, with the right hand, make a loop round the first two fingers of your left hand, winding clockwise (D).
Hold the loop in position with the left thumb. Now, with the needle in your right hand, put the point through the loop in your left hand, and use it to draw a length of yarn from the ball through (E).
Pull the yarn ends gently to form loop on needle (F). This is the first stitch. Put the needle with the loop into your right hand, take the shorter length of yarn in your left hand, and make a clockwise loop round thumb (G). Slip the point of the needle through this loop, from front to back (H), wrap the longer length of yarn with your right hand round the point of the needle, from back to front, draw the loop thus through with the needle and slide it off your thumb. Make it taut by pulling

gently on the yarn. Now make as many stitches as you need in a similar way. When the stitches are cast on, you can begin to knit at once. If the odd length of yarn is unwieldy. cut it about 5in. from the needle.
**Two-needle method.** This gives a 'looped' edging which can be useful if you need to pick up stitches along the edge afterwards. Make a slip loop, as described for Thumb Method, but make the loop only a few inches from the end of yarn. Put it on the left-hand needle. Put the point of the right-hand needle through stitch from front to back (J), wrap the yarn coming from the ball from the back round between needles and over right-hand needle. Pull yarn through loop with the right-hand needle to form stitch on the needle (K). Slip this stitch on to the left-hand needle so the yarn is at the front. Make as many more stitches as you need in a similar way. If you want a firm start to your work, it is best to work a knit row to begin with after casting on stitches, and before beginning the pattern. Work into the back of every stitch.

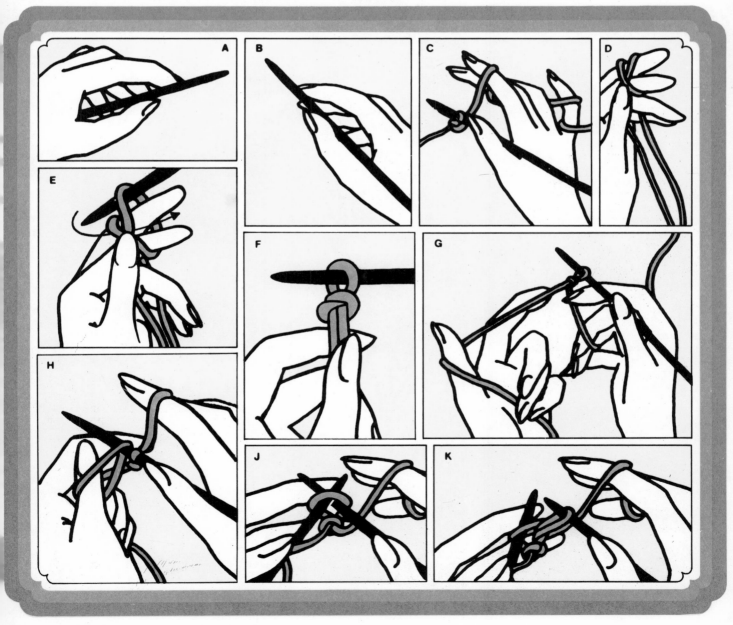

**Between stitch method.** This gives a twisted edge to the work, and is particularly useful for adding stitches in the middle of a piece of work—for shaping, for instance. Make a slip loop and first stitch, as for Two-needle Method. Now put the point of the right-hand needle between the 2 stitches and bring yarn forward and round the point of the right-hand needle (L). Draw yarn through space between stitches and slip this stitch on to the left-hand needle (M). Continue this way.

**Note.** If you are a tight knitter, both casting on and casting off should be done with a needle at least one size larger than the one used for the main part of the work—otherwise, you may break the edge when the garment is put on, or pulled over the head.

## Casting off

This is the term given to taking off stitches at the end of your work. Work 2 stitches keeping to the stitch pattern you are using. Slip the point of the left-hand needle under the first stitch worked and draw it over the second stitch, and off the needle (N). Work next stitch and in a similar way lift the previous stitch over it (O). Continue in this way along row until only one stitch remains. Break off the yarn a few inches from the stitch, remove needle from stitch, and carefully thread yarn end through stitch. Pull gently taut.

## The knit stitch

This is the first of the two basic stitches in knitting. Place the needle with stitches in the left hand, and keep yarn at the back of work. Put the point of the right-hand needle through the first stitch, from front to back, wrap the yarn from back to front between the needles and over right-hand needle (P). Turn the right-hand needle towards you and draw through the yarn to form loop on the needle (O). Let loop on left-hand needle drop. Continue in this way along the row until all stitches are worked. Now turn the work round, put the right-hand needle into your left hand, and start again.

*Sample of garter stitch*

When every row is worked in knit stitch, the fabric produced is made up of a series of small ridges (2 rows to each ridge) and this is called *garter stitch*. Our colour contrast bolero (see opposite) is worked entirely in this stitch.

## Decreasing

Shaping in knitting can be achieved either by increasing the number of stitches on the needle, or by decreasing (reducing) them. For this lesson we will deal with the simplest method of

shaping by decreasing: by taking 2 stitches together.

Put the point of the right-hand needle through 2 stitches on the left-hand needle instead of one and work them as if they were one stitch (R). Sometimes patterns will instruct you to work decreasing through the back of the stitch. This gives a slightly neater surface finish to your work. To do this, simply put the right-hand needle through the back of the 2 stitches instead of the front (S). Complete as for an ordinary knit stitch.

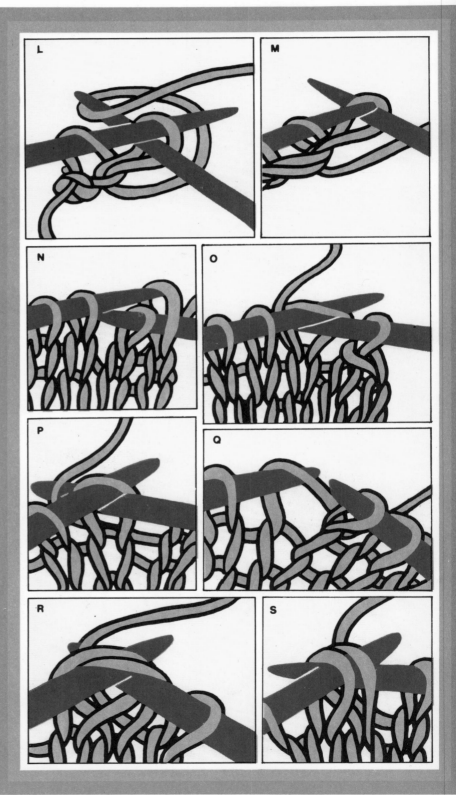

*Colour contrast bolero, worked entirely in garter stitch—instructions start after lesso*

## YOUR FIRST MAKE
### Smart garter stitch
# BOLERO

## MATERIALS YOU WILL NEED

9 (10, 11) oz. Emu Machine Washable Double Knitting in white, and 3 oz. in red. One pair each Nos. 8 and 10 (USA sizes 6 and 3) knitting needles.

## MEASUREMENTS

Finished bolero will comfortably fit a bust size 34 (36, 38) in.

## TENSION

5¼sts. and 10 rows to 1in. in garter stitch on No. 8 needles.

## ABBREVIATIONS

K., knit; st(s)., stitch(es); g.s., garter stitch; in., inch(es); tog., together; cont., continue.

## SIZE NOTE

Instructions in this pattern are given in size order, with larger sizes in brackets. Where only one set of figures occurs this refers to all sizes.

## TO MAKE
### Bolero back

With No. 8 needles and white yarn, cast on 94 (100, 106) sts. and work in g.s. (every row k.) until work measures 8¼ (9, 9¼) in.

### To shape armholes

**Next row:** cast off 5 sts., k. to end.
**Next row:** cast off 5 sts., k. to end.
***Next row:** k.2 tog., k. to last 2 sts., k.2 tog.
**Next row:** k. **
Repeat from * to ** 5 (7, 8) more times, when you should have 72 (74, 78) sts. remaining on the needle. Work straight in g.s. until armhole measures 7¼ (8, 8) in.

### To shape shoulders

**Next row:** cast off 10 sts., k. to end.
**Next row:** cast off 10 sts., k. to end.
**Next row:** cast off 9 (9, 10) sts., k. to end.
**Next row:** cast off 9 (9, 10) sts., k. to end. Cast off remaining sts.

### Bolero front

With No. 8 needles and white yarn, cast on 47 (50, 53) sts.
Work in g.s. for 8¼ (9, 9¼) in.

### To shape armholes and front slope

**Next row:** cast off 5 sts., k. to last 2 sts., k. 2 tog. (This is the front slope edge.)
***Next row:** k. to last 2 sts., k. 2 tog.
**Next row:** k.
**Next row:** k. to last 2 sts., k. 2 tog.
**Next row:** k. to last 2 sts., k. 2 tog.**

Repeat from * to ** 2 (3. 3) times more, when you should have 32 (32, 35) sts. remaining.

### For sizes 34 and 36 only
**Next row:** k.

### For size 38 only
**Next row:** k. to last 2 sts., k. 2 tog.

### For all sizes

**Next 2 rows:** k.
**Next row:** k. to last 2 sts., k. 2 tog.
****Next 3 rows:** k.
**Next row:** k. to last 2 sts., k. 2 tog.****
Rep. from *** to **** 11 (11, 12) more times when you should have 19 (19, 20) sts. remaining on the needle. Cont. straight in g.s. until armhole measures 7¼ (8, 8) in.

### To shape shoulder

**Next row:** cast off 10 sts., k. to end.
**Next row:** k.
Cast off rem. sts.

### Front band

With No. 10 needles and red yarn, cast on 10 sts.

Work in g.s. until the strip is long enough when slightly stretched to go up one centre front edge, round the back of neck and down other centre front edge. Cast off.

### Armhole bands
(make 2 alike)
With No. 10 needles and red yarn, cast on 7 sts.
Work in g.s. until strip is long enough when slightly stretched to go round armhole edge. Cast off.

## TO COMPLETE

Stitch shoulder seams and side seams of bolero. Sew Front Band in position round bolero centre front and neck edges, laying band slightly under the white edge before sewing.
Join the short edges of each Armhole Band strip together to form a circle. Stitch one band in place to each bolero armhole edge, again laying band slightly under the white edge before sewing.
Press lightly.
If wished, a hook and eye can be sewn to bolero centre front edges to fasten.

88

# KNITTING

## Lesson Two:
## The second basic stitch

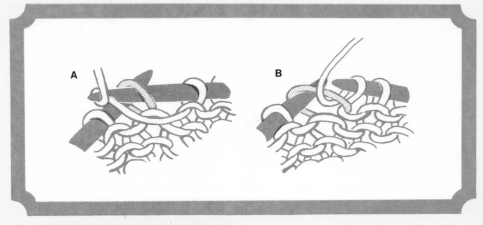

In lesson one you were introduced to the knit stitch and the garter stitch pattern which the knit stitch produces when worked on its own. The purl stitch is the second basic stitch of knitting, and once you have mastered it and learned to combine knit and purl in the same piece of work, the whole wonderful range of traditional knitting patterns will be at your fingertips.

## To work the purl stitch

For this stitch yarn is always kept at the front of the work. Put the needle with the stitches into your left hand. Keeping the yarn to the front, slip the point of the right-hand needle into the front of the first stitch on the left-hand needle in a right to left direction. Wrap the yarn round the right hand needle (A), then turn needle away from you and with the point draw through the loop you have just made. Slip this stitch on to the right hand needle (B). Let the original stitch drop. You have now worked a complete purl stitch. If you work every row in purl, you will produce a ridged pattern similar to garter stitch.

## Patterns combining the knit and purl stitches

### STOCKING STITCH

This is one of the most popular and widely used of all stitch patterns. It consists simply of alternate rows of knit and purl. The first and every odd-numbered row is worked in the knit stitch; the second and every even-numbered row is worked in the purl stitch. The knit side is the right side of work, the purl the wrong. *Reverse stocking stitch* is simply stocking stitch made up with the purl side as the right side, and the knit as the wrong side. The effect on the right side is similar to garter stitch, but the fabric is flatter.

### SINGLE RIB

This is worked on an even number of stitches. Each row is worked in the same

STOCKING STITCH

SINGLE RIB

DOUBLE RIB

FANCY RIB

way: knit the first stitch, purl the second, knit the third, purl the fourth, and so on to the end of the row. The yarn has to be taken to the front of the work after working the knit stitch, and taken to the back after forming the purl stitch. This produces a springy piece of fabric which is much narrower than stocking stitch worked on a similar number of stitches, but the fabric can be pulled out to approximately the same width if necessary. For this reason the single rib is an ideal pattern to use for any part of a garment which has to grip, such as the top of a sock, the hem and cuff of a sweater, or the neckline of a jumper or dress. Very often a pattern will instruct you to use a size smaller needle for a single rib section than that used for the main pattern, in order to give an even snugger fit.

Take particular care with casting on and casting off of ribbing sections. As these sections usually have to withstand a fair amount of strain (for instance, when a garment is taken on and off) the edge should be sufficiently springy to take the extra pull. If you are inclined to knit tightly, then it is a good idea to cast on and off with a size larger needle than that given in the pattern. When casting off ribbing, work the knit and purl stitches as you would normally do to maintain the continuity of the rib.

### DOUBLE RIB

This, like single rib, is also worked with an even number of stitches (preferably in multiples of four). Every row is worked alike: knit two stitches, purl two stitches, and so on to the end of the row. The fabric produced is slightly less springy than single rib. It is frequently used as an all-over pattern for a skinny sweater.

### FANCY RIBS

Knit and purl stitches can be used in an almost limitless number of combinations to give a variety of different rib patterns. Shown here is one variation: six knit stitches are alternated with two purl stitches. In the second and alternating rows, the sequence is reversed, and two knit stitches are alternated with six stitches. This gives a decorative and more sophisticated look to what is still basically a simple rib.

## MOSS STITCH

This is simply a single rib worked with an odd number of stitches. This means that on alternating rows you knit the stitches which were knit stitches on the previous row, and purl the stitches which were purl. This creates a 'stepped' effect and a regular, rather tweedy surface which is attractive for suits and coats. The fabric is a flat, not springy one like a normal rib. It can be worked with an even number of stitches if you wish, but in this case you have to start each row with the same stitch which finished the previous row: i.e. if you finished with a purl stitch, then the following row will start with a purl stitch.

# Decreasing—two more methods

In lesson one the simplest method of decreasing—by working two stitches together—was explained. According to the type of decrease you wish to work, and the pattern you are using, there are two further methods of shaping work by reducing the number of stitches:

### METHOD 1: PASSING SLIPPED STITCH OVER

In this, the first stitch on the left-hand needle is passed to the right-hand needle without being worked. The next stitch is then worked in the usual way, then the first (slipped) stitch is taken over the second one with the tip of the left-hand needle (as in casting off) (C).

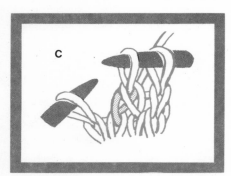

### METHOD 2: GROUP DECREASING

If it is necessary to decrease several stitches at once during the course of a pattern (for instance, at the shaping of a shoulder or an armhole) then you simply cast off the required number of stitches in the usual way, keeping the pattern correct by knitting the knit stitches, and purling the purl stitches while you cast off.

# How to increase

Shaping can also be achieved by increasing the number of stitches you are working with, and so giving greater width. This form of shaping can be done either within the body of the work, or at the edge. There are several methods to use:

### METHOD 1: WORKING TWICE INTO A STITCH

At the point where you wish the increase to occur, knit the next stitch in the normal way but do not take it off the left-hand needle. Put the point of the right-hand needle into the back of stitch and knit it again (D). Now take both stitches off at the same time. You can, of course, purl twice into the same stitch, or knit and purl into the front of the same stitch.

### METHOD 2: PICKING UP A LOOP

This is a neat way to increase in the middle of a row. Lift the loop between the stitch on the right-hand needle and the stitch on the left-hand needle, using the tip of right hand needle (E). Put it on to left-hand needle, then knit this stitch, working into the back of it.

### METHOD 3: WORKING INTO THE BASE OF THE NEXT STITCH

In this method, the right-hand needle is inserted into the fabric directly below the next stitch on the left-hand needle. Make stitch in the usual way by wrapping yarn round the needle, and then knit it (F).

### METHOD 4: YARN OVER THE NEEDLE

This technique makes a hole in the fabric and so is often used deliberately either to make a small buttonhole or as part of an openwork, lacy pattern. Between two knit stitches, the yarn is brought forward and the next stitch is worked without taking it back: this is called wool (or yarn) forward (G). Between two purl stitches, the yarn is wound round the needle once before the next stitch is worked: this is called wool (or yarn) round needle (H). Between a knit and a purl stitch the yarn is laid on the needle before the next stitch; this is called wool (or yarn) on needle (J).

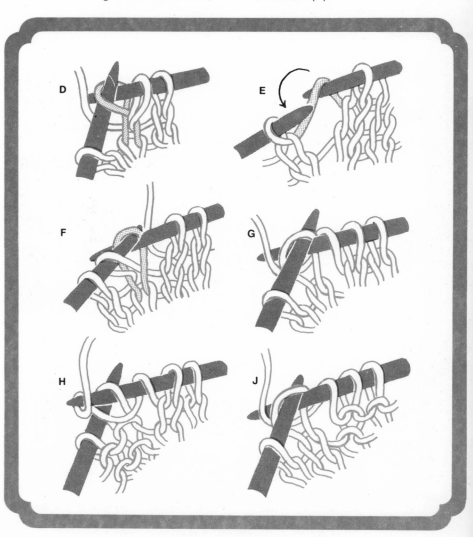

## METHOD 5: GROUP INCREASING

In a similar way as for group decreasing, when it is necessary to increase several stitches at once, the simplest method is merely to cast on these stitches. Ideally, the between stitch method or the two-needle method should be used, working the first row on the new stitches into the back of the stitch.

## Picking up stitches along an edge

Frequently a knitting pattern will instruct you to pick up stitches along an edge—down the side of a cardigan, perhaps, or round a neckline. To do this, use a fine needle (sometimes one that is a size smaller than the size you will use to work the edging) or a crochet hook. The first step however is to make sure you place your stitches evenly. If you are going to pick up, say, sixty stitches round a neck, mark the halfway point with pins, and then the quarters. Then you will know you have to pick up fifteen stitches between each pin. Holding the yarn in your right hand, put the needle or hook through the fabric, wrap the yarn round it, draw through a loop and knit it. Continue in this way all along the edge, working through the loops of the stitches formed when the main body of the design was worked. If the number of stitches picked up is a large one, and the area is curved or awkwardly shaped (for instance, round a V neck or a curved neckline) it is sometimes easier to use two or three needles from a set of four matched needles with points at each end.

### YOUR SECOND MAKES

## STOCKING STITCH CLASSICS

Begin now to build up an exclusive mix and match wardrobe of knitted clothes. Our versatile suit is designed to be right for any occasion, any weather, any age. Matching plaid patterned jacket and hat team with plain skirt, knickerbockers or trousers. Knit the whole ensemble, or just the items to suit your way of life. Instructions for the jacket are given in lesson five which deals with colour knitting; and instructions for the hat are in lesson six, with other designs worked on four needles. To wear with your skirt, knickerbockers or trousers now knit our trio of classic sweaters and matching cardigan.

# Knickerbockers, skirt and trousers

## MATERIALS YOU WILL NEED

**For knickerbockers:** 19 (20) oz. Wendy Double Knitting Wool; 1 yd. interfacing, 2 in. wide; one pair each Nos. 9 and 10 knitting needles (USA sizes 5 and 3); two 1-in. buckles; ¾ yd. boned petersham elastic, 1½ in. wide; a 10-in. zip fastener.
**For skirt:** 18 (19) oz. Wendy Double Knitting Wool; one pair each Nos. 9 and 10 knitting needles (USA sizes 5 and 3); ¾ yd. boned petersham elastic, 1½ in. wide; an 8-in. zip fastener; 2 hooks and eyes.
**For trousers:** 24 (26) oz. Wendy Double Knitting Wool; one pair each Nos. 9 and 10 knitting needles (USA sizes 5 and 3); ¾ yd. boned petersham elastic, 1½ in. wide; a 10-in. zip fastener.

## MEASUREMENTS

**Knickerbockers:** to fit hip size 36 (38) in., inside leg 19½ (20) in.
**Skirt:** to fit hip size 36 (38) in., length 26 in.
**Trousers:** to fit hip size 36 (38) in., inside leg 29 in.

## TENSION

6 sts. and 8 rows to 1 in. on No. 9 needles.

## ABBREVIATIONS

K., knit; p., purl; st.st., stocking stitch; st(s)., stitch(es); in., inch(es); t.b.l., through back of loop(s); inc., increase; dec., decrease; beg., beginning; rem., remain(ing); rep., repeat.

## SIZE NOTE

Instructions in this pattern are given in size order, with larger sizes in brackets. Where only one set of figures occurs this refers to all sizes.

# Knickerbockers

With No. 9 needles cast on 40 (42) sts. Work 3 rows in st.st., beg. with a p. row.
**First size only. Next row:** (k. twice into next 2 sts., k.1, k. twice into next 2 sts.) 8 times: 72 sts.
**Second size. Next row:** k. twice into first st., k.1, (k. twice into next 2 sts., k.1, k. twice into next 2 sts.) 8 times: 75 sts.
**Both sizes.** Work 19 rows in st.st. Leave sts. on a spare needle.
With No. 9 needles, cast on 35 (37) sts. Work 3 rows st.st., beg. with a p. row.
**First size only. Next row:** (k. twice into next 2 sts., k.1, k. twice into next 2 sts.) 7 times: 63 sts.
**Second size. Next row:** k. twice into first st., k.1, (k. twice into next 2 sts., k.1, k. twice into next 2 sts.) 7 times: 66 sts.
**Both sizes.** Work 19 rows in st.st.

**Next row:** k. across all sts. on needle, then across 72 (75) sts. on spare needle: 135 (141) sts.
Now cont. in st.st. until work is 19½ in. from beg. ending with a p. row. Now beg. shaping.***

**1st row:** cast off 4, k. 64 (67), k.2 tog., 65 (68) sts. Leave rem. 65 (68) sts. on a spare needle.
**2nd row:** p. to last 2 sts., p. 2 tog.
**3rd row:** k.2 tog., k. to end of row.
**4th row:** as 2nd row.
**5th row:** k.2 tog., k. to end.
**6th row:** work without shaping.
**7th row:** k.2 tog., k. to last 2 sts., k.2 tog. Work 3 rows without shaping.
**11th row:** k.2 tog., k. to end. Work 3 rows without shaping.
**15th row:** k. to last 2 sts., k.2 tog. Work 3 rows without shaping.
**19th row:** k.2 tog., k. to end. Work 5 rows without shaping.
**25th row:** k.2 tog., k. to last 2 sts., k.2 tog. Work 5 rows without shaping.
**31st row:** k.2 tog., k. to end. Work 5 rows without shaping.
**37th row:** k. to last 2 sts., k.2 tog. Work 3 rows with shaping.
**41st row:** k.2 tog., k. to end. Work 3 rows without shaping.

**45th row:** k. to last 2 sts., k.2 tog.
Work 5 rows without shaping.
**51st row:** k.2 tog., k. to last 2 sts., k.2 tog.
Work 5 rows without shaping.
**57th row:** k.2 tog., k. to end.
Work 5 rows without shaping.
**61st row:** k. to last 2 sts., k.2 tog.
Work 3 rows without shaping.
**65th row:** k.2 tog., k. to last 2 sts., k.2 tog.
Work 3 rows without shaping.
**69th row:** k. to last 2 sts., k.2 tog.
Work 3 rows without shaping.
**73rd row:** k.2 tog., k. to last 2 sts., k.2 tog.
Work 3 rows without shaping: 41 (44) sts.
Leave these sts. on a spare needle and return to 65 (68) sts. on first spare needle.
**1st row:** k.
**2nd row:** cast off 2 sts., p. to end.
**3rd row:** k. to end of row, k.2 tog.
**4th row:** p.2 tog., p. to end:
**5th row:** k. to last 2 sts., k.2 tog.
Work 3 rows without shaping.
**9th row:** k.2 tog., k. to last 2 sts., k.2 tog.
Work 7 rows without shaping.
Rep. last 8 rows 4 times.
**49th row:** k.2 tog., k. to end.
Work 5 rows without shaping.
**55th row:** k. to last 2 sts., k.2 tog.
Work 5 rows without shaping.
**61st row:** k.2 tog., k. to end of row.
Work 3 rows without shaping.
**65th row:** k. to last 2 sts., k.2 tog.
Work 3 rows without shaping.
**69th row:** k.2 tog., k. to last 2 sts., k.2 tog.
Work 3 rows without shaping.
**73rd row:** k.2 tog., k. to end.
Work 2 rows without shaping: 43 (46) sts.
**76th row:** patt. 10 (11), turn and work to end.
**78th row:** patt. 20 (22), turn and work to end.
**80th row:** patt. 30 (33), turn and work back.
**82nd row:** work across all stitches.
Cast off.

## LEFT LEG

This is worked as for Right Leg but with shapings reversed.
Begin by working the 35 (37)-st. section and leaving on spare needle, then work the 40 (42)-st. section.
At the correct time work across 72 (75) sts. and then across 63 (66) sts.
When you reach *** end with a k. row.
Now complete leg as for Right Leg, but read 'k.' for 'p.', and 'p.' for 'k.' throughout.

## BELT

With No. 10 needles cast on 158 (170) sts. Work in st.st. for 4¼ in.
Cast off.

## KNEE BANDS (make 2 alike)

With No. 10 needles cast on 80 (84) sts. K.1 row.

***Next row:** p. twice into first st., p. to end.
**Next row:** k. to last st., k. twice into last st.
Rep. these 2 rows then work 1 row without shaping.
**Next row:** k. to last 2 sts., k.2 tog.
**Next row:** p.2 tog., p. to end.
Rep. these 2 rows once.*
Work 1 row without shaping then rep. from * to * once.
Cast off.

## TO COMPLETE

Press all pieces separately. Join front of legs; join side seams and inner leg seams. Sew wide belt band to top of knickerbockers and interline with boned petersham elastic. Turn the belt inwards over the petersham and sew down on wrong side of work. Join the back seam leaving 10 in. open at top to take zip fastener.
Insert zip. Sew the small bands to the leg openings, the pointed edges to the front in each case. Place a strip of interfacing behind each band and fold it back inside over the interfacing. Sew down on the wrong side. To face the inside of the leg openings at the sides, make 2 strips of binding thus:
With No. 10 needles cast on 5 sts.
**1st row:** k.2 tog., k. to end, working twice into last st.

**2nd row:** p.
Rep. these 2 rows until strip is long enough to go all round opening.
Cast off and work another strip. Sew these strips neatly round leg openings. Sew a buckle to straight end of each band.
Press.

## Skirt

**MAIN PIECE (make 2 alike)**
With No. 10 needles cast on 142 (148) sts. Work 1 in. in st.st. ending with a k. row.
**Next row:** k. (this forms hem ridge).
Now beg. with a k. row, work a further 1 in. in st.st.
Change to No. 9 needles and cont. until work is 5 in. from hem ridge ending with a p. row.
**Next row:** k.2, (k.18, k.2 tog.t.b.l., k.6 (8), k.2 tog., k.18) 3 times, k.2: 136 (142) sts. Work a further 5 in., ending with a p. row.
**Next row:** k.2, (k.17, k.2 tog.t.b.l., k.6 (8), k.2 tog., k.17) 3 times, k.2: 130 (136) sts. Work 4 in., ending with a p. row.
**Next row:** k.2, (k.16, k.2 tog.t.b.l., k.6 (8), k.2 tog., k.16) 3 times, k.2: 124 (130) sts. Work 4 in., ending with a p. row.

*Short-sleeved, roll-necked jumper*

**Next row:** k.2, (k.15, k.2 tog.t.b.l., k.6 (8), k.2 tog., k.15) 3 times, k.2: 118 (124) sts. Work 1½ in., ending with a p. row.
**Next row:** k.2, (k.14, k.2 tog.t.b.l., k.6 (8), k.2 tog., k.14) 3 times, k.2: 112 (118) sts. Work 1½ in., ending with a p. row.
**Next row:** k.2, (k.13, k.2 tog.t.b.l., k.6 (8), k.2 tog., k.13) 3 times, k.2: 106 (112) sts. Work 1 in. ending with a p. row.
**Next row:** k.2, (k.12, k.2 tog.t.b.l., k.6 (8), k.2 tog., k.12) 3 times, k.2: 100 (106) sts. Work 1 in., ending with a p. row.
**Next row:** k.2, (k.11, k.2 tog.t.b.l., k.6 (8), k.2 tog., k.11) 3 times, k.2: 94 (100) sts. Work 1 in. ending with a p. row.
**Next row:** k.2, (k.10, k.2 tog.t.b.l., k.6 (8), k.2 tog., k.10) 3 times, k.2: 88 (94) sts. Work 1 in. ending with a p. row.
**Next row:** k.2, (k.9, k.2 tog.t.b.l., k.6 (8), k.2 tog., k.9) 3 times, k.2: 82 (88) sts. Work until skirt is 26 in. from hem ridge, or desired length. Cast off.

## TO COMPLETE

Join side seams, leaving left side open 8 in. at top for zip; insert zip. Cut boned petersham elastic to required length and attach to top inside of skirt with herringbone stitches. Finish with 2 hooks and eyes to fasten. Turn up hem and slipstitch into place. Press.

## Trousers

### RIGHT LEG

With No. 10 needles, cast on 107 (113) sts. Work 2 in. in st.st., ending with a k. row.
**Next row:** k. (this forms hem ridge). Now beg. with a k. row, cont. in st.st. for 2 in.
Change to No. 9 needles and work a further 3 in.
Inc. at each end of the next and every following 12th row until there are 135 (141) sts. Cont. until leg measures 29 in. from hem ridge ending with a p. row.**
Now shape as from *** of Right Leg on Knickerbockers.

### LEFT LEG

Work as for Right Leg until **, ending with a k. row.
Shape as for Left Leg of Knickerbockers, noting that 'k.' should be read for 'p.', and 'p.' for 'k.' throughout.

### BELT

Make as for Belt of Knickerbockers.

### TO COMPLETE

Join front, side and inner seams as for Knickerbockers. Attach Belt, and put in zip, as for Knickerbockers. Turn up hems of trouser legs and slipstitch on wrong side. Press.

# Matching Jumpers and Cardigan

## MATERIALS YOU WILL NEED

**For long-sleeved V-necked jumper** not illustrated: 11 (12, 12, 13) oz. Hayfield Beaulon 4-ply Fingering; one pair each Nos. 12 and 10 knitting needles (USA sizes 1 and 3); a cable needle.
**For V-necked cardigan:** 11 (12, 12, 13) oz. Hayfield Beaulon 4-ply Fingering; one pair each Nos. 12 and 10 knitting needles (USA sizes 1 and 3); a cable needle; 6 medium buttons.
**For short-sleeved, roll-necked jumper:** 8 (9, 10, 10) oz. Hayfield Beaulon 4-ply Fingering; one pair each Nos. 12 and 10 knitting needles (USA sizes 1 and 3); a cable needle; one set of four double-pointed No. 10 needles (USA size 3).

## MEASUREMENTS

**Both jumpers and the cardigan:** to fit bust size 34 (36, 38, 40) in.; length 22 (22½, 23, 23½) in.; sleeve seam of long-sleeved jumper and cardigan 17 in.; sleeve seam of short-sleeved jumper 2½ in.

## TENSION

7 sts. to 1 in. on No. 10 needles.

## ABBREVIATIONS

K., knit; p., purl; st.(s)., stitch(es); inc., increase; dec., decrease; in., inch(es); cont., continue; beg., begin(ning); rem., remain(ing); alt., alternate.

## SIZE NOTE

Instructions in this pattern are given in size order, with larger sizes in brackets. Where only one set of figures occurs this refers to all sizes.

## Long-sleeved Jumper

### BACK

With No. 12 needles, cast on 124 (130, 136, 142) sts. Work in k.1, p.1 rib for 1½ in.
Change to No. 10 needles and cont. in st.st. until work measures 14½ in., ending with a wrong-side row.

### To shape Raglan armholes

Cast off 6 (7, 8, 9) sts. at beg. of next 2 rows.
**Next row:** k.2, sl. next 3 sts. on to cable needle and leave at back of work, k. next st., then k.2 sts. tog. from cable needle, k.1, k. to last 6 sts., sl. next st. on to cable needle and leave at front of work, k.1, k.2 tog., then k. st. from cable needle, k.2.
**Next row:** p.
Rep. these last 2 rows until 46 sts. rem., ending with a right-side row.

### To shape neck

**Next row:** p.10, turn, finish this side first, leaving other sts. on a spare needle. Cont. to dec. at armhole edge as before, dec. 1 st. at neck edge on next and following 2 alt. rows, dec. at armhole edge only until all sts. are worked off. (Last few decs. will be made by k.2 tog. at end of rows.)
Return to sts. on spare needle, sl. centre 26 sts. on to holder for neckband, rejoin yarn to rem. sts. and work to correspond with other side, reversing all shapings.

### FRONT

Work as for Back until 92 (96, 100, 104) sts. rem. in armhole shaping, ending with a right-side row.

### Divide for neck

**Next row:** p.46 (48, 50, 52) sts., turn, finish this side first, leaving other sts. on a spare needle.
Still dec. at armhole edge as before, dec. 1 st. at neck edge on next and every 3rd row following until 15 sts. in all have been dec. at this edge. Dec. at armhole edge only until 2 sts. rem. Cast off.
Return to sts. on spare needle, rejoin yarn at inner edge and work to correspond with other side, reversing all shapings.

### SLEEVES (make 2 alike)

With No. 12 needles cast on 56 (58, 60, 62) sts. Work in k.1, p.1 rib for 2 in. Change to No. 10 needles and cont. in st.st., inc. 1 st. each end of 9th and every following 8th row until there are 88 (92, 96, 100) sts. on needle. Cont. without shaping until sleeve measures 17 in., ending with a wrong-side row.

### Shape top

*Cast off 6 (7, 8, 9) sts. at beg. of next 2 rows. Work 2 rows without shaping. Using the same method of dec. as for Back, dec. 1 st. at each end of next row, work 3 rows without shaping. Rep. these last 4 rows 1 (2, 3, 4) times more.
Rep. the 2 rows of armhole shaping as for Back until 6 sts. rem. Leave sts. on a spare needle.**

### TO COMPLETE

#### Neckband

Join raglan seams, leaving left back open. With right side facing, and No. 12 needles, pick up 6 sts. of left sleeve, 56 (58, 60, 62) sts. down left side of neck, 56 (58, 60, 62) sts. up right side of neck, 6 sts. of right sleeve and 7 sts. down right side of back neck, 26 sts. from back neck and 7 sts. up left side of back neck.
**Next row:** rib to within 2 sts. of centre, p.2 tog. through back of loops, p.2 tog., rib to end.
**Next row:** rib to within 2 sts. of centre st., k.2 tog., k.2 tog. through back of loops, rib to end.
Rep. these 2 rows 5 times more. Cast off in rib.

## To make up

Press gently with a cool iron over a dry cloth. Join remaining raglan seam and neckband. Join side and sleeve seams.

## Cardigan

### BACK

Work as for Back of Long-sleeved jumper, but cast off rem. sts. at neck edge.

### SLEEVES (make 2 alike)

Work as for Sleeves of Long-sleeved jumper, but cast off rem. sts. at top of sleeves.

### LEFT FRONT

With No. 12 needles cast on 56 (58, 60, 62) sts. Work in k.1, p.1 rib for 1½ in. Change to No. 10 needles and cont. in st.st. until work measures same as Back to armhole, ending with a wrong-side row.

### Shape armhole and front slope

**Next row:** cast off 6 (7, 8, 9) sts., k. to last 2 sts., k.2 tog.
Work 1 row. Cont. now to dec. at armhole edge as for back, at the same time dec. 1 st. at neck edge on 4th and every following 5th row until 11 sts in all have been dec. at this edge.
Dec. at armhole edge only until 2 sts. rem.
Cast off.

### RIGHT FRONT

Work as for Left Front, reversing all shapings.

### FRONT BORDERS

With No. 12 needles cast on 12 sts.

**1st row:** k.2, *p.1, k.1; rep. from * to end. Rep. this row until band will fit up left front, across top of sleeve and to centre back neck, slightly stretched. Cast off. Mark positions for 6 buttons on this front band, the first to come after ½ in., the 6th to come just before shaping for front slope and 4 more equally spaced between. Make right front band to correspond, making buttonholes to correspond with markers thus:
**Buttonhole row:** k.2, p.1, k.1, p.1, cast off 2 sts., rib to end. In the next row cast on 2 sts. above those cast off.

### TO COMPLETE

Press gently with a cool iron over a dry cloth. Join raglan seams. Sew on front borders neatly, with seams coming to centre back. Sew on buttons to correspond with buttonholes. Join side and sleeve seams.

## Short-sleeved Jumper

### BACK

Work as for Back of Long-sleeved jumper.

### FRONT

Work as for Back until 60 sts. rem. in armhole shaping, ending with a right-side row.

### Shape neck

**Next row:** p.19, turn, finish this side first, leaving other sts. on a spare needle. Cont. to dec. at armhole edge as before, dec. 1 st. at neck edge on next 5 rows. Dec. at armhole edge only until all sts. are worked off.
Return to sts. on spare needle, sl. centre 22 sts. on to a spare needle for collar, rejoin yarn to rem. sts. and work to correspond with other side reversing all shapings.

### SLEEVES (make 2 alike)

With No. 12 needles, cast on 74 (78, 82, 86) sts. and work in k.1, p.1 rib for 8 rows. Change to No. 10 needles and cont. in st.st., inc. 1 st. each end of next and every alt. row until there are 88 (92, 96, 100) sts. on needle. Work 1 row.

### Shape top

Work from * to ** of Long-sleeved jumper.

### TO COMPLETE

#### Collar

Join raglan seams. With right side facing, and the set of four No. 10 needles (see lesson six for hints on working with 4 needles), pick up 124 (128, 132, 136) sts. all round neck edge.
Work in rounds of k.1, p.1 rib for 4½ in. Cast off in rib.

#### To make up

Press gently with a cool iron over a dry cloth. Join side and sleeve seams. Fold collar in half to outside.

# KNITTING

## Lesson Three:
## Lacy patterns.

Now you can cast on and off, work flat fabrics such as stocking stitch and garter stitch, and also variations of ribs, it is possible to add another type of work to your repertoire: the lacy pattern.

In simple terms, lacy patterns are worked by setting holes or gaps at regular intervals into a solid knitted fabric. The pattern can be set in bands across the fabric or arranged in panels which run vertically. Open-work stitches can be achieved with equal success either by using fine, delicate yarns or thick, chunky ones. This type of knitting is suitable for making tablecloths and lace insertions, and also for baby garments, evening sweaters, lightweight summer jerseys and so forth. Lace patterns are also fascinating to knit!

### MAKING THE SPACES

As explained in lesson two, the basic way to make a hole in a plain fabric is to put the yarn over the needle. This will not only make a hole; it will also add a stitch. For this reason, two stitches are usually worked together to balance out the extra stitch, either just before or just afterwards. But this is not invariably the case. In some patterns, extra stitches are added on one row and taken off on the next, so a pattern is not necessarily faulty if you find more stitches on the needle at the end of one row than there should be. If the extra stitch is put on between two knit stitches, the yarn is brought forward and the next stitch made without the yarn being taken back. This is called 'yarn forward'. If the stitch is made between two purl stitches, the yarn has to be wound round the needle purlwise once before the second stitch is worked. This is called 'yarn round needle'.

Between a knit and a purl stitch the yarn is laid on the needle before the next stitch is made and this is called 'yarn on needle'. This technique is the basis of most lacy and openwork patterns. A few pattern variations are given below.

### FLORAL LACE

This is an all-over continuous pattern, suitable for fine or heavy yarn. Cast on stitches in a multiple of 6 plus 3 (e.g. 21).

**1st row:** k.1, * k.1, y.f., k.2 tog. t.b.l.,

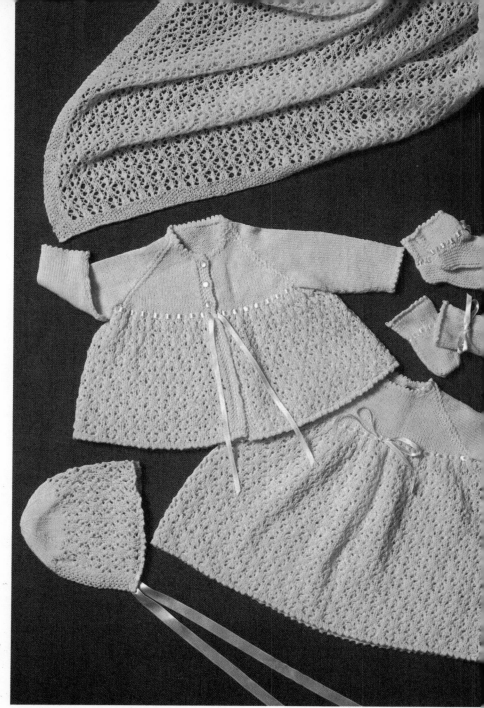

*Lacy-patterned layette for a new baby—instructions start opposite*

k.1, k.2 tog., y.f.; rep. from * to last 2 sts., k.2.
**2nd and all alt. rows:** p.
**3rd row:** k.1, * k.2, y.f., k.3, y.f., k.1; rep. from * to last 2 sts., k.2.
**5th row:** k.1, k.2 tog., * y.f., k.2 tog. t.b.l., k.1, k.2 tog., y.f., sl.1, k.2 tog., p.s.s.o.; rep. from * to last 8 sts., y.f., k.2 tog. t.b.l., k.1, k.2 tog., y.f., k.2 tog. t.b.l., k.1.
**7th row:** k.1, * k.1, k.2 tog., y.f., k.1, y.f., k.2 tog. t.b.l.; rep. from * to last 2 sts., k.2.
**9th row:** k.1, * k.2, y.f., k.3, y.f., k.1; rep. from * to last 2 sts., k.2.
**11th row:** k.1, * k.1, k.2 tog., y.f., sl.1, k.2 tog., p.s.s.o., y.f., k.2 tog. t.b.l.; rep. from * to last 2 sts., k.2.
**12th row:** p.
These 12 rows form one complete pattern. Repeat them until work is length required.

### PURSE STITCH

This is an entirely open stitch which is stretchy. For this reason it is not generally used for a complete garment but for panels between stocking stitch bands, for instance. It is particularly attractive when worked in a light yarn

and laid over a contrast colour (a baby dress over a contrast petticoat for instance). It is also good for rigid fabrics such as heavy cotton.
Cast on stitches in a multiple of 2.
**Every row:** k.1, * y.r.n., p.2 tog.; rep. from * to last st., k.l.
Continue working this row to length required.

## OPEN CLUSTERS

In this stitch the pattern is set in regularly spaced groups at 'stepped' intervals. It is frequently used for the bodice of a baby's dress or a matinée coat, or for an evening top.
Cast on stitches in a multiple of 10.
**1st row:** * k.2 tog., y.r.n., k.1, y.f., sl.1, k.1, p.s.s.o., k.5; rep. from * to end of row.
**2nd row:** * p.7, sl.1 purlwise, p.2; rep. from * to end.
**3rd row:** as first row.
**4th row:** as 2nd row.
**5th row:** k.
**6th row:** p.
**7th row:** * k.5, k.2 tog., y.f., k.1, y.f., sl. 1, k.1, p.s.s.o.; rep. from * to end.
**8th row:** * p.2, sl.1 purlwise, p.7; rep. from * to end of row.
**9th row:** as 7th row.
**10th row:** as 8th row.
**11th row:** as 5th row.
**12th row:** as 6th row.
These 12 rows form the pattern. Repeat them to length required.

## OPEN DIAMONDS

This is an attractive repeating all-over pattern which looks as effective worked in double knitting yarn as it does in 3-ply.
Cast on stitches in a multiple of 10 plus 2 (e.g. 32).
**1st row:** k.1, * y.f., sl.1, k.1, p.s.s.o., k.5, k.2 tog., y.f., k.1; rep. from * to last st., k.1.
**2nd and all alt. rows:** p.
**3rd row:** k.1, * k.1, y.f., sl.1, k.1, p.s.s.o., k.3, k.2 tog., y.f., k.2; rep. from * to last st., k.1.
**5th row:** k.1, * k.2, y.f., sl.1, k.1, p.s.s.o., k.1, k.2 tog., y.f., k.3; rep. from * to last st., k.1.
**7th row:** k.1, * k.3, y.f., sl.1, k.2, p.s.s.o., y.f., k.4; rep. from * to last st., k.1.
**9th row:** k.1, * k.2, k.2 tog., y.f., k.1, y.f., sl.1, k.1, p.s.s.o., k.3; rep. from * to last st., k.1.
**11th row:** k.1, * k.1, k.2 tog., y.f., k.3, y.f., sl.1, k.1, p.s.s.o., k.2; rep. from * to last st., k.1.
**13th row:** k.1, * k.2 tog., y.f., k.5, y.f., sl.1, k.1, p.s.s.o., k.1; rep. from * to last st., k.1.
**15th row:** k.1, * y.f., k.7, y.f., sl.1, k.2 tog., p.s.s.o.; rep. from * to last 2 sts., sl.1, k.1, p.s.s.o.
**16th row:** p.
These 16 rows form the pattern, and are repeated until work is length required. (*Note:* The edge stitch is used in the pattern in the 15th row.)

PURSE STITCH

OPEN CLUSTERS

OPEN DIAMONDS

VANDYKE STITCH

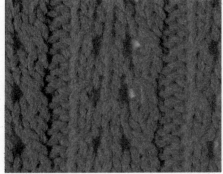
EYELET HOLES

## VANDYKE STITCH

This produces a zigzag fabric with a lacy construction. As the edge follows the zigzag line too, this stitch is attractive when used as a skirt edging. It is also possible to decrease within the ribs for shaping, so the stitch is often found on dresses, baby clothes and skirts. Rows of garter stitch can be used to break up the stitch at regular intervals.
Cast on stitches in a multiple of 12 plus 1 (e.g. 37).
**1st row:** * k.1, y.f., k.4, sl.1, k.2 tog., p.s.s.o., k.4, y.f.; rep. from * to last st., k.1.
**2nd row:** p.
These 2 rows form the pattern, and are repeated throughout until work is length required.

## EYELET HOLES

Although this is an open stitch, it is relatively tailored in appearance and is therefore suitable for men's sweaters as well as for fashion garments. It looks good in a heavy yarn.
Cast on stitches in a multiple of 7 plus 6 (e.g. 27).
**1st row:** k.2, * p.2., k.2 tog., y.f., k.1, y.f., k.2 tog. t.b.l.; rep. from * to last 4 sts., p.2, k.2.
**2nd row:** p.2, * k.2, p.5; rep. from * to last 4 sts., k.2, p.2.
**3rd row:** k.2, * p.2, k.5; rep. from * to last 4 sts., p.2, k.2.
**4th row:** as 2nd row.
These 4 rows form the pattern and are repeated throughout until work is length required.

## YOUR LACY-PATTERNED MAKE—

# BABY'S LAYETTE

## MATERIALS YOU WILL NEED

**For the dress:** 4 balls Patons Beehive Baby Wool 4 ply; 3 small buttons; $\frac{1}{4}$ in. wide ribbon. **For the jacket:** 4 balls of the same yarn; 3 small buttons; $\frac{1}{4}$ in. wide ribbon. **For bonnet:** 1 ball of the same yarn; $\frac{1}{2}$ in. wide ribbon. **For mitts and bootees:** 1 ball of the same yarn; $\frac{1}{4}$ in. wide ribbon. **Shawl:** 9 balls Patons Beehive 2 ply. **For all:** one pair each Nos. 8, 9, 10 and 12 knitting needles (USA sizes 6, 5, 3 and 1).

## MEASUREMENTS

**Dress:** to fit chest size 18—19 in.; length from top of shoulder 14in.; sleeve seam 1 in. **Jacket:** to fit chest size 18—19 in.; length at centre back 12 in.; sleeve seam $5\frac{1}{2}$ in. **Shawl:** approx. 48 in. square.

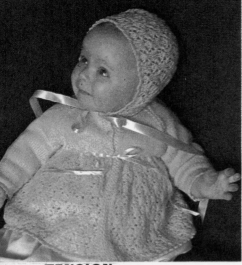

## TENSION

7 sts. and 9 rows to 1 sq. in. over st.st. on No. 10 needles.

## ABBREVIATIONS USED IN THIS PATTERN

K., knit; p., purl; st(s)., stitch(es); sl., slip y.fwd., yarn forward; y.r.n., yarn round needle; p.s.s.o., pass slip stitch over; tog., together; t.b.l., through back of loops; inc., increase by working into front and back of stitch; dec., decrease by working 2 sts. together; alt., alternate; rep., repeat; patt., pattern; in., inch(es).

## DRESS FRONT

With No. 10 needles and the two needle casting on method, cast on 103 sts.
**\*\* 1st row:** k.
**2nd row:** p.1, \* y.r.n., p.2 tog.; rep. from \* to end.
**3rd row:** k.
**4th row:** p.
**5th row:** make hem by knitting tog. 1 st. from needle and 1 loop from cast-on edge all across row. \*\*\*
**Next row:** p. \*\*
Change to No. 8 needles and lace patt. as follows:
**1st row:** \* k.1, y.fwd., sl.1, k.1, p.s.s.o., k.1, k.2 tog., y.fwd.; rep. from \* to last st., k.1.
**2nd and every alt. row:** p.
**3rd row:** \* k.2, y.fwd., k.3, y.fwd., k.1; rep. from \* to last st., k.1.
**5th row:** k.2 tog., \* y.fwd., sl.1, k.1, p.s.s.o., k.1, k.2 tog., y.fwd., sl.1, k.2 tog., p.s.s.o.; rep. from \* to last 7 sts., y.fwd., sl.1, k.1, p.s.s.o., k.1, k.2 tog., y.fwd., sl.1, k.1, p.s.s.o.
**7th row:** \* k.1, k.2 tog., y.fwd., k.1, y.fwd., sl.1, k.1, p.s.s.o.; rep. from \* to last st., k.1.
**9th row:** as 3rd row.
**11th row:** \* k.1, k.2 tog., y.fwd., sl.1, k.2 tog., p.s.s.o., y.fwd., sl.1, k.1, p.s.s.o.; rep. from \* to last st., k.1.
**12th row:** p.
These 12 rows form the patt.
Continue straight in patt. until Front measures 9¾ in., ending with right side facing, and *not* ending with a 4th or 10th row of patt.
Change to No. 10 needles and work as follows:
**Next row:** \* k.1, k.2 tog.; rep. from \* to last st., k.1: 69 sts.

**Next row:** \* p.2 tog., y.r.n.; rep. from \* to last st., p.1.
Continue in stocking stitch, shaping raglans as follows:
Cast off 4 sts. at beg. of next 2 rows.
**Next row:** k.1, k.2 tog.t.b.l., k.27, k.2 tog., k. to last 3 sts., k.2 tog., k.1: 58 sts.
**Next row:** k.1, k.2 tog.t.b.l., k. to last 3 sts., k.2 tog., k.1.
Rep. last 2 rows until 34 sts. remain, ending with right side facing.
**Shape Neck. Next row:** k.1, k.2 tog.t.b.l., k.9, turn and leave remaining sts. on a spare needle.
**Next row:** p. to last st., k.1.
**Next row:** k.1, k.2 tog.t.b.l., k. to last 2 sts., k.2 tog.
Rep. last 2 rows until 5 sts. remain, ending with right side facing.
**Next row:** k.1, k.2 tog.t.b.l., k.2 tog.
**Next row:** p. to last st., k.1.
**Next row:** k.1, k.2 tog.t.b.l.
**Next row:** p.1, k.1.
K.2 tog. and fasten off.
With right side facing, slip centre 10 sts. on to a safety-pin, rejoin yarn to remaining sts. and work to match first side, reversing all shapings.

## BACK

Work as for Front until 50 sts. remain in raglan shaping, ending with right side facing.

**Divide for Back Opening. Next row:** k.1, k.2 tog.t.b.l., k.24, turn and leave remaining 23 sts. on a spare needle.
**Next row:** k.4, p. to last st., k.1.
**Next row:** k.1, k.2 tog.t.b.l., k. to end.
Rep. last 2 rows once more.
**Next row:** k.4, p. to last st., k.1.
**Buttonhole row:** k.1, k.2 tog.t.b.l., k. to last 3 sts., y.fwd., k.2 tog., k.1.
**Next row:** k.4, p. to last st., k.1.
**Next row:** k.1, k.2 tog.t.b.l., k. to end.
Rep. last 2 rows 3 times more.
**Next row:** k.4, p. to last st., k.1.
Rep. last 10 rows once more, then buttonhole row again.
**Next row:** k.4, p. to last st., k.1: 13 sts.
Leave sts. on spare needle.
With right side facing, rejoin yarn to remaining 23 sts., cast on 4, k. across these 4 sts., k. to last 3 sts., k.2 tog., k.1.
Complete to match Left Side, reversing all shapings and omitting buttonholes.

## SLEEVES (make 2 alike)

With No. 12 needles and two needle casting on method, cast on 35 sts. and work as for Front from \*\* to \*\*
Change to No. 10 needles.
**Next row:** k., inc. 12 sts. evenly across row: 47 sts.
Work straight in stocking stitch, starting with a p. row, until sleeve seam measures 1 in., ending with right side facing.
**Shape Raglan.** Cast off 4 sts. at beg. of next 2 rows.
**Next row:** k.1, k.2 tog.t.b.l., k. to last 3 sts., k.2 tog., k.1.
**Next row:** k.1, p. to last st., k.1.
**Next row:** k.

**Next row:** k.1, p. to last st., k.1.
Rep. these 4 rows once more: 35 sts.
**Next row:** k.1, k.2 tog.t.b.l., k. to last 3 sts., k.2 tog., k.1.
**Next row:** k.1, p. to last st., k.1.
Rep. last 2 rows until 5 sts. remain, ending with right side facing.
Leave sts. on a safety-pin.

## TO COMPLETE

Block and press each piece lightly on wrong side, using a warm iron over a damp cloth.
Using a flat seam for raglans and a fine back-stitch seam for remainder, join raglan, side and sleeve seams.
With right side facing and No. 12 needles, start at top of Left Back and k.11, k.2 tog. from spare needle, k.5 sleeve sts. dec. 1 st. at centre, knit up 10 sts. down left side of neck, k.10 sts. from safety-pin inc. 1 st. at centre, knit up 10 sts. up right side of neck, k.5 sleeve sts. dec. 1 st. at centre, k.2 tog., k.11 from spare needle: 63 sts.
**\*\* Next row:** p.
**Next row:** k.
**Next row:** p.1, \* y.r.n., p.2 tog.; rep. from \* to end.
Work 2 rows st. st., starting with a k. row.
Cast off. \*\*
Fold Neckband to wrong side at picot and sl. st. neatly in position.
Catch button border to buttonhole border at base of opening. Press seams. Sew on buttons. Thread ribbon through holes at start of Yoke and tie in a bow at centre front.

## JACKET—BACK AND FRONTS

**(worked in one piece to armholes).**
With No. 10 needles and the two needle method, cast on 209 sts. and work as for Front of Dress from \*\* to \*\*
Change to No. 8 needles and working first 5 sts. and last 5 sts. in moss stitch work the 12 rows of lace patt. as on Front of Dress across 199 sts.
Your first 2 rows will read as follows:
**1st row:** k.1, (p.1, k.1) twice, \* k.1, y.fwd., sl. 1, k.1, p.s.s.o., k.1, k.2 tog., y.fwd.; rep. from \* to last 6 sts., k.2, (p.1, k.1) twice.
**2nd row:** k.1, (p.1, k.1) twice, p. to last 5 sts., (k.1, p.1) twice, k.1.
Continue thus in patt. until work measures 7¼ in., ending with right side facing and *not* ending with a 4th or 10th row of patt.
Change to No. 10 needles.
**Next row:** moss stitch 5, k.3, (k.2 tog., k.2) 8 times, (k.2 tog., k.1) 43 times, (k.2 tog., k.2) 8 times, k.3, moss stitch 5: 150 sts.
**Next row:** k.1, \* y.fwd., k.2 tog.; rep. from \* to last st., k.1.

**Divide for Back and Fronts. Next row:** moss stitch 5, k.30, cast off 8, k.64 (including st. on needle after cast off), cast off 8, k. to last 5 sts., moss stitch 5. Continue on first group of 35 sts. for Left Front, working in st. st. with moss stitch border, starting with a p. row and shaping raglan as follows:
**1st row:** moss stitch 5, p. to last st., k.1

**2nd row:** k.1, k.2 tog.t.b.l., k. to last 5 sts., moss stitch 5.
**3rd row:** as first row.
**4th row:** k. to last 5 sts., moss stitch 5.
Rep. first and 2nd rows until 22 sts. remain, ending with wrong side facing.
**Shape Neck. Next row:** cast off 8 sts., p. to last st., k.1.
Dec. 1 st. at neck edge on next and every alt. row until 5 dec. have been worked at neck edge, at the same time continue dec. 1 st. at raglan edge on next and every alt. row as before until 3 sts. remain, ending with right side facing.
**Next row:** k.1, k.2 tog.t.b.l.
**Next row:** p.1, k.1.
K.2 tog. and fasten off.
Rejoin yarn to next group of 64 sts. for Back and shape raglans as follows:
**1st row:** k.1, p. to last st., k.1.
**2nd row:** k.1, k.2 tog.t.b.l., k. to last 3 sts., k.2 tog., k.1.
**3rd row:** as first row.
**4th row:** k.
Rep. first and 2nd rows until 24 sts. remain, ending with right side facing.
Cast off.
Rejoin yarn to remaining group of 35 sts. for Right Front and shape raglan as follows:
**1st row:** k.1, p. to last 5 sts., moss stitch 5.
**2nd row:** moss stitch 5, k. to last 3 sts., k.2 tog., k.1.
**3rd row:** as first row.
**Next row (buttonhole row):** moss stitch 2, y.r.n., p.2 tog., moss stitch 1, k. to end.
Working a buttonhole on every following 12th row from previous buttonhole, continue repeating first and 2nd rows until 3 buttonholes in all have been worked.
Work 1 row, thus ending with right side facing : 22 sts.
Complete to match Left Front, reversing all shapings.

## SLEEVES (make 2 alike).
With No. 12 needles and the two needle casting on method, cast on 39 sts. and work as for Front of Dress from ** to **.
Change to No. 10 needles and continue in st. st., starting with a k. row, inc. 1 st. at each end of 3rd and every following 5th row until there are 53 sts.
Continue straight until sleeve seam measures 5½ in., ending with right side facing.
**Shape Raglan Top. 1st and 2nd rows:** cast off 4 sts., work to end.
**3rd row:** k.1, k.2 tog.t.b.l., k. to last 3 sts., k.2 tog., k.1.
**4th row:** k.1, p. to last st., k.1.
**5th row:** k.
**6th row:** as 4th row.
Rep. 3rd and 4th rows only until 5 sts. remain, ending with right side facing.
Cast off.

## TO COMPLETE
Press as for Dress.
Using a fine back-stitch seam for sleeve seams and a flat stitch for raglans, join seams.

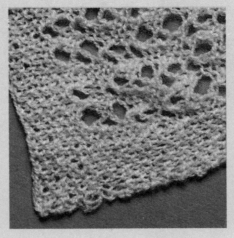

With No. 12 needles and right side of work facing, knit up 20 sts. from right side of neck, 25 sts. from back of neck and 20 sts. from left side of neck: 65 sts.
Work as for Neckband of Dress from ** to **
Fold Neckband to wrong side at picot and slip stitch neatly in position. Press seams. Sew on buttons. Thread ribbon through holes at start of Yoke to tie in a bow at centre front.

## BONNET
With No. 12 needles and the two needle casting on method, cast on 89 sts. and work as Front of Dress from ** to **.
**Next row:** p.8, * p.2, p.2 tog.; rep. from * to last 9 sts., p.9: 71 sts.
Change to No. 8 needles and working first 5 sts. and last 5 sts. in moss stitch, work 12 rows of lace patt. as on Dress across centre 61 sts., placing first 2 rows as for Jacket.
Continue until work measures 4½ in., ending with right side facing and *not* ending with a 4th or 10th row of patt.
Change to No. 10 needles and work as follows:
**Next row:** moss stitch 5, (k.5, inc. in next st.) 4 times, (k.3, inc. in next st.) 5 times, (k.4, inc. in next st.) 4 times, k.1, moss stitch 5: 84 sts.
**Next row:** moss stitch 5, p. to last 5 sts., moss stitch 5.
**Shape Crown. 1st row:** (k.10, k.2 tog.) 7 times.
**2nd and alt. rows:** p.
**3rd row:** (k.9, k.2 tog.) 7 times.
**5th row:** (k.8, k.2 tog.) 7 times.
Continue dec. in this way until 14 sts. remain.
Break yarn, thread through remaining sts. and fasten off securely.

## TO COMPLETE
Press as for Dress. Join seam from centre of crown to start of shaping. Press seam. Stitch ribbon to sides of Bonnet.

## MITTS (make 2 alike).
With No. 12 needles and the two needle casting on method, cast on 37 sts. and work as for Front of Dress from ** to **.
Change to No. 10 needles and st. st., starting with a k. row, until work.

measures 1½ in., ending with right side facing.
Work holes for ribbon:
**Next row:** k.1, * y.fwd., k.2 tog.; rep. from * to end.
**Next row:** p., dec. 3 sts. evenly across: 34 sts.
Continue in st. st., starting with a k. row until work measures 3½ in., ending with right side facing.
**Shape Top. 1st row:** (k.1, k.2 tog.t.b.l., k.11, k.2 tog., k.1) twice.
**2nd and every alt. row:** p.
**3rd row:** (k.1, k.2 tog.t.b.l., k.9, k.2 tog., k.1) twice.
**5th row:** (k.1, k.2 tog.t.b.l., k.7, k.2 tog., k.1) twice.
**7th row:** (k.1, k.2 tog.t.b.l., k.5, k.2 tog., k.1) twice.
Cast off.

## TO COMPLETE
Press as for Dress. Join seam. Press seam. Thread ribbon through row of holes at wrist.

## BOOTEES (make 2 alike).
Work as for Mitts to ***
**Divide for Foot. Next row:** k.23, turn.
**Next row:** p.12, turn.
Work 18 rows in st. st. on these 12 sts. for instep.
Break yarn.
With right side facing, rejoin yarn to inside edge of 11 sts. and knit up 14 sts along side of instep, k. across 12 sts. of instep, knit up 14 sts. along other side of instep, k. to end: 62 sts.
K.11 rows.
**Shape Foot. 1st row:** (k.1, k.2 tog., k.25, k.2 tog., k.1) twice.
**2nd and every alt. row:** k.
**3rd row:** (k.1, k.2 tog., k.23, k.2 tog., k.1) twice.
**5th row:** (k.1, k.2 tog., k.21, k.2 tog., k.1.) twice.
Cast off.

## TO COMPLETE
Press as for Dress. Join seam. Press seam. Thread ribbon through row of holes and tie in a bow.

## SHAWL
With No. 9 needles and 2 ply yarn, cast on 267 sts. and work 9 rows in moss stitch (every row * k.1, p.1; rep. from * to last st., k.1).
Change to lace patt. as on Dress with moss stitch borders as follows:
**Next row:** moss stitch 7, lace patt. 253, moss stitch 7.
**Next row:** moss stitch 7, p. to last 7 sts., moss stitch 7.
Continue thus until work measures 47 in. from start, ending with right side facing and not ending with a 4th or 10th row of patt.
Change to moss stitch over all sts. and work 9 rows.
Cast off in moss stitch.

## TO COMPLETE
Press lightly on wrong side using a warm iron over a damp cloth.

# KNITTING

## Lesson Four:
## Cable patterns

All the stitch types described so far have been flat stitches: that is, the fabric they produce has a smooth, flattish surface. It is possible, however, to work stitches with interesting, raised surfaces. These are not difficult to achieve, and once you have mastered the technique of 'textured' knitting, you will be able to produce some fascinating new patterns.

### The cable stitch

The best-known stitch which is used to give a raised effect is the cable, which is a twisted rope-like rib. The cable itself can vary in width according to the design being worked and it can twist in contrary directions, but basically the technique for making it is always the same. As well as your usual pair of knitting needles, you will also need a short needle, pointed at each

end, called a cable needle. Cable needles are usually available in a choice of two or three sizes. If possible, use a cable needle which is approximately the same size as the needles being used for the body of the work.

To work a cable 'twist', two or three stitches are slipped off the left-hand needle on to the short cable needle *before they are knitted*. This needle is either put to the back of the work or brought to the front, depending on which way the cable is to twist (A1 and A2). Two or three stitches are then knitted in the usual way, and finally the stitches on the cable needle are knitted off on to the right-hand needle. This completes the cable (B1 and B2).

It is customary to slip two, three or sometimes four stitches on to the cable needle; in other words, the complete cable pattern sequence consists of four, six or eight stitches. Instructions in a pattern will read: 'cable 8f.', which means that four stitches are slipped on to the cable needle and left at the front (f.) before the next four stitches are knitted, then the cable needle stitches are knitted. 'Cable 6b.' means that three stitches are slipped on to the cable needle and put to the back (b.) of the work before the next three stitches are worked.

This is the simplest kind of cable stitch; there are others, with the crossed sets of stitches going in different directions, or the twist being open-ended. It is also

possible, by means of knitting the second or third stitch on the left-hand needle before the first one or two, to produce a cabled effect in the knitting without having to use a separate cable needle. One of these 'mock' cables is illustrated on the following pages. It should be remembered that the cable itself is a rigid line in the fabric so, if you are designing any item which is to be cabled, this should be taken into account. Eight stitches in double knitting wool on No. 8 needles usually produce just under an inch and a half on normal stocking stitch, but if those eight stitches form a cable, then they will not stretch with the normal degree of elasticity and they will not measure so much as an inch and a half. Usually, the cables are set among ordinary ribs, against a background of purl stitches (two or three on each side of the cable). This makes them stand out more from the body of the work. If special thickness is desired, it is sometimes possible to use the yarn double for the cabled section alone. This is achieved by joining in a small extra ball of wool at the back of the cabled section and using it just for the few stitches involved on each row.

### Aran patterns

The cable is one of the most used group of stitches found in the traditional patterns which come from

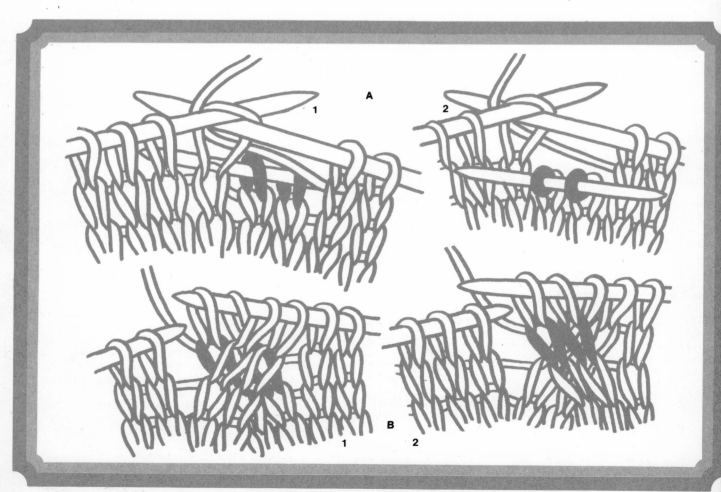

the Aran Islands, off the west coast of Ireland. These patterns are tremendously popular today not only for men's and boys' wear (as they were originally intended) but also for fashion garments for women—sweater dresses, jackets and jumpers, and trouser suits. Traditionally, Aran designs are worked in creamy-coloured wool called Bainin (pronounced Baw-neen) which is the Irish word for white, although the wool can be dyed to any colour. The Aran stitches originated approximately 500 years ago, when knitting was done with goose quills by the menfolk from wool spun by their women. Each family had its own design: each man his own pattern, and it was a matter of pride that a family should be known by its own variations on the traditional stitches, in a similar way that a Scottish clansman is identified by his tartan. Each stitch has a name and a meaning: some are of religious significance while others relate to the sea or the characteristics of the countryside. The cable represents the fisherman's ropes; the diamond, riches; the honeycomb, hard work and reward; the basket stitch, the profitable catch. The stitches are usually symmetrically arranged in panels from the centre; sometimes the sleeves are less heavily patterned than the body of the sweater or coat, but the general effect is always of richness and thick texture.

Do not be put off by the lengthy instructions that so often accompany these designs. Admittedly, Aran patterns cannot be worked with one eye on the television and little reference to the pattern, but they always are made up of a repeating number of rows—perhaps twelve, or six, or twenty-four. Once you have worked these repeats a few times you will be able to get on quite quickly. The patterns and stitches in themselves are *not* difficult but they do require concentration at first.

And a last word of warning: Aran yarn is usually thick and the fabric produced is heavy. If you are using a traditional, light colour, be sure that your lap is covered with a clean cloth to prevent soiling of the edge of the knitting.

# Some cable patterns

*Note. All samples illustrated are worked with double knitting yarn and No. 8 knitting needles (USA size 6).*

### THE BASIC CABLE

This is the basic eight-stitch design; the right-hand cable has the four stitches taken to the back, the left-hand cable has the four stitches taken to the front. You can see that the resulting cables run in contrary directions.
Cast on 30 sts.
**1st row:** k.2, p.3, k.8, p.4, k.8, p.3, k.2.
**2nd row:** p.2, k.3, p.8, k.4, p.8, k.3, p.2.

HONEYCOMB

**3rd row:** k.2, p.3, cable 8b., p.4, cable 8f., p.3, k.2.
**4th row:** as 2nd row.
Continue in this way, working a cable row on every 8th row from the first.

### WHEATEAR CABLE

This is a variant of the twisted rib, the twists going in different directions to produce a raised rib.
Cast on a basic 13 stitches for the rib. For this sample we have used 21 stitches, in order to provide a border.
**1st row:** k.1, p.3, k.13, p.3, k.1.
**2nd row:** p.1, k.3, p.13, k.3, p.1.
**3rd row:** k.1, p.3, cable 6b., k.1, cable 6f., p.3, k.1.
**4th row:** as 2nd row.
These 4 rows form the pattern.

BASIC CABLE

### OPEN CABLE

The cable itself occupies eight stitches. For this sample we used three purl stitches between each cable and a stitch at each end for the border.
Cast on 38 sts.
**1st row:** k.1, p.3, k.8, p.3, k.8, p.3, k.8, p.3, k.1.
**2nd row:** p.1, k.3, p.8, k.3, p.8, k.3, p.8, k.3, p.1.
**3rd row:** k.1, p.3, cable 4b., cable 4f., p.3, cable 4b., cable 4f., p.3, cable 4b., cable 4f., p.3, k.1.
**4th row:** as 2nd row.
Continue in this way, working a cable row on every 5th row from the first.

### MEDALLIONS

These attractive circular shapes are yet another version of the cable rib. To obtain the circular effect, the direction of the cabling is changed on alternate cable rows. Cast on 22 sts.
**1st row:** k.1, p.2, k.16, p.2, k.1.
**2nd row:** p.1, k.2, p.16, k.2, p.1.
**3rd row:** k.1, p.2, cable 8b., cable 8f., p.2, k.1.
Rep. 2nd and first rows 4 times, then 2nd row again: 9 rows.
**13th row:** k.1, p.2, cable 8f., cable 8b., p.2, k.1.
**14th row:** as 2nd row.
The next medallion can be worked immediately as in the sample, or at any desired interval. If cables are 8 or 12 stitches wide, then 5 or 7 rows of plain work should be worked, instead of 9.

### HONEYCOMB

This very popular stitch, often found in broad panels flanked by ribs or cables, is much simpler to work than may appear. It requires a multiple of 8 stitches.
Cast on 36 stitches (this includes edge stitches).

WHEATEAR CABLE

BOBBLE STITCH

**1st row:** k.1, p.1, k.32, p.1, k.1.
**2nd row:** p.1, k.1, p.32, k.1, p.1.
**3rd row:** p.1, k.1, * cable 4b., cable 4f.; rep. from * to last 2 sts., p.1, k.1.
**4th and alt. rows:** as 2nd row.
**5th row:** as first row.
**7th row:** k.1, p.1, * cable 4f., cable 4b.; rep. from * to last 2 sts., p.1, k.1.
**8th row:** as 2nd row.
These 8 rows complete the pattern.

## BOBBLE STITCH

Bobbles are extensively used in Aran and other types of decorative designs. They are set on a smooth base (usually stocking stitch) and can be of varying sizes, but the principle in making them is always the same. In our sample the bobbles are placed on every 5th stitch, in alternating steps. Cast on 33 sts.
**1st row:** * k.4, M.B. (make bobble: knit into the back and front of next stitch alternately 5 times. Now, turning the work backwards and forwards as would normally be done for successive rows, work 6 rows on these 5 sts. Using the point of the right-hand needle, slip the 5th then the 4th, then

3rd, then 2nd stitches over all the others until 1 stitch only remains on the needle. Knit this stitch), k.1; rep. from * to last 3 sts., k.3.
**2nd and alt. rows:** p.
**3rd and 5th rows:** k.
**7th row:** * M.B., k.4; rep. from * to last 3 sts., k.1, M.B., k.1.
**8th–11th rows:** rep. 2nd and 3rd rows twice.
**12th row:** p.
These 12 rows form the pattern. If you are working a 3 or 4 stitch bobble, work across the stitches for 2 or 4 rows instead of 6.

## MOCK CABLE

This is one of the many twisted stitches which look as though it has been cabled.
Cast on 25 sts.
**1st row:** * p.1, k.1; rep. from * to last st., p.1.
**2nd row:** * k.1, p.1; rep. from * to last st., k.1. Rep. these 2 rows once.
**5th row:** * p.1, cross 3 (k. the 3rd st. on the left-hand needle without removing it, p. the 2nd st. and k. the first st., then take all off the needle together); rep. from * to last st., p.1.
**6th row:** as 2nd row.
These 6 rows form the pattern.

# After-care of knitting

## WASHING YOUR WORK

Knitted garments have a long life if they are well cared for and this—especially with baby clothes and children's wear—means frequent washing. The quality of branded yarns sold today is so high that there should

MOCK CABLE

be few problems in laundering, but certain rules should still be observed. Never allow any knitted garment to get too dirty: ingrained dirt has to be rubbed clean and rubbing alters the structure of the fibres in the yarn and produces felting—the matted look which cannot be put right. Even a schoolboy's jersey that has been muddied thoroughly on the games field can be easily washed if you do it straight away, before the dirt has worked to 'settle' into the yarn.
Use a good-quality soap powder or detergent suitable for the type of water in your area( you may have found that an added water-softener produces good results). Have the water comfortably warm to the hand, and dissolve the washing agent thoroughly.
Immerse the garment in the water, and squeeze it gently. Try not to rub, which damages the fabric, and do not wring the knitting, as this will stretch it out of shape. Take it out of the soapy water and gently squeeze as much out as possible.
Rinse repeatedly, in water of the same temperature as that used for washing, until the water is clear. Squeeze the garment, roll it in a clean dry white towel and squeeze again, to get out as much water as possible. Then gently draw the garment into shape and dry it placed flat on the towel. If it is a small, light garment then it can be hung on a line or pulley to dry, but be sure that sleeves or trousers do not dangle, as water can run down to the lower edges and drag them out of shape.
Some yarn is now machine washable, which makes life a great deal easier for busy mothers. If you are using one of these yarns, then follow the yarn makers' instructions carefully, keep the water to the recommended temperature and if a particular washing agent has been specified, then use this.
Spin driers are certainly a great help in

OPEN CABLE

MEDALLIONS

laundering knitted garments. Used with care, they cut drying time dramatically. However, if the garment is in a delicate, open stitch or if you think that the design may stretch if spun-dried too rapidly, put the garment in a pillowcase before you start.

## STORING KNITWEAR

Knitwear should always be stored flat, whichever yarn has been used, since the weight of one garment can be considerable and the fabric will stretch. If you are putting garments away for any length of time, wash them, and wrap each one separately in a polythene bag, fold them lightly. Lay each one flat in a drawer. It is good sense, if you are storing woollens, to put in a few mothballs or moth-repellent crystals. Even knitteds in general use will benefit from being individually wrapped—fluffy yarns, such as Mohair and Angora, can 'shed' on to anything with which they are in contact.

## YOUR CABLE-PATTERNED MAKES

# ARAN SWEATERS FOR THE FAMILY

## MATERIALS YOU WILL NEED

**For adult's sweater:** 20 (22, 23, 23, 23, 25) 50 gr. balls. Mahonys Blarney Bainin Wool. One pair each Nos. 7, 9 and 10 knitting needles (USA sizes 7, 5 and 3). A cable needle.

**For optional belt:** one extra ball of yarn, a 2 in. buckle.

**For child's sweater:** 10 (11, 13, 14) 50 gr. balls. Mahony's Blarney Bainin Wool. One pair each Nos. 7, 9 and 10 knitting needles (USA: sizes 7, 5 and 3). A cable needle.

## MEASUREMENTS

**Adult's sweater:** to fit bust or chest size 34 (36, 38, 40, 42) in.; length 29 (29¼, 29¾, 27½, 28) in.; sleeve seam 18½ (18½, 19, 19½, 20) in.

**Child's sweater:** to fit chest size 25/26 (27/28, 29/30, 31/32) in.; length 18 (19½, 21, 22½) in.; sleeve seam 12½ (13½, 14½, 15½) in.

## TENSION

Over cross-rib pattern of side panel, 8 sts. measure 1¼ in.; 6 rows to 1 in. on all patterns.

## ABBREVIATIONS USED IN THESE PATTERNS

In., inch(es); st(s)., stitch(es); rep., repeat; k.f.b. or p.f.b., knit or purl into front and back of next stitch; beg.,

beginning; patt., pattern; C2L, cross 2 left (i.e. with wool at back pass needle behind first st., pull front loop of 2nd stitch through to back and k., then k. first stitch and slip both off needle); C2R, cross 2 right (i.e. with wool at back pass needle in front of first stitch, lift up 2nd stitch and k. then k. first stitch and slip both off needle); CP7, claw pattern 7 (i.e. slip next 2 sts. on cable needle and leave at back, k.1, then k.2 from cable needle, k. next stitch then slip next stitch on cable needle, leave at front, k.2 then k.1 from cable needle); C4B and C6B. cable 4 or 6 back (i.e. slip 2 or 3 sts. on cable needle and leave at back of work, k. next 2 or 3 stitches, then k. stitches from cable needle); C4F or C6F, cable 4 or 6 front (i.e. as for cable 4 or 6 back but leave cable needle at front of work); inc., increase; dec., decrease; patt., pattern; cont., continue.

# Adult's sweater

*Note. The first three sizes are tunic length for a woman, and the last two sizes are average length for a man. Any size can have either polo or deep crew neck.*

## PATTERN PANEL

This is worked over the centre 88 sts.
**1st row:** k.8, p.2, k.7, (p.2, k.4) 3 times, p.3, k.12, p.3, (k.4, p.2) 3 times k.7, p.2, k.8.
**2nd and alternate rows:** p.8, k.2, p.7, (k.2, p.4) 3 times, k.3, p.12, k.3, (p.4, k.2) 3 times, p.7, k.2, p.8.
**3rd row:** k.8, p.2, CP7, (p.2, C4F) 3 times, p.3, k.12, p.3, (C4B, p.2) 3 times, CP7, p.2, k.8.
**5th row:** C4B, C4F, p.2, k.7, (p.2, k.4) 3 times, p.3, k.12, p.3, (k.4, p.2) 3 times, k.7, p.2, C4B, C4F.
**7th row:** as 3rd.
**9th row:** C4B, C4F, p.2, k.7, (p.2, k.4) 3 times, p.3, C6F, C6B, p.3, (k.4, p.2) 3 times, k.7, p.2, C4B, C4F.
**11th row:** as 3rd row.
**13th row:** as first row.
**15th row:** as 3rd row.
**17th row:** as first row.
**19th row.** C4F, C4B, p.2, CP7, (p.2, C4F) 3 times, p.3, k.12, p.3, (C4B, p.2) 3 times, CP7, p.2, C4F, C4B.
**21st row:** k.8, p.2, k.7, (p.2, k.4) 3 times, p.3, C6F, C6B, p.3, (k.4, p.2) 3 times, k.7, p.2. k.8.
**23rd row:** as 19th row.
**24th row:** as 2nd.
These 24 rows form one patt.

## BACK

With No. 9 needles cast on 95 (103, 111, 111, 119) sts.
**1st row:** k.2, * p.1, k.1; rep. from * to last st., k.1.
**2nd row:** k.1, * p.1, k.1; rep. from * to end.

Rep. these 2 rows 5 times, then work first row.
**Inc. row (wrong side):** * k.f.b., (p.2, k.2) 2 (3, 4, 4, 5) times, (p.2, k.f.b.) twice, * p.3, p.f.b., p.3, k.f.b., (p.1, p.f.b.) twice, p.1,(k.f.b., k.1, p.f.b., p.1) 3 times, k.3, p.2, (.f.b., p.1) twice, p.f.b., p.2, k.3, (p.1, p.f.b., p.1, k.f.b.) 3 times, (p.1, p.f.b.) twice, p.1, k.f.b., p.3, p.f.b., p.3, then rep. from * to * 124 (132, 140, 140, 148) sts.
Change to No. 7 needles and patt.
**1st row:** p.2, (C2L, p.2) 4 (5, 6, 6, 7) times then work first row of patt. panel across next 88 sts., (p.2, C2R) 4 (5, 6, 6, 7) times, p.2.
**2nd row:** k.2, (p.2, k.2) 4 (5, 6, 6, 7) times, work 2nd row of patt. panel across next 88 sts., (k.2, p.2) 4 (5, 6, 6, 7) times, k.2. Cont. in patt. as now set, working the patt. panel as above over centre 88 sts. and keeping the 18 (22, 26, 26, 30) sts. in the cross-rib patt. as given on these 2 rows.
**For man's sweater (last two sizes):** work in patt. without any side shaping.

CROSS RIB

**For tunic-length woman's sweater:** shape sides as follows—dec. 1 st. at both ends of row on 16th and 24th row of first patt. and on 8th, 16th and 24th rows of 2nd and 3rd patts., then cont. without shaping until work is 17 in. Inc. at both ends of next row and again when work is 18 in. and 20 in.
**All sizes.** Cont. without shaping until work is 21½ (21½, 21¾, 18½, 18¾) in.: 114 (122, 130, 140, 148) sts.

**Armhole Shaping.** Cast off 6 sts. at beg. of next 2 rows then cast off 6 (8, 9, 10, 13) sts. at beg. of next 2 rows: 90 (94, 100, 108, 110) sts. Cont. without shaping until work is 28½ (28¾, 29¼, 27, 27½) in. ending with a wrong-side row.

**Neck and Shoulder Shaping.**
**1st row:** patt. 38 (40, 43, 46, 47) and leave these sts. on spare needle for

right back, cont. along row and cast off 14 (14, 14, 15, 16) sts. then patt. to end. Cont. on the 38 (40, 43, 46, 47) sts. now left on needle for left back and work 1 row straight. ** Cast off 4 sts. at beg. of next row and next alternate row. Now cast off 8 (8, 6, 6, 6) sts. for shoulder shaping at beg. of next row and 3 sts. at neck edge on following row. Rep. last 2 rows once (once, twice, twice, twice). Cast off remaining 8 (10, 9, 11, 12) sts. ** With wrong side facing rejoin yarn to inner edge of right back sts. Complete as given for left back from ** to **.

## FRONT

Work as for back until you have worked 8 (8, 10, 10, 10) rows fewer than on back up to start of neck shaping, thus ending on a wrong-side row.

### Neck and Shoulder Shaping.

**1st row:** patt. 39 (41, 44, 47, 48) and leave these sts. on spare needle for left front, cont. along row and cast off 12 (12, 12, 14, 14) sts. then patt. to end. Cont. on the 39 (41, 44, 47, 48) sts. remaining on needle for right front and work 1 row straight. *** Cast off 3 sts. at beg. of next row then dec. 1 st. at same edge on next 10 (10, 12, 12, 12) rows. Cast off 8 (8, 6, 6, 6) sts. for shoulder shaping at beg. of next row, then dec. 1 st. at neck edge on following row. Rep. last 2 rows once (once, twice, twice, twice). Cast off remaining 8(10, 8, 11, 12) sts. ***. With wrong side facing rejoin yarn to inner edge of left front sts. Complete as for right front from *** to ***

## SLEEVES (make 2 alike)

With No. 9 needles cast on 43 (43, 51, 55, 55) sts. and work 13 rows in rib as given for back.
**Sizes 34 and 36 inc. row:** k.f.b.,

* p.3, p.f.b., p.3, k.f.b., (p.1, p.f.b.) twice, p.1, k.3, p.2, (p.f.b., p.1) twice, p.f.b., p.2, k.3, (p.1, p.f.b.) twice, p.1, k.f.b., p.3, p.f.b., p.3, * k.f.b.: 56 sts.
**Size 38 inc. row:** k.f.b., p.2, k.2; rep from * to * of inc. row above, k.2, p.2, k.f.b.: 64 sts.
**Sizes 40 and 42 inc. row:** k.f.b., (p.2, k.f.b.) twice, then rep. from * to * of inc. row above, (k.f.b., p.2) twice, k.f.b.: 72 sts.
**All sizes.** Change to No. 7 needles and patt.
**1st row:** p.2, then for size 38 C2L, p.2; for sizes 40 and 42, (C2L, p.2) twice, then for all sizes k.8, p.2, k.7, p.3, k.12. p.3, k.7, p.2, k.8, then for size 38 p.2, C2R; for sizes 40 and 42 (p.2, C2R) twice, p.2. Cont. in patt. as now set at the same time inc. 1 st. at both ends of 5th, 11th, 17th, and 23rd rows of every patt. until there are 86 (90, 92, 104, 108) sts. working all extra sts. in the cross-rib patt. as on side panels of back, with C2L at beg. of row and C2R at the end. Cont. without shaping until work measures 18½ (18½, 19, 19½, 20) in. Place marker loops of contrast wool at each end of last row, then work 13 (15, 16, 18, 20) rows straight. Cast off 4 sts. at beg. of next 12 (12, 14, 16, 16) rows and 9 (11, 8, 10, 12) sts. at beg. of next 2 rows. Cast off remaining 20 sts.

## POLO COLLAR

With No. 9 needles cast on 129 (129, 137, 141, 141) sts. Work in rib as at beg. of back for 26 rows, then change to No. 10 needles and work 13 more rows in rib. Cast off in rib.

## CREW NECK

With No. 9 needles cast on 123 (123, 131, 135, 135) sts. and work in rib as

at beg. of back for 7 rows. Change to No. 10 needles and work a further 12 rows in rib. Change back to No. 9 needles and work 7 more rows. Cast off in rib.

## TO COMPLETE

Do not press. Join shoulder seams with backstitch. Press seams lightly. Sew cast-off edges of sleeves to sides of armholes and side edges of sleeves above markers to armhole casting off; remove markers and press seams. Join side and sleeve seams, and press. For polo collar, join sides beginning at cast-on edge and backstitching for three-quarters of the depth of the collar, thereafter making a flat seam. Press seam. With wrong side of collar facing right side of sweater and join at centre back, sew cast-off edge to neck edge with a flat seam. Lightly press and turn down the section worked on No. 9 needles to the right side. For crew neck, join ends of neckband and press seam; with right sides together and seam level with left shoulder seam, backstitch cast-on edge to neck edge. Press. Fold neckband in half to wrong side and slip stitch cast-off edge to seam.

## BELT

With No. 9 needles cast on 11 sts. and work in rib as for beg. of back until strip is long enough to give a comfortable fit round waist or hip, as desired, allowing an extra 4 in. for overlap. Cast off. Oversew cast-off edge to bar of buckle; at the other end turn in corners to wrong side and sew together to form a mitred end.

# Child's sweater

## PATTERN PANEL

This is worked over the centre 64 sts.
**1st row:** k.8, p.2, k.7, p.2, k.4, p.3, k.4, p.2, k.7, p.2, k.8.
**2nd and alternate rows:** p.8, k.2, p.7, k.2, p.4, k.3, p.12, k.3, p.4, k.2, p.7, k.2, p.8.
**3rd row:** k.8, p.2, CP7, p.2, C4F, p.3, k.12, p.3, C4B, p.2, CP7, p.2, k.8.
**5th row:** C4B, C4F, p.2, k.7, p.2, k.4, p.3, k.12, p.3, k.4, p.2, k.7, p.2, C4B, C4F.
**7th row:** as 3rd.
**9th row:** C4B, C4F, p.2, k.7, p.2, k.4, p.3, C6F, C6B, p.3, k.4, p.2, k.7, p.2, C4B, C4F.
**11th row:** as 3rd.
**13th row:** as first.
**15th row:** as 3rd.
**17th row:** as first.
**19th row:** C4F, C4B, p.2, CP7, p.2, C4F, p.3, k.12, p.3, C4B, p.2, CP7, p.2, C4F, C4B.
**21st row:** k.8, p.2, k.7, p.2, k.4, p.3, C6F, C6B, p.3, k.4, p.2, k.7, p.2, k.8.
**23rd row:** as 19th.
**24th row:** as 2nd.
These 24 rows form one patt.

LOBSTER CLAW

SMALL SINGLE CABLES

at each side in cross-rib patt. until work measures 12½ (13½, 14½, 15½) in.

**Armhole Shaping.** Cast off 5 sts. at beg. of next 2 rows and 4 (6, 7, 8) sts. at beg. of next 2 rows 66 (70, 76, 82) sts. Cont. without shaping until work measures 17½ (19, 20½, 22) in. ending with a wrong-side row.

**Neck and Shoulder Shaping.**
**1st row:** patt. 26 (28, 29, 32) sts. and leave on spare needle for right back, cont. along row and cast off 14 (14, 18, 18) sts. then patt. to end. Cont. on the 26 (28, 29, 32) sts. remaining for left back and work 1 row straight. ** Cast off 4 sts. at beg. of next row and next alternate row. Now cast off 6 (8, 8, 9) sts. for shoulder shaping at beg. of next row and 4 sts. at neck edge on following row. Cast off remaining 8 (8, 9, 11) sts. ** With wrong side facing rejoin yarn to inner edge of right back sts. and complete as given for left back from ** to **

## FRONT

Work as for back until you have worked 8 rows fewer than on back to start of neck shaping, thus ending with a wrong-side row.

**Neck and Shoulder Shaping.**
**1st row:** patt. 27 (29, 30, 33) sts. and leave on spare needle for left front, cont. along row, cast off 12 (12, 16, 16) sts., then patt. to end. Cont. on the 27 (29, 30, 33) sts. now on needle for right front and work 1 row straight. *** Cast off 3 sts. at beg. of next row, then dec. 1 st. at same edge on next 10 rows. Now keeping neck edge straight cast off for shoulder 6 (8, 8, 9) sts. at beg. of next row, work 1 row, then cast off remaining 8 (8, 9, 11) sts. *** With wrong side facing rejoin yarn to inner edge of left front sts. and complete as given for right front from *** to ***.

LARGE DOUBLE CABLE

## BACK

With No. 9 needles cast on 63 (71, 79, 87) sts. work in rib as on adult's sweater but work only 9 rows.
**Inc. row:** * k.f.b., (p.2, k.2) 0 (1, 2, 3) times, (p.2, k.f.b.) twice, * p.3, p.f.b., p.3, k.f.b., (p.1, p.f.b.) twice, p.1, k.f.b., p.1, p.f.b., p.1, k.3, p.2, (p.f.b., p.1) twice, p.f.b., p.2, k.3, p.1, p.f.b., p.1, k.f.b., (p.1, p.f.b.) twice, p.1, k.f.b., p.3, p.f.b., p.3, then rep. from * to *: 84 (92, 100, 108) sts. Change to No. 7 needles and patt.
**1st row:** p.2, (C2L, p.2) 2 (3, 4, 5) times, then work first row of patt. panel over next 64 sts., (p.2, C2R) 2 (3, 4, 5) times, p.2.
**2nd row:** k.2, (p.2, k.2) 2 (3, 4, 5) times, work 2nd row of patt. over next 64 sts., (k.2, p.2) 2 (3, 4, 5) times, k.2.
Cont. in patt. as now set working patt. panel in centre and 10 (14, 18, 22) sts.

BLARNEY KISS

## SLEEVES (make 2 alike)

With No. 9 needles cast on 35 (35, 39, 30) sts. and work 9 rows rib as for back.
**Inc. row:** * (k.f.b., p.2) once (once, (twice, twice), then for the two smaller sizes k.2 (for the two larger sizes k.f.b.), * then for all sizes (p.1, p.f.b.) twice, p.1, k.3, p.2, (p.f.b., p.1) twice, p.f.b., p.2, k.3, (p.1, p.f.b.) twice, p.1, then rep. from * to *: 44 (44, 52, 52) sts.
Change to No. 7 needles and patt.
**1st row:** p.2, (C2L, p.2) once (once, twice, twice), k.7, p.3, k.12, p.3, k.7, (p.2, C2R) once (once, twice, twice), p.2.
Cont. in patt. as now set, working the large double cable in centre and claw patt. over the groups of 7 sts. with side panels in cross-rib patt. but inc. 1 st. at both ends of every following 5th (5th, 6th, 5th) row until there are 66 (70, 76, 80) sts. keeping extra sts. at sides in the cross-rib patt. Cont. without shaping until work is 12½ (13½, 14½ 15½) in.
Place marker loops of contrast wool at each end of last row, then work 11 (13, 14, 15) rows straight. Cast off 4 4 sts. at beg. of next 12 (12, 14, 14) rows.
Cast off remaining 18 (22, 20, 24) sts.

## POLO COLLAR

With No. 9 needles cast on 105 (105, 113, 113) sts. and work in rib as on back for 18 rows, then change to No. 10 needles and work a further 9 rows.
Cast off in rib.

## CREW NECK

With No. 9 needles cast on 101 (101, 109, 109) sts. and work in rib for 5 rows. Change to No. 10 needles and work a further 8 rows. Change back to No. 9 needles and work 5 more rows. Cast off in rib.

## TO COMPLETE

Follow instructions given for adult's sweater.

# KNITTING

## Lesson Five: Colour work

Knitting designs which incorporate several colours look impressive but in fact they are easy to work, and quite often the simplest patterns are the most attractive. Multicolour work can range from a straightforward striped arrangement to a Fair Isle design which includes central motifs and fancy borders. Once you have grasped the basic techniques involved in working with more than one colour yarn, you will find it is not much more difficult to work a complex pattern than it is to work a simple striped one. As might be expected, the work is somewhat slower than straightforward single-colour knitting, but it is in many ways more interesting, and the results amply justify the extra time involved.

## Start with stripes

For the beginner, stripes are the easiest kind of multicolour work to try, and they can be used in a variety of arrangements.

Work in stocking stitch, and work an even number of rows in one colour; join in a second colour (without breaking off the first) and work a similar number of rows. Drop this second yarn and, taking care not to pull the yarn too tightly, take up the first colour again, and begin working with it. Always be careful not to drag on the yarns as they are looped up the side of your work in this way. When the

work is complete, the hanging end should be run into the fabric or else taken into the seam (be careful not to run the end into the contrast stripe or it may show through).

That is basic striping with two colours. Now try some variations. Use three colours in rotation, for an equal number of rows. Or try six rows of one colour, two of the second, four of the third, six of the first again. Or work in garter stitch: two rows of each colour will produce a fine, hairline stripe which is very effective. There is really no limit to the variations you can devise. And while you are experimenting, why not put the experiment to good use, and make something? Measure the width of a cushion, and take the tension of the yarn you are using. If it is double knitting and you are using No. 8 needles then you are probably getting $5\frac{1}{2}$ sts. to the inch. If the cushion is 10 in. wide, cast on 57 sts. (to allow a stitch at each side of the work for the seam). Now practise your striping, working different versions as you go, until the piece of work measures twice the depth of the cushion, and cast off. Stitch up the sides, put a zip in the third seam, and finish the whole thing off with a twisted cord or plait sewn all round the edges—and you have a gay cushion cover for a teenager's divan.

## Intricate colour patterns

Now you have mastered simple stripe patterns, move on to the more complicated colour designs such as Fair Isle knitting, chequered patterns and houndstooth, you have to use one of two techniques: weaving or stranding. Neither is difficult, but both must be practised.

**Weaving** colours together is usually

done when there are a fair number of stitches between colour batches. For instance, if you were working a pattern in which you knit 2 green, then 12 in white, then 2 green again; the green yarn has to be carried across the back of the 12 white stitches. It is difficult to do this and leave the yarn slack enough to stretch with the fabric in wear. So the green yarn is woven with the white, i.e. the green, which is not in use, is taken under the strand of white when you work the first stitch and over the white when you work the next and so on, all along the row. The same principle applies when you work a purl row (this type of colour design is usually worked in stocking stitch)—carry the two colours along at the same time, putting the colour not in use under the main yarn for the first stitch, over it for the second, and so on alternately all along (B1, 2 and 3). This is not a quick process but in time you get used to taking the two threads along together—some knitters like to carry each on a different finger of the right hand—and working them round each other.

**Stranding** is used when there are smaller gaps between the different coloured stitches: for instance, if you are working 2 white, 2 green, all along the row you can simply carry the yarn not in use across the back of the two stitches (A1 and 2).

It will be obvious that in some designs you may have to use a combination of stranding and weaving. For instance, if colours are arranged in blocks but set widely apart on a plain ground, you will need to strand the blocks, but weave between the blocks. Whichever method is employed, the golden rule is this: *never* pull the idle yarn taut. A little experiment will show what happens if the yarn is pulled even slightly too much. The fabric loses its flat surface and is caught up in ridges.

Not only is this ugly, but it pulls in the finished work so that the tension is wrong and there is no elasticity in the knitting. Only practice can ensure smooth, even working with several colours.

It sometimes happens that a second colour will be used only at one place in a design (perhaps a motif in the middle of the front of a jersey) in which case it is a waste of time and yarn to carry the second colour across on every row. In this case use a ball of the contrast yarn and keep this at the back of the work two or three stitches beyond where the motif occurs, stranding or weaving for a few stitches on each side of the motif to give the fabric the necessary firmness.

Patterns requiring more than one colour often are written exactly as for ordinary ones, but with the addition of initial letters to key the colours being worked. So the pattern which reads K.2G., 4B. would mean that you knit two stitches in green and four in blue and so on

(see our colour makes at the end of this lesson).

For other types of pattern, perhaps where one motif recurs across the whole fabric, it is usually easier to follow a chart, for a written pattern might be inordinately long. This is the method often used for Fair Isle designs. Charts may look frightening but in fact they are easy to follow, and are more reliable than a written pattern. You need remember only this: every square on the chart means a stitch; every horizontal row of squares is a row of knitting. The first will be a knit or right-side row, worked from right to left, the second a purl or wrong side row, worked from left to right.

If a design requires one contrast colour and the ground shade, the contrast is marked on the chart with a shaded square (or distinguished in some way from the plain ones). If there are several colours to be used, there are various ways of differentiating the squares. For instance, a cross inside the square

can be used for one colour, a dot inside the square for another, a diagonal line for a third and so on. The empty squares will represent the plain, basic shade (frequently natural or oatmeal in traditional Fair Isle designs). In this way you can see at a glance that your first row is worked in beige and red, the second in beige and green, and so on. A chart will usually give one complete repeat of a pattern rather than a whole row. If the repeat involves, say, 15 stitches your chart will probably show 16, with the last stitch an edge stitch. You will work this stitch at the *end* of the knit row and the *beginning* of the purl row. (Your pattern may specify a plain stitch at either end, in which case you work one at each end on every row.) If the design is for a motif—a star, perhaps, or an animal on a child's jersey—you may be told to work this motif after 10 plain stitches and with 10 plain stitches between each motif. This will ensure regular spacing of the motif across the finished work.

# Shortening or lengthening a knitted garment

It sometimes happens that you want to add or remove a few rows, or even inches, from a skirt or sweater, from sleeves or the legs of slacks. This is very simple to do on plain fabrics, such as ribs or stocking stitch, and even more elaborate designs can be undone by the more experienced knitter.

Undo the seam of the garment (let us say the sleeve seam). Now, at the chosen point (above the ribbing if you wish to lengthen or shorten the main fabric section) pull a thread at the edge of the fabric and draw it tight, right across the width of the work. Break this thread and gently draw the fabric out flat. You will now find that you can pull the the two pieces of fabric apart. Using a needle one size smaller than that used for the work, carefully pick up the stitches. You can now work a new ribbed band (if you are shortening the sleeve) or work some more main section and then work the ribbing (if you are lengthening it). In all cases, once the stitches are picked up change to the needle size originally specified for the design. Ribbing or stocking stitch can be worked either downward or upward, that is why it is possible to lengthen or shorten a garment made in these stitches. Anything more complex can be only shortened by the removal of some of the work and the addition of ribbing or a border stitch of some kind.

## Using yarn twice

It is possible to use yarn twice provided that it is in reasonable condition. For example, you might want to turn father's sweater into a waistcoat for junior. So long as you are using yarn of the correct thickness for the new pattern, and have weighed it to ensure that you have enough, here is how to set about it.

First, wash the garment and let it dry thoroughly. Now unpick all the seams carefully and, working from the top of each section downwards, undo the casting off and undo all the yarn. Wind this into loose skeins (round your knees or the back of a chair) and tie the hanks firmly. Soak these in warm water, squeeze them as dry as you can, and let them dry. Now wind them into loose balls of yarn, and you are ready to begin.

## Some colour samples

### BASIC STRIPES

This is the simplest multicolour pattern of all.
Our sample shows regular stripes,

**BASIC STRIPES**

**CHECKS**

worked in stocking stitch.
Cast on the desired number of stitches in green, and work 2 rows.
Do not break off yarn, but join in beige. Work 2 rows.
Drop beige yarn and take up green; work 2 rows.
Continue in this way, working alternate stripes of each colour.

### CHECKS

Cast on a number of sts. divisible by 8 (in our sample 32).
**Note.** P., purple; L., lilac.
**1st row:** * k.4P., 4L.; rep. from * to end.
**2nd row:** * p.4L., 4P.; rep. from * to end.
**3rd and 4th rows:** as first and 2nd rows.
**5th row:** * k.4L., 4P.; rep. from * to end.
**6th row:** * p.4P., 4L.; rep. from * to end.
**7th and 8th rows:** as 5th and 6th rows.
These 8 rows form the pattern. For checks of this size, it is necessary only to strand the yarn, taking care not to pull it too tightly.

### ZIG-ZAG STRIPES

This two-colour work is attractive used as the border for a sweater (set above welt or cuff ribbing) or spaced at intervals across the body of a garment.
Cast on a multiple of 4 sts.
**Note.** B., blue; R., red.
**1st-4th rows:** work in st.st. in B. Join in R.
**5th row:** k. * 1R., 3B.; rep. from * to end.

**ZIG-ZAG STRIPES**

**SLIP-STITCH CHECKS**

**6th row:** p.1R., * 1B., 3R.; rep. from * to last 3 sts., 1B., 2R.
**7th row:** k. in R.
**8th row:** p. * 3R., 1B.; rep. from * to end.
**9th row:** k.2B., * 1R., 3B.; rep. from * to last 2 sts., 1R., 1B.
**10th row:** p. in B.

### SLIP-STITCH CHECKS

This is a form of cheating! The finished effect is one of small checks, but in fact the yarn is neither stranded nor woven. Cast on an odd number of stitches, using white.
**1st row:** k.
**2nd row:** p. Join in green (G).
**3rd row:** with G., k.1, * sl.1 purlwise, k.1; rep. from * to end.
**4th row:** with G., * k.1, wool forward, sl.1 purlwise, wool back; rep. from * to last st., k.1.
These 4 rows form the pattern.
It is possible, of course, to create a bigger check by working two stitches in the dark contrast.

### RED AND WHITE SAMPLE

This is a motif worked in two colours from a simple chart. The blank squares are worked in white, the crossed squares in red. Work in stocking stitch throughout.

### RED, GREEN AND WHITE SAMPLE

This is a three-colour pattern, worked from a chart over 24 sts. The pattern repeats after 16 rows. Blank squares are white, crossed squares are red and dotted squares dark green. Work in stocking stitch throughout.

**RED AND WHITE SAMPLE**

**RED, GREEN AND WHITE SAMPLE**

**HOUNDSTOOTH**

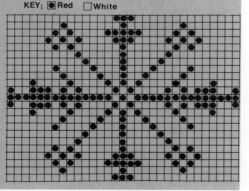

**Red and White Sample**
KEY; ■ Red □ White

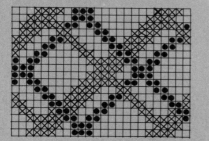

**Red, Green and White Sample**
KEY; ■ Red ⊠ Green □ White

## HOUNDSTOOTH

One of the most popular versions of checks, this stitch is easy to work and the yarn can be stranded at the back. Cast on a multiple of 4 sts.
**Note.** B., beige; G., green.
**1st row:** k.2B., * 1G., 3B.; rep. from * to last 2 sts., 1G., 1B.
**2nd row:** p. * 1B., 3G.; rep. from * to end.
**3rd row:** k. * 1B., 3G.; rep. from * to end.
**4th row:** p.2B., * 1G., 3B.; rep. from * to last 2 sts., 1G., 1B.
Rep. these 4 rows until work is length required.

## YOUR COLOUR PATTERN MAKES

# CHILDREN'S JERSEYS AND MATCHING CAPS

## MATERIALS YOU WILL NEED

**For fleur-de-lys striped jersey and cap:** 7 (8, 9) balls Hayfield Beaulon Double Knitting in cream, 3 balls each in amber, green and royal blue, 2 balls in red. One pair each Nos. 8 and 10 knitting needles (USA: 6 and 3).
**For Fair Isle jersey and cap:** 8 (9, 10) balls Hayfield Gaylon Double Knitting in main shade (emerald), 3 (4, 4) balls in Aran and 1 ball each in gold, blue and red. One pair each Nos. 7, 8 and 10 knitting needles. (USA: 7, 6 and 3).

## MEASUREMENTS

**Fleur-de-lys set:** to fit chest size 24 (26, 28) in.; length of jersey 15½ (17½, 19½) in.; sleeve seam 10½ (12, 13½) in.
**Fair Isle set:** to fit chest size 26 (28, 30) in.; length of jersey 18 (20, 22) in.; sleeve seam 11 (12, 13) in.

## TENSION

**Fleur-de-lys pattern:** 6 sts. and 7 rows to 1 in. over patt. on No. 8 needles.
**Fair Isle pattern:** 5½ sts. and 7 rows to 1 in. over st.st. on No. 8 needles.

## ABBREVIATIONS USED IN THESE PATTERNS

K., knit; p., purl; st(s)., stitch(es); in., inch(es); tog., together; inc., increase; dec., decrease; beg., beginning; cont., continue; rep., repeat; st.st., stocking stitch; foll., following; alt., alternate; rem., remain.
**For fleur-de-lys pattern:** C., cream; A., amber; G., green; B., blue; R., red.
**For Fair Isle pattern:** M., main colour; A., Aran; G., gold; B., blue; R., red.

## Fleur-de-lys jersey and cap

### FRONT

With No. 10 needles and C. cast on 81 (87, 93) sts. and work 8 rows in st.st., beg. with a k. row.
**9th row:** p. (this makes hem ridge). Change to No. 8 needles.
**10th row:** p.
**11th row:** k.3C., * k.3A., k.3C.; rep. from * to end.
**12th row:** p.1A., p.1C., p.1A., * p.4A., p.1C., p.1A.; rep. from * to end.
**13th row:** k. in A.
**14th row:** p. in A.
**15th row:** k. in A.
**16th row:** p.3A., * p.1A., p.1C., p.4A.; rep. from * to end.
**17th row:** k.3A., * k.3C., k.3A.; rep. from * to end.
**18th row:** as 16th.
Rep. 13th-15th rows.
**22nd row:** as 12th.
**23rd row:** k.3C., * k.3G., k.3C.; rep. from * to end.
**24th row:** p.1G., p.1C., * p.4G., p.1C., p.1G.; rep. from * to end.
Rep. 13th-22nd rows, but read G. for A.
**35th row:** k.3C., * k.3B., k.3C.; rep. from * to end.
**36th row:** p.1B., p.1C., p.1B., * p.4B., p.1C., p.1B.; rep. from * to end.
Rep. 13th-22nd rows, but read B. for A. Now work another 12-row stripe as before, keeping fleur-de-lys always correct and using R. as background colour. Introducing A. on the next row and working the background colours always in the sequence already established, cont. in same fashion to complete the 5th (6th, 7th) patt. stripe. Cont. in patt. and, keeping it correct, work shaping as follows:
Cast off 4 sts. at beg. of next 2 rows, then take 2 tog. at each end of every right-side row until there are 41 (45, 47) sts., ending with a p. row.
**Shape Front Neck.** K.2 tog., patt. 10 (12, 12); turn.
Cont. on these sts. in patt. dec. 1 st. at beg. of every row until 1 st. rem. Fasten off. Slip centre 17 (17, 19) sts. on spare needle and complete second half of neck to match first.

### BACK

Work as for Front, but omitting front neck opening and cont. to dec. until there are 29 (31, 33) sts. Leave on spare needle.

### SLEEVES (make 2 alike)

With No. 10 needles and C. cast on 38 (42, 46) sts. and work 11 rows in k.1. p.1 rib.
**2nd size:** inc. in last st. of last row: 43 sts.
**3rd size:** inc. in first and last sts. of last row: 48 sts.
**12th row:** * p.4, p. twice into next st.; rep. from * to last 3 sts., p.3: 45 (51, 57) sts.

Change to No. 8 needles and starting at the 11th row as given for Front, cont. in patt., inc. 1 st. at each end of every 8th row until there are 57 (63, 69) sts. Cont. in patt. until the 5th (6th, 7th) patt. stripe has been completed, i.e. matching exactly with Front and Back.

**Shape Top.** Keep patt. correct, follow instructions for shaping armholes for Front, cont. to dec. until there are 5 (7, 9) sts. Leave these sts. on spare needle.

## POLO COLLAR

Sew raglan seams, leaving seam between Back and Left Sleeve open. With right side of work facing, and using No. 10 needles and C., k. across sts. of Left Sleeve, pick up and k.10 (12, 12) down left side of neck, k. across centre front sts., pick up and k.10 (12, 12) up right side of neck, k. across sts. of Right Sleeve and sts of Back. Work one row in P. Now work in k.1, p.1 rib for 1½ in., then change to No. 8 needles and work another 2 in. Cast off loosely in rib.

## TO COMPLETE

Press st.st. sections. Join seam between Back and Left Sleeve. Join seam of polo collar. Sew side and sleeve seams; turn up hem and sew lightly.

## CAP

With No. 10 needles and C., cast on 98 (104, 110) sts. and work 9 rows in k.1, p.1 rib. Change to No. 8 needles and k.1 row, inc. 1 st. at end of row (this row forms hem ridge). Work 11th-16th rows of patt. as given for Front.
**Next row:** k.3G., * k.3C., k.3G.; rep. from * to end.
**Next row:** p.3G., * p.1G., p.1C., p.4G.; rep. from * to end. . . .
With G., k.1 row, p.1 row and k.1 row.
**Next row:** p.1G., p.1C., p.1G., *

p.4G., p.1C., p.1G.; rep. from * to end. Introducing B. on the next row and keeping the 6-row colour stripes correct with the fleur-de-lys, complete stripe in B. and then R. stripe, and then cont. in C. in st.st. to complete 40th (44th, 48th) row from cast-on edge.

**Shape Crown. 1st row:** (k.2 tog., k.31 (33, 35)) 3 times: 96 (102, 108) sts. Work 1 row p.
**2nd and alt. rows:** p.
**3rd row:** (k.2 tog., k.12 (13, 14), k.2 tog. through back of loops) 6 times.
**5th row:** (k.2 tog., k.10 (11, 12), k.2 tog. through back of loops) to end. Cont. to dec. thus by 12 sts. on every k. row until there are 12 (18, 12) sts. Break off yarn, thread through sts. and fasten off securely.

## TO COMPLETE

Sew seam at back. Turn ribbing inside and sew down lightly. Press, and finish with pompon in C. at point.

# Fair Isle jersey and cap

## FRONT

With M. and No. 10 needles, cast on 76 (82, 88) sts. and work 2 in. in k.1, p.1 rib, inc. 1 st. at end of last row. Change to No. 8 needles. Work in patt. with colours as follows:
**1st row:** k.1M., * k.1A., k.1M.; rep. from * to end.
**2nd row:** p.1M., * p.1A., p.1M.; rep. from * to end.
**3rd row:** as first row.
**4th row:** p. in A.
**5th row:** k.2A., * k.1A., k.1G.; rep. from * to last 3 sts., k.3A.
**6th row:** p.2A., * p.1A., p.1G.; rep. from * to last 3 sts., p.3A.
**7th row:** as 5th.

**8th row:** p.2A., * p.1A., p.5G.; rep. from * to last 3 sts., p.3A.
**9th row:** k. in A.
**10th row:** p.2A., * p.2A., p.3B., p.1A., rep. from * to last 3 sts., p. 3A.
**11th row:** k.2A., * k.3A., k.1B., k.2A., rep. from * to last 3 sts., k.3A.
**12th row:** as 10th row.
**13th row:** k.2A., * k.1A., k.5B., rep. from * to last 3 sts., k.3A.
**14th row:** as 10th row.
**15th row:** as 11th row.
**16th row:** as 10th row.
**17th row:** k. in A.
**18th row:** p.2A., * p.2R., p.1A.; rep. from * to end.
**19th row:** k.2A., * k.1R., k.2A.; rep. from * to end.
**20th row:** p.2A., * p.1R., p.2A.; rep. from * to end.
**21st row:** k.1R., k.1A., * k.2R., k.1A.; rep. from * to end.
**22nd row:** p. in A.
**23rd row:** as first.
**24th row:** as 2nd.
**25th row:** as first.
**26th row:** p. in M.
Work these 26 rows once more and then cont. in M. in st.st. until work is 12 (13½, 15) in. from beg. ending with p. row. (Length can be adjusted here, if required.)
**Shape Armholes.** Still working in M., cast off 3 (4, 5) sts. at beg. of next 2 rows: 71 (75, 70) sts.
**Next row:** k.2 tog., k. to last 2 sts., k.2 tog.
**Next row:** p.
Rep. these 2 rows until there are 57 (57, 57) sts. Leave these on spare needle.

## BACK

Work exactly as for Front.

## SLEEVES (make 2 alike)

With M. and No. 10 needles cast on 40 sts. and work 15 rows in k.1, p.1 rib.
**16th row:** p.1, * p. twice in next st., p.2; rep. from * to end: 53 sts. Change to No. 8 needles and work 52 rows of colour patt. as for Front. Then cont. in M. in st.st., and, for the 2nd and 3rd sizes only, inc. at each end of first and every foll. 3rd row until there are 59 (65) sts. Work straight until sleeve is 11 (12, 13) in. (or required length) from beg., ending with a p. row.
**Top of Sleeve.** Follow instructions for shaping armholes for Front until 33 sts. rem. Leave these on spare needle.

## YOKE

Sew raglan seams, leaving seam between Back and Left Sleeve open. Then, with right side of work facing, using No. 8 needles work across Left Sleeve: k.2 tog. M, * k.1A., k.1M.; rep. from * to last st., k. 1A., work across sts. for Front, k.1M., * k.1A., k1M.; rep. from * to end., work across Right Sleeve k.1A., * k.1M., k.1A.; rep. from * to end, work across Back, k.1M., k.1A., k.1M.; rep. from * to end: 179 sts.

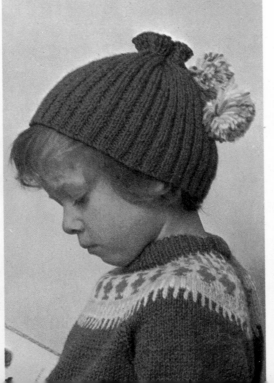

**2nd and 3rd rows:** work in colour patt.

**4th row:** using A., p.2 tog., p.7, (p.2 tog., p.8) 17 times: 161 sts

**5th, 6th, 7th and 8th rows:** work in colour patt.

**9th row:** using A. p.3, p.2 tog., p.3, (p.3, p.2 tog., p.4) 17 times: 143 sts.

**10th-16th rows:** work in colour patt.

**17th row:** using A, p.2 tog., p.1, (p.2 tog., p.2) 35 times: 107 sts.

**18th-21st rows:** work in colour patt.

**22nd row:** using A, p.2, (p.3, p.2 tog.) to end: 86 sts.

**23rd-26th rows:** work in colour patt. Complete in M., using No. 10 needles.

**Neck ribbing.** Work 8 rows in k.1, p.1 rib.

**Next row:** p. (this makes ridge on right side).

Work 6 rows in k.1, p.1, rib. Using a No. 8 needle, cast off loosely.

## TO COMPLETE

Press sections carefully and join seam between Back and Left Sleeve, joining sides of neck ribbing. Turn in ribbing on ridge row and hem inside. Join side and sleeve seams.

## Cap

With M. and No. 10 needles cast on 136 (144, 152) sts.

**1st row:** * k.2, p.2; rep. from * to end. Rep. this row 7 times more then change to No. 7 needles and continue to rib until work is 5½ (6, 6½) in. from beg. ending with a wrong-side row.

**Next row:** * k.2 tog., wool round needle, p.2 tog.; rep. from * to end: 102 (108, 114) sts.

**Next row:** * k.2 tog., p.1; rep. from * to end: 68 (72, 76) sts. Work for 1 in. in k.1, p.1 rib.
Cast off.

## TO COMPLETE

Sew seam at back of cap; make a cord of twisted wool in M. and thread through eyelet holes in cap, finishing each end of cord with a multicolour pompon. Press seam.

# PLAID JACKET

To team with your stocking stitch skirt, trousers and knickerbockers from Knitting, lesson one. Instructions for matching plaid deerstalker hat will be given in lesson six.

## MATERIALS YOU WILL NEED

20 oz. Wendy Double Knitting in main colour (to match colour used for skirt, trousers and/or knickerbockers), also 6 oz. dark green, 5 oz. paprika, 6 oz. brown and 5 oz. peppermint ice for plaid pattern (this quantity is sufficient to work plaid pattern for deerstalker hat as well). One pair each Nos. 9 and 10 knitting needles, with points at each end (USA: 5 and 3). 5 medium buttons.

## MEASUREMENTS

To fit bust size 35/37 in.; length 27 in.; sleeve seam 17½ in.

## ABBREVIATIONS USED IN THIS PATTERN

K., knit; p., purl; st(s)., stitch(es); in., inch(es); tog., together; beg., beginning; cont., continue; rep., repeat; inc., increase; dec., decrease; st.st., stocking stitch; t.b.l., through back of loop; patt., pattern; M., main; G., green; P., peppermint ice; B., brown; Pap., paprika.

## THE COLOUR PATTERN

**1st row:** k. in Pap.
**2nd row:** p. in Pap.
**3rd row:** in M. p.1, k.1, p.1, k.1, p.1, k.3, join in G. and k.3G., now in M. k.3, p.1, k.1, p.1, k.3, * in M. p.2, k.2, p.1, k.1, p.1, k.1, p.1, k.3, join in G. and k.3G., now in M. k.3, p.1, k.1, p.1, k.3 *; rep. from * to * 4 times ending last rep. k.1M.
*(Note: As the bands of k.3G. are continued up the entire garment it is probably easier to join in small balls of this colour at each point in the work where they are needed.)*
**4th row:** work back on the sts. as set, working k. sts. of 3rd row in p. and p. sts. of 3rd row in k., and working M. over M. sts. and G. over G. sts. Rep. 3rd and 4th rows twice more.
**9th row:** as 3rd row, but substituting B. for M. Break off B.
**10th row:** as 4th.
**11th row:** as 3rd.
**12th row:** as 4th row, but substituting P. for M. Break off P. Rep. 3rd and 4th rows 4 times more.
**21st row:** work over all sts. in G.
**22nd row:** work over all sts. in G. Rep. 21st and 22nd rows once. Rep. 3rd and 4th rows (using M.) twice more, then 3rd row once.
**30th row:** as 4th row but substituting B. for M. Rep. 3rd and 4th row once, using M.
**33rd row:** as 3rd row, but substituting P. for M. Break off P. Rep. 4th and 3rd rows once, using M.
**36th row:** as 30th. Rep. 3rd and 4th rows 3 times, using M. These 42 rows form patt.

## BACK

With No. 10 needles and M., cast on 114 sts. and work in st.st. for 1 in.,

ending with a k. row.
**Next row:** k. (this forms ridge for hemline).
Now beg. patt. and after 8 rows have been worked change to No. 9 needles and cont. for a further 4 rows. Now, keeping patt. correct, take 2 tog. at each end of next and every following 6th row until 9 decs. in all have been worked (96 sts.) then cont. straight until work is 9½ in. from hem ridge. Now inc. at each end of next and every following 8th row working 8 incs. in all until there are 112 sts., keeping patt. correct. Cont. until work is 17½ in. from hem ridge, ending with a wrong-side row.

**Shape Armholes.** Cast off 7 sts. at beg. of next 2 rows then take 2 tog. at each end of next 7 right-side rows (84 sts.) then cont. until work is 25½ in. from hem ridge ending with a wrong-side row.

**Shape Shoulders.** Cast off 7 sts. at beg. of next 6 rows and 8 sts. at beg. of next 2 rows. Cast off remaining 26 sts.

## LEFT FRONT

With No. 10 needles and M. cast on 92 sts. and work in st.st. for 1 in. ending with a k. row.
**Next row:** k. (this makes hem ridge). Now begin patt. working from 5th st. of patt. in brackets (i.e. p.1) followed by 3 full reps. After 8 rows have been worked change to No. 9 needles and work a further 4 rows. Take 2 tog. at beg. of next and every following 6th row until 9 decs. in all have been worked (83 sts.) then cont. straight until work is 9½ in. from hem ridge ending with a wrong-side row. Now, inc. at beg. of next and every following 8th row until 8 incs. have been worked (91 sts.) taking sts. into patt. Cont. until work is 17½ in. from hem ridge, ending with a wrong-side row.

**Shape Armholes.** Cast off 7 sts. at beg. of next row then take 2 tog. at beg. of next 7 right-side rows (77 sts.) then cont. until work is 25½ in. approximately from hem ridge and patt. matches that of Back, ending with a wrong-side row.

**Shape Shoulders.** Cast off 7 sts. at beg. of next 3 right-side rows, then cast off 8 at beg. of next right-side row. Cast off remaining 48 sts.

## RIGHT FRONT

Work as for Left Front, reversing the patt. and beg. with 3 full reps. followed by 20 sts. of last patt. When work is 3 in. from hem ridge ending with a wrong-side row make a buttonhole thus: patt. 11, cast off 6, patt. 14, cast off 6, patt. to end of row. Now on next row cast on 6 sts. above each group that has been cast off, taking these into patt. Cont. to complete as for Left Front, working a buttonhole every 4 in. from the first until five in all have been worked.

## SLEEVES (make 2 alike)

With No. 10 needles and M. cast on 56 sts. and work hem and ridge as for Back. Now begin patt., working last 3 sts. of patt. repeat, then 2 complete reps. of patt., then first 5 sts. of patt. Work 8 rows then change to No. 9 needles and work a further 4 rows. Now inc. at both ends of next and every following 8th row until 16 incs. in all have been worked (88 sts.) taking extra sts. into patt. Cont. until sleeve is 17½ in. from hem ridge ending with a wrong-side row.

**Shape Top.** Cast off 7 sts. at beg. of next 2 rows then take 2 tog. at each end of next 9 right-side rows, then at each end of every row until there are 18 sts. Cast off.

## POCKETS (make 2 alike)

With No. 9 needles and M. cast on 32 sts. and work in patt. beg. with last 3 sts. of patt. then one full rep. and 5 sts. of next patt. Cont. until work is 5½ in., ending with a right-side row.
**Next row:** in M., k. (this forms hem ridge).
Now in M. work 1 in. in st.st. on No. 10 needles. Cast off.

## TO EMBROIDER

Press the pieces carefully. Using a darning needle and chain stitch, work embroidery as follows: up the p.2 'gutters' work 2 rows in Pap. going over all colours. In the 3 gutters of 1 st. each work 1 row B., 1 row P. and 1 row B. Where there are 2 gutters of 1 st. each work 1 row of B. and 1 of P. (The lines of P. in all cases should be taken under the Pap. and G. horizontal lines.) Work in this way over all the pieces.

## TO COMPLETE

Join fronts of jacket to back at shoulder seams and set in sleeves. Turn front facings in and slipstitch down on wrong side. Neaten buttonholes and sew on buttons to correspond. Join side and sleeve seams. Turn up all hems and slipstitch into place; sew pockets on fronts, taking care to match patts.

## COLLAR

Now using M. and No. 10 needles, with right side of work facing, pick up 25 sts. evenly along the back of the neck and, beg. with a p. row, work 6 rows in st.st. picking up 5 sts. from the back of the neck at each end of the first 4 rows (45 sts.) and then picking up 6 sts. from the side of the neck to centre point of rever at the end of the next 2 rows (57 sts.). Now work until st.st. is 4 in.; mark this point. Now cont. in st.st. until work is 3½ in. from marked point, then cast off 6 sts. at beg. of next 2 rows and 5 sts. at beg. of next 4 (25 sts.). Cast off. Press collar lightly, double it over and slipstitch into position.

# KNITTING

## Lesson Six:
## Working in the round

The knitted fabrics which have so far been produced, although varying considerably in pattern, texture and style, have all been flat fabrics. Now it is time to learn the technique of knitting tubular fabrics. There are three principal ways of doing this: the four-needle method, round-needle method, and tubular work.

### Four-needle knitting

Probably the best-known way of working in the round is on a set of four matching needles. These needles are sold in sets in an equivalent range of sizes as pairs of needles, and each needle in the set is pointed at both ends. The four-needle method is usually employed in making fairly small objects, such as socks, gloves and polo collars.

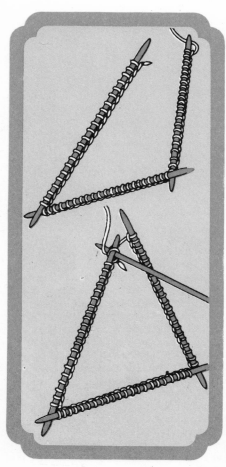

*Hooded evening cape knitted in sparkling silver yarn — instructions at the end of lesson.*

To cast on—let us say sixty stitches—cast on in the usual way using one needle. Now divide the stitches evenly (unless your pattern says otherwise) among three needles: twenty stitches on each. Form these three into a triangle and use the fourth needle to knit the stitches off the first needle. This releases a needle which in turn is used to knit the stitches off the second needle, and so on.

It is sometimes easier to work the first row on two needles in the usual way then to divide stitches, as this gives a slightly firmer edge to manipulate, and it is often difficult to avoid twisting the stitches on the first row when joining the first round; care should be taken at this point.

Another point to watch when working with four needles is to work firm stitches at the change-over from one needle to the other, otherwise there may be slack stitches in the finished fabric.

To produce a stocking stitch pattern in four-needle knitting it is not necessary to work purl rows, but simply a succession of knit rows. Ribbing is worked in the usual way, knit stitches set above knit, and purl stitches above purl.

## Round-needle knitting

This gives a similar finished effect to four-needle knitting (i.e. a continuous tube) and is worked in the same way, with all knit rows producing stocking stitch, but it is worked with only one needle which has a flexible centre section and two rigid points—the flexible centre allows the two rigid points to curve round to meet each other. You then work round and round on this single circular needle. These needles are available in a range of sizes similar to conventional needles and also in various lengths. The needle length you choose will depend on the pattern to be worked—the minimum number of stitches in the pattern must reach from one point of the needle to the other without stretching. Round needles are used mainly for large items such as skirts, dresses, sweaters and so on.

The great advantage of round-needle knitting is that no seams are necessary in the finished garment, and this gives a good hang to skirts and dresses. In fact, once a knitter is reasonably experienced, she can use a round needle for any sweater (working back and front together) as far as the armholes, where the work is divided into two halves for armhole and shoulder shaping. This can also, of course, be done on a skirt and, if the needle is small enough, for trousers.

To avoid confusion, if rounds have to be counted, it is helpful to tie a long coloured thread to the cast-on

first stitch. Then, each time the thread is reached in working, it is taken over the needle (although not knitted). In this way the contrast thread is taken up the work round by round, and counting is simple. This method can also, of course, be used for four-needle knitting. It is also helpful sometimes—especially when a fine yarn is being used—to work the first row after casting on straight across, by the use of a second needle, and to join up into rounds after the first row has been knitted.

## Tubular knitting

This produces a double fabric and is most often used for scarves. With two needles, cast on twice as many stitches as are needed for the finished width, and work as follows:
* k.1, y.fwd., s1.1 p.wise, y.back; rep. from * to end of the row. This row is repeated throughout. For casting off, knit two stitches together each time and slip stitches over each other in the usual way.

## Hints for a professional finish
### HEMS AND EDGES
Hems on knitted garments can be conventionally sewn, as in dress-making, or knitted into position.

**Plain hem.** This is usually worked in stocking stitch, even if the body of the garment is in a different stitch pattern. Cast on as usual and work the necessary number of rows in stocking stitch to give the depth of hem required. Often, if the entire garment is to be in stocking stitch, a ridge row is worked to form a defined edge. This is done by working a knit row where a purl row would normally be worked, or vice versa, to give a raised line.

**Knitted-up hem.** Cast on by the two-needle method (this gives a series of loops all along the edge). Work in stocking stitch for the desired number of rows, ending with a knit row. Now work a knit row for the ridge and, continuing in stocking stitch, beginning with a knit row, work another series of stocking stitch rows, to the same number as the first, and finish with a purl row.
**Next row:** fold up the hem and hold it behind the work on the needle. With the right-hand needle, slip point in the usual way into the first stitch on the left-hand needle and at the same time through the first loop at the cast-on edge. Knit them both together and take off the needle. Do this all along the row. Great care should be taken to start off with the very first loop on the cast-on edge and also not to miss a loop anywhere along the row, otherwise the hem will be dragged out of line. This gives a neat, permanent hem.

PICOT EDGE

KNITTED-UP HEM

VERTICAL HEM

**Picot edge.** This can either be sewn into position or knitted up as above. Instead of a ridge row, with right side facing, work: k.1, * y.fwd., k.2 tog; rep. from * to last st., k.1. Continue in the usual way. When the fabric is folded back to make a hem the effect is of a scalloped edge.

**Vertical hem.** On some jacket or cardigan patterns you are required to knit extra stitches at the inside edges of the fronts; these stitches are then folded back inside the fronts to form facings. A neat way of doing this is to work a slip stitch before the hem facing stitches begin on every right-side row. The slip stitch line is the fold-back line.

**Grafting.** This is the name given to the joining of two sets of stitches by the use of a sewing needle; it produces a virtually invisible seam and is preferred by some people for shoulder seams as well as for socks, facings and so on. Place the two pieces of knitting (which must have an equal number of stitches) together, right sides outside. Thread a tapestry needle with a length of yarn which will work the whole seam without having to be joined. * Slip the needle into the first stitch on the front needle as if you were going to knit it, and slip the stitch off, taking the wool through. Now insert the needle into the next stitch on the front needle as if you were going to purl it, draw the yarn through but leave the stitch on the needle. Put the needle through the first stitch on the back row of knitting as if to purl it and slip it off the needle, drawing the yarn through, then place the needle through the second back-row stitch, as if to knit it, pull the yarn through but leave the stitch on the needle. Repeat from * all along the row (A1 and 2). This produces an invisible join. Be careful not to pull the thread too tight or the tension will be distorted.

**Casting off two rows together.**
This technique is often used for sock toes. Place the two sets of stitches to be cast off together in the left hand and with the right-hand needle, put the point into the first stitch of the front needle and the first of the back. Knit this stitch and take the two stitches off the needles together. Do the same to the next two stitches, then take the first stitch on the right-hand needle over the second stitch in the usual way for casting off. Repeat all along the row (B).

## BUTTONHOLES

There are three ways of working these. If you want a **small** buttonhole (perhaps for a baby's garment) it is usual to work: y.fwd., and work 2 tog. at the point where the hole is required. The next row is worked normally.
For a **larger** buttonhole cast off a certain number of stitches at the specified point (perhaps four) and complete the row. On the next row, when you reach this point, turn the work round in your hands and cast on the number of stitches which were cast off in the previous row. Now reverse the work again and complete the row.
For a **vertical** buttonhole work as far as the point where you want the hole, then turn and work back. Work as many rows on these stitches as will give you the depth of buttonhole you require; leave yarn. Now join in yarn to the other set of stitches and work an equal number of rows on these. Work across all the stitches with the yarn left from the first set.

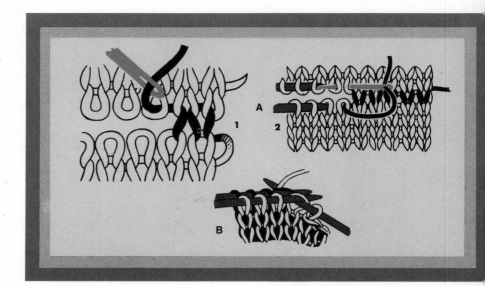

## PUTTING IN A LINING

Knitted garments are rarely lined, since they do not usually need it, and problems are created by putting a fabric which is basically stretchy above one which is rigid. But the one exception to this is the skirt—a knitted skirt is usually better for at least a half lining, because the lining takes the strain in wear and prevents 'seating'. For this reason, the lining should be made rather more close-fitting that would be the case in the lining of a fabric skirt.
Using the pieces of knitted skirt (before making up) as a pattern, cut out the lining, adding an allowance for hem and side seams. Sew the side seams and if necessary leave the left side open at the top to allow for a zip fastener. Neaten this opening. Turn in the top of the lining all round and ease it gently into the knitted waistband. Sew the hem of the lining. Stitch lining to knitting **only** at the waist.

## YOUR SIXTH MAKES

# TUBULAR KNITS

## Plus a special-occasion sparkling evening cape.

## Leg warmers

### MATERIALS YOU WILL NEED

5 oz. Hayfield Gaylon Double Knitting in red, 1 oz. in white. One pair of No. 9 knitting needles (USA: size 5), and one set of four double-pointed knitting needles No. 8 (USA: size 6). 1 yd. bias binding, 1 in. wide; ½ yd. elastic, ¾ in. wide. 10 small white buttons.

## MEASUREMENTS

Length from top to base of heel with top turned over is 13 in.

## TENSION

11 sts. and 15 rows to 2 in. on No. 8 needles.

## ABBREVIATIONS USED IN THIS PATTERN

St(s)., stitch(es); in., inch(es); k., knit; p., purl; sl., slip; p.s.s.o., pass slipped stitch over; beg., beginning; rep., repeat; inc., increase(d)(ing); dec., decrease(d)(ing); tog., together; patt., pattern; y.r.n., yarn round neeedle; ch., chain; d.c., double crochet; alt., alternate; t.b.l., through back of loop; PU 1, pick up and knit into loop before next stitch; R., red; W., white.

## TO MAKE (make 2 alike)

With R. and pair of needles, cast on 60 sts.
**1st-4th rows:** k. Join in W.
**5th row:** * k.2W., p.2R.; rep. from * to end of row.
**6th row:** * k.2R., p.2W.; rep. from * to end of row.
**7th row:** as 5th row.
**8th row:** with R. only, p. to end of row.
**9th row:** with R. only, k. to end of row.
**10th row:** * p.2R., k.2W.; rep. from * to end of row.
**11th row:** * k.2W., p.2R.; rep. from * to end of row.
**12th row:** as 10th row.
**13th row:** with R., k.
**14th row:** with R., p.
**15th-22nd rows:** as 5th-12th rows. Break off W.
With R. only, k. 6 rows, then work 2½ in. in k.1, p.1 rib. Transfer sts. from No. 9 needles to the set of four No. 8 needles, placing 20 sts. on each of three needles. Turn work so that wrong side of patterned top is outside and knit in rounds for 3½ in.

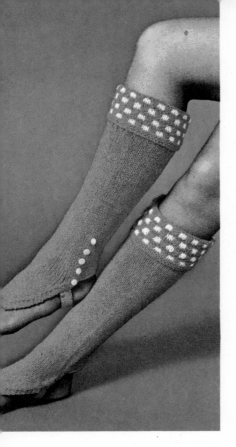

## Start Leg Shaping

**Next round:** ** k.2 tog., k. to last 2 sts. of round, sl.1, k.1, p.s.s.o. K.7 rounds straight **.
Rep. from ** to ** 4 times: 50 sts.
Continue without further shaping until work measures 13 in. from top of ribbing.

## Cast Off For Heel

K. to within 10 sts. of end of round. Cast off these 10 sts. also 10 sts. at beg. of next round: 30 sts.
Sl. the remaining 30 sts. on to one needle and k. across all sts. K. front as follows, working with only two No. 8 needles:

**1st row:** k.3, p. to last 3 sts., k.3.
**2nd row:** k.3, sl.1, k.1, p.s.s.o., k. to last 5 sts., k.2 tog., k.3.
**3rd row:** as first row.
**4th row:** k.
**5th and 6th rows:** as 3rd and 4th rows.
Rep. first to 6th rows once more then first to 5th rows. Rep. 2nd and 3rd rows until 14 sts. remain, ending with a 2nd row.
K. the next 6 rows and at the same time still dec. on alt. rows until 8 sts. remain. Cast off.

## TO COMPLETE

Stitch back seam of top turn-over. Press lightly using a warm iron and a damp cloth.
Divide elastic into two equal lengths and stitch one length to each sock, lower edges to fit underneath shoe. Face lower edges on inside with bias binding. Sew on 5 buttons to outside of each sock near lower edges (see illustration for position).

# Plaid deerstalker hat

### KNITTED ON FOUR NEEDLES

### MATERIALS YOU WILL NEED

4 oz. Wendy Double Knitting in main colour, also 6 oz. dark green, 5 oz. paprika, 6 oz. brown and 5 oz. peppermint ice for plaid pattern (this quantity is sufficient to work plaid pattern for matching plaid jacket as well—see Knitting, lesson five). One pair of No. 9 knitting needles, and a set of four No. 9 needles with points at each end (USA: size 5). ½ yd. heavy-weight interfacing, 32 in. wide.

### MEASUREMENTS

To fit average sized head.

### TENSION

6 sts. and 8 rows to 1 in. on No. 9 needles.

### ABBREVIATIONS USED IN THIS PATTERN

See Leg Warmers pattern; M., main shade; G., green; P., peppermint ice; B., brown; Pap., paprika.

### THE COLOUR PATTERN

**1st row:** k. in Pap.
**2nd row:** p. in Pap.
**3rd row:** in M., p.1, k.1, p.1, k.1, p.1, k.3, Join in G. and k.3G, now in M. k.3, p.1, k.1, p.1, k.3, * in M. p.2, k.2, p.1, k.1, p.1, k.1, p.1, k.3, join in G. and k.3G, now in M. k.3, p.1, k.1, p.1, k.3, * rep. from * to * 4 times ending last rep. k.1M.
*(Note. As the bands of k.3G. are continued up the entire garment it is probably easier to join in small balls of this colour at each point in the work where they are needed.)*
**4th row:** work back on the sts. as set, working k. sts of 3rd row in p. and p. sts of 3rd row in k., and working M. over M. sts. and G. over G. sts. Rep. 3rd and 4th rows twice more.
**9th row:** as 3rd row, but substituting B. for M. Break off B.
**10th row:** as 4th.
**11th row:** as 3rd.
**12th row:** as 4th row, but substituting P. for M. Break P. Rep. 3rd and 4th rows 4 times more.
**21st row:** work over all sts. in G.
**22nd row:** work over all sts. in G. Rep. 21st and 22nd rows once. Rep. 3rd and 4th rows (using M.) twice more, then 3rd row once.
**30th row:** as 4th row but substituting B. for M.
Rep. 3rd and 4th row once, using M.
**33rd row:** as 3rd row, but subsituting P. for M. Break off P.
Rep. 4th and 3rd rows once, using M.
**36th row:** as 30th.
Rep. 3rd and 4th rows 3 times, using M. These 42 rows form patt.

## CROWN

Using a set of four No. 9 needles and M. cast on 138 sts. and arrange in groups of 46 sts. on each of three needles. Work in patt., only working 6 repeats of 23 sts., (working 2G. instead of 3) for 10 rounds.
**1st dec. row:** (k.2 tog., k.19, k.2 tog. t.b.l.) 6 times. Work 9 rounds.
**2nd dec. row:** (k.2 tog., k.17, k.2 tog. t.b.l.) 6 times. Work 5 rounds.
**3rd dec. row:** (k.2 tog., k.15, k.2 tog. t.b.l.) 6 times. Work 5 rounds.
**4th dec. row:** (k.2 tog., k.13, k.2 tog. t.b.l.) 6 times. Work 3 rounds.
**5th dec. row:** (k.2 tog., k.11, k.2 tog. t.b.l.) 6 times. Work 3 rounds.
**6th dec. row:** (k.2 tog., k.9, k.2 tog. t.b.l.) 6 times. Work 1 round.
**7th dec. row:** (k.2 tog., k.7, k.2 tog. t.b.l) 6 times. Work 1 round.
**8th dec. row:** (k.2 tog., k.5, k.2 tog. t.b.l.) 6 times. Now work dec. rows without any rows between them.
**9th dec. row:** (k.2 tog., k.3, k.3 tog. t.b.l.) 6 times.
**10th dec. row:** (k.2 tog., k.1, k.2 tog. t.b.l.) 6 times.
**11th dec. row:** (sl.1, k.2 tog. t.b.l., p.s.s.o.) 6 times. Cast off tightly.

## BAND

Using two No. 9 needles and M. cast on 12 sts. and work in st.st. for 22 in. Cast off

## BRIM

Using two No. 9 needles and M. cast on 146 sts. and work thus:
**1st row:** k.1, (p.1, k.3, p.1, k.1, p.1, k.3, join in G. and k.3G., k.3, (p.1, k.1) twice, p.1, k.2, p.1) 6 times, k.1. Cont. on sts. as set in patt. for 4 more rows.

**6th row:** p. in P.
**7th row:** work in M. except for the 3 G. sts.
**8th row:** as 7th.
**9th row:** k. in B. except for 3 G. sts, and on first, 3rd, 4th and 6th G. groups of stitches, pick up and knit the loop between the first and 2nd and the 2nd and 3rd stitches, thus making 5 G. on these 4 stripes.
**10th row:** work in M.
**11th row:** work in patt. Now shape for brim thus:
**Next row:** patt. 26, y.fwd., sl.1 p. wise, y. back, turn, sl.1 p. wise, patt. to end.
**Next row:** patt. 23, and on G. stripe pick up and knit the loop between the first and 2nd sts. in G. and between 3rd and 4th sts. in M., y. fwd., sl.1 p. wise, yarn back, turn, sl.1 p. wise, patt. to end.
**Next row:** using Pap., k.22 working right across row inc. the G. sts., and inc. on each side of single M. st., y.fwd., sl.1 p. wise, yarn back, turn, sl.1 p. wise, and patt. to end.
**Next row:** using M. patt. 19, y.fwd., sl.1 p. wise, yarn back, turn, sl.1 p. wise, patt. to end.
**Next row:** cont. to work patt. in same way, ending 3 sts. before end of previous row until 22 rows have been worked. Now leave these sts. and all sts. as far as the end of the 2nd patt. rep. on the needle and start shaping for the front peak thus:
**Next row:** work to end of 4th patt., y.fwd., sl.1 p. wise, yarn back, turn and work towards 2nd patt. turning with a sl.st. as before 3 sts. from the end. Work in this way, working 3 sts. fewer at end of every row until patt. matches first set of brim incs. remembering to inc. on same rows 3 times in all. Sl. these sts. and those of 5th patt. on to right needle and work last patt. as for first to make 2nd side back peak, reversing shapings. Now with M., p. back all along row. Begin brim lining, all in M. and st.st.
**1st row:** k.13, y.fwd., sl.1 p. wise, yarn back, sl.1 p. wise, turn and patt. back. Cont. in this way working 3 sts. more on every alt. row for 5 more rows.
**7th row:** k.12, sl.1, k.2 tog., p.s.s.o., k.6, turn with sl.st. as before and p. back.
**9th row:** k.23 then turn with a sl.st. as before and p. back.
**11th row:** k.12, sl.1, k.2 tog., p.s.s.o., k. to 3 sts. more than on previous row, turn with a sl.st. and p. back.
Put these sts. and all other sts. as far as end of 2nd patt. and 10 sts. beyond on right-hand needle. Join in M. and work 26, y. fwd., sl.1 p. wise, yarn back, turn, sl.1 p. wise, p. 29, sl. and turn as before, k.32, sl. and turn as before, p. 35, sl. and turn as before, k.38, sl. and turn as before, p.41, sl. and turn as before.
**Next row:** sl.1, k.2 tog., p.s.s.o. above centre of both broad green stripes. Work 3 more rows, still working 3 more sts. at end of every row, then work 1 more dec. row making the decs.

immediately above those worked before; p. back, working 3 more sts. as before. Add these sts. to those on right needle and all remaining sts. except the last 14. Rejoin M. and complete this second half of peak to match the first half, reversing shapings. Break off yarn, rejoin at beg. of row and work 2 rows without shaping along all sts. On next row work last row of shapings above those on previous row then work a further 7 rows. Cast off.

## TO COMPLETE

Press all pieces well. On crown and brim work the embroidery as given for jacket in Knitting, lesson five, then backstitch two ends of brim together and backstitch crown to brim. Cut interfacing to match shape of brim, baste to brim then double under the plain lining of the brim and stitch down, covering seam. Slipstitch band to base of crown, covering join.

# Silver evening cape

## MATERIALS YOU WILL NEED

31 oz. Twilleys Goldfingering in silver. One pair each No. 8 and No. 9 knitting needles (USA: sizes 6 and 5). One crochet hook International Standard Size 4.00.

## MEASUREMENTS

To fit bust size 32-40 in.; length 60 in.

## TENSION

11 sts. and 14 rows to 2 in. on No. 9 needles.

## ABBREVIATIONS USED IN THIS PATTERN

See Leg Warmers pattern.

## MAIN SECTION
### (make 3 pieces alike)

Beg. at neck and with No. 12 needles cast on 57 sts. and work 4 rows in k.1, p.1 rib.
**Next row:** rib 4, * y.r.n., k.2 tog., rib 2; rep. from * to last 3 sts., rib 3.
Work a further 5 rows in rib.
**Next row:** work twice into every st.: 114 sts.
**Next row:** k.
Change to No. 9 needles and patt. thus:
**1st row:** k.
**2nd row:** k.
**3rd row (right side):** k.1, y.r.n. twice, (k.1, y.r.n. 3 times) 5 times, * k.6, (k.1, y.r.n. 3 times) 6 times; rep. from * to end, winding y.r.n. only twice for last st. of row.
**4th row:** k., dropping extra loops on long sts.
**5th row:** k.
**6th row:** k.

**7th row:** k.6, * (k.1, y.r.n. 3 times) 6 times, k.6; rep. from * to end.
**8th row:** as 4th.
These 8 rows form patt.
Cont. in patt. until work is 30 in., then change to No. 8 needles and cont. until work is 60 in. from beg. ending with 2 k. rows. Cast off loosely knitwise.

## HOOD

With No. 9 needles cast on 126 sts. and work in patt. beg. with 2 k. rows until work is 10 in., ending with 2 k. rows. Cast off **tightly** knitwise.

## TO COMPLETE

Do not press. Join sides of ribbed neckbands of 3 sections; with crochet hook join remaining edges of 3 sections working d.c. through both edges. Work a 2nd row of d.c. along joining seams to form a ridge. Fold hood double and join doubled cast-off edge to form back seam. Sew side edge of hood to cast-on edge of ribbed neckband, leaving 1 in. of band free at front edges. With 4 strands of yarn crochet a ch. 60 in. long and thread through neck holes to make tie.

# PATCHWORK

## Lesson One: Learning to make the patches

### Patchwork— perfect patchwork

Patchwork is unlike any other craft because it consists of making something beautiful out of scraps of fabrics which might otherwise be thrown away. Originally patchwork was a thing of beauty, created out of necessity. Our grandmothers and their mothers and grandmothers before them, faced with a lack of fabrics or the money to buy them, used to make new curtains, bed-covers, wallhangings, cushions and chair-backs from the contents of the rag bag. Or they took the best fragments from worn out or outgrown garments and used the good pieces to make new. Part of the fascination of patchwork is the fact that each patch evokes memories—of a favourite dress, a special occasion, a friend who perhaps passed on the piece of fabric . . . Patchwork at its worst has individual personality and at its best becomes a work of art and a family heirloom to hand on with pride. Now that it is not so necessary to economise, patchwork has become a friendly hobby! Many groups of women are coming together in 'sewing bees', where, over a cup of tea or coffee they sew their patches and exchange or share fabrics and designs. They may even join forces (as some Women's Institutes are doing) to make one large item, such as a quilt, between them. It is more usual to use brand new fabrics today—remnants purchased in the sales and by mail order, or the leftovers from dressmaking or soft furnishing. It is possible to buy manufacturer's sample books from local stores, when the range of fabric is outdated.

### Materials and tools

Patchwork is the only craft which does not need special tools or involve the purchase of a lot of new materials. The average home should contain at least the materials for a first simple piece of patchwork such as a cushion or a teacosy, but once you become addicted to the craft, it is possible to create the most wonderful designs with fabrics specially selected for their decorative

quality and their ability to be used together for maximum contrast and effect.

The ideal fabrics to use are those which are non-stretch, easy-fold and non-fray. Dress weight cottons such as gingham, poplin, cretonnes etc. are ideal for beginners to use, but many of the man-made fibres, silks, velvets and furnishing fabrics can be used equally successfully. Very thin or transparent fabrics are not really suitable as they have to be lined before they can be incorporated into the patchwork. Do not mix fabrics of different weights together in one piece of work—a heavy velvet patch next to a piece of lawn could cause the latter to tear. It is wise not to mix man-made fibres and natural fibres, although fabrics such as linen and cotton can be used together successfully. If mixing old and new fabrics, wash the new material before using to avoid shrinkage and do not use old fabric which is at all worn, since repairing worn-out patches can be a most unrewarding job.

**SEWING EQUIPMENT**—Pins and needles must be fine, between size 8 to 10, and cotton 60 to 100, or Terylene thread or Drima can be used instead. If using silk fabric or velvet a silk thread should be used. Traditionally only black or white thread was used to sew the patches together, but the predominant colour of the patchwork pieces can be used. A sharp pair of scissors with good points are necessary for cutting the fabric and a second pair for cutting the paper linings, and a piece of tailor's chalk or soft lead pencil to mark out the patches.

**FOR THE LININGS**—A fabric stiffener (Vilene) or stiff paper (old bank statements, thick envelopes or old Christmas and Birthday cards are ideal)

**TEMPLATES**—These are the foundation from which the papers are cut. They must be accurate and strong and it is possible to buy machine-made ones of metal alloy and plastic, but as it is not possible to buy every size and shape which might be needed, it is essential to know how to make your own templates. For this you need a strong fine cardboard, a sharp knife, school compass, protractor, metal ruler and a well sharpened HB pencil. If this is your first attempt at patchwork use the ready-made templates. In lesson two we show you how to make your own. There are two types of template—the 'solid' and the 'window' (figs A and B). The solid template represents the size of the finished patch and is used as the pattern for making the paper linings. The window is used as a means of choosing the exact piece of fabric and marking out the patches themselves. *The hexagon* is the easiest shape for a beginner to make and used in conjunction with the *diamond* or *triangle* it is possible to create a variety of designs. Our designs have been based on these three shapes.

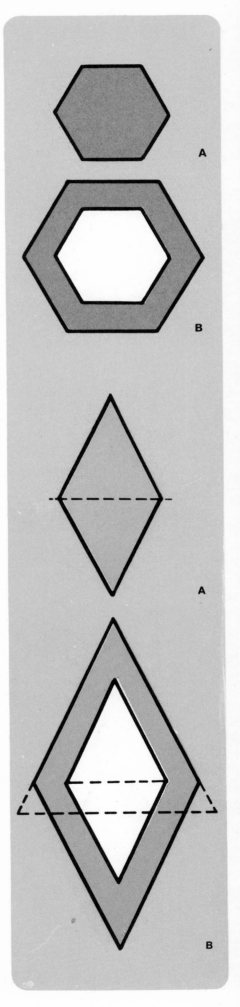

# Making the patches

First cut out the linings—either hold the template (A) against the paper and cut closely round it, or lay the paper on a flat surface, place the template on top and draw round it with a sharp pencil, and then cut out following the line. It is possible to cut more than one lining at a time, but as accuracy is very important (otherwise the finished work could pucker) it is best to cut only one lining paper at a time. Always use the template as the cutting guide—*do not* cut one lining from another.
Select the piece of fabric to be cut by using the window template (B) on patterned fabric, and moving it about to make sure you have chosen the most suitable piece, mark round the outside of the template with the soft pencil or tailor's chalk and then cut out the fabric. If you are working with a plain fabric you can use the solid template (A) allowing $\frac{3}{4}-\frac{3}{8}$ in. (1 cm.) turning all round. In cutting out any patch the straight of the material should run along one edge wherever possible. Cut out about two dozen patches (each one separately) before lining and tacking (basting). If fragile or sheer fabric is being worked, fabric stiffener can be used instead of a paper lining and this is usually retained as a permanent lining for the patches, but it does add

considerably to the weight of the work. Lay the lining paper on the wrong side of the fabric patch taking great care to place it centrally, pin in position, using one or two pins. These *must* be fine, as coarse pins leave permanent marks. Turn the fabric edge firmly over the paper, all round, pinching the turnings into place at the corners—if possible press with a warm iron as you go along. Tack (baste) with the back of the patch towards you, putting the needle through from back to front—tack (baste) as indicated (fig C) so the small stitch holds down the fold of fabric at the corners of the patch. To make sure you have folded accurately lay another lining paper on top of the patch—if a very small amount sticks out evenly all round, the patch is accurate. With the hexagon shape the corners should all tuck in quite neatly, but with the diamond and triangle shape there are sharp corners where the edge is likely to stick out. Pin the fabric fairly near the points with fine pins. Start folding at a blind corner, towards a sharp corner (fig D1). Take the projecting tip and fold it down, so the fold lies parallel to the edge of the paper lining (D2). Hold between left thumb and first finger and bring over to make a double fold and neat point. Pinch well and tack through with one tacking (basting) stitch, small enough to hold in position (D3). Complete a diamond patch by repeating the double fold at the second sharp point (D4).

# Sewing the patches together

Patches are usually joined together using a fine oversewing stitch on the wrong side, and as the stitches are not meant to be completely invisible, they must be neat and tidy! Pins are not used, so start by placing two patches, right sides together and starting at one corner use fine even stitches (about 16 to 20 stitches to the inch) sewing the fabric only and not the paper lining. As patchwork is plain sewing knots may be used, but they must be firm so the patches do not come apart. When the next corner is reached, unfold the patches and look at the work on the right side to make sure the line of stitches is really neat. Continue sewing the patches together as is convenient, depending on the shapes used (figs E1 and E2) taking great care to see the points come exactly together. Sometimes adjustment does have to be made, and where corners do not meet properly, the corner may have to be stitched and re-folded, or a new patch made, otherwise the finished work will be puckered. If this problem occurs frequently, then the papers must be inaccurate or the folding careless! Usually patches are sewn into units, then joined to similar sized units until the work is finished as this is easier than sewing single patches to a large heavy

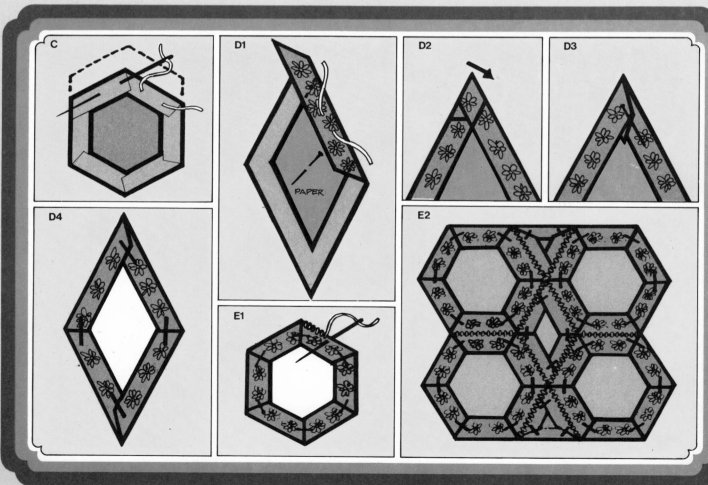

*The cushion (above) and the cushion and tea cosy (below) are all based on hexagon-shaped patches.*

**To make a patchwork cushion:** The colour, shape and design of the patches are up to you. Buy a cushion pad the size you require and make a paper pattern the exact size of the pad (no larger) so cushion will fit tightly. Make the front half from patches (we used hexagons as in lesson) to exactly fit the pattern using half-patches for the edge where necessary. Cut the back from toning plain fabric. Make up the cover as for an ordinary cushion (add piping if like in the plain colour), closing with a zip or press-studs. See embroidery, lesson six for more on cushion-making.

**To make a patchwork tea/coffee cosy:** Measure your pot then draw out the cosy shape on squared paper to fit. To make sure both sides are equal, fold down centre and cut out double. Work out patchwork design for both sides based on pattern. Sew patchwork pieces together. Make cosy from plain or toning fabric which is cut double and used to entirely cover 2 pieces of polyethylene foam about $\frac{1}{4}$ in. thick. Pin and try on pot before sewing. Appliqué patchwork design in position on both sides of cosy.

piece of patchwork. Half or part patches are cut to form the finished edge when the work is complete.

## Pressing the work and removing the papers

If a small piece of work is being done, it is usual to leave the papers, tacking (basting) removal and pressing until the end—with larger items such as a quilt, it is more practical to deal with a section at a time. First remove the tacking (basting) thread, then press the work on the *wrong side* with the iron setting appropriate for the type of fabric used, then remove the papers carefully. These can be used again and again, and if the edge has become slightly serrated it can be strengthened with one layer of Sellotape, but care must be taken to ensure this has not

made the paper any larger or the patchwork corners will not meet properly. *Note*—if fabric stiffener (Vilene) has been used instead of papers, this is usually left in, acting as an interlining.

## Finishing

Most patchwork needs to be lined because of the raw edges on the wrong side and it is worth while using a firm and closely woven fabric as this will double the life of the piece of work. Poplin, linen, twill, sateen (for curtain lining) are all suitable, and a quilt can be lined with a new sheet, but this should be washed and ironed first to allow for shrinkage. If the patchwork is made from used fabric, the lining should always be washed first. When making cushion covers, tea cosies etc. lining may not be necessary so long as the fabric used for the patches is firm.

## A word about design

The instructions given are for simple random patchwork, but once the patchwork bug has bitten you and you have made the first simple item, you will find you want to experiment with different fabrics to get the most pleasing design possible. Sketches based on graph paper are helpful, but the easiest way to work out a pleasing design is to make a quantity of patches from the various fabrics available and then move them about until you get an attractive balance of pattern, colour and tone—the patches can be pinned to a soft board or cork bath mat once the desired effect is obtained.

You should also try experimenting with different shapes altogether. For example a straight-forward four-sided diamond can be made into an attractive star design.

# PATCHWORK

## Lesson Two

**Jill Blake tells you more about the craft and we show you how to make a fabulous long evening skirt in patchwork.**

In the first lesson on patchwork we showed how to cut and join patches and how to make simple items using the basic shapes, the *hexagon*, the *triangle* and the *diamond*, but there are many other shapes which can be used in patchwork; the *square* for example is often used in conjunction with the *triangle* (our skirt is based on *squares*), the *pentagon*, the *octagon*, the *church window*, the *coffin*, and for really ambitious work, the *clamshell* shape (see diagram A). Templates can be purchased in all these shapes and in several different sizes, but as most of the geometric shapes can be used in conjunction with each other, you may

need a different size from the one available or if you are planning to cut only a few patches in an unusual shape, it seems hardly worthwhile purchasing a template, when it is quite simple to make your own.

## Making your own templates

To make your own templates you will need some strong fine card, a sharp knife, a school compass, a protractor, a ruler with a metal edge or metal ruler, a well-sharpened pencil, and a useful extra (particularly for square and rectangular templates)—a setsquare. There are two ways of making your own templates, and it is wise to practise with paper first to get an accurate drawing. To make a hexagon with a compass, pencil and ruler, set the compass to give a radius the required length of the hexagon sides. Make a circle (see diagram B1). Set the point of the compass at a (i.e. anywhere on the outline of the circle) and with the same radius draw an arc to cross it at b, set the compass point at b and with

the same radius draw another arc, c, and so on until 6 arcs have been made. The last arc should cross the circle at a. Join the points where they cross the circle with a ruler and pencil. Cut along these lines with a ruler and knife.

To make a hexagon with a protractor, ruler and pencil, draw a straight line p—q the required length of the side of the hexagon (see diagram B2). Using a protractor, make an angle of 120° at each end of this line, drawing in lines x—p and q—y and mark the same length as p—q. At these points make angles of 120° again and if the angles are correct, the last line will join up the figure to form a hexagon, so if it does not meet, try again! Cut as before with ruler and knife.

These templates would be the 'solid' type (see lesson one) but if you want to make the 'window' type of template, then there are also two alternative methods of making these. You can describe a second circle outside the first, with a radius ¼ in. to ¾ in. (1 cm.) longer and divide it in the same way, being careful to start at the right place on the outer circle by drawing a straight line from the centre (compass point) through a to the outer circle.

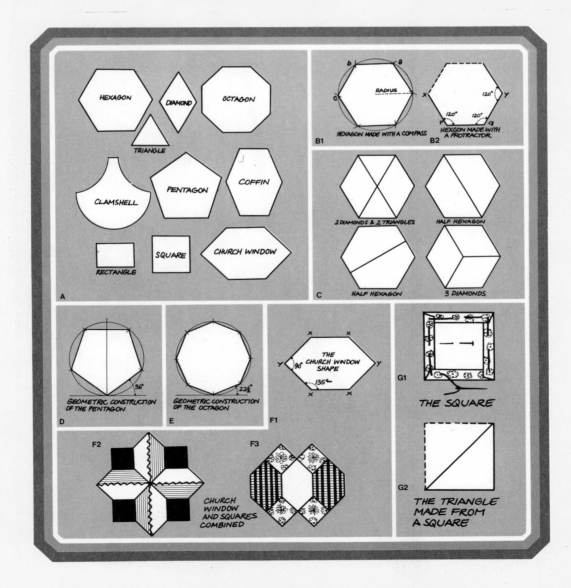

Draw in both hexagons as previously, cut out the inner and outer hexagons. A slightly less accurate way (but with the 'window' type of template accuracy is not quite so important) is to draw lines $\frac{1}{4}$ in. to $\frac{3}{4}$ in. (1 cm.) on the outside of the 'solid' template drawing, and to cut both out. Other templates can be made by dividing hexagons as shown in diagram C and these will all fit together with each other, or can be used in conjunction with a hexagon. Templates for the pentagon and the octagon can be made in a similar way to the hexagon. With the pentagon, five equal arcs are made with the compass on the circumference of the circle, or an angle of 36° (see diagram D). For the octagon, eight arcs are made on the edge of the circle, or an angle of $22\frac{1}{2}$° (see diagram E). The church window shape is really an elongated hexagon, and all the sides can be the same length as in diagram F1 or the sides x—x can be any length, but the four sides y—x must always be the same length. A protractor is necessary to make this template, the four angles at x are 135° and the two angles at y are 90° as shown. This is a particularly useful shape as it can be combined with square patches, so long as the sides of the square measure the same as the x—y measurement on the church window. Diagrams F2 and F3 show how to make up a pattern using these two shapes.

The square, rectangle and coffin shape are simple to make with a setsquare or a protractor, but the clamshell is rather harder to make than any of the others, particularly the 'window' template. I would suggest buying ready-made templates if you want to use this shape, and you can then scale the shape up or down by using squared paper, if you decide you want a different size.

## Working with squares and triangles

The square was frequently used in early patchwork, and it is still almost as popular as the hexagon and the diamond, because it can be combined with other shapes; with the church window shape (which has already been mentioned); with rectangles; with triangles. The template can be made by using a setsquare or a protractor, making the angle 90° and the triangle is made by cutting the square in half from corner to corner. Diagram G1 shows how square patches are tacked over the lining paper, and G2 how the square shape is cut to form the triangle. There are many traditional designs associated with squares and triangles which can be seen in early examples of the craft, but would look equally effective used in modern

patchwork. When only small scraps of fabric were available, *Roman squares* were made—these were based on oblongs, three different fabrics were cut into oblongs, sewn together to form a square and then set into a framework of darker patches, cut to the same width as each oblong (see diagram H). Today this idea could be copied for a cushion or nightdress case using ribbon instead of scraps of fabric.

Other traditional patterns include the *chequerboard* design, where light and dark squares are joined to create a chess or draught board effect. The fabric can be two plain contrasting colours or a plain and a patterned fabric used alternately (see diagram J) The triangle can also be used to create different patterns, some of which date back to the earliest examples of patch-work, but if modern fabrics are used, these can look surprisingly up-to-date. The *cotton reel* (diagram K1), the *windmill* (diagram K2) and the *basket* (diagram K3) are all particularly characteristic of American patchwork based on the triangle. The *basket* was usually appliquéed onto the centre of a cushion, coverlet etc. Traditionally only two fabrics were used, both in plain colours, but a patterned light fabric could be used to contrast with a plain dark fabric as shown on the *windmill* diagram.

## YOUR SECOND MAKE

# A LONG EVENING SKIRT IN PATCHWORK

When making patchwork garments the same rule applies as when making items for the home.—fabrics of different weights should not be mixed together.

We used silky-texture fabrics, brocade, some light-weight velvet and some fabric incorporating 'glitter' to give added richness—one or two pieces of 'silver' jersey fabric, left over from an evening top, were also used.

## MATERIALS YOU WILL NEED

to fit 24 in. waist
36 in. hips
44½ in. length
Enough interesting and varied fabrics of the same weight to make the equivalent of 4 yd. of 36-in. wide fabric; 4½ yd. of 32-in. wide stiffened dress weight lining fabric (Vilene); 5-in. square template or card to make one; 1¼ yd. of 1-in. wide petersham ribbon; 9-in. zip; 2 hooks and eyes or snap fastners; 5 yd. ½-in. wide ribbon to tone with fabric (we used turquoise velvet ribbon); 2¼ yd. fringed braid for hem, to tone with fabrics (we used turquoise lampshade fringe); 2½ yd. lining fabric.

## TO MAKE

This is made very simply with the stiffened lining fabric replacing lining papers. Using a template, cut out the fabric and the stiffened lining into 5-in. squares. Tack a square of lining onto the back of each patch (approximately 190 squares will be needed). Lay out the patches on a flat surface to form the front and back of the skirt, 9 squares wide by 10 squares long, grouping them in an attractive arrangement of colours, patterned and plain fabrics.

Tack each row of 9 squares together, allowing ¼ in. for seams. Press the seams flat, then tack and sew the strips of squares together to form a solid piece of patchwork material, pressing the seams open. As this is not the traditional method of preparing patchwork, the seams can be machined. If preferred the fabric can be prepared by the method described in lesson one, and the squares would then

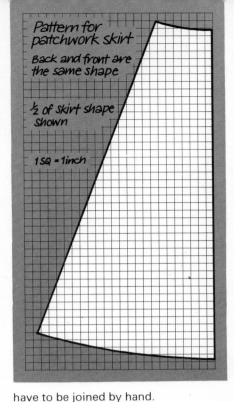

Pattern for patchwork skirt
Back and front are the same shape
½ of skirt shape shown
1 SQ = 1 inch

have to be joined by hand.

Make a pattern following the diagram, pin on the pattern pieces and cut the fabric for the skirt, folding the fabric in half as indicated, and making sure the top and bottom edges of the squares will meet at the side seams. Tack the side seams, allowing for the zip on the left-hand side. Fit and adjust if necessary. If more shaping is required at the waist, insert darts at each side edge of the centre back square. Machine seams and press open. For the waistband, cut out and sew one row of 9 squares (using pieces of material left over).

Cut a 3-in. band from the row of patchwork, allowing ½ in. for turnings, and long enough to fit waist with 2-in. overlap. Lay the band onto the top of the skirt, with ½-in. overlap on the back and 1½ in. at the front and with the *right sides* together tack and then sew along the top of the skirt. Press. Fold the waistband over the petersham stiffening. Tack and slipstitch into position on the wrong side of the skirt so the previous line of stitching is hidden. Turn in raw edges at end of band and slipstitch. Insert zip in left-hand side of skirt (see Sewing, lesson one) and attach waistband fastening (fastners or hooks and eyes). Adjust length of skirt if necessary, turn, tack and sew hem by hand. Measure side seam, cut ribbon to length and tack then sew down both side seams, very neatly so the stitches do not show. Tack and sew the ribbon and the fringe round the edge of the hem. Now make the lining. Fold the width of material in half, pin on pattern and cut. Sew side seams, press flat. Turn up narrow hem and machine stitch. Attach lining to waist of skirt with *wrong sides* together. Leave lining loose at sides and hem, but slipstitch neatly round zip opening.

H
1
K
2
3
J

# PATCHWORK

## Lesson Three:
## The 'Cathedral Window'

**Jill Blake tells you how to make this unusual patchwork design.**

The 'Cathedral Window' design is an American patchwork pattern which produces a pierced effect, almost like a coarse lace. The patterned fabric shows through the 'window' frame rather like the brightly coloured glass in a stained-glass church window, hence the name 'Cathedral Window'. The original foundation fabric was coarse feed sacks, but nowadays unbleached muslin or calico can be used to make the basic squares for this pattern. Naturally all the foundation squares must be of the same fabric, but the patterned centres can be as varied as you like, so long as you stick to the rule of using the same weight of fabric for all the patches. Plain jewel-bright material or small prints look best.

There are many advantages with this type of patchwork, particularly if the finished work is to be a bedcover or, as in our illustration, a daybed coverlet (another American innovation). The pierced squares make a very neat and decorative edge so there is no need to cut and shape extra patches specially for the edge of the work, and as the back will be very much neater than ordinary patchwork, it is not necessary to line the finished cover (although it will prolong its life if you do). It can also be worked in easy-to-manage sections, so you can take your work about with you, unlike conventional patchwork quilts (once you are past the initial stages), which do have to be worked at home with plenty of space to spread out the design.

## Constructing the patches

### FOR 'CATHEDRAL WINDOW' PATCHWORK

If you are using unbleached muslin or calico for the foundation, or any other fabric you suspect might shrink, wash and press. Bleached calico or poplin are other ideal fabrics which do not need preshrinking.

Cut a seven-inch square out of the foundation fabric and make $\frac{1}{2}$-inch turnings all round (A1). To simplify this, cut a template six inches square out of stiff card.

Fold muslin or calico in half with seam allowance on outside (A2). Sew edges together at sides from top open edge down $1\frac{1}{2}$ in. with close overcasting stitch, catching the edges of fabric only. Turn piece inside out and refold flat so seams are at the centre (B). Slip-stitch the two open edges together from the centre, out $1\frac{1}{2}$ in. each side, leaving ends open—**do not sew** through bottom fabric. You now have a $4\frac{1}{4}$ in. square. Turn square over and fold each corner of **this** square to the centre, and pin in place (C). You now have a 3-in. square. Secure the corners at the centre, two at a time, with small firm tacking stitches. Tack centre through all thicknesses. Make three more squares and seam two together with tiny oversewing stitches in the usual way. Join two more to first two to form a square. Cut out a two-inch square of cardboard and use this to cut the 'window' patches in the printed or coloured fabric. Place these over the diamond shapes formed by two adjoining patches (D). This is on the side of the work with **unstitched** folds. Trim the edges of the 'window' patch so it is fractionally smaller than the diamond shape and pin in position. Fold one edge of the diamond shape over on top of the print 'window' and slipstitch across, leaving about $\frac{1}{4}$ in. at the ends unstitched. Repeat with the next side tacking adjacent sides together $\frac{1}{4}$ in. from the ends. Continue round four sides in this manner. When four 'windows' have been put in you will notice that the touching points form tiny petals, also the sides of the windows form circles (E).

A 'window' patch is applied to every diamond shape except in the case of a half-square coming at the edge of an article. In this case the edges of the white and coloured cottons are turned in and neatly overstitched.

## Adapting the design

This design may be adapted to make all sorts of things—cushions, a long skirt, a table cover, or a magnificent edging to a pair of heavy curtains at a tall window. The squares may be made larger—for example a 9-in. foundation square will need window patches of 3-in. square.

The foundation fabric need not be white or off-white, this could be in a colour, with the printed fabric to tone or contrast.

A1

A2    ($\frac{1}{2}$ of A1)

B
($4\frac{1}{2}''$ sq)

C  (3″ sq)

D

E

# CATHEDRAL 'WINDOW' COVERLET

## MATERIALS YOU WILL NEED

To make a coverlet 64 in. by 80 in. — 2¼ yd. unbleached muslin, 72 in. wide, or the equivalent in calico, poplin, etc.; piece of firm card for templates; scraps of printed and/or plain fabric all in the same weight (cotton would be ideal); sewing thread to match foundation fabric.

## TO MAKE

Wash the muslin (or other foundation fabric if necessary) to pre-shrink, and press. To make this coverlet you will need 616 base squares, so mark the edge of the muslin into 7-in. wide pieces, clip and tear in strips across the width from selvedge to selvedge. Cut these strips into 7-in. squares. Cut a 6-in. template from the card and use this to turn in the edges as described under **Constructing the patches.**

Sew some of the foundation patches together in blocks of four. As working with all the same coloured fabric can become very boring, break off when you have a few blocks of four made and cut some of the 'window' patches from the patterned fabric using a 2-in. piece of card as a template. Stitch these to form the 'windows' as previously described. You will need to stitch the blocks of four together to form the coverlet 22 squares by 28 squares to get the desired size. Finish the edge as illustrated. The coverlet may be made larger or smaller by adding or subtracting squares in multiples of two.

# CROCHET

## Lesson One:
## Variations on a single stitch

### Get hooked on crochet with our easy-to-follow instructions and diagrams

Once the craft of crochet was used mainly to produce lacy mats, collars and cuffs, and simple decorative edgings. In recent years however the full potential of the craft has been discovered, and now it is used to make beautiful fashion garments for men and women, clothes for children and babies, and magnificent household accessories.

Crochet is supremely satisfying to do, for work grows quickly, and patterns are instantly effective. Also, as you use only a single stitch on the hook at a time, work is easy to handle and to carry around with you to do on a bus or a train, in the garden, or on the beach.

There is just one basic stitch to learn, and according to the way this one stitch is used and combined into groups or blocks, and also of course the yarn used, finished results can range from thick dense fabrics for coats and suits, to cobwebby lacy fabrics for tablecloths and baby garments.

## Yarns to use

Cotton yarns of all weights and types are particularly suitable for crochet work—the fine white cottons for lace work, the heavier, coloured ranges for fashion outfits and accessories. Many yarn manufacturers produce ranges of yarns in both natural and man-made fibres specially recommended for crochet. But now that crochet has become so versatile, virtually any yarn produced for knitting can be used with equal success for crochet work. As with knitting, the yarn should be chosen to suit the purpose for which the finished garment is intended.

## Crochet hooks

Crochet hooks are made in aluminium, plastic or bone for working with wools, heavy cottons and synthetic yarns; in steel for working with fine cottons.

Recently in an attempt to standardise the sizings of crochet hooks, a new range of numbered sizes has been introduced—the International Standard range. However some countries have as yet not converted to this new system, and of course there are still many patterns and hooks in existence marked in the old sizes. Our Crochet Hook and Knitting Needle chart gives full details of the new sizings, including equivalent sizes of hooks in old and new ranges.

## Tension

As with knitting, it is essential to check tension before commencing a pattern, as the success of your work depends on accurate tension measurement throughout. To check your tension, follow instructions as given for checking tension in Knitting, lesson one. If your sample square is too big, try using a size smaller crochet hook; if your sample is too small, then try a hook one size bigger.

## Making the first loop

For practise purposes, use a medium hook (International Standard Size 4.50 or 4.00) and a fairly thick yarn (e.g. double knitting) in a bright colour, so stitches are easy to see and control.

Make a slip loop thus: undo a few inches of yarn from the ball and make a loop, clockwise, round the first two fingers of your left hand (A). Take crochet hook in your right hand and push it through the loop thus formed (B), pull yarn through to make a loop on the hook itself (C). Pull gently on the shorter end of the yarn and this will tauten the yarn to make the first loop.

## Holding the work

There is no hard and fast rule about how you should hold the yarn and hook since most crochet workers adopt a method which is comfortable to them. It is important however to use a method which controls the yarn so it is paid out evenly and allows you to work smoothly. One recommended method is to loop the yarn round the little finger of your left hand, then take it across the palm and behind the forefinger (D). The yarn is then held over the forefinger while you work, the actual work being grasped between thumb and forefinger to steady it (E).

Hold the hook in your right hand between thumb and forefinger, as you would a pencil. Place your middle finger on top of hook to guide it. The first loop on the hook should be fairly near the tip of hook, so work can be more easily controlled (F).

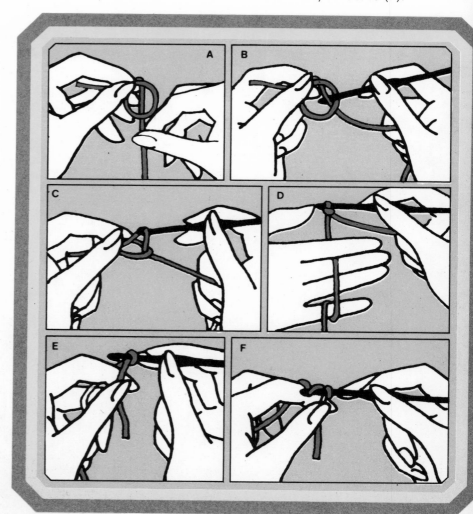

# The basic stitch: the chain

The chain is the foundation of all crochet work. With the first loop on the hook, pass the hook under the yarn on the left hand, and with the hook pull the yarn through the loop already on the hook (G). Let the first loop drop. Continue to make stitches in this way, and you will form a chain (H). Each time you pull yarn through the loop on hook counts as one chain. As the work grows, it will probably be necessary to change the position of the left hand so it is kept near the top of work.
Spend some time practising chains until you are able to produce regular stitches at a fairly even rate. To finish off the chain, cut the yarn a few inches from the work, pull out the hook, slip the yarn end through the final loop and pull gently. This will fasten off the work. When you make a large piece of crochet this end should be firmly darned in to the wrong side of work to prevent unravelling.
You can now do chain stitch with ease so learn the first few simple stitch variations.

## Slip stitch

It is unusual to use slip stitch (sometimes known as single crochet) for the whole body of a piece of work, but the stitch is useful as an edging or when you want to take off stitches during work. Make a chain, then put the hook through the first stitch to the left of the hook, catch the yarn with the hook and draw it through the stitch and the loop which is already on the hook. Continue thus in every stitch along the chain (J).

## Double crochet

This is an important stitch, used frequently both as a foundation stitch since it gives close, even work, and as a main pattern stitch. Make a chain. Miss the first stitch, and insert the hook into the second stitch to the left of the hook. Put the hook through both top loops of the stitch, catch hold of the yarn with the hook and pull it through stitch (K). There are now two loops on hook (L). Put the yarn over the hook and draw it through both loops to leave one loop on the hook (M). Continue in this way, working a double crochet into every stitch along the chain to the end.

## Trebles

There are several variants of the treble stitch which will be explained and illustrated in a later lesson. In this lesson we will deal only with the basic treble itself, and its simplest variation: the double treble. Treble gives a longer stitch than double crochet—used on its own it gives a firm fairly close fabric which is appropriate to most fashion garments; used in combination with chain stitches, a number of attractive open patterns can be produced. Make a chain. Pass the hook under the yarn and then insert the hook into the fourth stitch to the left of the hook and pull the yarn through. You now have three loops on the hook. Put

the hook under the yarn (N) and pull it through the first two loops on the hook. You now have two loops on the hook. Put the hook under the yarn again (O) and pull through to leave only one loop on hook (P). Continue in this way working a treble into every stitch in the chain.

# ouble treble

ke a chain. Pass the hook under the
rn twice, then insert hook into fifth
ain to the left of hook, yarn over hook
d draw through stitch (four loops on
ok). Yarn over hook and draw
ough two loops on hook, yarn over
ok and draw through other two loops
hook, yarn over hook and draw
ough remaining two loops (one loop
ly remains on hook) (Q). Continue in
s way, working a double treble into
ery stitch in chain.

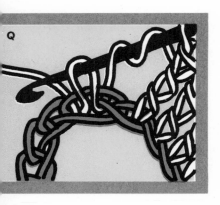

# ouble treble
roup

s consists of working four double
bles all into the same stitch or over a
gth of chain (known as a chain loop
en it forms part of a pattern). As each
uble treble is worked leave final
ch on hook. When four double
bles are worked, yarn over hook and
w through all four loops on hook to
ve only one. (R).

# MOTIF MATS AND TABLE RUNNER

## MATERIALS YOU WILL NEED

For every 2 single mats or motifs—2 oz.
Lister Prema Bulky Knitting. One
crochet hook International Standard
Size 7.00.

## MEASUREMENTS

Each single mat is 7½ in. square: long
runner is 7½ in. by 22½ in.

## TENSION

Each motif is 7½ in. square—try one
complete motif as a tension check.

## ABBREVIATIONS USED IN THIS PATTERN

Ch., chain; s.s., slip stitch; d.c., double
crochet; d.tr.gr., double treble group;
ch.loop, chain loop; ch.sp., chain space.

## TO MAKE EACH SINGLE MAT

Make 6 ch., s.s. to first ch. to join into a
ring.
**1st round:** (8 ch., 1 d.c. into centre
ring) 12 times.
**2nd round:** s.s. to centre of next loop,
*4 ch., (1 d.tr.gr., 3 ch., 1 d.tr.gr.) in
next loop, 4 ch., 1 d.c. in next loop,
3 ch., 1 d.c. in next loop; repeat from
* 3 times.
**3rd round:** s.s. to centre of 4 ch.loop,
* 4 ch., (1 d.tr.gr., 3 ch., 1 d.tr.gr.) in
next 3 ch.sp., 4 ch., 1 d.c. in 4 ch.loop,
4 ch., 1 d.tr.gr. in 3 ch.sp., 4 ch., 1 d.c.
in 4 ch.loop; rep. from * 3 times.
Fasten off.

## TO MAKE TABLE RUNNER

Follow instructions as given for Single
Mat, but make motif three times
altogether.
Stitch the three motifs together to form
long strip.

## Other ways to use your motifs

*Make 2 single motifs: use one as a
teapot mat, the other as a teapot grip
or kettle-holder.
*Join strips of motifs together and use
to edge a trolley cloth, or tablecloth.
*Make lots of motifs in assorted colours,
stitch together to form a big oblong and
use as a patchwork cot blanket.
*Join 12 motifs together to form a
square edging for a cushion cover.

*Make two 9-motif squares, stitch
together round three sides, add a plaited
handle to top open edges—and you
have an up-to-the-minute crocheted
bag. Add lining if wished.
*Join 4 motifs into a square, then make
4 more motifs and stitch one to the
centre of each side of the 4-motif
square, to give an attractive centre mat.

# CROCHET

## Lesson Two: Trebles and simple shaping

In lesson one you were introduced to the basic treble and its simplest variation. In fact there is a whole family of treble crochet stitches which all give the characteristic long, firm stitch. When worked close together, these stitches give a strong fabric with a fair amount of elasticity. It is also possible to arrange trebles in groups to form patterns.

## Other treble variations

### HALF TREBLE

Make a chain. Beginning with the second chain from the hook, pass the hook under the yarn held in the left-hand, insert the hook into the chain stitch, catch the yarn and draw it through the stitch. You now have three loops on the hook. Put the yarn over the hook and draw the yarn through all loops at the same time, so producing one loop. This is the half treble (A).

### TRIPLE TREBLE

Make a chain. Pass the hook under the yarn three times and, starting with the fourth chain from the hook, insert the hook into chain. Pull the yarn through with the hook. There are now five loops on the hook. Put the yarn over the hook and pull it through the two loops closest to the hook. This produces four loops. Yarn over the hook and pull through first two loops (three loops in all) yarn over the hook and pull through first two loops (two loops) yarn over hook and pull through both loops (B).

### QUADRUPLE TREBLE

Make a chain. Pass the hook under the yarn four times and, starting with the fifth chain from the hook, insert hook into the chain, pull the yarn through with the hook. There are now six loops on the hook. Pass the yarn over the hook and pull it through the two loops closest to the hook, thus producing five loops. Pass yarn over hook and pull through first two loops (four loops now), put yarn over hook and pull through first two loops (three loops), pass yarn over hook and pull through first two loops (two loops), pass yarn over hook and pull through these two loops (C).

### TREBLE BETWEEN TREBLE

When working consecutive rows of trebles it is usual to work the stitches into the top of the stitches on the previous row, but if a solid fabric is wanted, it is best to work the stitches into the spaces between the stitches of the previous row. This is a good stitch for rug making, husky cardigan or jackets—anything where you need close texture or warmth. Work a row trebles in the usual way, and work turning stitches at the end of the row (see below). Now in the next, and al subsequent rows, work trebles not in the top of the previous row but into the spaces between the stitches of th previous row.

### TREBLES AND SPACES

Trebles worked in groups, interspers with spaces, can be used to form all manner of different patterns. To work the variation illustrated overleaf, mak chain of a number divisible by 6 plus (i.e. 26). *1st row:* miss 2 chain, work treble into each of next 3 chain sts., miss 3 chains * work 3 chain, work 1 treble into each of next 3 chain, repe from * to end, work one treble into e of basic chain, 2 chain, turn. *2nd row* work 2 trebles into first space, * 3 chain, 3 trebles into next space, repe from * to last space, 3 chain, 1 treble into turning chain, 2 chain, turn (D). Repeat the 2nd row until work is leng required. This forms an open lattice-type pattern and it is possible, with a little ingenuity, to group the spaces and sets of trebles into little patterns within a solid treble design.

## To turn work

In rows of crochet a certain number chain stitches are added at the end o each row to bring the work into position for the next row. Then the work is turned so that the reverse sid is facing you. The number of 'turning chain', as they are called, depends u the stitch with which you intend to begin the next row. The following gi a general guide to the number of turning chain required for different stitches:

**double crochet:** 1 turning chain
**half treble:** 2 turning chain
**treble:** 3 turning chain
**double treble:** 4 turning chain
**triple treble:** 5 turning chain
**quadruple treble:** 6 turning chain
Frequently when turning chain are worked, this also stands as the first stitch in the row.

## Increasing

Shaping in crochet is achieved, as in knitting, by either increasing or decreasing the number of stitches in your work. There are three principal methods of increasing:

### METHOD 1

When only a single stitch has to be increased at one time, at the beginnin end or in the middle of a row, simply work two stitches into the same stitc at the point where you wish the increasing to appear. At the edges of

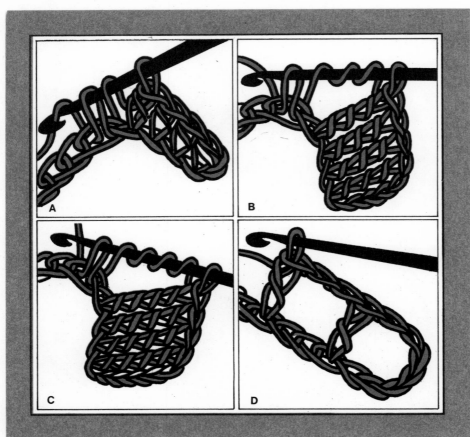

**ALF TREBLE**

**IPLE TREBLE**

**UADRUPLE TREBLE**

**REBLE BETWEEN TREBLE**

**REBLE AND SPACES**

the fabric work twice into either the first or last stitch.

## METHOD 2

When a group of stitches have to be increased (usually at the side of the work) the most usual method is to make a chain at the beginning of the row equivalent to the required number of stitches plus the necessary stitches for turning. For example, if you need five more stitches and are working double crochet which needs one turning chain, you make a chain of six stitches and work along on this, continuing across the main body of the work. It will be seen that if you want to increase at both ends of the same row, the increases are going to be unevenly 'stepped' if you make a chain at the beginning, work along, and then make a chain at the end and work back on it. So if you know you want to increase at each end on the same row, do it this way: on the row before the increasing, when the work is turned, make six chain and slip stitch over the first five chain, the last chain then becoming the first stitch of the row. On the next row, increase at the beginning, work to the end and work straight across the five stitches which have already been made.

## METHOD 3

If the width of work has to increase gradually (for instance, the skirt of a dress in an open-work pattern) then the most usual method is to change to a slightly larger hook and to continue to do this at regular intervals. In this way the work will gradually increase in overall size without the pattern being changed in any way.

## Decreasing

Again, there are three principal methods of reducing the width of your work:

## METHOD 1

If you are working a very close fabric (for instance double crochet on a fine hook) and want to lose one stitch within the work or at either end of the row, it is possible merely to miss out a stitch. At the end of a row, miss the last stitch but one; at the beginning of a row miss the second stitch. If the work is close there will be no ugly gaps.

## METHOD 2

When it is not possible to employ Method 1, two stitches are worked together. To do this with a treble pattern: put yarn on the hook, insert hook into first stitch, draw yarn through (three loops on hook); yarn on hook and pull through first two loops, leaving two loops on hook. Now put yarn round hook and insert into next stitch, draw yarn through, put yarn round hook, draw through first two

loops, yarn round hook, pull through all loops. In this way two stitches are combined. This can be done anywhere in the row, and any stitch can be decreased in this way. The method is simply not to complete the first stitch and then complete the two stitches together.

## METHOD 3

When a group of stitches have to be taken off (for instance, at the beginning of armhole shaping) this is done by working slip stitches over the required number of stitches, and then working the chain stitches needed to continue the row. For example, if you need two chain to turn at the end of each row, and you want to lose five stitches at the beginning of the row, do not work two chain at the end of the previous row, but slip stitch across the first five stitches and then work two chain and continue with the row in the usual way. If you want to decrease at the end of the row, simply work to within the number of stitches to be taken off, and turn work at this point, working back in the usual way.

**YOUR SECOND MAKES—**

# FRINGED SHAWL & PARTY SKIRT

## MATERIALS YOU WILL NEED

**For skirt:** of Patons Limelight Courtelle Crêpe 4-ply—6 (6, 7, 7) balls in brown, 6 (6, 7, 7) balls in gold and 6 (6, 7, 7) balls in mauve. One 8-in. zip fastener. Shirring elastic. **For shawl:** of the same yarn as for skirt, 8 balls in each colour. **For both:** crochet hooks International Standard Sizes 3.00 and 3.50.

## MEASUREMENTS

**Skirt:** to fit hip size 34 (36, 38, 40) in., length 28 (28½, 29, 29½) in. **Shawl:** 77 in. at widest point.

## TENSION

13 sts. and 8 rows measure 2 square in. on No. 3.50 hook.

## ABBREVIATIONS USED IN THIS PATTERN

Ch., chain; d.c., double crochet; h.tr., half treble; tr., treble; sp., space; sl.st., slip stitch; dec., decrease; beg., beginning; rep., repeat; patt., pattern; in., inch(es); B., brown; M., mauve; G., gold.

## SKIRT

**(back and front are both worked alike, so make 2 pieces the same).**
With No. 3.00 crochet hook, and G. (B., M., G.), make 86 (92, 98, 104) ch.

**Foundation row:** 1 h.tr. in 3rd ch. from hook, 1 h.tr. in each ch. to end: 85 (91, 97, 103) sts.

**Next row:** 3 ch., miss 2 sts., * 1 h.tr. in next st., 1 ch., miss 1 st.; rep. from * to end, ending with 1 h.tr. in 2nd of 2 ch.

Now commence patt. as follows:

**1st row (right side facing):** 2 ch., 1 h.tr. in the first ch.sp., * 1 ch., 1 h.tr. in next ch.sp.; rep. from * ending with 1 h.tr. in last ch.sp., 1 h.tr. in 2nd of 3 ch.

**2nd row:** 3 ch., * 1 h.tr. in next ch.sp., 1 ch.; rep. from * ending with 1 h.tr. in 2nd of 2 ch.

Now change to No. 3.50 hook and join in other colours. Repeating these 2 patt. rows, and carrying the yarn loosely up the side of the work, work in patt. of 1 row B., 1 row M., 1 row G., taking the stripes in sequence from whichever colour was the first to be used.

Continue until 8 pattern rows have been worked.

Commence shaping as follows:

**Next row:** 2 ch., (1 h.tr. in next ch.sp., 1 ch.) 8 times, * (1 h.tr., 1 ch.) twice in next ch.sp., (1 h.tr. in next ch.sp., 1 ch.) 7 (8, 9, 10) times; rep. from * twice more, (1 h.tr., 1 ch.) twice in next ch.sp., (1 h.tr. in next ch.sp., 1 ch.) 7 times, 1 h.tr. in last ch.sp., 1 h.tr. in 2nd of 3 ch.

Work 9 rows straight.

**Next row:** 2 ch., (1 h.tr. in next ch.sp., 1 ch.) 8 times, (1 h.tr., 1 ch.) twice in next ch.sp., (1 h.tr. in next ch.sp., 1 ch.) 8 (9, 10, 11) times, (1 h.tr., 1 ch.) twice in next ch.sp.,

(1 h.tr. in next ch.sp., 1 ch.) 9 (10, 11, 12) times, (1 h.tr., 1 ch.) twice in next ch.sp., (1 h.tr. in next ch.sp., 1 ch.) 8 (9, 10, 11) times, (1 h.tr., 1 ch.) twice in next ch.sp., (1 h.tr. in next ch.sp., 1 ch.) 7 times, 1 h.tr. in last ch.sp., 1 h.tr. in 2nd of 3 ch.

Work 9 rows straight.

Continue to work an increasing row every 10th row (working extra sts. between increase sts. as indicated above) until 9 increase rows in all have been worked: 157 (163, 169, 175) sts., then cont. straight until skirt measures approximately 28 (28½, 29, 29½) in., ending with a row in M. (G., B., M.). Change to No. 3.00 hook.

**Next row:** in G. (B., M., G.), * 2 ch., 1 d.c. in 2nd ch. from hook, sl.st. in ch.sp.; rep. from * to end, fasten off.

## TO COMPLETE

Join two sections together at side seams, leaving 8 in. opening at top of left side. Sew in zip to this opening. Run shirring elastic through waist section at back of work. Press lightly on wrong side, using a dry cloth and a cool iron.

## SHAWL

With No. 3.50 hook and G. (B., M., G.) make 5 ch., and join with sl.st. to form a ring.

**1st row:** 3 ch., (1 h.tr., 1 ch.) 3 times into ring, 1 h.tr. into ring: 9 sts. Join in B. (M., G., B.) and turn with 4 ch.

**2nd row:** in B. (M., G., B.) I h.tr. in first ch.sp., * 1 ch., 1 h.tr. in next ch.sp.;

rep. from * ending with 1 ch., 1 h.tr. 3rd of 4 ch.: 11 sts. Join in M. (G., B., M.) and turn with 4 ch.

**3rd row:** in M. (G., B., M.) work as 2nd row: 13 sts. Turn with 4 ch. in G. (B., M., G.). *Note:* Carry yarn loosely up side of work.

**4th row:** in G. (B., M., G.), (1 h.tr., 1 ch.) twice in first ch.sp., * 1 h.tr. in next ch.sp., 1 ch.; rep. from * to last ch.sp., (1 h.tr., 1 ch.) twice in last ch.sp., 1 h.tr. in 3rd of 4 ch.: 19 sts. Turn with 4 ch. in B. (M., G., B.). Rows 2—4 inclusive form the patt. Cont. in patt. and work a further 146 rows, thus ending with 1 row M. (G., B., M.): 503 sts.

**Next round:** in G. (B., M., G.), * 2 d.c. in next ch.sp., 1 d.c. in next ch.sp.; rep. from * along top edge then continue along sides working 2 d.c. into each row end all along.

**Next round:** in G. (B., M., G.) work d.c. along top edge, then work round sides as follows: * 1 ch., miss 1 st., 1 d.c. into each of next 2 sts.; rep. from * to end. Fasten off.

## TO COMPLETE

Cut a remaining yarn into 12 in. length and, using two or three strands together work a fringing as follows, alternating colours along the edges: fold cut threads in half, put crochet hook through ch.sp., pull doubled yarn halfway through ch.sp., slip cut ends of threads through the doubled end, and pull taut.

Trim fringes. Press as for skirt.

# CROCHET

## Lesson Three:

## Working lacy patterns

The one basic stitch of crochet—the chain—offers an infinite number of variations. By grouping long and short stitches, and varying the spaces in between them, it is possible to produce fascinating open-work, lacy patterns. Traditionally, open-work patternings are used for such items as mats, lace and fine shawls but very often these same stitches, worked in a heavy yarn and with a thicker hook, can be used successfully for fashion garments, for dresses, suits, jerseys and children's wear. All the samples illustrated here were worked with double knitting yarn and a size 3.50 hook: the patterns are firm in texture in spite of being open and light looking. It will be seen, after little practice, that many of these stitches are worked upside down— that is, each row as it is added frequently forms an attractive hem row (especially when the pattern has a curve or scallop shape in it) and that the pattern looks much better when the work is reversed. This can be useful, as it is very much easier to determine the length a garment is to be if you are working down towards the hem instead of up and away from it. Consequently, many designs for dresses and jackets are made in two sections: a yoke or upper bodice (often in a firm, close stitch) and then the skirt, which is worked from the lower edge of the bodice downwards towards the hem. This lesson's make—a child's lacy-patterned dress—is worked in this way. When a garment is made by this method it is a simple matter to shorten the skirt merely by undoing a few rounds or rows and fastening off again, or to add a few inches if required. Another advantage in the working of crochet is that it is as easy to work in rounds as it is back and forth in rows. For this reason, dresses are frequently made by having the yoke section worked in one piece, or two which are then sewn together, so that the skirt can be worked round and round in a continuous section. This eliminates side seams and means that patterning can be carried round without any break in the design. Sleeves are often made in this way as well.

### BUTTONHOLES

When working buttonholes in a crocheted fabric it is customary to use a band of double crochet, or some

her fairly close stitch, down the
...nts of cardigans or at the back
...ening of jumpers and dresses. If this
...nd is, say, five rows deep, the
...ttonhole is made on the third row by
...orking a few chain stitches and
...ssing the corresponding number of
...uble crochet in that row, resuming
...e working of double crochet after
...e chain stitches. The number of
...ain stitches will be governed by the
...e of the button to be used. On the
...lowing row, each chain stitch is
...ed as the foundation for a double
...ochet stitch. In this way, a slit is
...ade in the work.
...will be seen, therefore, that it is
...ssible to work these buttonholes
...herever required, and as it is not
...ual for patterns to say how many
...uble crochet should be picked up
...ong an edge, the worker is left to
...ace them at her own discretion. It is
...st done in this way: when the first
...ws have been worked, lay the work
...t flat and measure it. Decide where
...e buttons are to come, being sure
...measure between each one evenly,
...d mark the position of each with
...in. On the following row work the
...ain stitches above the pin.
...te: This gives an excellent finish
...r a knitted garment, as well as a
...ocheted one, and many people in fact
...efer a double crochet edge to a
...bed one.

## dgings

...dges of hems and cuffs, as well as
...eckbands, are easy to work in crochet
...ecause all that is necessary is to go
...und the space, sometimes with a
...er hook than was used for the body
... the work, working successive rows
...ccording to the pattern. Often a

BUTTONHOLES

pattern will not necessarily say how
many stitches exactly to work but will
specify 'a number divisible by four'
or something similar.
Care must be taken not to work too
many stitches, otherwise the edging
will be baggy; or for that matter too
few, otherwise it may be difficult to get
the garment over arm or head.
Judging the correct number comes with
practice, but any errors can usually be
spotted on the second or third round
or row, and rectified.
Plain bands of double crochet can be
effective at sleeve, hem or neck edge,
but it is just as simple to work a
decorative edging. A picot edge and a
shell edge are two of the most popular
decorative edgings.

### PICOT EDGE

This can be used on fine or thick
yarns, and adds a neat finish to virtually
any edge: neck, hem, cardigan front,
sleeve. It is usual to work one or two
rows of double crochet as a foundation.
**Next row:** * sl.st. into first 2 sts.,

SHELL EDGE

1 d.c. into next st., work 3 ch., then
work 1 d.c. into same st. as last d.c.;
rep. from * all round edge. If wished,
the bobbles can be spaced more widely
by working more sl.sts. between
each one.

### SHELL EDGE

This is slightly more decorative than a
picot edge. It is suitable for use on a
lacy pattern and forms a pleasant
scallop shape all round. It can be
worked directly into the fabric or on a
basis of one or two rows of double
crochet.
**Next row:** 1 sl.st., * miss 2 sts., work
5 tr. into next st., miss 2 sts., 1 sl.st.
into next st.; rep. from * all round.

## Lacy patterns

There are literally dozens of different
lacy patterns in crochet work, but only
a few can be shown here. All our
examples are fairly representative of
different kinds of open-work stitches

PICOT EDGE

TREBLE ARCHES

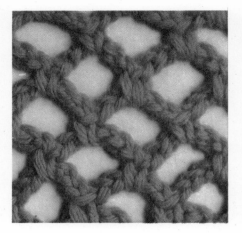

ARCHES

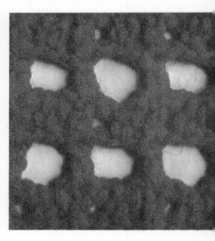

GRILL STITCH

in common use. There is one important point to remember when working open stitches: make a very loose chain to begin with. If this is not done, and a too-tight foundation worked, the open design will not fan out properly for the first few rows.

## TREBLE ARCHES

Although there is plenty of 'air' in this stitch it is close enough to be firm and therefore suitable for sweaters or trousers.
Make a chain to a multiple of 6 sts. plus 1 (i.e. 25).
**1st row:** 1 d.c. into 2nd ch. from hook, 1 d.c. into next st., * 3 ch., miss 3 sts., 1 d.c. into each of next 3 sts.; rep. from * to last 5 sts., 3 ch., miss 3 sts., work 2 d.c. into each of next 2 sts., 1 ch., turn.
**2nd row:** 1 d.c. into first st., * 5 tr. into 3 ch.sp., miss 1 d.c., 1 d.c. into next st.; rep. from * to end, turn.
**3rd row:** * 3 ch., 1 d.c. into each 3 centre tr. of group; rep. from * to end, 2 ch., 1 d.c. into last st., 3 ch., turn.
**4th row:** 2 tr. into 2 ch.sp., * 1 d.c. into centre of 3 d.c. of previous row, 5 tr. into 3 ch.sp.; rep. from *, 1 d.c. into centre of 3 d.c., 3 tr. in last sp., 1 ch., turn.
**5th row:** as first row, beg. with 2 d.c. Cont. in pattern repeating from 2nd row.

## ARCHES

This is one of the simplest of the open-work patterns, and can be used for dresses and sweaters. Care must be taken in matching the right size hook to the right yarn—if too large a hook is used a fabric will be produced which stretches easily. Simple experiment will show the wide variation in effect if thick yarn or fine cotton is used.
Work a chain to any length.
**1st row:** 1 d.c. into 3rd ch. from hook, * 5 ch., miss 3 ch., 1 d.c. into next ch., rep. from * to end, work 5 ch., turn.
**2nd row:** * 1 d.c. into centre of 5 ch. loop, 5 ch.; rep. from * to end.
Now repeat row 2 throughout.

## GRILL STITCH

This is a more geometric type of pattern, appropriate for clothing and also attractive for lace edgings on cloths, napkins and so forth. The pattern holds its shape well.
Make a chain to any length.
**1st row:** 1 tr. into 4th ch. from hook, * 3 ch., miss 3 ch., 1 tr. into next ch.; rep. from * to end, work 4 ch., turn.
**2nd row:** * 1 d.c. into 2nd st. of 3 ch. of previous row, 2 ch., 1 tr. on next tr., 2 ch.; rep. from * to end, 2 ch., 1 d.c., 5 ch., turn.
**3rd row:** * 1 tr. on next tr., 3 ch.; rep. from * to end, 1 tr. into 3rd ch. of 4 ch. of previous row. 4 ch., turn.
The pattern is formed by repeating rows 2 and 3 until work is length required

## FAN STITCH

There are many variations on the basic idea of two groups of stitches fanning out from a central point. This is a stitch pattern which is best worked downwards, as it forms a scalloped edge, and is very attractive used for skirts.
Make a chain in a multiple of 8 plus 5 (i.e. 29).
**1st row:** 3 tr. in 6th ch. from hook, * miss 2 ch., 1 tr. in next ch., miss 2 ch., 3 tr. in next ch., 2 ch., 1 tr. in next ch., 2 ch., 3 tr. in next ch.; rep. from * to last 7 sts., miss 2 ch., 1 tr. in next ch., miss 2 ch., 3 tr. in next ch., 2 ch., 1 tr. in last ch.
**2nd row:** 3 ch., 3 tr. in 2 ch.sp., 2 ch., * 1 tr. in tr., 2 ch.; 3 tr. in 2 ch.sp., 2 ch., 1 tr. in tr., 2 ch., 3 tr. in 2 ch.sp.; rep. from * to last group, 2 ch., 1 tr. in tr., 2 ch., 3 tr. in 2 ch.sp., turn.
**3rd row:** 3 ch., * 3 tr. in 2 ch.sp., 2 ch., 1 tr. in tr., 2 ch., 3 tr. in 2 ch.sp., 1 tr. in single tr.; rep. from * to last group, ending (2 tr., 2 ch., 1 tr.) in end sp., turn.
Now repeat rows 2 and 3 until work is length required.

## ARCH AND SHELL STITCH

This too is a stitch pattern which can be worked down or up, as it can form a

curved edge depending upon which row worked in is the last one. It is effective in any weight of yarn.
Make a chain in a multiple of 8 plus 3 (i.e. 27).
**Foundation row:** 1 d.c. in 2nd ch. from hook, 1 d.c. in next ch., * 3 ch., miss 2 ch., in next ch. work (1 tr., 3 ch. 1 tr.), 3 ch., miss 2 ch., 1 d.c. in next 3 ch.; rep. from * to end.
Now patt. thus:
**1st row:** 4 ch., * 7 tr. in 3 ch. between tr. of previous row, 3 ch., 1 d.c. in centre d.c., 3 ch.; rep. from * to end, ending 7 tr. in 3 ch. between tr., 3 ch., 1 d.c. in last st.
**2nd row:** 6 ch., * 1 d.c. in each of 7 tr., 3 ch.; rep. from * to end, ending 1 tr. in first of 4 ch.
**3rd row:** 3 ch., 1 tr. in same sp., * 3 ch., 1 d.c. in centre 3 d.c. of previous row, 3 ch., (1 tr., 3 ch., 1 tr.) in 3 ch.sp. rep. from * to end, ending 1 tr., 1 ch., 1 tr. in 3rd of 6 ch.
**4th row:** 3 ch., 3 tr. in 1 ch.sp., * 3 ch., 1 d.c. in centre d.c., 3 ch., 7 tr. in 3 ch. between tr.; rep. from * to end, ending 4 tr. in 3 ch.
**5th row:** 1 ch., 1 d.c. in 3 tr., * 3 ch., 1 d.c. in each of 7 tr.; rep. from * to end ending 1 d.c. in each of 4 tr.
**6th row:** 1 ch., 1 d.c. in 2nd d.c., * 3 ch., (1 tr., 3 ch., 1 tr.), in 3 ch.sp., 3 ch., 1 d.c. in centre 3 d.c.; rep. from * to end, ending 1 d.c. in last 2 d.c.
These 6 rows form patt., and should be repeated until work is length required.

FAN STITCH

ARCH AND SHELL STITCH

*Close up of yoke pattern*

*Close up of skirt pattern*

## YOUR LACY-PATTERNED MAKE

# LITTLE GIRL'S PARTY DRESS

## MATERIALS YOU WILL NEED

6 (7, 8, 9) balls Twilleys Stalite. One crochet hook International Standard Size 4.00. 4 small buttons.

## MEASUREMENTS

To fit chest size 22 (24, 26, 28) in.; length at centre back 17 (19, 21, 23) in.; sleeve seam 7½ (9, 10½, 12) in.

## TENSION

5 pattern repeats and 7 rows measure 3 square in. over yoke pattern.

## ABBREVIATIONS USED IN THIS PATTERN

St(s)., stitch(es); in., inch(es); patt., pattern; ch., chain; d.c., double crochet; tr., treble; sp., space; sl.st., slip stitch; beg., beginning; rep., repeat; cont., continue.

## YOKE

Make 112 (124, 130, 142) ch.
**1st row:** (1 tr., 1 ch., 1 tr.) in 4th ch. from hook, * miss 2 ch., (1 tr., 1 ch., 1 tr.) in next ch.; rep. from * to last 3 ch., miss 2 ch., 1 tr. in last ch: 36 (40, 42, 46) patt. groups.
**2nd row:** 3 ch., * (1 tr., 1 ch., 1 tr.) in next 1 ch.sp.; rep. from * ending 1 tr. in top of 3 ch.
This last row forms yoke patt. Work 1 row more in patt.
**Armhole dividing row:** 3 ch., work 7 (8, 9, 10) patt. groups, 1 tr. in next tr., sl.st. over next 4 groups for first

armhole, 3 ch., work 14 (16, 16, 18) groups, 1 tr. in next tr., sl.st. over next 4 groups for second armhole, 3 ch., work 7 (8, 9, 10) groups, 1 tr. in top of 3 ch. Work on last set of sts. for first side of back.
Cont. in yoke patt. until work measures 5½ (6, 6½, 7) in. from beg., ending at armhole edge.
**Next row:** 3 ch., work 3 (4, 4, 5) groups, 1 tr. in next tr., turn and fasten off.
Rejoin yarn to centre 14 (16, 16, 18) groups for front.
Work in patt. until work is 4½ (5, 5½, 6) in. from beg.
**Neck shaping row:** 3 ch., work 4 (5, 5, 6) groups, 1 tr. in next tr., turn. Work on these sts. only.
**Next row:** sl.st. over first group, 3 ch., patt. to end.
Work 1 row straight.
Fasten off.
Leave centre 6 (6, 6, 6) groups for centre front neck, rejoin yarn to last tr. of 6th group, 3 ch., patt. to end.
**Next row:** patt. to last group, 1 tr. in next tr., turn.
Work 1 row straight.
Fasten off.
Rejoin yarn to last 7 (8, 9, 10) groups for second side of back. Complete to match first side.

## SKIRT

**1st row:** work along right side of ch. edge of yoke thus:
1 d.c. in each of first 3 ch., * (6 ch., miss 1 ch., 1 d.c. in each of next 3 ch.); rep. from * to last 2 (2, 4, 4) ch., 6 ch., miss 1 (1, 3, 3) ch., 1 d.c. in last ch., sl.st. to first d.c. of row to form a ring: 27 (30, 31, 34) patt. reps.
Now patt. thus.
**1st round:** 1 d.c. in next d.c., * 7 tr. in 6 ch.sp., 1 d.c. in centre d.c. of 3 d.c. group; rep. from * to end, ending 7 tr. in last 6 ch.sp., sl.st. to first d.c.
**2nd round:** 5 ch., * 1 tr. in 2nd of 7 tr., 2 ch., (work 1 tr., 1 ch., 1 tr. in 4th of 7 tr.) in 2 ch., 1 tr. in 6th of 7 tr., 2 ch., 1 tr. in d.c., 2 ch.; rep. from *, ending sl.st. to 3rd of 5 ch.
**3rd round:** sl.st. over 2 ch., 1 tr., 2 ch. and 1 tr., 2 d.c. into 1 ch.sp., * 6 ch., 3 d.c. in next 1 ch.sp.; rep.

from * to end., ending 1 d.c. in first 1 ch.sp.
These 3 rounds form patt.
Cont. until work measures 17 (19, 21, 23) in. from shoulder edge, ending with a first round (adjust length here if required).
Fasten off.

## SLEEVES (make 2 alike)

Make 43 (49, 55, 58) ch.
**1st row:** as for Yoke: 13 (15, 17, 18) patt. groups.
Now rep. 2nd row of Yoke twice.
Still working in yoke patt., shape top as follows:
**Next row:** sl.st. over first group, 1 tr. in next tr., turn.
Work 1 row straight in patt.
Rep. last 2 rows until 4 (4, 5, 5) decrease rows have been completed with 5 (7, 7, 8) groups remaining.
Fasten off.
**Lower Sleeve. 1st row:** work along right side of ch. edge of upper sleeve as follows:
1 d.c. in each of first 3 ch., * 6 ch., miss 2 ch., 1 d.c. in each of next 3 ch.; rep. from * to last 2 (3, 4, 2) ch., 6 ch., miss 1 (2, 3, 1) ch., 1 d.c. in last ch., sl. st. to first d.c. of row to form a ring: 8 (9, 10, 11) patt. reps.
Now work in patt. as skirt until work measures 7½ (9, 10½, 12) in. from beg. of top shaping, ending with a first patt. round.
Fasten off.

## TO COMPLETE

Join shoulder seams.
**Neck and Back Border.** With right side of work facing, work in d.c. up left side of back opening, around neck and down right side of back opening. Work 2 rows more in d.c., working 3 d.c. into each corner d.c. at top of back opening and making 4 evenly-spaced buttonholes on last row on right side of back opening by working 2 d.c., 2 ch., miss 2 d.c. for each hole. Fasten off.

**To Make Up.** Press lightly. Join upper sleeve seams, then set in sleeves. Press seams. Sew on buttons to correspond with buttonholes.

# CROCHET

## Lesson Four:
## Multicolours and motifs

The use of a second colour can give a new dimension to crochet work, since it entirely alters the appearance of the simplest stitch. As a proof of this, try a small piece of any of the lacy stitches (or even plain ones) given in previous lessons: use one colour for the first row, then change to a different shade for the second, and continue in this way. Lacy patterns in particular look quite different and extremely effective when a second colour is added.

Working with two colours in crochet does not present the problems which may occur in two-colour knitting: technical details are much simpler. Nevertheless certain rules have still to be observed.

Usually, when a second colour is specified, it is used on the stripe principle: that is, equal horizontal bands of the new colour are slotted in between bands of the basic shade. If you are working a pattern which alternates two rows of each colour, it is very easy to carry the two colours up the side of the work, without breaking yarn off—for instance, if you are working in red, join in white by tying it loosely to the red yarn already in use and use the white for the next two rows. Then drop it and pick up the red again, being careful not to drag it too tightly. The two colours can be alternated all the way up the striped section with no trouble, and when the sewing up is done the joined ends are hidden by working them into the seam.

However, if the pattern specifies only one row of the extra colour, it may be easier to work with two balls of the basic shade and sometimes of both shades. Thus, if you are working from right to left in the usual way, you will first join in the white at the right-hand side of the work. You complete the white row and then need red again. Instead of breaking off the white, leave it, and join in a second ball of red. You work back in red. Perhaps you need one more row in red, so work it, and leave thread at the left-hand side, where you pick up the white again. Thus it is possible to use both colours without continually breaking and rejoining yarn. Whether this method is possible or not will depend on the individual pattern, but it is a point to watch as you can often save time both in work and in sewing up by the use of this technique.

If you are using a new colour at the start of the row, work the last loop of

Afghan square waistcoat with a knitted collar—instructions at end of lesson.

the last stitch in the previous row in the new colour: i.e. if you are finishing with a treble in red, make the last loop round the hook in white, so that you draw white through, and are ready to do your turning chain in the new colour. Joining colours at the end of a row presents no problems, but as crochet is often worked in rounds rather than rows it is sometimes impossible to change yarn except in the middle of a round. Here it is usually advisable to adopt the stranding principle. Cut away a few threads from the yarn a few inches from the end both of the old yarn and the new and rub the two ends together in your palms. This should produce a thread that is equal in thickness to the main yarn. Work this carefully and the join will not show. However, with some very fine yarns used in crochet—cotton, for instance—it is not always possible to do stranding effectively. In this case, there is no

alternative but to work with double thickness yarn for a few stitches (using yarn from both old and new balls) and to trim away excess ends afterwards or, if that is going to make an unsightly lump, to tie a knot at the back of the work. This is directly against all the rules—of course—but there are times when nothing else will do! The method is this: tie the new yarn loosely round the old, making a simple one-turn tie, and draw up the new yarn. This will leave two hanging ends. When the work is completed, these ends are either run in as they are (be careful to run colours into their matching backgrounds if you are working a two-colour pattern) or you undo the knot carefully and then run the ends in. Provided long enough ends are left, there is little likelihood of work unravelling.

The simplest two-colour stitch is shown on the next page in a striped fabric.

## SIMPLE STRIPES

Using colour A, make a chain.
**1st row:** beginning with the 3rd chain from the end, work a d.c. into every chain. Work a turning chain at the end.
**2nd row:** as first, but join in second colour at the end of the row.
Now cont. in stripes, working 2 rows of each colour alternately.

## WORKING MOTIFS

One of the most effective ways of using several colours in crochet is within motifs. The whole concept of the motif—squares, flowers and circles—is one that is well suited to crochet because, by the nature of the way the fabric is formed, it is easy to go round and round a central point, varying the shape and pattern of the outer borders as you do so.

Traditionally, multi-coloured motifs—sometimes called Afghan squares—are used for bedspreads, but today they have found a place in fashion, and are used for all kinds of garments, from straight scarves and stoles to skirts, waistcoats and cardigans. One of the great advantages of this form of crochet work is that it is easily portable—it can be taken anywhere (in a handbag for instance) with odd squares being worked in spare moments.

Another advantage is that odd bits and pieces of yarn can be used in this kind of work to great effect, and it is worth a beginner's while to try this motif work by making, say, a child's cot or pram blanket out of different colours. Of course, a bedspread or garment in a group of colours is effective in a different way: for instance, a blanket in pale blue, dark blue and white (the three colours being switched around in order within each square, perhaps, or used identically) all edged and joined with navy.

These motifs can, of course, be worked in one colour only if preferred, and many of them are so attractive in their design that they are shown to advantage in single colours. Examples of both multicoloured and plain motifs are illustrated here.

As well as square motifs, crochet can be used for flower shapes which have pointed or petalled edges. These are used either to trim basic items (dresses, cushion covers, belts and so on) or joined together, as in traditional lacy tablecloths. Floral shapes will not form a solid fabric as squares will, so the spaces between the motifs are usually filled in with smaller motifs or left open, to give an attractive lace fabric. This kind of design, laid over a plain dark table, or perhaps over a contrasting fabric has a charm of its own.

## JOINING THE MOTIFS

Floral-shaped motifs have to be joined at four (or it may be six or eight) points, depending on their shape. This is laborious but unavoidable. Some designs are so worked that motifs can be crocheted in a sequence and this cuts out some of the tedium, but there always has to be some sewing up. This *must* be done carefully, and preferably from the back of the work so that the joins are invisible. Use a blunt needle and the same yarn as has been used in the crochet work. If you are joining motifs each of a different colour, then use the invisible thread which can be bought from most haberdashery stores.

Multicoloured square motifs can be joined by sewing together, or by crocheting them together. First of all, pin the squares together, right sides facing. If you are sewing them together, join along the two edges by making over stitches fairly loosely, so that the two motifs can be opened out flat. If you are joining by crochet, the hook should be inserted into the loop at the edge of one square and then into the corresponding loop on the other square and make a slip stitch, taking both stitches at once. Alternatively, the stitches can be taken one by one in a zig-zag shape, first a slip stitch with a border stitch from square one, then the corresponding stitch from square two and so on, all along. It adds very much to the appeal of a multicoloured item if you use the same colour for the last round of every motif and also for the joining; the background colour acts as a foil for the shades used within the design, and gives it unity. All the samples shown here can be joined by one or other of these two methods. If a square or circle does not come up quite as large as you would like, then you can increase it by working extra rounds or borders of double crochet or trebles. Extra stitches will have to be worked into a circular design at regular intervals, and on a square one at the corners, to take in the extra size.

## Some sample motifs

### TRADITIONAL SQUARE

Make a chain in colour A of 6 ch., join into ring with sl.st.
**1st round:** 2 ch., 2 tr., 3 ch., * 3 tr., 3 ch. into ring; rep. from * twice, sl.st to first 2 ch., joining in colour B.
**2nd round:** sl.st. to first sp., (2 ch., 2 tr., 3 ch., 3 tr.) into first 3 ch.sp., * (1 ch., 3 tr., 3 ch., 3 tr.) into next 3 ch.sp.; rep. from * twice, joining with a sl.st. and joining in colour A.
**3rd round:** sl.st. to first sp., (2 ch., 2 tr., 3 ch., 3 tr.) into first 3 ch.sp., * 1 ch., 3 tr. into 1 ch.sp. (1 ch., 3 tr., 3 ch., 3 tr.) into each corner; rep. from * ending 1 ch., sl.st. to join, joining in colour B.
**4th round:** sl.st. to first sp., (2 ch., 2 tr., 3 ch., 3 tr.) into first 3 ch.sp., * 1 ch., 3 tr. into each 1 ch.sp., (1 ch., 3 tr., 3 ch., 3 tr.) into each corner; rep. from * ending 1 ch., sl.st. to join.
Fasten off.

### WHEEL CENTRE SQUARE

Using colour A, make 8 ch. and join into ring with sl.st.
**1st round:** 6 ch., * (1 tr., 3 ch.) 7 times into ring, sl.st. to join, joining in colour B.
**2nd round:** 2 ch., 3 tr., 2 ch. into first sp., * 4 tr., 2 ch. into next sp.; rep. from *, sl.st. to join, joining in colour C.
**3rd round:** 2 ch., 5 tr., 1 ch. into first sp., * 6 tr., 3 ch. into next sp., 6 tr., 1 ch. into next sp.; rep. from * 3 times, 6 tr., 3 ch. into next sp., sl.st. to join, joining in colour A.
**4th round:** 2 ch., 1 tr., 3 ch., 2 tr. into 3 ch.sp. at corner, * 3 ch., 1 d.c. between 3rd and 4th tr. of next group, 3 ch., 1 d.c. into 1 ch.sp., 3 ch., 1 d.c. between 3rd and 4th tr. of next group, 3 ch., (2 tr., 3 ch., 2 tr) into 3 ch.sp. at corner; rep. from * 3 times, sl.st. to join. Fasten off.

**SIMPLE STRIPES**

**TRADITIONAL SQUARE**

**WHEEL CENTRE SQUARE**

**OCTAGON**

**PLAIN COLOUR SQUARE**

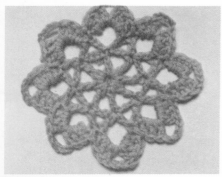

**SNOWFLAKE STAR**

**FLOWER WITH PETALS**

**MEDALLION**

## OCTAGON

Using colour A, work 6 ch. and join into ring with sl.st.
**1st round:** 2 ch., work 15 tr. into ring and join with sl.st., joining in colour B.
**2nd round:** (2 ch., 1 tr., 1 ch., 2 tr.) into first st., miss 1 st., * (2 tr., 1 ch., 2 tr.) into next st., miss 1 st.; rep. from * 6 times, sl.st. to join, joining in colour A.
**3rd round:** (2 ch., 1 tr., 1 ch., 2 tr.) into first ch.sp.; * 1 tr. between 4 tr. groups, (2 tr., 1 ch., 2 tr.) into next ch.sp.; rep. from * 7 times, 1 tr. between last 4 tr. group, 1 tr. to join, joining in colour B.
**4th round:** work 1 d.c. into each tr. and ch. Fasten off.

## PLAIN COLOUR SQUARE

Work 8 ch., joining into a ring with sl.st.
**1st round:** 2 ch., work 15 trs. into ring, join with sl.st. to 2nd of first 2 ch.
**2nd round:** 4 ch., (1 tr., 2 ch.) 15 times, join with sl.st. to 2nd of 4 ch.
**3rd round:** 2 ch., 2 tr. into first sp., 1 ch., (3 tr., 1 ch.) into each sp., sl.st. to join.
**4th round:** * (3 ch., 1 d.c. into next 1 ch.sp.) 3 times, 6 ch., 1 d.c. into next sp.; rep. from * to end, join with sl.st.
**5th round:** 2 ch., 2 tr. into first 3 3 ch.sp., 3 tr. into next two 3 ch.sps., * (5 tr., 2 ch., 5 tr.) into corner sps., 3 tr. into each 3 ch.sp.; rep. from * to end, join with sl.st.
**6th round:** 2 ch., work 1 tr. into each st., and 2 tr. into each 2 ch.sp. at each corner. Fasten off.

## MEDALLION

Work 6 ch. and join into ring with sl.st.
**1st round:** 2 ch., work 23 tr. into ring, join with sl.st. to 2 ch.
**2nd round:** 4 ch., 1 tr. into same st. as sl.st., 1 ch., * miss 2 sts., (1 tr., 2 ch., 1 tr.) into next st., 1 ch.; rep. from * 6 times, sl.st. to 2 ch. at beg. of round.
**3rd round:** 2 ch., (1 tr., 2 ch., 2 tr.) into first 2 ch.sp., * 1 d.c. into 1 ch.sp., (2 tr., 2 ch., 2 tr.) into next 2 ch.sp.; rep. from * 6 times, 1 d.c. into last 1 ch.sp., sl.st. to 2nd ch. of first 2 ch.
**4th round:** * (3 tr., 1 ch., 3 tr.) into 2 ch.sp., 1 d.c. on d.c. of previous round; rep. from * 7 times, sl.st. to join. Fasten off.

## FLOWER WITH PETALS

Work 8 ch. and sl.st. into a ring to join.
**1st round:** work 12 tr. into ring and join with sl.st.
**2nd round:** * work 6 ch. and beg. with 3rd ch. from hook, work a tr. into ch., (4 tr. in all), d.c. into next st.; rep. from * all round. Fasten off.
(Note: If petals are required to be more widely spaced, then work 1 or 2 sl.st. into trs. between each petal.)

## SNOWFLAKE STAR

Work 6 ch. and join into ring with sl.st.
**1st round:** 7 ch., (1 d.tr. into ring, 3 ch.) 7 times, sl.st. into 4th of 7 ch.
**2nd round:** 3 ch., * miss 3 ch., (1 tr., 6 ch., 1 tr.) into top of d.tr.; rep. from * ending last rep. miss 3 ch., 1 tr. into first d.tr., 6 ch., sl.st. into top of 3 ch.
**3rd round:** * (3 tr., 5 ch., 3 tr.) into next ch.sp., 1 sl.st. into 2nd tr.; rep. from * to end. Fasten off.

# HREE-COLOUR
# AISTCOATS

## ATERIALS YOU WILL NEED

**r fringed waistcoat:** 8 oz.
yfield Gaylon Double Knitting in
n, 6 oz. in Aran, 4 oz. in Bottle. One
chet hook International Standard
e 3.50. 4 medium buttons.

**r waistcoat with knitted collar:**
z. Hayfield Gaylon Double Knitting
Fern, 5 oz. in Aran, 4 oz. in Rust. One
chet hook International Standard
e 3.50. One pair of No. 10 knitting
edles. 3 medium buttons.

## ZE NOTE

ch waistcoat should comfortably
a bust size 34/36 in. If a size smaller
equired (e.g. size 32 in.) then use
ook one size smaller; if a size larger
equired, then use a hook one size
ger.

## EASUREMENTS

ch motif measures 3½ in. square.

## BBREVIATIONS USED
## THESE PATTERNS

, chain; s.s., slip stitch; tr., treble,
s)., space(s); d.c., double crochet;
., repeat; k., knit; st(s)., stitch(es);
t., garter stitch; in., inch(es); A.,
an; B., bottle; F., fern; R., rust.

## MAKE MOTIF

ther waistcoat)

th A., make 5 ch., and s.s. into ring.
t round: 3 ch., 2 tr. in ring, (3 ch.,
. in ring), 3 times, 3 ch., s.s. to 3rd
3 ch. Fasten off and join in B. (R. for
istcoat with knitted collar) to 3 ch.sp.
d round: 3 ch., (2 tr., 3 ch., 3 tr.) in
ne sp., * 1 ch., (3 tr., 3 ch., 3 tr.) in
xt 3 ch.sp.; rep. from * twice, 1 ch.,
to 3rd of 3 ch.
sten off and join in A. to 3 ch.sp.
d round: 3 ch., (2 tr., 3 ch., 3 tr.)
same sp., 1 ch., 3 tr. in 1 ch.sp.,
h., * (3 tr., 3 ch., 3 tr.) in 3 ch.sp.,
h., 3 tr. in 1 ch.sp., 1 ch.; rep. from *
ice, s.s. to 3rd of 3 ch.
sten off and join in F.
h round: 3 ch., (2 tr., 3 ch., 3 tr.)
same sp., 1 ch., (3 tr. in 1 ch.sp.,
h.) twice, * (3 tr., 3 ch., 3 tr.) in
h.sp., 1 ch., (3 tr. in 1 ch.sp., 1 ch.)
ice; rep. from * twice, s.s. to 3rd of
h.
sten off and rejoin F. to 3 ch.sp.
h round: 1 ch., work 3 d.c. in 3
sp., and 1 d.c. in each tr. and 1 ch.sp.
end, s.s. to 1 ch.
sten off.

## MAKE FRINGED
## AISTCOAT

ke 52 motifs in all.
w in all ends. Press each motif using
arm iron and damp cloth.
h F., join motifs by working d.c.
ough last row of 2 motifs together.

Join them in 4 rows of 10 each (as
shown in diagram, right). To centre 4
squares of last row add 2 rows of
4 motifs each. To first and 4th squares
of last row add 2 rows of 1 motif each,
joining the last motifs to 2nd and 9th
squares of last row of 10, as indicated
by arrows on diagram.
With right side of work facing and
with F., work 1 row of d.c. around
armholes. With A., work 2 rows d.c. up
right side of front, around neck, down
left side and across lower edge.
Work 2 further rows on front edges,
making 4 buttonloops on last row of
row of right front, the first to come 8 in.
up from lower edge, the 4th just below
neck edge and the other 2 spaced
evenly between.
**To make each buttonloop:** 2 ch.,
miss 1 st.
Press lightly. Sew on buttons to
correspond with buttonloops. Make a
knotted fringe along lower edge, using
2 strands of B. and 1 strand of A., each
strand 13 in. long, for each tassel.

## TO MAKE WAISTCOAT
## WITH KNOTTED COLLAR

Make 54 motifs in all. Join motifs as for
Fringed Waistcoat, but add a further
motif to the first and the 10th squares
of last row of 10 motifs.
**Collar.** With No. 10 knitting needles,
R. and with wrong side of work facing,
pick up and k. 24 sts. down right side
of neck. Work in g.st. in stripe sequence
of 2 rows R., 2 rows A., 2 rows F.

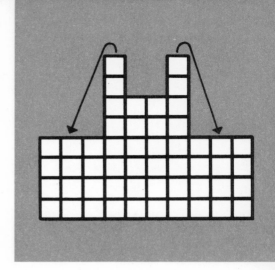

for 5¼ in. Cast off.
With wrong side of work facing and R.,
pick up and k. 50 sts. across back of
neck. Complete to match right side.
Work left side and 2 front edges of
neck as for right side.
Join seams.
With right side of work facing and F.,
work 1 row d.c. round armholes.
With R., work 4 rows d.c. down left
front, across lower edge and up right
front, making 3 buttonloops on last
row up right side, the first to come 11¼
in. up from lower edge the other 2
spaced at 2 in. intervals. Follow
instructions in Fringed Waistcoat
pattern for working buttonloops.
Press lightly. Sew on buttons to
correspond with buttonloops.

# CROCHET

## Lesson Five: Simple Tunisian work

**and some more motif designs**

Tunisian crochet — sometimes known as tricot crochet — employs a somewhat different technique from 'conventional' crochet, but it is a fascinating form of crochet, and easy to learn. In a way, the technique is halfway between knitting and crochet for it is the only form of crochet in which all the stitches in your work are on the hook at the same time. Patterns are usually designed in two rows: in the first row the stitches are taken on to the needle one by one; in the second row the stitches are worked off. The pattern is usually created by the way the stitches are worked in the second row.

The fabric produced from Tunisian crochet looks rather like knitting, and extra firm and stable in wear. It is in fact sometimes difficult to tell the difference between a piece of knitting and a piece of Tunisian crochet work.

*Colourful patchwork bedcover — instructions at end of lesson.*

The technique is particularly good for such items as skirts and jackets, where hardwearing qualities are essential. Open stitch variations are possible as well, but even the closed ones have interesting surface textures. Tunisian crochet is worked on special hooks which are usually about 12 in. long, have a knob at one end like a knitting needle, and a hook at the other like a normal crochet hook. They are obtainable in a range of sizes, from good handicraft shops and departments.

## To work plain Tunisian stitch

This is the basic stitch of the craft which is usually worked at the beginning of any design as it gives a firm edge.

Make a chain to the desired length. Now insert the hook into the second chain from the hook and draw the yarn through in the usual way. This forms the first stitch. Leave it on the needle. Insert the hook into the next chain and draw the yarn through. Continue in this way all along the chain, so that you have as many loops or stitches on the hook as there were chains in the foundation row (see diagram below). This is the first row; to work the second row, the work is not turned round as it is for conventional crochet.

**2nd row:** yarn round hook, and draw through the first stitch, * now yarn round hook and draw through next two stitches; rep. from * to end of row. Work 1 chain for the beginning of the next row.

**3rd row:** * insert the hook into the first vertical stitch and draw a loop of yarn through; rep. from * all along the row. Repeat 2nd and 3rd rows until work is length desired.

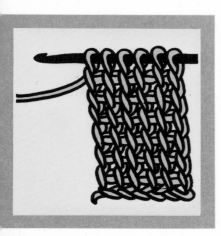

## Some stitch variations

### ALTERNATING STITCH

This is a firm stitch, which has a kind of basketweave appearance. Begin with 2 rows of the plain stitch.

**1st patt. row:** * insert the hook *between* the vertical stitches of the previous row, and draw a loop of yarn through; rep. from * all along the row.
**2nd patt. row:** as 2nd row of plain stitch.
Repeat first and 2nd patt. rows until work is length desired.

### STOCKING STITCH

This has a similar appearance to knitted stocking stitch but it is thicker, with more 'body' and is a good stitch for any garment that must hold its shape well (especially trousers and skirts). Begin with 2 rows of plain stitch.
**1st patt. row:** * insert the hook into the stitch below, i.e. between the vertical threads below the chain that was worked on row 2 and rep. from * all along.
**2nd patt. row:** as 2nd row of plain stitch.
Repeat first and 2nd patt. rows until work is length desired.

### LATTICE STITCH

This is a stitch which, while it is more open than the others illustrated here, is nevertheless firm and relatively stable. Begin with 2 rows of plain stitch.
**1st patt. row:** * insert the hook into the stitch below (as for stocking stitch) and draw a loop of yarn through, yarn round hook and pull through that stitch; rep. from * to end of row.
**2nd patt. row:** as 2nd row of plain stitch.

## Striped designs

It is possible to work striped designs in Tunisian crochet, and these are worked exactly as for ordinary crochet or knitting, with the yarn taken up the right-hand side of the work and an even number of rows of each colour being worked (if an uneven number is worked, then the yarn must be broken off and joined according to the specifications of the stripe).

### TO INCREASE

Increases can be made at either end of a row by working an extra loop through the chain of the previous row, usually after the first and before the last stitches. These stitches are then worked off in the usual way.

### TO DECREASE

Decreases can be made at any place in the row by drawing one loop through two stitches (i.e. inserting the hook through one stitch after another and then drawing one loop through both). This loop is then worked in the usual way on subsequent rows.

PLAIN TUNISIAN STITCH

ALTERNATING STITCH

STOCKING STITCH

LATTICE STITCH ▲
STRIPED DESIGN ▼

*Large square motif bedspread*

## TO FINISH OFF

Tunisian crochet can be left after a second pattern row and fastened off in the usual way; this will leave a chain stitch edge. If preferred, a firmer edge can be given—and this is useful for such edges as shoulder seams—by working a row of double crochet after the second row, working one double crochet into each stitch.

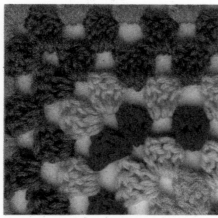

*Close up of large motif bedspread*

# MULTI-COLOURED BEDSPREADS

## Large square motif spread

### MATERIALS YOU WILL NEED

12 oz. double knitting yarn in main shade (we used a plum/purple colour), 3 oz. in each of seven contrasting colours (we used blue, green, pink, apricot, mauve, yellow and red), and 2 oz. of an eighth contrasting colour for the border (we used bright purple). One crochet hook International Standard Size 5.00.

### MEASUREMENTS

Finished bedspread measures approximately 6 ft. 6 in. by 4 ft. 9 in.

### TENSION

One large square measures 23 in. without border.

### ABBREVIATIONS USED IN THIS PATTERN

Ch., chain; tr., treble; d.c., double crochet; sp(s)., space(s); sl.st., slip stitch; rep., repeat; in., inch(es); M., main colour.

### SQUARE MOTIF

With any colour, work 4 ch., and join into ring with sl.st.
**1st round :** 3 ch., 2 tr. into ring, (3 ch., 3 tr. into ring) 3 times, 3 ch., join with sl.st. at top of 3 ch. Fasten off.
**2nd round :** join in another colour to a 3 ch.sp., and work 3 ch. for first tr., (2 tr., 3 ch., 3 tr.) all into the same sp., * (1 ch., 3 tr., 3 ch., 3 tr.) into next sp.; rep. from * 3 times, 1 ch., join into ring with sl.st. and fasten off.
**3rd round :** join in another colour to corner sp. and make 3 ch., then work (2 tr., 3 ch., 3 tr.) into the same sp., * 1 ch., 3 tr. into next sp., 1 ch., (3 tr.,

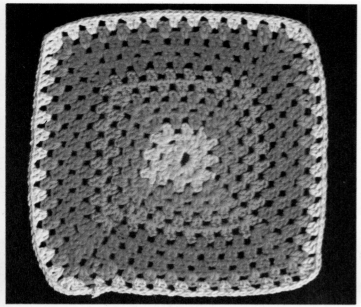

*The small motif may be worked in multicolours if wished*      *Close up of small square motif bedspread*

3 ch., 3 tr.) into corner sp.; rep. from *
twice, 1 ch., 3 tr. into next sp., 1 ch.,
join into ring. Fasten off.
**4th round:** join in another colour to
corner sp. and make 3 ch., then work
(2 tr., 3 ch., 3 tr.) into same sp., * (1 ch.,
3 tr. into next sp.) twice, 1 ch., (3 tr.,
3 ch., 3 tr.) into corner sp.; rep. from *
twice, (1 ch., 3 tr. into next sp.) twice,
1 ch., join into ring. Fasten off.
Work a further 20 rounds, working into
corner spaces as before and increasing
the number of groups of stitches along
each side as before. Change colours as
wished, but include a row of M. at
fairly regular intervals (see illustration).
Work 2 more squares in a similar way,
but vary the colour sequence of each.

## TO JOIN THE MOTIFS

The three squares are now joined in a
strip to form the lengthwise centre of
the bedspread. Work in this way:
Holding two squares together and
using M., put hook through first st. of
each and draw yarn through, yarn
round hook and draw yarn through.
Now putting hook through two lots of
edge sts. each time, work in d.c. all
along the edge of the 2 squares.
Repeat with 2nd and 3rd squares.

## SIDES

Lay the strip of joined squares flat, right
side up, and still using M., work along
one long side as follows:
Join yarn to first sp., work 3 ch., 2 tr.
in first sp., then work 3 tr. in each sp.
to end, work 2 ch. to turn.
Rep. this row 17 times, changing colour
for each row. Fasten off and work the
other long side in a similar way.

## TO COMPLETE

Join in yarn (any colour) at one corner
of bedspread and work all round the
four sides as for the long side, working
one round.

## BORDER

Join in the eighth contrasting shade at
one corner and work (1 d.c., 3 ch.,
1 d.c.) into each sp. all round. Fasten
off. Press lightly.

# Small square motif spread

## MATERIALS YOU WILL NEED

Each square motif requires 1 oz.
double knitting yarn either in mixed
colours (if you wish to make multi-
coloured squares) or all the same
colour (if you want to make plain-
coloured squares). You will also need
8 oz. double knitting yarn in white.
Crochet hook International Standard
Size 4.00.

## MEASUREMENTS

Finished bedspread measures
approximately 7 ft. by 8 ft.

## TENSION

One square measures 9 in.

## ABBREVIATIONS

See pattern for Large Square Motif
Spread.

## SQUARE MOTIF

Using any colour yarn, make a ch. of
4 and join in to a ring with a sl. st.
**1st round:** work 3 ch., then work 15
tr. into the ring, and join with a sl.st.:
16 sts into the ring altogether.
**2nd round:** * (2 tr., 1 ch., 2 tr.) into
sp. between first 2 tr., miss 2 tr., 1 ch.,
1 tr. into next sp., 1 ch., miss 2 tr.;

rep. from * 3 times more and join into
ring with a sl.st.
**3rd round:** * (2 tr., 1 ch., 2 tr') into
sp. between first 2 groups of tr., 1 ch.,
miss 2 tr., 2 tr. into next sp., 1 ch., miss
2 tr., work 2 tr. into next sp.; rep. from *
3 times more and join into a ring with a
sl.st
Rep. the last round, working twice
into each corner and into the spaces
along each side, working one more
each time until the round has been
worked with ten groups of 2 tr. along
each side. Fasten off.
Join in white yarn, and work another
round, inc. as before. This completes
12 rounds altogether. Fasten off.
Work 90 square motifs altogether,
using a different colour for each square
as desired.
To work multi-coloured motifs (see
close-up sample illustrated), work 2 or
3 rounds in one colour, fasten off, join
in another colour and work 2 or 3
rounds with it. Fasten off and join in a
third colour. Continue in this way,
keeping in pattern as for plain-
coloured motifs, but joining in new
colours as desired. Finish with a round
of white, as for the plain-coloured
motifs.

## TO COMPLETE

First join motifs into strips of 9 each,
alternating colours as wished. The
motifs may be joined either by
crocheting together or sewing them
together (see Crochet, lesson four).
Now join these strips together so
bedspread measures 9 squares across
(width), 10 squares down (length).

## BORDER

Join in yarn in any colour to one
corner and work one round of d.c.
round all four edges of spread. Fasten
off and join another colour of yarn.
Work another round of d.c. all round.
Fasten off

# CROCHET

## Lesson Six:
## Advanced Tunisian work and hairpin crochet

*Crochet your own family heirloom—instructions for this elegant lace tablecloth start at the end of lesson.*

## Advanced Tunisian work

Now that the simple stitches in Tunisian crochet have been mastered, it is possible to go on to some which are slightly more difficult. These can be used by themselves, or in combination with others, to produce fabrics with a variety of weaves and surface interest.

### PURL STITCH

This stitch, like Tunisian stocking stitch, produces an approximation of its knitted equivalent, although it is rather thicker and firmer in construction. Make a chain in the usual way. Now, in making the first foundation row, put the hook from back to front of the work through a chain, keeping the yarn *in front* of the work. The yarn is then taken round the hook, drawn through to the back of the work, and the loop left on the needle. This is repeated all along the row. The second row is worked as for the second row of Tunisian plain stitch.

**1st patt. row:** * keeping the yarn to

PURL STITCH

OPENWORK STITCH

RIBBED EFFECT PATTERN

OPEN RIB

the front of the work, insert the hook from right to left through the vertical stitch of the previous row, take the yarn round the hook and draw it through from front to back; rep. from * to end.

**2nd patt. row:** as 2nd row of Tunisian plain stitch.

## RIBBED EFFECTS

It is possible to combine stocking stitch—or any other of the stitches learned so far—with purl stitch to give a ribbed effect. This fabric will not have the elasticity of knitted ribbing, but can be used effectively nevertheless; it is a good all-over stitch and the ribs can be increased or decreased to allow for shaping on a skirt or dress.

There are plenty of variants possible; the one illustrated here combines stocking and purl stitches using two of each alternately throughout. .

## OPENWORK STITCH

This is similar to the traditional fancy crochet stitches worked with a conventional crochet hook.

Make a chain of desired length.

**1st foundation row:** as for foundation row on Tunisian plain stitch.

**2nd foundation row:** * make 3 ch., put the yarn round the hook and draw it through 5 loops (i.e. the 3 ch. just made and the next 2 loops on the hook), put the yarn round the hook and draw it through the loop thus formed; rep. from * to the end, finishing as usual with 1 ch.

Now work in patt. thus:

**1st patt. row:** work along the row making a loop through each chain stitch and also through the top of each group of sts.

**2nd patt. row:** as 2nd foundation row above.

These 2 patt. rows are repeated until work is length desired.

It should be noted that this stitch produces a scalloped edge after each 2nd row, so that if the work is arranged to go in a downward direction, a decorative edge is produced.

## OPEN RIB

This has a ribbed effect but there is a certain amount of space between the stitches, so that with fine yarn an open fabric is created.

Make a chain of desired length.

**1st foundation row:** * yarn round hook, insert hook into 2nd ch. from hook, draw through a loop, miss the next ch.; rep. from * to the end of row.

**2nd foundation row:** as for 2nd row of Tunisian plain stitch but after taking the yarn through the first st., take yarn through groups of 3 (not 2) stitches (i.e. counting the 'yarn round hook' as a stitch).

**1st patt. row:** as for foundation row, but putting hook under the horizontal threads, between the vertical loops of the previous row.

**2nd patt. row:** as for 2nd foundation row.

# Hairpin crochet

This type of work is sometimes called fork crochet. It is used to produce long strips of lacy fabric which can be used for insertion or edgings. Sometimes the strips are joined together to form a broad band of open work—for instance for a band above the hem of a skirt, or to edge a stole or tablecloth.

A special hairpin or prong is used for this work (available in a range of sizes from good handicrafts shops and departments). The width of the U-shaped prong determines the width of the finished work. This prong is used in conjunction with a crochet hook. See overleaf.

**Step 1.** Hold the prong, open end downwards, in the left hand; make a slip loop and put it over the right prong, keeping the knot in the centre, and put the yarn behind the right prong.

**Step 2.** Turn the prong from right to left so that the yarn is automatically taken behind the prong again. Using the crochet hook, put it through the original loop (A) yarn round hook and draw through a loop, yarn round hook and draw through a loop (in effect this is working a double crochet into each stitch) (B).

**Step 3.** Keeping the hook in the loop just made, and the yarn to the back of the prong, turn the prong from right to left once more, put hook under loop thus formed on left side of the prong, work a double crochet as before (C). The work continues with step 3 being repeated. (D). As the prong gradually fills with completed loops, the lower ones can be slipped off to give more room.

## TO FINISH OFF

Break yarn and pull it through the last loop, drawing it fairly tight.

## TO JOIN THE STRIPS

This can be done with matching or contrasting yarn. Lay the strips side by side and, with a conventional crochet hook, join loops by putting the hook through one loop from the left, one from the right and making a slip stitch (three loops on the hook) to join; rep. this all the way along. If preferred, the hook can be put through first a right-hand loop and then a left-hand loop, working a chain stitch between each, turning the loop when the hook is inserted so as to twist the stitch. This gives a more open join, which is appropriate to a lacy design.

149

# CROCHET YOUR OWN FAMILY HEIRLOOMS

## Elegant tablecloth

*illustrated at start of lesson*

### MATERIALS YOU WILL NEED

40 oz. Twilleys Lyscordet; one crochet hook International Standard Size 3.00.

### MEASUREMENTS

Finished tablecloth measures approximately 84 in. by 48 in.

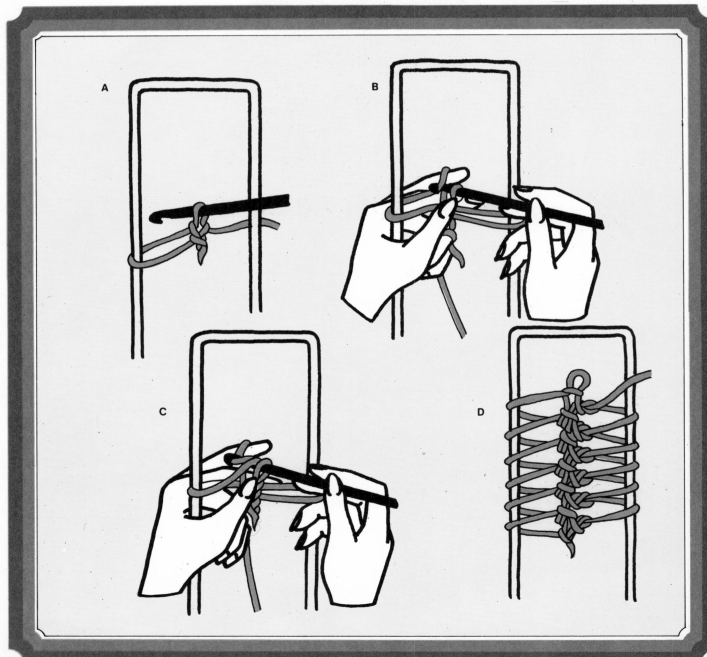

## TENSION

7 sts. to 1 in.

## ABBREVIATIONS USED IN THIS PATTERN

St(s)., stitch(es); in., inch(es); ch., chain; d.c., double crochet; tr., treble; d.c., double crochet; d.tr., double treble; sl.st., slip stitch; sp., space; rep. repeat.

## TO MAKE

With No. 3.00 hook make 336 ch.
**Foundation row:** 1 d.c. in 2nd ch. from hook, 1 d.c. in each ch. to end: 335 sts.
**Next row:** 1 ch., 1 d.c. in each d.c. to end.
Rep. last row once.
Now work in pattern as follows:
**1st row:** 3 ch., 1 d.tr. in 2nd d.c., 1 d.tr. in each of next 3 d.c., * (1 ch., miss 1 d.c., 1 d.tr. in next d.c.) 8 times, 1 ch., miss 1 d.c., 1 d.tr. in each of next 5 d.c.; rep. from * to end.
**2nd row:** 1 ch., 1 d.c. in each of first 5 d.tr., * (1 d.c. in 1-ch.sp., 1 d.c. in next d.tr) 8 times, 1 d.c. in next 1-ch.sp., 1 d.c. in each of next 5 d.tr.; rep. from * to end, working last d.c. in 3rd of 3 ch.
**3rd row:** 1 ch., 1 d.c. in each d.c. to end.
**4th row:** as 3rd row.
Rep. last 4 rows 4 times more.
**21st row:** as first row.
**22nd row:** as 2nd row.
Rep. these 2 rows 11 times more.
**45th and 46th rows:** as 3rd row.
These 46 rows form the pattern.
Continue in pattern until work measures 84 in.
Fasten off.
Press lightly.

*Note.* If wished, the crocheted fabric produced from this pattern may be used as a curtain instead of a tablecloth. In this case the pattern should be made up twice, to give a matching pair of curtains. To make a curtain of a different length, estimate 1 oz. of Lyscordet yarn to every 2¼ in. worked.

# Christening gown

## MATERIALS YOU WILL NEED

11 oz. Lister Lavenda 4 ply; crochet hooks International Standard Sizes 3.00 and 2.50; 3 small buttons; 1 yd. ribbon, 1 in. wide.

## MEASUREMENTS

Width all round at underarm 18 in.; length from top of shoulder 30 in.; sleeve seam 6 in.

## TENSION

1 pattern measures 2¼ in. on No. 3.00 hook.

## ABBREVIATIONS USED IN THIS PATTERN

See pattern for Elegant Tablecloth.

## BACK

With No. 3.00 hook, make 105 ch.
**1st row:** 1 tr. in 3rd ch. from hook, 3 ch., miss 2 ch., 1 d.c. in next ch., 3 ch., miss 2 ch., 1 tr. in next ch., * miss 2 ch., 5 tr. in next ch., miss 2 ch., 1 tr. in next ch., 3 ch., miss 2 ch., 1 d.c. in next ch., 3 ch., miss 2 ch., 1 tr. in next ch.; repeat from * to last ch., 1 tr. in end ch., 2 ch. (to count as first tr. on next row), turn.
**2nd row:** 1 tr. in next tr., (2 ch., 1 d.c. in 3 ch.sp.) twice, 2 ch., 1 tr. in next tr., * miss 2 tr., 5 tr. in next tr., miss 2 tr. in next tr., (2 ch., 1 d.c. in next 3 ch.sp.) twice, 2 ch., 1 tr. in next tr.; repeat from * to turning ch., 1 tr. in turning ch., 2 ch., turn.
**3rd row:** 1 tr. in next tr., 2 ch., (1 tr. in next 2 ch.sp) 3 times, 2 ch., 1 tr. in next tr., * miss 2 tr., 5 tr. in next tr., miss 2 tr., 1 tr. in next tr., 2 ch., (1 tr. in next 2 ch.sp) 3 times, 2 ch., 1 tr. in next tr.; repeat from * to turning ch., 1 tr. in turning ch., 2 ch., turn.
**4th row:** 1 tr. in next tr., 2 ch., 1 tr. in 2 ch. sp., miss 3 tr., 1 tr. in next 2 ch.sp., 2 ch., 1 tr. in next tr., * miss 2 tr., 5 tr. in next tr., miss 2 tr., 1 tr. in next tr., 2 ch., 1 tr. in 2 ch. sp., miss 3 tr., 1 tr. in next 2 ch.sp., 2 ch., 1 tr. in next tr.; repeat from * to turning ch., 1 tr. in turning ch., 2 ch., turn.
**5th row:** 1 tr. in next tr., miss 2 ch., 2 tr. in next tr., 1 ch., 2 tr. in next tr., miss 2 ch., 1 tr. in next tr., * 3 ch., miss 2 tr., 1 d.c. in next tr., 3 ch., miss 2 tr., 1 tr. in next tr., miss 2 ch., 2 tr. in next tr., 1 ch., 2 tr. in next tr., miss 2 ch., 1 tr. in next tr.; repeat from * to turning ch., 1 tr. in turning ch., 2 ch., turn.
**6th row:** 1 tr. in next tr., miss 2 tr., 5 tr. in 1 ch.sp., miss 2 tr., 1 tr. in next tr., * (2 ch., 1 d.c. in 3 ch.sp.) twice, 2 ch., 1 tr. in next tr., miss 2 tr., 5 tr. in next 1 ch.sp., miss 2 tr., 1 tr. in next tr.; repeat from * to turning ch., 1 tr. in turning ch., 2 ch., turn.
**7th row:** 1 tr. in next tr., miss 2 tr., 5 tr. in next tr., miss 2 tr., 1 tr. in next tr., * 2 ch., (1 tr. in next 2 ch.sp.) 3 times, 2 ch., 1 tr. in next tr., miss 2 tr., 5 tr. in next tr., miss 2 tr., 1 tr. in next tr.; repeat from * to turning ch., 1 tr. in turning ch., 2 ch., turn.
**8th row:** 1 tr. in next tr., miss 2 tr., 5 tr. in next tr., miss 2 tr., 1 tr. in next tr., * 2 ch., 1 tr. in 2 ch.sp., miss 3 tr., 1 tr. in 2 ch. sp., 2 ch., 1 tr., miss 2 tr., 5 tr. in next tr., miss 2 tr., 1 tr. in next tr.; repeat from * to turning ch., 1 tr. in turning ch., 2 ch., turn.
**9th row:** 1 tr. in next tr., 3 ch., miss 2 tr., 1 d.c. in next tr., 3 ch., miss 2 tr., 1 tr. in next tr., * miss 2 tr., 2 tr. in next tr., 1 ch., 2 tr. in next tr., miss 2 ch., 1 tr. in next tr., 3 ch., miss 2 tr., 1 d.c. in next tr., 3 ch., miss 2 tr., 1 tr. in next tr.; repeat from * to turning ch., 1 tr. in turning ch., 2 ch., turn.
**10th row:** 1 tr. in next tr. ( 2 ch., 1 d.c.

in 3 ch.sp.) twice, 2 ch., 1 tr. in next tr., * miss 2 tr., 5 tr. in 1 ch.sp., miss 2 tr., 1 tr. in next tr., (2 ch., 1 d.c. in 3 ch.sp.) twice, 2 ch., 1 tr. in next tr.; repeat from * to turning ch., 1 tr. in turning ch., 2 ch., turn.
The 3rd to 10th rows inclusive form the pattern. Continue in pattern until work measures 23 in. ending with a 4th row of pattern.

### Shape Waist

**1st row:** 1 tr. in next tr., miss 2 ch., 2 tr. in next tr., 1 ch., 2 tr. in next tr., miss 2 ch., 1 tr. in next tr., * miss 2 ch., 3 tr. in next tr., miss 2 ch., 1 tr. in next tr., miss 2 ch., 2 tr. in next tr., 1 ch., 2 tr. in next tr., miss 2 ch., 1 tr. in next tr.; repeat from * to turning ch., 1 tr. in turning ch., 2 ch., turn.
**2nd row:** 1 tr. in next tr., miss 2 tr., 5 tr. in 1 ch.sp., miss 2 tr., 1 tr. in next tr., * miss 1 tr., 3 tr. in next tr., miss 1 tr., 1 tr. in next tr., miss 2 tr., 5 tr. in 1 ch.sp., miss 2 tr., 1 tr. in next tr.; repeat from * to turning ch., 1 tr. in turning ch., 2 ch., turn.
Repeat 2nd row twice (working 5 tr. into centre tr. instead of in 1 ch.sp.).
**5th row:** 1 tr. in next tr., (miss 2 tr., 1 tr. in next tr.) twice, * miss 1 tr., 5 tr. in next tr., miss 1 tr., 1 tr. in next tr., (miss 2 tr., 1 tr. in next tr.) twice; repeat from * to turning ch., 1 tr. in turning ch., 2 ch., turn.
**6th row:** (1 tr. in next tr.) 3 times, * miss 2 tr., 5 tr. in next tr., miss 2 tr., (1 tr. in next tr.) 3 times; repeat from * to turning ch., 1 tr. in turning ch., 2 ch., turn.
Repeat 6th row twice.
**9th row:** miss next tr., 1 tr. in next tr., miss 3 tr., 5 tr. in next tr., miss 3 tr., 1 tr. in next tr.; repeat from * to last tr. and turning ch., miss 1 tr., 1 tr. in turning ch., 2 ch., turn.
**10th row:** 1 tr. in next tr., * miss 2 tr., 5 tr. in next tr., miss 2 tr., 1 tr. in next tr.; repeat from * to turning ch., 1 tr. in turning ch.
The 10th row forms the pattern for bodice. Continue in pattern until work measures 26½ in. (no turning ch. after last row).

### Shape Armholes and Divide for Back Opening

**1st row (right side facing):** slip st. over 8 tr., 2 ch., (miss 2 tr., 5 tr. in next tr., miss 2 tr., 1 tr. in next tr.) 3 times, 2 ch., turn. Work on these sts. only.
**2nd row:** * miss 2 tr., 5 tr. in next tr., miss 2 tr., 1 tr. in next tr.; repeat from * to end, 2 ch., turn.
Repeat 2nd row until work measures 29½ in. Fasten off. Return to sts. left for other side, rejoin yarn to centre tr.
**1st row:** 2 ch., (miss 2 tr., 5 tr. in next tr., miss 2 tr., 1 tr. in next tr.) 3 times, 2 ch., turn. Complete to correspond with first side.

### FRONT

Work exactly as for Back, until work measures 26½ in

*Close up of stitch pattern*

## Shape Armholes

**1st row:** slip st. over 8 tr., 2 ch., (miss 2 tr., 5 tr. in next tr., miss 2 tr., 1 tr. in next tr.) 6 times, 2 ch., turn.
**2nd row:** miss 2 tr., 5 tr. in next tr., miss 2 tr., 1 tr. in next tr.; repeat from * to end, 2 ch., turn.

*Close up of robe showing lower edging*

Repeat 2nd row until work measures 28½ in.

## Shape Neck

**1st row:** (miss 2 tr., 5 tr. in next tr., miss 2 tr., 1 tr. in next tr.) twice, miss 2 tr., 1 tr. in next tr., 3 ch., turn.

**2nd row:** miss 3 tr., 3 tr. in next tr., pattern to end.
**3rd row:** miss 2 tr., 5 tr. in next tr., (miss 2 tr., 1 tr. in next tr.) twice, miss 1 tr., 1 tr. in turning ch. Fasten off. Return to sts. left for other side. Rejoin yarn to next centre tr.
**1st row:** 2 ch., miss 2 tr., 1 tr. in next tr., pattern to end
**2nd row:** miss 2 tr., 5 tr. in next tr., miss 2 tr., 1 tr. in next tr., miss 2 tr., 3 tr. in next tr., miss 2 tr., 1 tr. in next tr., 2 ch., turn.
**3rd row:** (miss 1 tr., 1 tr. in next tr.) twice, miss 2 tr., 5 tr. in next tr., miss 2 tr., 1 tr. in end tr.
Fasten off.

## SLEEVES (make 2 alike)

With No. 3.00 hook, make 28 ch.
**1st row:** 1 d.c. in 2nd ch. from hook, 1 d.c. in each remaining ch.: 27 d.c.
**2nd row:** 1 d.c. in each d.c.
Repeat 2nd row 4 times.
**1st row:** 2 ch., miss first d.c., 1 tr. in next d.c., * miss next d.c., 5 tr. in next d.c., miss next d.c., 1 tr. in next d.c.; repeat from * to last d.c., 1 tr. in end d.c. 2 ch., turn.
**2nd row:** 1 tr. in next tr., miss 2 tr., 5 tr. in next tr., miss 2 tr., 1 tr. in next tr.; repeat from * to turning ch., 1 tr. in turning ch., 2 ch., turn. The 2nd row forms the pattern. Continue in pattern until sleeve measures 7 in. Fasten off.

## TO COMPLETE

Press each piece carefully. Sew shoulder seams. Sew sleeves placing first inch of sleeve seam into armhole. Sew side and sleeve seams.

### Back Opening

With No. 2.50 hook, work 1 row d.c. up left side of opening. With No. 2.50 hook, work 3 rows d.c. down right side of opening, working 3 buttonholes evenly on 2nd row. For each buttonhole work 2 ch., missing 2 d.c.

### Neck Edging

With No. 2.50 hook, work 2 rows d.c. evenly round neck edge.
3 ch., 4 tr. in first d.c., * miss 2 d.c., 1 tr. in next d.c., miss 2 d.c., 5 tr. in next d.c.; repeat from * all round, ending miss 2 d.c., 1 tr. in end d.c.
**4th row:** 1 d.c. in each of 2 tr., * 1 d.c., 3 ch., 1 d.c. in next tr., miss 2 tr.; repeat from * ending 1 d.c. in each of last 2 tr.

### Lower Edging

With No. 2.50 hook, work 1 row d.c. evenly round lower edge of gown. Work 3rd and 4th rows of sleeve edging. Fasten off.

### To Make Up

Press all seams. Sew on buttons to correspond with buttonholes. Thread ribbon through holes in pattern at waist and tie a bow at the front.

# TATTING

## Lesson One: Learning to use the shuttle

Tatting is a pleasant occupation requiring little concentration as, after continual repetition, the movements of the shuttle become almost mechanical. Once you have mastered the basic stitch, you will be able to make beautiful lace-like edgings and motifs to trim household and fashion accessories. Beginners should start with a fairly coarse crochet cotton, as this clearly shows the formation of the stitches, and how they build up a pattern.

## Tools and equipment

**Shuttle:** this is the basic tool of tatting, and it is possible to buy shuttles in bone, tortoiseshell or plastic. The one you choose is really a matter of personal preference, as each is as efficient as the others. Make sure however that the shuttle you select is not more than 2¾ in. long. A longer shuttle is inclined to be clumsy and can slow down the speed of your work. Shuttles are usually sold complete with a separate hook for joinings.
**Threads:** all forms of cotton threads, especially the finer varieties, are suitable for tatting. Coats chain Mercer-Crochet Nos. 10, 20, 40 and 60 are particularly recommended, and all these sizes are available in a good range of colours.
**You will also need:** scissors, a tape measure, good-quality pins.

## Winding the shuttle

Before you can begin work it is necessary to wind a length of your chosen yarn on to your shuttle. If there is a hole in the centre of the bobbin insert the thread through the hole and tie a knot, then wind the thread round the centre of the shuttle, taking care to wind evenly. Do not wind the thread beyond the edge of the shuttle. When working motifs it is a good idea to count the number of turns of thread round the shuttle so that the amount of thread used to make a single motif can be assessed. This will prevent unnecessary and perhaps ugly joinings of thread.

## Holding the shuttle

1. Hold the flat side of the shuttle in a horizontal position, between the thumb and the forefinger of the right hand. Allow approximately 15 in. of the shuttle thread to hang free from the back of the shuttle (A).
2. Grasp the free end of the shuttle thread between the thumb and the forefinger of the left hand (B).
3. Spread out the middle, third and little finger of the left hand and pass the thread over them (C).
4. Bring the thread round the fingers of the left hand to form a circle and hold it securely between the thumb and the forefinger (D).
5. Bend the third and little finger of the left hand to catch the thread against the palm (E).
6. Raise the middle finger of the left hand to 'open' the circle (F).
7. Adjust the thread so that the fingers do not feel strained and draw the shuttle thread out to its full length keeping the right and left hands at the same level (G).
8. Pass the shuttle thread round the back of the little finger of the right hand (H). Both hands are now in position to commence the basic stitch in tatting known as the Double Stitch.

## To work the double stitch

1. With the thread in position drop the middle finger of the left hand and move the shuttle forward passing it under the shuttle thread and through the circle (J).
2. Bring the shuttle back over the circle of thread and under shuttle thread (K).
3. Relaxing the fingers of the left hand, drop the thread from the little finger of the right hand and draw the shuttle thread taut with a sharp tug. (L).
4. Slowly raise the middle finger of the left hand, slide the loop into position between the thumb and forefinger. This completes the first half of the double stitch (M)
5. Now move the shuttle forward, dropping the shuttle and thread and passing the shuttle over the circle and back through between the circle and shuttle threads (N).
6. Drop the middle finger of the left hand (O).
7. Relaxing the finger of the left hand, draw the shuttle thread taut with a sharp tug (P).
8. Slowly raise the middle finger of the left hand to slide the loop into position next to the first half of the stitch. This completes the second half of the double stitch (Q).
9. Position hands and shuttle ready to begin next double stitch (R).

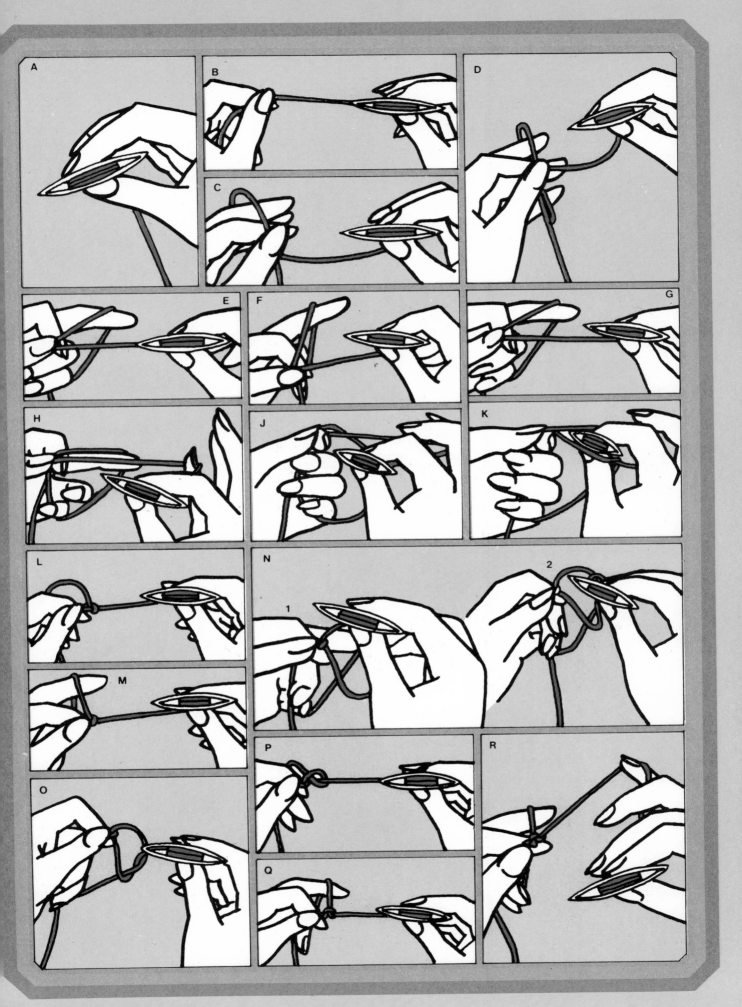

# Rings, picots and joinings

1. As each double stitch is formed, slide it along the circle of thread to meet the preceding double stitch. Hold them securely between the thumb and forefinger (S).
2. Make four double stitches, then make the first half of a double stitch, sliding it to within ¼ in. of the preceding stitch (T).
3. Complete the double stitch.
4. Slide the stitch along the ring to meet the first four double stitches. The small loop formed between the last two double stitches is a picot. The size of this may be altered as desired by adjusting the space left from the preceding stitch. Make three more double stitches. Make a second picot and four double stitches (U).
5. Holding the stitches securely between the thumb and forefinger of the left hand, draw the shuttle thread tight so that the first and last stitches meet to form a ring (V). In pattern instructions, the ring just completed would be written as: *R. of 4 d., 3 ps. sep. by 4 d.s., 4 d.s., cl.* —i.e. Ring of 4 double stitches, 3 picots separated by double stitches, 4 double stitches, clos
6. To make a second ring and a joining wind the thread round the left hand in position for another ring. Leaving a space of ¼ in. from base of previous ring, make four double stitches. Insert the hook through the last picot of the previous ring and pull the circle thread through, being careful not to twist it as you do so. Pass the shuttle through the loop. Slowly raise the middle finger of the left hand to draw up the loop (W). This stands as the first half of the next double stitch (a joining and one double stitch have now been completed). Work 3 d.s., 2 ps. sep. by 4 d.s., 4 d.s., cl. (second ring completed).

## Using ball thread and shuttle

Rings are made with the shuttle thread but chains in tatting are worked with the ball thread. Although some designs are made up of rings only, and others only contain chains, in general most designs consist of a combination of both chains and rings. It is therefore necessary to learn how to use the ball thread and shuttle thread together before beginning to follow a full set of pattern instructions.
1. Commence by tying the ends of the shuttle thread and the ball thread together. Make a ring, as described before.
2. Unlike rings, chains are made with the thread held across the back of the fingers of the left hand, winding it round the little finger to control tension (X).
3. A chain consists of a given number of double stitches worked over the ball thread with the shuttle. A chain may also include picots.

## Reversing

You will notice that the rounded end of the working ring or chain faces upwards. When working a design of rings and chains it is sometimes necessary to reverse your work. To do this, turn the ring or chain just completed face downwards—i.e. in the reverse position. The next ring or chain is then worked in the usual way having the rounded end facing upwards (Y).

## To finish off ends

Make a flat knot—e.g. a reef knot or a weaver's knot—close to the base of the last ring or chain. Do not cut off ends as the strain during working may loosen the knot. With a single strand of cotton, oversew the ends neatly to the wrong side of the work (Z).

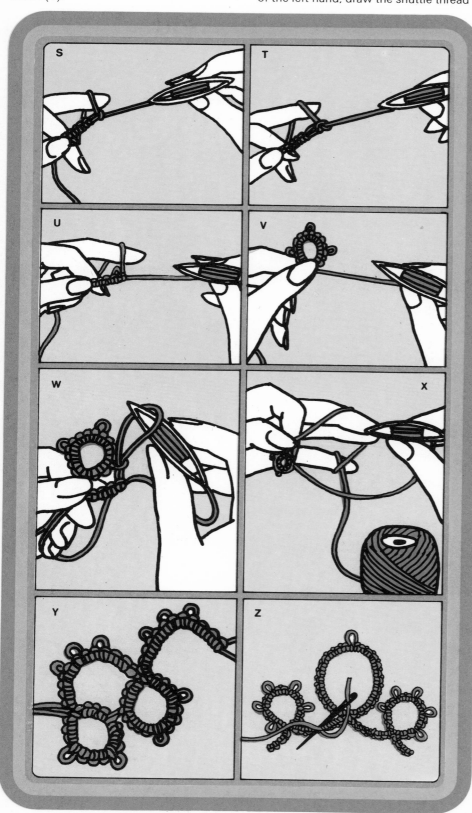

# EDGING FOR A HANDKERCHIEF AND A LACY COLLAR

## Handkerchief Edging

### MATERIALS YOU WILL NEED

1 ball Coats·Chain Mercer-Crochet No. 60; a tatting shuttle; a handkerchief to tone or contrast with thread shade.

### MATERIALS

Depth of edging: ⅝ in.

### TENSION

1 repeat measures ½ in. approximately.

### ABBREVIATIONS

D.s., double stitch; r., ring; ch., chain; p(s)., picot(s); sep., separated; cl., close; r.w., reverse work; rep., repeat.

### TO MAKE

Tie ball and shuttle threads together. R. of 3 d.s., 5 ps. sep. by 3 d.s., 7 d.s., join to last p. made, 3 d.s., 4 ps. sep. by 3 d.s., 3 d.s., cl., r.w.
*Ch. of 3 d.s., 4 ps. sep. by 3 d.s., 3 d.s., r.w. R. of 3 d.s., 2 ps. sep. by 3 d.s., 3 d.s., join to 3rd last p. on previous r., 3 d.s., 2 ps. sep. by 3 d.s., 7 d.s., join to last p. made, 3 d.s., 4 ps. sep. by 3 d.s., 3 d.s., cl., r.w.; rep. from * along side to next corner.
Ch. of 1 d.s., p., 1 d.s., r.w.
R. of 3 d.s., join to last p. on previous r., 3 d.s., 4 ps. sep. by 3 d.s., 7 d.s., join to last p. made, 3 d.s., 4 ps. sep. by 3 d.s., 3 d.s., cl., r.w.; rep. from first * 3 times more omitting last r. at end of last rep. and joining last p. on last r. to first p. on first r., join last ch. to base of first r.

### TO COMPLETE

Tie ends, cut and oversew neatly on wrong side. Damp and pin out to measurements. Sew neatly to edge of handkerchief.

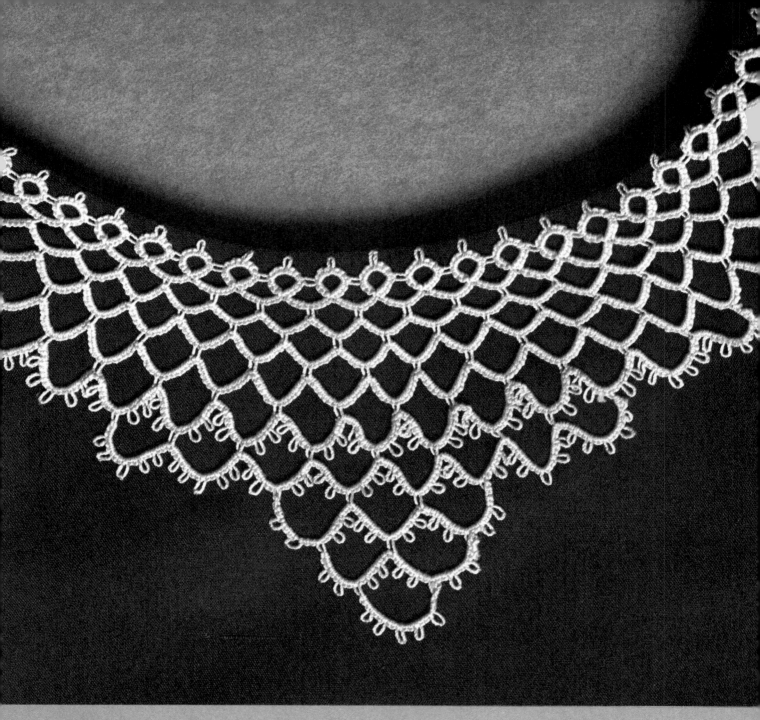

# Lacy collar

## MATERIALS

1 ball Coats Chain Mercer-Crochet No. 40; a tatting shuttle.

## MEASUREMENTS

Depth of collar at centre front: 3 in.

## TENSION

5 rings measure 1½ in.

## ABBREVIATIONS

See handkerchief edging pattern.

## TO MAKE

**1st row:** tie ball and shuttle threads together. R. of 4 d.s., 3 ps. sep. by 4 d.s., 4 d.s., cl., r.w. *Ch. of 4 d.s., p., 4 d.s., r.w.

R. of 4 d.s., join to last p. of previous r., 4 d.s., 2 ps. sep. by 4 d.s., 4 d.s., cl., r.w.; rep. from * 52 times more or for length required to fit round neck, having an even number of rs.
Tie ends, cut and oversew neatly on wrong side.

**2nd row:** tie ball and shuttle threads together, join to p. of first ch. on previous row.
*Ch. of 5 d.s., p., 5 d.s., join by shuttle thread to p. on next ch., rep. from * to end. Tie ends, cut and oversew neatly on wrong side.

**3rd row:** as 2nd row, having ch. of 6 d.s., p., 6 d.s.

**4th row:** as 2nd row, having ch. of 7 d.s., p., 7 d.s.

**5th row:** tie ball and shuttle threads together, join to 7th p. to left of centre. *Ch. of 3 d.s., 5 ps. sep. by 3 d.s., 3 d.s., join by shuttle thread to p. on next ch.; rep. from * 12 times more. Tie ends, cut

and oversew neatly on wrong side.

**6th row:** tie ball and shuttle threads together, join to centre p. of 3rd ch. on previous row.
*Ch. of 3 d.s., 5 ps. sep. by 3 d.s., 3 d.s., join by shuttle thread to centre p. on next ch.*; rep. from * to * 7 times more. Tie ends, cut and oversew neatly on wrong side.

**7th row:** as 6th row; rep. from * to * 3 times in all.

**8th row:** tie ball and shuttle threads together, join to centre p. on first ch. on previous row.
* Ch. of 3 d.s., 5 ps. sep. by 3 d.s., 3 d.s., join by shuttle thread to centre p. on next ch.; rep. from * once more. Tie ends, cut and oversew neatly on wrong side.

**9th row:** as 8th row, omitting 1 ch.

## TO COMPLETE

Damp and pin out to measurements.

# TATTING

## Lesson Two:

## Working with two colours

Working tatting with a single shuttle means that you are restricted to one colour of yarn only, and also you can only produce circular motifs. By using two shuttles together, each wound with a different coloured yarn, not only can you work interesting two-colour designs, but you can also make semi-circles and arcs which are not joined at their base by a thread.

## Using two shuttles

Wind each shuttle with your chosen yarn, and knot the ends of the two yarns together. The shuttles are now used alternately, according to the pattern being followed. If you are right-handed, then the shuttle not being used is put into the left hand. Take the thread from this shuttle over the middle and third fingers of the left hand, then wind it twice round the little finger. Let the thread and shuttle fall free. Use other shuttle in right hand, and work in a similar way as for single shuttle tatting (A).

When it is required to change to the contrast yarns, simply change positions of the two shuttles and proceed as before. If working in a pattern in which rings are separated by chains, when the chains are worked, the thread of the second shuttle should be held in a similar way as the ball thread is held when using ball thread and shuttle together (see Tatting, lesson one).

## To work a Josephine knot

This is a particularly pleasing decorative knot. It is very simple to work. Merely work the first half of a double knot (i.e. do not complete the second part of the double knot) continuously to a specified number of times (B1). When the knot has been worked the required number of times, draw up the thread to form an attractive circular motif (B2). The Josephine knot can be worked with only a few half knots to give a small finished knot, or with about 10 or 12 half knots to give a bigger finished knot. The Josephine knot can be used in the course of a design instead of a picot, or if wished simple picots and Josephine knots can be combined and either used alternately, or in any sequence wished.

## Joining threads

When working a design with ball thread and shuttle, a knot can be avoided at the beginning of the work by filling the shuttle and commencing the ring without cutting the thread. If a knot is unavoidable in the course of work. however, then tie ends together with either a reef knot or a weaver's knot close to the base of the last ring or chain. Do not cut off the ends, as the strain during working may loosen the knot.

**To tie a weaver's knot:** lay old yarn end across new yarn end, at right angles to it. Bring the end lying underneath up and over other end, then take it behind itself from left to right, and down over other end (C1). Bring other yarn end from right to left over the first end, and through the loop formed by it (C2). Draw knot tight.

## Left-handed workers

The directions for each stitch in tatting apply both to the right and left-handed worker. The left-handed worker however should work from right to left, and the shuttle will of course be held in the left hand. Place a pocket mirror to the left of each illustration and the exact working position will be reflected.

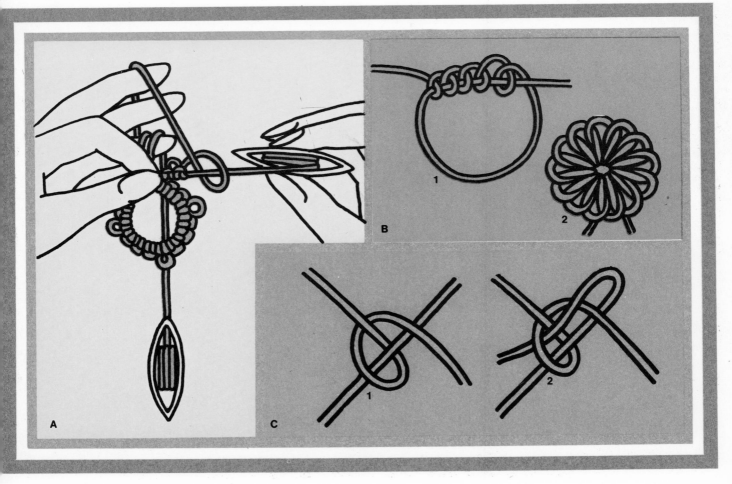

## YOUR TWO-COLOUR MAKE

# DRUM LAMPSHADE

## MATERIALS YOU WILL NEED

Of Coats Chain Mercer-Crochet No.
20 — 2 balls in main colour, and 2 balls
in a contrasting colour; a tatting shuttle;
2 lampshade rings, each 10 in. in
diameter, one with fitting; 1 card bias
binding for covering rings; 1 yd.
bonding parchment, 39 in. wide.

## MEASUREMENTS

Depth of finished shade is approximately
$10\frac{1}{2}$ in.

## TENSION

One motif is $2\frac{1}{8}$ in. in width.

## ABBREVIATIONS

D.s., double stitch; r., ring; ch., chain;
p(s)., picot(s); sm.p., small picot;
sep., separated; cl., close; r.w., reverse
work; rep., repeat; M., main colour;
C., contrast colour.
*Note:* This design can easily be
adapted to fit different sizes of
lampshades by working more or less
motifs on each row.

## FIRST STRIP
### First Motif

Fill shuttle with M.
**1st row:** using shuttle with M., and
ball of C., tie ball and shuttle threads
together; * r. of 9 d.s., sm.p., (4 d.s.,
p., 4 d.s., sm.p.) twice, 9 d.s., cl.,
r.w. Ch. of 4 d.s., p., 4 d.s., r.w.; rep.
from * 3 times more, join to base of
first r.
**2nd row:** ch. of 6 d.s., p., 6 d.s., *
join by shuttle thread to first sm.p. of
adjacent r. Ch. of 6 d.s., 2 ps. sep. by
d.s., 4 d.s., join by shuttle thread to
next sm.p. on same r. Ch. of 4 d.s.,
2 ps., sep. by 4 d.s., 6 d.s., join by
shuttle thread to next sm.p. on same
r. Ch. of 6 d.s., p., 6 d.s., join by
shuttle thread to base of same r.
Ch. of 4 d.s., p., 4 d.s., join by shuttle
thread to base of next r. Ch. of 6 d.s.,
join to p. on second last ch., 6 d.s.; rep.
from * omitting last ch. on last rep. and
joining last ch. to first ch. to correspond
Tie ends, cut and oversew neatly on
wrong side.

### Second motif

Work as for first motif for one row.
**2nd row:** ch. of 6 d.s., p., 6 d.s., join
by shuttle thread to first sm.p. of
adjacent r. Ch. of 6 d.s., p., 4 d.s., join
to corresponding p. on first motif,
4 d.s., join by shuttle thread to next
sm.p. on same r. of second motif.

Ch. of 4 d.s., join to next p. on first
motif, 4 d.s., p., 6 d.s., complete to
correspond with first motif. Make 3
more motifs or number required for
depth of lampshade joining each as
second motif was joined to the first.

## REMAINING STRIPS

Make 14 more strips, or number
required for circumference of lampshade, joining each to previous strip
in the same manner and joining last
strip to first strip to correspond.

## TO COMPLETE

Damp and pin out to measurements.
Bind lampshade rings tightly with bias
binding, overlapping edges so the rings
are completely covered. Cut bonding
parchment to the depth of tatting and
its length to measure 1 in. larger than
the circumference of the lampshade
rings. Overlap short ends of parchment
by 1 in. to form drum shape and glue
in position. Oversew parchment to
rings. Place tatting over drum shape
and sew neatly in position.

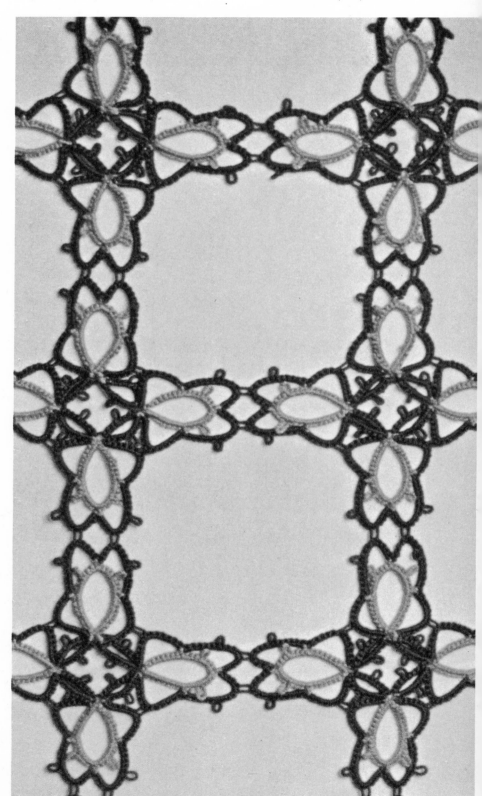

# TATTING

## Lesson Three
## Alternative working method

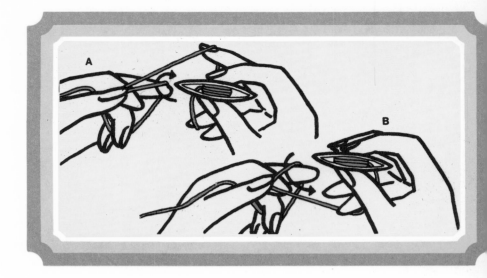

Now you have learned the basic way to hold the shuttle and to work the tatting stitches, try this alternative method of working: if this advanced method can be mastered a very much greater speed of working can be attained.

The shuttle should first pass under (A), then over the loop of thread around the left hand, while the thread is held tightly stretched by the little finger of right hand (B). In this way, the length of thread from the shuttle to the work itself must be very much shorter than in the first basic method. Practise working by this new method to see if you can accustom yourself to it.

# Laundering tatting

Use a warm lather of pure soap flakes and wash gently either by hand or by washing machine. If wished, the article may be spin-dried until it is damp, or left until it is half dry. Place a piece of paper, either plain white or squared, on top of a clean, flat board. Following the correct measurements as given in your pattern, draw the shape of the finished article on to the paper, using ruler and set-square for squares and rectangles and a pair of compasses for circles. With rustless pins, pin the tatting out to the pencilled shape, taking care not to strain the tatting. Pin out the general shape first, then finish by pinning each picot, loop or space into position.

When pinning out, make sure the pin is in the centre of each loop to form balanced lines.

When pinning scallops, make all the scallops the same size and regularly curved. Pull out all picots.

If the tatting requires a slight stiffening, use a solution of starch—1 dessertspoon to 1 pint of hot water—and dab lightly over the article. Raise the tatting up off the paper to prevent it sticking as it dries. When completely dry, remove the pins and press the article lightly with a hot iron.

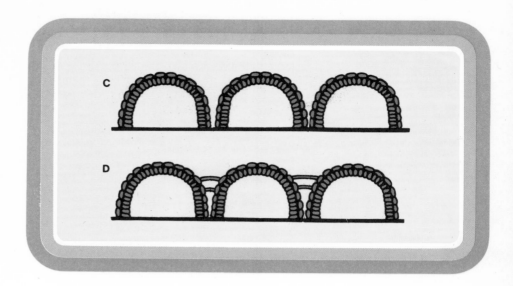

# Two simple edgings

## DETACHED SCALLOPS

Working with one shuttle, make 12 double stitches, then draw up the thread so that the stitches form a semi-circle. The first stitch of the next scallop must be made close enough to the last stitch of the preceding scallop so that it touches it. Continue in this way.

## JOINED SCALLOPS

With one shuttle make 4 double stitches, 1 picot, * 8 double stitches, 1 picot, 4 double stitches, close the scallop, 4 double stitches, draw the thread through the second picot of the previous scallop; rep. from * until edging is required length.

# TRIMMING FOR WEDDING HEADDRESSES

## MATERIALS YOU WILL NEED

**For bride's headdress:** 1 ball Coats Chain Mercer-Crochet No. 20 in white; plain white pillbox shape with veil.
**For bridesmaid's headdress:** 1 ball Coats Chain Mercer-Crochet No. 20 in deep pink (or colour wished); wired headband, 2 in. wide, in pale pink (or colour wished). **For both:** a tatting shuttle.

## MEASUREMENTS

Each complete motif is approximately 2 in. across at widest point.

## ABBREVIATIONS USED IN THIS PATTERN

D.s., double stitch; r., ring; s.r., small ring; l.r., large ring; ch., chain; p(s)., picot(s); sm.p., small picot; l.p., long picot; sep., separated; cl., close; r.w., reverse work; rep., repeat.

## TO MAKE MOTIF

**Outer Row.** Tie ball and shuttle threads together. * S.r. of 5 d.s., p., 5 d.s., cl., r.w. Ch. of 5 d.s., p., 5 d.s., r.w. L.r. of 5 d.s., 3 ps. sep. by 5 d.s., 5 d.s., cl., r.w. Ch. of 5 d.s., p., 5 d.s., r.w.; rep. from * 3 times more, join to base of first s.r. Tie ends, cut and oversew neatly on wrong side.
**Centre Row.** Tie ball and shuttle threads together. R. of 5 d.s., sm.p., 3 d.s., 3 l.p. sep. by 1 d.s., 3 d.s., sm.p., 5 d.s., cl., r.w.
* Ch. of 5 d.s., p., 5 d.s., r.w. R. of 5 d.s., join to last sm.p. on previous r., 3 d.s., 3 l.p. sep. by 1 d.s., 3 d.s., sm.p., 5 d.s., cl., r.w.; rep. from * 6 times more joining last sm.p. to first sm.p. to correspond.
Ch. of 5 d.s., p., 5 d.s., join to base of first r.
Tie ends, cut and oversew neatly on wrong side.
Make 16 complete motifs (i.e. outer row and centre row) in white for bride's headdress, plus one centre row only.
Make 7 complete motifs in pink for bridesmaid's headdress.

## TO COMPLETE

Damp and pin out outer rows to measurement given.
**Bride's Headdress.** Arrange 10 outer rows of motifs evenly round side of pillbox shape, positioning them so the tip of each alternate motif is near top of edge of pillbox shape, and the remaining motifs have lower point near bottom edge of pillbox. Sew neatly in place. Sew remaining 6 outer rows of motifs

evenly round top crown of pillbox. Now thread a length of yarn through ps. on each centre row of motifs, draw up to form a bell shape. Stitch a centre row in centre of each outer row. Stitch final centre row to centre of crown.

**Bridesmaid's Headdress.** Arrange outer rows of motifs evenly round headband and stitch neatly in place. Draw up centre rows of motifs, as for bride's headdress, and stitch in place in centre of each outer row.

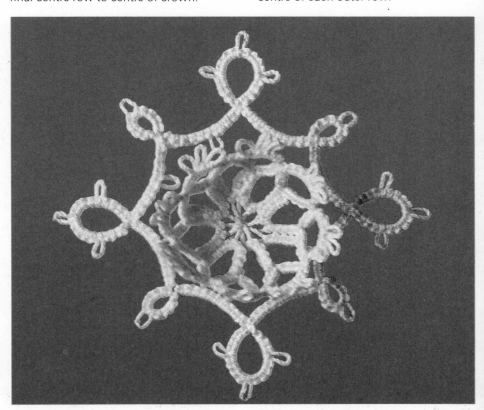

# MACRAMÉ

## Lesson One: Knots with a decorative purpose

**Joan Fisher introduces you to the fascinating craft of knotting.**

### What to use

Any yarn can be used to work macramé, depending on the article being made and the finished result required, but the most successful are the smooth, firm yarns which knot easily and do not slip. String is one of the best—and cheapest—materials of all. If you want a crisp finish with the knotting pattern clearly defined, then it is essential you use a firm material such as string, linen thread, nylon cord or any form of cotton. On the other hand if you prefer an all-over textural effect, then any knitting or crochet yarn, fine or thick, can be used. Rug wool is excellent for it is more substantial than ordinary knitting wools, and being thick makes up quickly. You will need a convenient-sized board to work on for small items, and any oddment of wood—preferably a soft one which will take pins easily—can be used, or a sheet of cork, or even several thicknesses of hardboard. If using a hard wood, it is a good idea to 'pad' it first with a sheet of foam plastic, or even a folded-up old towel. An expanse of wall makes an ideal working base for large items.

### Beginning work

As well as a working surface and a suitable yarn (string is best for practice purposes) you will need some pins, scissors and a tape measure.
Before you can begin knotting, your yarn must be cut into suitable lengths, and these are mounted on to another length of yarn, known as the **holding cord.** This is called **setting on threads.** The holding cord is sometimes used as part of the finished design—for instance, as a handle for a bag—or it can be withdrawn after knotting is complete. It is not always easy to join in new yarn in mid-knotting so it is important that working lengths are cut long enough for the complete design. As a very general guide if setting on each thread double (which is the usual method) then the thread should be cut to eight times the length required. For instance, if you are making a braid to measure 6in. long, then cut each thread 48in. If you are setting on threads singly then they should be cut to four times the finished length required.

① ② ③ ④

## How to set on threads

For practice purposes, cut a holding cord of about 12in., and 10 lengths of string, each 1 yard long. Tie a knot near one end of holding cord by taking the end over and round itself, and through the loop formed. This is known as an **overhand knot**. Pin the cord through this knot to your working surface near top left-hand corner. Stretch the cord horizontally across your working surface, tie a similar overhand knot near the other end of cord and pin it to your working surface (A).

Now take the first of your working cords, double it and insert looped end under holding cord from top to bottom. Bring loose ends down over holding cord and through the loop. Draw tight. Repeat with each length of string, positioning each doubled set-on string close to previous one (B). When you have finished you will then have 20 lengths of string hanging vertically from your holding cord, each measuring a little under 18in.

## The basic knots

### Half hitch

Work on the first 2 cords. To tie a half hitch from the left, hold right-hand cord taut, bring cord 1 in front of it then up and behind it from right to left. Bring through loop formed. Draw tight (C). Work on cords 3 and 4. To tie a half hitch from the right, merely reverse the knotting procedure: hold left-hand cord taut, and bring right-hand cord in front of it, then up and under it from left to right, and down through loop formed. Draw tight (D).

Work on cords 5 and 6. Tie a half hitch from the left, then tie a half hitch from the right. Continue in this way, alternating the direction of the knot each time, and drawing each knot close to the previous one. This forms a chain of knots known as the **single alternate half hitch chain** (E).

Work on cords 7, 8, 9 and 10. Tie half hitches alternately from the left and right, as for the single alternate half hitch chain, but this time use cords double, so first knot is tied with cords 7 and 8 over 9 and 10; the second knot is tied with cords 9 and 10 over 7 and 8. Continue in this way to form a chain of knots. This is known as the **double alternate half hitch chain** (F).

### Flat knot

The flat knot which is the second basic knot is tied in two parts as follows: work on cords 11, 12, 13 and 14. Hold cords 12 and 13 taut, take cord 11 under them and over 14. Take cord 14 over 12 and 13 and under 11. Draw tight (G). This is the first half of the flat knot, and is known as the **half knot**. If the half knot is tied continuously this produces an attractive twisted spiral of knots.

To complete the flat knot, still keeping 12 and 13 taut, bring cord 11 back

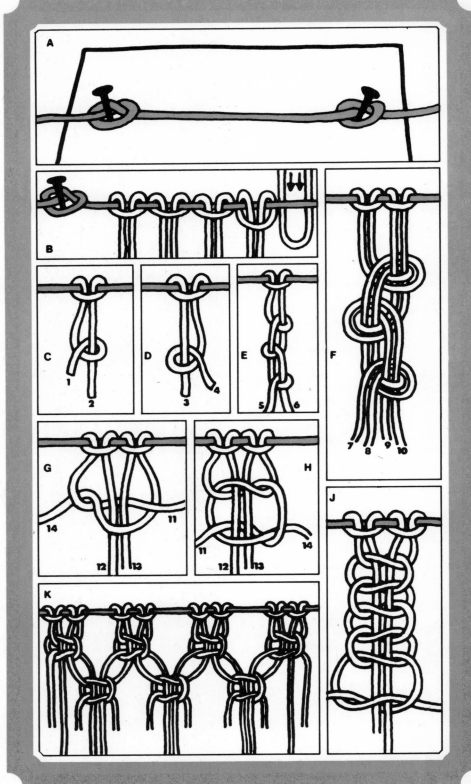

under 12 and 13 and over 14. Take 14 over 12 and 13 and under 11. Draw tight (H). Continue in this way to tie flat knots one below the other to form a chain. This is often known as a **Solomon's bar** (J)

### To work the alternate flat knot pattern

This pattern occurs frequently in all forms of macramé work, and is often used to form a fabric. It is worked on any number of knotting cords, provided the total number is a multiple of 4. Begin by tying flat knots with each group of 4 cords to the end of the row. In the 2nd row, leave the first 2 cords unworked, then tie flat knots with each group of 4 cords to the final 2 cords in row, leave these 2 cords unworked (K). The 3rd row is the same as the first, and the 4th row is the same as the 2nd. Continue in this way to build up a fabric. By tying knots and rows close together you create a dense fabric; space out knots and rows and you will achieve an open-work lacy fabric.

# Cording

This is a useful macramé technique for it can be used to create solid fabrics, to 'draw' outlines and figures, and to shape edges of work. It is based on the half hitch knot.

To practise cording on your set-on strings, cut a new length of string, approximately 1 yard long. Tie an overhand knot near one end of it, and pin it to your working surface immediately to the left of working cords. Lay it horizontally across working cords (L). This is known as **leader cord**, and as the knots are all tied on to this leader cord it is essential to keep it taut all the time—if necessary pin it to your working surface at the opposite side to keep it taut while you work. Now beginning with cord 1, take it up and over leader, and then down behind it, bringing end out to the left of the loop formed. Repeat sequence exactly with the same cord. This means you have tied 2 half hitches, or—as is more usually known—a **double half hitch**. Repeat with every cord along the row, pushing each half hitch as it is tied close to previous one (M). At the end of the row you should have a row of tiny loops along the leader cord all nestling close to each other.

To work the next row, place a pin in working surface at the end of the first row, take leader round the pin and place it horizontally across working cords, this time from right to left. Now tie double half hitches with each cord in turn, but this time as you are working from right to left, as each half hitch is tied you will bring the cord end down to the right of the loop formed (N). This is known as horizontal cording. Diagonal cording is worked in a similar way, except leader cord is placed at an angle across working cords. The leader for horizontal or diagonal cording may be a separate cord, or it can be one of the set-on cords (O).

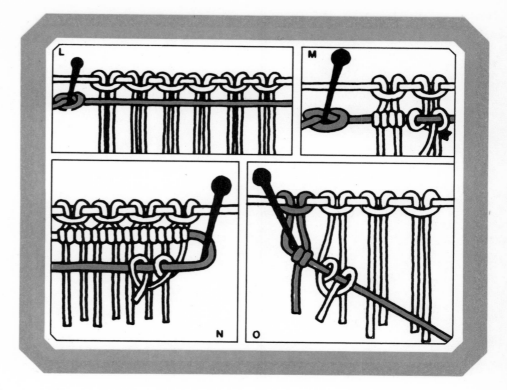

## YOUR FIRST MAKES

# MULTI-PURPOSE BRAIDS

*Braids 1 to 4 are illustrated on the previous page, braids 5 and 6 overleaf.*

**How to use your braids**

Make the braids as long as you wish to form belts, bracelets, chokers, hairbands, trimmings for lampshades, or to edge picture frames, to tie back curtains, as bell pulls, edgings for stools, or stitch strips of braids together to make an unusual and colourful table runner. All the braids shown here are made from ordinary coloured strings and twines obtainable from hardware stores and stationers. If you prefer, you can of course make the braids in any other yarn you choose to suit the purpose for which braid will be used.

## Braid 1

### MATERIALS

Mediumweight parcel string in 2 colours; plastic coated twine in 2 colours.

### PREPARATION

Cut 2 cords in each colour of parcel string, and in one colour of plastic-coated twine; cut 1 cord in 2nd colour of plastic-coated twine—each cord to measure at least 8 times the length of finished braid required. Set these on to a short holding cord (or directly on to bar of buckle if making a belt) in the following order: 1 cord in colour A parcel string, 1 cord in colour B parcel string, 1 cord in colour A plastic-coated twine, 1 cord in colour B plastic-coated twine, 1 cord in colour A plastic-coated twine, 1 cord in colour B parcel string, and 1 cord in colour A parcel string: 14 working cords.

### TO MAKE

Cut a separate leader cord in one of the strings (it does not matter which as it will not show in the finished design). Cut it to a manageable length to work with, and join in new lengths as required always at the beginning of a row of cording. Pin leader to left-hand side of work.
**1st–3rd rows:** close horizontal cording across all cords over leader (first row will be worked from left to right; 2nd row from right to left; 3rd row from left to right).
**4th row:** slant leader down to the left and work diagonal cording over it with all cords.

**\*Next row:** horizontal cording from left to right.
**Next row:** horizontal cording from right to left.
**Next row:** slant leader down to right and work diagonal cording over it with all cords.
**Next row:** horizontal cording from right to left.
**Next row:** horizontal cording from left to right.
**Next row:** slant leader down to the left and work diagonal cording over it with all cords.\*\*
Repeat from \* to \*\* until braid is length required. Finish with 3 rows of close horizontal cording as at the beginning. Trim leader ends to about $\frac{1}{2}$in. Press to back of work and secure to wrong side of a row of cording with a few neat stitches.

## Braid 2

### MATERIALS

Natural-coloured mediumweight parcel string; assorted colours of round and long beads.

### PREPARATION

Cut 3 cords each measuring at least 8 times the length of finished braid required. Pin these 3 cords to your working surface by their top loops, so one cord lies inside the other. Tie an overhand knot with all cords about 1in. from the triple loop: 6 working cords.

### TO MAKE

This design is a free one based on alternating sequences of flat knot chains (use double knotting cords, 2 central knotbearing core cords), the alternate flat knot pattern (having only a single knotbearing core cord in each knot), and chains of half knots (first half of flat knot tied continuously to form twisted spiral). Thread beads on to single or double cords between chains as required, or alongside the half knot spirals (on the cords not being used to tie spiral). Tie overhand knots above and below beads to keep them in place. If making a tie belt, when braid is length required, tie an overhand knot with all cords then thread at least 3 beads on to each individual cord, tying overhand knots between beads and after last one has been threaded on. Trim cord ends.

## Braid 3

### MATERIALS

Plastic-coated twine in 2 colours; natural-coloured mediumweight parcel string.

### PREPARATION

Cut 4 cords in plastic-coated twine colour A, 2 in colour B, 2 in parcel string Each cord should measure at least 8 times the required finished length of braid. Set these cords on to a short holding cord (or directly on to the bar of a buckle if making a belt) in the following order: 2 cords in colour A plastic-coated twine, 1 in colour B, 2 in parcel string, 1 in colour B plastic-coated twine, 2 in colour A: 16 working cords.

### TO MAKE

If wished, work a row of horizontal cording first as a foundation, using a separate leader (any cord). With cord 6 as leader slanting down to the left, work diagonal cording over it with cords 5, 4, 3, 2 and 1. Work a 2nd row of diagonal cording immediately below with cord 5 as leader and knotting over it cords 4, 3, 2, 1 and 6.
In a similar way work a double row of diagonal cording slanting down to the right, with cord 11 as leader for first row and knotting over it cords 12, 13, 14, 15 and 16. Cord 12 will then be leader for 2nd row and cords 13, 14, 15, 16 and 11 will be knotted over it.
Tie 2 flat knots with centre 4 cords (parcel string). Loop cords 3 and 4 round 2 left-hand cords of parcel string, and loop cords 13 and 14 round 2 right-hand cords of parcel string. Tie 3 more flat knots with centre 4 parcel string cords. Reverse direction of cord on far left (original cord 5) round a pin and work diagonal cording slanting down to the right with cords 6, 1, 2, 3 and 4.
Work a 2nd row of diagonal cording immediately below with cord 6 as leader and knotting over it cords 1, 2, 3, 4 and 5.
In a similar way work a double row of diagonal cording slanting down to the left, with cord 12 as leader for the first row, and knotting over it cords 11, 16, 15, 14 and 13. Cord 11 will then be

leader for the 2nd row and cords 16, 15, 14, 13 and 12 will be knotted over it. Now lay cord 11 across cord 6 and work cording over cord 11 with cord 6. Work another double-row diamond of diagonal cording in a similar way, letting cord 11 continue as leader for first row of cording on left-hand side of work; and cord 6 continue as leader for first row of cording on right-hand side of work. Chain of flat knots with parcel string cords continues behind linked point of cording diamond until it is long enough for cords 3 and 4 and 13 and 14 to be looped round it as before (probably another 3 flat knots in chain) Continue in this way until braid is length required.

## Braid 4

### MATERIALS

Mediumweight parcel string and plastic-coated twine in a contrasting colour.

### PREPARATION

Cut 4 cords in parcel string, 2 in plastic-coated twine, each cord to measure at least 8 times the length of finished braid required. Set them on to short holding cord (or directly to bar of buckle if making a belt) in the following order: 2 cords in parcel string, 2 in plastic-coated twine, 2 in parcel string: 12 working cords.

### TO MAKE

*Tie a single flat knot with the centre 4 cords (the plastic-coated twine cords). Now using cords 5 and 6 (plastic-coated twine) as a double leader slant these cords down to the left and work diagonal cording over them with cords 4, 3, 2 and 1 in turn. In a similar way slant cords 7 and 8 down to the right and work diagonal cording over them with cords 9, 10, 11 and 12.
Now criss-cross centre (parcel string) cords over each other, taking cords 3 and 4 first over 9 and 10, then under 11 and 12, and taking 1 and 2 under 9 and 10 then over 11 and 12.
Reverse direction of 5 round a pin, and work diagonal cording slanting down to the right with cord 6.
Now continuing with cords 5 and 6 as a double leader work diagonal cording slanting down to the right with cords 9, 10, 11 and 12.
In a similar way, reverse direction of cord 8 round a pin, and first work diagonal cording slanting down to the left over it with cord 7, then continue with both cords as a double leader and work diagonal cording slanting down to the left over them with cords 4, 3, 2 and 1.**
Repeat from * to ** until braid is length required.

## Braid 5

### MATERIALS

Mediumweight parcel string in 2 colours; plastic-coated twine in 2 colours.

### PREPARATION

Cut 4 cords in colour A, 4 in colour B, each cord to measure at least 8 times the length of finished braid required. Set these on to a short holding cord.
Set them on in the following order: 2 cords in colour A, 4 in colour B, 2 in colour A: 16 working cords.

### TO MAKE

Work in the alternate flat knot pattern until braid is half the length required. Now work a chain of flat knots over centre 2 cords, but change knotting cords as wished. Let cords not being used to knot form loops at sides of braid. Divide cords into 2 groups of 8 cords, and work a 4-row band of diagonal cording with each.
*Work 2 rows of horizontal cording, cord on left as leader. Then work a pattern panel to a depth of 1 in. across cords as follows: single alternate half hitch chain; flat knot chain; half knot spiral; flat knot chain; single alternate half hitch chain. ** Repeat from * to ** until braid is length required.

## Braid 6

### MATERIALS

Plastic-coated twine in 4 colours.

### PREPARATION

Cut 2 cords in each of 3 colours, 1 cord in 4th colour, each cord to measure at least 8 times the length of finished braid required. Set these on to a short holding cord (or directly on to bar of buckle if making a belt) in the following order: 1 cord in colour A, 1 in B, 1 in C, 1 in D, 1 in C, 1 in B, and 1 in A: 14 working cords.

### TO MAKE

*Work 8 rows of close diagonal cording slanting down to the right, using cord on far left as leader for each row, and stopping knotting on each row after 2nd cord in colour A has been knotted on to the leader.
**Next band:** work 8 rows of close diagonal cording slanting down to the left, using cord on far right as leader for each row and stopping knotting on each row after 2nd cord in colour in C (2nd group) has been knotted on to the leader.**
Repeat from * to ** until braid is length required.

5

6

# MACRAMÉ

## Lesson Two:

## Finishing ends and edges

**Joan Fisher tells you more about knotting and shows you to finish your work attractively.**

In macramé you are working with multiple strands of yarn—unlike knitting or crochet where you work with a single strand only—and therefore certain problems are involved in bringing your work to a neat conclusion. There are various possible methods you can choose from.

## Fringes

A fringe is by the far the simplest method of ending a macramé design. Simply trim the cord ends evenly to the depth required. The fringe may be left plain, or the cords may be knotted in any of the following ways:
1. Overhand knots in single cords, or pairs of cords (A).
2. Combine pairs of cords and tie in single alternate half hitch chains (B).
3. Combine groups of 4 cords in single flat knots (C).
4. Divide cords into equal groups and tie each group into a neat tassel with a collecting knot: to work a collecting knot, form a loop in the cord on the far right of the group at the point where the finished knot is to appear. Take the cord in front of the group from right to left, then round behind the group. Bring cord end down through the original loop and draw tight. Repeat this process several times to give a more substantial tassel (the more cords there are in the tassel, the greater number of loops in the collecting knot should be worked) (D).
5. Individual cords can be neatened with a coil knot: at the point where the finished knot is to appear form a loop, and then wind the cord several times round itself (E1). Pull cord on either side of these winds, and the winds will form into a solid corkscrew-like coil. The more winds you work, the deeper will be the finished coil knot (E2).
6. Beads may be threaded on to individual cord ends to give a decorative finish. Tie an overhand knot below each bead to hold it in place.

## Tassels

Cords may be combined into simple tassels with a collecting knot, as described above, or may simply be tied into groups with a single overhand knot. For a more substantial tassel however, work as follows:

1. Divide cords into equal groups (the number of tassels required). Now divide each group into two equal sets of cords.
2. Tie these two sets of cords together in the first half of a flat knot (without any central knotbearing cords) (F1).
3. Cut a number of cords (using either the same yarn as used for the design, or a contrasting one) to give the required thickness of finished tassel. Cut these cords to a little over double the measurement of tassel wanted.
4. Place these new cords together, double them, then loop them over the knotted group of cords. Adjust the new cords so they lie evenly over the half knot. If necessary add some more cords. Pull the half knot tighter to draw it in out of sight (F2).
5. Using one of the new cords, tie a collecting knot tightly round the entire set of cords (knotted ones and new ones). Position the collecting knot close to the 'head' of the tassel. Tie the collecting knot several times to give extra strength and to balance the finished tassel (F3).

## Clean-edged finish

If you want to end your knotting with a smooth edge (no fringe or tassel) ideally the design should finish with at least one (preferably more) rows of horizontal cording. Cord ends may then be neatened by any of the following methods:
1. Trim ends to within $\frac{1}{2}$ in. of last row of knots, or 1 in. if the yarn is inclined to fray easily. Turn work over and press the cut ends back on to wrong side of last row of knots. The ends may be secured in place by machine stitching across them, or working a row of running stitches by hand. Alternatively, if string is being used, a dab of fabric adhesive should hold the ends firmly in place.

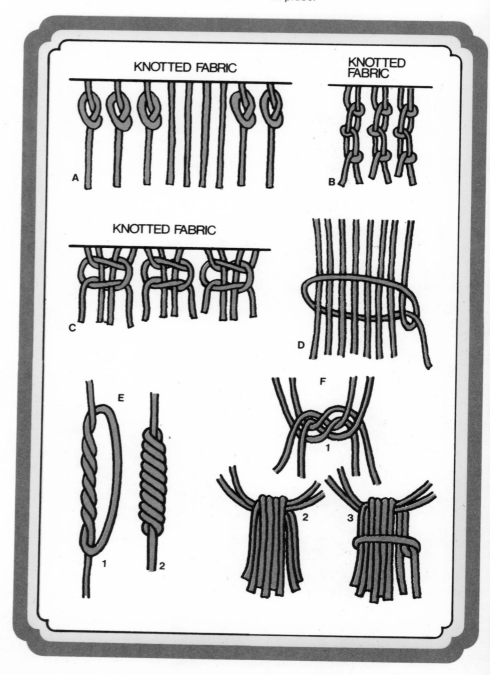

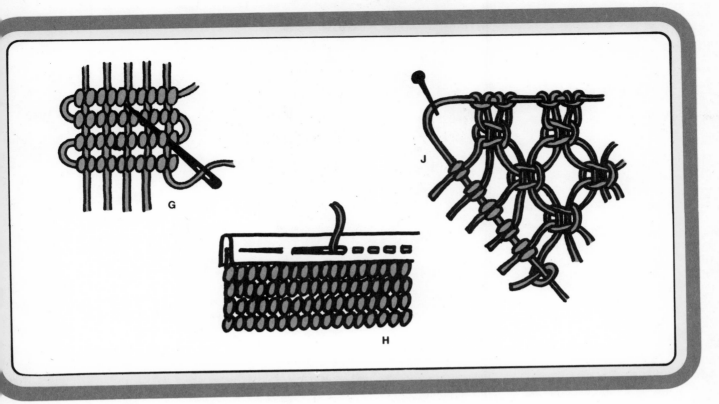

Do not trim cord ends. Turn work wrong side, then thread each cord turn on to a large-eyed darning needle and weave it through the back last few rows of knotting (G). Trim ends when sufficient weaving has been worked. If the cord is too thick to thread on to a needle, then use a crochet hook to pull ends through.

Trim ends and press to wrong side of work. Enclose complete edge in seam binding, in a colour to match or contrast with knotting yarn (H).

A complete lining may be made for a design—this is particularly suitable for knotted handbags and for fashion garments. Any design worked in knitting yarn should be fully lined to prevent the weight of the knots pulling the fabric out of shape. Make a paper pattern from the finished piece of knotting. Cut out lining fabric, adding in. to all edges for turnings. Press turnings to wrong side, then place lining to knotting, wrong sides together. Sandwich cord ends between lining and knotting. Slipstitch lining neatly in place round all edges.

## Finishing side edges

Most knotting patterns automatically give neatly-finished side edges. If separate leaders are used for rows of horizontal cording, these ends—and also those of the holding cord at the beginning—will have to be neatened. The easiest way to do this is to trim the ends to within ½ in. of knotting, then press to wrong side of work and secure on back of row of cording (or set-on edge) with a few neat running or machine stitches.

Alternatively a decorative touch can be added to your design by threading beads on to leader and holding cord ends. Push bead close to knotting, tie an overhand knot in cord end to hold in place and trim close to the knot. If a design has a sloping edge or other type of shaped edge, then leave holding cords long enough to use as leaders and work a row of diagonal cording down each side of work—use left-hand end of holding cord to work cording down left-hand side of work; right-hand holding cord for right-hand edge.

### YOUR MACRAME MAKE

# A GOLDEN SHAWL

### MATERIALS YOU WILL NEED

Nine 50-gram balls Twilleys Double Gold.

### MEASUREMENTS

Our shawl measures just under 4 ft. across at the widest edge; approximately 20 in. deep, excluding fringe. This measurement however is adaptable— see *Note* below.

### TENSION CHECK

Five double half hitches worked with double strand cords measure 1 in. (diagonal cording).

*Note:* This shawl is worked on the triangle principle: i.e. a predetermined number of working cords are set on to a holding cord (the number will depend on the depth of shawl required); only the first row of pattern will use all the working cords. Thereafter an equal number of cords are dropped at each end of every pattern row, so a regular triangle of pattern is gradually formed. From this you will see that only the centre cords are used to knot throughout the complete design and these cords therefore should be cut to the full length—8 times the finished length required, plus an allowance for fringe. The remaining cords can be cut proportionately shorter.

It is best to set on the central full-length cords to holding cord first, then set on cords to either side of this, gradually reducing the lengths by 2 or 3 in. each time right up to the top corners.

The size of your finished triangle will be governed by the number of cords you set on, and—as a very, very approximate guide—the depth of the triangle (to the point, excluding any fringe) is equal to about half the set-on edge (again excluding the fringe).

For example, if you wish to make a triangle to measure 25 in. deep, you will have to set on sufficient cords to give a measurement of 50 in. on the holding cord. Establish how many set-on cords are required to give a 1 in. measurement on the holding cord, then multiply this by 50 to give total number of cords required.

Each pattern repeat in our shawl uses 4 double cords (8 double working ends), so cords have to be set-on in a multiple of 4. But as each group of 4 double cords measure exactly 1 in. on the holding cord, this simplifies your calculations.

For each extra 1 in. measurement required on holding cord (or ½ in. of

171

awl finished depth, excluding fringe)
u simply set-on 4 extra double cords
rds are set-on double, and double
and working cords are used
oughout, to give extra stability to
e knotting.

**REPARATION**

t a double holding cord of 50 in.,
us double the measurement of fringe
quired (e.g. if you wish a 6-in. fringe,
en cut holding cord to 62 in.).
n holding cord to your working
rface—an expanse of wall is the
st working surface for a design of
s size. Cords are set-on double
e. 2 cut lengths are placed together
d treated as a single thickness).
u will require a total number of 174
uble set-on cords. Begin by cutting
cords each 13 ft. 6 in., plus measure-
ent of fringe required. Set these on
ntrally to holding cord. Now set-on
rds in groups of 4 double cords to
ther side of these central cords,
ducing the cut measurement of each
oup by 6 in. each time.
ne final group of 4 double cords at
e top left and top right corners will
en each be cut to 3 ft., plus measure-
ent of fringe. You should now have a
tal of 348 double working cords.
it is wished to make a larger or
naller shawl than the one shown,
en increase or decrease number of
t-on cords, and their cut lengths,
llowing instructions in *Note* p. 171

**O MAKE**

*ote:* Each double working cord will
e referred to as a single working cord
roughout instructions. Work on first
roup of 8 cords.
With cord 1 as leader slanting down
o the right, work diagonal cording
ver it with cords 2, 3 and 4.
With cord 8 as leader slanting down to
e left, work diagonal cording
ver it with cords 7, 6 and 5.
ink the 2 leaders by working a double
alf hitch (cording) with cord 8 over
ord 1. **
epeat from * to ** with each group
f 8 cords to end of row.
**Next row:** leave first 4 cords
nworked, then work pattern from
to ** on next group of 8 cords
cord 1 from first motif in previous
ow therefore continues as leader for
eft-hand edge of this 2nd-row motif;
ord 8 from 2nd motif on first row
ontinues as leader for right-hand
dge of this 2nd-row motif).
epeat pattern from * to ** with each
group of 8 cords to last 4 cords in
ow; leave these unworked.
**Next row:** leave first 8 cords
nworked, then work in pattern to
ast 8 cords; leave these unworked.
ontinue in this way, leaving 4 more
cords at each end unworked with
ach row.
t will be seen that the first and 8th
cords of every group remain as leaders
hroughout the design, and in fact

travel right across work.
Inevitably therefore some of these
cords will not be long enough to
complete the design. This could be
avoided by careful calculations when
measuring, cutting and setting-on
cords, but the mathematics involved
are fairly complex; it is easier in this
particular design merely to cut new
cords and introduce them as required.
As all the new cords will be introduced
in cording this is a fairly simple matter:
merely lay the end of the new cord
alongside the end of the old cord, and
work the next few double half hitches
in the pattern, over both ends together.
When the new cord is securely caught
in, let the old cord drop (the end can
be trimmed on wrong side of work
afterwards).
Eventually you will reach a row with
only one repeat of the pattern motif
in it: this completes the triangle.

**TO COMPLETE**

Trim fringe to depth required, including
the ends of holding cord as part of the
fringe.

# MACRAMÉ

## Lesson Three:
## Introducing beads

One of the easiest and most effective ways of adding extra interest to your knotting patterns is to introduce beads into the design. There is no complicated beading technique to learn—as with knitting or crocheted bead work—for the beads are simply slid on to your cord ends wherever you want a bead to appear in the design, then secure bead in place by tying an overhand knot immediately below it.

All sorts of beads may be used—china, plastic, metal or wooden, round, oblong or square. The shape and substance are immaterial provided the bead harmonises with the yarn you are using, and the design. Obviously, the bead must be suited to thickness of the yarn—small beads for fine yarn, big beads for chunky yarns. It is possible to thread quite thick cords through beads if the cord ends are bound tightly with fuse wire first of all. Finer yarns can have their ends dipped in colourless nail varnish, and allowed to dry—this will give a rigid end which will slip easily through the bead. The varnished end can be cut away afterwards when the design is complete. Sometimes it is possible to widen the hole in a bead by very gentle drilling.

### SOME WAYS TO USE BEADS IN A MACRAME DESIGN

In a flat knot pattern, beads may be threaded on to the central knotbearing cords between groups of knots (A). The knotting cords should be taken fairly tightly round either side of bead and then the next flat knot in the chain tied to hold the bead in place. Alternatively after working one flat knot, tie an overhand knot in the knotbearing cords, slide on the bead, tie another overhand knot with the central cords, then tie a flat knot below with all four cords.

A bead may form the central focal point in a motif—for instance in a cording diamond pattern, after working the top two 'arms' of the diamond, take all— or some—of the central cords through a bead, then complete remaining two 'arms' of the diamond (B).

In a flat knot chain, after a group of knots have been tied, thread a bead on to each knotting cord, then continue with flat knot chain (C).

Beads may also be threaded on to cord ends to give an attractive finish to a design. In this case merely tie an overhand knot beneath the bead and trim cord ends close to knot (D).

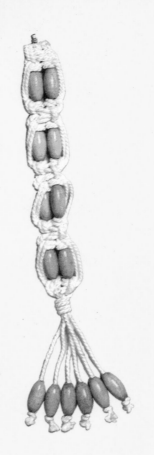

## YOUR BEADED MAKES

### Piping cord bracelet

#### MATERIALS YOU WILL NEE[D]

7 yd. piping cord No. 3; 14 large oval wooden beads; 1 large hook and eye.

#### TO MAKE

Cut cord into 3 lengths, each 6 ft. 6 in[.] and set these on to a very short holdin[g] cord: 6 working ends. Tie a multiend half knot (first half of the flat knot), using double strand knotting cords, 2 central knotbearing cords.

* Tie a half hitch from the left with cor[d] 1 and 2 over cord 3. Tie a half hitch from the right with cords 5 and 6 over cord 4.

Thread a bead on to cord 3, and a bead on to cord 4. Tie a half hitch from the left with cords 1 and 2 over cord 3, and a half hitch from the right with

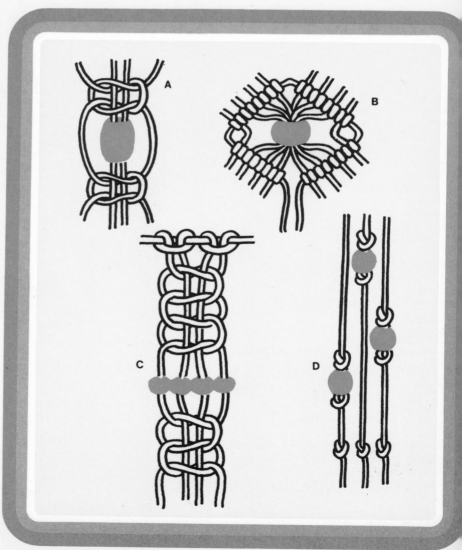

cords 5 and 6 over cord 4.
Tie a multiend flat knot, with double
strand knotting cords, 2 central knotbearing cords.
Repeat from * 3 times.
Tie a collecting knot 4 times round all
cords.
Leave about 2½ in. of cords unworked
then thread a bead on to each cord end.
Tie an overhand knot beneath each
bead, and trim cord ends close to
overhand knot.
Trim leader cord to about ½ in. at each
end, press to wrong side of work, and
stitch to secure. Sew hook to this end,
eye to other end, on back of last flat
knot tied.

# Pink and gold bracelet

### MATERIALS YOU WILL NEED

4 yd. gold cord; ½ yd. yellow dressing
gown cord; 28 long beads in shades of
pink and lilac; 1' hook and eye.

### TO MAKE

Cut gold cord into 2 equal lengths.
Place these together. double them, and
join by top loops to working surface.
Double yellow cord and place inside
gold cords, so there is a triple top loop,
with gold cords outside, yellow cord
on inside. Pin in place to working
surface. Tie 2 multiend flat knots, with
double strand knotting cords (gold
cords), 2 knotbearing central cords
(yellow cord).
Now thread 2 beads on to each outer
gold cord, arranging beads to form a
'V' shape, as shown in photograph
below. Tie a flat knot chain with centre
4 cords of 3 knots. Tie a multiend flat
knot, using double knotting cords
(gold cords), 2 knotbearing central
cords.
Continue in this way, tying a continuous flat knot chain in the centre,
and threading 2 beads on to outer
cords between the multiend flat knots,
until all the beads are used up.
Tie 2 more multiend flat knots to finish.
Trim cords to about ½ in. from last
knot, press to wrong side of work,
and secure with a few neat stitches.
Stitch a hook to one end of chain, eye
to other end.

## Red, brown and cream necklace

### MATERIALS YOU WILL NEED

11 yd. red mediumweight string; 29 oval wooden brown beads; 26 round cream beads.

### TO MAKE

Cut string into 3 equal lengths. Pin singly to your working surface so each strand is 1 in. higher than the one next to it.

Tie an overhand knot close to end of each cord. On first cord thread on 3 long beads, 3 round beads

On second cord thread on 3 long beads. On third cord thread on 2 round beads.

Now link cords by working a 3-end half knot spiral (first half of the flat knot)—use single strand outer knotting cords, only 1 central knotbearing cord. Tie 8 half knots in the spiral, and let spiral twist right round on itself after the 4th knot.

* Thread a long bead on central cord; tie a half knot with all 3 cords; thread a round bead on to central cord; tie a half knot; thread a long bead on central cord; then work another 8-half knot spiral.

Thread a round bead on central cord; half knot; thread a long bead on central cord; half knot; thread a round bead on central cords; work another 8-half knot spiral.

Repeat from * 4 times. Work another beaded motif, following the pattern sequence, and another 8-half knot spiral. Now link end of chain to beginning of chain by tying a multiend flat knot with all 6 ends, immediately below half knot spirals at beginning and end—use double strand knotting cords, central knotbearing cords. Finish ends by threading 3 round beads, 3 long beads on to one cord end; 3 long beads on to another end; and 2 round beads on to last end. Tie an overhand knot in each cord immediately below beads. Trim cords close to overhand knots.

## Red, white and blue choker

### MATERIALS YOU WILL NEED

11 yd. fine natural-coloured twine; 30 round red beads; 52 small round blue beads.

### TO MAKE

Cut yarn into 4 equal lengths. Pin singly to working surface so 3 cords are about 1½ in. longer than the 4th cord. Tie an overhand knot near end of each cord. On to each cord thread a red bead followed by a blue bead. From about 4 in. down from ends of longer cords, tie an overhand knot with all 4 cords.

* Thread 2 blue beads on to cord 1; thread a red bead on to cord 4.

Tie 3 flat knots with all 4 cords. Repeat from * until chain measures 18 in. from overhand knot (or length required), ending with a beaded sequence. Tie an overhand knot with all cords immediately below beads. Thread beads on to individual cord ends, tying overhand knots beneath each, to correspond with beaded ends at beginning of choker.

Trim cord ends close to overhand knots.

## Red choker

### MATERIALS YOU WILL NEED

1 hank Twilleys ''747' Orlon Sayelle (or any extra thick wool—rug wool could be used, although as it is not so 'chunky' as the '747' Orlon Sayelle it will not bulk up quite so much) ; 12 small black beads; 13 small white beads; 1 hook and eye.

### TO MAKE

Cut 2 lengths of yarn, each 4 yd. Place these together, double them and pin by their double top loop to your working surface.

* Tie a half hitch from the right with cord 4 over cords 3 and 2 together. Thread a white bead on to cord 4 (it may be necessary to bind the cord ends tightly with fuse wire in order for them to go easily through the beads).

Now tie a reversed half hitch with cord 4 over cords 3 and 2: i.e. take cord 4 under cords 2 and 3, and bring it up and over it to form loop. Draw knot tight.

Now tie a half hitch from the left with cord 1 over cords 2 and 3. Thread a black bead on to cord 1, then tie a reversed half hitch with cord 1 over cords 2 and 3 **.

Repeat from * to ** until choker is 16 in. (or length required).

Tie a tight flat knot to finish. Trim ends to about ¾ in. from last knot, press to wrong side of work, and secure with a few neat stitches.

Sew hook to one end of choker; eye to other end.

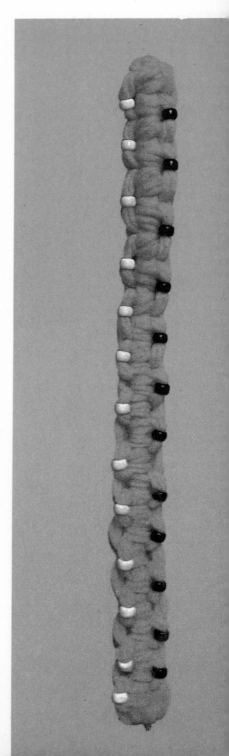

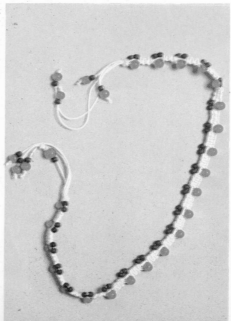

# Green pendant necklace

## MATERIALS YOU WILL NEED

1 ball mediumweight green string (gardening stores usually sell a suitable brand); 2 long dark green beads; 16 round bright green beads.

## TO MAKE

**Make main chain section first:** cut 3 lengths of string, each 6 yd. 1 ft. Place these 3 cords together, and thread one long dark green bead on to all the cords. Position bead at midway point of the triple thickness cords. Secure to your working surface by this point, then tie an overhand knot with all cords together about ½ in. below the bead.

Begin pattern: work a half knot spiral with cords 1, 2, 3 and 4, working 12 half knots altogether, and letting spiral twist round on itself after every 4th knot.

Now tie a similar half knot spiral using cords 3, 4, 5 and 6. Continue in this way tying half knot spirals alternately at the left and right of chain.

After 12 half knot spirals in all have been worked, work central beaded motif: thread a round bead on to cord 6. Tie a multiend flat knot just below bead, using single knotting cords, 4 central knotbearing cords. Continue in this way, threading a bead on to cord 6 then tying a multiend flat knot below it until 8 beads in all have been threaded on to chain. Do not tie a flat knot below the 8th bead. Work in half knot spiral pattern as before, working first spiral with cords 3, 4, 5 and 6.

After 12 spirals in all have been worked below beaded section, tie an overhand knot with all cords together. Leave about 1½ in. of cords unworked, and tie another overhand knot. Trim cord ends close to this knot.

**Work pendant section:** cut 8 new cords, each 1½ yd. Unpin chain section already worked from your working surface and repin it so the beaded section runs horizontally across the top of your working surface—the new cords will be set on directly to this part of the chain.

Thread each new cord in turn through a bead on the chain, having the midway point of the cord inside the bead. You will then have a total of 16 new working cords (the ends should hang down on opposite side of beads from the multiend flat knots worked in chain section).

With cord on far left as leader work a row of horizontal cording across all cords, immediately below the beads. Work a second row of horizontal cording immediately below the first row, using same leader.

With cord on far left as leader slanting down to the right, work diagonal cording over it with first 6 cords. In a similar way with cord on far right as leader slanting down to the left, work diagonal cording over it with 6 cords at right of work. Thread a single round bead on to 2 centre cords together, then work cording with the left-hand cord of this pair over the first leader (maintaining same slope of cording) and work cording with right-hand cord of centre pair over the second leader (again maintaining the same slope of cording).

Now link the 2 rows of cording at the centre 'V' point, by knotting left-hand leader over right-hand one.

Thread a round bead on to 6th cord from left-hand side, and thread a round bead on to 6th cord from right-hand side.

Continue with rows of diagonal cording, letting leader from left-hand side cross to become leader for right-hand side, and the previous right-hand leader become left-hand leader for the lower part of the cross-over cording motif. Let these lower arms of the cross-over cording motif pull in much tighter than upper arms (see photograph of pendant, above).

Thread a round bead on to 2 centre cords together. Work a chain of multiend flat knots with centre 8 cords: have double knotting cords, 4 central knotbearing cords; tie 3 knots in chain. Thread a long dark green bead on to centre 4 cords. Tie another multiend flat knot below to hold in place.

Work on first 4 cords: work a chain of 3 flat knots, thread 2 round beads on to centre 2 cords, tie a flat knot below to hold in place.

Work beaded and flat knot chain with last 4 cords to correspond with the first chain.

Now link the 3 chains together: tie an overhand knot with first 3 cords; tie an overhand knot with next 3 cords (combining one cord from first chain with 2 cords from second chain); overhand knot with next 4 cords; overhand knot with next 3 cords (combining 2 cords from centre chain with one cord from third chain); overhand knot with last 3 cords. Trim cord ends to about 3 in. below overhand knots.

# Tasselled pendant necklace

## MATERIALS YOU WILL NEED

11 yd. 6 in. striped cord; oddment of gold yarn.

## TO MAKE

Cut 2 strands of cord, each 4 yd., cut 2 strands of cord, each 1½ yd. Pin these cords singly to your working surface, so the 4-yd. cords are at outside edges, the 1½-yd. cords are in the centre.

Start knotting about 2 in. from cord ends: tie 3 flat knots; tie next flat knot about ½ in. below, then when the knot is complete push it up into place immediately below the previous knot —this will form loops (picots) at the sides of the chain, and is generally known as a flat knot with picots. Tie another flat knot, then follow with another flat knot with picots.

Now work in flat knot chain until chain is 30 in. long (or length required). Tie a flat knot with picots; a single flat knot; another flat knot with picots; and finish with 3 flat knots. Trim ends to about 2 in. from last knot. Unpin chain from working surface. Tie cord ends at the beginning of the chain in a half knot.

Now cut 15 strands of cord, each 10 in. Place these together and loop over the half knot just tied. Bind group of cords tightly together just below looped point using gold thread. Be sure to tuck in strands of half knot so they are completely hidden in the finished tassel.

# MACRAMÉ

## Decorative beginnings

**In this final macramé lesson, Joan Fisher explains how you can add interest to the start of a design.**

It is possible to set on cords to give a decorative start to your work—rather than just a plain straight edge. This is particularly useful when the set-on edge forms an important role in the finished design, such as the top edge of a bag or a shawl. A few of these decorative headings are described below.

### SIMPLE PICOT EDGE

Lay doubled cord under holding cord with the loop extending slightly beyond holding cord. Now work a double half hitch (cording) with the left-hand cord of the doubled pair. Pin top loop to working surface and work a double half hitch with right-hand cord. Repeat with each set-on cord, being sure to keep top picot loop the same size with each cord (A).

### OVERHAND PICOT EDGE

Double cord to be set on then in centre point tie an overhand knot. Pin cord to working surface through this overhand knot and place holding cord across working ends. Secure to holding cord with a double half hitch with each end below overhand knot (B).

### CHAIN PICOT EDGE

Double cord to be set on then from centre point down work alternate half hitch chain to length required. Attach to holding cord with double half hitches, as for overhand picot edge (C).

### FLAT KNOT PICOT EDGE

Double two cords to be set on and pin to working surface side by side, pinning at top loops. Tie a single flat knot with the four cords, attach to holding cord with double half hitches (D).

### SIMPLE SCALLOPED EDGE

Double three cords and pin to working surface by top loops, placing each cord inside the other to give a triple top loop. Lay holding cord across all cords and work a double half hitch with each over the holding cord (E).

## YOUR FOURTH MAKE

# FRINGED EVENING SKIRT

**Designed by Marjorie Craske**

### MATERIALS YOU WILL NEED

25 balls Wendy Tricel Nylon Double Knit Machine Washable yarn; two ¾-in. buttons.

### MEASUREMENTS

Our skirt was made to fit a waist size of approximately 24–26 in., hip size 36–38 in., but it is quite easy to adapt the instructions to fit any size, and any length required.

*Note.* As the major part of this design is worked 'in the round' it will not be possible to work on a flat surface. A suitable three-dimensional working base must be used instead. A dressmaker's dummy adjusted to your own size is the ideal working base as it is then an easy matter to shape the skirt as you work, knowing the resulting fit will be right for you.

### TO MAKE

**Waistband**
This is worked first, as a separate strip. As it is knotted flat, your usual flat working base may be used.
Cut 12 cords, each 8 times your waist measurement plus 8 in. (i.e. if your waist is 26 in., then cut cords to 18 ft. each). Set these centrally on to a double thickness holding cord of 12 in.
* Starting with cord on far left as leader work 6 rows of close horizontal cording, using same leader throughout. Divide cords into groups of 4, and work a chain of 2 flat knots with each group.**
Repeat from * to ** until waistband is long enough to fit comfortably round your waist, ending with a band of horizontal cording.
Work another 1 in. of horizontal cording (this will form underlap for waist fastening).
Unpin waistband from working surface. Trim cord ends to about 2 in. from end of knotting, press these to back of work and either weave the ends through last few rows of cording, or stitch neatly to back of work to hold in place.
With double holding cord on left of waistband, work half hitches with one cord over the other to 1 in. Work a similar chain of half hitches with double holding cord at right of waistband. Fold each chain to centre of

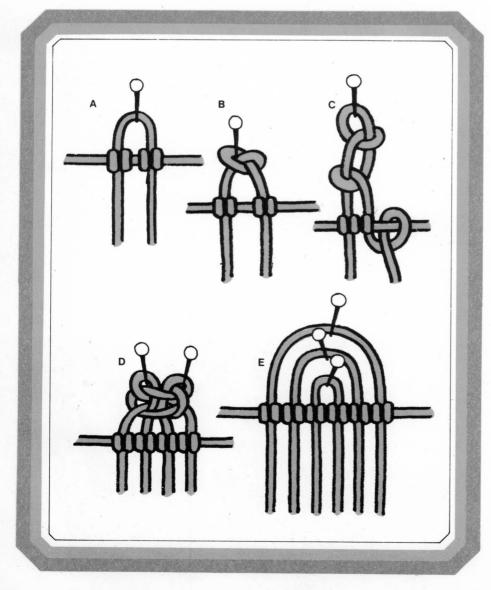

set-on edge and stitch neatly in place, trimming away excess cords—this forms two button loops.

## Main Section

Now pin waistband round three-dimensional working surface. If you are using a dressmaker's dummy, then pin it in place round waist of dummy. Cut 299 cords, 8 times the finished length of skirt required (or sufficient cords in a multiple of 3 plus 8 to fit size of waistband made). Set these directly on to lower edge of waistband—you will probably find the easiest way to set these cords on is to thread each individual cord on to a large-eyed darning needle and 'sew' it through waistband edge. This gives a total of 598 working ends.

Pattern is worked in the alternate flat knot pattern, with 6 cords to each knot (double knotting cords, 2 central knotbearing core cords). The first 16 cords at back waist opening edge however are used to work close horizontal cording to give an underlap for waist fastening. Begin knotting from this edge, using cord on far left as leader and working horizontal cording across next 15 cords, then proceed in 6-cord flat knots to end of row. Work 2nd row from right to left, working in alternate flat knot sequence and working 6-cord flat knots to last 15 cords. Now use cord on far left of last 6-cord flat knot worked as leader and work horizontal cording across last 15 cords. Continue in this way until underlap of horizontal cording is 4 in.

Now overlap front waist opening edge over back waist opening edge to 6 cords beyond the cording strip. Working in the round, and maintaining alternate sequence of flat knots, tie 6-cord flat knots right round, working with double cords where front edge overlaps back .

Back opening edge cords are now no longer used for knotting—if they are in the way then double them up and pin out of the way of knotting in progress. Continue in alternate pattern of 6-cord flat knots for another inch.

Now continue in alternate pattern of 4-cord flat knots, but gradually shape skirt over working base by increasing distance between knots and rows. As skirt gets longer, increase distance between knots and rows considerably (see skirt in our illustration).

When skirt is about 6 in. from final length required, work 4 rows of alternate 4-cord flat knots, keeping knots and rows fairly close together.

## TO COMPLETE

Trim cord ends to give a fringe of about 5 in., or length required.

Sew on buttons to back waistband to correspond with button loops. Trim cord ends at end of back waist opening underlap to about 2 in. Press to back of work, and secure with a few neat stitches, or else weave each cord end through back of cording rows.

# TAPESTRY NEEDLE-WORK

## Lesson One: Tent stitch

## Threads

The traditional threads to use for tapestry needlework are silk, wool and linen. It is possible however in a modern embroidery to use all manner of novelty, special-effect and other yarns: so long as the thread has hard-wearing qualities and is able to give good coverage to the canvas, then it is suitable for tapestry embroidery. The important rule to bear in mind is that the thread should never be finer than the woven threads of the canvas you are using, otherwise the canvas background will show through your stitches. Tapestry wool and crewel wool are both good-quality threads produced specifically for tapestry work. Stranded and pearl embroidery cottons can also be used successfully. The embroidery cottons and crewel wool may be used in single or multiple strands as required, to give adequate coverage to the canvas. Tapestry wool is only used in single strand. The Coats range of Anchor Tapisserie wool includes 200 attractive, fast-dyed shades. These are available in 15-yard skeins, and a certain number of selected shades are also available in 1-oz. (90-yard) hanks: these are useful when a large quantity of wool is required—for a background, for example. Sufficient grounding wool, as these threads are called, for a particular design should be purchased at the same time, as any slight change in the dye lots might be noticeable in the finished work.

## Canvas

The canvas is the ground on which you work your tapestry embroidery stitches. Although in the finished design no canvas will—or should—be visible, it is essential in order to give your design a long life, that a good-quality, hardwearing canvas is chosen. Basically there are two main types of canvas: single thread and double thread. In the double thread canvases, the warp and weft threads are arranged in pairs. The single thread canvases,

as a rule, are easier to work with, but if you wish to work tramming stitches (see right), then double thread canvas must be used.
Both types of canvas are graded according to mesh size. This is the degree by which the warp and weft threads are spaced out. A wide mesh will give fewer warp and weft threads to the inch; a fine mesh will give considerably more. In single canvas, the mesh size is referred to by the number of threads to the inch; in double canvas it is referred to by the number of holes to the inch. Mesh sizes range from 10 to about 32 threads or holes to the inch. There are also rug canvases available with only 3, 4 or 5 holes to the inch. These are excellent for working with thick wools, for quick bold designs.

## Frames

Tapestry embroidery stitches can be very roughly divided into straight stitches (i.e. those which follow the warp and weft lines of the canvas) and diagonal stitches (those which are worked across the canvas threads). If you intend to work only in straight stitches, then it is not necessary to mount your work on a frame, although many people find a frame does give greater comfort and flexibility. But if you eliminate all the diagonal stitches from your work, your designs almost inevitably will lack a certain amount of interest and variety. In fact all the traditional stitches of tapestry embroidery—tent, for example, cross and gobelin—are diagonal stitches. Unless your canvas is securely mounted in a frame, the strain of these stitches will gradually pull your canvas out of shape, and distort your design. For this reason it is essential a frame is used. Never use a circular embroidery frame for canvas work: only a rectangular slate frame. There are three basic types of frame to choose from, depending on the size and type of designs you intend to work on: a leader frame which is a simple rectangular frame and has to be supported against a table or other suitable surface; a table frame which has its own adjustable support and can be placed on any table top; and a floor frame which is a free-standing, fully-adjustable frame similar in principle to an artist's easel.

## Preparing your canvas

Your canvas should be cut to 3 in. larger than the embroidery you intend to work. It is important that canvas is mounted on your frame the correct way up—i.e. with selvedges at the sides.
Before mounting your canvas, or 'framing-up' as the process is known, measure the centre points both

horizontally and vertically of your canvas. Mark these points with lines of basting stitches running right across the canvas. Ordinary sewing cotton can be used for this basting. Now fold back $\frac{1}{2}$-in. turnings along top and bottom edges of canvas; baste to hold in place. Use tape, 1 in. wide, to bind these edges, and also the side edges of the canvas. Your canvas is now ready to frame-up.
For detailed instructions on framing-up, see Appliqué, lesson two.

## The stitches

### TRAMMING

This is an important tapestry embroidery technique which helps to give a rich appearance to your finished work, and also to increase the hardwearing qualities of the design. Tramming is really a sort of ground work: long stitches are laid across the canvas, before your begin the embroidery stitches. When the ground is completely covered with tramming, then the embroidery is worked over it thus giving a double covering of thread to the canvas. Tramming should be worked in the same colour and type of thread as the finished design.
To work **split trammed stitch**, which is the tramming stitch most suitable for covering large areas of canvas fairly quickly, bring the needle through from back to front of canvas at the point where a pair of vertical threads of your canvas cross a pair of horizontal threads. Work from left to right. Carry the thread along horizontally for a distance not greater than 5 in. then pass needle through the canvas at a similar crossing of threads (A).
Bring the needle back through one vertical thread of the canvas to the left on the same line, through the stitch just made, thus forming a split stitch. Continue in this way to cover entire area where tramming is required.

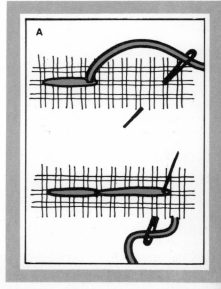

*Traditional tapestry cushion, chart and stitch details after lesson*

## Tent stitch

This stitch is sometimes known as petit point. It is worked without tramming and may either be worked on single canvas, or if worked on double thread canvas, then the threads of the canvas should be opened up so the stitches are worked over separate, single threads.

Bring needle out on the left-hand side of the area to be covered, and on the top part of the first stitch. Work from left to right. Pass needle diagonally down over one horizontal thread of the canvas, and one vertical thread to the left. Bring needle back out two vertical threads to the right and one horizontal thread up (B). Continue in this way.

When the first row is completed, work the second row from right to left. This time, in order to maintain same slant of stitch, the needle passes the crossed thread up and over and then under two vertical threads.

## TRAMMED TENT STITCH

This stitch is sometimes known as gros point. It is simply tent stitch worked over a tramming base. Tramming and tent stitch can be worked concurrently in the following way: work a trammed stitch from left to right, then pull the needle through and insert again up and over the crossed threads. Pull the needle through on the lower line two double threads to the left in readiness for the next stitch. Work tent stitch over the trammed stitch from right to left. When the stitch is covered bring needle out between a crossing of canvas threads on the line below, and repeat sequence working trammed stitch first from left to right, then tent stitch over it from right to left.

## YOUR FIRST MAKE

# TRADITIONAL CUSHION

## MATERIALS YOU WILL NEED

Of Coats Anchor Tapisserie Wool—21 skeins Petrol Blue 0850, 1 skein each Carnation 023, Magenta 065, Cyclamen 085 and 089, Violet 096 and 099, Lilac 0105 and 0107, Jade 0185 and 0187, Forest Green 0215 and 0217, Moss Green 0268, Muscat Green 0280 and 0281, Canary Yellow 0288, Amber Gold 0306, 0308, 0309, Tangerine 0314, Terra Cotta 0336, 0337, 0339 and 0340, Sage Green 0842 and 0843, Pink 0894 and 0895; ½ yd. double thread tapestry canvas, with 10 holes to 1 in., 19 in. wide; ½ yd. velvet or other suitable mediumweight fabric, 36 in. wide, to

match Petrol Blue background of embroidery; a Milward 'Gold Seal' tapestry needle No. 19; cushion pad approximately 16 in. square.

## MEASUREMENTS

Finished embroidery measures 16 in. square.

## DIAGRAM

The large diagram opposite give the complete centre flower motif Each background square on the diagram represents the double threads of the canvas.

## TO MAKE

Prepare canvas and frame-up, as described previously. Commence embroidery centrally, and work embroidery, following the diagram opposite and the guide to thread colours beside it. The blank arrows on the diagram mark the centre and should

coincide with your basting stitches. The main flower heads on the diagram have been outlined in order to make the design more clear. The embroidery is worked throughout in trammed tent stitch.

Continue background on all sides of the central flower motif until work measures 16 in. (Note. As you have only ½ yd. of canvas, 19 in. wide, you will not in this instance be able to have the usual minimum of 3 in. unworked canvas around the design.)

## TO COMPLETE

Trim canvas to within 1 in. of embroidery on side edges. Cut a square measuring 18 in. from backing fabric. Place embroidery and backing fabric together, right sides facing, and stitch close to the embroidery round three sides. Trim seams and turn cover to right side. Insert cushion pad, turn in seam allowance on remaining open edge, and slipstitch neatly together

### Colour key

| | | |
|---|---|---|
| CARNATION | FOREST GREEN (LIGHT) | TERRA COTTA (PALE) |
| MAGENTA | FOREST GREEN (DARK) | TERRA COTTA (LIGHT) |
| CYCLAMEN (LIGHT) | MOSS GREEN | TERRA COTTA (MEDIUM) |
| CYCLAMEN (DARK) | MUSCAT GREEN (LIGHT) | TERRA COTTA (DARK) |
| VIOLET (LIGHT) | MUSCAT GREEN (DARK) | SAGE GREEN (LIGHT) |
| VIOLET (DARK) | CANARY YELLOW | SAGE GREEN (DARK) |
| LILAC (LIGHT) | AMBER GOLD (LIGHT) | PETROL BLUE |
| LILAC (DARK) | AMBER GOLD (MEDIUM) | PINK (PALE) |
| JADE (LIGHT) | AMBER GOLD (DARK) | PINK (DARK) |
| JADE (DARK) | TANGERINE | |

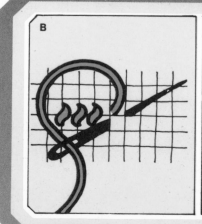

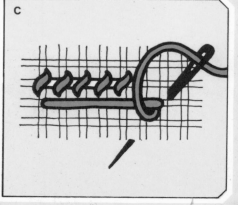

# TAPESTRY NEEDLE-WORK

## Lesson Two:
## Stretching your canvas

Unless only straight stitches are used in a design (i.e. those which follow the warp and weft lines of the canvas) even if your work is mounted in a frame, when a tapestry embroidery

*Satin stitch kneeler*

is complete it is advisable to stretch the canvas. This will help to restore the straight lines of the canvas, if the diagonal stitches have pulled it slightly out of true, and stretching will also help to give your finished design a professional look.

Stretching should be done after the embroidery is complete, but before trimming canvas prior to making it up into its finished form—handbag, picture, stool top, kneeler or whatever you have chosen to make.

## What you will need

A large wooden board; several sheets of blotting paper; small nails or drawing pins; a small sponge.

## Stretching canvas, step by step

1. Dampen the blotting paper and spread the sheets over the wooden board.
2. If the canvas is badly pulled out of shape, then dab over the back of it with a sponge soaked in cold water. Continue until the back of the canvas is evenly dampened.
3. Place canvas right side up on top of the damp blotting paper.
4. Now, beginning with top edge, make sure the edge is parallel with top edge of wooden board, then pin it at 1-in. intervals to the board. Do not pin the worked embroidery: only the outer border of unworked canvas.
5. When the top edge is pinned, pull opposite edge taut and pin along it. Make sure the grain of the canvas is absolutely straight before you insert the pins.
6. When top and bottom edges are securely pinned, then pin the two side edges in a similar way.
7. Leave canvas to dry completely. This may take several weeks with a heavy piece of work.
8. When you are satisfied canvas is dry, remove pins, and check to see if the stretching has restored canvas to its true shape. If it still seems to be distorted, however slightly, it is best to repeat the stretching process.

# Satin stitch on canvas

When a tapestry design uses satin stitch, it is usual to work these in blocks to form an allover pattern. If you are using single-thread canvas, then each block of satin stitches consists of 4 separate upright satin stitches, each worked over 4 horizontal threads of the canvas (A).
If you are using double-thread canvas, then each block will consist of 3 double satin stitches each worked over 3 double threads of the canvas (B).
The blocks of stitches are worked side by side to form horizontal lines of stitchery across the entire canvas (C).

# Hints on making kneelers

Normally a pattern chart for a kneeler design will give the complete design for the top of the kneeler, plus one long side and one short side. You must remember to add on the other two

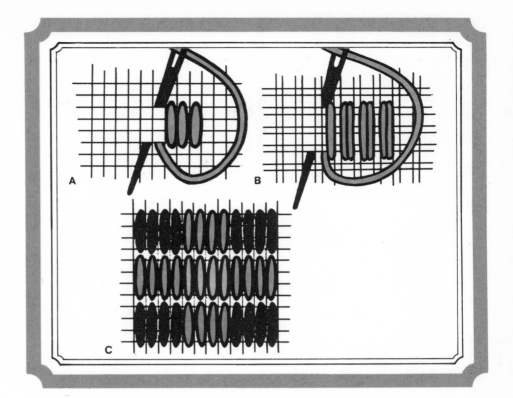

*Tent stitch kneeler*

sides to correspond with the sections given.

As a kneeler will have to withstand long and constant wear, it is important that a good-quality canvas and good strong yarn are used.

When preparing your canvas, as well as marking centres with basting stitches as usual, it is a good idea to mark out with further lines of basting total area embroidery will cover, indicating the centre (top) area of kneeler, and the four sides. The diagram, right, shows the shape you will embroider.

The pad you use for your kneeler should be very firm and solid—a dense rubber makes a good pad. It is important that the embroidered canvas fits tightly over the pad. If necessary stuff cotton wool or cushion stuffing into the corners to ensure a really good tight fit in all parts.

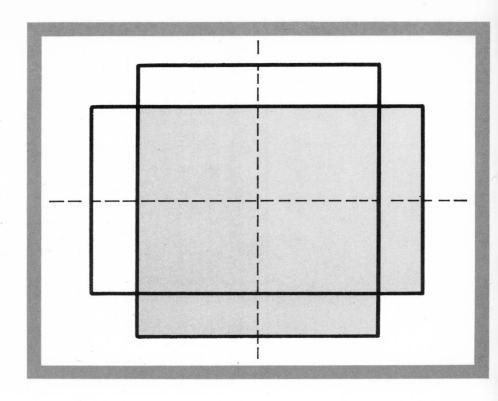

## TWO KNEELERS TO MAKE

# TENT STITCH KNEELER

## MATERIALS YOU WILL NEED

Of Coats Anchor Tapisserie Wool—16 skeins Dark Red 019, 8 skeins Bright Red 0335, 3 skeins each Mid Blue 0160, Light Grey 0397 and White 0402, 2 skeins Dark Blue 0148, 1 skein each Mid Moss Green 0268, Muscat Green 0280, Yellow 0306, Dark Grey 0399 and Black 0403. ¾ yd. double-thread tapestry canvas, 10 holes to 1 in.,

27 in. wide. Milward 'Gold Seal' tapestry needle No. 19. Pad approximately 11½ in. by 15 in. by 3 in. Piece of furnishing velvet or tailor's linen to match background of embroidery, 13 in. by 17 in., for base.

## MEASUREMENTS

Finished kneeler measures approximately 11½ in. by 15 in. by 3 in.

## DIAGRAM

The large diagram chart overleaf gives the complete pattern for the top of the

kneeler, one long side and one short. side. Each background square on the diagram represents the double threads of the canvas.

## TO MAKE

Prepare canvas and frame-up, as described in lesson one. The embroidery is worked throughout in trammed tent stitch (see also lesson one). Commence embroidery centrally at crossed basting stitches, and work embroidery, following the diagram overleaf and the guide to thread colours. The blank arrows on the

*Close up of tent stitch design*

*Close up of satin stitch design*

diagram mark the centre and should coincide with your basting stitches. Work the top and side sections as given in the diagram, then work each side section once more in required position.

## TO COMPLETE

Stretch canvas, as described in lesson. Trim unworked canvas to within ¾ in. of stitching, including the corner areas. Oversew to prevent fraying. With right sides facing, stitch corners close to the embroidery.
Turn embroidery right side out and fit over kneeler pad, stuffing corners if necessary to give a good tight fit (see hints on previous page).
Fold unworked borders of canvas to base of pad, and lace top and bottom edges together, and side edges together (see lacing instructions in Picture Framing, lesson one).
Turn in seam allowance on the fabric base to fit kneeler and stitch neatly in place, wrong sides together.

# SATIN STITCH KNEELER

*Illustrated at start of lesson*

## MATERIALS YOU WILL NEED

Of Clark's Anchor Tapisserie Wool—19 skeins Smoke 0985, 2 skeins each Geranium 013, Buttercup 0298, Tangerine 0314, and White 0402,

## COLOUR KEY

| | | | |
|---|---|---|---|
| ⊙ DARK RED | ⊡ MID BLUE | ⊞ YELLOW | ⊠ DARK GREY |
| | ▲ MID MOSS GREEN | ◉ BRIGHT RED | ☐ WHITE |
| ◣ DARK BLUE | △ MUSCAT GREEN | ◺ LIGHT GREY | ◼ BLACK |

1 skein each Carmine Rose 045, Cyclamen 089, Peacock Blue 0170, Jade 0187, Canary Yellow 0290, Amber Gold 0305, Violet 0417, and Pink 0892. ¾ yd. single-thread tapestry canvas, 18 threads to 1 in., 27 in. wide. Pad approximately 15 in. by 12 in. by 3¾ in. Piece of furnishing velvet or tailor's linen to match background of embroidery, 18 in. by 15 in., for base. Milward 'Gold Seal' tapestry needle No. 18.

## MEASUREMENTS

Finished kneeler measures approximately 15 in. by 12 in. by 3¾ in.

## DIAGRAM

The large diagram chart below gives the complete pattern for the top of the kneeler, one long side and one short side. Each background square on the diagram represents one block of 4 satin stitches worked over 4 threads of the canvas.

## TO MAKE

Prepare canvas, as described in lesson one. As only straight stitches are used in this design, it is not necessary to mount work in a frame, although you may find working more comfortable if you do use a frame.

The embroidery is worked throughout in blocks of satin stitches (4 satin stitches to each block, worked over 4 threads of the canvas).

Commence embroidery centrally, following the diagram below and the guide to thread colours. The black arrows on the diagram mark the centre and should coincide with your basting stitches. Work the top and side sections as given on the diagram, then work each side section once more in required position.

## TO COMPLETE

Trim unworked canvas to within ¾ in. of stitching and make up kneeler as described for tent stitch kneeler.

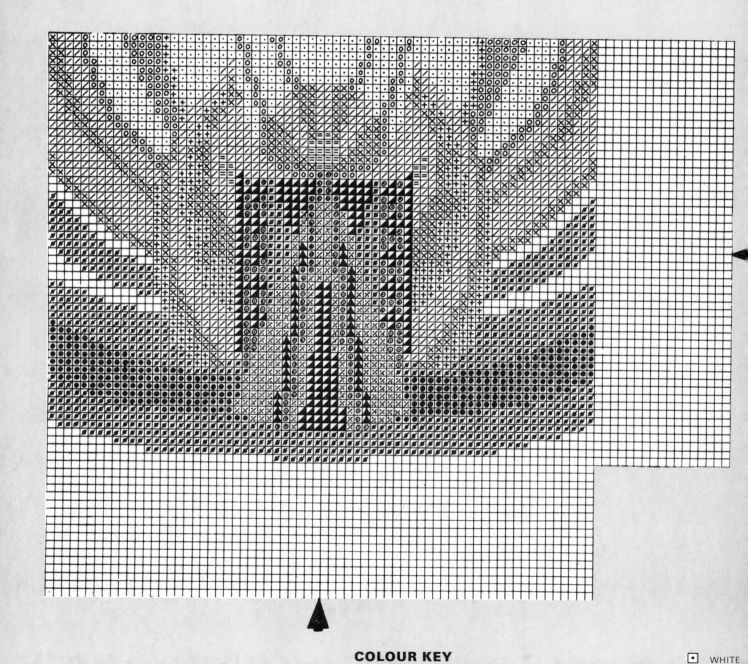

## COLOUR KEY

| ◩ GERANIUM | ◪ PEACOCK BLUE | ◹ BUTTERCUP | ◙ WHITE |
| ◉ CARMINE ROSE | ◣ JADE | ◎ AMBER GOLD | ◤ VIOLET |
| ◉ CYCLAMEN | ✚ CANARY YELLOW | ☒ TANGERINE | ▣ PINK |
| | | | ▢ SMOKE |

# RUG-MAKING

## Lesson One: Hooked rugs

**How to hook a rug and two contrasting designs for you to make.**

It is quite easy to 'get hooked' on rug-making particularly if you use the cut wool and latch hook method! The work grows quickly, the end product is a thick luxurious pile rug which will last a long time, and the cost will be very much less than for a bought rug of similar quality. Another advantage with this type of rug-making — two people can work on the same rug at the same time, starting at opposite ends of the canvas. As men have been known to find this craft soothing, your husband or boyfriend might agree to help, and it won't matter if you change ends—the finished rug will look as though it has been made by one person, unlike knitting, crochet and allied crafts where it often shows if another person helps with the work. Much the simplest method of making a hooked rug is to buy a kit, which already has the design printed on the canvas, and the correct amounts of wool (already cut) in each colour, are included, as well as full instructions and a rug hook. If, however, you prefer, you can buy plain rug canvas, use a charted design and make up the rug in your own colours (which you can do with our rugs if you prefer, following the charts overleaf), or if you are really creative you can buy canvas and wool and make up a design of your own! This can be fun if you want a striped or abstract design or something simple like a chequerboard effect, but if you have never made a rug before it is better to start with the kit or chart method.

## Materials and tools

### CANVAS

All hooked rugs are made on rug canvas, and there are various widths available from 12in. to 48in. The canvas is whitish and of the best quality cotton, with a selvedge down both sides (buy the very best canvas) and usually has nine holes to the square inch, with coloured lines (blue, red or brown) dividing up the canvas into squares, to make it easier to count out the holes when making a pattern.

Kit canvasses do not need these markings, because the design is printed directly on to the canvas and counting out the holes is unnecessary which is why this is the best method for beginners.

You need to buy a little extra canvas than required for the finished rug, because it is usual to turn over the canvas at both ends and work double for the first 5—6 rows, so allow an extra 6 to 9in. (kits allow for this turn over). Circular, semi-circular and oval rugs are usually worked on square or rectangular canvas and cut to shape after the rug is hooked.

### WOOL

The correct wool to use for hooked rugs is a coarse 6-ply rug wool. This is available ready-cut and done up in neat little round bundles or in skeins which can be cut to the required length by winding round a grooved wooden gauge and cutting with a sharp knife, razor blade in a holder, or scissors, or by using a patent device.

### TOOLS

A rug hook or latch hook (diagram A) is the only tool you will need if you are using ready-cut wool. Kit manufacturers supply one hook with each rug-making pack, but it is wise to have a second hook in case you can persuade somebody to help with the other end of the rug! These are easily obtainable from local handicraft shops. If you are buying skeins of wool and cutting your own, then you will need the wooden gauge already mentioned and a sharp knife, razor blade in a holder, or good pair of scissors (diagram B) or you could use the automatic cutter (diagram C). These are available from shops selling rug wool and canvas. You will also need a rug needle or crochet hook to finish the edges.

## Starting the rug

Lay the canvas on a table or other flat surface with the printed side up (if you are using a kit) and with the full length stretching away from you. As canvas is usually rolled up to bring it home, the purpose of the exercise is to flatten as much of it as possible to make working easier, so secure it with a heavy weight (pile of books) at intervals. Now, to prevent the cut ends from fraying, fold the end of the canvas over like a hem, right-sides together, for about 2in. or for the marked amount on the rug kit (diagram D) exactly matching each hole with the hole beneath. Crease the canvas sharply along the edge. It helps to tack the double thickness in position, or even to machine it. This 'hemmed' edge is worked double thickness.

Leave the outside edge of the canvas free and one square at either side next to the selvedge so they can be oversewn at the end. Start working the rug from left to right (or *vice versa* if you are left handed) and knot each square in the canvas. Keep working in parallel rows, don't be tempted to do patches of the pattern and then join them up, as this could give an uneven finish and it would be easy to miss a square here and there.

*Note:* If two persons are working on a rug at the same time from opposite ends of the canvas, crease and tack or machine both ends before starting. One person should use rug knotting method 1 and the other method 2 so the pile lays in the same direction, and both working to the same tension.

## Knotting or hooking the rug

There are two methods of making the knots in a hooked rug—the four-movement method (diagram E) and the five-movement method (diagram F). The first method is quicker, but the difference in methods effects the direction of the pile, which is why it is essential to use only one method if you are starting at one end of the canvas and working straight through to the other end, or to use the two methods if two people are working from opposite ends.

**For method 1,** or the four-movement method—

E1. Fold a cut length of wool in half, and hold it between the thumb and index finger of the left hand, loop round the neck of the latch hook, below the latchet.

E2. Still holding on to the ends of the wool, push the hook down through one square of the canvas and up through the one immediately in front.

E3. Put the two ends of the wool into the eye of the hook, turning the hook a little if necessary, and pull the hook back through the loop, giving it a flick upwards as you do so.

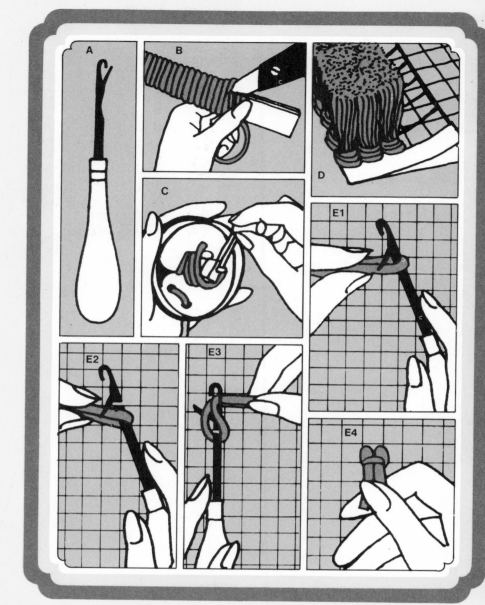

E4. Pull lightly on the two ends of the wool to tighten the knot.

**For method 2,** or the five-movement method—

F1. Push the latch hook under a double thread of canvas, until the latchet is through the canvas then catch the loop of a folded piece of wool in the hook.

F2. Pull the hook until the loop of wool comes under the canvas threads, holding on to the ends with thumb and index finger.

F3. Push the hook and latchet back through the loop of wool and catch the hook round both ends of the wool held in the fingers.

F4. Pull the hook back, bringing the wool ends through the loop.

F5. Pull lightly on the two ends of the wool to tighten the knot.

If you are working with a rug kit, or a ready-stencilled pattern and cut wool, this is all you need to know, so you can get knotting right away. When you start, work through the double thickness of the 'hem' and when you finish (if the rug is not being worked from both ends), stop about 10—12 rows from the end, crease sharply as for starting,

and tack or stitch down and knot your wool through the double thickness of canvas (see diagram G).

## Working from a chart

If you are designing your own rug, unless it is very very simple as previously suggested, you will need to make and work from a chart, or you can buy a chart or use one of ours. Each square on a chart represents a square on the canvas, and much the easiest method is to mark the design on your canvas with felt pen. If the design is multicoloured, then try to use a different felt pen for each colour, preferably in the same colour as the wool. Fold the hem over first, then count the number of squares on the chart and mark them correspondingly on the canvas. Once you have transferred the complete design, you are ready to begin. Remember to work from selvedge to selvedge, completing one row at a time, and hooking each square, changing the wool colour as

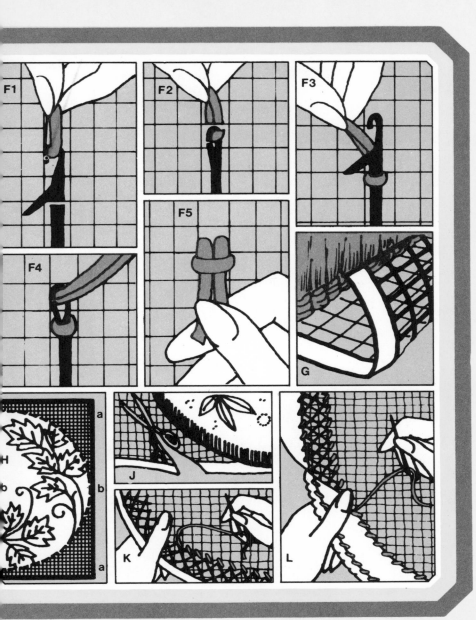

not right the way across the canvas, and if you are working from a chart or your own design, mark the edge of the circle, semi-circle or oval very clearly on the canvas before starting.

When you have knotted all the wool into the canvas, cut all round the canvas about 1½-2 in. from the edge of the design. *Do not* do this before the design is complete or the canvas will fray and the design go out of shape or, worse still, you will be unable to complete the rug because the holes towards the edge will disappear as the canvas frays. Fold the spare canvas underneath the rug and stitch down securely using one stitch to each square of canvas (diagrams J and K). Sew on binding tape, so it covers the stitched-down edge of the canvas, using two rows of stitching, one stitch to each square of canvas, ⅛ in. from each edge of the binding tape as shown (diagram L). Binding tape for rugs can be bought with the canvas and rug wool, but it is provided with kits where the design needs finishing in this way.

## Finishing touches

When the rug is completed, give it a good shake, then lightly brush the pile in one direction only to remove loose fibres. Now trim the pile lightly with a pair of sharp scissors. The 'hems' of the rug at either end should be nice and firm if you have followed our directions, but the selvedge edge is vastly improved if it is properly finished and strengthened. To finish the edges you will need skeins of rug wool to match the design—if possible work in one colour only—purple or brown for our two rugs for example.

### Backing

Many people like to back their home-made rugs. Not only does this preserve the fabric of the rug and help to prolong its life, it also helps keep it clean. Hessian is frequently used. This is cut slightly larger than the rug, and the raw edges turned in, then slipstitched to the back of the rug. Extra stitching can be made across the back of the rug for extra firmness, like large tacking stitches, but care must be taken to make sure they do not come through to the front of the rug and catch any of the tufts and pull them through to the back.

It is also possible to buy special non-slip backings, which can be sewn or stuck on—some are already adhesive, with a peel-off surface which is fixed to the back of the rug. This material can be purchased at handicraft shops and rug-making specialist shops.

### YOUR FIRST MAKES
**One in a traditional Paisley design in purple and turquoise. One in modern style in autumnal colours.**
Both these rugs can be bought in kit form. In each kit there is a printed rug

necessary. You must *not* fill in bits of the pattern or work all one colour first. If you have designed your own rug, by sketching it and painting in the colours, then the transferring of the design to the canvas is a little harder than working from a chart. Use squared paper to scale the design in inches, then transfer the design to graph paper so you can work out the knots per inch (3×3 holes so 9 squares), then transfer to the canvas and work as above.

## Quantities

With a kit, enough wool, rug canvas etc. are provided, and if you buy a chart instructions are given for quantities of wool needed, but if you are designing your own, remember a rug 72in. long by 36in. wide takes about 12¼ lb. of wool on coarse open rug canvas. A rug 54in. long by 27in. wide takes about 7 lb. You can see from this, a rug gets rather heavy with so much wool in it, so it is better to work on a flat surface pulling the work towards you as each row is finished, and supporting the worked end on your lap. When it gets too heavy, you can support the weight

on a chair or stool, or turn the work round and work the second half from the other end, using method 2 so all the pile lies in the same direction.

## Circular, semi-circular and oval rugs

If working from a kit or printed canvas, lay out the canvas on a table with selvedges (b) to left and right as in diagram H, and place weights (books) on the middle. Start with the short row nearest to you (a) and knot one piece of wool into each square in the design using either of the knotting methods previously described. You must work from one selvedge towards the other, so you start with a short row and few knots until you reach the centre of the rug where you will probably be working full width of the canvas. Again complete each row before starting the next, knotting every square in the design, and do not be tempted to work in patches, or by colour. Naturally you only work to the edge of the design and canvas, so you can follow the design quite easily; a rug hook; enough bundles of pre-cut rug wool to complete the design, and full instructions. All you have to do is fill in the coupon, and while you are waiting for your kit to arrive, read our first lesson on rug-making so you are ready to get hooking the minute the materials arrive! However, if you want to make the rugs yourself, following our chart and using plain rug canvas, you can do so.

## The Paisley Rug

### MATERIALS YOU WILL NEED FOR A RUG 27in. × 54in.

Piece of rug canvas 27 in. wide (this is standard width and allows for the selvedge) by 58 in. long (this allows a 2 in. turn over each end); 4½ lb. 6-ply rug wool for the background, or 36 packs of pre-cut wool; 3 lb. 6-ply rug wool for the design, or 23½ packs of pre-cut wool; wooden gauge and knife or scissors (if you are cutting your own

wool), or automatic cutter; latch hook; skein extra wool in background colour (for finishing the edges); crochet hook or rug needle.

### TO MAKE

If necessary, cut a good quantity of the wool in both colours as diagrams B and C, keeping the different colours in a separate box or bag. Fold the canvas each end to make the hem as described under 'Starting the Rug'. Work following the diagrams and instructions for 'Knotting or Hooking the Rug', working from left to right in parallel rows, knotting each square in the canvas and changing the wool colour when necessary. If you are working from the chart you should be able to plot each hole, but if you prefer you could use the chart to mark the design on the canvas in felt pen, which is easier to follow when you are working, but this method takes a little more time at preparation stage!
Continue hooking the rug, remembering to turn in the hem at the opposite end of the rug.

## The Modern Rug

### MATERIALS YOU WILL NEED FOR A RUG 27in. × 54in.

Piece of rug canvas 27 in. wide (this is standard width and allows for the selvedge) by 58 in. long (this allows a 2 in. turn over each end); 4 lb. 6-ply rug wool for the background, or 31 packs of pre-cut wool, 1½ lb. rug wool for dark stripe, or 12 packs of pre-cut wool; 1¼ lb. rug wool for light stripe, or 9½ packs of pre-cut wool; wooden gauge and knife or scissors (if you are cutting your own wool), or automatic cutter; latch hook; skein extra wool in background colour (for finishing the edges); crochet hook or rug needle.

### TO MAKE

Work following the chart, which can be transferred to the canvas with a felt pen if preferred, and follow the instructions and lesson given previously.

**SCALE: ONE SQUARE = ONE INCH**

# RUG-MAKING

## Lesson Two:
## Rugs from rags

**Margaret Seagroatt tells you how to utilize the contents of the rag bag to make woven and clip rugs. The clip technique can also be used to make cushions and our oval rug has two circular matching cushions.**

Rugs made from strips of material have been a feature of rural life in many countries for many years. The Scandinavians seem to have specialised in well-designed rugs from rags cut into long strips and woven on a loom and many examples of this craft can be seen in their homes today. Some of us may remember our grandmothers' 'clip' or 'peg' rugs, which were made, for reasons of economy, from short strips of fabric cut from used clothing. These rugs were usually rather dull in colour, presumably because they were made from the hardwearing woollen material cut from used trousers and overcoats in sober navy, greys, browns and black. Today such rugs, owing to the greater variety of tough materials available in many bight colours, can be very well designed and colourful.

## Materials

Before starting to design a rag rug, a large collection of materials should be accumulated. These may be either remnants of new fabric, left over from dressmaking, or old garments, bedspreads, curtains etc. If the material is worn, check to see it still has a reasonable amount of strength left by pulling the fabric taught between your hands. Weak fabric will quickly cause the rug to disintegrate, and it would be a pity to work in vain! Special care should be taken with old curtain material as this can be weakened by constant abrasion or by exposure to strong sunlight.
Next sort out the fabrics into types, separating the light cottons, rayons and synthetics from the heavier woollens and jersey fabrics. A second sorting into colours is then necessary as the designing of a rug depends on the

colours available (bearing in mind that the material *can* be dyed, particularly the lighter colours), and the finished weight required. For example our woven rug weighs only $\frac{3}{4}$ lb. while the heavier clip rug weighs 13 lb.

## Design

The design is limited to some extent by the fabrics available, but also by the method chosen. If you are making a woven rug the finished result is usually striped, although you can create a subtle effect by using different tones of one colour and starting with a pale tone and gradually working through to the deepest one. The rug we made is not a strictly symmetrical design of stripes. There is however, a colour scheme of related blues, ranging from dark navy through to turquoise and light blue, with an overall balance between the dark and light tones with occasional streaks of purple to enliven the dark stripes, and the pattern of the material gives a slight sparkle to the background colour. The strips are arranged in a haphazard manner so that both sides of the material show at random, and this again adds life to the design. If an exact symmetrical effect is required, the rags should be divided into equal quantities. Half the rug is then worked, and when the halfway mark is reached, the design is reversed, using the rest of the rags.
A clip rug gives much more scope for design, as strips of fabric are hooked into a canvas at random in varying directions, making the pile lie in a haphazard manner, accentuated by the difference in fabric texture. This allows the pile to cast interesting shadows which add to the effect. It is possible to make almost any type of design, but obviously simple bold shapes on a neutral or one-colour background look very effective and are more practical for a first attempt. You can work out a design in rough first, bearing in mind the position which the rug is to occupy in your home and the different fabrics which you have available. Such a design would then have to be transferred onto squared paper such as dressmaker's $\frac{1}{4}$-inch squared paper, or graph paper, and the design could then be transferred

to the rug canvas, or the canvas worked following the pattern on the squared paper.
Our clip rug and matching cushions are good examples of rug designing; the flowers in pinks, reds and purple are hooked in circles, which makes the pile lie like petals. These are in cotton, rayon and nylon, the tufts being longer than those of the off-white background, and overlapping to give a three-dimensional effect. The flower centres are hooked in nine strands of 4-ply knitting wool, cut shorter than the rest, the knots being close together to make the pile stand up, and still knotted in decreasing circles. The flowers are of different and quite random sizes, and each flower head is different, although in related colours, so small quantities of material may be utilized. This combination of texture, design and colour gives the rug a spontaneity and charm far removed from the rather utilitarian considerations of simply using up old scraps of fabric to make a rug!

## Preparation

What happens next depends on the type of rug you want to make. If you have decided on a **woven rug**, then you will need to cut long strips of material about 1 inch wide, depending on the thickness of the fabric (cut thinner fabrics wider). The ends should be cut diagonally (see Fig. A) and it is preferable to seam them as indicated. If the rug is to be washed frequently it is best to seam the strips into manageable lengths, otherwise the ends can fray out slightly and the rug begins to look untidy— very short strips not seamed together can also unravel The fabric should be the same weight for this type of rug— cottons, rayons etc. can be used together or woollen and knitted fabrics, but not mixed together in the same rug. The lighter fabrics pack down better in a woven rug as they have less resilience.
If the rags are to be used for a **clip rug** they should be cut into 6-inch to 8-inch strips approximately 1 inch wide. Keep the various colours and weights separate—a shoe box is an ideal place to store the cut pieces of fabric.

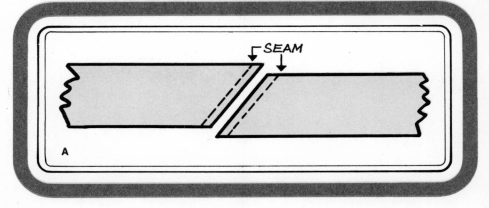

A

# To make a woven rug

The rug illustrated on p. 197, which measures 18×27 inches, is woven on a simple frame and does not require any more skill than darning. Many primitive people make the most beautiful and intricate materials on a similar frame. You may improvise your frame from an old iron bedstead, picture frame or you may construct your own. Rug frames may also be purchased.

To make the frame (Fig. B) for the rug illustrated (see last page of lesson) you will need the following materials: 2 pieces of 2-in. by 1-in. batten, 27 in. long; 2 pieces of 2-in. by 1-in. batten, 42 in. long; 2 pieces of 1-in. lathe, 27 in. long; 1 piece of 2-in. lathe, 18 in. long with notches cut at ends (see Fig. B1); 12 screws.

The short lengths should be screwed to the long ones to make a rectangular frame, using three screws at each corner, the long sides resting *underneath* the short ones.

You will then need yarn for the warp, which is the yarn stretched over the frame to make the ground for the rug. This may be string or soft cotton yarn such as dish-cloth cotton. The yarn is secured at one end (Fig. B2) and is then wound in a figure of eight round the frame, spacing it out to four or five threads to every inch. The frame could be marked out in inches to facilitate this. The yarn should be wound at an even tension, not too tight, but not too loose either, or the rug strips will not beat down adequately The end of the warp should be secured when the winding is complete (Fig. B3).

One of the lathes should then be 'darned' over and under each alternate warp thread (Fig. B4). When turned on its edge this forms the first 'shed' or space for inserting the weft. A small amount of the warp yarn should be wound round a shuttle (Fig. B1) made from the 18-inch strip of wood. This is inserted into the first 'shed' below the 'shed stick' and drawn through with the yarn, tucking the end round the last warp thread and back into the same 'shed' (Fig. B5). The 'shed' stick is then pushed up to the far end of the frame, and the second stick 'darned' in (Fig. B6). The weft is then drawn through the second 'shed' (Fig. B7) and the stick is withdrawn. The first stick may then be brought down again to push the two rows of yarn against one another. Twelve or so rows should be woven in this way, using a heavy table fork to beat the rows down to form a heading of approximately ¾ inch, according to the thickness of the yarn. Cut off the extra yarn and tuck in the end as before. Figure B shows the position of the sticks after three rows have been woven, the second stick ready in position for row four to be woven. After this preparation, the rag strips can be woven in. These may be pushed through by hand, using the 'shed' sticks as before, or if joined together, wound round the shuttle. The strips are used exactly like the yarn, and beaten down heavily every few rows to lie closely against one another. The closer the rows are beaten, the stronger and heavier the rug will be. The illustrated rug was beaten down at about six rows to the inch and is fairly light in weight for its size. The closer the weft, the less the warp will show— in other words, the more you beat down the rags, the less the yarn or dish-cloth cotton will show! Care must be taken not to pull the weft (the rag strips) too tightly or the rug will be narrower at one end than the other. When the design is complete, weave another heading from the warp yarn, identical with the first one. The rug may then be cut from the frame, and finished off by knotting the warp threads in a fringe, using overhand knots (Fig. C), three or four threads at a time. Your rug is now complete and ready to use.

# To make a clip rug

This technique is totally different from the one used for woven rugs. The clippings form a pile springing from a background of rug canvas, and the only equipment needed being a prodding hook of special design (Fig. D), the rug canvas and the rags, cut as previously described. It is easiest to use a rug canvas which is slightly stiffened and the rug illustrated was made on a ¼-inch mesh canvas. The prodder is a pointed piece of metal with a groove running almost up to the point. Into the groove fits a curved piece of metal which is kept closed by a spring. When the spring is depressed, the other end opens, the strip of rag is inserted and held when the spring is released. Figure D shows this process at the half-way stage. Prodding hooks can be purchased at craft shops or from certain suppliers by mail order.

There are several ways of making the knots in the canvas with the rags, but the following is the easiest method for the longer type of pile. The tip of the prodder is pushed into one of the holes in the mesh and then up again through the next hole. The prodder is held by one of the strands in the mesh going over it (Fig. E). The spring is

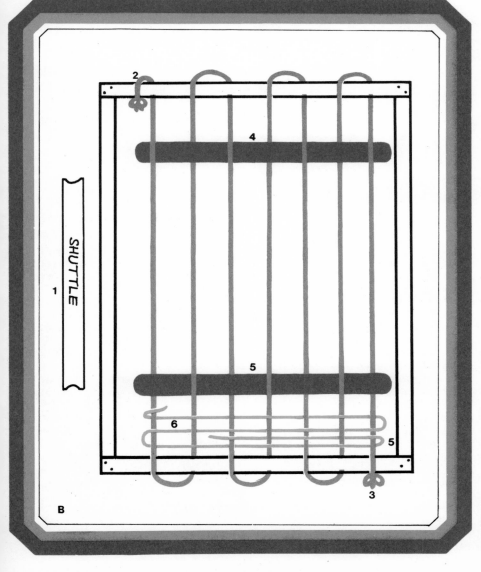

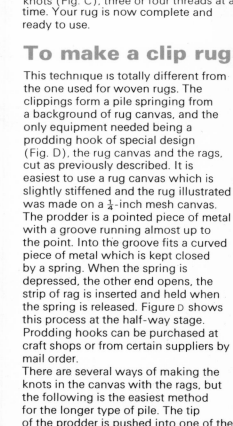

B

SHUTTLE

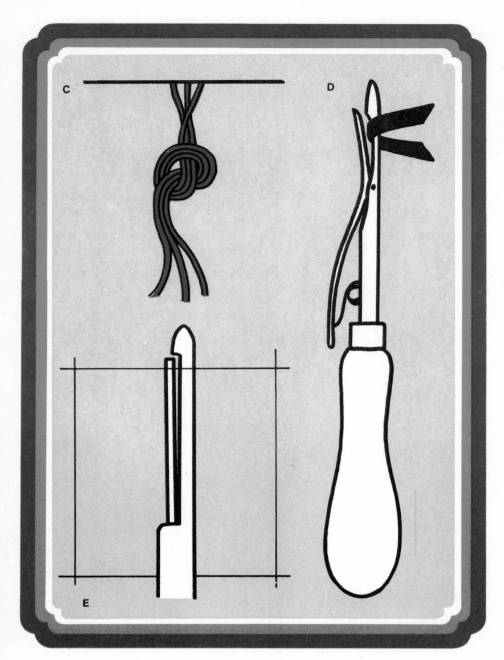

## YOUR SECOND MAKES

# A WOVEN RAG RUG

### MATERIALS YOU WILL NEED

$\frac{3}{4}$ lb.—1 lb. rags of a similar weight; 300 yards of yarn (string or soft dish-cloth cotton); frame and shuttle.

### TO MAKE

Divide the rags into colours and cut them into 1-in. wide strips or $1\frac{1}{2}$-in. wide strips if the fabric is very lightweight. Join where necessary to form manageable strips as previously described (Fig. A). Using the yarn prepare the frame with the warp (Fig. B) and weave the heading as explained previously. Weave the rag strips across the warp threads, going over and under exactly as if you were darning. Beat down the rag strips so 6 rows equals 1 in. Continue weaving until the rug is the required length. Weave another heading from the warp yarn, identical with the first one. Cut the rug from the frame and knot the warp threads into a fringe as previously mentioned (Fig. C).

# A COLOURFUL CLIP RUG

## For a girl's room

### MATERIALS YOU WILL NEED

2 yd. slightly stiffened rug canvas with $\frac{1}{4}$-in. mesh; crayon or pencil; about 13 lb. assorted rags, the majority in the background colour (see below); 3—4 hanks 4-ply knitting wool for flower centres; rug prodder (see section on making clip rugs); 2 yd. hessian or other backing materials; needle and thread.

### TO MAKE

Draw out an oval on the canvas with wax crayon or heavy pencil, leaving 2 in. all round to turn under. The oval should measure 60 in. at the longest and 32 in. at the widest part. If preferred the oval can first be drawn out on paper. Do this by drawing half on doubled paper and cutting the two thicknesses at once. Draw round plates, saucers or tin lids for the flower heads, allowing enough space between the shapes for the finished pile to spread without touching, e.g. about 2—3 in. apart.

then depressed, the loop of a doubled strip of rag inserted into the space. Releasing the spring, the loop is held and drawn through the mesh for about an inch, and then released from the prodder. The tip of the prodding hook is inserted into the loop and the cut ends gripped and drawn back through the loop to form a knot, which should be tightened with the hands. This may be done in any direction through the four sides of the square canvas mesh, or even at an angle through the corners. If no prodder is available, a stout hairpin or bent piece of wire could be used to pull the loop through, the ends then being pulled through the loop and tightened, but this of course, is a slower process.

When the rug is complete, the pile may be trimmed if necessary and the hem turned under and stitched to the underside of the rug, so that it does not show. A backing of hessian or other suitable strong non-slippery material should be cut to the same size as the rug, plus a 2-inch hem allowance. Turn the hem under, slipstitch to the rug all round the edge. Further stitching across the back helps hold the backing in place.

## Cleaning rag rugs

Rag rugs need cleaning once they are in constant use. The woven type may be washed in the ordinary way, and are flexible enough to be spun dry if they are not too large. Clip rugs should not be shaken violently or vacuum cleaned or the ends of the strips will fray. Sweeping with a clean broom will suffice for normal day-to-day cleaning, but this type of rug may also be washed by soaking in detergent for a few minutes and agitating until clean. Rinse well and hang in the open air to dry thoroughly. This should be done in hot sunny weather, as the rug is so heavy it will take some time to dry. The use of synthetic fabrics in this type of rug is practical if they are to be washed frequently as these

*A woven rag rug*

Cut the rags into strips 1-in. wide by 6—8 in. long. We used a mixture of wool and Crimplene rags in varying shades of white and off-white for the background and these were cut to the short length. The rags for the flowers were in tones of pinks, purples, plums, some plain, some patterned, in a mixture of cottons, rayons and nylons. These were cut to the longer length. The knitting wool was cut slightly shorter than the background rags, between 4—5 in.

Hook the rug using the prodder, as described in the section on making clip rugs, filling in the background first. The thickness of the rags dictate the distance between each knot,

but the knots should lie comfortably together without being crowded. When the material is thick it should not be necessary to knot each section in the mesh. Hook the strips at random in varying directions, making the pile lie in a haphazard manner. Knot the flowers in decreasing circles, and fill in the centre with the knitting wool— hook 9 strands at a time and as wool is much narrower than rags, each section in the mesh must be hooked. When the rug is completed, trim up any very uneaven pieces of rag, but part of the charm of this type of rug lies in the slight uneavenness of the pile, it should not look like a cropped lawn! Turn in the 2 in  hem.

Cut the backing hessian or other material 2 in. wider than the finished rug, turn in the hem and slipstitch the edge to the rug all round. Make some extra lines of stitches across the back to hold the backing securely in place. *Note:* cushions can be made in the same way based on a circle of canvas to look like a flower head. Hook in the same way as for the flowers on the rug with the centre of wool. Use a toning fabric for the backing to the cushion— one which is strong and attractive. Turn in a hem, and stitch very securely leaving an opening to insert a cushion pad, circle of foam or foam chippings. Stitch up opening or close with press studs or strip fastening.

# RUG-MAKING

## Edging stitches

There are two fairly basic edging stitches, either one would be perfectly suitable for most hooked rugs. One is the plaited stitch and the other is the crochet edging stitch. The first is worked with a needle and the second with a crochet hook.

### To work the plaited stitch method

**(Diagrams A1, A2 and A3; shown on double canvas.)**
Work from right to left, using a rug needle. Turn the selvedge over so you only sew over half the width, and with the right side of the work facing you:
1. Bring the needle through from the back of the canvas leaving about 3-in. of wool lying along the top edge of the work where it can be held in your left hand. This end of wool is covered by the stitches as you work along the canvas. Take the needle over the edge to the back of the canvas and bring it through again to the front, one hole to the left.
2. Take the needle over the edge of the work and back through the first hole.
3. Take the needle over the edge again and bring it through from the back to the front through the fourth hole along. Take it over the edge again as before and bring it back through the second hole to the right.
Continue working along the selvedge in this way, moving forward three holes and back two, passing the needle through from the back to the front of the canvas each time.
If you have not turned in a hem and the whole edge is to be worked this way, when you reach a corner, go back two holes, forward two, back one, forward

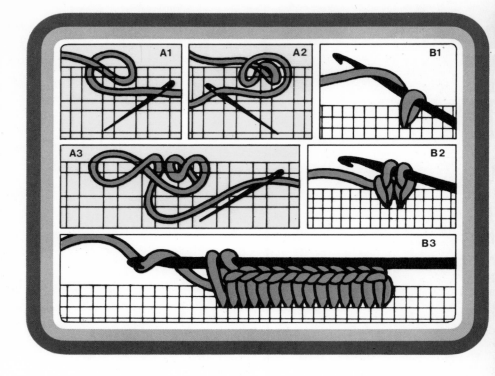

one and then continue again with step 1.

### To work the crochet edging stitch

**(Diagrams B1, B2 and B3; shown on single canvas.)**
Work from right to left and use a No. 5.00 (International Standard Size) crochet hook. Fold over the edge as for the plaited stitch method.
1. Push the crochet hook through the first hole and pull back a loop of wool leaving a piece hanging. (You can darn this into the back later.) With the loop still in the crochet hook, catch the wool from the back of the rug, over the top of the canvas and pull it through the loop.
2. Put the hook into the next hole and catch the wool from the back again and pull it through the hole. Then,

catching the wool from over the top, pull it through the two loops already on the hook.
3. Push the hook through the third hole and continue along the edge of the rug. To join the wool, always leave a long end free at the start and end of a length of wool, to darn in afterwards.
*Note:* Some experts prefer to work the edging stitches first—this is a matter of personal taste, but it does mean you will avoid having to unpick any of the work due to miscalculations! You can work either edging stitch all the way round the rug if you prefer, in which case the 'hem' of the cut ends can be edged like the selvedge, but to make doubly sure the end is firm, the first rows of tufts will still be knotted into double-thickness canvas. It is usual to turn the raw edges of pile rugs over on to the right side, as previously mentioned. With embroidered rugs the raw edges are turned over to the wrong side.

# FUN WITH FABRIC AND FELT

## Lesson One:

## Book markers and book cover

Book-markers are such fun to make and are ideal for small Christmas or birthday presents, or for a stall at a bazaar or fête. They can be as simple or as decorative as you like, and the easy ones can be made in minutes. There is no need to stitch the trimmings in place, you can use an all-purpose fabric adhesive (Copydex) for quick results. If you are making some of the other exciting things in this book, then you will probably have a few pieces of fabric or left-over trimmings already to hand, otherwise look out for bargains at the Sales or on the remnant counter. Ribbon, felt, leather and braid are the best materials to use for the base of the marker—because they don't fray, with trimmings of lace, ribbon, braid, or motifs cut from felt. All our book-markers are easy-to-copy and we hope you will enjoy using our techniques to make some original designs of your own. We have included an embroidered marker in cross-stitch for those who like more delicate work.

## To make our markers

*illustrated overleaf*

**From left to right . . .**

1. About 12 in. red ribbon is edged with narrow white *broderie anglaise*, stuck in place with fabric adhesive.
2. A variation on the same theme, but the centre of the marker is decorated with a 9-in. row of lace flowers and trimmed top and bottom with a motif cut from a piece of lace.
3. A 12-in. strip of dress fabric 3 in. wide is folded double lengthways, the ends cut on the slant, the raw edges turned in and stuck down with fabric adhesive.
4. A piece of blue felt, 9 in. long by 3 in. wide is trimmed to an attractive pointed shape top and bottom and decorated with lace motifs which echo the shape. These can be stuck in position with fabric adhesive or stitched very neatly, in which case back the marker with a contrasting coloured felt

to hide the stitches on the reverse side.
5. Cut a piece of felt 10½ in. long and 2½—3 in. wide with pinking shears. Trim the bottom to a point and fringe the top by making 5 cuts with the pinking shears down about ¾ in. from the top. Trim with braid, a gilt button and heart-shaped motifs in felt, stuck on with fabric adhesive.
6. A piece of chamois-leather is cut into an interesting shape, about 8½ in. long with pinking shears. The 'totem pole' design is made with felt-tipped pens.
7. A piece of plaited woollen braid, 1½—2 in. wide and about 12 in. long is fringed top and bottom and trimmed down the centre with narrow zig-zag braid, stuck on with fabric adhesive.
8. White evenweave linen marker is embroidered in cross-stitch in blue and black stranded embroidery cotton. Follow the chart (below), then fringe the ends. The edge is worked in satin stitch.

## To work cross stitch

Bring the needle through on the lower right line of the cross and insert at the top of the same line, taking a stitch through the fabric to lower left line (A1). Continue to the end of the row in this way. Complete the other half of the cross (A2). It is important that the upper half of each stitch lies in one direction. Stitches can be worked from left to right or right to left.

## To work satin stitch

Satin stitch can be used to fill in a shape, but when used for edging, as here, the stitches are worked in a straight line. Make straight stitches close together as shown. The number of threads over which the stitches are worked may vary. This stitch may be worked from left to right, or right to left (B).

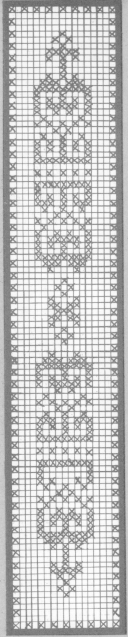

Without fringe this marker measures 7¾ in. Make each cross stitch over two threads in each direction. Border is straight satin stitch.

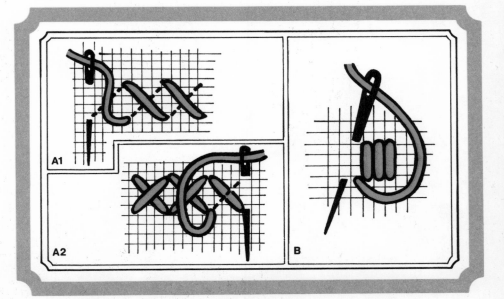

## To make our felt book cover

Precious books which are read over and over again, can sometimes become scuffed once they have lost their dust jacket. Here is a pretty and practical felt 'jacket' which can be made to fit any size book. If you like you can adapt the idea to cover telephone directories or the Radio and Television Times—just slip a cardboard stiffener into the pockets front and back.

### MATERIALS YOU WILL NEED

Brown paper (for pattern); enough felt to wrap right round the book and allow a good 3-in. tuck-in for front and back cover; contrasting felt for spectacle pocket and trim; matching or contrasting sewing thread; fabric adhesive (Copydex).

### TO MAKE

First measure the book to be covered and make a paper pattern. This should allow ½-in. turning top and bottom and a good 3-in. tuck-in on each side (more if the book is large). Remember the opening and closing of the book places strain on the spine of the book so the finished felt 'jacket' should not fit too tightly. If the book has a dust jacket this can be used to help make the pattern. Place pattern on the felt and cut out.

Turn in slightly less than the ½-in. turning top and bottom and machine or hand sew in matching or contrasting thread. Fit 'jacket' round book and turn in tuck-in and pin in position top and bottom to make sure the fit is not too tight and the book can be easily opened. Oversew top and bottom of front and back of tuck-in to front and back covers, forming pockets into which the front and back covers of the book will slip.

Measure spectacles and cut a suitable sized pocket for them. Stick or stitch in place on the front of the cover. Other trims can be added such as a flower motif cut out of felt and stuck or stitched in place. Alternative trimming could be the book owners initials, a butterfly, leaves, hearts, fruit etc., or something which ties in with the book title.

# FABRIC CRAFT

## Lesson One:

## Working with fabrics as a creative craft

**Valerie Janitch has some gay ideas to take advantage of the current fabric scene. All items in this feature are designed by her unless otherwise stated.**

Fabrics have never been more exciting. I find the only problem when working with fabric is to choose just one or two from the tempting array of interesting textures, subtle weaves, delicious colours and patterns!

## Design around your fabric

With most of the designs in this lesson, I have let the fabric take over—using it, not just as a piece of cloth to make the item, but exploiting the particular *quality* of the fabric in each case. First I chose a suitable fabric for the particular article which I had in mind (choosing by weight, texture, washability etc., rather than by colour and design), then I looked *at* it— really *at* it and *into* it for inspiration. Incidentally, by letting the fabric do much of the work, you have to do very little more to create a striking design! For example, the oven glove and mitts exploit a bold pattern, which I have picked out as colourful embroidery. The Cheshire Cat cushion was suggested by chintzy dress cotton which looked like those serene flower-painted china cats which gaze smugly out of the windows of antique shops. Some gaily coloured scraps of printed cotton and felt which I had hoarded from some other fabric work seemed just right for a collection of pin cushion mice.

## Basically simple

Most of these designs are not difficult to make, and they can be sewn by hand or machine. I have planned

them with children in mind, and even the young ones can make some of the simpler items—Mother can lend a helping hand with the slightly more difficult designs and with the cutting out!
You will find fabric craft great fun and the end results make ideal presents or items for bazaars and sales-of-work.

## Materials and equipment

All you will need, apart from the basic fabric and trimmings where necessary, are the things you use for home dressmaking and/or embroidery:— scissors, thimble, tape measure, needles, pins, sewing thread and in *some* cases, fabric adhesive. You will also need squared paper (or white paper, pencil and ruler to make your own grid) for making the pattern.

## Enhancing the fabric

When a fabric has a bold pattern of its own, it can look doubly effective if part of the design is picked out in embroidery, or by the addition of cord, braid, ric-rac, scraps of lace and other trimmings which can be bought by the yard at haberdashery counters. It is always worth hoarding remnants of fabric and trimmings, or picking them up cheaply at Sale time if you intend to do much fabric craft.
One of the easiest ways to enhance fabric is by using *couching*. Although this is one of the techniques used in embroidery, you don't have to be an expert embroideress to couch! *Couching* simply means laying a decorative thread, strand or cord on top of the fabric and then catching it into position every so often with tiny stitches in matching cotton. The distance between the stitches depends on the thickness of the strand you are couching—it is important that the intervals be evenly spaced—about

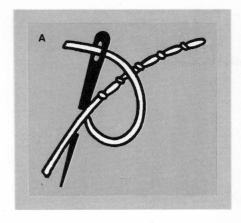

$\frac{1}{4}-\frac{1}{2}$ in. apart is a general average. (See diagram A). Unless the strand to be couched is too thick to take through the fabric, thread one end through a large tapestry needle and take it down through the fabric at the beginning of the line to be couched, securing the end on the wrong side. When you reach the end of the couching, finish off in the same way. Prevent the cut ends of thicker strands (ric-rac braid for example) from fraying with just a touch of fabric or PVA adhesive (Copydex or Sellobond).
The luncheon mats, which look so expensive, are a typical example of how effective this treatment can be—the Spring-leaf design is made entirely from couched textured wool, although it looks like the most professional hand embroidery—and it is much quicker to do!

## YOUR SECOND MAKES

## Spring-leaf luncheon mats

Hand-embroidered linen place mats are very expensive. Even if you make your own, the linen is costly and the embroidery time-consuming. These

mats cheerfully admit to being a quick cheat, but they are none the less attractive for that! A linen-textured dress fabric ('Topeka' by Moygashel) makes the mat, and you can get 6 out of a yard. Nubbly-textured wool is couched to make the fake embroidery. We used Patons' Four Seasons in Courtelle, but there are lots of suitable yarns—Twilley's Flexette for example, or you can make your mats an *all* fabric creation by couching threads drawn from a heavy woven tweed dress or furnishing fabric.

## MATERIALS YOU WILL NEED

1 yd. suitable linen-textured fabric (see above); matching sewing thread; sheet of squared paper or plain paper, pencil and ruler; tissue paper; nubbly-textured wool for couching (see above); matching thread.

## TO MAKE

Cut each mat 12 in. deep by 16 in. wide, following the thread of the fabric. Draw two or three threads $\frac{1}{2}$ in. away from each cut edge. Zig-zag stitch inner edge of fabric against drawn threads to prevent fraying and form hem-stitched edge of fringe. Rule a sheet of paper into inch squares (or use ready-squared paper) and draw leaf pattern following diagram (B). Then trace on to thin tissue paper — making one for each mat. Cut out round edge of leaf.
To work each mat, tack the tissue leaf into place at the left-hand side, 1 in. from inner edge of fringe at the side, and $1\frac{1}{2}$ in. below the top.
Couch the side veins, working through the tissue paper, beginning at the tip of a vein, on one side, couching a 'V' shape and ending at the tip on the other side.
Beginning at the top of the centre vein, couch down and 1 in. beyond bottom tip of leaf, for stalk, then turn wool and couch back alongside stalk, continuing round the outside edge of the leaf. When you have completed one line of couching continue round the stalk and all round the outside again, to form a double line, then take wool up centre vein and finish at tip where you began. Tear away tissue paper (remove obstinate bits with tweezers), and draw threads all round edge of mat to form fringe. Press carefully on the wrong side of the mat, according to fabric, using a damp cloth.

# Oven mitts and glove

If you have any pieces left over from your kitchen curtains, make one or both of these to match. If you are buying fabric, look amongst the gay dress prints or kitchen curtain fabric ranges. It is worth buying really strong, washable fabric for both these items.

## MATERIALS YOU WILL NEED FOR MITTS

Sheet of paper, ruler, pencil or ready-squared paper; greaseproof or tracing paper; $\frac{1}{4}$—$\frac{1}{2}$ yd. 36-in. wide gaily printed fabric for mitt ends; matching sewing thread; black Anchor stranded embroidery cotton; black ric-rac braid; 8 white lace daisies; $\frac{1}{2}$ yd. plain fabric to tone with mitt ends; Courtelle wadding to pad; bias binding to tone.

## TO MAKE

Rule a sheet of paper into inch squares (or use ready-squared graph paper), and draw the pattern following diagram (C). Trace onto the greaseproof or tissue paper and cut out. Lay the traced cut-out over the fabric, moving it about until the design visible is just as you want it. Pin the tracing down and cut out. Cut the second mitt end in a similar way. The two ends need not be identical, in fact it is more fun if they are not. Work the couching according to your fabric. We used black stranded embroidery cotton (do not split), black ric-rac braid and white lace daisies as illustrated.
Make up the mitts as follows:
Cut a backing piece for each embroidered mitt using the paper cut-out as a pattern. With the wrong sides together, tack round the edge of each mitt. Then bind the straight edge on each as shown.
Cut two lengths of plain fabric 27 in. long by 9 in. wide, and one or two thicknesses of Courtelle wadding to pad. Tack the wadding between the two pieces of fabric, right sides outside. Place the mitts, right side up, on top of the strip, one at each end, and tack into place. Join all the way round, following rounded edge of mitts, with zig-zag stitch. Trim raw edges and corners, then bind all round, as illustrated.

## MATERIALS YOU WILL NEED FOR GLOVE

Sheet of paper, ruler, pencil or ready-squared paper; greaseproof or tracing paper; $\frac{1}{4}$ yd. 36-in. wide gaily printed fabric for back of glove; black Anchor stranded embroidery cotton; guipure lace daisy; lace trimmings to tone with glove; $\frac{1}{4}$ yd. 36 in. wide plain fabric for palm of glove; matching sewing thread; Courtelle wadding to pad; bias binding to tone.

## TO MAKE

Rule a sheet of paper into inch squares (or use ready-squared graph paper) and draw pattern following diagram (D). Trace onto greaseproof or tissue paper and cut out. Lay the traced cut-out over your fabric, moving it about until the design visible underneath is in just the position you want it. Pin the tracing down and cut out. Work the couching, etc., to complement your fabric, we picked out a central motif with the couched black embroidery cotton (do not split), a guipure lace daisy, and lace across the cuff.
Using the paper cut-out as a pattern, cut another piece of fabric to back the embroidered side of the glove, and another two pieces for the palm in a toning or contrasting fabric—whichever you please. Also cut one or two thicknesses of Courtelle wadding. Place these between the two palm pieces of fabric (wrong sides together) and tack round the edge. Tack the embroidered and backing pieces together without padding. Bind the cuff edge on both halves of the glove. Tack the two pieces together, right sides outside, then join all round outer edge with zig-zag stitch. Trim the raw edges, then bind all round, as illustrated.

# Cheshire Cat cushion

If you make him in chintzy flowered cotton he'll purr his way contentedly into your favourite armchair, or grace a teenagers' bed. He could be made without his stuffing and used as a nightdress or pyjama case!

## MATERIALS YOU WILL NEED

Sheet of paper, ruler, pencil or ready-squared paper; greaseproof or tissue paper; ¾ yd. 36 in. wide flowered cotton fabric; piece of black felt 2 in. by 3 in.; 2½ yd. black Russian braid; 6 in. black silk fringe (1 in. deep); 2 yd. black cord edge insertion; ½ yd. patent fastening (Velcro); Courtelle wadding and Kapok for inner cushion; fabric adhesive (Copydex) or PVA adhesive (Sellobond).

## TO MAKE

Rule a sheet of paper into inch squares (or use ready-squared graph paper), and draw out the pattern following diagram (E1).
Fold a sheet of greaseproof, or good quality tissue paper in half and place the fold against the lefthand edge of the pattern. Trace the outline, paws and features etc. Now turn the tracing over and trace the lines through on to the other half of the pattern, omitting tail.
Tack the tracing to the right side of your fabric (do not cut out).
Trace pattern for nose following diagram (E2) and cut out in the black felt.

Following the lines, and stitching through the paper, outline the inner ears, mouth, paws and tail with Russian braid—either couching it into position, or stitching neatly along the centre of the braid. (Prevent cut ends from fraying with a tiny dab of PVA adhesive). Stitch a 2½ in. length of fringe into place for each eye, and appliqué the nose into position. Stitch cord edge all round outline of cat, the *outer* corded edge of the insertion towards the centre of the cushion. Carefully tear away the tracing, removing any obstinate bits with tweezers. Cut out, ½ in. outside insertion cord, and press. To make the back, fold a piece of fabric 20 in. long by 18 in. wide down the centre, and cut. Turn in each centre edge 1½ in. Stitch patent fastening (Velcro) to each side, then place them together to join, so that the back fabric is in one piece, with the (joined) opening down the centre. A zip fastner or press studs could be used instead, or a strip of hooks and eyes used for chair covers. With right sides together, pin the front to the back, centres matching, trim back level with front. Join front and back all round outer edge of cushion, following stitching line of cord edge insertion. Turn to right side and press. Make an inner cushion the same size as the cover from the Courtelle wadding (to emphasise shape) and stuff lightly with the Kapok, unless the cat is to be used as a nightdress case.

## Mousie-mousie pin cushions

Make these from left-over scraps of gaily patterned fabric. They're quick and cheap to make as well as being gay *and* useful which makes them particularly popular for bazaar items.

## MATERIALS YOU WILL NEED FOR EACH MOUSE

Sheet of paper, ruler, pencil or ready-squared paper; piece of soft cotton 5½ in. by 9 in.; piece of toning or contrasting felt 5 in. by 4 in.; piece stiff card; Kapok for stuffing; ¼ yd. lacing cord; fabric adhesive (Copydex); tracing paper; scrap of black felt.

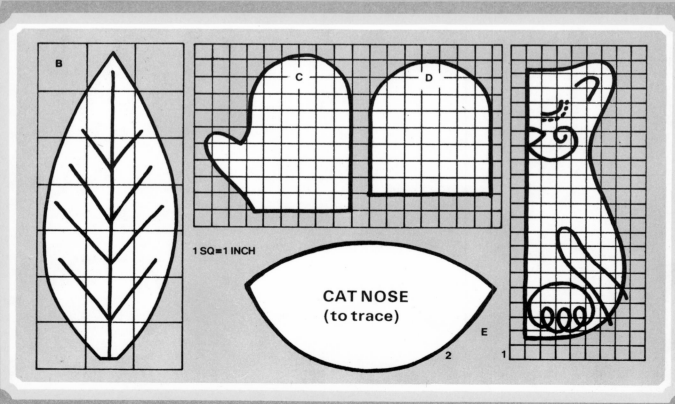

1 SQ = 1 INCH

CAT NOSE
(to trace)

## TO MAKE

Rule the paper into inch squares (or use ready-squared graph paper) and draw out the pattern following the diagram (F1). Add the markings. Cut the body twice and the base once in the printed cotton and the head twice in felt. Cut the base again in stiff card, $\frac{1}{4}$ in. smaller all round than the pattern. $\frac{1}{4}$ in. turnings are allowed for all seams. With the right sides together, and matching notches, circles and straight edges, carefully join the felt heads to each side of the body. Clip seam. With right sides together, join the two halves of the mouse all round the curved edge, leaving straight lower edge open. Clip seam. With right sides together, and matching sides and centres, join the front (pointed) half of the base round the lower edge. Clip seam and turn to right side.

Partially stuff mouse with Kapok, then push card inside, setting it smoothly against the base. Turn the raw back edge of the base over the card and stick. Finish stuffing mouse.

Cut a 9 in. length of lacing cord; knot one end and seal the fraying other end with fabric adhesive (Copydex) to form a point. Slip-stitch one side of back edge of body to base, as far as the centre back seam. Insert knotted end of cord, stitch securely and then finish slipstitching body to base.

Trace patterns (F2) for the features. Cut the ear twice in felt. Place each flat against the cotton body, the straight edge of the ear level with the head and body seam, centred at each side. Slipstitch firmly into place, then pull forward over the face as shown.

Cut the eyes and nose in black felt, and stick to face as illustrated.

## Felt cat sewing tidy

### Designed by Kate Verdun

As this cat is made from felt and fabric adhesive there is practically no stitching at all, so he is particularly suitable for the younger members of the family to make. Hanging up behind the door he is a practical addition to the sewing cupboard, or he could be used in a child's room to hold pencils, rubbers and ruler.

### MATERIALS YOU WILL NEED

$\frac{1}{4}$ yd. 36 in. wide felt in a bright colour; fabric adhesive (Copydex); squared paper; wadding or Kapok (to fill head); scraps of felt and embroidery cotton (for features); ribbon for neck; brass curtain hook.

### TO MAKE

Cut a strip of felt 5 in. wide and 30 in. long to make the base of the cat, and curve at one end to make the top of the head. Fold back the opposite end to make two deep pockets, and stick

the pocket seam and then the edges with the fabric adhesive (Copydex). Cut out the shape for the cat's haunches in the squared paper following diagram (G1) and the head following diagram (G2). Cut out the haunches in one thickness of felt and the head in two thicknesses of felt. Stick the haunches to make the front pockets as illustrated, sticking pocket seams first, then the side edges. Stick the sides and top of the head pieces together and leave until dry, then pad the head (this can be used for pins, needles etc.), sticking the neck seam to keep the padding in place. Stick the head onto the felt 'body'. When quite dry, stick on features made from felt and embroidery cotton as shown. Stick a ribbon round the neck and stitch the hook to the back of the head to hang the tidy.

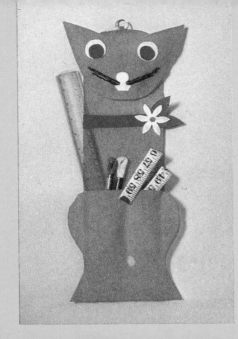

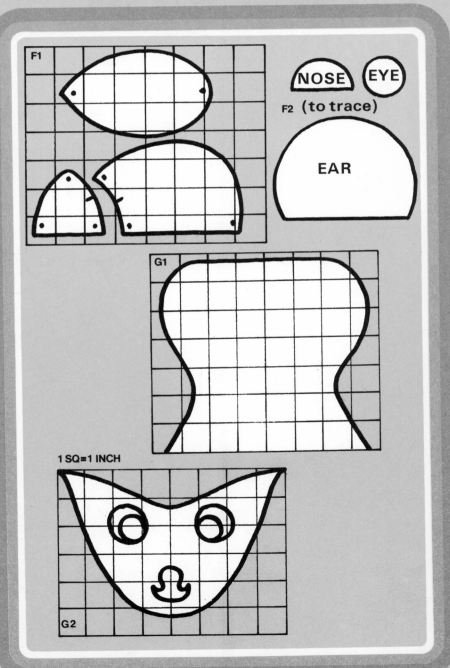

# FELTCRAFT

## Lesson Two:
## Using felt decoratively to create clothes and accessories

As we said in previous lessons, felt is very easy to work with because it does not fray. This is why we also used if for our appliqué aprons (Appliqué, lesson one). Because it is so relatively easy to handle, it is particularly suitable for children to use, and it can be either sewn or stuck.

## Materials and tools

Felt can be purchased in a number of different ways. It can be bought by the yard in various widths from specialist handicraft suppliers, local handicraft shops and departmental stores, as well as being available by mail order. It is also possible to buy small 6-inch squares of felt in bright colours, from handicraft and needlecraft specialist shops and from the haberdashery departments in most large stores. These squares are relatively inexpensive and are ideal for making small flowers or for appliquéing onto larger items.

Sharp dressmaker's scissors are necessary for cutting large pieces of felt, but a small pair of really sharp ones are ideal for cutting more intricate shapes. Obviously small children should not be allowed to

handle very sharp scissors, so they will need help with the cutting. Pinking shears are not really much good for cutting felt, and in any case are not necessary as it does not fray.

Pins tend to leave a mark in felt, so it is wise to draw round the pattern with tailors' chalk and cut out following the chalk line.

Special fabric adhesive (Copydex) is ideal for sticking felt, but it can also be hand or machine stitched. Set the tension fairly loosely on the machine, as you would for sewing a fairly heavy furnishing tweed, otherwise the felt can pucker.

## Be practical

If you are thinking of using felt to make a garment, remember it cannot be washed very successfully and should be dry-cleaned. This makes it suitable for gay fashion extras like our waistcoat, or accessories, such as hats, belts and bags, but it is not really suitable for

trousers or a dress! Felt can be used to make a very attractive evening skirt particularly if you choose one of the extra wide ones, for say a circular or semi-circular skirt.

Felt can also be used most successfully in home furnishing, for cushions, wallhangings, as an appliqué design on nursery curtains, or as a fringed table cover to completely conceal an old circular table — giving it a new lease of life.

**YOUR SECOND MAKES**

# FELT FLOWERS

Small scraps of felt are required for making these felt flowers, and so left-over scraps or small 6-inch squares are suitable. Colours depend on your personal taste — we used naturalistic colours suggesting the actual flowers themselves, but shapes and colours can

be changed and adapted to create any number of fantasy flowers.

## MATERIALS YOU WILL NEED

Scraps of felt (see above); all-purpose adhesive (Copydex); needle and thread to tone with felts; in some cases wire or stiffening.

## TO MAKE THE BASIC FLOWER

There is a basic method for making stems, leaves and flowers which was used to make all our felt flowers. The basic design can then be adapted to create the various different kinds.

**To make stems:** Cut a strip of green felt 4½ in. long by ¾ in. wide. Roll into a tubular stem shape. Oversew along the edge. To make the stem more rigid, a piece of soft wire can be inserted into the tubular stem, and the bottom sewn up. This enables the stem to be bent into any desired shape.

**To make leaves:** Cut out two leaf shapes and stick them together with an all-purpose adhesive (Copydex). Make sure the edges are firmly stuck. Oversew approximately 1 in. at the base of the leaf to the bottom of the stem.

**To make basic flower:** Cut the sepal shapes and petals according to flower required. Cut a small cross in the middle of each sepal shape and each set of petals. Push the petals and then the sepal shapes gently onto the stem. Secure the shapes to the stem with a few small stitches, or if preferred, stick in position.

## TO MAKE THE DAISY

Use white felt for petals, one or two shades of yellow for sepals, and green felt for the leaves. Make following the basic instructions.

## TO MAKE THE PANSY

Use shades of purple, violet and pink felt for the petals, cream, yellow and black for the centre and green for the leaves and stem. Make following the basic instructions.

## TO MAKE THE KINGCUP

Use yellow felt for the petals, grey, black and pale yellow for the centre and green for the leaves and stem. Make as the basic flower.

## TO MAKE THE ANEMONE

Use pink and purple felt for the petals, black for the centre and green for the leaves and stem. Make as before.

## TO MAKE THE MARIGOLD

Use orange or vivid yellow felt for the petals, and centre, and green for the leaves and stem. Make as before. These designs can be adapted to make many other flowers.

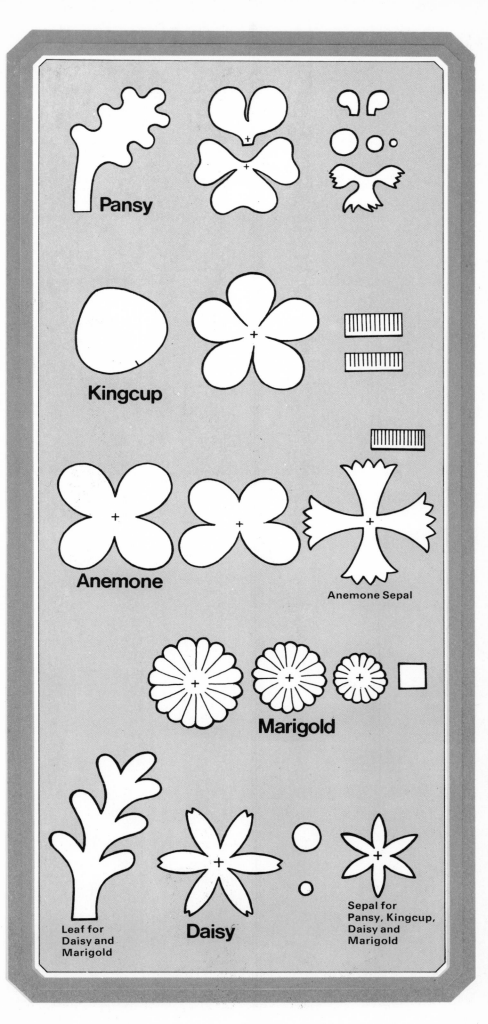

Pansy

Kingcup

Anemone

Anemone Sepal

Marigold

Leaf for Daisy and Marigold

Daisy

Sepal for Pansy, Kingcup, Daisy and Marigold

# WAY-OUT FELT WAISTCOAT

This will fit size 34 in. to 36 in. bust, to adjust the patterns to fit other sizes see Sewing, lesson one.

## MATERIALS YOU WILL NEED

Squared paper; tailors' chalk; 2 yd. bright coloured felt (we used pink); all-purpose fabric adhesive (Copydex); embroidery transfer for 'embroidered' design to taste (we used simple flowers); stranded embroidery cotton (see instructions); 4 yd. braid for trimming.

## TO MAKE

Transfer pattern onto squared paper, (scale 1 square to 1 inch). Cut out. Place on felt, draw round pattern with tailors' chalk and cut out.

Stick darts and seams with the fabric adhesive (Copydex) using the *dry* method. This is done as follows. Coat both edges of the fabric to be stuck and leave until transparent (Copydex is white in the tube) which usually takes about 15 to 20 minutes. Press the two coated surfaces together firmly. If necessary weight down with something heavy, leave until dry. When the waistcoat is ready, transfer your chosen embroidery design onto the felt with a warm iron and decide which colour stranded embroidery cotton you will use for the various pieces of the

design. Cut them to size following the lines of the design. Put on one side. Using a paint brush, cover the lines of the transfer with the adhesive as neatly as possible and not too thickly. When nearly dry, lay the strands of embroidery cotton carefully and firmly onto the adhesive. The result—instant appliqué. Other pieces of felt could be used in this way if preferred, rather than the stranded cotton. Finish the waistcoat by cutting the braid into strips for the waistcoat edges and armholes. Seal the cut ends with the adhesive (Copydex) and then stick the braid onto the waistcoat as illustrated, again using the *dry* method of sticking. **Note:** Care must be taken to see that the adhesive (Copydex) is not allowed to get onto other parts of the felt as it is very difficult to remove.

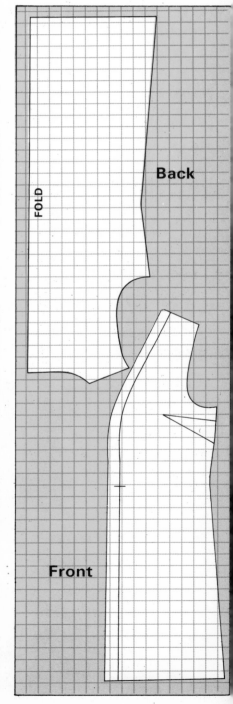

FOLD

Back

Front

210

# PICTURE FRAMING

## Step-by-step to framing fabric pictures

**Prudence Nutall, author of 'Picture Framing for Beginners', tells you how to frame your embroidered, appliqué and tapestry pictures and how to frame your collages, saving yourself expensive picture framing charges. Her instructions can be adapted to frame other pictures, too, and if you follow our step-by-step guide to picture framing you should soon be a competent framer!**

Anyone who has completed a fabric picture will realise the necessity of having it framed if they want to display it properly. After all the work of making, it seems a waste to put it away in a drawer where no one else can see it. As the majority of pictures cannot be cleaned satisfactorily, they must also be protected by glass before any dust or dirt spoils them. This is, of course, particularly true if you live in a city, as the greasy grit which comes into every house soon leaves a dull film on everything.

Having a picture framed professionally can be an expensive business, due primarily to the high cost of labour, as every picture has to be treated individually and the work can never be hurried. If you have a co-operative male member of the family who enjoys making things, he might be persuaded to help you to frame your own pictures, or even do it himself. Otherwise, with time and patience it should not be too difficult to tackle it yourself. The results can be very rewarding, and the initial layout on

tools will soon be paid back by the money saved.

## Choose the frame to suit the picture

Firstly, you must decide whether or not the picture is suitable for framing. Large hangings which would be too heavy or expensive to frame are best displayed by suspending from a length of dowelling at the top, with another fixed to the bottom to weigh the hanging down. This means, of course, that they are not protected by glass, but the large frame required would be difficult to make. It is easier to begin on a smaller picture, and when you have successfully mastered that to go on to something larger.

It might be helpful to visit any local exhibitions of fabric pictures to study the frames, and see which ones you think are most successful in displaying the work to its best advantage. There is, in fact, a wider choice of possibilities than might be realised initially, both in

the selection of mouldings and in the finishing and colouring of frames.
If you live near a large city, some of the larger stores have fabric pictures in their gallery departments, or your local Public Library may have illustrations in books on fabric collage which will also be helpful. It is worth getting ideas to set your mind working before you start. Picture framing is more of an art than it might appear. A successful frame can really transform a picture, by displaying it well, whereas a bad frame is merely a distraction. This does not mean to say that an elaborate frame is always the best, sometimes a very simple moulding is all that is needed for the best effect.
As with most things, experience is the best teacher. And trust your own judgement—after all, the picture is yours and is probably going to hang in your own home, so choose something that you like yourself.

## Deep frames

As most fabric pictures have some depth, it is usually necessary to have a double frame so that the glass can be sandwiched between the two frames and kept clear from the picture, rather than flattening it down. This can be

achieved in three ways. If the depth of the picture is not too great, a fillet of wood about $\frac{3}{8}$-inch wide and $\frac{1}{4}$-inch deep can be put inside the frame to lift the glass up a little way. With a deeper relief, an inner frame which has a slope about $1\frac{1}{2}$-inch wide and 1-inch deep will keep the glass further away, and act as a mount to the picture. This is suitable with pictures up to about 20 inches by 15 inches, otherwise the effect is too heavy (see illustration). For very deep relief, or three dimensional objects, a box frame can be made with sides cut to the required depth.
An important point to make with a double frame is to have a contrast of widths—with a sloping inner frame a narrow outside moulding looks best, and a fillet is best with a wide frame to give the effect of a narrow inner border.

## Small pictures

Small, elaborate pictures look best with a wider frame, or a slope to act as a mount rather than being constricted by a narrow frame. A simple picture surrounded by a lot of background is better with a narrower moulding, to avoid looking too clumsy. Colours for

frames which are referred to in the section on 'Preparation' should be kept neutral so as not to compete with the picture. Subtle greys and browns are better than bright colours which attract the eye to the frame. Gilt frames bring out the warmth of reds and yellows, and silver mouldings look pleasing with blues and greens. Fillets are most effective if painted with black or white matt emulsion paint as a contrast to the picture, giving the effect of a narrow margin all round.
Consider also where the picture is to hang, as although the primary consideration should be what is best suited to the picture, it is also helpful to take into account the room setting, whether modern or traditional, and not, say, to use a decorated gilt moulding in a modern room.

## Using existing frames

There is also the possibility that you might already have an existing frame that could be used—if it is too large, it can always be cut down to the right size to fit your picture. Unfortunately the days have passed when it was possible to find beautiful maple frames selling very cheaply in junk unless you are lucky enough to live in some remote area where the dealers have not yet penetrated. However, it is still worth looking out for frames in a reasonable condition, and even if the finish is not particularly good they can be treated to give a satisfactory result.

## Tools and materials

The first requirement is a steady surface on which to work. If you do not already have a workbench, a large table will do, and the top can be protected by a sheet of heavy hardboard which will also give a level surface.
The most important tool is a mitre-box to cut the corners to an accurate angle of 45°. Prices of mitre-boxes vary considerably, the cheapest being a simple beechwood box without ends which has 4 slots cut in at angles of 45° (A). The moulding is laid in the box and the saw fitted in the slots to cut through the moulding at the same angle. With this box, care has to be taken to keep the saw upright so the sides of the slots do not get eaten away—if they become too wide the saw will wobble about and the mitres become less accurate. The steel mitre-cutter (B) has clamps to hold the moulding in position while the mitres are being cut, and being heavier it does not tend to move around. It also can be screwed to a workbench. With both these pieces of equipment a 12-inch tenon saw is used, and this will also cut the hardboard.

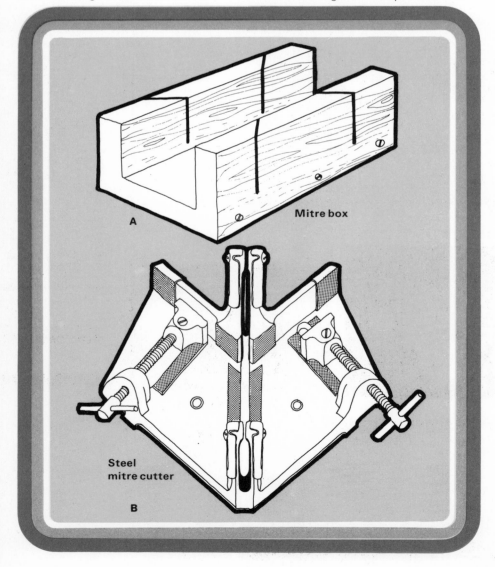

**Mitre box**

A

**Steel mitre cutter**

B

## FRAMING FABRIC PICTURES IN 20 SIMPLE STEPS

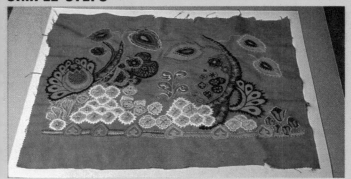

1. Trim fabric to approximate size required, and cut card slightly larger.

2. Make sure fabric is smooth and there are no knots on the back. Paste card, *not* fabric, using vegetable paste. Coat evenly and use plenty of paste thickly for heavy plastic, less paste and a lighter coating for thin fabric.

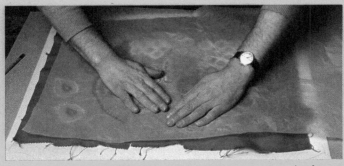

3. Place on card, taking care not to get any paste on the front of the picture, and cover the surface of the fabric with tissue paper. Start from the middle and press firmly with your hands on top of the tissue paper to make sure you remove all the air bubbles. Work out towards the edge, feeling carefully for any bumps. You could give the fabric a final going-over with a felt roller (available in good decorators' shops) but in this case it is not advisable as it would squash the embroidery flat. Leave for 24 hours.

4. Measure the picture horizontally and vertically to check on the size of frame required.

5. Put moulding in mitre block and cut through with a saw to make neat angled corners.

6. Make the holes for the nails in the frame with a bradawl. Glue the two short ends to the two long ends with woodworking adhesive, make sure the edges fit properly (feel with the fingers) and put into a clamp or vice to dry.

7. Tap in 1-inch panel pins as shown while the half-frame is still in the clamp. Tap firmly but carefully to within $\frac{1}{16}$ inch of frame, then use a punch. This prevents the frame from being bruised. Join the other corners.

A lightweight hammer is best for joining and fitting, to be used with the recommended nails. Synthetic resin glue can be bought in a container with a narrow neck so that it can be applied without waste when joining the mitred corners. Small clamps can be bought to hold the corners steady when the frame is drying.

You will also need an accurate rule for measuring the moulding, the glass and the background. A try-square, though not essential, is useful when testing the angles of the frame to ensure a correct angle of 45°

A trimming knife with replaceable blades is best for cutting card and trimming the backing paper and the blade should always be sharp. A bradawl is helpful for marking the screw holes when fixing the hanging fittings, and a screwdriver is also needed. Finally you will need fine sandpaper for rubbing down the corners and smoothing rough wood, and Brummer Stopping for filling any holes.

Mouldings are the lengths of wood from which frames are made. Manufacturers who sell to the trade do not usually deal in amounts under 100 feet of any one type, which would be more than is generally required unless you intended to make a lot of frames, but they do of course have the widest selection.

Local do-it-yourself shops are probably the best source, and though your choice may be limited by what is available, even the plainest wood mouldings can be stained or painted to give a variety of finishes. It is best to know what you *can* get before finally deciding on your frame.

Glass can be bought from glaziers and it is wise to get them to cut it to size for you once you have decided on the dimensions of the picture. Before you order your glass, look at our step-by-step pictures and read 'Fitting together and hanging' overleaf.

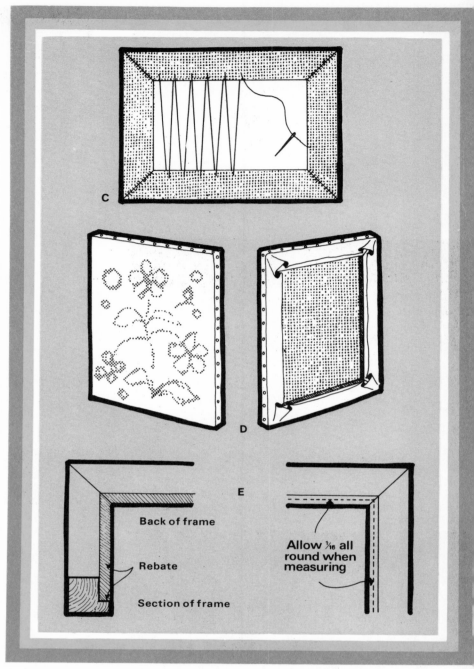

Back of frame

Rebate

Section of frame

Allow ¹⁄₁₆ all round when measuring

## Preparation of work to be framed

All fabric pictures must first be prepared for framing by being laid out or stretched on to card (press back of fabric first if necessary). This is to remove any creases or unevenness, and also to give a rigid backing with which to work.

There are various ways of doing this depending on the background material. Pictures with a felt background can be laid on to a larger piece of card which has been pasted with a vegetable paste. This will not damage the felt, and as this material is slightly stretchy the work can be eased to the right size when laying. Afterwards the card can be trimmed back to the edge of the picture.

Pictures with a silk or other delicate background are best treated in the following way. Cut a piece of card the exact size of the area of the picture to be shown in the frame. Do not forget that about ¼ in. all round the picture will be covered by the rebate of the frame—this is the channel in the moulding that holds the picture in the frame. Fold the edges of the material over the card and secure at the back with long stitches in both directions, stretching the work tightly but without pulling it out of shape, and paying special attention to the neatness of the corner (see C).

Another method can be used with light, closely woven material such as fine canvas. Again, cut a piece of thick card the exact size of the picture allowing for the rebate. Fold the material over the card and trim any excess, leaving about 1 inch all round. Fix through the edge of the card with fine dressmakers' pins at intervals of about ½ inch, again stretching the material as you work. This method is not satisfactory with silky materials, when the pins would split the fibre, or with heavy materials when the pins would not be strong enough to hold the fabric.

Heavy tapestry work is a bit harder as it should be fixed to a wooden stretcher to make it really taut. A stretcher is like a flat frame made from 1-inch by ½-inch wood with mitred corners, the exact size of the picture. The work is stretched tightly over this—use household pliers if extra pulling pressure is required, and tack the canvas to the outside edge of the stretcher (see D).

Having prepared the work, it next has to be measured to find the size of the frame. Remember that the measurements are to the inside of the rebates of the frame, so that the picture doesn't just drop through the opening (see E). Remember also when

# FRAMING FABRIC PICTURES IN 20 SIMPLE STEPS

8. Cut glass to fit frame, remembering it must just slip inside the frame. *Note*: unless you are an expert glass cutter or picture framer it is better to have this done for you.

9. Fit glass over picture and square up. Mark cutting line on the fabric.

10. Cut edge off fabric and card cleanly, using hardboard as a backing so you don't score your work surface.

11. Choose fillet which is to fit inside frame. A fillet is a piece of wood $\frac{1}{4}$ in. x $\frac{1}{2}$ in. and it prevents the glass from squashing pictures which have a raised surface. Cut fillet to fit inside frame, glue corners and pin with single pin. Paint white or desired colour.

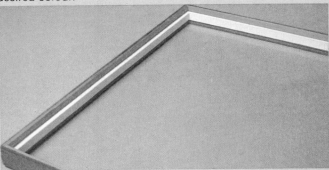

12. Put frame face downwards with glass in it and place fillet inside to check fit.

13. Cut backing card to the same size as the finished picture and fix hooks or backing plate on it.

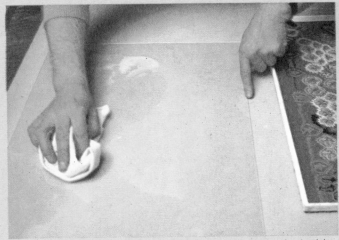

14. Check that everything fits together, then clean the inside of the glass with proprietary glass or mirror cleaner.

15. Fit picture back into frame, place backing card in position and clean front of glass.

16. Turn picture face down (protect glass) and pin backing in position by carefully tapping in the pins at an angle as shown. Place one pin in the centre of each side.

17. File or sandpaper corners of the frame if necessary, then fill with Brummer Stopping. Touch up moulding if necessary.

18. Seal the back of the frame with brown masking tape or sticky tape 2 inches wide.

19. Tuck and press in tape as shown, cut and trim.

20. Your picture is now ready for its cord and to be hung in position.

you mark the moulding to add twice the width of the moulding to the actual measurements that you have taken. If you are making a double frame, start with the inner frame first, then when this is finished it will be easier to take the measurements for the outer frame. A fillet inside the frame can be added afterwards, and if this is cut to fit tightly the four lengths need not be joined at the corners but can just be wedged into place when the picture and frame are fitted together.

## Making the frames

Read these instructions first and then look at the step-by-step picture guide. Having checked the measurements, now to making the frame. The moulding can first be cut into lengths a little longer than you require, as it can be unwieldy to try to saw the mitre on a very long piece of wood. Mark the outside measurements in pencil. The mitres should be cut very carefully, as the ultimate success of the frame depends on the accuracy of the corners, and in getting a true rectangle. Saw the mitres from the top of the moulding to the bottom, so that any splitting of the wood will occur on the inner edge, and the outside corners will stay clean. Keep the saw straight and vertical. Having prepared all the four

lengths of moulding, join the frame in the following way. First join one long and one short side into an L-shape. The long side should be fixed in a vice, (if you have one) the cut edge coated with a synthetic resin glue (Evo-stick) and the mitred edge of the short side brought up to it. The corners should then be nailed with nails long enough to pass through one side of the moulding and halfway through the other. Veneer pins will do on a very narrow moulding where thick nails would split the wood, on a heavy moulding use oval nails. When hammering in the nails, hold the short edge slightly below the longer, as the force of the hammer will then bring the joint together correctly. This is a complicated manoeuvre, and as the two sides of the frame must be kept level when being fixed together you will probably need an extra pair of hands when doing this!

Having completed the first joint, join the other two pieces into a second L, and finally join the two L's together to finish the frame. Clamps can be used to hold the corners while drying. When the frame is completed it should be left to dry undisturbed for a few hours. Then the corners can be sanded if they are a bit ragged, and any holes filled with Brummer Stopping.

If you have used a plain whitewood moulding, it can be finished in a

variety of ways. In any case, if the wood is at all rough it should first be rubbed down with a fine sandpaper to give a smooth surface. If you want to leave the wood plain, it can just be lightly waxed and polished with a good quality white wax, or it can first be stained with a wood stain to the required colour, and then waxed and polished. Painting a frame is quite a useful disguise if the corners are not very accurate and have gaps in the joints. The spaces can be filled in with Brummer Stopping, left to dry and then sanded down to the right level. Two coats of emulsion paint should be sufficient to give a good finish, and this can also then be waxed and polished to protect the surface. As mentioned earlier, it is advisable not to paint frames in strong colours but to keep to neutral shades.

Don't throw away odd pieces of mouldings, as they are useful for experimenting with different finishes, so that you can try out a colour against a picture before colouring the whole frame.

## Fitting together and hanging

When the frame is finished, the glass and the backboard should be assembled so that everything can be fitted together.

Picture glass is clearer and thinner than window glass and without the flaws, and is known as 18-ounce glass It is probably easier to buy it cut to size from a glazier or hardware shop, as it is difficult to cut without some experience, and wastage is expensive. When measuring the size, check very carefully, remembering that the glass must be very slightly smaller than the picture to allow it to drop easily into the frame. Hardboard can also be bought cut to size, but it is more economical to get a large sheet and cut it yourself. In this case the glass can be used as a template for the backboard, by laying it on a piece of hardboard and marking round the outside before cutting. Before you start to assemble the frame, make sure that everything is clean and free from dust. Examine the picture to see that there are no ends of thread still attached. The glass can be given a final light polish with methylated spirits to remove any marks—be careful not to get any fingermarks on the *inside* of the glass which cannot later be removed. Fix everything together (see F) and nail lightly into the frame from the back using $\frac{3}{4}$-inch panel pins. If you hold a small block of wood against the frame while you are nailing, it will give a more rigid surface to work against; care must be taken to hammer lightly so that the glass does not break. Finally seal round the back of the frame with brown sticky paper to give a neat finish and as a protection against dust. If you want to be able to remove the picture easily from the frame, the backboard need not be nailed in but secured with small turnscrews which are screwed to the back of the frame and hold the backboard in place. The sticky paper is then, of course, omitted. When choosing the fixtures for hanging the picture (see G) make sure they are strong enough to take the weight of the picture. Small screw eyes are generally suitable for a medium-sized frame if the moulding is wide enough to take them without splitting the wood. Two holes should be marked with a bradawl about one third of the way down each side and the fittings screwed in. If the moulding is too narrow to have anything screwed into it, back hangers can be fitted into the backboard before the frame is assembled—two slits are cut with a trimming knife about 2 inches down from the top and 2 inches in from the sides of the backboard. The hinges are then pushed through and the two flanges opened out and hammered flat on the inside of the backboard. Picture wire for hanging can be bought from most hardware shops or nylon cord can be used, but *never* use string—even as a temporary measure—it will fray and break.

All that remains is to hang the picture on a picture hook—not too high above eye level—stand back and admire your work!

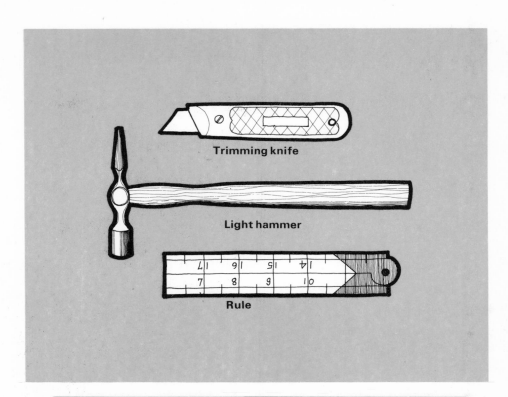

Trimming knife

Light hammer

Rule

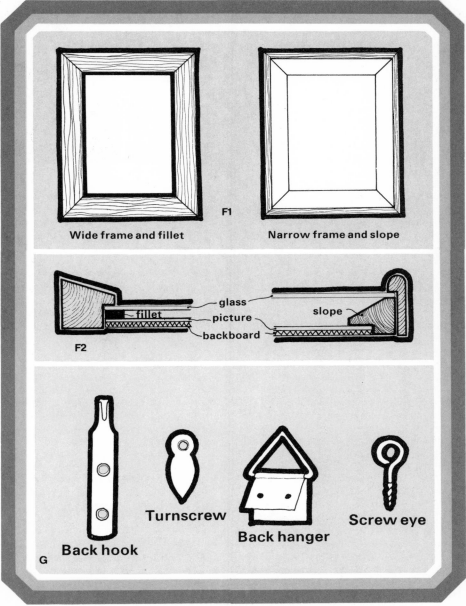

Wide frame and fillet    Narrow frame and slope

F1

glass
fillet
picture
slope
backboard

F2

Back hook    Turnscrew    Back hanger    Screw eye

G

# LEATHER-WORK

## Lesson One:
## Working with leather

Working with leather can be most rewarding, particularly as leather garments and accessories are so costly, and making your own can be relatively inexpensive.

## Materials

Leather is made from the skin of an animal and is usually bought in the shape of that animal. Each whole shape is called a 'skin' and the centre part (the back of the animal) tends to be thicker and stronger than at the edges. It is important to remember this when cutting out pattern shapes. There are many different kinds of leather, but we have used the softer ones made from the skins of sheep and goats because they are easier to work with. **Sheepskin** is usually the cheapest to buy and is often embossed with patterns to make it look like a more expensive type of skin. It is dyed to a wide range of colours. **Goatskin** is often called 'Morocco', but this is the name given to the dyeing and finishing, not the place of origin! It is usually firmer in texture than sheepskin. **Pigskin** is more expensive and it is best to wait until you are quite practised at making things from leather before you use it. The distinguishing marks of three little holes in a row (where the bristles grow) are often imitated on other skins, but you can always tell the real thing if you look carefully. The groups vary slightly on different parts of the pigskin, but machine-made holes are symmetrical. **Calfskin** is also rather expensive, but beautifully smooth and supple. **Hide** is the name given to the heavier, stiffer type of leather which is obtained from cows, and generally used for the soles of shoes, suitcases and similar items. Hide is often split into several layers and these are called 'skivers'; they can be fairly thick or as thin as paper—the thin ones are mainly used for lining purses and wallets. **Suede** is not from a particular animal, but is soft leather that has been specially treated on the flesh side to give it a pile like velvet. When using suede, pattern pieces should be cut with the pile all running in the same direction, as with velvet.

SPECIAL NOTE

All types of leather and suede should be stored flat or rolled up. If you roll several inside each other they should be interleaved with tissue paper, and suede should have the velvet side protected. Never fold leather or tie it up with string or rubber bands. It could become permanently bruised or marked and would be unusable.

## Tools

In order to cut good clean edges, a sharp craft knife or razor-blade in a holder is essential. Scissors should not be used as they tend to crush the edge of the leather and tear the fibres, leaving an unsightly, uneven, 'fuzzy' edge. Blades should be renewed as soon as they become the slightest bit blunt. Proper leather knives can be bought from craft shops if you intend to do a lot of leather work and these can be sharpened regularly on an oilstone.
You will also need a good cutting surface, and a board can be made from the smooth side of a piece of hardboard. When this becomes too scored, it should be discarded and a new piece used.

A stitchmarker should be used to space the stitches, and again these can be bought from craft shops and look a bit like a flat dinner fork. The marker is placed with the prongs in position on the leather and tapped with a mallet through the leather into the cutting board. A sharp dressmakers' tracing wheel will serve just as well for the beginner if it is kept carefully on the stitching line. If the leather is very thin, you can use an unthreaded sewing machine to mark the stitch-holes.

## Cutting out

Paper patterns should always be made for every part of the garment or item to be made, including duplications of similar shapes. The patterns should then be laid on the right side of the skin so that you can check to see if there are any flaws to be avoided. Draw around each shape with a sharp pencil. Patterns should never be pinned to either leather or suede as the pin marks will remain permanently imprinted on it. Cut out the shapes with the knife or razor blade in a holder, taking care to keep the blade at right angles to the leather to avoid undercutting.

# Placing pieces together

As leather cannot be pinned or tacked, alternative methods must be found to hold the pieces together while sewing. On suede, a sticky tape (Sellotape) can be used, but this would tear the face of smooth leathers, so spring-type clothes pegs or bulldog clips (not too fierce a spring) are good alternatives.

# Sewing

Pure silk thread can be used for thin leathers and strong linen thread for the heavier types. Thread for hand sewing should be waxed with candle or beeswax before stitching, as this will enable it to slide more easily through the leather. If you are sewing by machine, set the stitches to medium size and slacken off the tension a little. Too large a stitch will look unsightly, and smaller ones may tear the leather. If you have difficulty in feeding the leather smoothly under the foot of the machine, place a layer of tissue paper each side of the skin, stitch through it and then tear it away afterwards. Avoid stretching the leather too much as you pass it under the foot of the machine or the seam will be pulled out of shape. If seams cross each other, it is a good idea to trim away the surplus from the first seam before stitching the second, as this will prevent the extra thickness from getting jammed under the foot of the machine and spoiling the line of stitching.

If you are sewing by hand, first mark the stitch holes as described in the section on tools, then use a saddlemaker's needle to stitch a straight line of stitches, return along this line, going through the holes the opposite way, so you have a continuous line of stiches on both sides of the seam, looking like machine stitches.

# Sticking

Sometimes it is necessary to stick rather than stitch the leather. The best type of adhesive to use is a rubber-based one (Copydex) which is flexible and will not cause the leather to become too stiff and hard. Great care must be taken not to get any adhesive on the face of suede, since it will soak in and leave a nasty shiny mark which is impossible to remove. Always apply the adhesive sparingly to both surfaces, and wipe away any surplus from the face of the leather immediately. Take care to avoid getting anything on the glued surfaces, particularly the ends of threads, which will show through when the two pieces are glued together.

# Pressing

Great care must be taken not to damage the skin. Do not use steam, but press with a warm, dry iron over a press cloth or thick pad of brown paper. Do not rub the iron up and down, just press down fairly firmly on it.

## YOUR FIRST MAKES

# BELTS AND BAG
## Plaited silver belt

### MATERIALS YOU WILL NEED

A strip of soft silver leather at least 24 in. by 3¾ in. (depending on waist size); rubber based adhesive (Copydex); white or grey sewing thread small scrap of extra silver leather for tassels.

### TO MAKE

Using a ruler and sharp craft knife, divide the silver leather into three strips at least 24 in. by ¾ in. and one strip 1¼ in. wide. Rule a line down the centre of the wrong side of each ¾-inch narrow strip. Coat the back of one strip lightly with the adhesive and fold the edges to the centre line all the way down. Repeat with the other two. With the right sides facing you, gather the three strips together and clip firmly through all layers. Carefully plait strips together down entire length, keeping right sides of each one facing you all the time to avoid twisting, Secure each end with a few stitches. Divide the remaining length of leather into two 12-inch long strips and rule a centre line down the back of each. Lay one strip face down and spread with a little adhesive. Lay the plaited strip, face down with the end overlapping the end of the plain strip by ½ in. Fold the edges of the plain strip into the ruled line down each side, trapping the end of the plait. Press firmly into position and allow the adhesive to dry thoroughly. Repeat with the other 12-inch strip at the other end of the plait. Cut two 2-inch by 1½-inch strips of leather and fringe 1¼ in. of the 1½ in. width. Wind round the ends of the belt, securing in place with adhesive, to make the fringe tassels.

# Patchwork leather belt

### MATERIALS YOU WILL NEED

Strip of red leather at least 6½ in. by 3½ in.; strip of red leather at least 18 in. by 2½ in.; strip of navy leather at least 18 in. by 2½ in.; strip of turquoise leather at least 18 in. by 2½ in.; piece of calico 36 in. by 3½ in.; rubber based adhesive (Copydex); red silk sewing thread; 2-in. wide buckle without a prong

### TO MAKE

Make a pattern from the large shape shown in the diagram (scale 1 square to 1 inch). Use this to cut out a shape from the 6½ in. by 3½ in. piece of red leather. Cut the other leather into 1-in. wide strips lengthways, then use the small shape on the diagram to cut out 13 red,

14 navy and 13 turquoise shapes. Rule a line down the centre of the calico strip, then place the large red leather shape on the calico with notch on centre line and end opposite notch at the end of strip. Arrange the small shapes on the calico strip in two rows with one short edge to the edge of the strip. Start one row with navy, then red, then turquoise. Start the other row with turquoise, then navy, then red. Continue this sequence down the entire length of the belt. Stick all the shapes carefully in place with the adhesive. When this is thoroughly dry, stitch diagonally across the belt, close to each patch with the red silk, then top stitch round the edges of the belt and make a double row of stitching down the centre (this is decorative but also prevents the patches lifting during wear). Trim the long edges of the belt straight with a sharp craft knife and ruler, then fold the edges to the centre on the wrong side down the entire length and stick in place, folding the large red shape on dotted lines as shown in the diagram to form blunt angular point. When the adhesive is thoroughly dry, slip the buckle onto the end of the belt opposite the point, trim surplus leather from this end and stick in place with the adhesive.

# Turquoise shoulder bag

## MATERIALS YOU WILL NEED

A whole skin turquoise leather; $\frac{1}{2}$ yard wide black buckram stiffening 36 in. wide; rubber based adhesive (Copydex) turquoise silk thread.

## TO MAKE

Make patterns from the diagram (scale 1 square to 2 inches) and use these to cut out one of each shape from the leather. Also cut out a strip of leather 30 in. by $1\frac{1}{2}$ in. for the handle. Using the diagrams follow the dotted lines to make a pattern for the lining. Cut out in the buckram. Using the adhesive sparingly, stick the buckram shapes in place on the wrong side of the leather shapes as shown on the diagram and leave to dry thoroughly. Clip into hem allowance around top of shape A from **o** to **o** as shown on the diagram. Coat hem allowance lightly with adhesive and press smoothly down over buckram to make a neat hem and leave to dry thoroughly. Turn top hem allowance of piece B in the same way and the short ends of piece C. Spread a little adhesive on the seam allowance around base of

piece A from **o** to **o** and stick one long side of piece C onto this with wrong sides together, matching * and **o**s and easing smoothly round curves. When thoroughly dry, stitch all round edge of piece A about $\frac{1}{8}$ in. from the edge in the turquoise thread (by hand or machine). Stitch round a second time about $\frac{1}{8}$ in. from the first line for extra strength and decoration. Carefully trim edge of seam around base of bag with a sharp craft knife. Coat seam allowance of piece B and stick and stitch to other side of piece C in the same way, matching symbols and working two lines of stitching as before. Trim seam as before.

To make the handle, rule a line down the centre of the wrong side of the leather strip, coat lightly with adhesive and fold edges to centre down the entire length. When the adhesive is thoroughly dry, stitch down each side about $\frac{1}{8}$ in. from the edge to strengthen and decorate strap. To attach the handle to the bag, turn under about $\frac{1}{2}$ in. at each end and stick in place. Position the ends of the handle at the sides of the bag about $2\frac{1}{2}$ in. from top and stitch into place using large strong needle and doubled thread. Stitch through handle and side of bag very strongly with stab stitches.

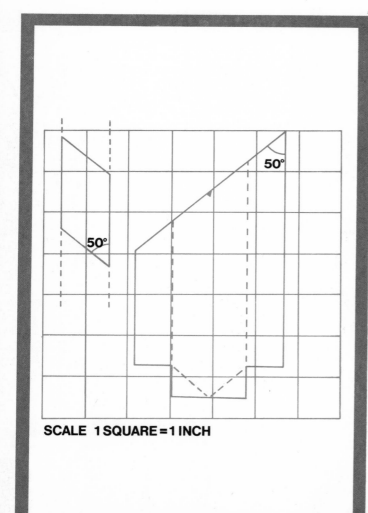

SCALE 1 SQUARE = 1 INCH

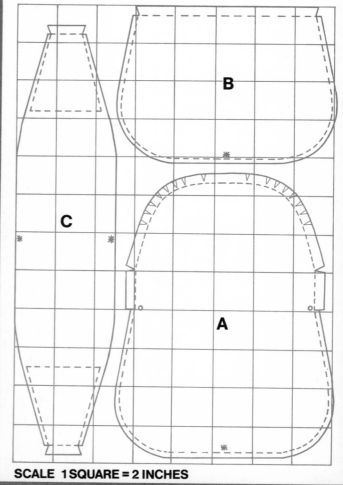

SCALE 1 SQUARE = 2 INCHES

## Lesson Two:

# Working with leather—further techniques and lots more things to make

In lesson one we explained the basic techniques and gave you a simple belt, bag and plaited belt to make. Now we go on to more complicated items, including a suede waistcoat.

## Working with suede

Suede is smooth and supple and has a velvet-like pile—it has been specially treated to give it this finish. Suede marks easily so it needs particular care in handling. Store it rolled with the plush side *inside*, preferably interleaved with tissue paper. When sticking this leather take care not to get any of the adhesive on the front or it will stick to the pile and leave a mark. When cutting out garments and other items in suede, remember to cut them so the pile lies in one direction only, just as you would with a pile fabric. If suede is being stitched with a sewing machine, it may be necessary to protect the pile with tissue paper, which can be stitched through, and then torn away when the seam is completed.

## Obtaining leather

There are now many sources for obtaining leather; local handicraft shops usually stock some, there are leather specialists in most large towns and many department stores have a selection available. Much the best way to buy leather is to go to one of these sources of supply and choose your own skins by the feel and look—buy the one which pleases you personally. Part of the charm of leather is its natural marking or graining, which gives it that individual quality.

If you cannot go to leather, then it can come to you! Many leather suppliers and handicraft specialists will supply leather by mail order, and they usually send you small samples before you order, as a guide to colour and texture. Once you have become experienced in working with leather and decide the craft is definitely your particular *forte*, it may be cheaper to buy an entire

cow hide. You will find it is of medium thickness and uniform quality at the centre, or back part of the animal, while the neck portion is rather thick and the stomach part rather thin, so you will have at least three different grades of leather with which to work. Remember not to mix the different grades in one piece of work, for just like fabric, if different weights are mixed together in one garment the heavier weight drags on the lighter weight and causes it to weaken and eventually tear.

## Alternative methods of joining leather

In lesson one we mentioned simple methods of stitching leather, both by hand and machine, and ways of sticking leather. There are other ways of joining leather to produce a decorative effect which becomes an integral part of the item being made.

**Saddle Stitching** is one of the best-known decorative stitches. It is usually done in a light-coloured thread or a colour which contrasts with the leather. Use heavy waxed linen thread and two needles. Push the first needle in from front to back, the second through from back to front, then pull both threads taut. Now push the first needle in from back to front and the second needle from front to back (through the same holes) and pull both threads taut. Continue until the seam is finished — both sides of the work will have a neat line of running stitches. Try not to have to join the thread along the length of a seam unless absolutely essential. If the leather is rather thick or coarse and stitching seems laborious, punch very small holes in the leather with an awl before starting to stitch.

**Lacing** is a more elaborate way of joining pieces of leather and is generally used for the sides of wallets, writing cases, purses and book covers. It can also be used very effectively to edge a leather photograph frame or mirror frame, and can also be used as a decorative edging for the top and sides of a leather wastepaper basket or lamp base.

There are several different types of lacing but the basic principle is the same. First make holes in the leather, evenly spaced, and fairly near the edge. You can use a lacing chisel which makes slits, or a punch which makes holes. There is a special punch available which makes one hole and marks the following one, so you are sure the holes will be equidistant. Laces are available ready-cut from the same sources as leather, or you can cut your own. To make lacing easier, trim the end of the lace to a diagonal point. Again, try not to join the lace along the length of a seam, so cut it plenty long enough to allow for the top overlapping

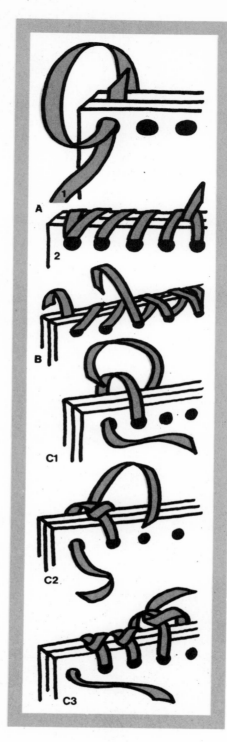

(this is why this technique is best used on smaller items). If you must join the lace, carefully pare away the edges of both old and new lace until they are thin and wedge-like and stick with adhesive, overlapping by about ¾ in. Leave to dry completely before using.
**Spiral Stitch** is shown in diagrams A1 and A2, and it consists of running a single lace, in a spiral, through the holes in the leather. If you have a problem hiding the ends of the lace, you can make the first and last loop a double one as shown.
**Cross Stitch** is shown in diagram B and is a variation on spiral stitch. Simply lace once with spiral stitch, then bring another lace back in the same way through the same holes, but in the

opposite direction. Laces of a different colour can be used.
**Buttonhole Stitch** is shown in diagrams C1, C2 and C3. The lace is taken through and under the loop formed by the lace (following the arrow) and forming a decorative 'knot' at the top as shown.

## Embossing

**Embossing** is a method of decorating leather so it has a textured surface and the design looks as though it has been stamped into the surface. The leather is dampened first, then placed over a plywood board or other firm surface. A small hammer or mallet is then used to impress the shapes into the leather. In some cases, the shapes are cut out of hardwood (pinewood), but for more delicate work, large nailheads are filed down and these are tapped onto the damp leather to create an embossed design.

| Quantities chart — | E.I. Skins | Domestic Skins |
|---|---|---|
| Maxi-length Coat | 10 | 8 |
| Midi-length Coat | 9 | 7 |
| Mini-length Coat | 7 | 6 |
| Three-quarter Jacket | 7 | 6 |
| Jacket | 6 | 5 |
| Bolero | 4 | 3 |
| Waistcoat | 2 | 2 |
| Maxi Skirt | 5 | 4 |
| Midi Skirt | 4 | 3 |
| Mini Skirt | 2 | 2 |
| Cat Suit | 10 | 8 |
| Trousers | 5 | 4 |
| Dresses | 4 | 3 |
| Hot Pants | 2 | 2 |

## YOUR SECOND MAKES

### Suede waistcoat
illustrated on previous page

#### MATERIALS YOU WILL NEED

Brown paper, pencil and ruler; 1 or 2 skins of brown suede (or other colour) depending on size; matching silk thread; adhesive (Copydex).

#### TO MAKE

Square up the brown paper in 2-inch squares and transfer the diagram (each square represents 2 inches) to the paper. Cut out. Using the brown paper template as a pattern, cut out the shapes in the suede, reversing the front and back to make a left and right side. (If skin is large enough it might be possible to cut the back in one piece, placing the middle of the back pattern to a central fold in the suede).
*Note:* It is vital to cut the suede with the pile all running in the same direction, otherwise some of the pieces will look a slightly different colour. If

possible arrange the pattern on the suede so the grain is running from top to bottom on all sections. With right sides together, stitch the back of the waistcoat down the centre back with a $\frac{1}{2}$-in. seam. Open out the seam on the wrong side, press as flat as possible with your thumb and stick flat with adhesive (Copydex). Fasten off the threads, at top and bottom of the seam, by tying very firmly. Stitch the darts in the waistcoat fronts as indicated on the diagram; clip into dart to point as shown on diagram, open out and stick flat with the adhesive. Stitch side and shoulder seams as back seam, fastening off threads securely and opening out flat and sticking.

Turn the hem allowance around arm-holes, neck and front of waistcoat to the inside, clip into hem where necessary and stick in place with the adhesive (Copydex). There is no need to turn over two thicknesses of hem when working with leather.

Trim the lower edge of the waistcoat into a fringe below the dotted line, by cutting the edge into $\frac{1}{4}$-in. wide strips.

*Note:* To make this pattern larger—to fit 36-in. bust for example, add an extra $\frac{1}{2}$ in. to the side and shoulder seams. For additional alterations to the pattern see Sewing, lesson one.

# Flower-trimmed spectacle case

## MATERIALS YOU WILL NEED

Squared paper; fabric for lining to tone with suede; two pieces of red

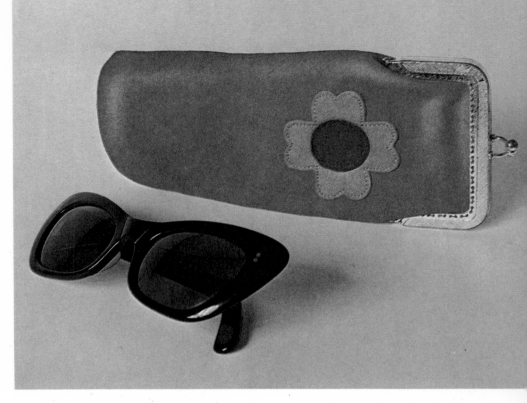

suede at least 8 in. by $4\frac{1}{2}$ in.; scraps of yellow and blue suede; adhesive (Copydex); matching red, yellow and blue silk sewing thread; gilt spectacle case frame $3\frac{1}{4}$ in. wide.

## TO MAKE

Make a template from the diagram (1 square to 1 inch) and use this to cut two shapes from the lining fabric. Trim off the top part of the template along the dotted line and use the pattern again, minus this hem allowance, to

cut two shapes from the red suede. Cut out the two flower motifs from yellow suede, and two circles (use a small coin as template) from the blue suede. Centre the blue circles onto the yellow flower shapes and stick in place with the adhesive (Copydex), and when thoroughly dry, stitch round the edge of the circles with blue silk. Position the flower shapes on the main red shapes and stitch in place with the yellow silk thread, after first sticking in position.

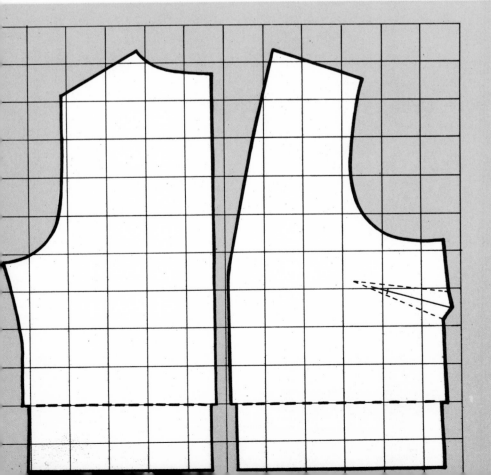

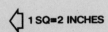 1 SQ=2 INCHES

1 SQ=1 INCH

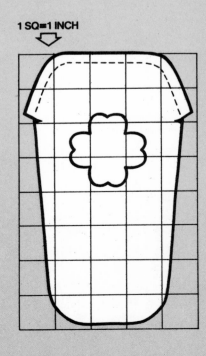

Place the red shapes together, with the *right* sides inside and stitch together along sides and base from notch to notch. Turn right side out. Stitch lining together from notch to notch in the same way, trim seam to ¼ in. with pinking shears, then turn top hem allowance over to the *wrong* side and tack in place. Fit lining inside case and slipstitch top edges together from notch to notch.

Spread a little adhesive around the inside of the frame and press case top into this carefully and leave to dry thoroughly. When adhesive is dry, stitch carefully in place through the holes in the frame, using running stitches in double red silk.

## Comb and nail file case

### MATERIALS YOU WILL NEED

Squared paper; piece of red leather at least 6 in. by 4 in.; adhesive (Uhu); red silk sewing thread; small metal comb 5¼ in. long; small nailfile 4 in. long.

### TO MAKE

Make a template from the diagram (1 square to 1 inch) and cut out the shape from the leather. Trim off the top part of the template, along the dotted line as shown. Use this trimmed template to cut out a second shape from the leather. Cut out the inner template shape and use this to cut out a third piece of leather. Spread a very thin line of the adhesive (Uhu) along

the sides, and lower edge of the smallest piece of leather and position this very carefully on the right side of the medium-sized piece of leather. When this adhesive is thoroughly dry, carefully stitch around the sides and base, close to the edge of the smallest shape. Draw the threads through to the wrong sides and knot securely before trimming off the surplus. Spread a thin line of adhesive along the sides and lower edge of the *wrong* side of the front section of the comb case, and position onto the back section with the *wrong* sides together. When the adhesive is thoroughly dry, stitch as before, but draw threads through to the right side, knot securely, trim, then tuck surplus down inside the case. Re-trim the edges of the case with a sharp craft knife. Insert comb and nailfile in case.

## Two-tone watch strap

### MATERIALS YOU WILL NEED

Squared paper; strip of navy-blue leather at least 6½ in. by 2½ in.; red and navy-blue silk sewing thread; strip red leather at least 10 in. by ½ in.; adhesive (Copydex); ½-in. wide buckle.

### TO MAKE

Make a template from the diagram (1 square to 1 inch) and use this to carefully cut out a shape from navy-blue leather. Stitch around the shape, as close to the edge as possible, with red silk thread, then re-trim the edges if necessary with a very sharp craft

knife. Trim one end of the red leather strip into an angled point, then carefully stitch down each side and around the pointed end with navy-blue thread. Re-trim edges if necessary. Make a hole using a large darning needle, about ¾ in. from the straight end of the strap, slip buckle onto strap and push buckle prong through this hole. Trim end of strap to tapered shape and stick down behind buckle with adhesive (Copydex). Place strap on wrist to gauge position for holes in strap. Make holes with a large darning needle. Carefully cut ½-in. wide strips across main navy-blue shape where indicated by lines on diagram. Thread red strap through these and through lugs of watch.

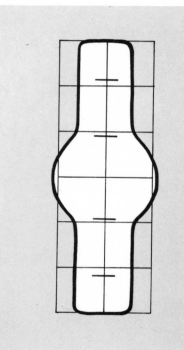

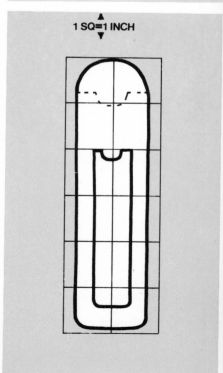

1 SQ=1 INCH

# Simple things to make in
# LEATHER AND SUEDE

## Luggage label

### MATERIALS YOU WILL NEED

Approximately 6 in. by 8 in. snakeskin or other firm leather; strong card for stiffening; ½-in. brass buckle; fabric glue; mica or celluloid.

### TO MAKE

Cut 2 pieces of leather, each 3 in. by 4 in. In the centre of one, mark and cut out a rectangular window, leaving a ½-in. border all round, for the front of the label.
Cut the stiffening card to measure 2½ in. by 3½ in., and glue centrally on to wrong side of back section of label. Glue both sections of leather together, round 2 long and 1 short side, spreading only a thin line of glue at the very edge of each piece. Press together to adhere well. Stitch all round these 3 sides, about ⅛ in. from the outer edge.

One end is left open for the address card to be slotted in.
Cut a slot about ¾ in. long, through both pieces of leather along the open end. Cut leather for the strap 1 in. wide and 6 in. long. Spread glue over entire back. When set, fold strap in half lengthways and press down very firmly all along. Cut one end to a neat point, and stitch all round the strap.

Attach buckle at straight end, and stitch end down on to strap. Thread pointed end through slot in label, ready to attach to a suitcase. Cut mica or celluloid to fit and slot in place.

## Pen or pencil holder

### MATERIALS YOU WILL NEED

Cylindrical tin or similar container; white or coloured paint for the inside; small paint brush; strip of leather, the length to be the circumference and the width the height of the cylinder, plus ¼ in. for overlap; glue (a type suitable for use on fabric or plastics is best); gold braid edging long enough to go round the cylinder twice, plus 2 in. for turnings; a different gold braid, long enough to go round the cylinder once plus 1 in. for turnings; ruler and pencil; glass paper.

### TO MAKE

Rub the glass paper over the outer surface of the tin to roughen, thus helping adhesion of the glue. Paint the inside of the tin, and leave overnight to dry.
Measure the tin and, using the ruler, mark the outline very accurately on the leather. Cut out carefully, with smooth straight edges. Spread glue all over the wrong side of the leather, and over outer surface of the tin. Leave for 10–15 minutes for glue to set dry to the touch. Position short end of leather band upright on the tin very carefully

as it will adhere on impact. Work round tin, smoothing leather and avoiding air bubbles.

The end of the leather band should overlap the starting upright edge by about $\frac{1}{4}$ in., so spread a $\frac{1}{4}$ in. wide strip of glue along the outside of the starting edge. Leave aside for glue to set and then smooth down very firmly and neatly.

Cut the longer piece of gold braid into two lengths, each measuring the circumference of the tin, plus 1 in. for turnings.

Spread a layer of glue round the top edge of the pen holder, the width being the same as the width of the braid. Spread glue along wrong side of braid. Leave both aside for glue to set. Stick braid all round top, turning starting and finishing ends under neatly, near where the leather cover is joined. Work all round, pressing braid to leather very firmly.

Glue gold braid round the bottom edge, using exactly the same method and, finally, the remaining length round the centre of the pen holder.

## Money bag

### MATERIALS YOU WILL NEED

2 rectangles of soft leather, each 5 in. by 6 in.; fabric glue; approximately 1 yd. thin strong cord.

### TO MAKE

Cut one 5-in. edge of one rectangle into $\frac{1}{2}$ in. deep points all along for top decoration. Spread a thin line of glue round the other three edges,

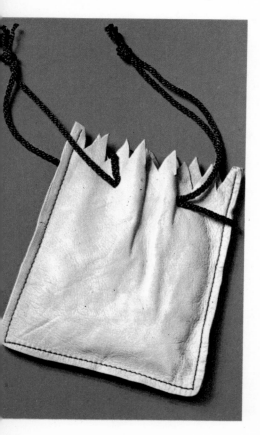

on wrong side of leather. Repeat both stages for other rectangle, and leave until glue is set.

Place one down upon the other, matching points along top, with wrong sides facing. Press all round glued edges to ensure good adhesion. Machine or hand-stitch down sides and along the bottom, on right side, about $\frac{1}{8}$ in. from edge. Finish off stitching very securely.

Punch two holes at the top on front and back of purse. They should be about 2 in. apart and about $1\frac{1}{4}$ in. down from the tops of the points.

Cut the cord into two lengths. Thread one length round the top, through the holes. Tie ends together tightly. Thread the other length through the holes in the opposite direction to ensure that the purse closes by pulling the cords separately, one in each hand. Tie the ends of the second cord together tightly.

Trim edges if necessary, and round off the bottom corners.

## Bookmarker

### MATERIALS YOU WILL NEED

2 in. by 12 in. strip of maroon suede; 2 in. by $10\frac{1}{2}$ in. strip of pink suede; fabric glue; 6 round templates with different diameters (use bottle tops, small coins, thimbles or counters, and draw round on to the suede).

### TO MAKE

Cut the maroon suede to size accurately, then the pink suede. Round off the top end of the latter, and cut the bottom end to a point about 1 in. deep. Mark 6 different sized circles on the wrong side of the pink strip, varying from $\frac{3}{4}$ in. to $1\frac{1}{2}$ in. Cut out holes very neatly.

Lay the pink strip right side up on the right side of the maroon strip, with the pink point about $1\frac{1}{8}$ in. from one end of the maroon. The top of the pink should be about $\frac{3}{8}$ in. down from the edge of the maroon. Holding the pink on to the maroon very carefully, mark round the inside of each circle the curved top edge and the bottom point. Separate the two strips.

Spread glue all over the back of the pink strip and leave to set. Spread glue over maroon strip, on right side, but leaving the circles, the top edge and corners and the bottom section below the point all quite free from glue. Leave to set.

When ready, place the pink piece down on the maroon, and starting at the top work down carefully, matching all edges and marked areas. Press down firmly to ensure good adhesion all over.

To make the fringe, cut the maroon suede at the bottom into narrow strips about $\frac{1}{8}$ in. wide. Make each cut up to the edge of the pink point, being careful not to snip the pink by mistake.

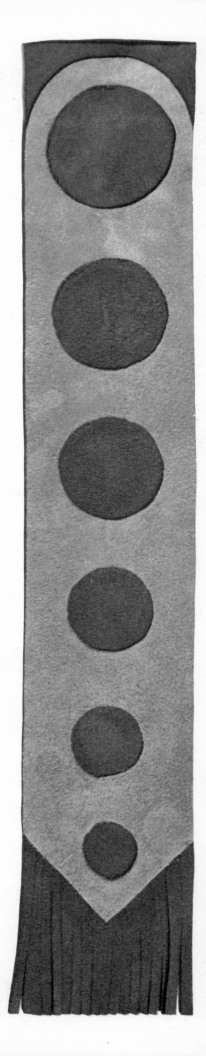

## Photograph frame

### MATERIALS YOU WILL NEED

6 in. by 7 in. firm leather (non-stretching); $3\frac{1}{2}$ in. by 6 in. thin strong card for lining; fabric glue; 6 in. by 7 in. mica or celluloid to protect the photograph; knife for cutting leather; thin card for pattern; matching polish.

### TO MAKE

Draw the pattern on to the card from the diagrams given (i.e. outer section and inner frame). Cut out each piece. Lay the card templates on to wrong side of leather and mark one large outer piece and two inner frame pieces. Cut out each part.
From the thin strong card, cut one lining for each inner frame—they must match in size exactly.
Spread glue all over back of one inner frame and one card lining. Leave to set and then press both together, matching edges and corners exactly. Repeat for other inner frame. Spread a very thin line of glue round inside edge

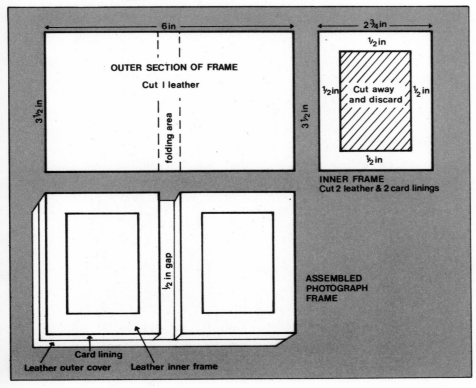

**6 in**

OUTER SECTION OF FRAME

Cut I leather

$3\frac{1}{2}$ in

folding area

**$2\frac{3}{4}$ in**

$\frac{1}{2}$ in

$\frac{1}{2}$ in    Cut away    $\frac{1}{2}$ in
and discard

$3\frac{1}{2}$ in

$\frac{1}{2}$ in

INNER FRAME
Cut 2 leather & 2 card linings

$\frac{1}{2}$ in gap

ASSEMBLED
PHOTOGRAPH
FRAME

Card lining
Leather outer cover    Leather inner frame

of large outer piece of leather, omitting the $\frac{1}{2}$-in. gap at centre top and bottom, where the fold will come. Spread a very thin line of glue round the outer side and top and bottom edges on the card side of each inner frame. When glue has set, press each inner frame on to outer frame, matching all edges and corners very carefully. Hand or machine-stitch all round outer edge in a continuous line, to hold all sections firmly together.

Cut pieces of mica or celluloid to size and slot into place behind each inner frame. Polish frame lightly, especially round the edges.

## Key ring tags

### MATERIALS YOU WILL NEED

**For each tag:** key ring fitting; scraps of suede or leather; fabric glue.

### TO MAKE SIMPLE TAG

Cut 2 pieces of strong leather, each $1\frac{3}{4}$ in. by $2\frac{1}{4}$ in., and a piece of firm card about $\frac{1}{4}$ in. smaller all round. Round off the top of each leather piece. Cut a small piece of leather $\frac{1}{2}$ in. by 1 in., fold in half lengthways and glue together. Loop through the ring, and join both ends together with a dab of glue. Glue card on to wrong side of one section of leather tag. Then glue one side of ends of loops (already through the ring) on to this. Glue other section of tag in place, so that the card and the ends of the loop are sandwiched between. When glue has set, stitch all round and fasten off neatly and firmly. Make the crescent motif by marking a $1\frac{3}{4}$-in. circle on the back of a small piece of white leather and marking a $\frac{7}{8}$-in. circle inside it, against the edge. Cut out the crescent shape only and glue to one side of the tag. Repeat for the other side, but attach the crescent the other way up. If preferred the crescents may be glued and stitched on the leather before making up the tag.

## TO MAKE THE FRINGED TAG

Cut a piece of suede 4 in. deep and 5 in. wide. Cut fringing $2\frac{1}{4}$ in. deep along one longer side, making each strand $\frac{1}{8}$ in. wide. Spread glue all along both surfaces of unfringed area and leave to set.

Cut a strip of leather 1 in. by 9 in. and spread the wrong side with glue. When set, fold in half lengthways to make a double strap $\frac{1}{2}$ in. by 9 in. Slip through tag fitting, so that ring comes into centre strap.

Glue inside surfaces of strap together, starting $\frac{1}{2}$ in. down from loop, and spreading for $1\frac{1}{4}$ in. downwards. Spread glue over corresponding outer surfaces of strap, and stick down one end of fringed piece of leather so that ends of strap are level and parallel with bottom edge of fringing. Now roll up the fringed piece, starting at one short end, very tightly, with the strap in the centre. The already-glued area on the main fringed piece will stick together very well if pressed down firmly as you roll up. Cut the strap ends in the core into fringes to match the rest.

Cut a piece of suede approximately $2\frac{3}{4}$ in. by $3\frac{1}{2}$ in. Spread glue along wrong side of both short ends and join together when set. Cut looped fringes along folded edge, $\frac{1}{8}$ in. wide and up to within $\frac{1}{4}$ in. of joined edge. Spread a $\frac{1}{4}$-in. line of glue along top edge, on wrong side, and stick round other roll (attached to ring fitting) $\frac{1}{4}$ in. down from top edge. Cut a strip of contrasting leather $\frac{1}{4}$ in. by 2 in. and stick this round the top of the first roll, above the second roll, to finish off neatly. Ease up the looped fringes to resemble a bell.

# PAPERWORK

## Lesson One: Fun with paper

**Valerie Janitch shows just how versatile paper can be and designs a complete parade of paper people for you to make.**

Paper has tremendous potential as a craft material and it is only when one begins to think objectively about it that one realises just how versatile it is. The wide variety of different papers which are now available, in different colours, textures, designs and weights increases the scope even more. It is clean and pleasant to work with, generally quite inexpensive and needs no special tools—for this reason it is ideal for keeping children amused and happy for hours, which is why several designs, including the parade of paper people on the next page, are aimed to appeal to children.

One of the joys of working with paper is that it is cheap and disposable, allowing you to ring the changes with paper lampshades, fill the house with exotic and highly-colored flowers all the year round; and make special decorations for birthdays and other festivities, which can be thrown away with the rest of the party debris! In the following pages there are plenty of ideas for both, but for this first lesson I have turned paper into people to demonstrate the variety of paper available and some of the techniques one can use.

## Getting the materials

Sources of paper are inumerable and as has already been mentioned, the variety is surprisingly wide. Most of the necessary materials can be found in local art shops or stationers, or you probably already have plenty of different sorts of paper around the house. A visit to the stationery chain store will provide rolls of cartridge paper (white and coloured) special packs of tissue and crêpe paper, scrap books (a useful source of rough-grained paper), origami papers, children's play packs (including sticky-backed, shiny paper), decorative

gift-wrap, pretty flowered writing pads and deep tone paper napkins . . . as well as adhesives, clips, fasteners, sticky tabs and labels (often very handy), poster paints and drawing equipment.

Modern adhesives simplify things too; gone are the days of making your own flour paste, or having to use messy gums and glues and waiting an age for them to dry. I have recommended particularly suitable adhesives for each type of paperwork, but special brands are not essential. You can use an all-purpose adhesive (Copydex), wallpaper paste which can be made up in small quantities (Polycell) and clear glues (Sellobond or Bostik).

You will need scissors, which you keep for cutting paper only and in addition, a sharp cutting knife (for adults only). I find one which also scores particularly suitable. It is most important to ensure sharp creases when folding paper. Sharp pencils, a pair of school geometry compasses, a ruler (with metal edge or a metal rule if possible), a setsquare, brushes for paste and paint and you're all set to go! Working with paper is such fun, and the materials are so inexpensive, if you make a mistake you can afford to throw away the ruined effort and start again. The best way to learn is to start making, no need to read through pages of techniques and instructions first, so make your first basic paper person and then go on to make some more, giving each one an individual personality. You will see from our parade of paper people overleaf how the basic figure has been adapted to create seven characters.

# PARADE OF PAPER PEOPLE

Your people will depend on the papers you use; in fact paper people are a kind of three-dimensional collage and I have designed the various characters specifically to introduce as many different treatments and papers as possible. First of all, begin by making a basic figure, which you can adapt to make it look like any character. You will find white cartridge paper just right for this.

*Note:* If children are making the figures, they could use the core of a toilet paper roll or core of kitchen paper roll.

## MATERIALS YOU WILL NEED

Sheet of cartridge paper about 9 in. by 12 in.; thin card; flesh-coloured paper or poster paint; paper fasteners; black felt pen or Indian ink; adhesives (Copydex; or clear Sellobond).

## TO MAKE THE BASIC FIGURE

Decide the height and diameter of your figure, then roll the sheet of cartridge paper into a cylinder, cutting down the height if necessary. To measure the diameter accurately, cut a circle of the required size from a piece of thin card. Roll the cartridge paper so the circle just fits inside, fix each end temporarily with a paper clip. Sketch out the position of the face roughly, features and clothes,

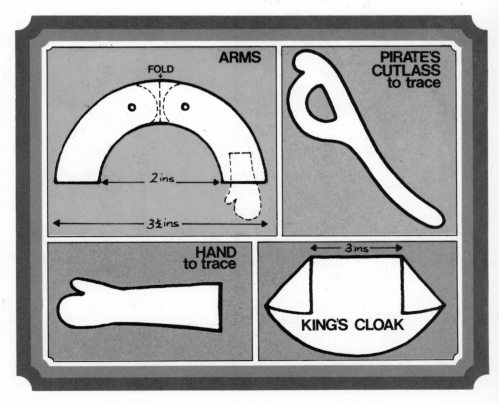

then either stick a strip of flesh-coloured paper, or paint round the face area, overlapping a little above and below (it is often easier to open out the paper again to do this, at the same time drawing in the features, but make sure you indicate the features on the *cylinder* as they will look different when rolled, if you draw them flat). Re-roll the cylinder when the paint is dry and stick with adhesive down the back.

Cut and stick the strips of paper round the cylinder for the clothes. Always begin with the face, then continue in the 'order of dressing' so where one garment meets another, you make and stick the underneath one first, cutting slightly wider than necessary, to overlap. Stick the strip for the next garment neatly over this overlap. Finally add hair if necessary—this can be cut from paper or wool or embroidery silk can be used, or the hair can be drawn on, according to the figure. Then add the arms.

Make the hands and arms, trace two hands as diagram. Cut in flesh-coloured paper or white paper and paint them. Then draw a 3½-in. diameter semi-circle on the 'sleeve' paper (same colour as the main garment) with a 2-in. diameter semi-circle inside. Cut out, fold in half and stick, inserting a hand piece as you do so (thumb towards the inside of the curve). If your 'sleeve' paper is very thin, cut the shape in card and cover with the coloured paper. Round off the straight folded edge, using scissors, and shortening the arm to suit your figure if necessary. Punch a hole ¼ in. from the top. Push a paper fastener through, making a slit in the cylinder where it should join the body. Open out the prongs of the fastener, then push together again to push through the slit. They should spring open again inside the cylinder sufficiently to enable you to open them out with the point of a pair of scissors.

# To make Professor Snodgrass

Make the basic figure by rolling a piece of cartridge paper to make a cylinder 8 in. tall by 1½ in. diameter.

## MATERIALS FOR TRIMMING

Thin card for hat brim; green hat-covering paper; grey paper for trousers; black paper for shoes; yellow paper for waistcoat; white paper for collar; scrap brown tissue-paper for beard; wallpaper for jacket and arms; contrasting wallpaper or patterned paper for bow tie and hat band.

Cut a circle of thin card 3 in. in diameter and cut a 1½-in. diameter hole in the centre, to form the hat brim. Mark basic cylinder 2½ in. from top for position of brim, mark 1 in. below for face and either paint with flesh-coloured paint or stick on flesh-coloured paper (see basic figure) slightly overlapping above and below the marked lines.

Stick hat-covering paper to each side of the brim, cutting away the inner circle on one side, but leaving a ¼-in. overlap round inner edge when covering the second side. Snip this to form tabs all the way round, then fold up tabs and slide brim gently down over the cylinder to marked line, sticking the tabs above the brim, to hold it in position. Cut a 2-in. diameter circle in the hat paper and draw a 1½-in. diameter circle in the centre. Cut edge into V-shaped tabs, being careful not to go too near the inner circle. Stick over the top of

the cylinder by glueing the tabs only, to form the top of the hat. Cut a 2-in. deep strip of hat-covering paper large enough to go round the cylinder and stick this round to form the rest of the hat, completely covering the tabs at top and bottom. Cut a 3-in. deep strip of grey paper for the trousers and stick in position with lower edge of paper and cylinder level. Draw a black line to mark centre division as illustrated. Stick a $\frac{3}{8}$-in. strip of black paper round the lower edge for shoes. Cut a 2-in. deep strip of yellow paper and fold in half to cut pointed fronts for waistcoat, stick in position over trousers, and draw in buttons and watch-chain as shown. Stick a $\frac{1}{2}$-in. wide strip of white paper between face and waistcoat for the collar and complete the features if you have not already done so, then crumple a strip of brown tissue-paper 1 in. wide by about 15 in. long and stick round face and below brim of hat for beard and hair.

Cut a piece of wallpaper 4 in. by 2 in. for the jacket, and stick into position at a slight angle as shown, so the lower edges stick out slightly. Make and fix the arms and hands as for the basic figure.

Finally cut a bow tie 1$\frac{1}{2}$-in. wide and about $\frac{1}{2}$ in. deep narrowing at the centre, from the patterned paper and stick in position and cut a $\frac{1}{2}$-in. wide strip from the same paper for the hat band and stick in position.

# To make the Fairytale King

Make the basic figure by rolling a piece of cartridge paper to form a cylinder 7$\frac{1}{2}$ in. tall by 1$\frac{3}{4}$ in. diameter.

## MATERIALS FOR TRIMMING

Royal blue paper for robes; red paper napkin for cloak; white paper tissue for ermine trimming; grey scrap-book paper for beard and hair; narrow strips of different coloured paper for belt, hem of robe and base for crown; gold foil for main part of crown and jewels; coloured foil for jewels.

Make face as for Professor Snodgrass

and paint or cover with flesh-coloured paper and draw in eyes only. Cover cylinder from neck to bottom with Royal blue paper. Make cloak by cutting a 7-in. diameter circle from the red paper napkin folded in half with the ends folded down again as diagram. Leave 3 in straight across centre to stick across the back. Cut a 7-in. by 2-in. wide strip from the white paper tissue and mark with black felt pen for ermine trim, folding corners inside at each end. Stick cloak in position. Make hair and beard from grey scrap-book paper, fringe the end and curl gently over the blunt side of a knife blade by drawing gently and firmly between the thumb and the blunt blade (or ruler edge). Stick in position, then cut moustache and eye brows. The edges of the moustache can be curled. Stick in position. Measure 5 inches down from the top of the cylinder and stick narrow strip of paper for belt in position, then stick strip of purple paper round top and pink strip round bottom of cylinder. Make the crown by sticking a strip of gold foil 1$\frac{3}{4}$ in. deep by 6 in. long to some white stiff paper. Cut out three points, as illustrated, to come at the front and sides, leaving a $\frac{1}{2}$-in. overlap at the back. Stick in position over the purple strip so this shows between the points. Cut small jewels from coloured foil and use them to decorate the crown, belt and hem of robe.

# To make Captain Cutlass

Make the basic figure by rolling a piece of cartridge paper to form a cylinder 6 in. tall by 2 in. diameter.

## MATERIALS FOR TRIMMING

Red paper for shirt; green paper for trousers; strip black paper for shoes and brown belt; light blue paper for jacket and arms; scraps white paper doily for cravat and cuffs; brown scrap-book paper for beard and black scrapbook paper for hat and patch; white paper for skull and crossbones; gold and silver foil for belt and cutlass.

Make the face as previously described and cover with flesh-coloured paper or paint and mark in features. Cut strip red paper 2 in. by 7 in. and green paper 2$\frac{1}{2}$ in. by 7 in. Stick shirt, trousers and shoes and make the dividing line for legs as for Professor Snodgrass. Make the belt from $\frac{3}{8}$-in. wide brown strip of paper. Cut light blue paper 3 in. by 4$\frac{1}{2}$ in. and make coat as for the Professor and the arms as for basic

figure. Add the cravat and cuffs cut from the doily. Cut an oval from the brown scrap-book paper 4 in. across and cut in half, trim centre to fit face and trim outside edge to look like points of beard. Stick in place. Retain small leftover piece of brown paper and shape to cover back of head as hair. Stick in position. Make the hat from two pieces of black paper, 4 in. wide and 2 in. high. Trim to shape and stick white skull and crossbones on the front. Draw in teeth, nostril and eye sockets on skull with black pen. Stick the two side pieces of the hat together only for about $\frac{1}{2}$ in. in from the end. When dry, open out the centre portion of the hat and stick in position over the top of the head. Complete Captain Cutlass with his cutlass. Trace outline shown and cut from a piece of thin card or white paper. Cover the blade with silver foil and the handle with gold foil. Cut his buckle $\frac{1}{2}$ in. wide and $\frac{3}{4}$ in. deep and stick on top of the belt. Finally add eye patch cut from black paper and complete features on face.

# To make the Upstairs Maid

## MATERIALS FOR TRIMMING

Grey-blue paper for dress and arms; brown tissue-paper for hair; white doily for apron and cap; white paper tissue for cap; bright yellow tissue-paper for duster; drinking straw for duster handle.

Make face as for other figures. Cut grey-blue paper 4 in. by 7 in. and stick round cylinder to make dress. Make arms as basic figure. Cut brown tissue-paper to measure 4 in. by 10 in., crumple one long edge into gathers, stick *inside* the top edge of the cylinder, bring the remainder smoothly down and draw round to the back, gather together to form a bun and stick in position. Study the design of the doily and cut a suitable piece, probably from the centre, to make the apron and stick in place. Cut two small pieces for collar, two more for cuffs and stick in place. To make the cap, cut a strip of doily 8 to 10 in. long and not more than 1 in. deep and gather slightly. Stick *inside* cylinder on top of hair so the frill looks like the edge of the cap. Gather the edges of a paper tissue, push inside the cylinder and fluff out to form the top of the cap and stick. To make the duster, cut a piece of yellow tissue-paper 6 in. by 1 in. and fold widthways into twelve.

Leave the lower edge joined, cut a feather shape, open out the paper and curl round a blunt knife blade (as king's beard). Cut a 2-in. length from a drinking straw and stick the lower edge of the yellow tissue-paper round and round the end, fluff up duster and stick to hand.

# To make Crazy the Clown

Make the basic figure by rolling a piece of cartridge paper to form a cylinder 5 in. tall by 2 in. diameter.

## MATERIALS FOR TRIMMING

Gift-wrap paper for costume and arms; green paper for bow tie; brown shiny paper for boots; card and purple paper for hat; paper flower cut from magazine; narrow strip yellow paper for ribbon; orange paper for hair; white paper for eyes, nose and mouth.

Make face as for other figures. Cut strip of gift-wrap paper 3 in. by 7 in. and stick round cylinder. Make arms as for basic figure. Cut bow tie 2 in. wide and 1 in. deep and narrow at the centre to form bow. Mark on spots with black pen and stick in position. Cut 1 in.-diameter semi-circles in brown shiny paper and stick on for boots. Make the hat from the purple paper and card as for the Professor, but fix brim only $\frac{1}{2}$ in. down from the top of the cylinder. Trim with the narrow (1 cm.) ribbon and flower. Cut two pieces of orange paper 1 in. square and cut to make fringes of hair, stick to the side of the head by a small tab, bent backwards. Cut eyes and nose from white paper—three circles $\frac{5}{8}$-in. diameter, stick in position, circle with black pen and make crosses for eyes and colour nose red. Make mouth from white paper, cut $1\frac{1}{4}$ in. wide and $\frac{1}{2}$ in. deep. Draw in grin and outline edge with black pen.

# To make Mr. Horridge the Headmaster

Make the basic figure by rolling a piece of cartridge paper to form a cylinder 6 in. tall by $1\frac{3}{4}$ in. diameter.

## MATERIALS FOR TRIMMING

White paper for shirt; brown scrap-book paper for trousers and hair; black strip of paper for shoes; scrap wallpaper for jacket and arms; black crêpe paper for gown; card and black paper for mortarboard.

Make face as for other figures,

drawing in features. Cut a strip of white paper 2 in. by 7 in. and stick on for shirt. Draw in collar and tie and colour tie. Cut strip of brown scrap-book paper 3 in. by 7 in. for trousers and stick in position. Draw line for legs and stick on $\frac{3}{8}$-in. wide strip black paper for shoes. Cut strip of wallpaper $2\frac{1}{2}$ in. by $4\frac{1}{2}$ in. for the jacket and stick on as for the Professor. Make arms as for basic figure. Cut black crêpe paper 3 in. by $5\frac{1}{2}$ in. turn back 1 in. at each edge and stick in position over jacket. About $\frac{1}{2}$ in. should show of the jacket front edges, under the black. Pull the lower edge of the crêpe paper slightly to stretch it so it stands well away from body. Cut $\frac{1}{2}$-in. wide strip of brown paper for hair, fringe and curl as previously described and stick in position. Complete by making the mortarboard. Cut a $2\frac{1}{2}$-in. square of card and cover with black paper. Cut a strip of black paper $\frac{3}{4}$ in. deep by $6\frac{1}{2}$ in. long, stick round the top of the cylinder so half overlaps the hollow centre, cut into tabs. Stick top of mortarboard into position centrally with one point directly over his nose— the tabs help keep the top in position.

# To make Mr. Haddock the Fishmonger

Make the basic figure by rolling a piece of cartridge paper to form a cylinder $6\frac{1}{2}$ in. tall by $1\frac{3}{4}$ in. diameter.

## MATERIALS FOR TRIMMING

White paper for overall and arms; blue-white striped paper or blue paper for apron; card and yellow paper for boater; shiny black paper for band and shoes; brown scrap-book paper for hair, moustache; grey paper for fish. Make face as for other figures, drawing in features. Cut a strip of white paper $4\frac{1}{2}$ in. by 6 in. and stick on cylinder for overall. Make arms as for basic figure. Cut striped or blue paper $2\frac{1}{2}$ in. by 3 in. for apron. If you need to stripe the apron, cut strips of white paper $\frac{3}{8}$ in. wide and 3 in. long and stick across the blue paper to form equal stripes. Stick apron in position. Make the boater as the Professor's top hat, cutting the brim $2\frac{3}{4}$ in. in diameter with a hole $1\frac{3}{4}$ in. in the centre and fix $\frac{5}{8}$ in. down from the top of the cylinder. Trim with a shiny black band and bow (1 cm.) and stick a strip $\frac{3}{8}$ in. wide round the bottom of the cylinder for shoes. Draw in line for legs below apron. Cut hair as for Mr. Horridge, but fringe curl and stick so the hair curls upwards just under the brim of the hat. Cut moustache and stick in position, make fish and stick onto right hand.

# PAPERWORK

## Lesson Two:

**Valerie Janitch shows you how to make more things in paper.**

In lesson one I told you about the variety of different papers and cards available and showed you how to make a parade of paper people. As I said in that first lesson, the easiest way to learn about paperwork is to experiment and to make various items from different papers and cards, using alternative techniques—after all, paper is so inexpensive you can afford to make a few mistakes and throw them into the waste paper basket—I show you how to make one from old newspapers in this feature! New readers can start here with the first of the makes, but to recap, you will need the following tools and materials, apart from as many varied papers as possible. The materials which I used are listed under each make, but of course you can use completely different papers and/or colours to get the effect *you* want.

### YOUR SECOND MAKE

## Mobiles
## Maypole dancers
## Waste paper basket
## Collar for floral decoration

## Midnight mobile

Witches on broomsticks and a glowing crescent moon would be a marvellous Hallowe'en decoration, or a decoration for childrens' bedrooms.

### MATERIALS YOU WILL NEED

5 pipe cleaners ($6\frac{1}{2}$ in. long); $5 \times \frac{5}{8}$-in. diameter papier maché or polystyrene balls for heads (or use a wooden ball, bead or button); cotton to tone with pipe cleaners or fine wire; black crêpe paper; flesh-coloured poster paint; grey tissue paper; black cartridge paper; brown crêpe paper; five round lolly sticks or drinking straws; fluorescent yellow paper; black paint; a lampshade ring about 10-in. diameter; black cotton; clear sticky tape (Sellotape); clear glue (Sellobond); rubber-based all-purpose adhesive (Copydex); wall-paper paste.

### TO MAKE

Make the witches first. Cut a pipe cleaner in two—one piece $4\frac{1}{2}$ in. long and the other 2 in. Bend the longer piece in half for the body. Push the bent end up into the ball you are using for the head, but do not secure.
Fix the remainder of cleaner across the body for arms, binding it firmly into place just below the head (remove head once position is marked) with cotton (or fine wire).
Cut a 4in. diameter circle of black crêpe paper for the dress. Fold this in half *along the grain*, then bring each side of the folded edge together so that the circle is now in quarters, but *do not crease fold*. Snip off the folded corner at the centre, then open out paper. Push the pipe cleaner body down through the centre hole, bringing the paper right up under the arms; now re-fold in half along the grain so that the fold is straight across the body and gently push the centre of the double semi-circle between the two pipe cleaners which form the body, so that each folded side comes round to hang straight down the front of the body, a pipe cleaner 'leg' inside (see diagram A). Cut a 2-in. diameter circle

A

for the sleeve, fold and snip the centre as for the dress, bring this down over bent top of the body until it is level with the arms, then push through body until it is level with the arms, then push through body as before so that arms are inside the front folds (see diagram A).

Fix the head in place and paint. Cut a $2\frac{1}{2}$-in. diameter semi-circle of grey tissue paper, soak in the wallpaper paste, stick the straight edge over the top of the head and smooth down to form hair.

To make the witch's hat, cut a $2\frac{1}{2}$-in. diameter semi-circle of black cartridge paper and form into a cone shape to fit neatly onto the head, stick. Stick two pieces of the black paper together to form double thickness, then cut a 1-in. diameter circle for brim, with a hole in the centre about $\frac{5}{8}$ in. in diameter (this will depend on the size of the head and consequent size of the cone). Push down over top of cone and adjust size if necessary, stick and when dry, stick hat to head.

To make the broom, cut a strip of brown crêpe paper $1\frac{1}{2}$ in. wide by about 9 in. long, with the grain running widthways. Gather together to ressemble twigs, then wire round the end of the lolly stick or drinking straw.

Fold a piece of black catridge paper in half for the cat, trace the diagram B for the pattern, then cut in double thickness paper, placing lower edge along the fold, open out and punch holes for eyes on one side only, stick fluorescent yellow paper to other side of head so it will show through the holes as eyes. Fix the cat round the broomstick and fix underneath with sticky tape so that the cat remains firmly in position.

Sit the witch over the top of the broomstick. Make four more witches. Thread a fine needle with black cotton, make a large knot in the end, then push up through the paper just behind the back of the witches neck and then through the point of the hat to hang. Draw round a section of the outer rim

of the lampshade ring on the yellow fluorescent paper, to come about one third of the way up the side of the ring, draw round the edge of a large plate to form the inner curve, and cut out crescent so formed. Paint the lampshade ring black. When it is dry fix the crescent to the ring with clear glue (as illustration) and then attach the witches to the frame with the black cotton. Tie another piece of black cotton onto the top of the frame to suspend it.

## Snowflake mobile

This is an unusual and very effective mobile to hang in front of a window or other source of light. The light shining through the coloured tissue paper gives the impression of a stained glass window. The adhesive which I suggest has a nozzle top which is most useful when fixing tissue paper.

### MATERIALS YOU WILL NEED

Black cartridge paper: different coloured tissue papers (colours optional); PVA adhesive (Sellobond); black cotton; sticky tape (Sellotape); 14–15 in. garden cane; wire to suspend mobile.

### TO MAKE

Use thick black paper—medium-weight but not too heavy. For each snowflake, cut a 4-in. diameter circle from the black paper. Fold in half across the centre, then carefully fold again into quarters, with the folded edges exactly together. We cut eight snowflakes. Snip out shapes to form a pattern up each folded side, finishing the top with a point, or the lowest part of a curve as in diagram C. Now open out the circle and very carefully fold into quarters again, this time exactly between the previous folds, so that they all fall together in the middle of your new quarter. Snip and finish the folded edge as before, making sure you are not left with any large areas un-cut, but allowing at least $\frac{3}{8}$ in.

between each cut-out. Open out and press the circles flat with a warm iron. Cut out pieces of coloured tissue paper to fit the sections of your design as illustrated on the mobile. You can use two or three different colours as on our mobile, or for a simpler effect, just one piece of coloured tissue paper can be cut to fit the black snowflake. The cut edges must overlap the black area round the section which you are covering. You will find if you are using different coloured tissues, that you can cut two and often all four sections of each colour at the same time. Spread a little PVA adhesive over the black area of the snowflake (with the nozzle type this is easy and makes no mess) and press the tissue smoothly into place (this will be the back of the snowflake). Join the snowflakes to each other with two strands of cotton, side-by-side, $\frac{1}{2}$ in. apart, so they are about 2 to 3 in. apart. Join three together in this way for the two outside edges of the mobile and two for the centre. Leave at least 12 in. of double cotton at the top to suspend from the cane.

Make slip knots to tie the snowflakes to the cane, adjust and tie when in correct position. Hold in place with a strip of sticky tape. Pass a piece of wire about 3 ft. long through the centre of the bamboo cane, twist to form a loop to hang the mobile.

## Maypole dancers

Although they look so different, the basic figures of the Maypole dancers are very similar to the witches on the Midnight Mobile. They would make a charming party table decoration—or just imagine them dancing round a little May Queen's birthday cake covered in white icing with pink candles the only top decoration on the cake, apart from the central Maypole

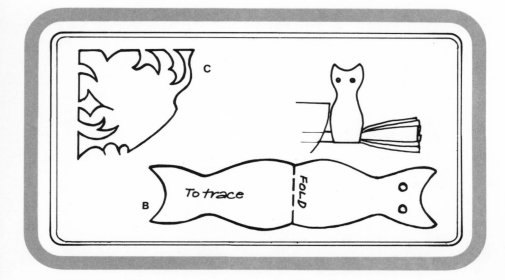

(in this case use a steel knitting needle) with a dancer going to each place. She could perhaps hold the place name? Each small guest could take hers home with her.

## MATERIALS YOU WILL NEED

9 pipe cleaners (6½ in. long); pink paper tissues; wallpaper paste (Polycell); white or pink cotton or fine wire; 6 ¾-in. diameter papier maché or polystyrene balls for heads (or use a wooden ball, bead, button—or Plasticine); pink and white crêpe paper; paper doilies, flesh-coloured poster paint; brown tissue paper; black ink. For the maypole see making instructions.

## TO MAKE

Make the dancers first by bending a pipe cleaner in half to measure 3¼ in. for body and legs, with a 3 in. length for arms. Cut a piece of pink tissue 2 in. by 4 in. and roll lengthways round the arm piece; stick join and soak each rolled end in the wallpaper paste before smoothing flat and cutting hand shape at tip. Wind cotton tightly round wet wrist and leave until dry; then remove so that indentation remains.

Push the bent end of the body into the ball for the head, slip the arms through the body, close under the head and secure in position with cotton or wire, remove head. Cut a piece of white crêpe paper 9 in. long by 2 in. with the grain running widthways. Gather one long edge and draw up tightly round the body, level with the bottom of the legs.

Cut a similar piece of crêpe paper, in pink, and 2½ in. wide, gather as before and fix over the petticoat, again level with the feet.

Now cut a section from the edge of a doily 2 in. in depth and about 7 in. wide. Soak thoroughly in paste, then pinch inner edge together over top of pink skirt, securing with cotton and sticking join at the back. Gently shape the lower edge with the fingertips, so that it dries as illustrated. Cut a 1½-in. diameter circle of pink crêpe, make a hole in the centre and slip down over the top of the body to form sleeves and bodice. Cut a circular motif from the doily, about 1 in. in diameter, make a hole in the centre and slip over the pink circle.

Paint the head pink with the flesh-coloured poster paint and fix in position. Cut a 3½-in. diameter circle of brown tissue paper for the hair. Paste very thoroughly, then fold about ¾ in. off centre, place centre of straight edge across top of head (shorter part underneath) and smooth down sides and back flicking up ends as illustrated. Draw in black dots for eyes. Make five more dancers.

**To make the Maypole:** you can use a foil-covered pea-stick, or a knitting needle stuck in a firm base, or even a candystriped drinking straw. Cut 'ribbons' from narrow strips of pink and white crêpe paper and attach to the top of the Maypole—each dancer can hold the end of a 'ribbon'

# Newspaper waste paper basket

If your waste paper basket is always full of old newspapers use some of them to weave a novel new basket. We saved the colour sections (across two pages) from the larger newspapers to make this one. Alternatively it is fun to use ordinary black and white newsprint for the horizontal rings and plain black paper for the vertical strips, giving a chequered effect.

## MATERIALS YOU WILL NEED

A suitable grocery carton (see below), or thick card and sticky tape (Sellotape) to make your own; old newspapers as above; wallpaper paste (Polycell); rubber-based adhesive (Copydex); coloured sticky tape (Sellotape Trendy-mend), or coloured paper.

## TO MAKE

Find a carboard carton about 6 in. square by 10 in. high or make a suitable one from thick card taped together with the sticky tape.

Open out the double-page widths of newspaper, fold neatly over and over into long 1½-in. wide strips and stick with wallpaper paste. For a carton this size you will need eight strips for the vertical weave. If your carton is a different size, measure the width of the sides and use sufficient strips to cover them when placed side-by-side with a very slight space between each. Mark the centre on each strip, then weave together, four (or the number you need) in each direction, at the centre, so that the remaining length of each strip extends equally in four directions like a cross.

Measure the remaining strips horizontally round the carton, so that they slide up and down easily, stick the overlap and remove. Stick the base of the carton over the woven newspapers, then bring the strips up at each side and slide rings down, two at a time, weaving the vertical strips neatly up through them as illustrated. Press each ring down firmly above the previous one, continuing up to the top.

Cut the remainder of the vertical strips about 3 in. above the top of the basket, then turn neatly over the edge and stick down inside. Neaten the cut edges inside the basket with coloured sticky tape or coloured paper.

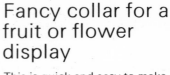

# Fancy collar for a fruit or flower display

This is quick and easy to make, and you can adjust the measurements to any size you wish—to encircle a plain round bowl of fruit or flowers. Use it the way up we show, or turn it over, according to the contents of the vase. Our version is comparatively small, to display a little posy of early spring flowers.

## MATERIALS YOU WILL NEED

Thin card; gold, silver or coloured foil (we used gold); wallpaper paste (Polycell); pins.

## TO MAKE

Cut a circle in card and cover with foil paper (we cut a 5-in. diameter circle). Then draw a smaller circle in the centre (3½ in. diameter) and mark the outer circle into eight equal sections. Cut away centre circle and trim the outer edge with pinking shears if you have them.

Now cut two circles of foil paper, twice as large as the original circle (10 in.) and stick them back-to-back with the wallpaper paste. Pink edge with shears as before. Draw a smaller circle in the centre (6 in.) and fold in half exactly across the centre and crease sharply. Open out and fold across the centre again so the folds form a cross exactly at right angles. Open out and fold a third and fourth time, exactly between previous folds. Turn paper over and repeat again, these folds falling exactly between the first set (see diagram D).

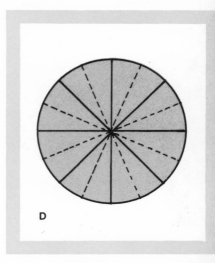

D

Open out paper and cut away centre circle, then re-fold outer edge in a star shape and cut a slit (¾ in.) in each outer fold, ½ in. above the lower edge. Carefully fit the card circle round the star and slot into the cuts, each point of the star falling at a marked point on the rim. Secure with a pin pushed up through the rim inside the fold of each point.

# PAPERWORK

## Lesson Three

**Designed by Valerie Janitch**

Paper lampshades are the 'in' thing at the moment! They are quick and easy to make and it is possible to get a really widely contrasting range of designs. One of the great advantages of working with paper—it is so inexpensive you can literally ring the changes every time the shades look grubby or you want a change of colour scheme. Once you have your frame or a pair of rings, you can make a new shade as often as you please—for practically no cost.

## YOUR THIRD MAKES

## Aquarium shade

This is fun as either a hanging or a table lampshade. The underwater scene is effective unlit—and changes character completely when lit. All the shapes are cut free-hand—and it's simple enough for children to make themselves, with only a little supervision.

## MATERIALS YOU WILL NEED

Lampshade parchment; two 10-in. diameter lampshade rings, one with a pendant or gimbal fitting; adhesive (Copydex or clear Sellobond); pale blue, pale lilac and olive green tissue papers—with scraps in other colours to tone with fishes; wallpaper paste (Polycell); thick papers in dull colours; coloured foil papers for fishes; clear varnish (optional).

## TO MAKE

Cut a piece of lampshade parchment 9 in. deep by 33 in. long. Oversew to rings round top and bottom; trim and stick join.
Cut the 'wave' shapes about 5 in. long by 1¼ in. wide (see illustration) in pale blue and lilac tissue. Paste over the parchment with wallpaper paste (Polycell), slightly overlapping, as illustrated.
Cut the 'pebbles' in thick coloured papers (you can use pages from a scrapbook) and paste all round lower edge, overlapping as illustrated.
Cut long wavy strips of olive green tissue for seaweed and paste one over another as illustrated.
Cut fish shapes in coloured foil papers

and punch small circles for eyes.
Cut fins and tail in toning tissue. Position fish round the shade, as illustrated, holding in place with a dab of paste in the centre: then paste on fins and tail, so that edges overlap behind body, before sticking the body into place. Finish with a coat of clear varnish if liked.

## Cut and slotted shades

Stiff paper is an obvious material for inexpensive lampshades, and is ideal for smart shades made entirely by cutting and slotting different papers together. Once you've made one you will find endless variations suggesting themselves, offering exciting scope for dramatic colour combinations. Remember one important thing, or you will be disappointed. A really professional finish depends entirely on accurate measuring, scoring and careful cutting. I find it useful to work out my design on graph paper, using that as a pattern to cut the paper: then it *must* be accurate!

## Cerise and white curves

### MATERIALS YOU WILL NEED

Graph paper; stiff cerise-coloured paper; 9-in. diameter pendant lampshade ring; thin white card or heavy paper; adhesive (Copydex); white sewing cotton.

### TO MAKE

Draw out the shape in diagram B1 along a strip of graph paper, making it as long as possible, and marking carefully as shown (each square representing ½ inch). Cut out and use as a template to cut three strips of coloured paper, each about 45 in. long. Mark and cut ¼-in. deep slots along both sides of one strip, and along one side only of the other two. Score broken lines carefully.
Cut two strips of white card or paper 1½ in. wide and about 32 in. long, cutting ¼-in. deep slots at 1½-in. intervals along both sides (exactly opposite each other, as diagram B2). To assemble, fold the coloured paper along creases and slot in and out of the slots in the white bands, alternating the position of the three rows as illustrated. Trim ends of all five strips to match, and stick overlap to form a circle of ten coloured sections in each row. Fix pendant ring to inside of upper white circle, and tie at intervals with white cotton.

## Layers of pleats

Pleated strips are slotted together to form a small fluted shade—ideal for

porch or hall: add more strips to make it longer, if you like.

### MATERIALS YOU WILL NEED

Heavy coloured paper 30½ in. by 8 in. and plain white paper 20 in. by 4 in.; adhesive (Copydex); two 6-in. diameter lampshade rings, one with pendant fitting; sewing thread.

### TO MAKE

Carefully measure a sheet of paper 30½ in. by 8 in. deep as diagram C (scale, each square represents 1 inch). Rule into four 2-in. wide horizontal strips and mark vertical broken lines 1 in. apart: score these A-A on one side of the paper and B-B on the reverse.
Cut into four long strips, then cut ¼-in. deep slots exactly halfway between the scored lines (see diagram) along both edges of two strips and along one edge of the other two (for top and bottom).
Fold into pleats, then carefully slot the pleated strips together, alternating folds as illustrated. Trim ½ in. overlap at end of each strip and stick behind other end to join.
Cut a piece of white paper 20 in. long by 4 in. deep. Stitch pendant and plain rings round top and bottom edges and stick join.
Slip pleated shade over the white cylinder: it should grip sufficiently to hold itself in place, but may be taped here and there if liked.

## Chinese lantern

So simple—but so effective. Contrast a light, bright colour in the centre with a dark outside paper.

### MATERIALS YOU WILL NEED

Two 7-in. diameter lampshade rings, one with pendant fitting; stiff paper 23 in. by 8 in. in light colour, and 23 in. by 13 in. in dark contrast; adhesive (Copydex).

### TO MAKE

Oversew the rings round top and bottom edges of light-coloured (inside) papers, and stick join.
Score and fold the dark paper lengthways (see diagram D) and then rule lines at 1-in. intervals, ending 1 in. from top, cut edge. Holding the folded paper together firmly, cut from folded edge along each line to within 1 in. of cut edge.
Open out folded paper and stick one edge round top of cylinder, overlapping ½ in. above. Then stick lower edge round bottom of cylinder, overlapping ½ in. as before. Finally, stick join.

## Gift-wrap lighting

There are some enchanting designs available in gift-wrap paper—or you

can make your own patterned paper. It's so cheap you can have a complete change whenever you feel like it at very little cost. The delicate flower fairies drum is sweet for a nursery table lamp—the more vivid narrow cylinder is pretty for a pendant fitting in a little girl's room.

## Nursery lampshade

### MATERIALS YOU WILL NEED

Thin white card; gift-wrap paper; wallpaper paste (Polycell); two 8-in. diameter lampshade rings, one with gimbal (or pendant) fitting; 1½ yd. narrow braid; adhesive (clear Sellobond or Copydex); sewing thread.

### TO MAKE

Cut a piece of card 6 in. deep by 27 in. long. Place over gift-wrap paper to decide how to show the design to the best advantage—mark outline and cut. Paste gift-wrap to card with wallpaper paste.
When dry, oversew to rings round top and bottom, then trim and stick join. Stick braid trimming round upper and lower edges, to hide stitches.

## Flowers for a little girl
### MATERIALS YOU WILL NEED

Thin white card; gift-wrap paper; wallpaper paste (Polycell); sewing thread; two 7-in. diameter lampshade rings, one with pendant (or gimbal) fitting; 1½ yd. narrow braid; adhesive (clear Sellobond or Copydex).

### TO MAKE

Cut a piece of card 9 in. deep by 23 in. long.
Now follow directions for the nursery shade.

## Straws in a circle

Ordinary drinking straws make an unusual but couldn't-be-easier paper lampshade. Choose a gay colour scheme like our red-white-and-blue theme—or plain white for a more sophisticated shade suitable for a porch (in which case, bands of braid about an inch from each edge would be attractive).

### MATERIALS YOU WILL NEED

Thin white card; two 6-in. diameter lampshade rings, one with pendant (or gimbal) fitting; sewing thread; adhesive (Copydex); double-sided sticky tape (Sellotape); 2 packets of drinking straws; braid (optional).

### TO MAKE

Cut a piece of thin card 1 in. shorter than the depth of your straws, by 20 in. long. Oversew to rings round top and bottom, then trim and stick join.
Run a band of double-sided tape round the top and bottom edges, with another round the middle of the cylinder.
Pulling away the backing strip a little at a time, press each straw, one at a time, firmly against the bands of tape, overlapping ½ in. at each end, so that it is securely held.
Trim with bands of braid, if liked.

B 1  EACH SQUARE = ½"  2

30½'
A B A B A B A B A B A B A B A B A B A B A
C
8"
EACH SQUARE = 1" (C & D)

D
6½"
23"
FOLD

# Woody cottage

Paper collage (just like the Paper People in lesson one) is a fascinating craft, and makes an intriguing lampshade for the nursery. This design might be too hard for children to tackle, but they would be delighted if Mummy or Daddy made it for them. We used a ceiling rose, upside down, for the base, so the shade almost touches the table and the light glows through making the cottage look as though somebody is inside with the lights on!

*Note:* The bulb must be of low wattage to prevent scorching the shade, and the lampshade might be better made up as a hanging shade for very young children, who might be too inquisitive about the inner workings of the lamp at eye level!

## MATERIALS YOU WILL NEED

White cartridge paper, card or lampshade parchment; black cartridge paper; paper and ruler or ready-squared paper (old arithmetic book); adhesive (Copydex or Sellobond PVA adhesive); yellow ochre poster paint; coloured papers; gift-wrap paper or greetings cards printed with flowers; black felt pen; green, pink and red tissue paper; white paper doily; strong sewing thread or cotton; two 8-in. diameter lampshade rings, one with pendant or gimbal fitting; 4-in. diameter ring for top; brown crêpe paper.

## TO MAKE

Cut a strip of white cartridge paper, card or parchment $5\frac{1}{2}$ in. deep and $27\frac{1}{2}$ in. long. Cut another strip in black paper the same size. Rule a sheet of paper the same size into $\frac{1}{2}$-in. squares (or use pages from a squared exercise book) and copy the diagram E, or design your own cottage.

Hold in position securely with paper clips and place pattern over the black cartridge paper, edges level, and very carefully prick the corners of the windows, lantern and diamond in the front door, marking the paper underneath. Then using a sharp knife, cut these parts away (but keep the pieces) Now stick the black paper to the back of the white strip—edges level. Prick the corners of the windows etc. as before, but this time from the black side, to indicate the position on the right side. Turn over, pencil in outlines and rule windows into $\frac{1}{4}$-in. squares. Avoiding windows etc. (by holding original black shapes over them), colour the walls with the yellow ochre poster paint—putting this on unevenly to look like rough plaster. You can use a small sponge or piece of cotton wool, or even your finger, rather than a brush.

Cut $\frac{1}{4}$-in. wide strips of blue paper and stick above and beside lower windows to form frame, as indicated. Cut the shutters to size and stick beside upstairs windows as indicated. Mark on window ledges and shutter lines.

Cut out window boxes and fill with flowers cut from gift-wrap or cards. Cut front door in brown with slightly larger piece of blue paper for the surround, cut window in door before you stick in position.

Draw in hinges, knocker, bolt, bell, lantern, key and name as illustrated. Cut the back door in blue, with brick red tiles above and stick in place. Cut the nesting box in brown, stick in place and draw in roof etc.

To make the creeper, cut 1-in. wide strips of green tissue paper. Crumple quite tightly, then lay a trail of adhesive—not *too* much, but more than the usual thin smear—on a piece of flat green tissue. Press the crumpled strip down onto it, making sure it is well held.

When dry, gently tear away the backing at each side, then stick in position as indicated by the broken lines on the wall of the cottage.

For the roses, cut a strip of tissue, 1 in. by 3 in. Fold in half lengthways, but do not crease. Then coil round into a tight rosette, twisting and flattening the strip as you do so. Press firmly down into a blob of adhesive on another piece of tissue and leave until quite dry before tearing away the surrounding backing as before. Stick in position. Stick coloured paper behind the lantern and either paper or pieces of white doily behind the windows for curtains and blind.

Stitch lower edge round pendant or gimbal ring, then stitch top edge round plain ring and stick join. Cut a 30-in. length of brown crêpe paper 20 in. wide. Fold in half lengthways (across the grain, shiny side inside). Place the folded crêpe over the shade, covering the outside, fold level with the top edge. Oversew round top of shade, then gently draw up so that the crêpe stands stiffly up above the shade. Fold over, bringing the top edges down to overlap the shade $\frac{1}{2}$ in. Crease fold, then open out paper again and slip small ring over crêpe before turning paper down again, gathering it over the ring held inside the fold. Distribute gathers evenly, stick join and gently stretch the crêpe forming lower edge of roof.

Cut water butt in brown paper, draw lines and stick over join. Cut brick red flower pots and stick into place, filling with flowers as for window boxes. Make a long strip of crumpled green tissue paper as for creeper, about $1\frac{1}{4}$ in. wide and stick round the lower edge to cover the stitches.

# String-bound shade

This is an ideal way of re-using an old lampshade frame, and it is so easy to make, children could quite easily cope. There are so many different types of string available now (see our Macramé lessons), it is possible to ring the changes with several string-bound shades. We used a natural coloured sisal string.

## MATERIALS YOU WILL NEED

A lampshade frame with lamp fitting, a suitable size for your lamp (we used a 10-in. diameter drum frame); white enamel paint (optional); binding for top and bottom rings; large ball of sisal string (about 80 yards); adhesive (Copydex).

## TO MAKE

Wipe the frame, then paint if necessary (if using an old frame this may not need painting, or if the frame is already nylon-coated). When dry, bind the rings with the binding. Keeping the string in the ball, knot the end firmly round one ring (preferably the lower), and start binding the string round and round the frame from top to bottom, keeping it as taut as possible, making sure each strand fits closely up against the next, but without overlapping. Unwind the ball of string as you work, but keep the working end short.

Bind the frame completely and tie off firmly. If you do have to join the string, knot firmly to the lower ring. To trim the shade measure the circumference. Take six lengths of string twice the circumference, knot at one end and pin to a board, plait the strands to required length, allowing a $\frac{1}{2}$ in. overlap, knot and trim. Stick round top of shade, repeat for bottom of frame.

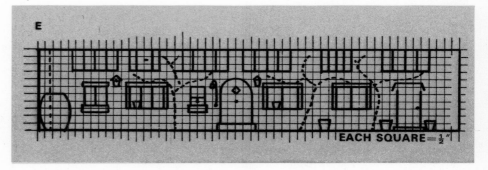

E

**EACH SQUARE = $\frac{1}{2}$"**

# PAPERWORK

## Lesson Four:

## Pretty paper flowers

**Valerie Janitch shows you how to fill the house with colourful blooms — all the year round.**

Paper can be used for the most fabulous flowers — and when you know how, even quite elaborate specimens are usually very easy to make. If you have been following the earlier lessons on paperwork, you will already be familiar with the techniques of working with paper, and making flowers is not very different from other branches of the craft. Some of my designs — like the happy funflowers — were designed with children in mind. The more complicated ones, involving the use of wire, are more suitable for grown-ups to make!

## Papers

It is a good idea to get to know your papers first — some are much more suitable for making flowers than others, and there are a few basic methods to learn before you begin.

**Crêpe paper** is the most versatile — its silky finish and stretchability can create very realistic petals and leaves. The better quality papers have more sheen and greater stretch, so it's worth paying a little more for crêpe paper for flowers. Usually the darker the paper the easier it is to see the sheen; on the very pale papers it is often difficult to tell which is the dull side — but don't worry. It is important to cut it with the grain running in the right direction.

**Tissue paper** is good for delicate blooms (look at our chrysanthemums) and comes in a very wide range of colours, so it is possible to get nearer to the original colour of the flower if you want to. It is crisp and easy to handle, and twists, folds and fringes very well.

**Face tissues** can be used most effectively in flower making, and a box of assorted colours can be turned into a veritable flower garden!

## Wires

Florists' wire is ideal, but can be difficult to get unless you are near a wholesaler who supplies the trade. If you have to compromise, any fine

wire, medium fuse wire, PVC covered garden wire or insulating wire can be used, or ordinary galvanised wire—medium gauge.

## Adhesives

There are many adhesives sold by stationers which are suitable for sticking paper. It is wise to choose the adhesive to suit the particular job, and obviously those which are neat to handle are the most practical. An all-purpose adhesive (Copydex) a PVA adhesive with a neat nozzle top (Sellobond PVA adhesive), an adhesive which works like a lipstick (Sellostic) and wallpaper paste (Polycell) are the four which I find most useful and I have recommended the one I consider most suitable under each 'make'.

## Techniques

There are several basic techniques which, once you have learned them, can be used for most paper flowers.
**Petals:** Once you have your basic shape you can often cut out several petals at the same time. Hold the paper together with paper clips while you cut out the petals, to prevent the layers from shifting.
**Cupping:** Holding the petal, place your thumbs in the centre and gently stretch the crêpe paper so that it forms a cupped, petal shape.
**Frilling:** Gently stretch the cut edge of the crêpe paper to form a frill.
**Curling:** Gently stroke the paper between your thumb and the blade of a blunt knife—the heavier your paper the firmer you stroke.
**Leaf veins:** You can mark these effectively by placing the leaf face down on a padded surface and 'drawing in' the veins with the point of a knitting needle or orange stick.

# YOUR FOURTH MAKES

## A bunch of daisies

## Autumn glory chrysanthemums

## Rose in a pot

## Frilly carnations

## Happy funflowers!

## Oriental poppies

## Bunch of daisies

Simple and unsophisticated, these fresh-looking daisies are easy to make, and are ideal for mass-production. We used two greens with the white, but the darker shade would do for both centre and stem, or you could have an all-yellow centre.

### MATERIALS YOU WILL NEED

Cotton wool; pipe cleaners; PVA adhesive (Sellobond); light green, emerald green, lemon yellow and white crêpe paper.

### TO MAKE

Stick a tiny piece of cotton wool on to the tip of a pipe cleaner and mould it round into a firm ball the size of a large pea. Cut a 2-in. diameter circle in light crêpe paper, spread adhesive all round the edge, then place centre over cotton wool, bring edges down and stick below cotton wool.
Cut two 6-in. long strips, 2 in. wide, one in light green and the other yellow (grain width-ways, as arrows—diagram A). Fold in half lengthways (broken line), shiny side inside. Cut a close fringe, ¼-in. deep, along the folded edge on each side, then open out and refold, shiny side outside, along line of previous fold—but do not crease. Stick the strips together along the lower edge, fringed edges level. Wind the double strip, yellow inside, round and round the covered centre, sticking along base.
Cut two 2½-in. by 9-in. strips of white crêpe paper, grain as arrows (diagram B). Cut down, at ½-in. intervals, to ½ in. from lower edge: snip off corners at tip of each petal. Stick together along lower edge, so that each cut between two petals on the top piece falls directly over the centre of the petal underneath. Wind round and round base of centre, sticking lower edge and keeping it absolutely level.
Cut three leaves in emerald crêpe paper, 3 in. long by ½ in. wide: shape tips. Then cut a 12 in. long strip, ¾ in.

wide—grain running *across*. Stick one end round base of petals, then wrap round and round—then slowly twist it round and down the stem—binding in leaves as you go, by wrapping the base of each round the pipe cleaner and then winding strip over it. Secure at base. Open out the petals and stroke gently against the blade of a blunt knife to curl them round slightly, as illustrated.

## Autumn glory chrysanthemums

I used 'Rainbow' tissue paper for these realistic chrysanthemums—you can make four different blooms from one sheet 20 in. by 30 in. But plain tissue would do just as well (in which case just ignore the references to shading in instructions).

### MATERIALS YOU WILL NEED

Yellow-bronze shaded ('Rainbow' by Elgin Court) or plain tissue paper (see above); PVA adhesive (Sellobond); plastic covered garden wire; olive green crêpe paper.

### TO MAKE

Cut a 30-in. long strip of tissue paper 5 in. deep. Fold in half lengthways. Now fold the strip in half in the other direction, then in half again—and again, to measure 3¾ in. by 2½ in. Holding the folded edges together, cut down from this edge to within ¾ in. of lower edge, making your cuts fairly close together. Unfold and cut the strip into four equal lengths. Then, on each piece, carefully open out the fringed fold and smooth it gently to flatten, then bring the lower edges together again *against* the previous fold, without re-creasing, to form a looped edge. Having done this, stick the four sections together along the lower edges, one on top of another—darker side of each uppermost. Now, with the lighter side inside, roll the strip up loosely, sticking the lower edge and keeping it absolutely level, as the centre tends to ride up inside: if you *do* lose the centre, rescue it with the tip of your scissors and pull it down before squeezing the base together firmly. Cut a 36-in. length of wire and bend it in half. Fix this loop round the base of the flower, close under the petals, then twist the wire until the flower is tightly gripped. Bring the two ends of the wire down to form stalk. Cut a 1-in. wide strip of green crêpe paper and bind base of flower and then stem, as in the instructions for daisies. Cut a crêpe leaf from the pattern (diagram C), and stick round stalk.

## Rose in a pot

A single, giant rose makes a stylised decoration with a very professional look—though it's surprisingly simple to make. We used three shades—pale pink, mid pink and deep red. But this isn't essential: two shades, or even only one, will still make a spectacular rose—though much of the effect is in the shading, so try to use at least two shades. You can also make a smaller, less full-blown, rose by simply following the directions for the ten (X) centre petals—or a medium-size bloom by adding the eight (Y) petals, but ignoring the outer (Z) ones.

## MATERIALS YOU WILL NEED

Thin card; pale pink, mid-pink, deep red, yellow and olive green crêpe paper; adhesives (Sellostic, Copydex); cotton wool; a thin garden stake 12–18 in. long; fine wire; 9-in. long florists' wire (or any thicker, but flexible, wire); cardboard; black paper; a 5-in. plastic flower pot; Plasticine.

## TO MAKE

Using thin card, draw and cut out the petal pattern in the diagram (D) three times—to the following measurements:

   (X) 2½ in. wide by 3½ in. deep
   (Y) 3 in. wide by 4 in. deep
   (Z) 4 in. wide by 5 in. deep

With the grain running up and down (see arrows) cut ten (X) petals in *double* crêpe—deep red on top, mid-pink behind (dull surfaces together—shiny outside). Using adhesive (Sellostic), stick each pair of pink and red petals together at tip, sides and base.

In the same way, cut and stick together eight (Y) petals mid-pink on top, pale pink behind. Finally, cut six (Z) petals—pale pink both on top and behind.

Beginning with six pale pink (Z) petals, cup the centre of each as instructed. Then cup the *lower* half of the eight (Y) petals—turning each petal over and cupping the *upper* half from the back—so that the tip of the petal curls over backwards.

Finally, cup the upper and lower parts of the ten (X) centre petals in the same way—making the tips curl over even more.

Wrap a small piece of cotton wool round the tip of the garden cane: cut a 2-in. diameter circle of yellow crêpe, put adhesive (Copydex) on the edge and stick neatly over the cotton wool. Now take one (X) petal and roll it (lengthways) round the yellow tip of the stick, sticking the base of the petal round the stick below. Follow with another (X) petal, half overlapping the first—and then continue sticking the remaining eight round the stalk in the sale way (lower edges always level). Now wire the base, to hold securely, and push the petals gently together with your cupped hands.

Then stick the eight (Y) petals over the centre ones, overlapping and wiring just as before. Finally, add the six outer (Z) petals, wire, and then re-cup to emphasise the shape.

Draw the leaf shape (E) 3½ in. wide by 5 in. deep. Then cut four times in green crêpe, grain running as arrowed. Using adhesive (Sellostic) down the centre and round the edges, put two leaf shapes together with a 9-in. length of florists' wire down the middle, extending below base of leaf. Then stick another paper leaf to each side: trim edge all round. Mark veins as instructed.

Wrap and stick a little cotton wool over the stuck and wired base of the petals. Then cut a long, 1-in. wide strip of green crêpe—with the grain running across. Stick one end firmly over it and then slowly twist it round and down the stick: tape the wire to the stick so that the base of the leaf is about 5 in. below the flower, then continue binding stick and wire with green crêpe, securing firmly at the base. Cut a 5-in. diameter circle of card to fit inside rim of pot and cover with black paper. Make a hole in the centre and push stick through. Fix a large lump of Plasticine on the end of the stick to weight (adjusting length first if necessary), and fit rose and card into pot.

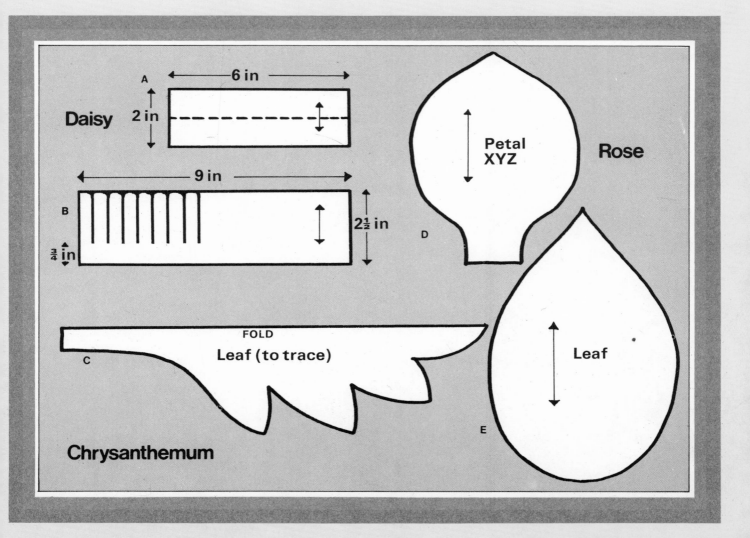

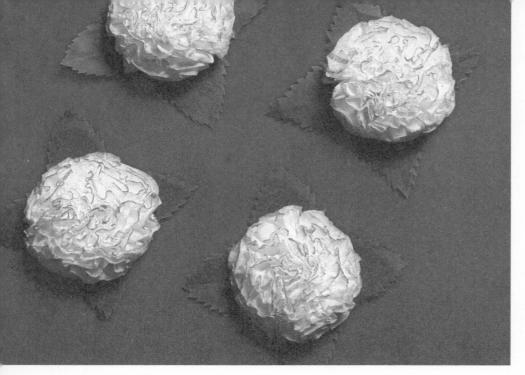

## Frilly carnations

These pretty carnations would be such a charming way to welcome your guests to the dinner table—put one at each place setting.

### MATERIALS YOU WILL NEED

White (or coloured) face tissues (Scotties); green tissue paper; fine wire; water colours; adhesive (Copydex).

### TO MAKE

Place two face tissues together and fold in half lengthways: cut along fold, forming four two-ply layers. Fold—widthways—every ½ in., concertina fashion, then twist wire round centre. Carefully separate the plies of the tissues, starting with the top ones and gently pulling each layer up towards the centre—be very careful to avoid tearing the tissue. Trim shape neatly.

Paint an area of very wet water colour on a flat sheet of glass or other non-absorbent surface. Holding the base of the carnation, gently dab the edges of the petals into the colour so that a little is absorbed. Leave to dry. Cut a 5-in. square of green tissue paper for the leaves. Fold across diagonally—and again (broken lines in diagram F1). Fold resulting triangle in half as broken line in diagram F2. Cut a jagged edge as diagram F3. Open out and stick carnation in the centre.

## Happy funflowers!

These cheerful little pot plants smile and nod in the slightest breeze: the children will love making—and proudly displaying—them.

### MATERIALS YOU WILL NEED

Thin card; coloured paper for petals and centres, and green paper for leaves;

wallpaper paste (Polycell) or adhesive (Copydex); green crêpe or tissue paper; pipe cleaners; fine wire; tiny flower pots (peat root pots); Plasticine; face tissues.

### TO MAKE

Make a pattern in thin card to cut the petal shape (squared arithmetic book or graph paper will help, but is not essential). Rule a 4-in. square as diagram (G1), then add horizontal, vertical and diagonal lines—all crossing at the centre. With the point of a pair of compasses at this centre point, draw a 3-in. diameter circle. Now, with the point of the compasses at each point where a line crosses the circle, draw a 1½-in. diameter circle. Cut out round the outer edge of each small circle. Use this template to cut each flower in coloured paper stuck to thin card. Draw a 2-in. diameter circle in a contrasting paper for the centre, marking a ⅝ in. radius curve for the mouth, and stick to centre of flower. Draw the mouth and eyes with a felt pen.

Trace the leaf shape (G2) and cut four times. Bind one whole pipe cleaner, and two halves, with crêpe or tissue paper. Stick one end of the long cleaner behind the flower, covering it with a circle of green paper. Stick two shapes together for each leaf, the tip of a short cleaner between. Wire the other ends of the leaf stalks closely round the main stalk, 2 in. from the bottom. Flatten a ball of Plasticine to fit inside top of pot; push stalk through centre, adding more Plasticine for weight if necessary. Wrap a tissue round base of stalk to pad out pot, fit inside and push down firmly.

## Oriental poppies

Make these great big blooms in dramatic colours—just a few make a fabulous display.

### MATERIALS YOU WILL NEED

Face tissues; black and green crêpe paper for centre and stem; coloured crêpe paper for petals; 12-in. florists' wire; adhesive; 18-in. long thin garden cane; sticky tape; bleach (this is optional).

### TO MAKE

Roll a face tissue into a neat ball, hooking one end of the florists' wire round the centre to hold firmly. Then cut a 4-in. diameter circle of black crêpe paper and cover the tissue smoothly, gathering in the edges round the wire and sticking. Cut a 2½-in. wide by 20-in. long strip of black crêpe, along the grain. Fold along the centre to measure 20 in. by 1¼ in. Fold in half across the grain, then in half again. Snip along the folded edges at ¼-in. intervals—about ½ in. deep. Dab adhesive (Copydex) along the strip below the snipped edge and stick round the black centre ball. Then repeat with two more similar

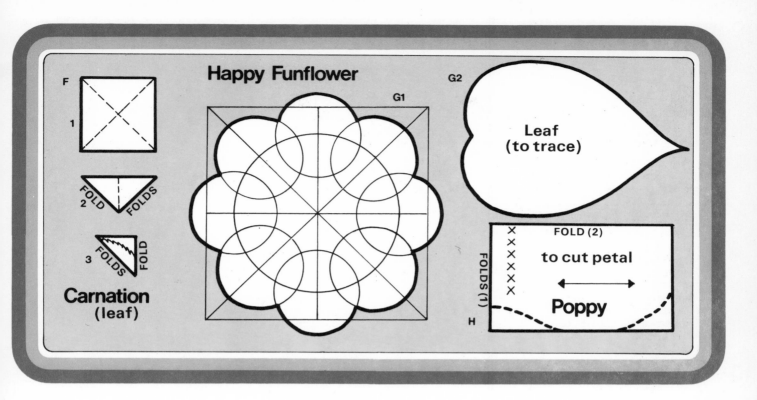

**Happy Funflower**

F
1

FOLD
2
FOLDS

FOLDS
3
FOLD

**Carnation**
**(leaf)**

G1
G2

Leaf
(to trace)

FOLD (2)
to cut petal
FOLDS (1)
Poppy
H

strips of snipped black crêpe.
Cut a 6 in. by 20 in. strip of crêpe
paper, along the grain, to make two
petals. Fold in half across the grain, and
cut. Fold one of these pieces in half
across the grain again, keeping the two
pieces together so that the petal is
double. Fold this in half along the
grain and then cut as indicated by
broken line in diagram H. Open out last
fold and dab a line of adhesive
(Copydex) about 1 in. above the
folded base of the petal, following the
line of X's on the pattern. Stick this to
lower edge of black centre, gathering in
each side with the finger-tip to stick
the bunched base of the petal round
half of the black centre. Make a second
petal and stick round other half of
centre. Make two more petals and stick
lower edges round the first pair,
positioning the centre of each new
petal between the first two. Repeat
with four more sets of petals—six pairs
in all—sticking securely round over
previous ones, and alternating positions
as before. Now press the thumbs
gently down into each petal to cup
centre, then frill top edges. Turn the
poppy upside-down and coat the
inside of the black centre with
adhesive (Copydex) before stuffing in
face tissues to make a firm round
base to the flower—adding more
adhesive as necessary.
Align the protruding wire along one end
of the garden cane, and tape securely
into place. Cut a 1-in. wide strip of
green crêpe paper across the grain and,
beginning just above the base of the
outside petals, bind back of flower and
stalk.
To obtain a variegated effect, hold
the flower upside-down and brush
lightly with a few drops of diluted
bleach to remove patches of colour.

# COLLAGE

## Lesson One:
## Basic techniques

**Valerie Janitch starts you off on a fascinating pastime which everyone can enjoy.**

Collage is such fun because there are so few rules—and it's often possible to break those! Collage is simply the application of different shapes and decoration on a background, to build up a picture or design. What you use, and how you do it, is entirely up to you! Our designs show how different collages can be—and there are more variations to come in future lessons. The flexibility collage offers for individual choice of treatment and personal expression means that, if you are artistic, you will want to create your own designs. But the examples here show different treatments, and I shall describe just how I created them, for guidance. Collage is so personal— depending on what you yourself have available—that you won't want to follow my ideas and materials exactly—I shall tell you what I used only so that you can substitute an appropriate alternative.

The essential *tools* are few: pencil, ruler, paper (including paper for tracing), large scissors, and small, pointed embroidery scissors, pins, a sharp craft knife (Rexel Versicut)—and possibly compasses and a set square.

### Materials

These can be almost anything— depending on whether you like a delicate, pretty effect, or something more robust. I hoard fabric cuttings and samples, coloured paper (including colour pages from newspapers and magazines), all trimmings . . . braid, lace, ribbon, sequins, beads, buttons, artificial and everlasting flowers, bits of fur, feathers, wools, string, shells, interesting pastas, cord, raffia, gift wrappings, foliage, seeds . . . In fact, you reach a point when you're terrified to throw *anything* away! Often I buy some major components of a design—then find all the "bits and pieces" amongst my own collection. I store everything in see-through polythene bags: as your collection grows, the less you will need to buy. The large stores are the best hunting ground for fabrics and trimmings, but market stalls and your local grocer and hardware shop are all ideal sources of material.

I use three *adhesives*: for heavier fabrics and most trimmings, a special fabric adhesive which does not mark the fabric (Copydex), a wallpaper paste for paper and light fabrics (Polycell) and a clear all-purpose adhesive (Sellobond) for hard objects needing a firm bond. Double-sided adhesive tape (Sellotape) is invaluable for certain delicate jobs.

One cannot generalise on *backgrounds*, but I am specially fond of textured fabrics—coarse weaves and uneven linen (or Moygashel) and rough hessian to set off the subject. Don't hurry to decide on your background: often it will suggest itself when you have collected together the bits and pieces of your design.

You will probably have no difficulty choosing *subjects*—but keep the basic design simple, and not too small: this gives more scope for development and detail. If you need inspiration, just look at greetings cards (many of which are themselves printed reproductions of collage pictures): posters, magazines, children's books, catalogues . . . sometimes a piece of fabric will suggest a theme. Ideas are everywhere: just remember to keep the basic design simple.

### YOUR FIRST MAKES

## TWO SIMPLE PICTURES
## The bridal couple

To avoid starting with a formidable blank sheet, I suggest experimenting on a purchased greetings card or other illustration. Work your collage on this— using the original faces and background

(this is quite legitimate!)—and be guided by the picture for your choice of materials (see our illustration).
This is how I turned the card on the left into the collage on the right: it introduces a variety of treatments and materials—and the method described applies to all collage
Begin by studying your subject. I left the background to form a hazy, out-of-focus setting for the figures. Always start with the basic garments or the central object: in this case the man's suit and the girl's dress and veil.
Make a pattern on tracing or grease-proof paper, tracing the outline carefully: try to keep your patterns simple, and just go straight through areas you will later be covering with another layer of collage. I chose black felt for the suit—but if you use a fabric which frays, back it with iron-on fabric stiffener (Vilene) before cutting. Pin the pattern to the fabric and cut the shape out accurately. I traced and cut the girl's dress in blue flock-spotted organza, and her veil—in three pieces—in a fine cotton lace. *Don't* stick anything down yet.
When you reach a similar stage, place the pieces in position on the illustration and plan your intended treatment, making notes of any ideas which occur to you. As the man's lace collar and cuffs appear from inside his suit, I stuck scraps of lace over the lace in the picture, the inner edge overlapping the jacket illustration. Then I stuck the suit into place using a fabric adhesive (Copydex). Then came the girl's dress, soaking the fabric thoroughly in wallpaper paste (Polycell) before pressing it into position.
Next came some scalloped lace trimming for the skirt and bodice. The bow on her shoulder is narrow satin ribbon, and the decoration green guipure lace daisies, each with a pink velvet forget-me-not stuck in the centre. I stuck all this with fabric adhesive.
Now for the hair. *His* first. I generally use stranded embroidery cotton, cutting each six-strand piece to length and soaking it thoroughly in paste before sticking it into position, beginning at the outer edge. The girl's was great fun: first I did the tendrils which appear from *under* the main sweep of hair—the top ends overlapping the final sweep so that they would be covered. Then the front curves round with the cut ends of each length to be hidden later by the flowers—as will the top ends of the back hair. I use tweezers and pointed scissors to guide the strands—and plenty of paste is essential!
Now came the veil. But I didn't feel the fine lace showed up enough. I tried heavier alternatives—which spoilt the effect: so I cut some narrow lace trimming in half and used each side to edge the veil, leaving the hair still visible through the fine lace.
The flower stalks are narrow strips of green raffia, the bouquet first built up with crumpled green tissue paper,

covered with leaves cut from taffeta ribbon, and pink lace daisies with velvet forget-me-not centres. The flowers in her hair have a few tiny seed pearls fixed into place at the end—with added sparkle in the silver sequin on her ear.

## Straw daisy circlet

Colourful straw-daisies (helichrysums) can be bought from florists—but they are very easy to grow from seed in a sunny garden—and are very attractive used in collage. Here they are combined with coloured statice and fluffy brown grass-heads in a charming wall decoration which is simplicity itself to do. I chose a pink colour scheme—but golden straw-daisies with yellow and white statice (or dyed glixia flowers) and green grass-heads would be effective too—on a vivid green mount. First I covered a 7½-in. square of card with a 10-in. square of linen-like fabric (Moygashel)—mitre corners, take excess neatly over edges and stick to back—then drew a light pencil circle, diameter 6½ in., on the fabric.
Now I was ready to plan my arrange-

ment: I chose pink-toned straw-daisies, alternating with deep pink and white statice—set off by the brown grass. I wired each tiny bunch of statice and grass together like a miniature sheaf, grass at the top, with fine wire: it helps to wire the grass and first flower heads by winding the wire tightly round under the heads, then wiring in each following flower head separately. Cut the stems of the completed bunch ½–¾ in. below final wire. A circle this size takes about ten groups, according to the size of the straw-daisies and your bunches.
Arrange the straw-daisies in a circle to decide their relation to each other: larger alternating with small, light with dark. Then stick a bunch firmly to the linen with clear all-purpose adhesive (Sellobond) along the line of the circle: pin temporarily to hold in position till dry if necessary, then stick a straw-daisy over the stalks, closely followed by another bunch—and another straw-daisy, until the circle is complete.
To border the linen, pick a fabric in a strong shade which emphasises your colour scheme and, for an arrangement this size, cover a 10½-in. square mount as previously described, and then stick on the linen-covered board.

247

# COLLAGE

## Lesson Two

**Valerie Janitch takes you forward to more ambitious designs.**

Assuming you are now keen to continue—if not already addicted to—the fascinating craft of collage, here are some more advanced, and very effective examples of the contrasting forms from which you can choose. But again—especially as you become more experienced—I must stress, as in Collage, lesson one, how personal collage is. Even if you base your pictures on mine, the different materials and trimmings which *you* use will be what makes the finished work so rewarding and individual.

I have chosen subjects which I hope will inspire you to adapt and design similar collages of your own—following the details of my treatment only for guidance. But if you want to reproduce your own version of any of these, there are diagrams and full instructions for working them—together with notes of the materials I used for mine. In all cases I used either wallpaper paste (Polycell), fabric adhesive (Copydex), clear adhesive (Sellobond) or double-sided sticky tape (Sellotape)—depending on the weight and type of thing I wished to stick.

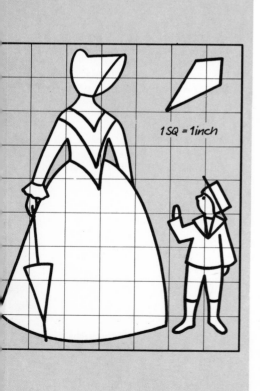

1 SQ = 1inch

**YOUR THIRD MAKES**

## Three costume collages and collage with pasta and pulses

### Victorian Costume Collage

#### A Windy Day
A comparatively simple design in fabric and allied materials: cuttings from a summer frock made Mama's gown, an evening dress her bonnet—and her sailor son wears an old cotton skirt and a garden raffia boater. Identifying your own bits is half the fun of collage!

#### MATERIALS YOU WILL NEED
**For Mama—**

Tracing paper; soft and hard pencil (or carbon paper); white cartridge paper; pink face tissue; wallpaper paste (Polycell); scraps of lace, ribbon and satin; all-purpose fabric adhesive (Copydex); coloured card for background; patterned fabric for dress; narrow braid; embroidered motif; drop pearl; cocktail stick; nail varnish or paint; guipure lace daisy.

**For The Little Boy—**

Pink face tissue; brown stranded embroidery cotton; piece natural raffia; black stranded embroidery cotton; scraps of gingham, cotton poplin, white and black felt; black Russian braid; black ink.

**For the background**
Scrap white chiffon and striped fabric; soft embroidery thread; scraps coloured ribbon; green guipure lace daisies; multicoloured lace flowers and artificial forget-me-nots.

#### TO MAKE

To copy this design, rule a sheet of tracing paper into 1-in. squares and draw the figures following the diagram. Rub over the back of the paper with a soft pencil and then transfer the lines to white cartridge paper by drawing over them again with a hard point (or use carbon paper). Then cut each figure out.

First of all, paste a piece of pink face tissue over Mama's neck and hand, overlapping the edges. Then stick narrow lace round her neck and along the lower edge of her bonnet. (We used pale green ribbon inside her bonnet brim, then stuck lace *behind* the front edge, overlapping as illustrated, and trimmed the inner edge as the neck). Cut the bonnet in satin, then take the narrow white band of ribbon right over the top to the back. At this point, trim the cut edge and stick the paper figure on to the background of pale grey card. Trace a paper pattern for her dress following the diagram, then cut it carefully in flowered cotton and paste into position, trimming the cuffs and hem with lace, then edge the cuffs and neck with narrow silk braid cut in half, using the same braid—full width— along the hem. (We cut similar pink braid in half for the bodice detail trimming).

A short piece of narrow white ribbon, with a knot in the centre, made her bonnet strings, and an embroidered motif the trimming. A drop pearl and a cocktail stick painted with nail varnish, and more satin for her parasol, trimmed with a scrap of lace and a guipure daisy.

Now for the little boy. Make face and hands from a pink face tissue like his mother's, then cut hair from brown stranded embroidery cotton. Soak each length thoroughly in wallpaper paste, then stroke into position, the ends following the hairline and overlapping the hat. The crown of his hat—but *not* the brim is added at this point—use a short piece of natural raffia.

At this point stick the figure into position on the background—slightly overlapping Mama, as illustrated. Then finish off the hat with more raffia for the brim, and trim it with black soft embroidery cotton.

A scrap of gingham makes his dickey, then trace patterns following the diagrams for his suit, collar and boots, cutting them in cotton poplin, and white and black felt respectively. The edge of the collar and ties are soft embroidery cotton again, but the lower edge and cuffs are edged with black Russian braid. A spot of black ink for his eye, and he is complete.

Cut the clouds from white chiffon and the kite in striped cotton, using white soft embroidery thread for the string, and knotting scraps of coloured ribbon on to the tail. Finally, a double row of green guipure daisies, cut in half, makes the edge of the flower border, with multi-coloured lace flowers and artificial forget-me-nots above.

# Tudor costume collage

### Queen Elizabeth I as a Young Girl (1546)

Historical costume is always a popular subject, and gives exciting scope for collage—especially the Tudor period, with its rich fabrics and extravagant ornamentation. It isn't difficult to find illustrations and reproductions of contemporary paintings in books and elsewhere, to inspire you: I couldn't resist a portrait of Queen Elizabeth I as a girl of thirteen, by an unknown artist. I have retained the original colours, but substituted crushed velvet for the rich brocade of her gown in the painting, and simplified the lavish trimming, which would have looked too heavy if copied in detail in this size.

The most important thing to study, in costume collage, is the order in which you do each section—always remembering the basic rule to begin with the

underneath parts, overlapping the edges which will later be covered by other parts of the design.

I suggest you find a picture which particularly appeals to you, adapting it as I have done: but you might find it helpful to experiment with mine first, to see the order in which I have applied each section. One thing to note—when I refer to left and right, mean *yours* and not hers!

## MATERIALS YOU WILL NEED

Tracing paper; soft and hard pencil (or carbon paper); white cartridge paper; pink face tissue; wallpaper paste (Polycell); stranded embroidery cotton (for hair); scrap satin; scrap brocade and velveteen; all-purpose fabric adhesive (Copydex); crushed velvet (for dress); dark green card for background; scrap pink suede and green leather (for book); scraps narrow white ribbon; small red glass bugle beads; scrap guipure lace; soft black embroidery cotton; narrow gold braid; tiny seed pearls; dark glass beads; gold bugle beads; three tiny oval pearls; tiny coral beads; $\frac{1}{2}$-in. diameter gold sequin; black ink.

## TO MAKE

Use 1-in. squares to scale up the design and then transfer it to white cartridge paper as before (Windy Day). Cut out. Begin with her face and neck, using a pink face tissue, stick in position. Then the hair, use stranded embroidery cotton, soaked in paste, following the

hairline—followed by rose satin for her headdress. (If you like, you can now stick the figure to the background, although we did not do so yet).

Trace a paper pattern and cut her kirtle (underskirt) in cream and gold brocade, overlapping the edge at each side—and the left sleeve lining in deep red velveteen. Next cut both sides of the skirt, and also the bodice, in crushed

1 SQ = 1 inch

velvet: then the right sleeve lining in velveteen. Cut the left and right inner sleeves, in the kirtle fabric, and finally the sleeves themselves in crushed velvet. We found *this* a good point to mount the figure on its dark green background.

To make the hands, cut them in white paper—following the broken lines so that they are joined. Cover in pink face tissue. Cut the whole book in pink suede, followed by the cover in green leather—leaving the pink visible only as the page edges and fix in position between her hands, then stick the whole into position on the design. Now finish off the inner sleeves with strips of narrow white ribbon to represent the slashing, decorated with rubies made of small red glass beads. Her cuffs are guipure lace, edged with black soft embroidery cotton.

The basic figure is now complete, so stick narrow gold braid round the neck and lower edge of the bodice, as a base for tiny seed pearls, alternating with dark glass beads on top. She wears more tiny pearls round her neck, and her headdress is edged with pearls and gold beads. Her cross is made up of bugle beads and three tiny oval pearls, and tiny coral beads make her rings. A ½-in. diameter gold sequin and a pearl surrounded by red beads form the pomander which hangs down her kirtle, suspended by a chain of tiny beads and pearls. Finally, mark the features in black ink.

# Edwardian costume collage

### Ascot

Although essentially another costume collage, this one is in a very different form. Instead of using portraits, we have fashion plates of this era to guide us—and all the emphasis is on the fabric and clever blending of colour. I have chosen this subject to demonstrate the use of lace, and the effectiveness of a subtle colour scheme, compared to the rich, colourful, be-jewelled Tudor period. Again, I give the order in which I worked, so you can follow my design.

## MATERIALS YOU WILL NEED

Tracing paper; soft and hard pencil (or carbon paper); white cartridge paper; piece deep cream moiré ribbon 3½ in. wide (or taffeta or moiré fabric), ¼ yd. cream and deep brown lace 2½ in. wide; ¼ yd. 2½ in. wide cream lace; all-purpose fabric adhesive (Copydex); scrap coffee-coloured ribbon; ½ yd. coffee-coloured and deep brown lace 1 in. wide; ½ yd. black lace ½ in. wide; dark brown satin ribbon; sage green felt stuck to a piece of card; toothpick; scrap narrow cream ribbon.

## TO MAKE

Use 1-in. squares to scale up the design and then transfer it to white cartridge paper as before (Windy Day). Cut out. Begin by cutting off the top of her left

arm along the line of her back, and cover with deep cream moiré ribbon (any scrap of similar fabric, watered silk or taffeta would be equally effective). Let the fabric overlap the edge which joins her body, and cover the moiré with a scrap of cream lace. Then use the overlap to stick *behind* the body, replacing the arm in its previous position. Then cut a strip of moiré for her back, down to the bow of her bustle, carefully placing the marking of the moiré to the best effect. After this, cut the right arm, again using moiré and cream lace—with a scrap of coffee tafetta ribbon for her glove, and coffee lace trimming the cuff and neck. The full sweep of her bustle as it forms a train is moiré—and also the top section of her skirt, immediately below the band of ribbon. Then cut carefully up between the side of the train and the skirt—to the top of the highest frill. To make the frills, cut the entire frill section off along the line of the top frill. Then cut off the top frill, along its lower edge, and cover it with coffee lace, the lower edge of the lace just overlapping the top and each side about ½ in. This top surplus is stuck behind the skirt, so that the frill is back in its former position. Cut off and cover the next frill in the same way—using deep brown lace—and replace it by sticking the surplus behind the top frill.

Continue with the remaining frills in the same way, alternating coffee and deep brown, until the lowest. Make this a black one. Fold the overlapping lace at the front neatly round and stick it to the back of the figure, doing each frill separately, beginning with the lowest. The excess on the inside is tucked smoothly behind and stuck to the back of her train.

1 SQ = 1 inch

Mask the cut edge of the train with a scrap of cream lace (indicated by broken line), then stick slightly gathered deep brown lace round (behind) the lower edge, as illustrated.

Cut the front sweep of the bow, the two ends and the bow itself, in three separate pieces of paper, covering each with dark brown satin ribbon, and sticking them into position in that order. Following the edge and the motif, cut deep brown lace into convenient shapes to cover the hat, sticking one on top of another so that the edge of the lace just overlaps all round the edge of the hat, finishing with a single motif in the centre to hide the cut ends. For the cream border, cut narrow lace into pieces to stick behind the hat, leaving just the edge visible all round.

Only at this stage is she ready to mount on the background of sage green felt covered card. The parasol is cut in paper and covered with remaining scraps of moiré and cream lace, the top edged first with coffee and then deep brown lace, stuck behind the paper to overlap the top as illustrated. Wooden toothpicks make the handle and ferrule, and a tiny bow of narrow cream ribbon trims the base.

# Flowers in the sun

### Collage with Pastas and Pulses

Pastas and pulses and rough materials make a more robust collage which is great fun to do. Vary your composition to suit yourself. My only guidance is the basic formation of the flower—you can decide the size, the design and the arrangement—just use my examples to spark off your own ideas. First decide the size and background you require: I used a coarsely woven dark brown Moygashel dress fabric stuck on to card. Then plan your flowers: draw a circle on a piece of tracing paper the size you want the finished flower to be. Trace the angles in the diagram, matching centres of angles and circles exactly. Extend each line to meet the edge of the circle. Cut out and arrange this and your other flowers as you want them on the background. Trace leaves and draw buds from diagram, adding these to your design. Move the tracings about until you are satisfied with your arrangement, then plan your treatment of the different flowers, and make notes. Mark the centre and five outer points of each flower with chalk, wax crayon or felt pen (making sure the marks will eventually be covered). Add lines of stems, indicate positions and leaves and outline the buds. Remove the tracings. Now place and decide the arrangement of the assorted items you plan to use for each flower. When this is to your satisfaction, stick firmly into place with plenty of clear adhesive (Sellobond).

I gave the largest flower (5 in. diameter) a 1¼-in. diameter centre of coiled thin piping cord, then built up the shape of the flower with butter beans, stuck a

line of yellow split peas up the centre of each petal, then soaked the fabric with a liberal amount of adhesive before sprinkling pearl barley over the remainder of each petal, pressing it firmly down into the adhesive. When thoroughly dry, shake gently to remove surplus.

The centre flower is 4 in. in diameter; it has a 2-in. diameter centre of yellow split peas, the outline is macaroni, and the petals are rice grains.

The top flower (3½ in. diameter) has a 2½-in. diameter centre of coiled thick piping cord and the petals are outlined with a thinner cord—then filled in with yellow split peas round a line of green split peas. The buds are green split peas, the bud itself outlined in Russian braid filled in with pearl barley. I used rough hessian webbing for the leaves. This frays the moment one cuts it, so I made the leaves like this: trace the pattern and cut it out. Pin this to the webbing, then make a thin trail of white PVA adhesive (Sellobond) on the hessian, all round the edge of the pattern. Remove the pattern and press wool or other edging into the adhesive to form the shape of the leaf. When dry, cut out level with the outer edge of the leaf. Finally, I stuck a row of green split peas up the centre.

Before fixing the leaves, stick the stems into place. I used lacing cord for the thick stem, with Russian braid for the stalks of the leaves—hiding the ends neatly whenever possible.

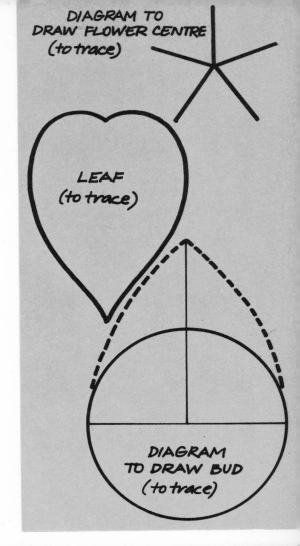

DIAGRAM TO DRAW FLOWER CENTRE (to trace)

LEAF (to trace)

DIAGRAM TO DRAW BUD (to trace)

# COLLAGE

## Lesson Three
## Make use of natural materials

**Valerie Janitch continues her instructions on this simple craft.**

I have already described how this easy craft — which is particularly suitable for children, who can make up really imaginative collages using all sorts of oddments from around the home — requires minimum tools and virtually no expense.

You can make up attractive pictures using small items from the kitchen and from your work bag, and, as shown on this page, even the garden can be used as a source of materials.

This wise old owl illustrates how to use natural materials to combine in a striking, almost three-dimensional picture.

First I covered my backing (a piece of strong card 21 in. by 18 in.) with rough hessian. Then I assembled the various materials I planned to use, and kept re-arranging them until I was satisfied with the effect. The inexpensive straw oval table mat had originally suggested an owl in my mind — and the similar round drink mats followed as ideal eyes — with dark wooden buttons sewn with natural garden raffia, for the pupils. Honesty petals made his fluffy chest — and here I used double-sided Sellotape to attach each delicate circle — as well as the cockade of fluffy grassheads above.

He needed wings, which I made from bunches of dyed grass (oats or similar seed-heads would be just as suitable), and attached to each side of the mat — before sticking on the eyes, followed by a walnut shell for his beak. I found a piece of cork bark for him to stand on, and a couple more walnuts for his legs, with bits of filbert shell for his claws. With the addition of fir cone ears (I cut away the backs to make a flat surface), the parts were ready to stick to the hessian once I had decided the ideal position using clear all-purpose adhesive (Sellobond) throughout. Now I was ready to do the background — provided by a packet of bay leaves from a health food shop: the flowers are everlasting straw daisies (helichrysums), grown in my own garden!

# COLLAGE

## Lesson Four:

## More robust collages, and the use of heavier techniques

In previous lessons you have been shown how to make pretty pictures using various collage techniques and how to create really decorative costume collage. The materials used have all been rich in colour and texture, but confined mostly to fabric, trimmings from the haberdashery counter, dried flowers and pulses. However it is possible to use a much wider variety of items in collage to create more robust pieces, and the theme of this type of design is usually an abstract one.

## Variety

In this lesson we have asked several different designers to make collages using their own ideas to create an interesting and unusual picture. You can see the results in the completely different collages in this feature. An 'assemblage' or picture built up with interesting textures; abstract metal collages; a hedgehog wall-hanging in hessian and leather and an unusual treatment for a proprietory filler and bottle glass.

Once you have started to think along these slightly more abstract lines you will be surprised with the ideas you can adapt for use in collage. These are the sort of designs which you don't sit down and work out or draw before you start. Once you have the materials, the design usually suggests itself, and you will find working with the actual bits and pieces which are to form the finished collage is a very satisfying way of starting a picture. After all surely that is what craft is all about—being able to adapt natural resources to produce something attractive which enhances the original material, and hopefully the end result is a work of art!

## 'Assemblage' technique

This is an accepted form of collage, and one which can be adapted to the use of many different materials. The word simply means an assembly of found materials which are formed into a satisfying arrangement—and which can be completely abstract or grouped

to form a picture within a picture. You can use almost anything for this type of collage technique—bits of metal like the inside of a watch or clock or a collection of nuts and bolts; dried, pressed leaves; bottle tops; a collection of wine labels; newspaper cuttings; plastics such as Perspex—in fact anything which inspires you to be creative!

This type of heavier collage does sometimes demand different types of adhesive from those used in the previous lessons. For example, metal insides from a clock would not stay on hessian very long if they were stuck with wallpaper paste! For this type of collage, the heavy duty adhesives have to be used—for example our metal panels were created by sticking the various nuts, bolts, cogs and wheels onto the background with an epoxy resin adhesive.

## YOUR FINAL MAKES

## Abstract 'assemblage'

## Textures in metal

## Plaque in plaster

### FUN FOR CHILDREN TO MAKE

## Hedgehog wall-hanging

## Abstract 'assemblage'

**Designed by Valerie Janitch**
This is created from materials in different textures, and the finished result suggests the roughness and the soft and subtle colours of the countryside.

## MATERIALS YOU WILL NEED

A piece of pine panelling about 9 in. by 16 in., or a piece of stiff card and woodgrain paper; green tapestry wools; small piece hessian webbing; piece rough bark; piece fine canvas; 2 fluffy grass heads; piece of golden-brown lacing cord; green feather; green stranded embroidery cotton; garden raffia; scrap green corduroy; twist of dishcloth cotton; thin string; small piece of dark brown linen; green bay leaf (dried); scrap golden-brown suede; adhesive (clear Sellobond); small screw eyes and wire for hanging (optional).

## TO MAKE

If necessary stick paper onto card using a wallpaper paste (Polycell), and leave to dry. Knot the tapestry wools, fray the hessian webbing and sick together before sticking onto the background. Stick the rough bark onto the canvas and stick into place. Stick the grass heads in position. Coil the lacing cord and stick in place. Stick the feather down. Twist the embroidery cotton into a pleasing shape and stick down. Knot a piece of garden raffia and stick onto a scrap of green corduroy and stick in position. Twist the dishcloth cotton and string together as shown and stick to the linen, then stick in place. Finally stick the bay leaf onto the suede and stick in position.
This collage could be framed, or if it has been made on a wood panel the screw eyes can be inserted into the back and the picture suspended on fine wire.

## Textures in metal

**Designed by Daphne Bradley**
Both these collage panels were built on a simple frame with hessian stretched over it and the cleaned metals stuck in position. The metals you choose depend entirely on what you have available. The insides of an old clock or watch do make a most attractive picture, but are rather small and delicate so the finished result is a fairly small collage. If you want something larger then you can use nuts, bolts, nails, screws etc. even adding a small tool or two. An old metal Meccano set

would provide some interesting pieces for a collage of this type.

## MATERIALS YOU WILL NEED

Battens for making the frame (size will depend on the size the finished picture is to be); piece of hessian large enough to go over the frame and be tacked behind frame; nails or screws and tacks; spray paint optional (U-Spray); assorted metal objects; epoxy resin adhesive (Power Pack); screw eyes and wire for hanging.

## TO MAKE

First make the frame from the battens, stretch the hessian over the frame so the front is perfectly taut, and tack hessian to back of frame. If liked the hessian can then be sprayed a colour, or sprayed partly with coloured and partly with metallic spray paint (U-Spray) and left to dry thoroughly. The collage would look very effective if the whole area were sprayed orange and left to dry, then if part of the hessian was sprayed silver, with a few touches of black, creating an interesting textured background for the metal.

Leave to dry thoroughly, then arrange the metal in a pleasing shape and stick in position with the epoxy resin (Power Pack). When dry, fix the screw eyes in position in the back of the frame and hang with wire.

*Note:* If very heavy metal objects are stuck onto a background, the hessian would tear if it was stretched on a frame. In this case, stick the hessian to a panel of hardboard. Mirror plates would be needed for hanging to take the weight.

## Plaque in plaster

### Designed by Eileen Geipel

This was made using a metal household tray as the mould—the attractive marbled effect is created by mixing in poster colour, but not stirring it too thoroughly.

### MATERIALS YOU WILL NEED

Tray 14 in. by 18 in.; household foil to cover tray; enough strong string to coil round and almost cover tray as well as provide a loop for hanging the picture—about 4 ft. to 6 ft.; sticky tape (Sellotape); brown and green bottle;

few pebbles; scant handful coffee beans; few odd beads; small piece gold cord; piece plain paper same size as tray; 16 cupfuls proprietory filler (Polyfilla); 10 cupfuls cold water poster colour (orange, yellow and red); clear varnish.

## TO MAKE

Cover tray with foil to prevent it spoiling. Slit foil across 3 in. from top edge. Slide loop of string (centre of length) through slit in foil and close slit with the sticky tape (Sellotape). The loop of string will be used to hang the picture. Coil the remaining string round on the foil, so it will become embedded in the plaster.

Now break the bottles to give you the fragments of coloured glass. The most sensible way to do this is to wrap them in an old blanket or piece of newspaper, place on a pathway (away from children and pets) and smash with a hammer. Don't completely pulverize them or the fragments will be too small to work with. Arrange the glass fragments, the pebbles, the coffee beans, the beads and the cord on the piece of plain paper until you get a pleasing result—or you can simply follow our design. As the broken glass will be sharp, use thick gardening gloves when handling it, or a pair of tweezers.

Measure filler (Polyfilla) into a bowl and measure the water into another. Melt a little orange paint in the water. Add filler to water and stir with large spoon or old whisk until completely free from lumps. Pour some of mixture into the tray making sure the string is well embedded into it. Continue to pour in the mixture until the tray is *almost* full. There should still be a good bit of the mixture left. Put some of this into an old saucer, mix in some more orange paint until it is fairly bright—do not stir up too much, so the effect will be marbled, and spread this mixture over part of the surface of the picture using a flexible knife, rather like applying butter icing to a cake. Add some red paint to some more of the mixture and repeat the process, and then do the same thing with yellow paint—as the colours mix with each other they blend into one another in the most fascinating way.

Now arrange the items on the surface of the picture, following the plan laid out on the paper. If necessary press down slightly into the wet mixture, but not too much or they could disappear! Leave to set for at least 48 hours. Carefully remove from the tray by lifting the foil, and taking great care not to damage the edges. Leave for another 36 hours before touching. Then remove foil from the back of the picture. Varnish and hang.

## FUN FOR CHILDREN TO MAKE

## Hedgehog wall-hanging

### Designed by Jane Buckle

This collage can be made with scraps of multi-coloured leather which are available in bags of off-cuts from most leather suppliers, or if you decide to use one colour, alternate the rough and smooth sides of the leather to get an interesting texture. Choose coloured hessian for the background to tone or contrast with your leather.

### MATERIALS YOU WILL NEED

Piece of hessian 31 in. square; piece of

white felt 16 in. by 10 in.; 2 dowel
rods 35 in. long; needle and white and
yellow sewing thread; piece of leather
(half a skin) or bag of pieces;
adhesive (Copydex); piece of cord
for hanging picture.

## TO MAKE

Press hessian to make sure there are no
creases. Turn two opposite sides under
and make a 1½ in. hem, tack, press and
hem. Turn the other two opposite
sides under 2 in., and hem as before.
Make a pattern for the body following
the diagram (A) and cut out of white
felt. Position on the hessian and sew
in place using very small stitches. Press
to make sure it is absolutely flat.
Cut the pieces of leather into small
pieces (the approximate size is shown

on the diagram). However, these need
not all be the same size and shape as
irregularity adds to the effect of the
spines. Now glue into position on the
white felt one by one. Each piece
should have a thin coating of glue all
over the surface which is to be stuck
down. Start from the head end and
work from head to tail, sticking the
spines on the outer edges of the body
first. Press each piece firmly onto the
felt, and where they overlap the hessian
make sure they are really well stuck.
Each spine should overlap another so
no piece of felt shows through.
Following the diagram, cut out the
nose and eye in a piece of leather (we
used black) and stick into position as
shown. Insert dowels into hems and
stitch, making a second hem so they
are held firmly. Attach cord and hang.

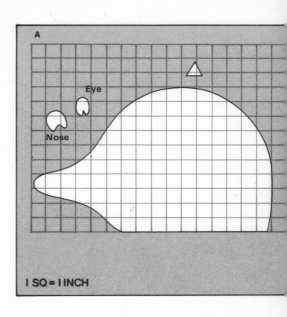

A

Eye

Nose

I SQ = I INCH

# BASKET-WORK

## Lesson One:
## Making your own shopping basket

Making baskets is probably one of the earliest crafts known to man. From traces found by the archeologists we know the early North American Indians used baskets as moulds for clay cooking pots, the imprint of the basketweave showing clearly on the clay. Specimens of coiled and plaited basketwork have been found in the Nile Delta, some date back as early as 8000 BC.

Many museums throughout the world have a collection of basketwork, usually shown alongside early pottery, and the common factor seems to be that baskets have always been made of any material available, and design and type are largely dependent on this. Baskets are usually associated with 'bringing home the shopping' as they are nearly always used for carrying or holding things. Many are in common use by builders; fishermen (lobsterpots are inverted baskets!); laundries; potteries; glass foundries; chemical companies and farmers (think of those potato baskets). There are decorative baskets too, for cradling a wine bottle, holding flowers and fruit, bringing bread rolls to the table, hanging up house plants, to name a few, and what about wickerwork lampshades, wastepaper baskets, work baskets, cribs for small babies, pet baskets, picnic hampers, cane carpet beaters, all of which are decorative as well as being functional?

### MATERIALS YOU WILL NEED

There are several different materials used for basketmaking including willow or osier, cane, wicker, and seagrass, raffia and rushes all come under the 'suitable materials' heading as they can all be used for basketmaking. It is possible to obtain most of these materials in various thicknesses, lengths and textures, and also in almost any colour as they are often specially dyed. Basketwork usually looks most effective when the natural colour, from cream to soft brown, rather than the bright colours are used, although some people like to mix the dyed and the natural material together in one piece of basketwork. We used the natural coloured cane for our 'shopper',

contrasted with vivid green wooden beads between the lengths of cane. All these materials should be readily available from local handicraft shops.

## YOUR FIRST MAKE
## A fun 'shopper' from string, cane and wooden beads

### MATERIALS YOU WILL NEED

**For the bag:**
Ball of smooth, fine string or twine (at least 64 ft. in length); curtain ring for base, 3 in. diameter; 128 wooden beads ($\frac{1}{4}$-inch necklace beads are best); 232 lengths of cane $1\frac{1}{2}$ in. long by $4\frac{1}{2}$ mm. in diameter No. 15; 1 medium-sized bodkin or hairpin if necessary.

**For the handle:**
18 large wooden beads $\frac{1}{2}$ in. in diameter; 10 lengths of handle cane $\frac{1}{2}$ in. long by 1 cm. in diameter.

### TO MAKE

Cut 16 pieces of string 4 ft. long and loop each piece of string through the base ring once to form two equal 2 ft. lengths. Arrange into eight sets of four strings (i.e. two loops in each set) and thread each set of four strings through a small bead. The string should push through quite easily, but use a bodkin or hairpin if necessary. Knot the four strings together close to the bead. Divide each set of four strings

into two pairs and thread each set of strings through a $1\frac{1}{2}$-in. cane and small bead. Split each pair of strings into single strings and thread a cane tube onto each string. Group the strings in pairs (as shown in diagram A) and thread a bead onto each pair of strings. A diamond-shaped pattern of canes and beads has now been formed. Repeat the process as in the diagram, five more times to make the body of the bag in a continuous diamond pattern. Divide the strings into four consecutive sets of eight. Taking each set in turn, thread a cane onto each pair of strings and bring the ends of each pair of canes together to complete the diamond and thread the four strings through the remaining beads (there should be 8 left). Thread the remaining lengths of $1\frac{1}{2}$-in. cane onto each group of four strings (there should be 8 left).

The handle is now formed (as diagram B) by threading a large bead onto the string. There are now four sets of eight strings, each set passing through large bead. Thread large beads and $\frac{1}{2}$-in. cane onto each set of eight strings as shown in the diagram, to make approximately 4 in. in length. Tie each adjacent set of eight strings together tightly to complete the two handles (as shown in diagram) and tuck the cut ends of string out of sight inside a bead hole.

*Note:* If you are unable to buy cut lengths of cane, buy long pieces and cut to the required size with cane snips, a very fine saw—e.g. a fretsaw, or a sharp craft knife.

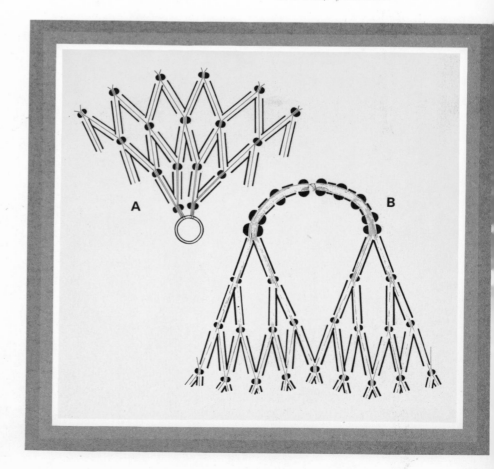

# BASKET-WORK

## Lesson Two:
## Materials and techniques

**Working with cane, weaving it into decorative and useful articles, is an ancient craft which is easy and satisfying to learn. Anne Hulbert explains the basic techniques of the craft, and gives five attractive basketwork designs to make up.**

## Materials

### CANE
There are two principal types of cane you can use:
**Centre cane** is a round cane varying in thickness from 1 mm. to 10 mm. It is easy to use, and suitable for beginners. The higher the size number, the thicker the cane.
**Lapping cane** is flat on one side and slightly rounded on the other. It is available in various widths, and adds an attractive variation to your weaving. It is also used for wrapping round basket handles for, being flat, it gives a smooth and comfortable grip.
Cane is a very brittle material which cracks and splinters when worked dry, so it is essential to use it damp. To make it pliable, soak it for about five minutes before using. Prevent it from drying out during working by an occasional dampening with a wet cloth. Cane is sold by the pound in coils, and is available from handicraft shops and suppliers, and in some of the larger stores too.
Natural-coloured cane and bleached cane can both be obtained. Bleached cane is very white, and can look most attractive used in combination with the natural colour.
You can dye your finished basketwork to any colour you like, or spray paint it. It is a good idea to varnish a dyed basket in order to retain the colour.

## Bases
Ready-made bases are recommended for the beginner and are available in many different shapes and sizes. They are supplied with holes drilled all round the edges, but there should always be an odd number of holes. You can, if you wish, make your own bases from plywood, using a 3/32 in. bit to drill the holes, which should be about $\frac{3}{4}$ in. apart and about $\frac{1}{4}$ in. from the edge.
Whether you buy or make your base, it is a good idea to protect the surface from water or other marks when working or using the article later. It may be covered with self-adhesive plastic, or painted, or varnished. Never allow wooden bases to become damp, or they will warp.
Although cane bases are a little more complicated to work, they look very professional and are really much more attractive. Instructions for two such bases are therefore included with this lesson's makes.

## Tools and equipment
Only a few basic tools are needed, and these are all available from a cane supplier.
**Side cutters** for trimming off ends of cane close to the weaving, and generally for cutting cane.
**Round-nosed pliers** for squeezing the cane stakes before bending at acute angles when working borders.
**Cane bodkin** or a domestic skewer, for easing spaces in the weaving for the insertion of byestakes or handles.
**Ruler (2 ft.)** for measuring stakes, and your work.
**Small knife** with a sharp point for splitting cane when necessary for woven bases.
**Clothes peg** to hold down weaving canes if you have to leave the work.
**Bowl or bucket of water,** and a damp cloth.

## Techniques and methods
There is not space here to describe all the many techniques which can be used in basket-making, but the following should give a good basic grounding in the craft.
**Stakes.** These are the upright canes which form the foundation for the weaving, and should be cut from thicker cane than the weaving cane. When cutting stakes, allow for the height of the basket plus allowances for foot and top borders (see A).
**Bye stakes.** These are additional stakes to give extra strength to the basket. They are inserted into the

*Waste paper basket, picnic basket and fruit or roll basket. Instructions start overleaf.*

weaving, close beside the original, after the 'upsetting' stage (see below), and must touch the base. They should be level with the original stakes all round the top of the work. In simple basketry, these pairs of stakes are treated as single stakes throughout the work. Bye stakes are not always necessary with small baskets.

**Weavers.** These are the finer weaving or working canes. Do not pull them too tight, just let them lie naturally. Press the weaving down firmly at intervals, to keep the work the same height all round. Always work from left to right, and keep your weaver under 3 yd. long to prevent tangling.

**Foot border.** This is the border worked on the underside of a ready-made base to secure the ends of the stakes. Damp the required number of stakes, and insert them through the base holes, leaving about 4 in. projecting on the underside. Hold the work upside down and, with the round-nosed pliers, squeeze each stake level with the base. Take one stake, bend it over to the right behind the second stake, in front of the third stake, and leave the end to rest against the back of the fourth stake (see B). Continue all round in this manner, taking each stake in its turn. When you reach the beginning, ease the first stakes up with the bodkin, and ease the last stakes through in their turn to complete the border.

Turn the base right side uppermost and press it down on to the foot border just completed, pulling the side stakes gently to ensure that the foot border is really close to the underside of the base. Work round the stakes, easing each one outwards, before commencing weaving, to start shaping your work.

**Waling (3 rod).** This is a very strong and firm method of weaving. Generally, it is worked with three weavers. Place the ends of three weavers in three adjacent spaces between the stakes, and leaving the ends on the inside. Take the left-hand weaver, pass it in front of the second and third stakes, behind the fourth, and out to the front. In doing this, it will also pass over the two right-hand weavers (see C). Work all round, always using the left-hand weaver, until the right-hand weaver falls in the space to the left of the space holding the first weaver (see D). For the next row, take the right-hand weaver and pass it in front of the next two stakes, behind the next one, and out at the front. Next, work the middle weaver, and lastly the left-hand weaver in the same manner. This 'reversal' of weaving must be done on each row at exactly the same point and ensures that each row of waling is complete and level.

When the required number of rows have been worked, finish off the waling with the same method as used to finish each row, but this time you will have to ease up the woven work with a bodkin for easy passage of the final weaving ends.

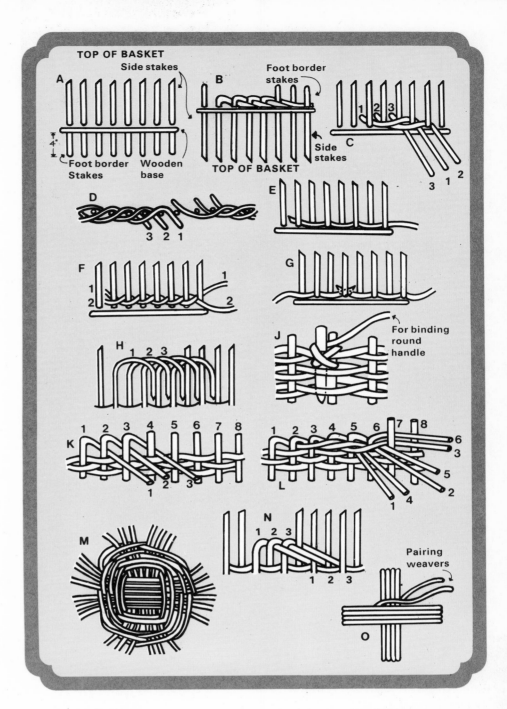

**Upsetting.** This is the term used for the initial weaving of the sides of a basket. It is the stage which sets the shape and firmness of the basket, and waling is the weave generally used. It is when the required number of rows of upsetting are worked that the bye stakes, if used, are inserted.

**Randing.** This is the simplest form of weaving. One weaver only is used, being passed in front of one stake and behind the next, alternately (see E). Randing, worked with two canes at once looks very attractive. They should be kept flat, with one above the other, as with one weaver.

**Pairing.** This is worked by weaving two weavers alternately. It is a fairly strong weave, and may be used for upsetting on small baskets. Forming a firm weave makes it suitable for a trivet or platter (see F).

**Joining weavers.** To add a new weaver when the old has run out, always leave the old weaver behind a stake on the inside of the basket. Insert the end of the new weaver above it, behind the same stake, also on the inside. Continue weaving as before, and join will not show on the right side (see G).

**Trimming ends.** Make sure that all ends are on the inside of the work. Clip off, leaving enough for the end to rest on its correct stake. Always cut at a slant.

**Singeing.** Cane gets 'hairy' when being worked, and can be singed off if you move a flame very quickly over the work. Be careful to avoid blackening the work.

**Maintenance of finished articles.** Brush gently to remove dust. The basketwork, but not wooden bases, may be swished in warm, soapy water, rinsed well, and left to dry.

# YOUR BASKET-WORK MAKES

## Plant pot holder

### MATERIALS YOU WILL NEED

Approx. 4 oz. No. 6 natural cane for: 23 stakes, each 20 in. long, and 23 bye stakes, each 13 in. long. Approx. 3 oz. No. 3 natural cane for upsetting/pairing. Approx. 12 yd. lapping cane for randing. Round base, 6 in. in diameter, with 23 holes.

### MEASUREMENTS

Finished pot holder is approx. 7 in. high, with a top diameter of approx. 7 in.

### TO MAKE

1. Paint, varnish or cover one surface of base as required.
2. Cut and prepare required number of stakes.
3. Work foot border, following diagram B.
4. Place basket right side up.
5. For upsetting, weave 5 rows of pairing, using No. 3 natural cane (see F).
6. Point off one end of each bye stake, and insert in the weaving beside each original stake.
7. Weave·5 rows of pairing, using No. 3 natural cane.
8. Tuck ends down into weaving, each beside a stake, to fasten off neatly and securely.
9. Trim off each pair of stakes to a point, and about 5 in. above the last row of weaving.
10. Place basket upside down in water for a few minutes to dampen the stakes only.
11. With the round-nosed pliers, squeeze each pair of stakes level with last row of weaving.
12. To start the scallop border, take one pair of stakes, arch it gently over to the right and in front of the next two pairs. Insert the ends down into the weaving, close beside the 4th pair of stakes, leaving a scallop about 1¼ in. high (see H). Continue making scallops all round the top.
13. Ease basket into shape and leave to dry out thoroughly.
14. Trim off all spare ends at a slant as necessary on the inside of the basket.

## Picnic basket

### MATERIALS YOU WILL NEED

Approx. 8 oz. No. 6 natural cane for: 47 stakes, each 26 in. long, and 47 bye stakes, each 20 in. long. Approx. 10 oz. No. 3 natural cane for weavers. A base, 4½ in. by 16 in., with 47 holes. 2 lengths No. 25 handle cane, each approx. 22 in. Approx. 4 yd. lapping cane for binding handles.

### MEASUREMENTS

Finished picnic basket is approx. 11½ in. high, 16 in. long.
*Note:* This size is big enough to hold a picnic flask at each end, with a standard-sized tin and cups between them.

### TO MAKE

1. Paint, varnish or cover one surface of base as required.
2. Cut and prepare required number of stakes.
3. Work foot border, following diagram B.
4. Place basket right side up.
5. For upsetting, weave 2 rows of 3-rod waling, using No. 3 cane (see diagrams C and D).
6. Point off one end of each bye stake and insert in the weaving beside each original stake.
7. Weave 84 rows of randing, using No. 3 cane (see diagram E).
8. Weave 2 rows of 3-rod waling using No. 3 cane.
9. Weave 8 rows of randing using 2 weavers together.
10. Weave 2 rows of 3-rod waling.
11. Trim off stakes to a point and about 6 in. above the last row of weaving.
12. Place basket upside down in water for a few minutes to damp the stakes only.

### HANDLES

Take one piece of handle cane and point it at both ends for about 2 in. Soak to make it pliable. Push one end firmly down into the weaving about 6 in. from end of basket. Make a hole in the handle cane (about 2 in. from point) from front to back and just under the top waling. Repeat for other end of handle. Point one end of lapping cane, and push end through the hole. Tuck this end into the weaving. Bring the other end to the front under the waling and to left of handle cane. Cross over to right, round top of waling, down the back, out at front right through waling, over top of waling at left and down the back. This forms a neat cross, and may be worked over a second time. Do not cut off the long end.
Wind this long end closely and firmly round the handle cane until other end is reached. Point end of lapping cane and thread it through hole at end of handle cane. Work another cross to

match the first one. Repeat for other basket handle, and do avoid a join in the lapping cane (see diagram J).

## TOP BORDER

With the round-nosed pliers, squeeze each pair of stakes level with the last row of weaving (see diagram K).
Bend over stake 1 behind 2.
Bend 2 behind 3.
Bend 3 behind 4.
Following diagram L carefully, pass stake 1 over 2 and 3, in front of 4, behind 5, and out to the front.
Bend 4 down alongside 1. Repeat for stakes 2 and 3.
Pass 4 in front of 7, behind 8, and out to the front. Bend 7 down alongside it as before.
There must always be three pairs of ends coming out at the front. The fifth from the right in this set is the one which is taken in front of the next upright stake, behind the next one, and out at the front. The left-hand cane of each pair is the one left pointing outwards.
Continue working all round top of basket, working neatly round handles as you come to them, until only one stake remains upright.
Ease up the beginning stakes with the bodkin, making room for the final canes to pass through.
Finish off the pattern in sequence, and passing under beginning stakes as necessary.
Clip off all ends close to the border.

## Waste paper basket

### MATERIALS YOU WILL NEED

Approx. 8 oz. No. 8 natural cane for: 29 stakes, each 26 in. long, 29 bye stakes, each 14 in. long. Approx. 8 oz. No. 6 natural cane for weavers. Approx. 5 oz. No. 6 bleached cane for weavers. Round base, 8 in. in diameter, with 29 holes.

### MEASUREMENTS

Finished waste paper basket is approx. 10¼ in. high, with a top diameter of 10¼ in.

### TO MAKE

1. Paint, varnish or cover one surface of base as desired.
2. Cut and prepare required number of stakes.
3. Work foot border, following diagram B.
4. Place basket right side up.
5. For upsetting, weave 3 rows of 3-rod waling, using No. 6 bleached cane (see diagrams C and D).
6. Point off one end of each bye stake, and insert in the weaving beside each original stake.
7. Weave 27 rows of randing, using No. 6 natural cane (see diagram E).
8. Weave one row of 3-rod waling, using No. 6 bleached cane.
9. Weave another 27 rows of randing, using No. 6 natural cane.

10 Weave 1 row of 3-rod waling, using No. 6 bleached cane.
11. Weave a third band of 27 rows of randing, using No. 6 natural cane.
12. Finish with 1 row of 3-rod waling, using No. 6 bleached cane.
13. Trim off each pair of stakes to a point, and about 5½ in. above the last row of weaving.
14. Place basket upside down in water for a few minutes to damp the stakes only.
15. Work scallop border exactly as for Plant Pot Holder.
16. Ease basket into shape and leave to dry out thoroughly.
17. Trim off all spare ends at a slant as necessary, on the inside of the basket.

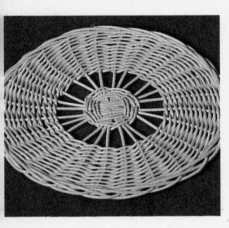

## Trivet

### MATERIALS YOU WILL NEED

Approx. 1½ oz. No. 6 natural cane for 12 stakes, each 16 in. long. Approx. 1½ oz. No. 3 natural cane for weavers.

### MEASUREMENTS

Finished trivet measures 8 in. in diameter.

### TO MAKE

Cane bases are a little more difficult to make, but once you have learned the basic process you will be able to make basketwork articles in any size or shape you choose, and not be restricted by the sizes of ready-made bases available. A cane base is also much lighter than a wooden one.
1. Cut the No. 6 cane into 16-in. stakes.
2. Make a slit about 1 in. long through the centre of 6 stakes.
3. Thread the other 6 stakes through these slits, sliding them close together to form a cross (see diagram M).
4. Bend a long length of No. 3 weaver cane in half and slip the loop over one group of 6 stakes (see diagram M).
5. Work 2 rows of pairing, treating each group of 6 stakes as one.
6. Divide stakes into 8 groups of 3.
7. Work 2 rows of pairing, treating each group of 3 stakes as one.
8. Fasten off weavers by tucking ends into the weaving.
9. Start the next round of weaving 1 in. from the last, to form the open work.
10. Bend the length of No. 3 weaver in half and slip loop round a stake.

11. Work 12 rounds of pairing, over single stakes. Leave ends at back.
12. Place in water to damp stakes.
13. With the round-nosed pliers, squeeze each stake close to the last row of pairing.
14. To start the edging, take one stake, bend it down to the right, behind the next stake, in front of the 3rd and 4th stakes, and pass it to the back behind the 5th stake.
15. Continue all round until the starting stakes are reached. Ease these first stakes upwards with the bodkin to enable the last working stakes to be woven through, completing the edging pattern (see diagram N).
16. Ease trivet into shape and leave to dry out thoroughly.
17. Cut off spare ends at a slant at the back of the trivet.

## Fruit or roll basket

**A more advanced design.**

### MATERIALS YOU WILL NEED

Approx. 8 oz. No. 8 bleached cane for: 8 stakes, each 56 in. long, and 32 bye stakes, each 28 in. long. Approx. 4 oz. No. 4 natural cane for centre weaving.

### MEASUREMENTS

Finished basket is approx. 3 in. high, with a top diameter of 9 in.

### TO MAKE

1. Cut the No. 8 bleached cane into eight 56-in. stakes.
2. Make a slit about ¾ in. long through the centre of 4 stakes.
3. Thread the other 4 stakes through these slits, sliding them close together to form a cross (same method as shown in diagram M but fewer stakes).
4. Bend a long length of No. 4 natural cane in half, and slip the loop over one group of 4 stakes (diagram O).
5. Weave 4 rows of pairing, treating each group of 4 stakes as one.
6. Divide stakes into 8 groups of 2 stakes.
7. Weave 4 rows of pairing, treating each group of 2 stakes as one.
8. Divide into single stakes (16).
9. Weave 4 rounds of pairing.

10. Trim one end of each bye stake to a point.
11. Insert each bye stake into the weaving, placing one each side of each original stake.
12. Weave 4 more rounds of pairing, at the same time easing stakes upwards to make slightly concave. By this time the basket should measure about 5½ in. across.
13. Place work in water to damp the stakes.
14. With the round-nosed pliers, squeeze each stake level with last row of pairing.
15. Work sides by interweaving the actual stakes and finishing with a plait round the outer edge of the base.
16. Work round the outside of the basket from left to right with a group of 3 stakes. From now on, each group of 3 stakes will be considered as one stake.
17. Bend it up and over towards the right to form an arch 3 in. above the last row of pairing.
18. Pass this stake (1) in front of next stake (2) behind the third, in front of the fourth, behind the fifth and in front of the sixth to face you at the top edge of the base pairing.
19. Work all round bringing in each stake (group of 3) in its turn, and weaving the last stakes into the first stakes to complete the pattern.
20. All free ends are now used for working the base plait.
21. Place basket in water to damp the ends of stakes again if they have dried out.
22. Working from left to right, take one stake (one group of 3) and ease over to the right. Pass it under the next stake (2), over the following stake (3), and inside against the 4th stake.
23. Take the next stake and repeat the same interweaving.
24. Continue all round, until the starting ends are reached. Ease the last few canes under the first ones, using a bodkin if necessary. Ends should be slanting towards the centre of the underneath surface of the base.
25. Leave basket to dry out thoroughly.
26. Trim all ends off at a slant.
*Note:* When base plait is being worked, make sure that arched sides are not pulled out of place. They must keep their 3 in. height.

# LAMPSHADE MAKING

## Lesson One:

Our lampshades for you to make in fabric and paper are designed to give as much variety as possible and to fit in with different types of decor.
For the traditionally minded there is a swathed chiffon shade in deep pink, trimmed with plum bobble fringe. For those who like really bold shades— a cylinder made from sheer linen curtain fabric, and if you prefer classic simplicity—a ribbon-velvet striped shade. For the young and houseproud there are lots of shades; some geometric and boldly coloured; others sweetly pretty—all made inexpensively from paper. There's a string-bound shade too, and a shellcraft lamp shaped like a bird.

## Lampshades

The importance of light fittings and lampshades is often underestimated in planning a decoration scheme. Shades in particular can be renewed with comparatively little outlay and can quickly give a 'face lift' to a room. Fashions in furnishings change and so do fashions in lampshades, although many of the traditional shapes are always in fashion. We have tried to keep a balance between traditional and modern in our selection of shades, and a balance between designs for table lamps and pendant fittings—however most of the designs are interchangeable, depending on the type of frame you buy.

### CHOOSING THE FRAMES

The choice of lampshade frames can be bewildering as most handicraft shops have a wide selection—or you may have an old shade which you want to recover. The important thing to remember when buying the frame is the position it is to occupy in the room. If it is to go on a table lamp, then try to take the lamp with you when you get the frame—you can then test it on the actual lamp and judge the full effect of shape and size. If it is to be a pendant lampshade, then the larger the room, the larger the shade can be— also the amount of light and the wattage of the bulb is important here—it you need a strong good light, then don't have a narrow cylindrical shade (bulb would burn it for a start), have a fairly wide shade, preferably one lined with white, to give extra reflected light.

### PREPARING THE FRAME

Buy the best you can afford and make sure the metal joints are smooth—if necessary file them carefully before using. Some lampshade frames are now available ready-painted or even nylon coated and these are ready to use, but if you are buying a simple metal frame then it should be painted before use to prevent the metal from rusting. The alternative is to bind the shade, and this is done when a fabric shade is being made, so the material can be stitched to it.
If painting the frame (fabric or paper shade) use a colour which will tone as near as possible with the finished shade —a small tin of quick-drying enamel paint sold in handicraft shops is ideal for this purpose. Leave to dry for at least 48 hours before using the frame. If binding the frame (fabric shade only) then the rings (top and bottom of shade) must be bound; all struts to which material is to be stitched; the pair of struts opposite each other on shades where material may be pinned in position, must all be bound. The struts of a shade without internal lining may be bound *or* painted, whichever you prefer. It is usual to bind the rings first and then the struts.
*Rings*—allow twice the circumference when buying the binding.
*Struts*—allow twice the length for $\frac{1}{4}$-in. tape or one-and-a-half for any other binding.

### LINING LAMPSHADES

It is usual to line fabric lampshades but not paper ones. The purpose of the lining is to hide the struts (particularly in a hanging shade), to give extra light-filtering quality to the fabric (chiffon, lace, etc.) and to increase the amount of reflected light—i.e. a white lining for a dark shade. A lining can also be used to give extra warmth—a peach, apricot or pink lining to a white or blue shade for example.

### MATERIALS AND EQUIPMENT

Apart from the actual frame, very little equipment is necessary for making lampshades. A pair of sharp scissors, needles, pins and a thimble are essential. The needles should be short so they do not get broken when striking the frame—No. 5 or 6 are recommended, and the fine lillikins pins are the best type to use. The choice of materials for the shade depends on the room, the type of shade you have in mind and the amount of money you want to spend. With paper shades, enough suitable paper, a little adhesive or sewing thread and perhaps some fringe for trimming and you are all set to go. With fabric shades you will need the binding tapes, and fabric for lining as well as the material for the actual shade. With a soft shade (fabric), the trimming is more likely to be important, and a decorative braid can be used to trim the top and a luxurious fringe to trim the bottom.

# SHADES IN FABRIC

**Designed by Pauline Janitch**

## Swathed pleated chiffon shade

The most elegant type of traditional shade, this takes time, patience and a good many pins, but it is well worth the effort. Choose a deep colour to emphasise the dramatic shading of the chiffon when the lamp is lit. Use a toning satin for the lining, with the *shiny* side facing the chiffon.

### MATERIALS YOU WILL NEED

10-in. diameter bowed Empire lamp-shade frame, preferably nylon coated (see Preparing the Frame); enough lampshade binding tape to bind all the frame; 1 yd. crêpe-backed satin (for lining); 1 yd. 36-in. wide silk chiffon (for shade); sewing silk to tone; 1 yd.

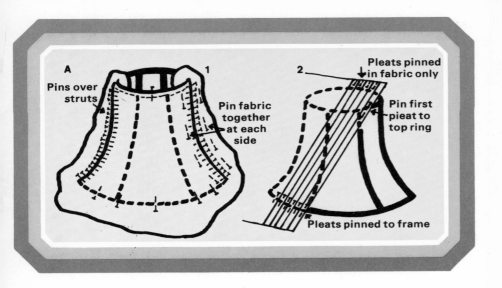

toning silk fringe; 1½ yd. silk braid to match; fabric adhesive (Copydex).

## TO MAKE

Bind the outside of the frame (not the inner or top fittings), winding the tape round and round, at an angle, edges overlapped, so that the wire is completely covered. Bind all but one of the vertical struts, finishing off each end securely and neatly—then bind the top (beginning at the un-bound strut), continue down strut and finally bind bottom ring.

Next make the lining. Fold the satin diagonally across the centre, shiny side *inside*, and pin edges. Pin this triangle of double fabric over half your frame, as diagram A1. Keep pulling gently and adjusting until the fabric is absolutely smooth over the frame. Mark the line of the two pinned side struts in pencil. Pin the fabric together at each side of marked struts, and cut away excess about 2 in. above and below top and bottom edges: then remove pins and fabric from frame (leaving pins at each side of struts holding fabric together). Stitch the fabric together, neatly, along the pencil lines, trim close to seam, then turn to the other (satin) side and finish each side as a run-and-fell seam. Put lining to one side. Now to pleat. Divide your fabric width-ways into three 12-in. deep strips, each 36 in. wide (you can calculate the amount of chiffon you need by multiplying the circumference of the frame by three). Remove the selvedges, then turn under one of these short edges the width you want your pleat (about ⅜ in.). Pin this pleat to the top and bottom rings as shown in diagram A2: if your frame has six panels, stretch the fabric diagonally across 1½ panels—if it has eight panels, stretch the fabric across two panels. Make another pleat, close to the first, and pin next to it on the bottom ring: folding the pleat along the line of the fabric, pin the fold in the *fabric* only, just below the top edge: do not pin to top ring yet. Continue pleating and pinning to the bottom ring—and

pinning each pleat in the fabric at the top—until you reach the next strut. As the top ring is considerably smaller than the bottom, the pleats will obviously need to overlap: you can now see how much the top pleats must overlap to distribute them evenly round an equivalent section of the top ring to that covered at the bottom. Pull each pinned pleat taut and pin to top ring, overlapping as described. Pleat the next section in the same way, and continue until half the frame is covered. Join in each new strip of fabric by turning under the raw edge, as before, and pinning this first pleat over the raw edge at the end of the previous strip. Now oversew the top pleat securely to the frame, removing pins as you do so, but *do not sew* the first two pleats—just leave them pinned. Once the top pleats are firmly attached in position, adjust and re-pin bottom pleats if necessary, before stitching securely into place as the top.

Pleat the remaining half of the frame in the same way, lifting the first two pleats and pinning over the raw end of the very last pleat, to make a neat join. Oversew securely as before. Cut away surplus fabric close to top and bottom rings.

Place the lining inside the shade, shiny satin against the chiffon, pinning seams to rings at top and bottom, and then pulling the surplus fabric over the top and bottom rings and pinning over trimmed edge of chiffon. Keep adjusting and re-pinning at top and bottom until the lining is absolutely smooth. Then oversew securely to both rings before trimming away surplus fabric close to stitches. Stitch fringe round lower edge, then stick braid round top of shade, and over the edge of fringe round the bottom of the shade.

## Sheer linen cylinder

Scandinavian sheer linen curtaining, with an interesting woven texture,

makes the simplest of tall shades for a big lamp. The trimming is unusual and hand-made—from dishcloth cotton! This shade has no struts as it is made with 2 lampshade rings.

### MATERIALS YOU WILL NEED

Piece of bonding parchment at least 18 in. by 46 in.; ½ yd. sheer linen curtain fabric (48 in. wide); sewing thread to tone; two 14-in diameter lampshade rings, one with a standard or table lamp fitting; unbleached dishcloth cotton; adhesive (Copydex or Sellobond).

### TO MAKE

Cut the bonding parchment 18 in. deep by 46 in. long. Bond the fabric to the treated surface (shiny side) by ironing it smoothly into place, using a damp cloth, and placing the selvedge level with one side edge. When cool and firmly fixed, trim the edges. Roll into a cylinder and place rings in top and bottom.

Oversew shade to rings and stick the join as unobtrusively as possible. Cut six 4-yd. lengths of dishcloth cotton and double each to measure 2 yd. Divide into pairs, to make three sets of 4 strands each. Tie the looped ends together and plait neatly. Repeat twice more. Stick one plait round the top edge, and two round the bottom as illustrated.

# LAMPSHADES

## One in wool and parchment — one knotted in macramé string over fabric

### Cats' cradle lampshade

**Designed by Valerie Janitch**

This rough, tweedy textured lampshade looks like hand weaving, yet it is easy to make and looks very effective, particularly with the light shining through it. Choose wool mixtures in toning shades to complement your colour scheme. I used Sirdar Candytwist in blue-mauve and turquoise-green mixtures.

### MATERIALS YOU WILL NEED

Lampshade parchment; two 9-in-diameter lampshade rings, one with pendant or gimbal fitting; clear adhesive (Sellobond); two balls (or more if liked) toning wools: fabric or white PVA adhesive (Copydex or Sellobond).

### TO MAKE

Cut a piece of lampshade parchment 6 in. deep by 30½ in. long. Oversew to rings round top and bottom, trim edges and stick join.

Wind first one, and then the second, wool horizontally round and round the outside of the shade at uneven angles over the whole area: pull taut, but not tight, so that it holds firmly in place. Secure ends at one edge. Then wind each wool vertically over and over at uneven angles all the way round, as illustrated: secure as before. To trim each edge, twist two 2½-yd. length of each colour (more if you have used a thinner wool) and double into a loose cord. Stick over edge, securing ends carefully.

### Macramé lampshade

### MATERIALS YOU WILL NEED

3 balls of medium-weight natural string; a drum lampshade frame, 6½ in. deep, with a top diameter of approx. 7½ in.; ½ yd, lining fabric, 36 in. wide; tape to bind lampshade frame; 1¼ yd. narrow elastic.

### TO MAKE

Bind struts of lampshade frame neatly and firmly with tape. Cut strip of lining fabric to fit round lampshade frame, plus ½ in. on each short edge for turnings and ½ in. at top and bottom edges.

Right sides together, stitch short edges together. Press seam open. Make a 1 in. casing at top and bottom edges (leave a gap in each casing so elastic may be threaded through). Fit lining over lampshade, wrong side of lining against outside of frame. Stitch lining to taped frame round top and bottom rings, taking fairly easy, loose stitches through the tape. Thread elastic through top and bottom casings of lining to draw it in snugly above and below frame.

Now cut 102 lengths of string, each 4 ft. 6 in., plus depth of fringe required (e.g. if you wish a 2-in. fringe round finished lower edge of lampshade, then cut string to lengths each 4 ft. 8 in.). Cut a holding cord approx. 2 ft. 6 in.

Set cords on to holding cord by usual method: 204 working ends. Now on right side of lampshade, position holding cord (with its set-on cords) round top edge of frame. Tie ends of holding cord together firmly, then stitch holding cord right round to lining. Trim ends of holding cord and tuck in loose ends behind set-on cords nearest to them. Space out set-on cords so they are evenly distributed round frame.

Cut a separate leader, about 2 ft. 6 in. and work horizontal cording over it with all cords immediately below set-on edge. Tie ends of leader cord together firmly, trim and tuck in ends as for holding cord.

Now begin knotting pattern:

**1st pattern panel.** Divide cords into groups of 4 each. With each group work a half knot spiral (first half of flat knot tied continuously) to a depth of 1 in. (about 12 half knots).

**2nd pattern panel.** Divide cords into groups of 12 each. * Work on each group of 12 as follows: with cord on far left as leader slanting down to the right, work diagonal cording over it with first 5 cords. With cord on far right as leader slanting down to the left, work diagonal cording over it with remaining 5 cords. Link tip of 'V' by tying a flat knot with centre 4 cords. Now combine the 6 cords on the right of one group with the 6 cords on the left of the next group and work a similar 'V' of diagonal cording, linked at the tip with a flat knot. ** Repeat from * to ** once, so a band of cording diamonds has been completed.

**3rd pattern panel.** Divide cords into groups of 4 each, as for first pattern panel, and work a half knot spiral with each group to a depth of about 2½ in. Cut a separate leader, approx. 5 ft. long, and work 2 rows of horizontal cording over it with all cords immediately below half knot spirals. After second row is completed tie ends of leader together firmly (on wrong side of macramé). Trim and tuck in ends as before.

### TO COMPLETE

Stitch macramé to lampshade lining round lower edge. Trim fringe to depth required.

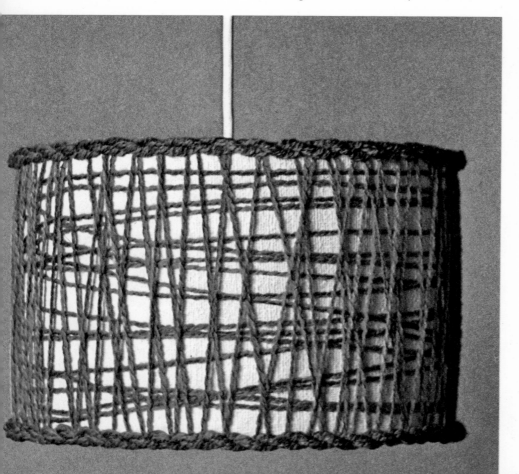

# JEWELLERY

## Lesson One:

## Simple jewellery to make from beads and sequins.

**Anne Hullbert tells you how to make some original jewellery, using the beads you may well already have lurking in the bottom of the button tin, or which you can buy cheaply from a haberdashery counter.**

Jewellery can be expensive to buy, particularly costume jewellery, and even then it is not always easy to find exactly what you want in the right colour and correct size. Yet it is possible to make some very pretty pieces of jewellery yourself without using costly tools, techniques or materials. You will find it easy to create something original, and inexpensive too! Once you have started experimenting, you can go on to create some really exciting pieces. Basically there are not many techniques to learn to produce this type of jewellery—it is wise to sort out the beads you have into types and colours, and if possible, keep them in clear containers, so you can see at a glance exactly what you have available. One of the little nail and screw holders sold for amateur carpenters would be ideal.

Tweezers of the delicate eyebrow type are useful for handling beads, and you will need some strong threads—a very fine nylon which is thin enough to go through the holes in the smallest beads, yet strong enough to take the weight is a wise choice.

Button thread is good for some beads with large holes. Needles also need to be thin, and the eye must not protrude too much. It is sometimes possible to wax the end of a thread to make it stiff, so it can be threaded through the bead without having to use a needle.

### YOUR FIRST MAKES

## Green, glittery hairband or choker

## Jet necklace

## Pretty pink glass eardrops and bracelet

## Green, glittery hairband or choker

This is made from an Alice band, bought ready-covered with velvet. Sequins and silvery beads are stitched along it to give a wonderful sparkle. Wear it as a hairband or clip-on choker round the neck. You could make a pair to match!

### MATERIALS YOU WILL NEED

Velvet-covered headband in your own colour choice (we used vivid emerald green); 12 cup sequins $\frac{1}{2}$ in. in diameter; 12 flower sequins $\frac{1}{2}$ in. in diameter; 25 thin silver beads $\frac{1}{2}$ in. long; matching threads.

### TO MAKE

Stitch each sequin on to the band through the little hole in the centre. Start at the centre front to ensure the design is symmetrical. Then apply the beads by running a thread through the centre of the bead and then through the fabric. As can be seen from the illustration, the flower sequins are alternated with the circular sequins and a bead is placed vertically between them.

## Jet necklace

Jet is a hard coal-like substance. It was much used in Grandmother's day for mourning jewellery, but has long since gone out of fashion. However it is now making a comeback and old pieces of Victorian jewellery can often be picked up on market stalls, in junk shops and at jumble sales, quite cheaply. It is sometimes damaged, or heavier than the jewellery we like nowadays. It is usually quite simple to undo this old jewellery and remake the jet into pieces suitable for today.

Because jet has a wonderful glitter, beads make a really striking necklace as can be seen from our example.

### MATERIALS YOU WILL NEED

Strong black button thread; necklace clasp; needle for threading; black jet beads (number will depend on the length of the necklace you want or the number of beads available—we used about 145).

## TO MAKE

Attach one end of the thread to one side of the necklace clasp, using the loops provided. Thread beads on to button thread, this can be knotted between each bead if desired, to make a really strong necklace. When the necklace is the required length, attach the remaining piece of clasp to the other end and take the loose end of thread back through the last 2 or 3 threaded beads.

*Note:* When threading a lot of beads it is easiest if you make a little channel of stiff paper or newspaper and set the beads out along this, then you can pick them up one by one on the needle very quickly and easily.

# Pretty pink glass eardrops and bracelet

These look particularly pretty in artificial lighting, and the eardrops swing about when you wear them. Again the beads used were 'finds' from a bygone age, but similar beads can still be bought in the shops.

## MATERIALS YOU WILL NEED FOR EARDROPS

Strong thread; sewing needle; 16 long pink glass beads; 16 round glass beads; about 120 tiny pearl beads; 2 ear clips (the perforated sort on to which you can thread beads easily).

## TO MAKE

Pass one end of thread through needle and tie the other end through a hole at the edge of the ear clip. Pass needle through 3 tiny pearl beads, one long pink glass bead, 2 tiny pearl beads, 1 round glass bead and lastly 1 tiny pearl bead. Now take the needle round the outside of the last tiny pearl, pass it back through all the beads just threaded to emerge again at the beginning. Take needle through to back of the ear clip and bring out at front again at the next hole round edge of clip.

Continue threading each 'drop' at evenly spaced intervals all round edge of clip until 8 have been completed. Tie end securely at back. Thread needle with fresh thread and stitch tiny pearl beads in all the remaining spaces on the clip and between the 'drops'. Do this by taking the needle through a hole, through a bead, back through the hole again and on to the next hole. Make sure all threads are securely fastened off.

*Note:* If the perforated section of your ear clip is a separate piece, use a plastic adhesive to stick it to the clip. Apply glue to back of beaded/perforated section and to flat part of the clip. Leave to dry for a few moments, then press both firmly together. Leave overnight to set.

## MATERIALS YOU WILL NEED FOR BRACELET

Strong thread; 2 sewing needles; 12 long pink glass beads; 10 round glass beads; 3 larger round glass beads; small pearl beads (about 100).

## TO MAKE

Cut a length of thread and pass a needle on to each end. Pass one needle through a tiny bead and slide it down to centre of thread, this is the starting bead. The 2 needles are used throughout and the threads cross over inside each long glass bead. Work following the diagram (A). The method of bead threading is very quick and simple and is easily adapted to suit all shapes and sizes of beads, the method being always the same.

When threading the long beads, pass one needle and thread through from right to left, and the other through from left to right. Pull the threads taut each time to ensure that the beads are nice and close together.

To make the toggle which fastens the bracelet, pass both threads through 4 tiny pearl beads. Pass one thread through a large glass bead from right to left and the other through the same glass bead from left to right. Take the right-hand thread and pass it through a second large glass bead and a tiny pearl bead. Now take the thread round the outside of the tiny bead and back through the second glass bead. Remove the needle and leave the end loose.

Now take the left-hand thread from the first glass bead and pass it through a (third on the left) glass bead, and a

tiny pearl bead. Take the thread round the outside of the tiny bead and back through the third and first glass beads to meet the other loose end. Slide off the needle and tie both ends together in a tight knot. With the eye end of a needle, push knot inside a bead and dab a little glue in the hole to secure it. To fasten the bracelet, pass the glass bead bar right through the loop of tiny beads made at the beginning.

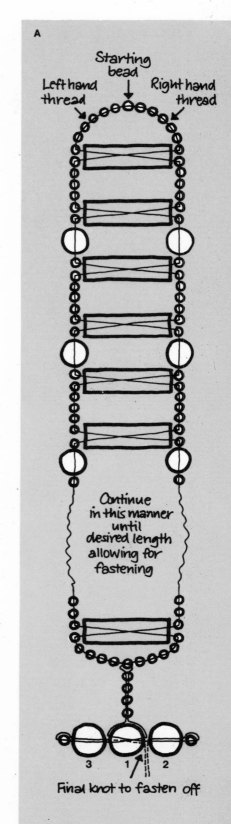

# JEWELLERY

## Lesson Two:
## Working with silver
By Joanna Bruning

## What you will need

**Sheet silver:** this is sold specially for jewellery work in flat sheets of standard gauge thickness and it is usually priced by the weight; 12 or 14 gauge is adequate for rings, and 14 or 16 gauge for bracelets, unless very heavy pieces are required. The backing for brooches and pendants is usually made from thinner silver, 8 or 10 gauge. For bezels (the band which holds in the stone) use 6 gauge.

**Silver wire:** used for making chains, loops, narrow bracelets, neckbands and so forth, this is sold in a wide variety of standard gauge sizes, and can be round, half-round or square in section. Round and square hollow tube is also available.

**Jeweller's findings:** this is a term used to describe readymade fittings for all types of jewellery, such as brooch pins, earring hooks and screws, cuff link ends, jump rings for links, and bolt rings for clasps. A selection of these is very useful, especially for beginners as it is possible to make inexpensive pieces of jewellery easily and quickly.

**Gemstones:** for beginners, **cabochon** cut stones are best—there are gemstones which have been polished and shaped for setting but have not been faceted; they are much easier to set than faceted stones. Faceted stones require a delicate claw setting, but cabochon need only a simple setting (or bezel, as it is known).

**Solder:** this can be bought in strips or in sheet form and is graded by its melting point: hard, medium and easy.

**For cutting:** a piercing saw with adjustable saw frame, jeweller's saw blades, a V-block and clamp, a 3—4 in. vice, jeweller's snips.

**For filing and shaping:** fine emery paper, 600 grit paper, at least two large files (half-round and flat) and at least four needle files (round, half-round, triangular and flat), a triblet (this is a tapered steel spike also known as a ring mandrel) and a vice large enough to hold it, small round-nosed pliers, small flat-nosed pliers, jeweller's ring pliers (one jaw round and one flat), a hide (or wooden) mallet, a jeweller's planishing hammer, a hand drill and drill heads, a ring clamp.

**For annealing and soldering:** a piece of asbestos sheeting, a charcoal block, a gas/air blow torch, pointed tweezers, paint brushes, flux (traditionally a flux paste is made by rubbing a lump of borax in a little water in a rough-textured borax dish, but ready-made

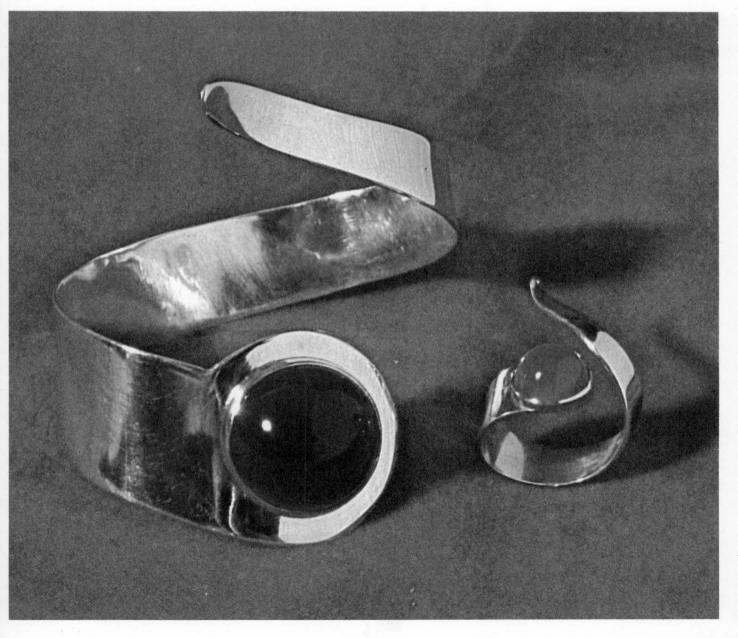

liquid flux is available as an alternative), iron binding wire.

**For cleaning and polishing:** an acid solution made from one part sulphuric acid to ten parts distilled water (both available from dispensing chemists)— make this by adding the acid to the water, *never* the other way round as water added to acid gives off chemical heat and can even cause an explosion; keep the solution in an ovenproof glass or pottery container with lid. You will also need brass or copper tongs, tripoli polish, jeweller's rouge, a set of polishing buffs, a flat or curved burnisher, Water of Ayr stone.

**Note:** a complete set of tools could be an expensive outlay for a beginner. If you want to try out the craft first of all before committing yourself to too much expense, it is a good idea to enrol for a day or evening class at a local school or college. Most of the equipment will then be provided at the class—cutting and filing can be easily done at home in your own time, soldering and machine polishing at the class.

If you do intend to buy a complete set of tools, equipment and materials, most of the specialised equipment (tools, findings, silver and gemstones) can be bought from jewellers' supply companies by mail order. Other items can be bought from good ironmongers or do-it-yourself shops.

# Basic techniques

## CUTTING SHEET SILVER

Using dividers or a fine point, rule and lightly score the line to be cut. Always cut on the outside of the line you have marked. Fine gauge silver can be cut with jeweller's snips but for heavier gauges and thick wire use a piercing saw. When fitting the blade make sure that the teeth face outwards and down towards the handle. To obtain the correct tension (the blade should 'ping' when plucked), loosen first the nuts at both ends of the frame, then insert the blade in the top and tighten it. Compress the whole frame slightly by pressing the top edge against the workbench, and keeping it compressed insert the loose ends of the blade and tighten the bottom nut. Release pressure on the frame gradually. Always keep the blade perpendicular to the sawing surface and cut on the downward stroke. Heavy pressure is not necessary and will break the blade. To support the sheet silver while cutting, a hardwood V-board clamped to the table or workbench is useful. For cutting thick wire or tube use a small vice to hold it, first lining the jaws with leather so that they do not mark the silver.

## ANNEALING

Sheet silver cannot be shaped without first being heated and then rapidly cooled—a process known as annealing. This softens the metal so that it can be hammered or bent without damage. Put the silver on an asbestos sheet and heat it quickly with a blow torch until it turns dark red in colour. A yellow-red colour is a danger sign, showing that the silver is on the point of melting. Try to avoid overheating when annealing or soldering as this can cause dull grey firestains which become visible after polishing and are difficult to remove.

Pick up the hot metal with tweezers and hold it under cold water. The silver will harden as it is hammered; when it becomes difficult to work, repeat the annealing process.

Silver wire is not always annealed—for instance, a round-wire neckband such as used on the pendant design in the designs to make, should be hard and springy. If the wire were annealed it would be too soft for its purpose.

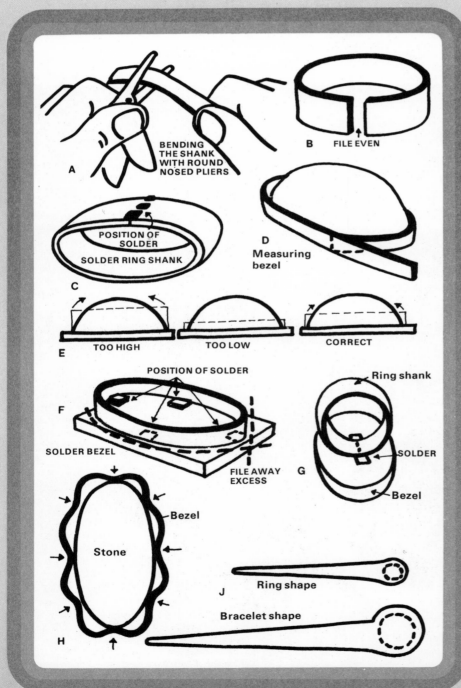

A BENDING THE SHANK WITH ROUND NOSED PLIERS

B FILE EVEN

C POSITION OF SOLDER / SOLDER RING SHANK

D Measuring bezel

E TOO HIGH — TOO LOW — CORRECT

F POSITION OF SOLDER / SOLDER BEZEL / FILE AWAY EXCESS

G Ring shank / SOLDER / Bezel

H Bezel / Stone

J Ring shape / Bracelet shape

## SHAPING AND FILING SILVER

For simple jewellery the flat silver is shaped by twisting or curving it with pliers or over triblets. Pliers for bending silver must have smooth polished jaws; serrations will cause dents and roughness. Round-nosed pliers are used for curves, flat-nosed pliers for angles. When hammering silver over a triblet to bend it, use a hide or wooden hammer—a metal hammer would mark the surface. The metal planishing hammer is used to stretch and thin silver; it is useful if you have made a ring too small and have to enlarge it.

When using a file on straight edges, work at a diagonal to the filing surface with a long even stroke. File from the tip of the file to the handle.

## SOLDERING SILVER

Molten solder will only flow into a join if it has been carefully fluxed. Apply flux to the surfaces to be soldered with a paint brush, having first made sure that the surfaces are free from dust and grease by sanding them with clean, fine emery paper. Always file joints to fit as accurately as possible—if there are gaps, the solder can run between them on to the visible surface and at best the join will be lumpy, at worst incompletely soldered. Choose the type of solder to be used most appropriate to the design: if the design requires soldering a number of times begin with hard solder, go on to medium and last of all use easy solder. Clean the solder, cut it into tiny pieces about $\frac{1}{32}$ in. square and coat them with flux by picking them up and positioning them with a flux-moistened brush. Several small pieces melt more easily than one large one. An even heat over the whole area to be soldered is essential for a successful result. Begin by quickly rotating the flame around the outside of the area without touching the silver. The flux will probably foam a little as it is heated and this can dislodge the solder, so have a pair of pointed tweezers ready to reposition it if necessary. A white crust will form on the fluxed surface. This indicates that the flux has hardened, and the area to be soldered can now be heated directly. Rotate the flame slowly over it until you see the solder melt and flow into the join. After soldering the metal will be discoloured and must be cleaned before further work can be done.

## CLEANING SILVER AFTER SOLDERING

The work is put in the acid solution (pickle) to remove discolouring oxides and the remains of the flux. The acid is very corrosive so try to avoid splashing and keep it in a well-ventilated place because of acid fumes. Leave the work in the pickle until it is clean—it will then appear a dull whitish colour. When you take it out, rinse it in cold water or the traces of acid will continue to eat into the metal.

Never use steel or iron tongs to put the silver into the acid as a copper deposit will form on it. Similarly if iron binding wire was used to hold the work together for soldering, it must all be removed before pickling. If you do not have brass or copper tongs, use bent pieces of strong silver wire.

## SURFACE FINISHING

A good machine polisher is an expensive piece of equipment, and not necessary for the beginner since it is possible to obtain a high degree of finish by hand-polishing.

Remove any scratches or dents by rubbing lightly with fine emery paper—a piece that has been worn almost smooth is ideal. Wash and dry the work and rub hard and evenly with a felt buffing stick charged with tripoli polish, changing the direction constantly. Any firestain will become noticeable at this point and should be removed with fine emery paper or Water of Ayr stone. Take a second buff and polish with jeweller's rouge. Places which cannot be reached by the buffs can be polished by rubbing with a flat or curved burnisher and a little cake rouge. Or you can use a piece of soft string coated with rouge.

## YOUR SILVER MAKES

# RINGS, PENDANTS AND A BRACELET

**Jewellery designed by Jane Withers**

## Labradorite ring

*Note*. The techniques described in detail for this design apply also to the other designs.

1. Cut a piece of 15 gauge silver to the required length and width. A very wide shank will cut uncomfortably when the finger is bent, so it is better to underestimate the width rather than overestimate. If you do not have a ring sizer you can measure the length required by bending a piece of stiffish paper round the large knuckle of the finger on which you wish to wear the ring, and then marking the overlap. Add about $\frac{1}{8}$ in. to this length to allow for the thickness of the silver.

2. Anneal the silver as described on previous page, then using a hide hammer, tap it against the triblet to round it and bring the ends together. Alternatively, jeweller's pliers can be used to do this (A). Bend the ends back and forth and over and under each other—you will find that a spring develops which will hold the ends firmly together. Check the final shape and adjust if necessary using a triblet.

3. File the join so that the edges fit evenly (B) (no light should be seen

between them—use a flat file for this). Flux and solder the join (C) using hard solder and clean away discolouration and the remains of the flux by putting the ring in the acid solution.

4. To make the bezel, measure the circumference of the stone with paper (D), cut a strip of 6 gauge silver, anneal it, round it and solder it with hard solder. Clean it in acid. The height of the bezel is important (E): if it is too low it will not hold the stone, if too high the bezel will have to be bent too far in over the surface of the stone and may buckle as a result. Fine silver (pure silver without alloys) is often used for bezels because it is very soft and bends more easily over the stone. The bezel should be made to fit the stone as accurately as possible but not so tightly that the stone sticks and cannot be pushed though it easily.

5. File the bottom of the bezel so it sits evenly on a flat surface. Check that the top and bottom edges are parallel.

6. This ring has a solid base to the stone. Cut a rectangular piece of 8 gauge silver slightly larger than the stone, solder the bezel to it with medium solder, clean it in acid and file away the excess to give a neat edge (F).

7. Before soldering the ring shank to the completed bezel and base, file a narrow flat area along the line of the original hard solder so that the ring will stand upright on the upside-down bezel. The ring shank is made from half-round wire. Position it carefully in the centre of the bezel and solder it with easy solder (G). Clean it in acid.

8. Remove all marks and traces of solder by filing with needle files and fine emery paper. Clean and polish the ring thoroughly before setting the stone If the stone is translucent it will be necessary to prevent the silver underneath it from tarnishing as this will spoil the appearance of the stone in time. The surface of the silver can be coated with colourless varnish, or a piece of aluminium foil cut to size and placed under the stone can be used instead.

9. Setting the stone. Hold the ring in a ring clamp, and using needle files and

271

emery paper file the top $\frac{1}{16}$ in. of the outside edge of the bezel to about half its original thickness. Put the stone in position and using a short curved burnisher, push the bezel in against the stone at opposing points in at least eight places (H). Now move the burnisher slowly round the bezel pressing it in firmly and evenly down against the stone. Polish again to give the ring a final finish.

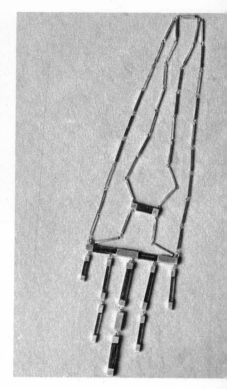

## Silver ring

This ring is made from scraps of sheet silver fused together. This is done by arranging the scraps in a strip on a charcoal block, painting them liberally with liquid flux, and heating until the metal begins to melt and to blend. The resulting strip is then formed into a ring, cut to size and soldered with easy solder.

## Chalcedony ring and bracelet

Use 12 gauge sheet silver for the ring; 14 gauge sheet silver for the bracelet. Cut the basic shapes, to size required, as shown in diagram J on previous pages. Bend the shapes round and shape them before adding the bezels. To fit a bezel to a curved surface, the bottom edge has to be carefully filed to fit the curve.
A ring of wire is soldered inside the bezel to make a level support for the stone.

## Silver wire pendant

This is made from different sizes of round silver wire. Texture is added to the pendant by cutting with a silicone carbine wheel fitted to an electric drill.

## Tourmaline pendant

The chain is made from equal lengths of square section silver wire, the links from jump rings. A coating of jeweller's rouge at the point where the links touch is needed to prevent the links fusing together when the second one is soldered into position. The pendant is made from two sizes of square hollow tube. To fit the stones three sides were cut away and the tourmalines glued into position with special jeweller's glue.

## Amethyst ring

The high bezel is made from 14 gauge sheet silver and shaped at the bottom to follow the curve of the ring shank. A wire ring and claws to support and hold the stone are soldered inside it. Before the stone is set, the bezel is given additional weight and texture with small silver balls and very fine silver wire twisted and woven around it and fused together.

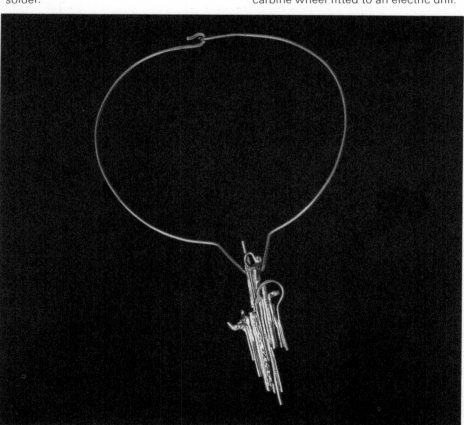

# TOYMAKING

**Making soft toys is a rewarding and fascinating hobby. Anne Hulbert introduces you to the basic principles of the craft, and gives six delightful toys to make.**

## MAKING PATTERNS FOR THE TOYS

The patterns are presented here in miniature form, on a squared grid. Each square on the grid equals 1 inch. To make your full-size patterns, use either 1-in. graph paper, or divide large sheets of strong plain paper into 1-in. squares. Copy the diagrams on to your paper, following the instructions for preparing a pattern in Sewing, lesson one. Cut out all the pieces required for each toy. It is a good idea to glue the patterns on to thin card, as they are then much easier to draw round on to the fabric. By making card templates in this way, the pattern can then be used over and over again, if required.

## CUTTING OUT FABRICS

The long arrows usually marked on pattern pieces indicate the straight grain of the fabric (if it has one). When cutting out, keep these arrows parallel with the threads in your fabric. If using fur fabric, the pile should run down the toy.

When choosing fabric for your toys, you will find an allover pattern is more economical and easier to work out than a fabric with a printed pattern running in one direction only.

Where two identical pattern pieces of irregular shape are required, do remember to reverse the template. Simply turn the template over to the other side and draw round it for the second pattern part required.

If possible, always cut pattern pieces from single thickness fabric. Fabrics tend to move when a double thickness is cut through, and this could distort one of the pattern pieces. It is also more economical to mark each piece on single fabric—the parts required can be placed closer together and fitted in more easily than if cutting from doubled fabric.

## STITCHING

For all body seams of toys, two rows of stitching are recommended. This ensures a strongly-made toy each time. On fur fabric, cotton and plastic fabrics, $\frac{1}{4}$-in. turnings are allowed for. Felt and suede seams are stitched together $\frac{1}{8}$ in. from the edge.

## FILLINGS FOR THE TOYS

Cut foam is only really suitable as a filling for fur fabric toys. It tends to give a bumpy appearance to toys made of cotton or smooth fabrics, but the bumps do not show under a fur pile. Kapok is the best all-purpose filling material. It is soft and light and easy to use for toys made of cotton or of corduroy, and it is easy to achieve a smooth appearance in the finished toy.

# Fur fabric owl

## MATERIALS YOU WILL NEED

Piece of brown fur fabric, 15 in. by 24 in.; piece of white fur fabric, 14 in. by 16 in.; 12-in. square of red felt; piece of brown felt, 2 in. by 4 in.; approx. 8 oz. Kapok or other suitable filling; fabric glue.

## MEASUREMENTS

The finished owl is approx. 9½ in. high, 11 in. wide.

## TO MAKE

Make and cut out your templates for all pattern pieces. Cut out all parts required in felt and fur fabric.

**Body.** With right sides facing, baste and stitch front and back body together from A round top and down to B.
Tack and stitch in bottom gusset, matching AA and BB. Leave gap open from C to D for turning and filling. Turn to right side and fill carefully so that the toy is a good shape but light and soft for a small child to hold. Stitch gap closed.

**Face.** Spread a little fabric glue on eyes and pupils and glue in position on face as shown on pattern. Oversew each piece neatly. Spread a little glue all round edge of back of face and glue on to body in position on pattern. Oversew all round carefully, using small stitches.
With wrong sides facing, stitch both beak pieces together ⅛ in. from edge. Leave open from E to F. Fill carefully with stuffing. Pin in position indicated on face and stitch all round very firmly.

**Wings.** With right sides facing, baste and stitch two wing sections together, leaving gap open from J to K. Turn to right side and insert enough filling to puff the wings out a little. Stitch gap closed. Spread a little glue on inside of wing and hold in place on body, as shown in picture. Stitch on firmly, carefully picking up body fabric and wing fabric alternately with the needle. Repeat for other wing.

**Feet.** With wrong sides facing, stitch two feet sections together ⅛ in. from edge, leaving open from G to H. Apply a little glue along from G to H, and glue to body in position on front seam of bottom gusset as shown in pattern. Stitch firmly in place. Repeat for other foot.
Using the eye end of a needle, go over all fur fabric seams, picking out any fur pile that has become caught in the stitching. Brush the fur pile of the forehead downwards to fall over edge of white face piece. Brush over rest of owl to fluff up the pile, and plump him into shape.

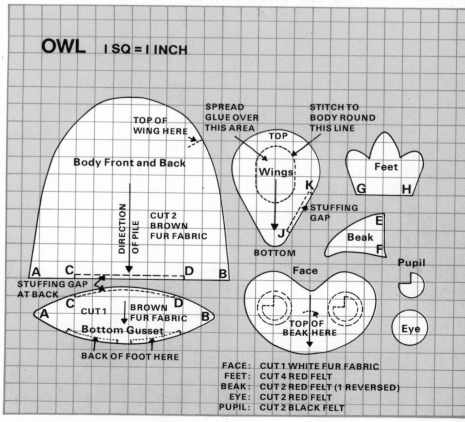

# Hedgehog

## MATERIALS YOU WILL NEED

Piece of beige felt, 15 in. by 19 in.; piece of purple felt, 6 in. by 11 in.; piece of white felt, 1½ in. by 2½ in.; piece of black felt, 1 in. by 2 in.; approx. 2 oz. (in total) of beige, cream and purple wool scraps; approx. 8 oz. Kapok or other suitable filling; fabric glue.

## MEASUREMENTS

Finished hedgehog is approx. 10 in. long, 5½ in. high.

## TO MAKE

Make and cut out your templates for all pattern pieces. Cut out all pieces required in felt.

**Body.** With wrong sides of felt facing, stitch sides together from A, round the top and down to B. Stitch in base, also on right side, leaving gap open from E to F for filling. Stuff until a good firm shape is obtained and stitch up gap.

**Face.** Spread a little fabric glue on eyes and pupils and glue in position as shown. Oversew neatly all round each piece. Take the nose piece and run a gathering thread all round the edge. Place a small piece of stuffing in the centre and draw up. Add more stuffing as you work, to achieve a firm round nose. Stitch firmly to face at A. Run 3 strands of purple wool through the face to make whiskers. Cut them about 4 in. long, and knot at each side against the face to prevent them slipping out.

**Feet.** Stitch 2 foot pieces together with wrong sides facing. Leave open from C to D. Insert a little stuffing to make the foot slightly rounded. Oversew gap and stitch foot to body in position shown. Repeat for other foot.

**Spines.** Cut the wool scraps into approx. 3¼ in. lengths. Take 3 strands together and fold in half (mix up the

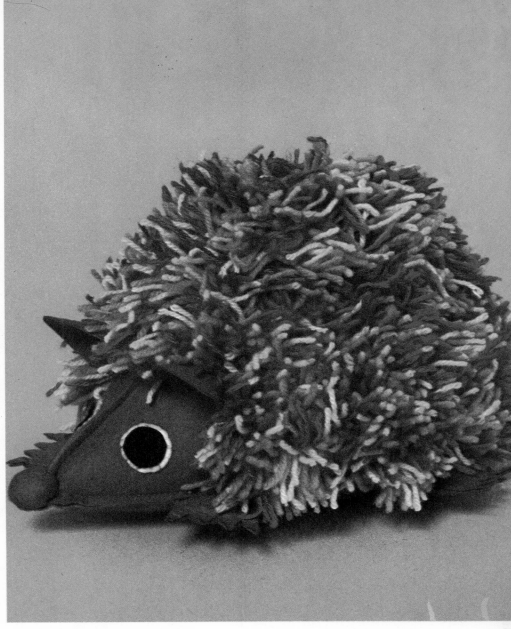

colours well). Stitch bundles at the fold to body sides and top of hedgehog until he is well covered. Work as far as line G to H on face.

**Ears.** Sew ears in position indicated on the head, curving them round slightly at the base.

Trim spines if necessary to make the hedgehog well rounded, and brush off excess filling.

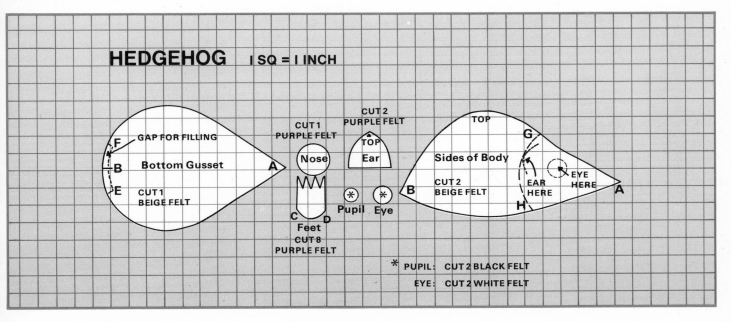

# Rice-filled frog

## MATERIALS YOU WILL NEED

Piece of printed needlecord, 9 in. by 15 in.; piece of plain needlecord, 9 in. by 15 in.; 11 oz. rice; 2 black beads; funnel made from a strip of card.

## MEASUREMENTS

Finished frog is approx. 13 in. long, 7 in. wide.

## TO MAKE

Make and cut out your templates for the pattern pieces. Cut out both pieces required for the frog. With right sides facing, stitch fabric round entire frog, leaving gap open from A to B for turning. Clip carefully at curves and corners. Turn to right side, pushing the feet well out to get a good shape. The blunt end of a pencil, used gently, will help you to do this. Place the end of the funnel in the filling gap and pour in rice. Stitch up gap neatly.
Sew the bead eyes in position, as shown in diagram. Run a thread across inside the head from one bead to the other and draw up slightly, to sink them into the head a little.
'Knead' over the frog, making sure that the rice filling will slide in and out of the legs freely.

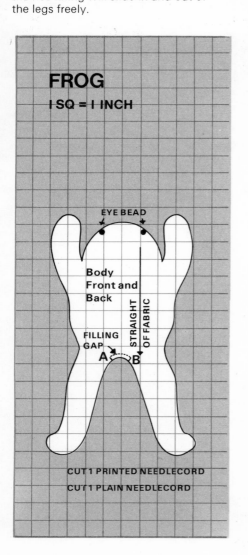

FROG

1 SQ = 1 INCH

EYE BEAD

Body Front and Back

STRAIGHT OF FABRIC

FILLING GAP

A    B

CUT 1 PRINTED NEEDLECORD
CUT 1 PLAIN NEEDLECORD

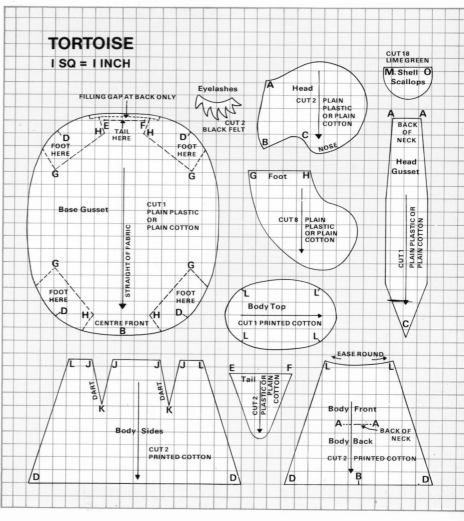

TORTOISE

1 SQ = 1 INCH

FILLING GAP AT BACK ONLY

Eyelashes
CUT 2
BLACK FELT

CUT 18
LIME GREEN
M. Shell O
Scallops

A    Head
CUT 2    PLAIN
PLASTIC
OR PLAIN
COTTON
B    C
NOSE

A    A
BACK
OF
NECK

Head
Gusset

D    H    TAIL    F    H    D
FOOT    HERE    FOOT
HERE    HERE
G    G

Base Gusset

CUT 1
PLAIN PLASTIC
OR
PLAIN COTTON

STRAIGHT OF FABRIC

G    Foot    H

CUT 8    PLAIN
PLASTIC
OR PLAIN
COTTON

CUT 1    PLAIN PLASTIC OR PLAIN COTTON

G    G
FOOT    FOOT
HERE    HERE
D    H    H    D

CENTRE FRONT
B

C

L    L
Body Top
CUT 1 PRINTED COTTON
L    L

EASE ROUND

L    J    J    J    J    L
DART    DART
K    K

Body Sides

CUT 2
PRINTED COTTON

D    D

E    F
Tail
CUT 2    PLASTIC OR PLAIN COTTON

L    L
Body Front
A    A    BACK OF
NECK
Body Back
CUT 2    PRINTED COTTON
D    B    D

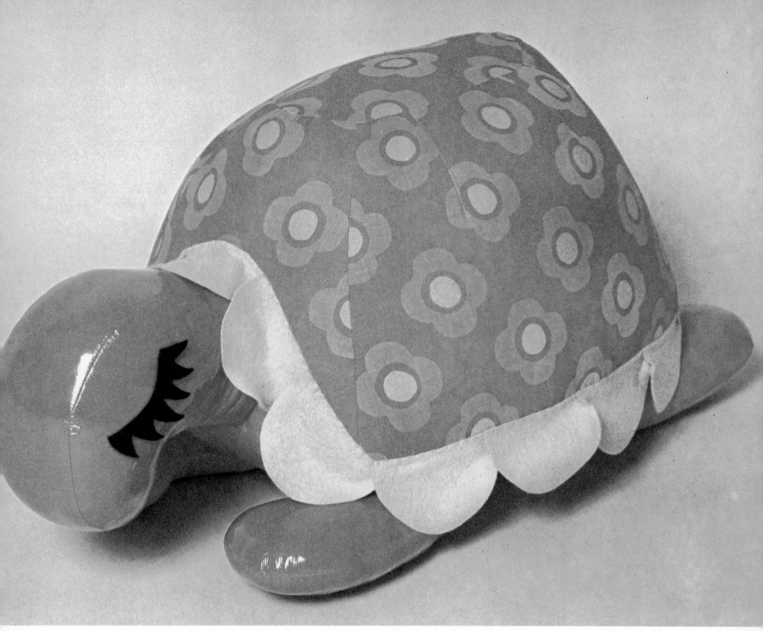

# Tortoise pouffe

## MATERIALS YOU WILL NEED

Piece of printed cotton, 23 in. by 36 in.; 36-in. square of plain stretchy plastic (not the stiff variety); 4-in. square of black felt; piece of lime felt, 10 in. by 18 in.; 4 lb. Kapok; fabric glue and glue suitable for sticking plastic.

## MEASUREMENTS

The finished pouffe is 14 in. high, 12 in. wide, not including his head.

## TO MAKE

Make and cut out your templates for all pattern pieces. Cut out all parts required for the tortoise.

**Body.** With right sides facing, baste and stitch up darts on body sides, from JJ to K. Baste and stitch body sides to back and front, from L to D, with right sides facing. In doing this, make sure that the side pieces are opposite each other.

Baste and stitch in base gusset, matching D at side seams to D on the base. Leave gap open at back as shown on the pattern. Baste and stitch

in body top, easing it round as you work. Match side seams to each L, as shown on pattern. Turn to right side. Fill carefully with stuffing, until very firm indeed, keeping a good even shape. Stitch up gap neatly.

**Head.** Place both head pieces together, right sides facing. Baste and stitch gusset between them, running from A at back of neck, all round front of face to C under the chin. Stitch seam from B to C after both sides of gusset are stitched in place. Turn to right side, and fill firmly with stuffing. Leave open at neck. Turn $\frac{1}{4}$ in. under all round. Stitch to head, matching B to centre front base seam and AA to AA on body front, as shown on pattern. Push in more stuffing as you work round neck to ensure that neck is very firm.

Spread a little plastic adhesive on back of lashes, and glue in place on face. There is no need to stitch as well. If you use plain cotton for the head, then glue the lashes in place with fabric glue and backstitch along $\frac{1}{4}$ in. from top edge.

**Tail.** With right sides facing, stitch tail pieces together, leaving gap open from

E to F. Turn to right side. Fill firmly with stuffing. Turn under $\frac{1}{4}$ in. all round opening, and stitch to back end of body as indicated.

**Legs.** Place 2 leg pieces together, right sides facing. Stitch all round, leaving open from G to H. Turn to right side and fill firmly with stuffing. Oversew across gap. Spread a little plastic adhesive on upper side of foot, towards the back, and stick to base, front legs pointing forwards and back legs pointing backwards. If cotton fabric is used, stick with fabric glue instead. Stitch on firmly.

**Shell scallops.** Spread a thin line of fabric glue along straight edge of each scallop. Start at the back of the neck and apply them down to D on base seam, glueing them on. Overlap each one by about $\frac{1}{4}$ in. Glue them along base line all round rest of body. When all are in place, oversew along top edge of each scallop. You may not need to use as many as 18 scallops: it depends on how fully you have stuffed the tortoise, but try pinning them round first to see how they fit round.

Brush off excess stuffing and plump the tortoise into shape.

# Dog

## MATERIALS YOU WILL NEED

Piece of green printed cotton, 27 in. by 45 in.; piece of green felt, 10 in. by 12 in.; piece of white felt, 3 in. by 3½ in.; piece of black felt, 3 in. by 4 in.; 2-in. square of pink felt; approx. 1½ lb. Kapok; fabric glue.

## MEASUREMENTS

Finished dog is 12 in. high, 2z in. long, from tip of tail to nose.

## TO MAKE

Make and cut out your templates for all pattern pieces. Cut out all pieces required in cotton and felt.

**Body.** With right sides facing, stitch head gusset to face gusset from A to A at forehead. Stitch face gusset to underbody gusset from D to D at throat.
Place head and body pieces together with right sides facing. Pin the completed gussets in between, very carefully matching AA, BB, CC and DD. Baste and stitch together all round, leaving gap open for stuffing at one side of underbody gusset seam. Stitch across back of dog from B to C. Clip curves and corners carefully. Turn to right side and fill very firmly with stuffing. Stitch up gap.

**Legs.** With right sides facing, stitch 2 leg pieces together all round, leaving top open. Clip curves. Turn to right side and fill very firmly with stuffing. Run a gathering thread round the top opening. Draw up enough to keep stuffing from falling out, and fasten off. Stitch leg to underbody as indicated in pattern. Work twice round very firmly. (N.B. Feet must point forward!)

**Eyes.** Spread a little fabric glue on the back of each eye piece. Stick in place as indicated and hem stitch all round each piece.

**Nose.** Glue in place as indicated, and hemstitch all round.

**Tongue.** Spread a thin line of glue along straight edge. Stick in position indicated, facing forward. Stitch along edge with stab stitch.

**Ears.** Make a tuck at the top of each ear, hold in place with a little glue. Stitch to top of head by oversewing in position indicated.

**Tail.** Fold tail in half lengthwise, with right sides facing, meeting F and F. Stitch along from F to E. Turn to right side and fill firmly with stuffing. Turn under ¼ in. all round opening, and stitch to end of body in position indicated. The tail should follow in a straight line, continuous with the back of the dog.
Plump him into shape, brush off excess filling, and bend his tongue forward.

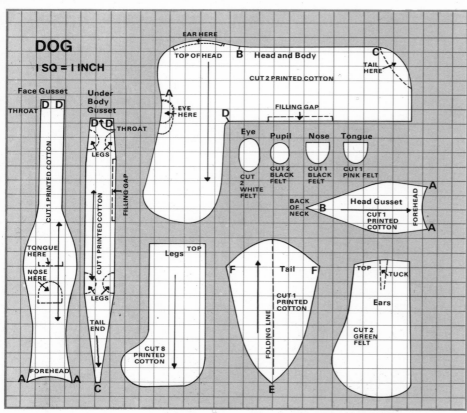

DOG

I SQ = I INCH

Face Gusset

THROAT D D

Under Body Gusset

D D THROAT

LEGS

CUT 1 PRINTED COTTON

FILLING GAP

CUT 1 PRINTED COTTON

TONGUE HERE

NOSE HERE

LEGS

TAIL END

FOREHEAD

A A

C

EAR HERE

TOP OF HEAD B Head and Body

CUT 2 PRINTED COTTON

A

EYE HERE

D

FILLING GAP

C

TAIL HERE

Eye

CUT 2 WHITE FELT

Pupil

CUT 2 BLACK FELT

Nose

CUT 1 BLACK FELT

Tongue

CUT 1 PINK FELT

BACK OF NECK B

Head Gusset

CUT 1 PRINTED COTTON

FOREHEAD

A

A

Legs TOP

CUT 8 PRINTED COTTON

F Tail F

CUT 1 PRINTED COTTON

FOLDING LINE

E

TOP TUCK

Ears

CUT 2 GREEN FELT

*Note: If you find that the legs splay out slightly, you can catch them together with double thread. Stitches should be high up between each pair of legs.*

# Bean-filled lion

## MATERIALS YOU WILL NEED

Piece of printed cotton, 13 in. by 18 in.; piece of orange felt, 4 in. by 8 in.; piece of tan felt, 2 in. by 3 in.; piece of pink felt, 1 in. by 1½ in.; piece of brown felt, 1 in. by 2 in.; 18 oz. haricot beans; fabric glue; double knitting wool; funnel made from a strip of card.

## MEASUREMENTS

The finished lion is approx. 9½ in. high.

## TO MAKE

Make and cut out your templates for all pattern pieces. Cut out all parts required for the lion.

**Paws.** For each paw, stitch 2 pieces together, wrong sides facing, leaving gap open from C to C. Insert a little filling and baste across gap. Repeat for other paws. Tack each one in place, as indicated on pattern, and include in side seams of body (see below).

**Body.** Join front body piece to side and back. With right sides facing, baste and stitch together down both sides from A to B. Stitch in face piece, matching D at chin to D on front of body. Ease it round the curves carefully as you work. Clip at 1-in. intervals all round the seam allowance.
Stitch in base, easing it round, and leaving gap at back for turning and filling. Clip in 3 or 4 places round the seam allowance. Turn to right side, push all seams well out to make a good shape. Place the end of the funnel in the filling gap and pour in haricot beans. Stitch up gap neatly.

**Face.** Using only a little fabric glue, stick nose, mouth and eyes in positions indicated in pattern. Oversew neatly around each piece, but stab stitch along the mouth.
Run 3 strands of wool, each about 5 in. long, through the top of the mouth on the nose piece for whiskers. Knot each one at each side and close against face to prevent them being pulled out.

**Mane.** Work this all round seam line of the face and use one long strand of wool: fasten end of wool to fabric; make 2 loops, each about 1½ in. long, and stitch the 'in-between' loop to the fabric seam. Continue working in this way all round seam, making only one row of loops. Vary their length between 1½ in. and 2 in., and stitch them very close together.
When finished, leave the loops of wool uncut, to give a curly effect.

**Tail.** Make a plait 7 in. long, using 9 strands of wool. Bind round with thread 1 in. from cut end, and fluff out ends of wool. Stitch other end to back of body at the base seam.

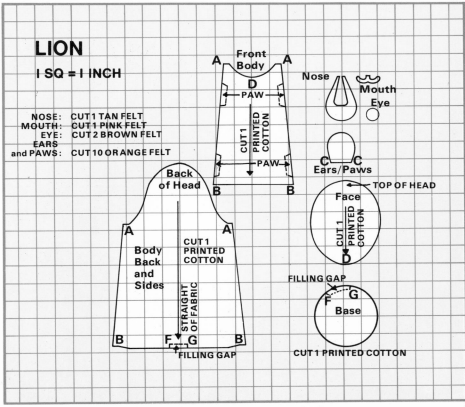

LION

1 SQ = 1 INCH

NOSE: CUT 1 TAN FELT
MOUTH: CUT 1 PINK FELT
EYE: CUT 2 BROWN FELT
EARS and PAWS: CUT 10 ORANGE FELT

Front Body

PAW

CUT 1 PRINTED COTTON

PAW

Back of Head

Nose

Mouth

Eye

Ears/Paws

TOP OF HEAD

Face

CUT 1 PRINTED COTTON

FILLING GAP

Body Back and Sides

CUT 1 PRINTED COTTON

STRAIGHT OF FABRIC

FILLING GAP

Base

CUT 1 PRINTED COTTON

# Hatmaking

**Louise Silver introduces you to the craft of millinery.**

Hatmaking is no more difficult than any other form of home sewing, once one or two simple basic rules have been learned and understood.

## Materials to use

Most good-quality fabrics can be used to make hats although the choice may be limited according to the type of hat you want to make—a flower-patterned silk, for instance, would scarcely be suitable for a country-style deerstalker, nor would a sturdy tweed be suitable for a veil-trimmed concoction for a wedding.

In general the heavier, stiffer fabrics work best—felt is ideal and easy to work for a beginner as it is fray-free, easy to cut and to shape, and edges need no binding. Corduroy and tweed are also good.

Good quality interfacing is usually used to line the various pieces for your hat, to give extra 'body' and stiffening. Either the iron-on or sew-on variety of interfacing may be used; for a hat

which requires only light stiffening, or where a reasonably stiff fabric is being used, then a lightweight sew-in interfacing, or a soft iron-on interfacing may be used. For a hat which requires a more rigid finished shape, or if the fabric is inclined to droop, then mediumweight sew-in or firm iron-on interfacing should be used.

For hand-stitching No. 7 straw needles are best for most general purposes. Sewing thread should be chosen to suit the fabric, or use a multipurpose thread. Ready-made linings in a variety of styles and sizes can be bought from most large stores. These linings are simply slipped inside your finished hat and stitched neatly in place. Using one of these ready-made linings will give an attractive professional look to your finished hat.

## Cutting fabric on the cross

One of the most important basic rules of hatmaking is that all woven materials must be cut on the cross. To do this lay your fabric flat, with short ends at the sides. Fold bottom left-hand corner up to meet top edge. Cut off this triangle. Pattern pieces are now cut with the grain line (straight arrow) running parallel with the cut edge on fabric. It may be necessary when sewing your fabric pieces together to ease the pieces cut on the cross gently into place. Always cut seam allowance to $\frac{1}{4}$ in. unless otherwise instructed.

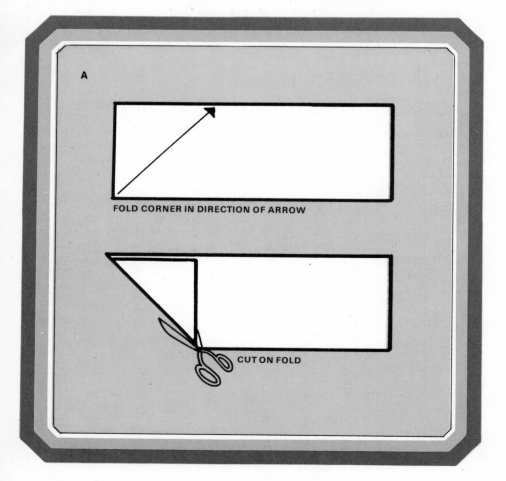

A

FOLD CORNER IN DIRECTION OF ARROW

CUT ON FOLD

# Your hat makes

## Tammy hat

### MATERIALS YOU WILL NEED

$\frac{1}{2}$ yd. fabric, 36 in. wide (we used checked linen-like fabric); $\frac{1}{2}$ yd. interfacing, 32 or 36 in. wide (iron-on or sew-in); 2 ft. petersham ribbon, 1 in. wide; 1 ready-made lining; 1 large flat button.

### TO MAKE

Cut fabric on the cross as explained in lesson. The diagram overleaf gives the single pattern piece you will need. Each square on the diagram represents 1 in. Following instructions in Sewing, Lesson one, prepare a full-size diagram. Cut out the pattern pieces six times, placing the piece on single thickness fabric, and making sure arrow on piece runs parallel with the cross of the fabric (the cut edge after the triangle section has been trimmed away). Add $\frac{1}{4}$ in. to all edges for seam allowance. Cut pattern piece six times from interfacing. Place each interfacing section on a fabric section, on the wrong side. Iron in place if using iron-on interfacing, or baste together round outside edges. Stitch dart in each section by bringing cut edges together, right sides facing, and stitching $\frac{1}{4}$ in. from the edges. Open dart seam and press well.

Now with right sides together, stitch sections together round curved edges. Press lower part of seams only. Turn the shape to the right side and turn in $\frac{1}{2}$ in. hem round entire lower edge. Baste. This is the headline. Pin petersham ribbon right round this turned-in seam allowance at headline, and invisibly sew in place.

Place button right side down on a left-over piece of fabric, run a gathering thread in a circle all round button $\frac{1}{2}$ in. bigger than the button. Pull thread up tight so fabric encloses button, and finish off. Cut away surplus fabric. Pin fabric-covered button to centre of tammy where the joins meet and stitch invisibly in place.

Place lining inside tammy and slipstitch in place to inside of headband. Press edge very lightly.

## Brimmed hat

### MATERIALS YOU WILL NEED

$\frac{3}{4}$ yd. felt, 36 in. wide (we used peacock blue); $\frac{3}{4}$ yd. interfacing, 32 or 36 in. wide (iron-on or sew-in); 2 ft. petersham ribbon, 1 in. wide; 1 ready-

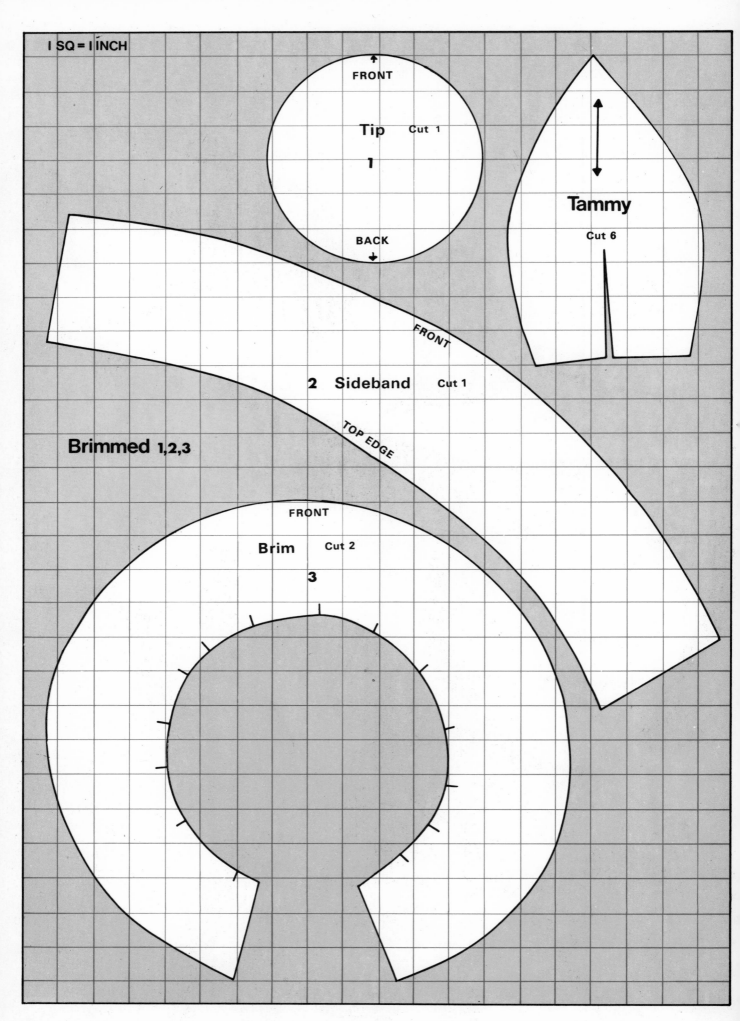

I SQ = I INCH

FRONT

**Tip** Cut 1

**1**

BACK

**Tammy**

Cut 6

FRONT

**2 Sideband** Cut 1

TOP EDGE

**Brimmed 1,2,3**

FRONT

**Brim** Cut 2

**3**

made lining; 2 hanks tapestry wool (we used ochre yellow).

## TO MAKE

The diagram opposite gives the three pattern pieces you will need: brim, sideband, and tip. Each square on the diagram represents 1 in. Following instructions in Sewing, lesson one, prepare a full-size diagram for all the pattern pieces.

Fold the felt in half lengthwise, and pin brim pattern section to felt. Cut out. Cut same section once from interfacing. Place both felt sections together, then place interfacing on top. Machine stitch right round outer edges. Open out underneath layer of felt, then join centre back seam. Turn opened-out felt section over on top of interfacing, so brim is now right way side out (the interfacing is then sandwiched between the two felt sections). Baste through all thicknesses.

Now machine stitch right round outer edge ⅛ in. from the edge. On inner edge, make ½-in. slits at 2-in. intervals (as marked on pattern diagram). Bend this into an upstanding rim to form the headband. If necessary press very lightly on wrong side with a dry cloth over the iron. The brim is now complete.

For the crown, cut out one sideband and one tip from felt, and also from interfacing. Baste interfacing to wrong side of felt.

Right sides together, stitch centre back seam of sideband. Press open.

Right sides together, pin sideband to tip easing slightly to make it fit. Machine stitch ¼ in. from edge.

Turn complete crown section to the right side and turn under ½ in. round lower edge. Pin all round.

Place centre seam of crown to centre back seam of brim pinning crown to brim. Slipstitch neatly all round.

For trimming cut both hanks of wool open, make a 3-in. loop in both hanks, linking them before binding the short ends tightly to the main length of wool. Place centre of loops to centre front of crown, arrange the trimming round crown. Finish at centre back with a double knot, stitch trimming invisibly into place. Sew headband and lining in place as for tammy hat.

## Cloche cap

### MATERIALS YOU WILL NEED

½ yd. fabric, 36 in. wide (we used pink satin); ½ yd. interfacing, 32 or 36 in. wide (iron-on or sew-in); 2 ft. petersham ribbon, 1 in. wide; 1 ready-made lining; 1 box of sequins, and 1 box of small beads, or any trimming wished (we used blue beads and long curved sequins).

### TO MAKE

Cut fabric on the cross as explained in lesson. The diagram overleaf gives

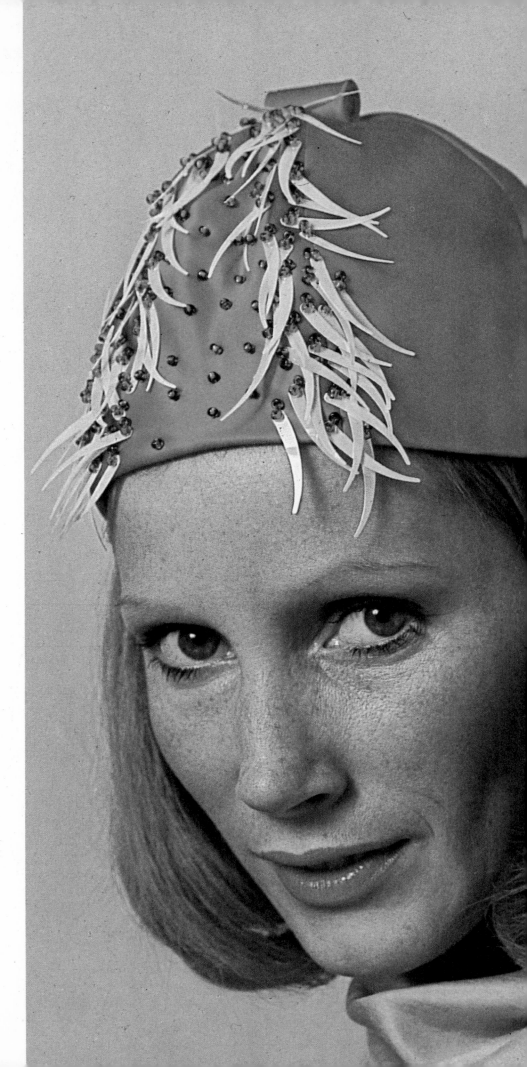

the three pattern pieces you will need. Each square on the diagram represents 1 in. Following instructions in Sewing, Lesson one, prepare a full-size diagram. Cut out the pattern pieces: one of section 1, two of section 2, three of section 3, placing the pattern pieces on single thickness fabric, and making sure arrow in each piece runs parallel with the cross of the fabric (the cut edge after the triangle section has been trimmed away). Add $\frac{1}{4}$ in. to all edges for seam allowance.

Cut the same pattern pieces in interfacing (no seam allowance). Place each interfacing section on the appropriate fabric section, on the wrong side. Iron in place if using iron-on interfacing, or baste together round outside edges. With right sides together, pin the sections together, as indicated in diagram right, and machine stitch down curved edges. Press seams open and turn shape to the right side. Turn in $\frac{1}{2}$ in. hem round lower edge and baste. This is the headline.

Beginning at the midway point of the centre No. 3 section (centre back) place petersham ribbon round the turned-in seam allowance and

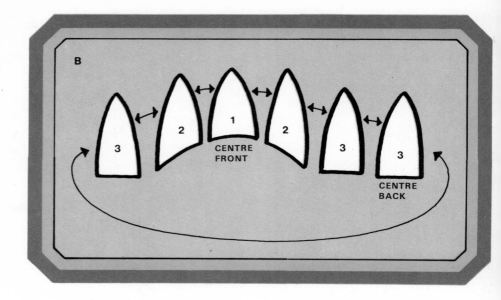

invisibly sew in place.

To trim pick up one sequin and two beads at a time on your needle and sew in place, trimming down each side of the two front seams. Fill in the centre front section with single beads only. For the centre top trimming cut a piece

of fabric, $8\frac{1}{2}$ in. by $6\frac{1}{2}$ in. Fold in three lengthwise and roll tightly, turn in hem and sew invisibly to centre of hat where seams meet.

Place lining inside hat and slip stitch in place to inside of headband. Press edge very lightly.

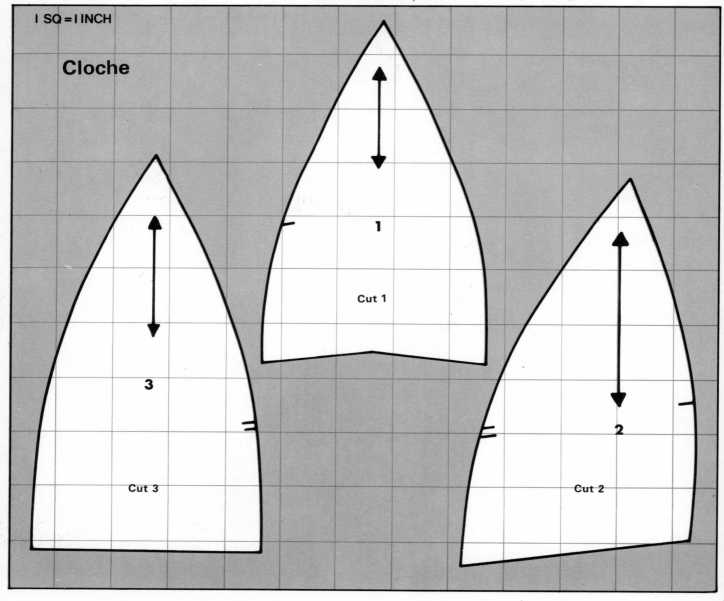

I SQ = I INCH

Cloche

# DICTIONARY OF YARN TYPES

**Acrylic Yarns** (e.g. Acrilan, Courtelle, Orlon). Acrylics are man-made fibres, made from products gained from coal and oil refining processes. It is possible when manufacturing these fibres to produce a very lightweight knitting yarn by causing some fibres to shrink and bunch up giving a larger diameter yarn than in wool or nylon for the same weight. There is therefore more yardage in a ball of acrylic fibre of equal weight. Yarns of this type produce lightweight garments which feel soft and wash easily.

**Angora.** A fluffy type of yarn popular for delicate knitwear, and originally spun from the hair of the Angora goat but now more usually spun from rabbit wool, and mixed with nylon. The synthetic mixture produces a fabric which is less soft and fluffy than pure Angora but the yarn will not shed hairs so much as the pure yarn.

**Baby Yarns.** These delicate yarns are usually made from the finest and softest botany wool, or sometimes from man-made fibres, usually in 2-ply, 3-ply or 4-ply weights, loosely twisted and dyed in pastel shades. The yarns are usually shrink resistant.

**Bainin Wool.** The traditional creamy coloured wool used for Aran knitting. Bainin (pronounced Baw-neen) is the Irish word for white, but the wool can be successfully dyed to any colour.

**Bouclé.** A 'textured' yarn which is good for suits and dresses. The bouclé effect is produced by severely over-twisting some of the plys of the basic yarn until they cockle up into clusters as in a tightly-twisted ball of string. These clusters are then bound in place by the other plys of ordinarily spun yarn or by a special binder thread. Fabrics knitted from this yarn possess a raised cluster texture which gives a two-tone effect even if the yarn is only in one colour.

**Cashmere.** A luxury natural fibre which although expensive knits up into beautiful, long-lasting classic garments. It is wonderfully soft and fine to the touch.

**Cotton.** Another natural yarn which is popular for lightweight summer knitted and crocheted garments. Cotton yarns are hard-wearing and wash well. They are particularly suited to crochet work.

**Crepe.** These are tightly-twisted multi-ply yarns which when knitted or crocheted produce a smooth fabric with an interesting textured surface.

**Double Knitting Yarns.** These are among the most popular yarns used today for knitting, and also often for crochet work as well. They may be either in natural or synthetic fibres, are quick to knit yet not too bulky. The name double knitting was originally given because when the yarns were first produced they were approximately double the thickness of 3-ply qualities.

**Fancy Yarns.** These yarns possess special effects which have been created by a combination of colours and spinning techniques. The 'fancy' quality may be in the texture of the yarn, or in its colouring, or a combination of both. Sometimes natural and man-made fibres are combined in one yarn.

**Fingering.** This term refers to a smoothly-twisted quality suitable for fine-textured garments.

**Linen.** A natural, hardwearing fibre which is often spun into knitting and crochet yarns. Sometimes these yarns have a novelty finish, similar to bouclé.

**Machine Washable Yarns.** There are many ranges of yarns available which wash well, not only by hand but by washing machine as well. Normally full washing instructions are given on the label for each yarn type. These should be carefully followed if you wish to get the best and longest wear from your garments.

**Man-made Fibres.** It is only in comparatively recent years that yarns have been produced for knitting and crochet work which are not connected with natural fibres at all, but are manufactured scientifically. There are three basic types of man-made fibres : nylon, acrylic and tri-acetate. See separate entries for each.

**Marls.** These are obtained by twisting together different colours of yarns after the spinning.

**Mixtures.** These are spun from a combination of colours dyed and mixed together in an early stage of the spinning process.

**Mohair.** This soft featherlight yarn comes from the hair of the Angora goat. It is very strong and yet light in weight and has an attractive fluffy appearance which makes it useful for special effects. The yarn is more suitable for knitting than crochet, and ideally should be knitted on fairly big needles so the light quality of the yarn is retained.

**Nylon.** A strong fibre which was the first man-made fibre to be used extensively in knitting and crochet yarns. It is made from the chemicals found in coal, air and water. As it is a very white fibre, it can be dyed successfully to brilliant white and vivid fluorescent shades. It is resistant to mildew and bacteria, and it is mothproof. Nylon can be used on its own to produce a knitting or crochet yarn, or it can be combined with wool or rayon to give the advantages of both fibres. As nylon is inclined to 'cling', it is best to make up your garment in a size larger than usual to give ease of movement.

**Orlon.** Another man-made fibre, known as an acrylic yarn. Garments made up in Orlon keep their shape well even after many washings. For best results, knit Orlon yarns fairly firmly.

**Tri-acetate.** Tricel is a tri-acetate fibre and is made chiefly from trees and oil but it is still relatively new to hand knitting and crochet yarns.

**Wool.** There are hundreds of different breeds of sheep in the world producing thousands of different types of wool. These can very broadly speaking be divided into the two following categories :

**1. Botany wool.** This comes from pure-bred Merino sheep, and is considered to be the finest of all wool. From such fleeces the softest qualities are spun.

**2. Crossbred wool.** This wool from crossbred sheep has a coarser tougher fibre suitable for the spinning of the harder wearing qualities of yarn.

# COMPARISON CHARTS

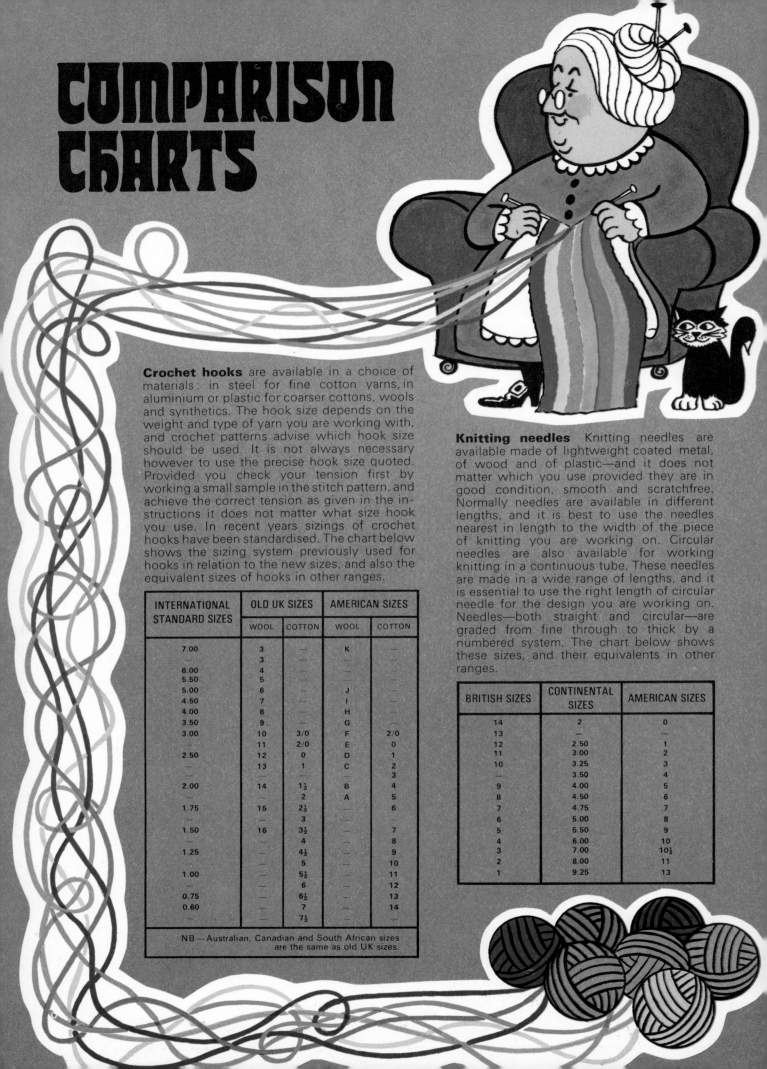

**Crochet hooks** are available in a choice of materials: in steel for fine cotton yarns, in aluminium or plastic for coarser cottons, wools and synthetics. The hook size depends on the weight and type of yarn you are working with, and crochet patterns advise which hook size should be used. It is not always necessary however to use the precise hook size quoted. Provided you check your tension first by working a small sample in the stitch pattern, and achieve the correct tension as given in the instructions it does not matter what size hook you use. In recent years sizings of crochet hooks have been standardised. The chart below shows the sizing system previously used for hooks in relation to the new sizes, and also the equivalent sizes of hooks in other ranges.

**Knitting needles** Knitting needles are available made of lightweight coated metal, of wood and of plastic—and it does not matter which you use provided they are in good condition, smooth and scratchfree. Normally needles are available in different lengths, and it is best to use the needles nearest in length to the width of the piece of knitting you are working on. Circular needles are also available for working knitting in a continuous tube. These needles are made in a wide range of lengths, and it is essential to use the right length of circular needle for the design you are working on. Needles—both straight and circular—are graded from fine through to thick by a numbered system. The chart below shows these sizes, and their equivalents in other ranges.

| INTERNATIONAL STANDARD SIZES | OLD UK SIZES | | AMERICAN SIZES | |
|---|---|---|---|---|
| | WOOL | COTTON | WOOL | COTTON |
| 7.00 | 3 | — | K | |
| | 3 | — | | |
| 6.00 | 4 | — | | |
| 5.50 | 5 | — | | |
| 5.00 | 6 | — | J | |
| 4.50 | 7 | — | I | |
| 4.00 | 8 | — | H | |
| 3.50 | 9 | — | G | |
| 3.00 | 10 | 3/0 | F | 2/0 |
| | 11 | 2/0 | E | 0 |
| 2.50 | 12 | 0 | D | 1 |
| — | 13 | 1 | C | 2 |
| | | | | 3 |
| 2.00 | 14 | 1½ | B | 4 |
| — | | 2 | A | 5 |
| 1.75 | 15 | 2½ | | 6 |
| — | | 3 | | |
| 1.50 | 16 | 3½ | | 7 |
| — | | 4 | | 8 |
| 1.25 | | 4½ | | 9 |
| — | | 5 | | 10 |
| 1.00 | | 5½ | | 11 |
| — | | 6 | | 12 |
| 0.75 | | 6½ | | 13 |
| 0.60 | | 7 | | 14 |
| — | | 7½ | | |

NB—Australian, Canadian and South African sizes are the same as old UK sizes.

| BRITISH SIZES | CONTINENTAL SIZES | AMERICAN SIZES |
|---|---|---|
| 14 | 2 | 0 |
| 13 | — | — |
| 12 | 2.50 | 1 |
| 11 | 3.00 | 2 |
| 10 | 3.25 | 3 |
| — | 3.50 | 4 |
| 9 | 4.00 | 5 |
| 8 | 4.50 | 6 |
| 7 | 4.75 | 7 |
| 6 | 5.00 | 8 |
| 5 | 5.50 | 9 |
| 4 | 6.00 | 10 |
| 3 | 7.00 | 10½ |
| 2 | 8.00 | 11 |
| 1 | 9.25 | 13 |

# KNITTING YARN TENSION GUIDE

**The following measurements all refer to 1 square inch**

## PATONS YARNS

**Brilliante 2-ply** 8 sts. and 10 rows on No. 10 needles.

**Limelight Baby, Brilliante 3-ply** $7\frac{1}{2}$ sts. and $9\frac{1}{2}$ rows on No. 10 needles.

**Limelight Crepe 4-ply, Cameo Crepe, Quickerknit** 7 sts. and 9 rows on No. 10 needles.

**Brilliante Quickerknit** $6\frac{1}{2}$ sts. and $8\frac{1}{2}$ rows on No. 8 needles.

**Ninepin** $6\frac{1}{4}$ sts. and 8 rows on No. 9 needles.

**Fiona** $6\frac{1}{4}$ sts. and $8\frac{1}{2}$ rows on No. 10 needles.

**Piccadilly** $5\frac{3}{4}$ sts. and $7\frac{1}{2}$ rows on No. 8 needles.

**Four Seasons, Promise** $6\frac{1}{2}$ sts. and $8\frac{1}{2}$ rows on No. 10 needles.

**Limelight Double Crepe, Brilliante D.K., Term Time D.K.** 6 sts. and 8 rows on No. 10 needles.

**Capstan** $5\frac{1}{2}$ sts. and $7\frac{1}{2}$ rows on No. 10 needles.

**Camelot** $4\frac{3}{4}$ sts. and $7\frac{1}{2}$ rows on No. 8 needles.

**Doublet** $4\frac{1}{2}$ sts. and $5\frac{3}{4}$ rows on No. 6 needles.

## WENDY YARNS

**Peter Pan 3-ply** $8\frac{1}{2}$ sts. and 11 rows on No. 11 needles.

**All 4-ply yarns** 7 sts. and 9 rows on No. 10 needles.

**All double knitting yarns** 6 sts. and 8 rows on No. 8 needles.

**Peter Pan Bri-nylon Quickerknit** $5\frac{1}{2}$ sts. and 7 rows on No. 8 needles.

**Peter Pan Courtelle, Quickerknit** $5\frac{1}{2}$ sts. and $7\frac{1}{2}$ rows on No. 8 needles.

**Diabolo** $4\frac{1}{4}$ sts. and $5\frac{1}{4}$ rows on No. 5 needles.

## SIRDAR YARNS

**All 3-ply yarns** 8 sts. and 10 rows on No. 10 needles.

**All 4-ply yarns** $7\frac{1}{2}$ sts. and $9\frac{1}{2}$ rows on No. 10 needles.

**All double knitting yarns** 6 sts. and 8 rows on No. 8 needles.

**Double bouclé** 5 sts. and 7 rows on No. 7 needles.

## EMU YARNS

**All 4-ply yarns (including Diadem)** $7\frac{1}{2}$ sts. and $9\frac{1}{2}$ rows on No. 10 needles.

**All double knitting yarns** $5\frac{1}{2}$ sts. and 8 rows on No. 8 needles.

**Baby Quickerknit Courtelle (and also Bri-nylon)** $5\frac{1}{2}$ sts. and 8 rows on No. 9 needles.

**Triple Knit** $4\frac{1}{2}$ sts. and $5\frac{1}{2}$ rows on No. 6 needles.

## LISTER YARNS

**All 3-ply yarn** $7\frac{1}{2}$ sts. and 10 rows on No. 10 needles.

**All 4-ply yarns (including Bel Air Starspun)** 7 sts. and 9 rows on No. 10 needles.

**Nursery Time Baby Quick Knitting** 6 sts. and 8 rows on No. 8 needles.

**All double knitting yarns** $5\frac{1}{2}$ sts. and 7 rows on No. 8 needles.

**Prema Bulky Knitting** $3\frac{1}{2}$ sts. and 5 rows on No. 3 needles.

## HAYFIELD YARNS

**All 4-ply yarns** 7 sts. and 9 rows on No. 10 needles.

**All double knitting yarns** $5\frac{1}{2}$ sts. and 7 rows on No. 8 needles.

## TWILLEY YARNS

**Goldfingering** $7\frac{1}{2}$ sts. and 10 rows on No. 10 needles.

**Lyscordet** $7\frac{1}{2}$ sts. and 10 rows on No. 10 needles.

**Crysette** 7 sts. and 10 rows on No. 10 needles.

**Note.** As yarn qualities and weights do vary from time to time, the above is only an approximate guide. It is always advisable to check your tension every time against the tension measurement quoted in a particular pattern.

# METRIC EQUIVALENTS

Although Imperial Standard measurements are used throughout the lessons and patterns in Handicrafts for All, it is a simple matter to convert these figures to give the equivalent metric measures.

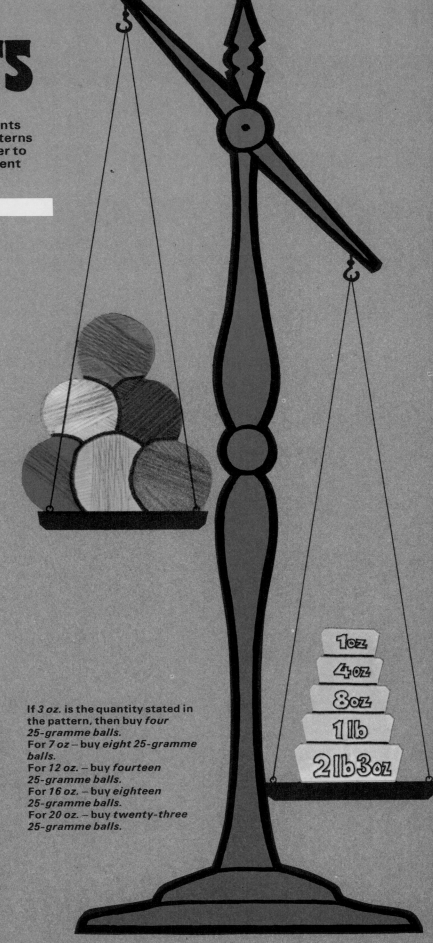

### Linear measurements
Converting inches, feet and yards to centimetres and metres.
1 inch = 2.54 centimetres
6 inches = 15.2 centimetres
1 foot = 30.48 centimetres
1 yard = 0.914 metre (just over 91 centimetres)
1 yard 4 inches = 1 metre

### Usual abbreviations
in., inch or inches
ft., foot or feet
yd., yard or yards
cm., centimetre or centimetres
m., metre or metres

### Weights
Converting ounces and pounds to grammes and kilogrammes
1 ounce = 28.35 grammes
4 ounces = 113.4 grammes
8 ounces = 226.8 grammes
1 pound = 454 grammes
2 pounds 3 ounces = 1 kilogramme (1,000 grammes)

### Usual abbreviations
oz., ounce or ounces
lb., pound or pounds
g., gramme or grammes
kg ., kilogramme or kilogrammes

## Knitting and crochet yarn
Many yarn manufacturers are now selling their yarn in 25-gramme balls where before they sold it in ounce quantities. But as this conversion is an approximate one – i.e. the exact conversion for 1 ounce is 28.35 grammes – if you require to buy a large number of gramme balls to work a pattern where the yarn quantity is given in ounces, it will be necessary to buy slightly more balls in the gramme weight than you would have done in the ounce measure. The following gives an approximate guide as to the number of gramme balls you should buy to give adequate yarn for a pattern where the quantity is specified in ounces.

If *3 oz.* is the quantity stated in the pattern, then buy *four 25-gramme balls.*
For *7 oz* – buy *eight 25-gramme balls.*
For *12 oz.* – buy *fourteen 25-gramme balls.*
For *16 oz.* – buy *eighteen 25-gramme balls.*
For *20 oz.* – buy *twenty-three 25-gramme balls.*

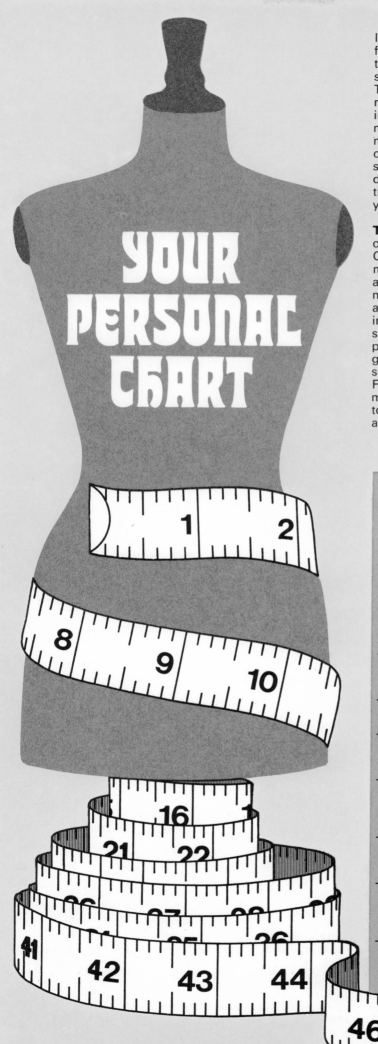

In order to establish the right paper pattern size for your figure, and also the points where the standard sized pattern will have to be adapted to give a good fit, it is necessary to keep a careful record of your body measurements. These are the actual measurements of your body and will not be the measurements of the pattern which has extra inches added for 'ease' of fit. Ideally always check your measurements over a slip and the underwear you normally wear. Measure the body at the points listed on the chart below by holding the tape measure comfortably snug but not tight. Record your measurements and the date taken on the chart. Check your measurements from time to time and record any changes in order to keep your measurement chart and your pattern size up-to-date.

**To select your pattern size** For a dress, blouse, suit or coat, select the pattern size by the bust measurement. Compare your bust measurement with the high bust measurement on the chart. In most cases there should be about a 2 in. difference. If there is a difference appreciably more than 2 in. between your high bust measurement and your bust measurement this means your bust is full in relation to your frame and you may select the pattern size according to the high bust measurement. Alter the pattern to fit bust measurement if necessary. This will give you a good fit through the chest, neckline, shoulders and armholes.

For a skirt or trousers, select the pattern size by the waist measurement. If your hips are much larger in proportion to your waist, select the size by the hip measurement, and alter at the waist.

# Dress Making Measuring Guide

| BODY POINT | WHERE TO MEASURE | YOUR MEASUREMENTS |
|---|---|---|
| High bust | Directly under the arms, then straight across the back bringing tape above the fullest part of the bust. | |
| Bust | Across fullest part of the bust. | |
| Waist | Around the natural waistline. | |
| Hips | Around the fullest part of the body which is usually about 9 in. below natural waistline. | |
| Back waist length | From the prominent bone at the nape of neck to the natural waistline. | |
| Front waist length | From base of neck at the front to natural waistline. | |
| Shoulder | From centre of back of neck to point where armhole seam would normally begin. | |
| Armhole | From top of shoulder around underarm and back up to top of shoulder. Keep arm resting lightly against body. | |
| Underarm measurement | From underarm to wrist bone. Hold arm straight out as you measure. | |
| Trouser inside leg | From crutch to ankle bone (or just below if you like long trousers). Stand with legs slightly apart while you measure. | |
| Trouser crutch depth | From centre front of natural waistline, down under crutch then back up to centre back of natural waistline. | |

# SEWING GUIDE
## Needle, thread and stitch

| Fabric Type | Thread | Needles | | No. of machine stitches per inch |
|---|---|---|---|---|
| | | Hand | Machine | |
| **Sheer:** net, lace, organdy, voile, chiffon | 70–100 mercerised cotton ; silk ; Terylene | 9, 10 | Fine | 16–20 |
| **Lightweight:** gingham, chambray, sheer wool, taffeta, crêpe | 60–70 mercerised cotton ; silk ; Terylene | 8, 9 | Fine | 12–16 |
| **Mediumweight:** poplin, faille, flannel, jersey, broadcloth, piqué, chintz | 50–60 mercerised cotton ; silk ; Terylene | 7, 8 | Medium | 12–14 |
| **Medium heavy:** corduroy, velveteen, denim, sail-cloth, suitings, felt, terry cloth | 36–40 mercerised cotton ; Terylene | 6 | Medium coarse | 10–12 |
| **Heavy:** coatings, fur fabrics, drapery fabrics | 40 mercerised cotton | 4, 5 | Coarse | 8–10 |
| **Very heavy:** canvas, duck, upholstery fabrics | Heavy-duty mercerised cotton | 1, 2, 3 | Coarsest | 6–8 |
| **Stretch fabrics** | Terylene ; multipurpose threads ; silk | 9, 10 | Fine | 15 |

**Note.** Ideally, your thread shade should be slightly darker than your fabric colour. Mercerised cotton, in light, medium and heavy weights, is a good all-purpose thread ; silk threads should be used for sewing woollen and silk fabrics. Spun Terylene is suitable for all synthetics and also for stretch fabrics. There are good-quality multipurpose threads available which can be used for all fabric types and weights.

**Basic stitch lengths**
There are four stitch lengths which are most generally used and each has a special purpose, as follows :
**Regulation stitch** – from 12 to 16 per inch, depending on the type of fabric. Fine and lightweight fabrics use shorter lengths.
**Basting stitch** – usually the longest stitch on your machine.
**Ease stitch** – about 10 to the inch. Used for easing-in fullness evenly (e.g. round the head of a sleeve when setting it into an armhole).
**Reinforcement stitch** – about 20 to the inch. Used in areas that need strengthening.

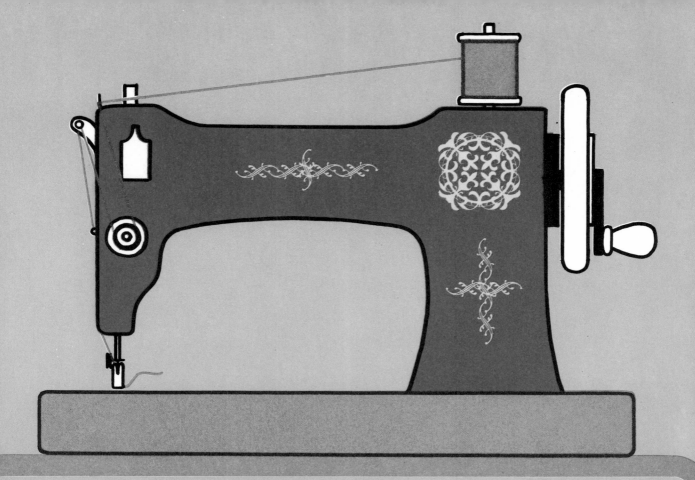

# BASIC NEEDLECRAFT EQUIPMENT

### For cutting
Small pair of embroidery scissors for clipping seams and snipping threads. Medium-sized pair of scissors for trimming seams. Bent-handled, well-sharpened cutting shears. Pinking shears for finishing seams.

### For marking
Dressmakers' tracing paper in light and dark shades. Tracing wheel to be used in conjunction with the tracing paper. Tailors' chalk in white and a selection of colours. Chalk pencils.

### For sewing
Sewing machine – a model to suit the type of sewing you intend to do. For instance if you intend only to do fairly plain sewing, then it is a waste of money to buy an expensive machine capable of producing a variety of decorative stitching.
Needles – good selection of hand and machine needles in different sizes.
Threads – in a variety of weights, colours and types. Always use thread one shade darker than the fabric colour you are using.
Stitch unpicker – very useful for undoing seams quickly.
Thimble – it should fit your middle finger comfortably.
Stiletto – for punching holes when making eyelets.

Bodkin – for running drawstrings in casings.
Hem marker – useful for marking an even hemline on a dress or skirt.

### For pressing
Iron – preferably one capable of steam and dry pressing.
Ironing board and sleeve board – both should be well padded.
Pressing cloths – different weights and fibres should be on hand for use with different fabrics.
Tailor's 'ham' or cushion – used for pressing areas that need shaping such as curved seams or darts.
Velvet board – for pressing velvet, velveteen and other similar pile fabrics.

### Other useful equipment
Rulers – in 12 in., 18 in. and 36 in. lengths.
Tape measure – with inch and centimetre markings.
Pins – good-quality steel ones are best.
Dress form – the perfect guide to making well-fitting garments.
Beeswax – useful for strengthening thread, especially for sewing on buttons. Beeswax can be bought in a special holder with grooves – the thread is simply pulled through the grooves in order to wax it.

# DICTIONARY OF FABRIC TERMS

**Fibre terms** Most fashion fabrics are made from yarns which in turn are made from either natural or man-made fibres.

Natural fibres, produced from animal or vegetable sources, include:

**Cotton** – natural vegetable fibre from cotton plant seed pod.

**Linen** – natural vegetable fibre from the flax plant.

**Silk** – natural animal fibre from cocoon of the silk worm.

**Wool** – natural animal fibre from the fleece of the sheep or lamb.

Man-made fibres are divided into two principal groups:

**Cellulose group** – this includes rayon, acetate and triacetate. Processed from the natural fibrous portions of wood pulp. Although they have a natural base, it is through chemistry that the fibres are obtained.

**Synthetic group** – this is a term used loosely for all man-made fibres. Actually the term includes only the fibres that are chemically created, such as nylon, polyester, acrylic, spandex and many others.

A **blend** is a yarn or fabric that combines the characteristics of two or more fibres, natural or man-made.

## Fabric terms

**Bonded.** A term applied to a single fabric that is a combination of two fabrics that have been sealed together back to back with a bonding agent of resin or glue.

**Bouclé.** Any fabric made from a bouclé yarn which has loops or knots in it; woven or knitted to give a nubby, uneven surface texture.

**Crêpe.** Fabric of any fibre with a crinkled or grainy surface formed by weaving various combinations of highly twisted yarns. Georgette and crêpe de chine are sheer crêpes; satin crêpe is a heavy crêpe.

**Crinkled.** Fabric with a wrinkled or puckered effect obtained in construction, chemically or with heat setting. Seersucker, which has crinkled stripes, is made by weaving some threads slack, others tight. The blistered surface of plissé and the crêpe-like crinkle of cotton georgette are obtained by chemically shrinking sections of the fabric.

**Eyelet and embroidery.** Any fabric may have embroidered detail or decorative needlework designs applied by hand or machine. Eyelet has open-punched patterns with machine-embroidered buttonhole stitch on edges.

**Felt.** Non-woven fabric made of matted fibres of wool, fur or mohair, often mixed with cotton or rayon.

**Jacquard.** Fabrics with a special weaving pattern that produces a raised design, often reversible to either side. Damask patterns stand out from the ground with a contrasting lustre. Brocade has heavy raised figures on a contrasting surface, often using gold and silver threads.

**Knits.** Fabrics made by interlocking loops of one or more yarns. Main types are jerseys (circular knits) and tricots (warp or flat knits). Single knits, such as jersey, drape softly but do not hold their shape as well as the double knits (made of two or more yarns). Knit fabrics are machine or hand-made of all fibres and blends, often in textures and patterns that simulate woven fabrics. They have a natural stretch or elastic quality.

**Lace.** This 'fabric' is technically not a fabric as it has no ground, is not woven, knitted or felted, but is a delicate openwork, consisting of a web of fine threads formed into a design.

**Laminated.** Term usually associated with fabric that is joined to a backing of synthetic foam. It provides insulation and warmth with little weight or bulk.

**Napped.** Fabrics with a 'third dimension'. Some of the hairy or downy fibres are brought to the surface and then are either brushed for a soft effect or pressed flat to give a sheen. Many napped fabrics reflect a different light in each direction so all pieces of a garment must be cut with the nap running in the same direction.

**Nubbed or Slubbed.** Fabrics distinguished by a roughness or unevenness in their weaves which may be due to natural thick-and-thin areas in the yarn such as in silk douppion, honan and tussah. Linen has a slightly slubbed effect due to occasional thicker places in the yarn. Rayon fabrics are often made with nubs and slubs to simulate a natural unevenness.

**Pile.** Pile fabrics are woven with an extra set of looped yarns, raised on the surface and clipped to stand up and form the special rich textures of fabrics such as velvet, velour and velveteen. Terry cloth is a pile fabric with uncut loops.

**Pique.** True piques are woven with lengthwise or crosswise ribs, or both. Sculptured cottons with novelty patterns are sometimes classified as piques.

**Plaids.** Pattern of coloured stripes or bars crossing each other at right angles, printed or woven in any fabric.

**Prints.** A general term for any fabric that has a printed pattern or design applied after the fabric is made.

**Quilted.** Two layers of fabric stitched together with a padding between.

**Sheers.** Any very thin fabric with a transparent quality, generally a plain weave. There are three principal types of sheer fabrics: soft sheers, which include chiffon; semi-soft sheers, which include voile, lawn and batiste; crisp sheers, which include organdie and dimity.

**Stretch.** Specially constructed texturised yarns woven in fabric to allow it to stretch when pulled then bounce back into shape. Stretch qualities add comfort, shape retention and wrinkle-resistance.

**Tweed.** Fabric of rough, unfinished appearance generally with a mixed colour effect but may be plain colours, checks and plaids.

**Twills.** There are several types of twill weaves. The basic twill runs up from left to right in a diagonal line. Variations include herringbone, also known sometimes as chevron.

**Vinyl.** Fashion 'fabric' of expanded vinyl (a type of plastic) popular for rainwear and other garments because it is permanently waterproof, cleans with damp cloth. Vinyl-coated fabrics are also available in which a base fabric – usually a printed or solid plain-weave cotton – is coated with a thin layer of vinyl.

# GUIDE TO INTERFACINGS

GUIDE TO INTERFACINGS

## Woven Interfacings

| FABRIC | WHERE TO USE | SPECIAL POINTS |
| --- | --- | --- |
| Batiste | Use to interface dresses, blouses and other garments in lightweight fabrics. | Shrink before using. |
| Calico (unbleached) | To give a backing to a loosely-woven fabric, or to add substance without stiffness. | Shrink before using. |
| Canvas | Available in stiff and soft finishes. Use the stiff canvas to interface heavy-weight fabrics, jackets and coats ; use soft canvas to interface lightweight fabrics. | Should be dry cleaned. |
| Lawn | To interface summer dresses in cotton and other washable lightweight fabrics. | Washable. |
| Net | Use to give backing to sheer fabrics. | Synthetic nets are washable. Others should be dry cleaned. |
| Organdie | Use to give a crisp finish to lightweight fabrics. | Washable. |
| Taffeta | Use to give a crisp finish to mediumweight fabrics (good for evening dresses and skirts). | Washable and dry cleanable. |

## Non-woven Interfacings

| | | |
| --- | --- | --- |
| Soft iron-on | Use on lightweight fabrics for small areas of stiffening only — e.g. collars, cuffs and pockets. Not advisable for use with silk, some synthetics and pure white fabrics. | Washable. |
| Firm iron-on | For use on medium and heavyweight fabrics in small areas — e.g. belts, hat brims. | Washable. |
| Lightweight sew-in | Use with all light and mediumweight fabrics where a soft stiffening is required — use on collars, cuffs, facings, behind buttonholes, pockets and waistbands. Strips of interfacing can also be used to ensure a permanent knife edge appearance to a pleat. Cut to the length of the knife pleat less hem, then machine to the pleat backing. | Washable. |
| Mediumweight sew-in | Use with medium and heavier weight fabrics, and wherever a firmer stiffening is required. | Washable. |

**Note.** Woven interfacings have grain and should be cut either with or against this grain, according to the pattern layout you are using.
Non-woven interfacings have no grain and can be cut in any direction.
An interfacing should never be heavier than the main fabric.
To apply an iron-on non-woven interfacing cut interfacing to $\frac{1}{16}$ in. less than the size of the pattern piece to be interfaced. Lay the powdered (rough) side of interfacing to wrong side of fabric. Fuse with hot iron (preferably steam) directly on smooth side of interfacing. Press evenly all over. Leave for a few minutes to cool. When applying sew-in interfacing, cut interfacing to same size as pattern piece, then place interfacing in position to wrong side of pattern piece. Baste round edges and trim interfacing close to stitching. Proceed with making up of garment in the usual way.
Always choose interfacing with similar properties to the main fabric — for instance if you are using a washable fabric, then be sure to choose a washable interfacing.

# PRESSING GUIDE FOR FABRICS

## Basic fabrics
**Cotton** The easiest fabric type of all to press. Lightweight cotton requires a heat setting similar to that used for silk (cool); heavyweight cotton requires a heat setting similar to that used for linen (fairly hot). Moisture is generally used, but the fabric should be pressed completely dry. Press first with steam, then press with the steam off.

**Rayon** Use a low heat. The steam iron usually supplies sufficient moisture. Press from the wrong side and use a dry cheesecloth, steam iron cloth or a drill cloth.

**Linen** Treat as for cotton, with a fairly high heat setting, and usually more moisture. Press until the fabric is dry.

**Wool** Sensitive to excesses of pressure, moisture and heat. It requires a moist heat, but should not be pressed when it is very damp or completely dry. When pressing napped surfaces or soft textures on the right side, use wool or wool sewn to a drill cloth as a press cloth.

**Silk and man-made fibres** Use minimal amounts of pressure, moisture and heat. Most fabrics made with these fibres may be pressed without a press cloth, but it is safer to use a thin press cloth to protect the fabric.

## Fabric textures
**Glossy** Fabrics such as glazed chintz and polished cotton are pressed on the right side without a pressing cloth and with little or no moisture.

**Dull-finished** These fabrics are pressed on the wrong or the right side using the proper press cloth for the specific fabric.

**Napped or pile** Fabrics such as fleece, deep-pile fake furs, corduroy and velvet must be steamed rather than pressed to prevent the nap or pile from flattening. Press in the direction of the nap.

**Raised-surface designs** These fabrics are pressed on a softly-padded board from the wrong side. Light pressure is best on woven or embossed fabrics, but heavier pressure is used to emphasise the design on embroidered fabrics.

## Special fabrics
**Knits** Press lengthwise, lifting and lowering the iron to avoid stretching the fabric. Always use a press cloth. When you press seams, place strips of brown paper under the seam allowance to prevent seam impressions from showing through to the right side of the garment.

**Lace** Lay the lace face down on a wool press cloth or on a Turkish towel to avoid flattening the raised design. Cover lace with a thin press cloth to prevent iron from catching in the lace.

**Laminates** Press with iron temperature set for outer fabric. Press over a press cloth or a sheet of brown paper so the iron will not stick to the foam backing.

**Leather** Use a dry iron (no steam) on a warm setting, and press over a sheet of brown paper or a press cloth.

## General hints
Always press with the point of the iron in the direction of the grain of the fabric. Press waistline seams towards the bodice. When pressing sleeve head, lay the top of sleeve seam over the edge of the sleeve board with sleeve side up and press seam allowance only. Baste pleats before pressing. When pressing hems, lift iron rather than gliding and work towards grain.

## Yarns
Pressing plays an important part in the appearance of a well-finished knitted or crocheted garment. Each piece of the garment should be pinned out to the correct shape and size right side downwards on a thick pressing blanket, care being taken to keep the stitches and rows of the fabric running in straight lines. This will ensure that no part of the fabric is unduly stretched. Plenty of pins should be used and these should be inserted from the outer edge towards the centre of the work. The closer the pins the straighter the pressed edge will be. First, omitting all ribbed portions, press the main part of the work using a damp cloth and a warm iron. Wait a few moments until the steam has settled then remove the pins from the edges of the main part and close the ribbed portions until the knit stitches only are showing. Pin the ribbing closely, inserting the pins downwards from the top of the ribbing and upwards from the lower edge. Press lightly but firmly and after allowing the steam to settle, remove the pins.

**Wool** Pure wool yarns usually need a fairly hot iron, but never push the iron backwards and forwards or allow it to stay in the same place for more than a second or two. Use a dabbing action letting the steam from the damp cloth do most of the work. When the garment is well pressed, dry it off by substituting a dry cloth for the damp one and pressing over this.

**Man-made fibres** Press with a warm iron over a dry cloth. No pressing at all is required for certain synthetic yarns – e.g. Courtelle, Acrilan, Tricel and Orlon. Read the label on the yarn for specific pressing instructions.

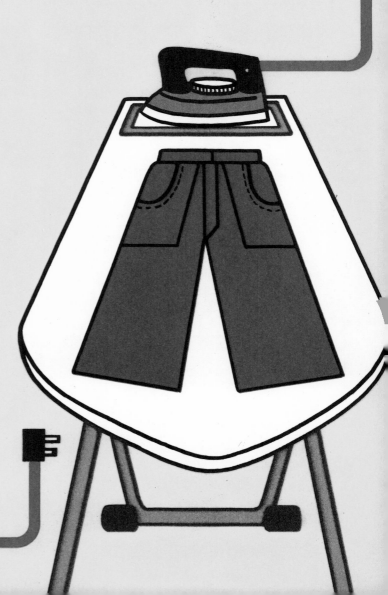

# GUIDE TO PAPER PATTERN SIZES

Most commercial paper patterns are grouped into six different figure types for adult fashion garment patterns. Each grouping then has an individual range of sizes. To determine which figure type and size you are, first take your body measurements carefully and accurately. Take the measurements snugly but not too tightly in a simple, well-fitting dress or slip and proper foundation garments. Your figure type is based on two measurements—your height and your back waist length. Once you have established which figure type is yours, then compare your body measurements with those listed on the chart for that particular figure type. The measurements quoted on the charts all refer to actual body measurements—allowance for ease of fit is always added to the actual pattern. When buying a pattern for a coat or suit, buy the same size as you would for a dress pattern. Do not purchase a larger size. When buying a pattern for a maternity garment buy the same size as you used before pregnancy.

The following sizing charts are based on those approved by the Measurement Standard Committee of the Pattern Fashion Industry.

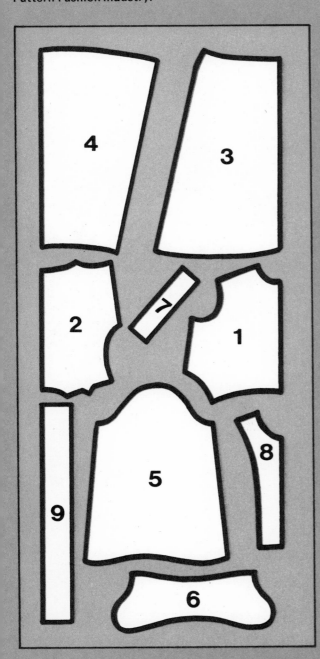

**MISSES** Misses' patterns are designed for a well-proportioned and developed figure ; about 5 ft. 5 in. to 5 ft. 6 in. without shoes.

| SIZE | 6 | 8 | 10 | 12 | 14 | 16 | 18 | 20 |
|---|---|---|---|---|---|---|---|---|
| BUST | 30½ | 31½ | 32½ | 34 | 36 | 38 | 40 | 42 |
| WAIST | 23 | 24 | 25 | 26½ | 28 | 30 | 32 | 34 |
| HIP | 32½ | 33½ | 34½ | 36 | 38 | 40 | 42 | 44 |
| BACK WAIST LENGTH | 15½ | 15¾ | 16 | 16¼ | 16½ | 16¾ | 17 | 17¼ |

**MISS PETITE** This size range is designed for the shorter Miss figure ; about 5 ft. 2 in. to 5 ft. 4 in. without shoes.

| SIZE | 6mp | 8mp | 10mp | 12mp | 14mp | 16mp |
|---|---|---|---|---|---|---|
| BUST | 30½ | 31½ | 32½ | 34 | 36 | 38 |
| WAIST | 23½ | 24½ | 25½ | 27 | 28½ | 30½ |
| HIP | 31½ | 33½ | 34½ | 36 | 38 | 40 |
| BACK WAIST LENGTH | 14½ | 14¾ | 15 | 15¼ | 15½ | 15¾ |

**JUNIOR PETITE** Junior Petite patterns are designed for a well-proportioned, petite figure ; about 5 ft. to 5 ft. 1 in. without shoes.

| SIZE | 3jp | 5jp | 7jp | 9jp | 11jp | 13jp |
|---|---|---|---|---|---|---|
| BUST | 30½ | 31 | 32 | 33 | 34 | 35 |
| WAIST | 22½ | 23 | 24 | 25 | 26 | 27 |
| HIP | 31½ | 32 | 33 | 34 | 35 | 36 |
| BACK WAIST LENGTH | 14 | 14¼ | 14½ | 14¾ | 15 | 15¼ |

**YOUNG JUNIOR/TEEN** This size range is designed for the developing pre-teen and teen figures ; about 5 ft. 1 in. to 5 ft. 3 in. without shoes.

| SIZE | 5/6 | 7/8 | 9/10 | 11/12 | 13/14 | 15/16 |
|---|---|---|---|---|---|---|
| BUST | 28 | 29 | 30½ | 32 | 33½ | 35 |
| WAIST | 22 | 23 | 24 | 25 | 26 | 27 |
| HIP | 31 | 32 | 33½ | 35 | 36½ | 38 |
| BACK WAIST LENGTH | 13½ | 14 | 14½ | 15 | 15⅜ | 15¾ |

**WOMEN'S** Women's patterns are designed for the larger, more fully mature figure ; about 5 ft. 5 in. to 5 ft. 6 in. without shoes.

| SIZE | 38 | 40 | 42 | 44 | 46 | 48 | 50 |
|---|---|---|---|---|---|---|---|
| BUST | 42 | 44 | 46 | 48 | 50 | 52 | 54 |
| WAIST | 35 | 37 | 39 | 41½ | 44 | 46½ | 49 |
| HIP | 44 | 46 | 48 | 50 | 52 | 54 | 56 |
| BACK WAIST LENGTH | 17½ | 17⅝ | 17¾ | 17⅞ | 17¾ | 17⅞ | 18 |

**HALF-SIZE** Half-size patterns are for a fully developed figure with a short back waist length. Waist and hips are larger in proportion to bust than other figure types ; about 5 ft. 2 in. to 5 ft. 3 in., without shoes.

| SIZE | 10½ | 12½ | 14½ | 16½ | 18½ | 20½ | 22½ | 24½ |
|---|---|---|---|---|---|---|---|---|
| BUST | 33 | 35 | 37 | 39 | 41 | 43 | 45 | 47 |
| WAIST | 27 | 29 | 31 | 33 | 35 | 37½ | 40 | 42½ |
| HIP | 35 | 37 | 39 | 41 | 43 | 45½ | 48 | 50½ |
| BACK WAIST LENGTH | 15 | 15¼ | 15½ | 15¾ | 15⅞ | 16 | 16⅛ | 16¼ |

# DECORATIVE BORDERS

## POMPONS

Cut two circular pieces of cardboard the same size as required for finished pompon, place these together and cut a hole through the centre – the larger the hole the thicker the finished pompon will be. Now wind yarn evenly round cardboard discs passing the yarn through the central hole each time until the cardboard is covered. Continue to wind yarn round until the hole is almost completely full. Break off the yarn and then cut through yarn and outer rim of cardboard. Tie a length of yarn round the centre between the card discs to secure, and slip cardboard discs off. Shake pompon well and trim if necessary.

## FRINGES

A fringe can be used as a decorative edging for both household and fashion designs. Any number of yarn strands can be used in each 'knot' of the fringe – with thin and fine yarns you will probably want quite a lot of strands in each knot, but with heavy and thick yarns you may only need a few. Ideally there should always be an even number of strands per knot.

### To make a single knotted fringe

Cut the required number of strands each to double the measurement of finished fringe required plus 1 in – i.e. if you want a finished fringe of 4 in., then cut strands to 9 in. Place the strands together, and then double them. Insert a crochet hook into the edge of the fabric where you wish the fringe to appear, and use the hook to catch hold of the strands by the doubled loop. Draw loop through fabric's edge. Remove hook, and draw the strand ends down through the loop. Pull gently tight so the knot is formed immediately below edge of fabric. Continue in this way along fabric, making a knot at $\frac{1}{2}$-in. intervals until the edge is complete. Trim the fringe evenly.

### To make a double knotted fringe

Cut the required number of strands each to double the measurement of finished fringe required plus 3 in. Insert strands into fabric edge and make a single knot, as described above. Now take half the number of strands from each of two adjacent knots, and tie these together with a single overhand knot (the knot used when setting-on cords in macramé – see Macramé, lesson one). Continue in this way along fringe. This second row of knots should be approximately $\frac{1}{2}$ in. below the first row. If wished, a third row of knots can be added (strands should be cut another 2 in. longer for this) – in the third row each knot is formed with the strands which were grouped together in the first row.

## To make a macramé fringe

Cut cords to eight times the length of finished fringe required. Double each cord and set on directly to the edge of the fabric by pulling the cord through the edge with a crochet hook. When all the cords are set on, work in any macramé pattern as wished. The alternate flat knot pattern is particularly effective, or for a more ornate fringe work in bands of different knotting patterns – perhaps a 1-in. band of half knot spirals, followed by 'triangles' of alternate flat knot pattern (each triangle worked over, say, sixteen cords). Finish by 'framing' the sides of each triangle with a row of diagonal cording. Trim cord ends to give a plain fringe below the knotting, following the shape of the triangles if wished.

## TASSELS

To make a simple, plain tassel wind yarn several times round a piece of cardboard cut to the length of finished tassel required. Thread a short length of yarn below loops at top of card, draw up loops and tie length of yarn to secure. Cut through bottom loops and remove card. Tie another short length of yarn round tassel about $\frac{1}{2}$ in. from the top.

To make a macramé tassel, see Macramé, lesson two.

## TWISTED CORDS

It is difficult to make a successful twisted cord on your own – ideally you should have someone to help you. Cut the required number of strands of yarn to give the thickness of cord you want, and cut each strand to three times the finished length of cord required. Place the strands together, and you take hold of one end, and your helper should take hold of the other. Keeping the yarn taut twist the strands towards the right until a firm twist has been obtained. Fold yarn in half lengthways and knot together the loose ends. Smooth to an even cord.

## PLAITS

The easiest plait to work is with three strands of yarn or cord, but multiple-strand plaits can also be successfully – and effectively – worked. Use single strands of yarn, or long narrow strips of knitted fabric for a bulkier plait. To make a five-strand plait, lay the five strands flat, and working from right to left take each strand in turn and weave it over and under the others. Continue in this way until plait is length required. Machine stitch across ends at start and finish of plait to prevent it coming undone.

# STAINS— SIMPLE HOME REMEDIES

| STAIN | WASHABLE FABRICS | NON-WASHABLE FABRICS |
|---|---|---|
| Alcohol (beer, wines and spirits) | Dampen the fabric, then sprinkle it with borax. Pour warm water over, then launder the fabric in the usual way. | Sponge gently with a solution of borax – one dessertspoon to ½ pint warm water. |
| Blood | Soak in cold water for at least an hour, then launder in the usual way. | Sponge with cold water. |
| Candle wax | Scrape off excess wax then melt away the remainder by pressing with a warm iron over a sheet of blotting paper. If necessary, apply a grease solvent. | As for washable fabrics. |
| Chocolate | Scrape off excess. Apply glycerine to the stain and soak for half-an-hour. Launder in the usual way. | Use a proprietary dry cleaner, or apply borax solution as for alcohol stains. |
| Coffee, Tea | Treat as for chocolate. | Treat as for chocolate. |
| Cod liver oil | Treat immediately with a proprietary dry cleaner or grease solvent. If necessary soak for ten minutes in a solution of equal parts of hydrogen peroxide and water. Launder as usual. | Treat at once with a proprietary dry cleaner or grease solvent. |
| Crayon | Treat with carbon tetrachloride or a grease solvent. Launder as usual. | Treat with carbon tetrachloride or a grease solvent. |
| Egg, Gravy, Milk | Wash in warm sudsy water. Rinse well. When dry remove any remaining stain with a dry cleaner or grease solvent. | Sponge carefully with warm suds. Remove suds with a clean white cloth wrung out in warm water. When dry remove any remaining stain with a dry cleaner or grease solvent. |
| Fruit juices | Treat as for alcohol stains. Sponge with methylated spirits. Launder as usual. | Treat as for alcohol stains. Sponge with methylated spirits. |
| Grease, Fats, Oil | Apply a dry cleaner or grease solvent. For stubborn stains, cover stain with clean blotting paper then press with a warm iron. This draws out the stain. Launder as usual. | Apply a dry cleaner or grease solvent. If necessary, use blotting paper and iron treatment as for washable fabrics. |
| Ice cream | Soak in warm suds then launder in as hot water as the fabric can stand. | Sponge with warm suds. When dry apply a dry cleaner or grease solvent. |
| Ink | **Ball-point:** Sponge with methylated spirits then launder as usual.<br>**Writing ink:** Rinse in cold water and then launder as usual. If the stains persist treat with oxalic acid.<br>**Red ink:** Soak in a solution of ammonia diluted in warm water for an hour. Launder as usual. | **Ball-point:** Sponge with methylated spirits.<br>**Writing ink:** Sponge with methylated spirits.<br>**Red ink:** Sponge with methylated spirits, or treat as for alcohol stains. |
| Iron mould, Rust | Soak in a solution of oxalic acid (one teaspoon of acid to half a pint of warm water) for a few minutes. Rinse and launder as usual. | Treat with a proprietary stain remover. |
| Jam | Wash in warm soapy water. If stain still remains treat as for alcohol stains. | Sponge with warm soap suds. Treat any remaining stain as for alcohol stains. |
| Mildew | Soak in a solution of hydrogen peroxide – equal parts of 20 vol. peroxide and water. Launder as usual. | Difficult to remove, but try rubbing over the mildewed area with lemon juice and salt, then leave the fabric to bleach in the sun. |
| Paint | Loosen hardened paint with a little vaseline or lard. Sponge stain with pure turpentine and then launder as usual. | Treat as for washable fabrics but instead of laundering rub the area with a little methylated spirits. |
| Milk | Soak in cold water, then launder in hot soapy water. | Treat with carbon tetrachloride then sponge with cold water. |
| Perspiration | Sponge stains with a vinegar and water solution – one tablespoon vinegar to a pint of cold water. Launder as usual. | Sponge with methylated spirits and dry with a soft cloth. |
| Tar | Scrape off as much as possible then treat with lighter fuel or eucalyptus oil. | As for washable fabrics. |

# SPECIAL INFORMATION

In case of difficulty, the following alternative products and addresses may be useful:

Adhesives: leather: Duall 88
              fabric and paper work: Craft Glue
              clear: Bostik Clear or Instant Grip
              impact: Araldite
              PVA white: Aquadhere
              woodworking: Bear brand

Crochet hooks: old UK sizes and some Continental sizes are available.
Pre-cut lengths of cane: use the same diameter in hollow plastic.
Filling for toys etc: cotton wadding or Dacron filling.
Wood filler: any proprietary brand.
Wools and yarns: refer to manufacturers' addresses below.
Tapisserie wools and stranded cottons: for substitute colours refer to manufacturer or colour cards available in stores and needlework shops.
Prodding hook: use a coarse crochet hook or make one from a piece of firm wire such as a wire coathanger.

## Useful addresses

If you have difficulty in obtaining any of the yarns or materials quoted in this book, please contact the appropriate manufacturing company as listed here:

Coats' Anchor tapisserie wools, Coats' Anchor soft embroidery, Mercer cottons, Clarks' Anchor stranded cottons, Patons' knitting wools:
    Coats Patons (Aust) Ltd
    Ferntree Gully Road
    Mount Waverley Vic 3149

Rug wools, canvasses, rug needles, transfers, huckaback, embroidery and needlework requirements, macramé twines, tapestry designs:

    Semco Pty Ltd
    Cheltenham Road
    Black Rock Vic 3193

Leather supplies, punches, needles, threads, lacings, adhesives etc:
    Porter and Co
    203 Castlereagh Street
    Sydney NSW 2000

Sewing patterns, tracing paper and wheels, carbon paper, graph paper and all sewing information:
    Simplicity Patterns Pty Ltd
    95 Bonds Road
    Punchbowl NSW 2196

Handicraft adhesives, basketwork, lampshade frames and parchments, patchwork templates, felt etc:
    Arbee Handcraft Centre Pty Ltd
    127 York Street
    Sydney NSW 2000

Cartridge and tissue papers etc:
    Swain and Co Pty Ltd
    330 George Street
    Sydney NSW 2000

Silver and all requirements for silver jewellery making:
    Australian Silvercraft Centre Pty Ltd
    104 Bathurst Street
    Sydney NSW 2000

Twilleys' yarns and Mahonys' Blarney Blainin wool:
    Panda Yarns Pty Ltd
    1 Belgium Street
    Richmond Vic 3121

Sirdar wools:
    Sirdar Wools (Aust) Pty Ltd
    38 Kenneth Street
    Longueville NSW 2066

Emu and Lincoln wools:
    Lincoln Mills (Aust) Ltd
    Lincoln Cleckheaton Yarns
    209 Australia Street
    Newtown NSW 2042

If Wendy and Hayfield and Lister yarns are not readily available, substitute any good quality yarn in the required ply, provided that it achieves the tension quoted in the pattern.

Quarter wave stitch 38